MACROECONOMICS

Seventh Edition

David C. Colander

Middlebury College

 **McGraw-Hill**
Irwin

Boston   Burr Ridge, IL   Dubuque, IA   New York   San Francisco   St. Louis
Bangkok   Bogotá   Caracas   Kuala Lumpur   Lisbon   London   Madrid   Mexico City
Milan   Montreal   New Delhi   Santiago   Seoul   Singapore   Sydney   Taipei   Toronto

Dedicated to the memory of Frank Knight and
Thorstein Veblen, both of whose economics have significantly
influenced the contents of this book.

MACROECONOMICS

Published by McGraw-Hill/Irwin, a business unit of The McGraw-Hill Companies, Inc., 1221 Avenue of the Americas, New York, NY, 10020. Copyright © 2008, 2006, 2004, 2001, 1998, 1995, 1993 by The McGraw-Hill Companies, Inc. All rights reserved. No part of this publication may be reproduced or distributed in any form or by any means, or stored in a database or retrieval system, without the prior written consent of The McGraw-Hill Companies, Inc., including, but not limited to, in any network or other electronic storage or transmission, or broadcast for distance learning.

Some ancillaries, including electronic and print components, may not be available to customers outside the United States.

This book is printed on acid-free paper.

1 2 3 4 5 6 7 8 9 0 DOW/DOW 0 9 8 7

ISBN   978-0-07-334366-2
MHID   0-07-334366-8

Executive editor: *Douglas Reiner*
Developmental editor: *Karen Fisher*
Marketing manager: *Melissa Larmon*
Media producer: *Lynn M. Bluhm*
Senior project manager: *Susanne Riedell*
Senior production supervisor: *Carol A. Bielski*
Designer: *Cara David*
Senior photo research coordinator: *Jeremy Cheshareck*
Photo researcher: *Keri Johnson*
Lead media project manager: *Brian Nacik*
Cover design: *Eric Kass, funnel*
Cover photo: *Eric Kass, funnel*
Interior design: *Pam Verros, pv design*
Typeface: *10.3/12 Goudy*
Compositor: *Aptara*
Printer: *R. R. Donnelley*

Library of Congress Cataloging-in-Publication Data

Colander, David C.
    Macroeconomics/David C. Colander.—7th ed.
        p. cm.
    Includes index.
    ISBN-13: 978-0-07-334366-2 (alk. paper)
    ISBN-10: 0-07-334366-8 (alk. paper)
    1. Macroeconomics. I. Title.
HB172.5.C638 2008
339—dc22

2007030174

ABOUT THE AUTHOR

David Colander is the Christian A. Johnson Distinguished Professor of Economics at Middlebury College. He has authored, coauthored, or edited over 40 books and over 150 articles on a wide range of economic topics.

He earned his B.A. at Columbia College and his M.Phil. and Ph.D. at Columbia University. He also studied at the University of Birmingham in England and at Wilhelmsburg Gymnasium in Germany. Professor Colander has taught at Columbia University, Vassar College, and the University of Miami, as well as having been a consultant to Time-Life Films, a consultant to Congress, a Brookings Policy Fellow, and Visiting Scholar at Nuffield College, Oxford. In 2001–2002, he was the Kelley Professor of Distinguished Teaching at Princeton University.

He belongs to a variety of professional associations and has been president of both the History of Economic Thought Society and the Eastern Economics Association. He has also served on the editorial boards of the *Journal of Economic Perspectives*, *The Journal of Economic Education*, *The Journal of Economic Methodology*, *The Journal of the History of Economic Thought*, *The Journal of Socio-Economics*, and *The Eastern Economic Journal*. He is chair of the AEA Committee on Electronic Publishing and a member of the AEA Committee on Economic Education.

He is married to a pediatrician, Patrice, who has a private practice in Middlebury, Vermont. In their spare time, the Colanders designed and built their oak post-and-beam house on a ridge overlooking the Green Mountains to the east and the Adirondacks to the west. The house is located on the site of a former drive-in movie theater. (They replaced the speaker poles with fruit trees and used the I-beams from the screen as support for the second story of the carriage house and the garage. Dave's office and library are in the former projection room.)

"Imagine . . . a textbook that students enjoy!"
That comment, from Glen Waddell, who teaches at Purdue, was e-mailed to me as I was struggling to write the preface to an earlier edition. That comment still captures what I believe to be the most distinctive feature of my book. I've always felt that the books students read in their courses should speak to them and be as enjoyable as possible to read. Those beliefs continue to be the guiding principle for my writing.

For Those Who Are New to the Book

For those of you who haven't used earlier editions, let me briefly describe where I see this book fitting in the panoply of top-selling books. Principles books are often categorized as old-style or new-style. In old-style books, short-run stabilization comes before growth; generally the books have a Keynesian activist macro policy flavor. New-style books do growth before stabilization, often with little coverage of stabilization issues, such as multiplier analysis; these new-style books generally have a Classical laissez-faire, macro-policy flavor.

This book is new-style in organization—it puts the long run first—but it is not new-style in terms of coverage; it presents stabilization as an important issue, and it doesn't have the laissez-faire flavor of some new-style books. I like to think of the flavor of this book as neither old- nor new-style, but instead cutting-edge style. Much of the conceptual foundations for the theory underlying it is derived from the new work in behavioral economics, non-linear dynamics, complexity, and strategic game theory.

The Cutting-Edge Style

Within this cutting-edge style work, everything is less certain than in either the new- or the old-style theory. Cutting-edge theory recognizes that Keynes and Keynesians had some important policy insights that need to be part of what we teach. However, it also recognizes that much of Keynesian policy was oversold, and that Keynesians underestimated government failure. So while theory may not tell us that laissez-faire is a desirable policy, a study of history and politics and the complexity of the system warns us about activist policy, even when our hearts tell us that government action is needed. Both these views show through in the presentations.

The Colloquial Style

Another way in which principles books are classified is on the easy–medium–difficult spectrum. This book is definitely in the medium range. Based on writing style alone, it would probably be placed in the easy range, but since it tackles difficult conceptual topics that will challenge even the brightest students, it should be considered a medium-range text. Why do I choose that combination? Because I believe that most students have the ability to understand economic concepts even though on exams it often appears as if they have serious problems. In my opinion many of those problems are not conceptual; rather, they are problems in motivation, reading, and math. The economics found in principles courses is not students' highest priority; it certainly wasn't mine when I was 18. I'm continually amazed at how many supposedly not-so-good students are conceptually bright. The reality is that most principles books bore this Internet generation. To teach them effectively, we've got to get their attention and hold it.

One way I try to get students' attention is to use a colloquial style. The book talks to students and makes them feel that the textbook is a second teacher who is urging them on to study harder, and is trying to explain the material to them. That colloquial style helps with one of the biggest problems in the course—getting students to read the book. Some professors don't always like the style, but even some of them have written to me to say that they use the book anyway because their students read it. And if the students have read the book, teaching is more rewarding.

A Focus on Policy

Another way the book relates to students is through its focus on policy. This book is not written for future economics majors. Most students aren't going to go on in economics. It is written for students who will probably take only one or two economics courses in their lifetime. These students are interested in policy, so I present the basics of economic reasoning as it relates to policy questions. This discussion presents policy as students see it in the news: policy questions are seldom clear-cut; to present policy any other way is unfair to students.

Institutions and History

This book also differs from some of the others in that it emphasizes the importance of institutions and history. Modern work in game theory and strategic decision making is making it clear that the implications of economic reasoning depend on the institutional setting. To understand economics requires an understanding of existing institutions and the historical development of those institutions. In a principles course, while we don't have time to present much about history and institutions, we can at least let students know that these issues are important. And that's what I try to do.

Openness to Various Views

While I present standard economics in the book, I present it in such a way that it is open to many different points of view. Thus, the book doesn't present the material as "the truth" but simply as the conventional wisdom, the learning of which is a useful hurdle for all students to jump over. To encourage students to question conventional wisdom, there is a set of questions at the end of each chapter—Questions from Alternative Perspectives—that includes questions written by economists from a variety of different perspectives. These include Post-Keynesian, feminist, Austrian, Radical, Institutionalist, and religious questions. The radical questions come from the Dollars and Sense Collective, a group with whom I've worked to coordinate their *Readers* (www.dollarsandsense.org/bookstore.html) with this text. I also often integrate Austrian ideas into my class; I find that *The Free Market* (www.mises.org/freemarket.asp) is a provocative resource. I often pair an article in *The Free Market* with one in *Dollars and Sense* in my assignments to students for supplementary reading. Having students read both Radical and Austrian views and then contrast those views with their own, generally middle-of-the-road, views is, for me, a perfect way of teaching the principles course. (If I have radicals and libertarians in the class, I argue in favor of middle-of-the-road views.) If you like to teach the course emphasizing alternative views, you might want to assign the brief survey of different approaches to economics in the "Preface for the Student" close to the beginning of the course, and then have the students answer, or at least discuss, the alternative perspective questions at the end of each chapter.

A Focus on the Modeling Method

As Robert Solow has said, for better or worse economics is a modeling science, and an important aspect of any introductory book is to introduce students to models and the modeling approach to understanding the world. My book does that, but its approach is slightly different than most of the other top introductory books. My book follows Alfred Marshall's approach to economics, which sees economics more as an approach to problems than as a body of confirmed truths. In my view, *it is the modeling method, not the models* that are most important to teach our students. In my presentation of models, I carefully try to guide students in the modeling method, rather than having them memorize truths from models. I carefully emphasize the limitations of the models and the assumptions that underlie them, and am constantly urging students to think beyond the models. This approach pushes the students a bit harder than the alternative, but it is, in my view, the best pedagogical approach.

For Those Who Have Used the Book Before

Those of you who have used earlier editions will find that this seventh edition has the same basic structure and tone as the sixth. The reason is that the book has reached an equilibrium—I made the book consistent with the standard presentations, but I also have kept enough of the historical and institutional approaches, and enough of the informal, student-friendly writing style, to make the book distinctive. I guess the process of reviewing and rewriting does finally lead to something like a steady-state equilibrium.

This is not the book I would have written for myself (my perspective often strays from conventional wisdom), but it is a book that I'm proud of, and one that reflects my views given the constraints of the market. Since optimizing subject to constraints is a central lesson of economics, it's not surprising that I would take that approach in writing this book.

Still, I want students to question everything and understand that economics is far more than what is presented in a textbook. Thus, I continually search for ways to challenge them to question. One of my latest attempts is to put together a book of essays that explores what we economists teach and why we teach it. The book is called *The Stories Economists Tell*. You can find the introductory essay to that book on the book's Web site (www.mhhe.com/economics/colander7e). If you are considering using my textbook for your class and want to know more about my views on teaching economics, you can get a free copy of the book by contacting your McGraw-Hill representative.

Changes from the Last Edition

The guiding principles of this revision were to make it

    simpler,

    shorter,

    more organized, and

    more applicable to the real world.

Toward those ends, I simplified complicated discussions where possible, cut some of my beloved tangents, moved material around to keep each chapter more narrowly focused on a particular topic, and added more real-world examples throughout. Let me briefly outline some of the major changes.

In the intro section (Chapters 1–5) I reworked the presentation in Chapters 2 and 3 so each is shorter and more focused, with Chapter 2 discussing trade and international issues and Chapter 3 discussing institutions. I simplified Chapter 7, the national income accounting chapter; it now focuses on the basics, and does not discuss the more esoteric aspects of national income accounting. In the growth chapter (Chapter 8), I added a discussion of the market for loanable funds to better tie the interest rate into the analysis, and cut the growth policy discussion to make the chapter shorter. In the money and financial markets chapter (Chapter 11), I added discussions of the supply and demand for loanable funds and of the supply and demand for money, setting up a discussion of the yield curve in the next chapter on monetary policy. I felt that this change was needed because the yield curve and the difference between the long- and the short-term interest rate are becoming increasingly central to discussions of monetary policy.

I also eliminated the term approximate real-world money multiplier, and cut much of the appendix on types of financial institutions, both in response to review suggestions. I then changed Chapter 12 to focus on monetary policy and open market operations, retitling the chapter "Monetary Policy." In the chapter on inflation (Chapter 13), I shortened the discussion of alternative views of inflation, tightening and simplifying the presentation. I completely reorganized and rewrote much of Chapter 14, which had been about aggregate demand policy, but is now about fiscal policy alone.

I have also updated facts, figures, discussions, and end-of-chapter questions to keep the book as up-to-date and relevant as possible. The economy and economics are constantly evolving, which means that the text must change to reflect the changing institutions, data, and evolving thinking in the profession. Where interest has changed, I changed the discussion, and where the chapter organization was not tight, I tightened it.

Finally, I have made some design and pedagogical changes. Each chapter now begins with a photograph that connects with an example that begins the chapter, making the presentation more visually appealing to students. I changed the names of boxed features to "A Reminder," "Added Dimension" and "Real-World Application" to more closely match their content. I also added learning objectives to questions, and identified some of the more challenging questions as "difficult." Overall, it is a substantial revision that I believe will make the book more teachable to a broader group of students.

Changes by Chapter[1]

Intro Chapters

- **Chapter 1 (Economics and Economic Reasoning):** I added an example of economic reasoning from Steven Levitt's book, *Freakonomics*, and a box on the costs and benefits of addressing or not addressing global warming.

- **Chapter 2 (The Production Possibility Model, Trade, and Globalization):** I reorganized the presentations in Chapters 2 and 3 so that Chapter 2 focuses more on trade and international issues and Chapter 3 focuses on institutions. Specifically, the role of government in the economy is moved from Chapter 2 to Chapter 3, and the discussion of globalization is moved from Chapter 3 to Chapter 2. I also deleted the box "Dealing with Math Anxiety" and added a new box on insourcing.

- **Chapter 3 (Economic Institutions):** This chapter was reorganized to focus more on economic institutions. The discussion of the roles of government that was previously in Chapter 2 was moved here, and the globalization discussion that was here was moved to Chapter 2. I updated the discussion of socialism to include a discussion of Hugo Chavez's "21st century socialism." I deleted a number of boxes and made the chapter shorter.

- **Chapter 4 (Supply and Demand):** I replaced the example that illustrates a shift in supply versus a movement along the supply curve with an example from Hurricane Katrina in 2005. I moved the discussion of what equilibrium isn't after the discussion of excess supply and excess demand.

- **Chapter 5 (Using Supply and Demand):** I shortened the initial presentation so that the chapter now begins with three real-world examples, two of which are new to this edition. I deleted the discussion of the market for advertising and moved the presentation of the exchange rate market to later in the chapter.

Macro Chapters

- **Chapter 6 (Economic Growth, Business Cycles, Unemployment, and Inflation):** I reorganized the chapter and added discussions of global warming

---

[1]A more in-depth discussion of the changes can be found on the professor's portion of the book's Web site (www.mhhe.com/economics/colander7e).

and of the distinction between real and nominal interest rates.

- **Chapter 7 (Measuring the Aggregate Economy):** I renamed and significantly simplified the chapter to provide a greater focus on the components of aggregate income and production without getting bogged down in the details of the technical relationship between the two. The chapter is shorter and much simpler.

- **Chapter 8 (Growth, Productivity, and the Wealth of Nations):** I deleted much of the discussion of government policies to promote growth in order to shorten the chapter and make it more focused. I moved the discussion of micro credit and the Grameen Bank to a box. I added a discussion of the importance of the loanable funds market in translating saving into investment.

- **Chapter 9 (The Aggregate Demand/Aggregate Supply Model):** I combined the graphs in the discussion of equilibrium in the *AS/AD* model, so that the text discussion is closer to the graphs. I also shortened the box discussing why prices are inflexible.

- **Chapter 10 (The Multiplier Model):** I incorporated the contents of the box about using taxes instead of government expenditures as a way to shift the *AE* curve into the text. I also added a table to Figure 10-5 to make the presentation clearer.

- **Chapter 11 (The Financial Sector and the Demand for Money):** I added a discussion of the determination of the long-term and short-term interest rates as a prelude to the addition of the yield curve in Chapter 12. I deleted boxes, redesigned tables, and eliminated the term approximate real-world money multiplier. I cut the section on regulation of banks.

- **Chapter 12 (Monetary Policy):** I reorganized the chapter to concentrate on monetary policy. I revised the chapter to reflect the reality that (1) monetary policy today is executed primarily through open market operations and (2) the focus of monetary policy is on the short-term interest rate. I added a discussion of the yield curve and possible limits to the Fed's ability to control the economy. I added a new box on central bank independence.

- **Chapter 13 (Inflation and the Phillips Curve):** I tightened up the discussion of inflation, money, and the Phillips curve. I shortened the discussions of different schools' views of inflation, and added a discussion of fighting inflation with reference to the *AS/AD* model. I modified and deleted a number of boxes and added a box on inflation targeting.

- **Chapter 14 (Fiscal Policy and Public Finance):** I reworked this chapter significantly so that it focuses on economists' changing views of the efficacy of fiscal policy over time. It now includes an in-depth discussion of the Ricardian equivalence theorem that ties together early Classical views of fiscal policy with modern New Classical views. This chapter now provides students with an overview of economists' approach to fiscal policy from the Classical approach to the modern dynamic stochastic general equilibrium approach.

- **Chapter 15 (Politics, Deficits, and Debt):** I provided an additional example of calculating the passive deficit, added a box on Social Security and the deficit, and used the *AS/AD* model to illustrate the real problem that aging baby boomers pose for the economy.

- **Chapter 16 (International Trade Policy, Comparative Advantage, and Outsourcing):** I changed the learning objectives to better fit the discussion, and added a discussion of the Doha round of WTO trade negotiations.

- **Chapter 17 (International Financial Policy):** I updated the chapter and added a box on Iceland's struggle to slow inflation.

- **Chapter 18 (Macro Policy in a Global Setting):** I updated data and examples.

- **Chapter 19 (Macro Policies in Developing Countries):** I updated the chapter and added a box on the Doha Round and the Millennium Development Goals.

A Final Comment

A number of my friends keep asking me why I spend so much thought and time on what goes into the book. The answer is that I care about teaching economic ideas, which I think is the most important job that society has assigned to academic economists. Research is nice, but good teaching is priceless, and if the writing and the ideas in this book contribute to good teaching, then I'm happy. As I get older, I find that I'm happier with less grandiose goals, and to have turned a few students on to economics seems like a worthwhile legacy.

Ancillaries

McGraw-Hill has established a strong history of top-rate supplements to accompany this book, and this seventh edition strives to carry on the tradition of excellence.

Study Guide

The study guide—written by myself, Doug Copeland, and Jenifer Gamber—provides a review of the concepts from each chapter. It gives students options to match a variety of learning styles: short-answer questions, matching terms with definitions, problems and applications, multiple-choice questions, brainteasers, and potential essay questions. To make the guide a true study tool, each answer includes an explanation of why it is correct. In addition, the answers to the even-numbered end-of-chapter questions can be found in the study guide (as well as on the book's Web site).

Instructor's Manual

This book boasts one of the strongest Instructor's Manuals on the market, and Keith Jakee of Florida Atlantic University has worked incredibly hard to maintain the high standard set in previous editions. Elements include

- Chapter Overview, which provides a quick review of each chapter.
- What's New, which helps instructors modify established lecture notes from edition to edition.
- Lecture Modules, which provide bite-sized lecture modules by learning objective for quick reference to key concepts and graphs in each chapter for lectures.
- Addressing Common Areas of Difficulty in the Classroom, which reviews areas students often find difficult in the chapter and sometimes provides an additional classroom exercise for more practice.
- Real-World Applications, which provide contemporary, real-world economic examples of chapter concepts.
- Student Problem Sets, which include five to eight short-answer and problem-type questions to be assigned for homework to help students prepare for the exam.

The Instructor's Manual also includes an essay about how to meet the unique challenges of teaching large classes. The Instructor's Manual is available in print, on the Instructor's Resource CD-ROM, and on the instructor's portion of the book's Web site, www.mhhe.com/colander7e.

Test Banks

Test Banks A and B contain about 4,000 unique questions for instructors to draw from in their classrooms—a great resource for all professors, and especially for departments with multiple sections. Robert Schenk of Saint Joseph's College of Indiana, James Wetzel of Virginia Commonwealth University, Karla Morgan of Whitworth College, and

Rimma Shiptsova of Utah State University–Logan worked diligently for months to make sure that this revised version is clear and useful. Each question is categorized by chapter learning objective, level of difficulty (easy, medium, hard), skill being tested (recall, comprehension, application), and type of question (word problem, calculation, graph). In addition, James Chasey has tagged the questions that are best suited for a high school Advanced Placement course for those using the book in AP sections.

Questions were reviewed by professors and students alike to make sure that each one was effective for classroom use, and each new question was reviewed by Jenifer Gamber for accuracy, clarity, and consistency with the textbook.

Test Bank C, revised by David Horlacher of Middlebury College, now consists of approximately 300 short-answer questions, essay questions, and graphical and mathematical problems. Questions vary in level of difficulty and type of skill being tested. Test Bank C is available in print and on the Instructor's Resource CD-ROM. Testbanks A, B, and C are available both in print form and in the EZ Test electronic test-generator on the Instructor's Resource CD-ROM.

McGraw-Hill's Homework Manager Plus™

McGraw-Hill's Homework Manager Plus is a complete, Web-based solution that includes and expands upon the actual problem sets found at the end of each chapter and features algorithmic technology that provides a limitless supply of online, self-graded assignments and graphing exercises, tied to the learning objectives in the book. McGraw-Hill's Homework Manager can be used for student practice, graded homework assignments, and formal examinations, all easily integrated with your course management system, including WebCT, Blackboard, and Desire2Learn.

McGraw-Hill's Homework Manager content can be delivered over the Web, automatically grading and storing results in a private grade book. Detailed results let you see at a glance how each student does on an assignment or an individual problem. This valuable feedback also helps you gauge how the class is performing overall.

For more information on this and other digital solutions, including Aplia, please contact your McGraw-Hill sales representative or Melissa Larmon at melissa_larmon@mcgraw-hill.com.

PowerPoint Presentations

Doris Bennett of Jacksonville State University has prepared an extensive slide program that includes all text exhibits and key concepts, as well as a narrated option to provide additional review. Each chapter has been scrutinized to ensure an accurate, direct connection to the textbook and concepts. This presentation is available on the Instructor's Resource CD-ROM and on the textbook's Web site.

Overhead Transparencies

We offer all key text exhibits in full-color acetate form for use with overhead projectors.

Classic Readings in Economics

This collection includes selections from the writings of economists such as Smith, Marx, Hayek, and Veblen, who have raised questions that changed the direction of economic thinking. This material is especially useful for courses that stress the importance of economic ideas.

Dollars and Sense Readers

While not directly an ancillary to the book, the *Dollars and Sense* readers are annotated to fit with chapters of this book for professors who want to supplement the text with a radical perspective. Contact your McGraw-Hill representative for more information.

Economics: An Honors Companion

The *Honors Companion* presents mathematical techniques that underlie numerous basic economic concepts. It presupposes a solid student background in algebra and geometry and some familiarity with basic calculus, thereby giving *Macroeconomics, Seventh Edition,* flexibility for use in more rigorous classes.

Package Pricing

To help lower costs of using ancillaries, McGraw-Hill has developed a variety of separate packages in which the book can be bought together with the ancillaries for a price that is close to the price of the book alone. Each of these packages has a separate ISBN number. For information on these packages, contact your McGraw-Hill sales representative, or Melissa Larmon at melissa_larmon@mcgraw-hill.com.

www.mhhe.com/economics/colander7e

The Online Learning Center to accompany Colander's seventh edition is a Web site full of exciting new content that follows the text chapter by chapter and provides a number of useful study tools:

- Learning Objectives provide an at-a-glance list of what concepts students need to master.
- Chapter Summaries give an overview of the chapter.
- Pretests help students assess areas for further study.
- Practice Exercises give students the opportunity to test what they have learned using fill-in-the-blank, short-answer, and graphing quesitons.
- Interactive graphs provide students with additional practice working with graphical material in the chapter.
- Post-tests help students know if they are ready for the exam.
- Flash cards can be flipped for quick recall of key terms.
- PowerPoint Presentations, now with narration, are another great way to review the chapter material.
- Web Notes bring the chapter alive. These are keyed to the Web Note symbol in the margin of the text.
- Web Questions provide active links for Web Questions in the text.

Web Note

Kit Taylor of Bellevue Community College has updated the Web Notes from the book; this feature extends the text discussion onto the Web. Web Notes are flagged in the margin and links are on the book's Web site. In addition, a *New York Times* Web feed presents students with economics-related news headlines.

On the book's Web site, instructors will find downloadable PowerPoints, the Instructor's Manual, Sample Syllabi, a link to Dave Colander's own Web site, and Help for AP courses by James Chasey. The entire Web site content also can be delivered through PageOut or within a course management system (i.e., WebCT, Desire2Learn, or Blackboard).

Assurance of Learning Ready

Many educational institutions today are focused on the notion of assurance of learning, an important element of some accreditation standards. *Macroeconomics, 7e* is designed specifically to support your assurance of learning initiatives with a simple, yet powerful, solution.

Each test bank question for *Macroeconomics, 7e* maps to a specific chapter learning outcome/objective listed in the text. You can use our test bank software, *EZ Test,* to easily query for learning outcomes/objectives that directly relate to the learning objectives for your course. You can then use the reporting features of *EZ Test* to aggregate student results in similar fashion, making the collection and presentation of assurance of learning data simple and easy.

AACSB Statement

McGraw-Hill Companies is a proud corporate member of AACSB International. Recognizing the importance and value of AACSB accreditation, the authors of *Macroeconomics, 7e* have sought to recognize the curricula guidelines detailed in AACSB standards for business accreditation by connecting selected questions in the *Macroeconomics, 7e* test bank to the general knowledge and skill guidelines found in the AACSB standards. While *Macroeconomics, 7e* and its teaching package make no claim of any specific AACSB qualification or evaluation, we have labeled selected questions according to the six general knowledge and skills areas. It is important to note that the statements contained in *Macroeconomics, 7e* are provided only as a guide for the users of this text.

People to Thank

Let me conclude this preface by thanking the hundreds of people who have offered suggestions, comments, kudos, and criticism on this project since its inception. This book would not be what it is without their input. So many people have contributed to this text in so many ways that I cannot thank everyone. So, to all the people who helped—many, many thanks.

I specifically want to thank the seventh edition reviewers, whose insightful comments kept me on track.

A. F. Alhajji
Ohio Northern University

Gerald Bialka
University of North Florida

Taggert T. Brooks
University of Wisconsin–La Crosse

M. Neil Browne
Bowling Green State University

Gregory DeFreitas
Hofstra University

James Frew
Williamette University

Shelby Frost
Georgia State University

Doris Geide-Stevenson
Weber State University

Kirk D. Gifford
Brigham Young University–Idaho

Julia Heath
University of Memphis

Jannett Highfill
Bradley University

Alexander Holmes
University of Oklahoma

Gail Hoyt
University of Kentucky

Scott Hunt
Columbus State Community College

Fadhel Kaboub
Drew University

Rodney Kingery
Hawkeye Community College

Andrew Kohen
James Madison University

Fred May
Trident Technical College

Karla Morgan
Whitworth College

Steve Pecsok
Middlebury College

Larry L. Ross
University of Alaska–Anchorage

Abdulhakeem Salaam
Park University

Garvin Smith
Daytona Beach Community College

Gokce Soydemir
University of Texas–Pan American

Carol O. Stivender
University of North Carolina–Charlotte

Travis K. Taylor
Christopher Newport University

Dale Thompson
University of St. Thomas

Deborah Thorsen
Palm Beach Community College

Don Uy-Barreta
De Anza College
University of California–Santa Cruz Extension

In addition to the comments of the formal reviewers listed above, I have received helpful suggestions, encouragement, and assistance from innumerable individuals via e-mails, letters, symposia, and focus groups. Their help made this edition even stronger than its predecessor. They include James Wetzel, Virginia Commonwealth University; Dmitry Shishkin, Georgia State University; Amy Cramer, Pima Community College–West; Andrea Terzi, Franklin College; Shelby Frost, Georgia State University; Doris Geide-Stevenson, Weber State University; James Chasey, Advanced Placement Economics Teaching Consultant and Homewood-Flossmoor High School (ret.), David Tufte, Southern Utah University; Eric Sarpong, Georgia State University; Jim Ciecka, DePaul University; Fran Bradley, George School; Ron Olive, University of Massachusetts–Lowell; and Rachel Kreier, Hofstra University.

I want to give a special thank you to the supplements authors. Jenifer Gamber expertly guided the ancillary team of Doris Bennett, Jacksonville State University; Robert Schenk, Saint Joseph's College of Indiana; James Wetzel, Virginia Commonwealth University; Rimma Shiptsova, Utah State University–Logan; Karla Morgan, Whitworth College; James Chasey, Advanced Placement Economics Teaching Consultant and Homewood-Flossmoor High School (ret.); Keith Jakee, Florida Atlantic University; Kit Taylor, Bellevue Community College; Doug Copeland, Johnson County Community College; and David Horlacher of Middlebury College. They did an outstanding job.

I'd also like to thank the economists who wrote the alternative perspective questions. These include Ann Mari May of the University of Nebraska–Lincoln, John Miller of Wheaton College, Dan Underwood of Peninsula College, Ric Holt of Southern Oregon University, and Bridget Butkevich of George Mason University. I enjoyed working with each of them, and while their views often differed substantially, they were all united in wanting questions that showed economics as a pluralist field that encourages students to question the text from all perspectives.

I have hired numerous students to check aspects of the book, to read over my questions and answers to questions, and to help proofread. These include Yan Min Choo, John Meyer, Zach Colander, Yunfei Ren, Hasat Cakkalkurt, Tom Brush, Dinesh Palhak, Tizzy Dominguez, Zhen Chen Wu, Yan Oak, Tugce Erten, Rachel Butera, Vijay Chowdhari, Eric Elderbrock, Elliott Fox, Catherine Horner, Saad Ahmed Khan, Kate Macfarlane, Andrew Matson, Allison Shanholt, and Yuki Yoshida. I thank them all.

A special thank-you for this edition goes to two people. The first is Jenifer Gamber, whose role in the book cannot be overestimated. She helped me clarify its vision by providing research, critiquing expositions and often improving them, guiding the ancillaries, and being a good friend. She has an amazing set of skills, and I thank her for using them to improve the book. The second is Karen Fisher, who came into this project as it was ongoing and with her hard work, dedication, and superb ability made it possible to get the book done on time, even during a period of turmoil. She and Jenifer are two amazing women.

Next, I want to thank the entire McGraw-Hill team, including Douglas Reiner, the executive editor; Susanne Riedell, the senior project manager; Cara David, the designer; Brian Nacik, the media project manager; Lynn Bluhm; the media producer; Carol Bielski, the production supervisor; and Melissa Larmon, the marketing manager. All of them have done a superb job, for which I thank them sincerely.

Finally, I want to thank Pat, my wife, and my sons, Kasey and Zach, for helping me keep my work in perspective, and for providing a loving environment in which to work.

Preface for the Student: Alternative Perspectives

This book is written for you, the student. It's meant to give you a sense of what economics is, how economists think, and how they approach policy problems. There's only so much that an introductory text can cover, which means that much is left out. That includes much of the subtlety of economic thinking. So if you have a problem swallowing some of the ideas, and you believe that there's more to the issue than is presented in the text, rest assured; generally you're right. Hard choices have to be made for pedagogical purposes—issues have to be simplified and presentations curtailed. Otherwise this would be a 1,200-page book and much too heavy to carry around in a backpack.

Economics as a Method of Reasoning, Not the Truth

This book is what would be called mainstream (it presents the conventional wisdom of economists) both because I'm mainstream and because most economists are as well. But pedagogically, I also believe that students learn by questioning—to say, no, that's not right, that's not the way I see things, and then to compare their way of thinking with the conventional way. Despite my being mainstream, I'm by nature also a skeptic, and in terms of pedagogy often find myself in sympathy with Joan Robinson, a famous economist, who argued that "the purpose of studying economics is not to acquire a set of ready-made answers to economic questions, but to learn how to avoid being deceived by economists." So, to encourage questioning everything, I don't present models and insights of economists as the truth (the field of economics is far too complicated to have arrived at a

single truth) but as a set of technical hurdles, reasoning processes, and arguments that students should know, and that will help prepare them to deal with economic issues. Economics primarily teaches you how to approach problems; it does not provide definitive answers about what is right and what is wrong. It is a method, not a set of truths.

Alternative Perspectives in Economics

One of the pedagogical choices I made in writing the book was to concentrate almost exclusively on the mainstream view. I strongly believe that focusing on that view is the best way to teach the course. However, I also believe that students should be aware of the diversity in economics and know that the mainstream view is not the only view out there. In fact, there are probably as many views out there as there are economists. Still, for a majority of economists, the concepts presented in this book are an acceptable pedagogical simplification of the myriad views held by economists.

Some economists, however, don't find aspects of what is presented in this text to be an acceptable simplification. They wouldn't necessarily say that the presentation is wrong; they are more likely to see it as misleading, or as diverting the discussion away from other, more relevant, issues. These economists are generally called nonmainstream or heterodox economists. A heterodox economist is *one who doesn't accept the basic underlying model used by a majority of economists as the most useful model for analyzing the economy.*

In this preface, I will briefly introduce six heterodox economic approaches to give you a sense of how their analyses differ from the mainstream analyses presented in this book. The six heterodox approaches are Austrian, Post-Keynesian, Institutionalist, Radical, feminist, and religious. Below are brief descriptions of each group, written with the help of the team of alternative-perspective economists.

Austrian Economists

Austrian economists believe in methodological individualism, by which they mean that social goals are best met through voluntary, mutually beneficial interactions. Lack of information and unsolvable incentive problems undermine the ability of government to plan, making the market the best method for coordinating economic activity. Austrian economists oppose state intrusion into private property and private activities. They are not all economists from Austria; rather, they are economists from anywhere who follow the ideas of Ludwig von Mises and Friedrich von Hayek, two economists who were from Austria.

Austrian economists are sometimes classified as conservative, but they are more appropriately classified as libertarians, who believe in liberty of individuals first and in other social goals second. Consistent with their views, they are often willing to support what are sometimes considered radical ideas, such as legalizing addictive drugs or eliminating our current monetary system—ideas that most mainstream economists would oppose. Austrian economists emphasize the uncertainty in the economy and the inability of a government controlled by self-interested politicians to undertake socially beneficial policy.

One proposal of Austrian economists will give you a flavor of their approach. That proposal is to eliminate the Federal Reserve System and to establish a free market in money—a policy that would leave people free to use any money they want and that would significantly reduce banking regulation. In a sense, their proposal carries the Classical argument in favor of laissez-faire to its logical conclusions. Why should the government have a monopoly of the money supply? Why shouldn't people be free to use whatever money they desire, denominated in whatever unit they want? Why don't we rely upon competition to prevent inflation? Why don't we have a free market in money? Well-known Austrian economists include Peter Boettke, Veronique de Rugy, Mario Rizzo, David Gordon, Israel Kirzner, Peter Leeson, Chris Coyne, Steve Horwitz, Roger Garrison and Roger Koppl.

Institutionalist Economists

Institutionalist economists argue that any economic analysis must involve specific considerations of institutions. The lineage of Institutionalist economics begins with the pioneering work of Thorstein Veblen, John R. Commons, and Wesley C. Mitchell. Veblen employed evolutionary analysis to explore the role of institutions in directing and retarding the economic process. He saw human behavior driven by cultural norms and conveyed the way in which they were with sardonic wit and penetrating insight, leaving us with enduring metaphors such as the leisure class and conspicuous consumption. Commons argued that institutions are social constructs that could improve general welfare. Accordingly, he established cooperative investigative programs to support pragmatic changes in the legal structure of government. Mitchell was a leader in developing economics as an empirical study; he was a keen observer of the business cycle and argued that theory must be informed by systematic attention to empirical data, or it was useless.

Contemporary Institutionalists employ the founders' "trilogy"—empirically informed evolutionary analysis directed toward pragmatic alteration of institutions shaping economic outcomes—in their policy approach. Examples include indicative planning—a macroeconomic policy in which the government sets up an overall plan for various industries and selectively directs credit to certain industries; and income support programs, including those assuring employment for all willing. Well-known Institutionalists include Greg Hayden, Geoff Hodgson, Anne Mayhew, James Peach, and Ronnie Phillips.

Radical Economists

Radical economists believe substantial equality-preferring institutional changes should be implemented in our economic system. Radical economists evolved out of Marxian economics. In their analysis, they focus on the lack of equity in our current economic system and on institutional changes that might bring about a more equitable system. Specifically, they see the current economic system as one in which a few people—capitalists and high-level managers—benefit enormously at the expense of many people who struggle to make ends meet in jobs that are unfulfilling or who even go without work at times. They see the fundamental instability and irrationality of the capitalist system at the root of a wide array of social ills that range from pervasive inequality to alienation, racism, sexism, and imperialism. Radical economists often use a class-oriented analysis to address these issues and are much more willing to talk about social conflict and tensions in our society than are mainstream economists.

A policy favored by many Radicals is the establishment of worker cooperatives to replace the corporation. Radicals argue that such worker cooperatives would see that the income of the firm is more equitably allocated. Likewise, Radical theorists endorse policies such as universal health care insurance that conform to the ethic of "putting people before profits."

There are a number of centers of Radical thought, including The Political Economy Research Institute, The New School for Social Research, and some campuses of the University of Massachusetts. A good place to find Radical views is the *Dollars & Sense* magazine. Well-known Radical economists include Lourdes Beneria, Sam Bowles, Arthur MacEwan, Robert Pollin, Gerald Epstein, Anwar Shaik, Michael Reich, Richard Wolff, and Stephen Resnick, as well as a number of feminist economists who would be considered both Radicals and feminists.

Feminist Economists

Feminist economics offers a substantive challenge to the content, scope, and methodology of mainstream economics. Feminist economists question the boundaries of what we consider economics to be and examine social arrangements surrounding provisioning. Feminist economists have many different views, but all believe that in some way traditional economic analysis misses many important issues pertaining to women.

Feminist economists study issues such as how the institutional structure tends to direct women into certain types of jobs (generally low-paying jobs) and away from other types of jobs (generally high-paying jobs). They draw our attention to the unpaid labor performed by women throughout the world and ask, "What would GDP look like if women's work were given a value and included?" They argue for an expansion in the content of economics to include "women as practitioners and as objects of study" and for the elimination of the masculine bias in mainstream economics. Is there such a bias? To see it, simply compare the relative number of women in your economics class to the relative number of women at your school. It is highly likely that your class has relatively more men. Feminist economists want you to ask why that is, and whether anything should be done about it.

The historical roots of feminist economics can be found in the work of such authors as Mary Wollstonecraft, John Stuart Mill, Harriet Taylor Mill, and Charlotte Perkins Gilman. Feminist economics has expanded significantly in the past 15 years and has emerged as an influential body of thought. Well-known feminist economists include Myra Strober, Diana Strassmann, Barbara Bergmann, Julie Nelson, Jane Humphries, Marianne Ferber, Randy Albelda, Nancy Folbre, and Heidi Hartmann.

Religious Economists

Religion is the oldest and, arguably, the most influential institution in the world—be it Christianity, Islam, Judaism, Buddhism, Hinduism, or any of the many other religions in the world. Modern science, of which economics is a part, emphasizes the rational elements of thought. It attempts to separate faith and normative issues from rational analysis in ways that some religiously oriented economists find questionable. The line between a religious and nonreligious economist is not hard and fast; all economists bring elements of their ethical considerations into their analysis. But those we call "religious economists" integrate the ethical and normative issues into economic analysis in more complex ways than the ways presented in the text.

Religiously oriented economists have a diversity of views; some believe that their views can be integrated reasonably well into standard economics, while others see the need for the development of a distinctive faith-based methodology that focuses on a particular group of normative concerns centered on issues such as human dignity and caring for the poor.

One religious perspective that is represented by a defined group in the U.S. economics profession is Christianity, and a number of Christian economists have joined together in the Association of Christian Economists (ACE). Its stated goal is "to encourage Christian scholars to explore and communicate the relationship between their faith and the discipline of economics, and to promote interaction and communication among Christian economists." Centers of ACE are Pepperdine University, Calvin College, and Gordon College. Leading Christian economists include Kurt Schaefer, Andrew Yuengert, and Stephen Smith.

Many of the religious alternative perspective questions that we provide in the text are from the Judeo-Christian perspective, the perspective most familiar to U.S. students. However, we intersperse some questions from other religious perspectives, both to show the similarity of views and to encourage students to think in a multicultural framework.

Post-Keynesian Economists

Post-Keynesian economists believe that uncertainty is a central issue in economics. They follow J. M. Keynes's approach more so than do mainstream economists in emphasizing institutional imperfections in the economy and the importance of fundamental uncertainty that rationality cannot deal with. They agree with Institutionalists that the study of economics must emphasize and incorporate the importance of social and political structure in determining market outcomes.

While their view about the importance of uncertainty is similar to the Austrian view, their policy response to that uncertainty is quite different. They do not see uncertainty as eliminating much of government's role in the economy; instead, they see it leading to policies in which government takes a larger role in guiding the economy.

One of their policy proposals that gives you a flavor of their approach is tax-based income policies—policies in which the government tries to directly affect the nominal wage- and price-setting institutions. Under a tax-based income policy, any firm raising its wage or price would be subject to a tax, and any firm lowering its wage or price would get a subsidy. Such a plan, they argue, would reduce the upward pressure on the nominal price level and reduce the rate of unemployment necessary to hold down inflation. Well-known Post-Keynesian economists include Paul Davidson, Jamie Galbraith, Barkley Rosser, John Cornwall, Shelia Dow, Malcolm Sawyer, Philip Arestis, Victoria Chick, Jan Kregel, and Geof Harcourt.

Consistency of the Various Approaches

A characteristic of almost all heterodox economists of all types is that their analyses tend to be less formal than mainstream analysis. *Less formal* doesn't mean better or worse. There are advantages and disadvantages to formality, but *less formal* does mean that there's more potential for ambiguity in interpretation. It's easy to say whether the logic in a formal model is right or wrong. It's much harder to say whether the logic in an informal model is right or wrong because it's often hard to see precisely what the logic is. The advantage of an informal model is that it can include many more variables and can be made more realistic, so you can discuss real-world problems more easily with that model. Nonmainstream economists often want to talk about the real world, which is why they use informal models.

Often, after I discuss the mainstream and heterodox approaches, some student asks which is right. I respond with a story told by a former colleague of mine, Abba Lerner:

> "But look," the rabbi's wife remonstrated, "when one party to the dispute presented their case to you, you said, 'You are quite right,' and then when the other party presented their case you again said, 'You are quite right.' Surely they cannot both be right?" To which the Rabbi answered, "My dear, you are quite right!"

The moral of the story is that there's nothing necessarily inconsistent among mainstream and heterodox economists' approaches. Their approaches are simply different ways of looking at the same event. Which approach is most useful depends on what issues and events you are analyzing. The class analysis used by Radicals is often more appropriate to developing countries than it is to the United States, and, in analyzing developing countries, many mainstream economists also include class fights in their approach. Similarly, Austrian analysis provides more insight into the role of the entrepreneur and individual in

the economy than does mainstream analysis, while Post-Keynesian and Institutionalist analyses are useful when considering major institutional changes.

The distinctions between heterodox and mainstream economists can be overdone. One economist may well fall into two or three different groupings and use a combination of various analyses.

I follow the work of heterodox economists carefully. Their writing is often more interesting than mainstream writing, which can often get rather technical and boring. But in this book, I present primarily mainstream views. I do that because that's what I see as the job of the principles of economics course. My goal, however, is to present those views to you, not to indoctrinate you with those views, and throughout the text I include some challenges to the standard views. At the end of each chapter, I also include some questions that challenge the view presented in the chapter. These questions are written by representatives of different heterodox groups. I also encourage you to look for these other views in your outside reading. The *Dollars and Sense* companion the book has Radical critiques and *Free Market*, an Austrian newsletter found at www.mises.org/freemarket.asp, has Austrian critiques. There are many other sources and Web sites for heterodox groups. Exploring these sites and learning about the many different views that are competing in the marketplace for ideas make your economics course more interesting.

A Concluding Thought

There are many ways to explore economics, and in your exploration, the textbook is only a map. You and your professor determine what you discuss and learn and what path you will take. Ultimately, that's the way it has to be. Most of you are in this course for the grade—college is a way of progressing up the ladder. That's how it was for me. But the process also can be transforming; it can change how you look at issues, how you think, and who you are. The economics courses I took were especially important in determining who I have become.

Much of the principles course is what I call hurdle jumping—calisthenics of the mind. It is a set of mind-strengthening exercises. Separately, each is not especially relevant, but combined, they help turn your weak cranial muscle into a strong muscle better able to handle the problems that life throws at you. So, do the work, even if it seems boring; follow your professor's reasoning, even if you don't agree with what he or she is arguing; and keep thinking. Read newspapers and try to apply the lessons, deciding when they apply and when they don't. But, in the process, be happy—enjoy the moment, because that moment will never be again.

BRIEF CONTENTS

CONTENTS

PART II

MACROECONOMICS

Section I
Macroeconomic Problems

Section II
The Macroeconomic Framework

8 Growth, Productivity, and the Wealth of Nations 176

9 The Aggregate Demand/Aggregate Supply Model 201

10 The Multiplier Model 227

Section III
Money, Inflation, and Monetary Policy

11 The Financial Sector and the Demand for Money 257

12 Monetary Policy 290

■ Contents ■

LIST OF BOXES

(continued)

A REMINDER

Introduction: Thinking Like an Economist

Part I is an introduction, and an introduction to an introduction seems a little funny. But other sections have introductions, so it seemed a little funny not to have an introduction to Part I; and besides, as you will see, I'm a little funny myself (which, in turn, has two interpretations; I'm sure you will decide which of the two is appropriate). It will, however, be a very brief introduction, consisting of questions you may have had and some answers to those questions.

Some Questions and Answers

Why study economics?
Because it's neat and interesting and helps provide insight into events that are constantly going on around you.

Why is this book so big?
Because there's a lot of important information in it and because the book is designed so your teacher can pick and choose. You'll likely not be required to read all of it, especially if you're on the quarter system. But once you start it, you'll probably read it all anyhow. (Would you believe?)

Why does this book cost so much?
To answer this question, you'll have to read the book.

Will this book make me rich?
No.

Will this book make me happy?
It depends.

This book doesn't seem to be written in a normal textbook style. Is this book really written by a professor?
Yes, but he is different. He misspent his youth working on cars; he married his high school sweetheart after they met again at their 20th high school reunion. Twenty-five years after graduating from high school, his wife went back to medical school and got her MD because she was tired of being

treated poorly by doctors. Their five kids make sure he doesn't get carried away in the professorial cloud.

Will the entire book be like this?
No, the introduction is just trying to rope you in. Much of the book will be hard going. Learning happens to be a difficult process: no pain, no gain. But the author isn't a sadist; he tries to make learning as pleasantly painful as possible.

What do the author's students think of him?
Weird, definitely weird—and hard. But fair, interesting, and sincerely interested in getting us to learn. (Answer written by his students.)

So there you have it. Answers to the questions that you might never have thought of if they hadn't been put in front of you. I hope they give you a sense of me and the approach I'll use in the book. There are some neat ideas in it. Let's now briefly consider what's in the first five chapters.

A Survey of the First Five Chapters

This first section is really an introduction to the rest of the book. It gives you the background necessary so that the later chapters make sense. Chapter 1 gives you an overview of the entire field of economics as well as an introduction to my style. Chapter 2 focuses on the production possibility curve, comparative advantage, and trade. It explains how trade increases production possibilities but also why, in the real world, free trade and no government regulation may not be the best policy. Chapter 3 gives you some history of economic systems and introduces you to the institutions of the U.S. economy. Chapters 4 and 5 introduce you to supply and demand, and show you not only the power of those two concepts but also the limitations.

Now let's get on with the show.

1 Economics and Economic Reasoning

AFTER READING THIS CHAPTER, YOU SHOULD BE ABLE TO:

1. Define economics and list three coordination problems that an economy must solve.
2. Explain how to make decisions by comparing marginal costs and marginal benefits.
3. Define opportunity cost and explain its relationship to economic reasoning.
4. Explain real-world events in terms of economic forces, social forces, and political forces.
5. Differentiate between microeconomics and macroeconomics.
6. Distinguish among positive economics, normative economics, and the art of economics.

When an artist looks at the world, he sees color. When a musician looks at the world, she hears music. When an economist looks at the world, she sees a symphony of costs and benefits. The economist's world might not be as colorful or as melodic as the others' worlds, but it's more practical. If you want to understand what's going on in the world that's really out there, you need to know economics.

I hardly have to convince you of this fact if you keep up with the news. Unemployment is down; the price of gas is up; interest rates are down; businesses are going bankrupt . . . The list is endless. So let's say you grant me that economics is important. That still doesn't mean that it's worth studying. The real question then is: How much will you learn? Most of what you learn depends on you, but part depends on the teacher and another part depends on the textbook. On both these counts, you're in luck; since your teacher chose this book for your course, you must have a super teacher.[1]

What Economics Is

Economics is *the study of how human beings coordinate their wants and desires, given the decision-making mechanisms, social customs, and political realities of the society.* One of the key words in the definition of the term "economics" is *coordination*.

---

[1] This book is written by a person, not a machine. That means that I have my quirks, my odd sense of humor, and my biases. All textbook writers do. Most textbooks have the quirks and eccentricities edited out so that all the books read and sound alike—professional but dull. I choose to sound like me—sometimes professional, sometimes playful, and sometimes stubborn. In my view, that makes the book more human and less dull. So forgive me my quirks—don't always take me too seriously—and I'll try to keep you awake when you're reading this book at 3 a.m. the day of the exam. If you think it's a killer to read a book this long, you ought to try writing one.

Coordination can mean many things. In the study of economics, coordination refers to how the three central problems facing any economy are solved. These central problems are

1. What, and how much, to produce.
2. How to produce it.
3. For whom to produce it.

How hard is it to make the three decisions? Imagine for a moment the problem of living in a family: the fights, arguments, and questions that come up. "Do I have to do the dishes?" "Why can't I have piano lessons?" "Bobby got a new sweater. How come I didn't?" "Mom likes you best." Now multiply the size of the family by millions. The same fights, the same arguments, the same questions—only for society the questions are millions of times more complicated. In answering these questions, economies find that inevitably individuals want more than is available, given how much they're willing to work. That means that in our economy there is a problem of **scarcity**—*the goods available are too few to satisfy individuals' desires.*

Scarcity has two elements: our wants and our means of fulfilling those wants. These can be interrelated since wants are changeable and partially determined by society. The way we fulfill wants can affect those wants. For example, if you work on Wall Street, you will probably want upscale and trendy clothes. Up here in Vermont, I am quite happy wearing Levi's and flannel.

The degree of scarcity is constantly changing. The quantity of goods, services, and usable resources depends on technology and human action, which underlie production. Individuals' imagination, innovativeness, and willingness to do what needs to be done can greatly increase available goods and resources. Who knows what technologies are in our future—nannites or micromachines that change atoms into whatever we want could conceivably eliminate scarcity of goods we currently consume. But they would not eliminate scarcity entirely since new wants are constantly developing.

So, how does an economy deal with scarcity? The answer is coercion. In all known economies, coordination has involved some type of coercion—limiting people's wants and increasing the amount of work individuals are willing to do to fulfill those wants. The reality is that many people would rather play than help solve society's problems. So the basic economic problem involves inspiring people to do things that other people want them to do, and not to do things that other people don't want them to do. Thus, an alternative definition of economics is that it is the study of how to get people to do things they're not wild about doing (such as studying) and not to do things they are wild about doing (such as eating all the lobster they like), so that the things some people want to do are consistent with the things other people want to do.

A Guide to Economic Reasoning

People trained in economics think in a certain way. They analyze everything critically; they compare the costs and the benefits of every issue and make decisions based on those costs and benefits. For example, say you're trying to decide whether a policy to eliminate terrorist attacks on airlines is a good idea. Economists are trained to put their emotions aside and ask: What are the costs of the policy, and what are the benefits? Thus, they are open to the argument that security measures, such as conducting body searches of every passenger or scanning all baggage with bomb-detecting machinery, might not be the appropriate policy because the costs might exceed the benefits. To think like an economist involves addressing almost all issues using a cost/benefit approach. Economic reasoning also involves abstracting from the "unimportant" elements of a question and focusing on the "important" ones by creating a simple

Three central coordination problems any economy must solve are what to produce, how to produce it, and for whom to produce it.

The coordination questions faced by society are complicated.

The quantity of goods, services, and usable resources depends on technology and human action.

Economic reasoning is making decisions on the basis of costs and benefits.

model that captures the essence of the issue or problem. How do you know whether the model has captured the important elements? By collecting empirical evidence and "testing" the model—matching the predictions of the model with the empirical evidence—to see if it fits. Economic reasoning—how to think like an economist, making decisions on the basis of costs and benefits—is the most important lesson you'll learn from this book.

The book *Freakonomics* gives examples of the economist's approach. It describes a number of studies by University of Chicago economist Steve Levitt that unlock seemingly mysterious observations with basic economic reasoning. For example, Levitt asks the question: Why do drug dealers on the street tend to live with their mothers? The answer he arrives at is that it is because they can't afford to live on their own; most earn less than $5 an hour. Why, then, are they dealing drugs and not working a legal job that, even for a minimum-wage job, pays over $6.00 an hour? The answer to that is determined through cost/benefit analysis. While their current income is low, their potential income as a drug dealer is much higher since, given their background and current U.S. institutions, they are more likely to move up to a high position in the local drug business (and *Freakonomics* describes how it is a business) and earn a six-figure income than they are to move up from working as a Taco Bell technician to an executive earning a six-figure income in corporate America. Levitt's model is a very simple one—people do what is in their best interest financially—and it assumes that people rely on a cost/benefit analysis to make decisions. Finally, he supports his argument through careful empirical work, collecting and organizing the data to see if they fit the model. His work is a good example of "thinking like an economist" in action.

Economic reasoning, once learned, is infectious. If you're susceptible, being exposed to it will change your life. It will influence your analysis of everything, including issues normally considered outside the scope of economics. For example, you will likely use economic reasoning to decide the possibility of getting a date for Saturday night, and who will pay for dinner. You will likely use it to decide whether to read this book, whether to attend class, whom to marry, and what kind of work to go into after you graduate. This is not to say that economic reasoning will provide all the answers. As you will see throughout this book, real-world questions are inevitably complicated, and economic reasoning simply provides a framework within which to approach a question. In the economic way of thinking, every choice has costs and benefits, and decisions are made by comparing them.

Marginal Costs and Marginal Benefits

The relevant costs and relevant benefits to economic reasoning are the expected *incremental*, or additional, costs incurred and the expected *incremental* benefits that result from a decision. Economists use the term *marginal* when referring to additional or incremental. Marginal costs and marginal benefits are key concepts.

Web Note 1.1
Costs and Benefits

A **marginal cost** is *the additional cost to you over and above the costs you have already incurred*. That means not counting **sunk costs**—*costs that have already been incurred and cannot be recovered*—in the relevant costs when making a decision. Consider, for example, attending class. You've already paid your tuition; it is a sunk cost. So the marginal (or additional) cost of going to class does not include tuition.

Similarly with marginal benefit. A **marginal benefit** is *the additional benefit above what you've already derived*. The marginal benefit of reading this chapter is the *additional* knowledge you get from reading it. If you already knew everything in this chapter before you picked up the book, the marginal benefit of reading it now is zero. The marginal benefit is not zero if by reading the chapter you learn that you are prepared for class; before, you might only have suspected you were prepared.

Marginal Cost and Marginal Benefit

Economic Knowledge in One Sentence: TANSTAAFL

Once upon a time, Tanstaafl was made king of all the lands. His first act was to call his economic advisers and tell them to write up all the economic knowledge the society possessed. After years of work, they presented their monumental effort: 25 volumes, each about 400 pages long. But in the interim, King Tanstaafl had become a very busy man, what with running a kingdom of all the lands and all. Looking at the lengthy volumes, he told his advisers to summarize their findings in one volume.

Despondently, the economists returned to their desks, wondering how they could summarize what they'd been so careful to spell out. After many more years of rewriting, they were finally satisfied with their one-volume effort, and tried to make an appointment to see the king. Unfortunately, affairs of state had become even more pressing than before, and the king couldn't take the time to see them. Instead he sent word to them that he couldn't be bothered with a whole volume, and ordered them, under threat of death (for he had become a tyrant), to reduce the work to one sentence.

The economists returned to their desks, shivering in their sandals and pondering their impossible task. Thinking about their fate if they were not successful, they decided to send out for one last meal. Unfortunately, when they were collecting money to pay for the meal, they discovered they were broke. The disgusted delivery man took the last meal back to the restaurant, and the economists started down the path to the beheading station. On the way, the delivery man's parting words echoed in their ears. They looked at each other and suddenly they realized the truth. "We're saved!" they screamed. "That's it! That's economic knowledge in one sentence!" They wrote the sentence down and presented it to the king, who thereafter fully understood all economic problems. (He also gave them a good meal.) The sentence?

There **A**in't **N**o **S**uch **T**hing **A**s **A** **F**ree **L**unch—
TANSTAAFL

Comparing marginal (additional) costs with marginal (additional) benefits will often tell you how you should adjust your activities to be as well off as possible. Just follow the **economic decision rule:**

If the marginal benefits of doing something exceed the marginal costs, do it.

If the marginal costs of doing something exceed the marginal benefits, don't do it.

As an example, let's consider a discussion I might have with a student who tells me that she is too busy to attend my classes. I respond, "Think about the tuition you've spent for this class—it works out to about $40 a lecture." She answers that the book she reads for class is a book that I wrote, and that I wrote it so clearly she fully understands everything. She goes on:

> I've already paid the tuition and whether I go to class or not, I can't get any of the tuition back, so the tuition is a sunk cost and doesn't enter into my decision. The marginal cost to me is what I could be doing with the hour instead of spending it in class. I value my time at $75 an hour [people who understand everything value their time highly], and even though I've heard that your lectures are super, I estimate that the marginal benefit of your class is only $50. The marginal cost, $75, exceeds the marginal benefit, $50, so I don't attend class.

I congratulate her on her diplomacy and her economic reasoning, but tell her that I give a quiz every week, that students who miss a quiz fail the quiz, that those who fail all the quizzes fail the course, and that those who fail the course do not graduate. In short, she is underestimating the marginal benefits of attending my classes. Correctly estimated, the marginal benefits of attending my class exceed the marginal costs. So she should attend my class.

If the marginal benefits of doing something exceed the marginal costs, do it. If the marginal costs of doing something exceed the marginal benefits, don't do it.

Q-1 Say you bought a share of Sun Microsystems for $100 and a share of Cisco for $10. The price of each is currently $15. Assuming taxes are not an issue, which would you sell if you need $15?

Economics and Passion

Recognizing that everything has a cost is reasonable, but it's a reasonableness that many people don't like. It takes some of the passion out of life. It leads you to consider possibilities like these:

Economic reasoning is based on the premise that everything has a cost.

- Saving some people's lives with liver transplants might not be worth the additional cost. The money might be better spent on nutritional programs that would save 20 lives for every 2 lives you might save with transplants.

- Maybe we shouldn't try to eliminate all pollution, because the additional cost of doing so may be too high. To eliminate all pollution might be to forgo too much of some other worthwhile activity.

- Providing a guaranteed job for every person who wants one might not be a worthwhile policy goal if it means that doing so will reduce the ability of an economy to adapt to new technologies.

- It might make sense for the automobile industry to save $12 per car by not installing a safety device, even though without the safety device some people will be killed.

You get the idea. This kind of reasonableness is often criticized for being cold-hearted. But, not surprisingly, economists disagree; they argue that their reasoning leads to a better society for the majority of people.

Q-2 Can you think of a reason why a cost/benefit approach to a problem might be inappropriate? Can you give an example?

Economists' reasonableness isn't universally appreciated. Businesses love the result; others aren't so sure, as I discovered some years back when my then-girlfriend told me she was leaving me. "Why?" I asked. "Because," she responded, "you're so, so . . . reasonable." It took me many years after she left to learn what she already knew: There are many types of reasonableness, and not everyone thinks an economist's reasonableness is a virtue. I'll discuss such issues later; for now, let me simply warn you that, for better or worse, studying economics will lead you to view questions in a cost/benefit framework.

Opportunity Cost

Putting economists' cost/benefit rules into practice isn't easy. To do so, you have to be able to choose and measure the costs and benefits correctly. Economists have devised the concept of opportunity cost to help you do that. **Opportunity cost** is *the benefit that you might have gained from choosing the next-best alternative*. To obtain the benefit of something, you must give up (forgo) something else—namely, the next-best alternative. The opportunity cost is the value of that next-best alternative; that is a cost because in choosing one thing, you are precluding an alternative choice. The TANSTAAFL story in the box embodies the opportunity cost concept because it tells us that there is a cost to everything; that cost is the next-best forgone alternative.

Opportunity cost is the basis of cost/benefit economic reasoning; it is the benefit that you might have gained from choosing the next-best alternative.

Opportunity Cost

Let's consider some examples. The opportunity cost of going out once with Natalie (or Nathaniel), the most beautiful woman (attractive man) in the world, is the benefit you'd get from going out with your solid steady, Margo (Mike). The opportunity cost of cleaning up the environment might be a reduction in the money available to assist low-income individuals. The opportunity cost of having a child might be two boats, three cars, and a two-week vacation each year for five years, which are what you could have had if you hadn't had the child. (Kids really are this expensive.)

Examples are endless, but let's consider two that are particularly relevant to you: what courses to take and how much to study. Let's say you're a full-time student and at the beginning of the term you had to choose five courses. Taking one precludes taking some other, and the opportunity cost of taking an economics course may well be not taking a course on theater. Similarly with studying: You have a limited amount of time to spend studying economics, studying some other subject, sleeping, or partying. The more time you spend on one activity, the less time you have for another. That's opportunity cost.

Notice how neatly the opportunity cost concept takes into account costs and benefits of all other options, and converts these alternative benefits into costs of the decision you're now making.

The relevance of opportunity cost isn't limited to your individual decisions. Opportunity costs are also relevant to government's decisions, which affect everyone in society. A common example is what is called the guns-versus-butter debate. The resources that a society has are limited; therefore, its decision to use those resources to have more guns (more weapons) means that it will have less butter (fewer consumer goods). Thus, when society decides to spend $50 billion more on an improved health care system, the opportunity cost of that decision is $50 billion not spent on helping the homeless, paying off some of the national debt, or providing for national defense.

Opportunity costs have always made choice difficult, as we see in the early-19th-century engraving, "One or the Other."

The opportunity cost concept has endless implications. It can even be turned upon itself. For instance, it takes time to think about alternatives; that means that there's a cost to being reasonable, so it's only reasonable to be somewhat unreasonable. If you followed that argument, you've caught the economic bug. If you didn't, don't worry. Just remember the opportunity cost concept for now; I'll infect you with economic thinking in the rest of the book.

Economic and Market Forces

The opportunity cost concept applies to all aspects of life and is fundamental to understanding how society reacts to scarcity. When goods are scarce, those goods must be rationed. That is, a mechanism must be chosen to determine who gets what.

Let's consider some specific real-world rationing mechanisms. Dormitory rooms are often rationed by lottery, and permission to register in popular classes is often rationed by a first-come, first-registered rule. Food in the United States, however, is generally rationed by price. If price did not ration food, there wouldn't be enough food to go around. All scarce goods must be rationed in some fashion. These rationing mechanisms are examples of **economic forces,** *the necessary reactions to scarcity.*

One of the important choices that a society must make is whether to allow these economic forces to operate freely and openly or to try to rein them in. A **market force** is *an economic force that is given relatively free rein by society to work through the market.* Market forces ration by changing prices. When there's a shortage, the price goes up. When there's a surplus, the price goes down. Much of this book will be devoted to analyzing how the market works like an invisible hand, guiding economic forces to coordinate individual actions and allocate scarce resources. The **invisible hand** is *the price mechanism, the rise and fall of prices that guides our actions in a market.*

Societies can't choose whether or not to allow economic forces to operate—economic forces are always operating. However, societies can choose whether to allow market forces to predominate. Social, cultural, and political forces play a major role in deciding whether to let market forces operate. Economic reality is determined by a contest among these various forces.

Q.3 John, your study partner, has just said that the opportunity cost of studying this chapter is about 1/34 the price you paid for this book, since the chapter is about 1/34 of the book. Is he right? Why or why not?

Q.4 Ali, your study partner, states that rationing health care is immoral—that health care should be freely available to all individuals in society. How would you respond?

When an economic force operates through the market, it becomes a market force.

Economic reality is controlled by three forces:

1. Economic forces (the invisible hand).
2. Social and cultural forces.
3. Political and legal forces.

Economics in Perspective

All too often, students study economics out of context. They're presented with sterile analysis and boring facts to memorize, and are never shown how economics fits into the larger scheme of things. That's bad; it makes economics seem boring—but economics is not boring. Every so often throughout this book, sometimes in the appendixes and sometimes in these boxes, I'll step back and put the analysis in perspective, giving you an idea from whence the analysis sprang and its historical context. In educational jargon, this is called *enrichment*.

I begin here with economics itself.

First, its history: In the 1500s there were few universities. Those that existed taught religion, Latin, Greek, philosophy, history, and mathematics. No economics. Then came the *Enlightenment* (about 1700), in which reasoning replaced God as the explanation of why things were the way they were. Pre-Enlightenment thinkers would answer the question "Why am I poor?" with "Because God wills it." Enlightenment scholars looked for a different explanation. "Because of the nature of land ownership" is one answer they found.

Such reasoned explanations required more knowledge of the way things were, and the amount of information expanded so rapidly that it had to be divided or categorized for an individual to have hope of knowing a subject. Soon philosophy was subdivided into science and philosophy. In the 1700s, the sciences were split into natural sciences and social sciences. The amount of knowledge kept increasing, and in the late 1800s and early 1900s social science itself split into subdivisions: economics, political science, history, geography, sociology, anthropology, and psychology. Many of the insights about how the economic system worked were codified in Adam Smith's *The Wealth of Nations*, written in 1776. Notice that this is before economics as a subdiscipline developed, and Adam Smith could also be classified as an anthropologist, a sociologist, a political scientist, and a social philosopher.

Throughout the 18th and 19th centuries, economists such as Adam Smith, Thomas Malthus, John Stuart Mill, David Ricardo, and Karl Marx were more than economists; they were social philosophers who covered all aspects of social science. These writers were subsequently called *classical economists*. Alfred Marshall continued in that classical tradition, and his book, *Principles of Economics,* published in the late 1800s, was written with the other social sciences much in evidence. But Marshall also changed the questions economists ask; he focused on those questions that could be asked in a graphical supply/demand framework.

This book falls solidly in the Marshallian tradition. It sees economics as a way of thinking—as an engine of analysis used to understand real-world phenomena.

Marshallian economics is primarily about policy, not theory. It sees institutions as well as political and social dimensions of reality as important, and it shows you how economics ties in to those dimensions.

Social, cultural, and political forces can play a significant role in the economy.

Q.5 Your study partner, Joan, states that market forces are always operative. Is she right? Why or why not?

Let's consider an example in which social forces prevent an economic force from becoming a market force: the problem of getting a date for Saturday night. If a school (or a society) has significantly more people of one gender than the other (let's say more men than women), some men may well find themselves without a date—that is, men will be in excess supply—and will have to find something else to do, say study or go to a movie by themselves. An "excess supply" person could solve the problem by paying someone to go out with him or her, but that would probably change the nature of the date in unacceptable ways. It would be revolting to the person who offered payment and to the person who was offered payment. That unacceptability is an example of the complex social and cultural norms that guide and limit our activities. People don't try to buy dates because social forces prevent them from doing so.

Now let's consider another example in which political and legal influences stop economic forces from becoming market forces. Say you decide that you can make some money delivering mail in your neighborhood. You try to establish a small business, but suddenly you are confronted with the law. The U.S. Postal Service has a legal exclusive right to deliver regular mail, so you'll be prohibited from delivering regular mail in competition with the post office. Economic forces—the desire to make money—led you to want to enter the business, but in this case political forces squash the invisible hand.

Often political and social forces work together against the invisible hand. For example, in the United States there aren't enough babies to satisfy all the couples who desire them. Babies born to particular sets of parents are rationed—by luck. Consider a group of parents, all of whom want babies. Those who can, have a baby; those who can't have one, but want one, try to adopt. Adoption agencies ration the available babies. Who gets a baby depends on whom people know at the adoption agency and on the desires of the birth mother, who can often specify the socioeconomic background (and many other characteristics) of the family in which she wants her baby to grow up. That's the economic force in action; it gives more power to the supplier of something that's in short supply.

If our society allowed individuals to buy and sell babies, that economic force would be translated into a market force. The invisible hand would see to it that the quantity of babies supplied would equal the quantity of babies demanded at some price. The market, not the adoption agencies, would do the rationing.[2]

Most people, including me, find the idea of selling babies repugnant. But why? It's the strength of social forces reinforced by political forces.

What is and isn't allowable differs from one society to another. For example, in Cuba and North Korea, many private businesses are against the law, so not many people start their own businesses. In the United States, until the 1970s, it was against the law to hold gold except in jewelry and for certain limited uses such as dental supplies, so most people refrained from holding gold. Ultimately a country's laws and social norms determine whether the invisible hand will be allowed to work.

Social and political forces are active in all parts of your life. You don't practice medicine without a license; you don't sell body parts or certain addictive drugs. These actions are against the law. But many people do sell alcohol; that's not against the law if you have a permit. You don't charge your friends interest to borrow money (you'd lose friends); you don't charge your children for their food (parents are supposed to feed their children); many sports and media stars don't sell their autographs (some do, but many consider the practice tacky); you don't lower the wage you'll accept in order to take a job away from someone else (you're no scab). The list is long. You cannot understand economics without understanding the limitations that political and social forces place on economic actions.

In summary, what happens in a society can be seen as the reaction to, and interaction of, these three forces: economic forces, political and legal forces, and social and historical forces. Economics has a role to play in sociology, history, and politics, just as sociology, history, and politics have roles to play in economics.

Economic Terminology

Economic terminology needs little discussion. It simply needs learning. As terms come up, you'll begin to recognize them. Soon you'll begin to understand them, and finally you'll begin to feel comfortable using them. In this book, I'm trying to describe how economics works in the real world, so I introduce you to many of the terms that occur in business and in discussions of the economy. Whenever possible I'll integrate the introduction of new terms into the discussion so that learning them will seem painless. In fact I've already introduced you to a number of economic terms: *opportunity cost, the invisible hand, market*

Economic forces are always operative; society may allow market forces to operate.

Web Note 1.2
Society and Markets

What happens in society can be seen as a reaction to, and interaction of, economic forces, political forces, social forces, and historical forces.

---

[2]Even though it's against the law, some babies are nonetheless "sold" on a semilegal market, also called a gray market. At the turn of the century, the "market price" for a healthy baby was about $30,000. If it were legal to sell babies (and if people didn't find it morally repugnant to have babies in order to sell them), the price would be much lower, because there would be a larger supply of babies. (It was not against the law to sell human eggs in the early 2000s, and one human egg was sold for $50,000. The average price was much lower; it varied with donor characteristics such as SAT scores and athletic accomplishments.)

forces, economic forces, just to name a few. By the end of the book, I'll have introduced you to hundreds more.

Economic Insights

Economists have thought about the economy for a long time, so it's not surprising that they've developed some insights into the way it works.

These insights are often based on generalizations, called theories, about the workings of an abstract economy. Theories tie together economists' terminology and knowledge about economic institutions. Theories are inevitably too abstract to apply in specific cases, and thus a theory is often embodied in an **economic model**—*a framework that places the generalized insights of the theory in a more specific contextual setting*—or in an **economic principle**—*a commonly held economic insight stated as a law or general assumption.* To see the importance of principles, think back to when you learned to add. You didn't memorize the sum of 147 and 138; instead, you learned a principle of addition. The principle says that when adding 147 and 138, you first add $7 + 8$, which you memorized was 15. You write down the 5 and carry the 1, which you add to $4 + 3$ to get 8. Then add $1 + 1 = 2$. So the answer is 285. When you know just one principle, you know how to add millions of combinations of numbers.

Theories, models, and principles are empirically tested (as best one can) to ensure that they correspond to reality. Because economics is an observational, not a laboratory, science, economists cannot test their models with controlled experiments. Instead, economists must carefully observe the economy and try to figure out what is affecting what. To do so they look for natural experiments, where something has changed in one place but has not changed somewhere else and compare the results in the two cases. An example of a natural experiment was when New Jersey raised its minimum wage and neighboring state Pennsylvania did not. But even in cases where there is a natural experiment, it is impossible to hold "other things constant," as is done in laboratory experiments, and thus the empirical results in economics are often subject to dispute.

While economic models and principles are less general than theories, they are still usually too general to apply in specific cases. Theories, models, and principles must be combined with a knowledge of real-world economic institutions to arrive at specific policy recommendations.

> Theories, models, and principles must be combined with a knowledge of real-world economic institutions to arrive at specific policy recommendations.

The Invisible Hand Theory

Knowing a theory gives you insight into a wide variety of economic phenomena even though you don't know the particulars of each phenomenon. For example, much of economic theory deals with the *pricing mechanism* and how the market operates to coordinate *individuals' decisions.* Economists have come to the following insights:

When the quantity supplied is greater than the quantity demanded, price has a tendency to fall.

When the quantity demanded is greater than the quantity supplied, price has a tendency to rise.

Using these generalized insights, economists have developed a theory of markets that leads to the further insight that, under certain conditions, markets are efficient. That is, the market will coordinate individuals' decisions, allocating scarce resources to their best possible use. **Efficiency** means *achieving a goal as cheaply as possible.* Economists call this insight the **invisible hand theory**—*a market economy, through the price mechanism, will tend to allocate resources efficiently.*

Theories, and the models used to represent them, are enormously efficient methods of conveying information, but they're also necessarily abstract. They rely on simplifying

> **Q-6** There has been a superb growing season and the quantity of tomatoes supplied exceeds the quantity demanded. What is likely to happen to the price of tomatoes?

Winston Churchill and Lady Astor

There are many stories about Nancy Astor, the first woman elected to Britain's Parliament. A vivacious, fearless American woman, she married into the English aristocracy and, during the 1930s and 1940s, became a bright light on the English social and political scenes, which were already quite bright.

One story told about Lady Astor is that she and Winston Churchill, the unorthodox genius who had a long and distinguished political career and who was Britain's prime minister during World War II, were sitting in a pub having a theoretical discussion about morality. Churchill suggested that as a thought experiment Lady Astor ponder the following question: If a man were to promise her a huge amount of money—say a million pounds—for the privilege, would she sleep with him? Lady Astor did ponder the question for a while and finally

Lady Astor

answered, yes, she would, if the money were guaranteed. Churchill then asked her if she would sleep with him for five pounds. Her response was sharp: "Of course not. What do you think I am—a prostitute?" Churchill responded, "We have already established that fact; we are now simply negotiating about price."

One moral that economists might draw from this story is that economic incentives, if high enough, can have a powerful influence on behavior. But an equally important moral of the story is that noneconomic incentives also can be very strong. Why do most people feel it's wrong to sell sex for money, even if they might be willing to do so if the price were high enough? Keeping this second moral in mind will significantly increase your economic understanding of real-world events.

---

assumptions, and *if you don't know the assumptions, you don't know the theory*. The result of forgetting assumptions could be similar to what happens if you forget that you're supposed to add numbers in columns. Forgetting that, yet remembering all the steps, can lead to a wildly incorrect answer. For example,

$$
\begin{array}{r}
147 \\
+\ 138 \\
\hline
1{,}608
\end{array}
$$ is wrong.

Knowing the assumptions of theories and models allows you to progress beyond gut reaction and better understand the strengths and weaknesses of various economic theories and models. Let's consider a central economic assumption: the assumption that individuals behave rationally—that what they choose reflects what makes them happiest, given the constraints. If that assumption doesn't hold, the invisible hand theory doesn't hold.

Presenting the invisible hand theory in its full beauty is an important part of any economics course. Presenting the assumptions on which it is based and the limitations of the invisible hand is likewise an important part of the course. I'll do both throughout the book.

Economic Theory and Stories

Economic theory, and the models in which that theory is presented, often developed as a shorthand way of telling a story. These stories are important; they make the theory come alive and convey the insights that give economic theory its power. In this book I present plenty of theories and models, but they're accompanied by stories that provide the context that makes them relevant.

At times, because there are many new terms, discussing theories takes up much of the presentation time and becomes a bit oppressive. That's the nature of the beast. As

Theory is a shorthand way of telling a story.

Albert Einstein said, "Theories should be as simple as possible, but not more so." When a theory becomes oppressive, pause and think about the underlying story that the theory is meant to convey. That story should make sense and be concrete. If you can't translate the theory into a story, you don't understand the theory.

Microeconomics and Macroeconomics

Economic theory is divided into two parts: microeconomic theory and macroeconomic theory. Microeconomic theory considers economic reasoning from the viewpoint of individuals and firms and builds up to an analysis of the whole economy. **Microeconomics** is *the study of individual choice, and how that choice is influenced by economic forces.* Microeconomics studies such things as the pricing policies of firms, households' decisions on what to buy, and how markets allocate resources among alternative ends. Our discussion of opportunity cost was based on microeconomic theory. The invisible hand theory comes from microeconomics.

> Microeconomics is the study of how individual choice is influenced by economic forces.

As we build up from microeconomic analysis to an analysis of the entire economy, everything gets rather complicated. Many economists try to uncomplicate matters by taking a different approach—a macroeconomic approach—first looking at the aggregate, or whole, and then breaking it down into components. **Macroeconomics** is *the study of the economy as a whole.* It considers the problems of inflation, unemployment, business cycles, and growth. Macroeconomics focuses on aggregate relationships such as how household consumption is related to income and how government policies can affect growth.

> Macroeconomics is the study of the economy as a whole. It considers the problems of inflation, unemployment, business cycles, and growth.

Consider an analogy to the human body. A micro approach analyzes a person by looking first at each individual cell and then builds up. A macro approach starts with the person and then goes on to his or her components—arms, legs, fingernails, feelings, and so on. Put simply, microeconomics analyzes from the parts to the whole; macroeconomics analyzes from the whole to the parts.

Microeconomics and macroeconomics are very much interrelated. What happens in the economy as a whole is based on individual decisions, but individual decisions are made within an economy and can be understood only within that context. For example, whether a firm decides to expand production capacity will depend on what the owners expect will happen to the demand for their products. Those expectations are determined by macroeconomic conditions. Because microeconomics focuses on the individual and macroeconomics focuses on the whole economy, traditionally microeconomics and macroeconomics are taught separately, even though they are interrelated.

> **Q-7** Classify the following topics as macroeconomic or microeconomic:
>
> 1. The impact of a tax increase on aggregate output.
> 2. The relationship between two competing firms' pricing behavior.
> 3. A farmer's decision to plant soy or wheat.
> 4. The effect of trade on economic growth.

Economic Institutions

To know whether you can apply economic theory to reality, you must know about economic institutions—laws, common practices, and organizations in a society that affect the economy. Corporations, governments, and cultural norms are all examples of economic institutions. Many economic institutions have social, political, and religious dimensions. For example, your job often influences your social standing. In addition, many social institutions, such as the family, have economic functions. I include any institution that significantly affects economic decisions as an economic institution because you must understand that institution if you are to understand how the economy functions.

> To apply economic theory to reality, you've got to have a sense of economic institutions.

Economic institutions differ significantly among countries. For example, in Germany banks are allowed to own companies; in the United States they cannot. This helps explain why investment decisions are made differently in Germany as compared to the United States. Alternatively, in the Netherlands workers are highly unionized, while in the United States they are not. Unions in the Netherlands therefore have the power

Economists and Market Solutions

Economic reasoning is playing an increasing role in government policy. Consider the regulation of pollution. Pollution became a policy concern in the 1960s as books such as Rachel Carson's *Silent Spring* were published. In 1970, in response to concerns about the environment, the Clean Air Act was passed. It capped the amount of pollutants (such as sulfur dioxide, carbon monoxide, nitrogen dioxides, lead, and hydrocarbons) that firms could emit. This was a "command-and-control" approach to regulation, which brought about a reduction in pollution, but also brought about lots of complaints by firms that either found the limits costly to meet or couldn't afford to meet them and were forced to close.

Enter economists. They proposed an alternative approach, called cap-and-trade, that achieved the same overall reduction in pollution but at a lower overall cost. In the plan they proposed, government still set a pollution cap that firms had to meet, but it gave individual firms some flexibility. Firms that reduced emissions by less than the required limit could buy pollution permits from other firms that reduced their

emissions by more than their limit. The price of the permits would be determined in an "emissions permit market." Thus, firms that had a low cost of reducing pollution would have a strong incentive to reduce pollution by more than their limit in order to sell these permits, or rights to pollute, to firms that had a high cost of reducing pollution and therefore reduced their pollution by less than what was required. The net reduction was the same, but the reduction was achieved at a lower cost.

In 1990 Congress adopted economists' proposal and the Clean Air Act was amended to include tradable emissions permits. An active market in emissions permits developed and it is estimated that the tradable permit program has lowered the cost of reducing sulfur dioxide emissions by $1 billion a year. Economists used this same argument to promote an incentive-based solution to world pollution in an agreement among some countries to reduce world pollution known as the Kyoto Protocol. You can read more about the current state of tradable emissions at epa.gov/airmarkets.

---

to agree to keep wages lower in exchange for more jobs. This means that government policies to control inflation might differ in these two countries.

Economic institutions sometimes seem to operate in ways quite different than economic theory predicts. For example, economic theory says that prices are determined by supply and demand. However, businesses say that they set prices by rules of thumb—often by what are called cost-plus-markup rules. That is, a firm determines what its costs are, multiplies by 1.4 or 1.5, and the result is the price it sets. Economic theory says that supply and demand determine who's hired; experience suggests that hiring is often done on the basis of whom you know, not by market forces.

These apparent contradictions have two complementary explanations. First, economic theory abstracts from many issues. These issues may account for the differences. Second, there's no contradiction; economic principles often affect decisions from behind the scenes. For instance, supply and demand pressures determine what the price markup over cost will be. In all cases, however, to apply economic theory to reality—to gain the full value of economic insights—you've got to have a sense of economic institutions.

Economic Policy Options

Economic policies are *actions (or inaction) taken by government to influence economic actions*. The final goal of the course is to present the economic policy options facing our society today. For example, should the government restrict mergers between firms? Should it run a budget deficit? Should it do something about the international trade deficit? Should it decrease taxes?

I saved this discussion for last because there's no sense talking about policy options unless you know some economic terminology, some economic theory, and something about economic institutions. Once you know something about them, you're in a position to consider the policy options available for dealing with the economic problems our society faces.

Policies operate within institutions, but policies also can influence the institutions within which they operate. Let's consider an example: welfare policy and the institution of the two-parent family. In the 1960s, the United States developed a variety of policy initiatives designed to eliminate poverty. These initiatives provided income to single parents with children, and assumed that family structure would be unchanged by these policies. But family structure changed substantially, and, very likely, these policies played a role in increasing the number of single-parent families. The result was the programs failed to eliminate poverty. Now this is not to say that we should not have programs to eliminate poverty, nor that two-parent families are always preferable to one-parent families; it is only to say that we must build into our policies their effect on institutions.

Some policies are designed to change institutions directly. While these policies are much more difficult to implement than policies that don't, they also offer the largest potential for gain. Let's consider an example. In the 1990s, a number of Eastern European countries replaced central planning with market economies and private ownership. The result: Output in those countries fell enormously as the old institutions fell apart. While most Eastern European economies have rebounded from their initial losses, some countries of the former Soviet Union have yet to do so. The hardships these countries continue to experience show the enormous difficulty of implementing policies involving major institutional changes.

Objective Policy Analysis

Good economic policy analysis is objective; that is, it keeps the analyst's value judgments separate from the analysis. Objective analysis does not say, "This is the way things should be," reflecting a goal established by the analyst. That would be subjective analysis because it would reflect the analyst's view of how things should be. Instead, objective analysis says, "This is the way the economy works, and if society (or the individual or firm for whom you're doing the analysis) wants to achieve a particular goal, this is how it might go about doing so." Objective analysis keeps, or at least tries to keep, subjective views—value judgments—separate.

To make clear the distinction between objective and subjective analysis, economists have divided economics into three categories: *positive economics, normative economics,* and the *art of economics*. **Positive economics** is *the study of what is, and how the economy works*. It asks such questions as: How does the market for hog bellies work? How do price restrictions affect market forces? These questions fall under the heading of economic theory. **Normative economics** is *the study of what the goals of the economy should be*. Normative economics asks such questions as: What should the distribution of income be? What should tax policy be designed to achieve? In discussing such questions, economists must carefully delineate whose goals they are discussing. One cannot simply assume that one's own goals for society are society's goals.

The **art of economics,** also called political economy, is *the application of the knowledge learned in positive economics to the achievement of the goals one has determined in normative economics*. It looks at such questions as: To achieve a certain distribution of income, how would you go about it, given the way the economy works?[3] Most policy discussions fall under the art of economics.

To carry out economic policy effectively, one must understand how institutions might change as a result of the economic policy.

Q-8 True or false? Economists should focus their policy analysis on institutional changes because such policies offer the largest gains.

Q-9 John, your study partner, is a free market advocate. He argues that the invisible hand theory tells us that the government should not interfere with the economy. Do you agree? Why or why not?

Positive economics is the study of what is, and how the economy works.

Normative economics is the study of what the goals of the economy should be.

The art of economics is the application of the knowledge learned in positive economics to the achievement of the goals determined in normative economics.

---

[3]This three-part distinction was made back in 1891 by a famous economist, John Neville Keynes, father of John Maynard Keynes, the economist who developed macroeconomics. This distinction was instilled into modern economics by Milton Friedman and Richard Lipsey in the 1950s. They, however, downplayed the art of economics, which J. N. Keynes had seen as central to understanding the economist's role in policy.

Economics and Global Warming

A good example of the central role that economics plays in policy debates is the debate about global warming. Almost all scientists are now convinced that global warming is occurring and that human activity such as the burning of fossil fuel is the cause. The policy question is what to do about it. To answer that question, most governments have turned to economists. The first part of the question that economists have considered is whether it is worth doing anything, and in a well-publicized report commissioned by the British government, economist Nicholas Stern argued that, based upon his cost/benefit analysis, yes it is worth doing something. The reason: because the costs of not doing anything would likely reduce output by 20 percent in the future, and that those costs (appropriately weighted for when they occur) are less than the benefits of policies that can be implemented.

The second part of the question is: what policies to implement? The policies he recommended were policies that changed incentives—specifically, policies that raised the costs of emitting greenhouse gases and decreased the

cost of other forms of production. Those recommended policies reflected the economist's opportunity cost framework in action: if you want to change the result, change the incentives that individuals face.

There is considerable debate about Stern's analysis—both with the way he conducted the cost/benefit analysis and with his policy recommendations. Such debates are inevitable when the data are incomplete and numerous judgments need to be made. I suspect that these debates will continue over the coming years with economists on various sides of the debate. Economists are generally not united in their views about complicated policy issues since they differ in their normative views and in their assessment of the problem and of what politically can be achieved; that's because policy is part of the art of economics, not part of positive economics. But the framework of the policy debate about global warming is the economic framework. Thus, even though political forces will ultimately choose what policy is followed, you must understand the economic framework to take part in the debate.

In each of these three branches of economics, economists separate their own value judgments from their objective analysis as much as possible. The qualifier "as much as possible" is important, since some value judgments inevitably sneak in. We are products of our environment, and the questions we ask, the framework we use, and the way we interpret the evidence all involve value judgments and reflect our backgrounds.

Maintaining objectivity is easiest in positive economics, where you are working with abstract models to understand how the economy works. Maintaining objectivity is harder in normative economics. You must always be objective about whose normative values you are using. It's easy to assume that all of society shares your values, but that assumption is often wrong.

It's hardest to maintain objectivity in the art of economics because it can suffer from the problems of both positive and normative economics. Because noneconomic forces affect policy, to practice the art of economics we must make judgments about how these noneconomic forces work. These judgments are likely to reflect our own value judgments. So we must be exceedingly careful to be as objective as possible in practicing the art of economics.

Policy and Social and Political Forces

When you think about the policy options facing society, you'll quickly discover that the choice of policy options depends on much more than economic theory. Politicians, not economists, determine economic policy. To understand what policies are chosen, you must take into account historical precedent plus social, cultural, and political forces.

Q-10 Tell whether the following five statements belong in positive economics, normative economics, or the art of economics.

1. We should support the market because it is efficient.

2. Given certain conditions, the market achieves efficient results.

3. Based on past experience and our understanding of markets, if one wants a reasonably efficient result, markets should probably be relied on.

4. The distribution of income should be left to markets.

5. Markets allocate income according to contributions of factors of production.

Web Note 1.3
The Art of Economics

18

In an economics course, I don't have time to analyze these forces in as much depth as I'd like. That's one reason there are separate history, political science, sociology, and anthropology courses.

While it is true that these other forces play significant roles in policy decisions, specialization is necessary. In economics, we focus the analysis on the invisible hand, and much of economic theory is devoted to considering how the economy would operate if the invisible hand were the only force operating. But as soon as we apply theory to reality and policy, we must take into account political and social forces as well.

An example will make my point more concrete. Most economists agree that holding down or eliminating tariffs (taxes on imports) and quotas (numerical limitations on imports) makes good economic sense. They strongly advise governments to follow a policy of free trade. Do governments follow free trade policies? Almost invariably they do not. Politics leads society in a different direction. If you're advising a policy maker, you need to point out that these other forces must be taken into account, and how other forces should (if they should) and can (if they can) be integrated with your recommendations.

Conclusion

There are tons more that could be said by way of introducing you to economics, but an introduction must remain an introduction. As it is, this chapter should have

1. Introduced you to economic reasoning.
2. Surveyed what we're going to cover in this book.
3. Given you an idea of my writing style and approach.

We'll be spending long hours together over the coming term, and before entering into such a commitment it's best to know your partner. While I won't know you, by the end of this book you'll know me. Maybe you won't love me as my mother does, but you'll know me.

This introduction was my opening line. I hope it also conveyed the importance and relevance that belong to economics. If it did, it has served its intended purpose. Economics is tough, but tough can be fun.

Summary

- The three coordination problems any economy must solve are what to produce, how to produce it, and for whom to produce it. In solving these problems, societies have found that there is a problem of scarcity.

- Economic reasoning structures all questions in a cost/benefit framework: If the marginal benefits of doing something exceed the marginal costs, do it. If the marginal costs exceed the marginal benefits, don't do it.

- Sunk costs are not relevant in the economic decision rule.

- The opportunity cost of undertaking an activity is the benefit you might have gained from choosing the next-best alternative.

- "There ain't no such thing as a free lunch" (TANSTAAFL) embodies the opportunity cost concept.

- Economic forces, the forces of scarcity, are always working. Market forces, which ration by changing prices, are not always allowed to work.

- Economic reality is controlled and directed by three types of forces: economic forces, political forces, and social forces.

- Under certain conditions, the market, through its price mechanism, will allocate scarce resources efficiently.

- Economics can be divided into microeconomics and macroeconomics. Microeconomics is the study of individual choice and how that choice is influenced by economic forces. Macroeconomics is the study of the economy as a whole. It considers problems such as inflation, unemployment, business cycles, and growth.

- Economics can be subdivided into positive economics, normative economics, and the art of economics. Positive economics is the study of what is, normative economics is the study of what should be, and the art of economics relates positive to normative economics.

Key Terms

art of economics (16)
economic decision
   rule (7)
economic force (9)
economic model (12)
economic policy (15)

economic principle (12)
economics (4)
efficiency (12)
invisible hand (9)
invisible hand
   theory (12)

macroeconomics (14)
marginal benefit (6)
marginal cost (6)
market force (9)
microeconomics (14)
normative economics (16)

opportunity cost (8)
positive economics (16)
scarcity (5)
sunk cost (6)

Questions for Thought and Review

1. Why does the textbook author focus on coordination rather than on scarcity when defining economics?   LO1

2. List two recent choices you made and explain why you made those choices in terms of marginal benefits and marginal costs.   LO2

3. At times we all regret decisions. Does this necessarily mean we did not use the economic decision rule when making the decision? (Difficult)   LO2

4. What is the opportunity cost of buying a $20,000 car?   LO3

5. Suppose you currently earn $30,000 a year. You are considering a job that will increase your lifetime earnings by $300,000 but that requires an MBA. The job will mean also attending business school for two years at an annual cost of $25,000. You already have a bachelor's degree, for which you spent $80,000 in tuition and books. Which of the above information is relevant to your decision whether to take the job? What other information would be relevant?   LO3

6. Suppose your college has been given $5 million. You have been asked to decide how to spend it to improve your college. Explain how you would use the economic decision rule and the concept of opportunity costs to decide how to spend it.   LO2, LO3

7. Economists Henry Saffer of Kean University, Frank J. Chaloupka of the University of Illinois at Chicago, and Dhaval Dave of Bentley College estimated that the government must spend $4,170 on drug control to deter one person from using drugs and the cost that one drug user imposes on society is $897. Based on this information alone, should the government spend the money on drug control?   LO2

8. Name three ways a limited number of dormitory rooms could be rationed. How would economic forces determine individual behavior in each? How would social or legal forces determine whether those economic forces become market forces?   LO4

9. About 90,000 individuals in the United States are waiting for organ transplants, and at an appropriate price many individuals would be willing to supply organs. Given those facts, should human organs be allowed to be bought and sold?   LO4

10. Prospect theory suggests that people are hurt more by losses than they are uplifted by gains of a corresponding size. If that is true, what implications would it have for economic policy? (Difficult)   LO6

11. Give two examples of social forces and explain how they keep economic forces from becoming market forces.   LO4

12. Give two examples of political or legal forces and explain how they might interact with economic forces.   LO4

13. What is an economic model? What besides a model do economists need to make policy recommendations?   LO6

14. Does economic theory prove that the free market system is best? Why? (Difficult)   LO6

15. List two microeconomic and two macroeconomic problems.   LO5

16. Name an economic institution and explain how it affects economic decision making or how its actions reflect economic principles.   LO4

17. Is a good economist always objective? Why?   LO6

Problems and Exercises

18. You rent a car for $29.95. The first 150 miles are free, but each mile thereafter costs 15 cents. You drive it 200 miles. What is the marginal cost of driving the car? LO2

19. Calculate, using the best estimates you can:
    a. Your opportunity cost of attending college.
    b. Your opportunity cost of taking this course.
    c. Your opportunity cost of attending yesterday's lecture in this course. LO3

20. A *Wall Street Journal* article recently asked readers the following questions:
    a. An accident has caused deadly fumes to enter the school ventilation system where it will kill five children. You can stop it by throwing a switch, but doing so will kill one child in another room. Do you throw the switch?
    b. Say that a doctor can save five patients with an organ transplant that would end the life of a patient who is sick, but not yet dead. Does she do it?
    c. What is the difference between the two situations described in *a* and *b*?
    d. How important are opportunity costs in your decisions? LO3

21. Economist Steven Landsburg argues that if one believes in the death penalty for murderers because of its deterrent effect, using cost/benefit analysis we should execute computer hackers—the creators of worms and viruses—because the deterrent effect in cost saving would be greater than the deterrent effect in saving lives. Estimates are that each execution deters eight murders, which, if one valued each life at about $7 million, saves about $56 million; he estimates that executing hackers would save more than that per execution, and thus would be the economic thing to do. (Difficult)
    a. Do you agree or disagree with Landsburg's argument? Why?
    b. Can you extend cost/benefit analysis to other areas? LO2

22. Tyler Cowen, an economist at George Mason University, presents an interesting case that pits the market against legal and social forces. The case involves payola—the payment of money to disk jockeys for playing a songwriter's songs. He reports that Chuck Berry was having a hard time getting his music played because of racism. To counter this, he offered a well-known disk jockey, Alan Freed, partial songwriting credits, along with partial royalties, on any Chuck Berry song of his choice. He chose *Maybellene,* which he played and promoted. It went on to be a hit, Chuck Berry went on to be a star, and Freed's estate continues to receive royalties.
    a. Should such payments be allowed? Why?
    b. How did Freed's incentives from the royalty payment differ from Freed's incentives if Chuck Berry had just offered him a flat payment?

    c. Name two other examples of similar activities—one that is legal and one that is not. LO4

23. In 1999 Royal Philips Electronics paid $180 million to buy 20-year naming rights of the Atlanta, Georgia, stadium, home of NBA's Atlanta Hawks. University of Massachusetts Professor Timothy D. DeSchriver and Drexel University Professor Paul E. Jensen analyzed naming rights. In their study, what was the likely impact of each of the following on a corporation's willingness to pay to name a stadium? (Difficult)
    a. An existing team is relocating to the stadium.
    b. The stadium is in a highly populated area.
    c. The stadium's current name is the Staples Center and has had that name for 20 years. LO3

24. Economics is about strategic thinking, and the strategies can get very complicated. Suppose you kiss someone and ask whether the person liked it. You'd like the person to answer "yes" and you'd like that answer to be truthful. But they know that, and if they like you, they may well say that they liked the kiss even if they didn't. But you know that, and thus might not really believe that they liked the kiss; they're just saying "yes" because that's what you want to hear. But they know that you know that, so sometimes they have to convey a sense that they didn't like it, so that you will believe them when they say that they did like it. But you know that . . . You get the picture. Economists have studied such issues; you can find a discussion of similar issues on George Mason University Economist Tyler Cowen's Web site (www.gmu.edu/jbc/Tyler). (Difficult)
    a. Should you always be honest, even when it hurts someone?
    b. What strategies can you figure out to avoid the problem of not believing the other person? LO3

25. Individuals have two kidneys, but most of us need only one. People who have lost both kidneys through accident or disease must be hooked up to a dialysis machine, which cleanses waste from their bodies. Say a person who has two good kidneys offers to sell one of them to someone whose kidney function has been totally destroyed. The seller asks $30,000 for the kidney, and the person who has lost both kidneys accepts the offer.
    a. Who benefits from the deal?
    b. Who is hurt?
    c. Should a society allow such market transactions? Why? LO4

26. State whether the following are microeconomic or macroeconomic policy issues:
    a. Should U.S. interest rates be lowered to decrease the amount of unemployment?
    b. Will the fact that more and more doctors are selling their practices to managed care networks increase the efficiency of medical providers?

c. Should the current federal income tax be lowered to reduce unemployment?

d. Should the federal minimum wage be raised?

e. Should Sprint and Verizon both be allowed to build local phone networks?

f. Should commercial banks be required to provide loans in all areas of the territory from which they accept deposits? LO5

27. Go to two stores: a supermarket and a convenience store.

a. Write down the cost of a gallon of milk in each.

b. The prices are most likely different. Using the terminology used in this chapter, explain why that is the case and why anyone would buy milk in the store with the higher price.

c. Do the same exercise with shirts or dresses in Wal-Mart (or its equivalent) and Saks (or its equivalent). LO4

28. State whether the following statements belong in positive economics, normative economics, or the art of economics.

a. In a market, when quantity supplied exceeds quantity demanded, price tends to fall.

b. When determining tax rates, the government should take into account the income needs of individuals.

c. What society feels is fair is determined largely by cultural norms.

d. When deciding which rationing mechanism is best (lottery, price, first-come/first-served), one must take into account the goals of society.

e. California currently rations water to farmers at subsidized prices. Once California allows the trading of water rights, it will allow economic forces to be a market force. LO6

29. Adam Smith, who wrote *The Wealth of Nations*, and who is seen as the father of modern economics, also wrote *The Theory of Moral Sentiments*. In it he argued that society would be better off if people weren't so selfish and were more considerate of others. How does this view fit with the discussion of economic reasoning presented in the chapter? (Difficult) LO3

Questions from Alternative Perspectives

1. Is it possible to use objective economic analysis as a basis for government planning? (Austrian)

2. In "Rational Choice with Passion: Virtue in a Model of Rational Addiction," Andrew M. Yuengert of Pepperdine University argues that there is a conflict between reason and passion.

a. What might that conflict be?

b. What implications does it have for applying the economic model? (Religious)

3. Economic institutions are "habits of thought" that organize society.

a. In what way might patriarchy be an *institution* and how might it influence the labor market?

b. Does the free market or patriarchy better explain why 98 percent of secretaries are women and 98 percent of automobile mechanics are men? (Feminist)

4. In October of 2004, the supply of flu vaccine fell by over 50 percent. The result was that the vaccine had to be rationed, with a priority schedule established: young children, people with weakened immunity, those over 65, etc., taking priority.

a. Compare and contrast this allocation outcome with a free market outcome.

b. Which alternative is more just? (Institutionalist)

5. The textbook model assumes that individuals have enough knowledge to follow the economic decision rule.

a. How did you decide what college you would attend?

b. Did you have enough knowledge to follow the economic decision rule?

c. For what type of decisions do you not use the economic decision rule?

d. What are the implications for economic analysis if most people don't follow the economic decision rule in many aspects of their decisions? (Post-Keynesian)

6. Radical economists believe that all of economics, like all theorizing or storytelling, is value-laden. Theories and stories reflect the values of those who compose them and tell them. For instance, Radicals offer a different analysis than most economists of how capitalism works and what ought to be done about its most plaguing problems: inequality, periodic economic crises with large-scale unemployment, and the alienation of the workers.

a. What does the radical position imply about the distinction between positive economics and normative economics that the text makes?

b. Is economics value-laden or objective and is the distinction between positive and normative economics tenable or untenable? (Radical)

Web Questions

1. Find an employment Web page (an example is www.monster.com) and search for available jobs using "economist" as a keyword. List five jobs that economists have and write a one-sentence description of each.

2. Use an online periodical to find two examples of political or legal forces at work. Do those forces keep economic forces from becoming market forces?

3. Using an Internet mapping page (an example is www.mapquest.com), create a map of your neighborhood and answer the following questions:
   a. How is the map like a model?
   b. What are the limitations of the map?

c. Could you use this map to determine change in elevation in your neighborhood? Distance from one place to another? Traffic speed? What do your answers suggest about what to consider when using a map or a model?

Answers to Margin Questions

The numbers in parentheses refer to the page number of each margin question.

1. Since the price of both stocks is now $15, it doesn't matter which one you sell (assuming no differential capital gains taxation). The price you bought them for doesn't matter; it's a sunk cost. Marginal analysis refers to the future gain, so what you expect to happen to future prices of the stocks—not past prices—should determine which stock you decide to sell. (7)

2. A cost/benefit analysis requires that you put a value on a good, and placing a value on a good can be seen as demeaning it. Consider love. Try telling an acquaintance that you'd like to buy his or her spiritual love, and see what response you get. (8)

3. John is wrong. The opportunity cost of reading the chapter is primarily the time you spend reading it. Reading the book prevents you from doing other things. Assuming that you already paid for the book, the original price is no longer part of the opportunity cost; it is a sunk cost. Bygones are bygones. (9)

4. Whenever there is scarcity, the scarce good must be rationed by some means. Free health care has an opportunity cost in other resources. So if health care is not rationed, to get the resources to supply that care, other

goods would have to be more tightly rationed than they currently are. It is likely that the opportunity cost of supplying free health care would be larger than most societies would be willing to pay. (9)

5. Joan is wrong. Economic forces are always operative; market forces are not. (10)

6. According to the invisible hand theory, the price of tomatoes will likely fall. (12)

7. (1) Macroeconomics; (2) Microeconomics; (3) Microeconomics; (4) Macroeconomics. (14)

8. False. While such changes have the largest gain, they also may have the largest cost. The policies economists should focus on are those that offer the largest net gain—benefits minus costs—to society. (16)

9. He is wrong. The invisible hand theory is a positive theory and does not tell us anything about policy. To do so would be to violate Hume's dictum that a "should" cannot be derived from an "is." This is not to say that government should or should not interfere; whether government should interfere is a very difficult question. (16)

10. (1) Normative; (2) Positive; (3) Art; (4) Normative; (5) Positive. (17)

The Production Possibility Model, Trade, and Globalization

Economics is a science of thinking in terms of models, joined to the art of choosing models which are relevant to the contemporary world.

—*J. M. Keynes*

Every economy must solve three main coordination problems:

1. What, and how much, to produce.
2. How to produce it.
3. For whom to produce it.

In Chapter 1, I suggested that you can boil down all economic knowledge into the single phrase "There ain't no such thing as a free lunch." There's obviously more to economics than that, but it's not a bad summary of the core of economic reasoning—it's relevant for an individual, for nonprofit organizations, for governments, and for nations. Oh, it's true that once in a while you can snitch a sandwich, but what economics tells you is that if you're offered something that approaches free-lunch status, you should also be on the lookout for some hidden cost.

A key element in getting people to recognize that lunches aren't free is the concept of opportunity cost—every decision has a cost in forgone opportunities—which I introduced you to in Chapter 1. Economists have a model, the production possibility model, that conveys the concept of opportunity costs both numerically and graphically. This model is important for understanding not only opportunity cost but also why people specialize in what they do and trade for the goods they need. Through specialization and trade, individuals, firms, and countries can achieve greater levels of production than they could otherwise achieve.

The Production Possibilities Model

The production possibilities model can be presented both in a table and in a graph. (Appendix A has a discussion of graphs in economics.) I'll start with the table and then move from that to the graph. Opportunity cost can be seen numerically with a **production possibility table**—*a table that lists a choice's opportunity*

AFTER READING THIS CHAPTER, YOU SHOULD BE ABLE TO:

1. Demonstrate opportunity cost with a production possibility curve.
2. State the principle of increasing marginal opportunity cost.
3. Relate the concept of comparative advantage to the production possibility curve.
4. State how, through comparative advantage and trade, countries can consume beyond their production possibilities.
5. Explain how globalization and outsourcing are part of a global process guided by the law of one price.

Q-1 In the graph below, what is the opportunity cost of producing an extra unit of good X in terms of good Y?

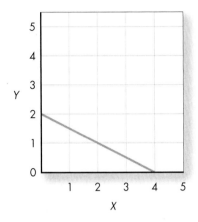

The production possibility curve is a curve measuring the maximum combination of outputs that can be obtained from a given number of inputs.

costs by summarizing what alternative outputs you can achieve with your inputs. An **output** is simply *a result of an activity*, and an **input** is *what you put into a production process to achieve an output.* For example, your grade in a course is an output and your study time is an input.

A Production Possibility Curve for an Individual

Let's consider the study-time/grades example. Say you have exactly 20 hours a week to devote to two courses: economics and history. (So maybe I'm a bit optimistic.) Grades are given numerically and you know that the following relationships exist: If you study 20 hours in economics, you'll get a grade of 100; 18 hours, 94; and so forth.[1]

Let's say that the best you can do in history is a 98 with 20 hours of study a week; 19 hours of study guarantees a 96, and so on. The production possibility table in Figure 2-1(a) shows the highest combination of grades you can get with various allocations of the 20 hours available for studying the two subjects. One possibility is getting 70 in economics and 78 in history.

Notice that the opportunity cost of studying one subject rather than the other is embodied in the production possibility table. The information in the table comes from experience: We are assuming that you've discovered that if you transfer an hour of study from economics to history, you'll lose 3 points on your grade in economics and gain 2 points in history. Thus, the opportunity cost of a 2-point rise in your history grade is a 3-point decrease in your economics grade.

The information in the production possibility table also can be presented graphically in a diagram called a production possibility curve. A **production possibility curve (PPC)** is *a curve measuring the maximum combination of outputs that can be obtained from a given number of inputs.* It is a graphical presentation of the opportunity cost concept.

A production possibility curve is created from a production possibility table by mapping the table in a two-dimensional graph. I've taken the information from the table in Figure 2-1(a) and mapped it into Figure 2-1(b). The history grade is mapped, or plotted, on the horizontal axis; the economics grade is on the vertical axis.

As you can see from the bottom row of Figure 2-1(a), if you study economics for all 20 hours and study history for 0 hours, you'll get grades of 100 in economics and 58 in history. Point A in Figure 2-1(b) represents that choice. If you study history for all 20 hours and study economics for 0 hours, you'll get a 98 in history and a 40 in economics. Point E represents that choice. Points B, C, and D represent three possible choices between these two extremes.

Notice that the production possibility curve slopes downward from left to right. That means that there is an inverse relationship (a trade-off) between grades in economics and grades in history. The better the grade in economics, the worse the grade in history, and vice versa. That downward slope represents the opportunity cost concept: you get more of one benefit only if you get less of another benefit.

The production possibility curve not only represents the opportunity cost concept but also measures the opportunity cost. For example, in Figure 2-1(b), say you want to raise your grade in history from a 94 to a 98 (move from point D to point E). The

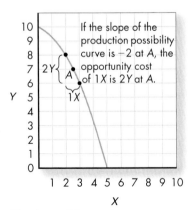

If the slope of the production possibility curve is −2 at A, the opportunity cost of 1X is 2Y at A.

The slope of the production possibility curve tells you the opportunity cost of good X in terms of good Y. You have to give up 2Y to get 1X when you're around point A.

---

[1]Throughout the book I'll be presenting numerical examples to help you understand the concepts. The numbers I choose are often arbitrary. After all, you have to choose something. As an exercise, you might choose different numbers than I did, numbers that apply to your own life, and work out the argument using those numbers.

A Production Possibility Table and Curve for Grades in Economics and History

The production possibility table (**a**) shows the highest combination of grades you can get with only 20 hours available for studying economics and history. The information in the production possibility table in (**a**) can be plotted on a graph, as is done in (**b**). The grade received in economics is on the vertical axis, and the grade received in history is on the horizontal axis.

Hours of Study in History	Grade in History	Hours of Study in Economics	Grade in Economics
20	98	0	40
19	96	1	43
18	94	2	46
17	92	3	49
16	90	4	52
15	88	5	55
14	86	6	58
13	84	7	61
12	82	8	64
11	80	9	67
10	78	10	70
9	76	11	73
8	74	12	76
7	72	13	79
6	70	14	82
5	68	15	85
4	66	16	88
3	64	17	91
2	62	18	94
1	60	19	97
0	58	20	100

(a) Production Possibility Table

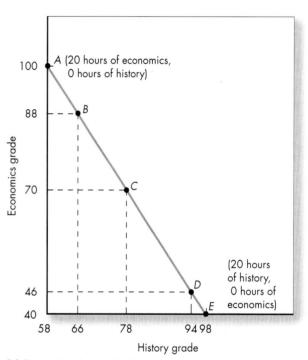

(b) Production Possibility Curve

opportunity cost of that 4-point increase would be a 6-point decrease in your economics grade, from 46 to 40.

To summarize, the production possibility curve demonstrates that

1. There is a limit to what you can achieve, given the existing institutions, resources, and technology.
2. Every choice you make has an opportunity cost. You can get more of something only by giving up something else.

Production Possibilities Curve

Increasing Marginal Opportunity Cost

In the study-time/grade example, the opportunity cost of trade remained constant; you could always trade two points on your history grade for three points on your economics grade. This assumption of an unchanging opportunity cost made the production possibility curve a straight line. Although this made the example easier, is it realistic? Probably not, especially if we are using the PPC to describe the choices that a society makes. For many of the choices society must make, opportunity costs tend to increase as we choose

The principle of increasing marginal opportunity cost tells us that opportunity costs increase the more you concentrate on the activity.

more and more of an item. Such a phenomenon is so common, in fact, that it has acquired a name: the **principle of increasing marginal opportunity cost**. That principle states:

> *In order to get more of something, one must give up ever-increasing quantities of something else*

In other words, initially the opportunity costs of an activity are low, but they increase the more we concentrate on that activity.

A production possibility curve that exhibits increasing marginal opportunity costs is bowed outward, as in Figure 2-2(b).

Why are production possibility curves typically bowed outward? Because some resources are better suited for the production of certain kinds of goods than other kinds of goods. To understand what that means, let's talk about the graph in Figure 2-2(b), which is derived from the table in Figure 2-2(a). This curve represents society's choice between defense spending (guns) and spending on domestic needs (butter).

Suppose society is producing only butter (point A). Giving up a little butter (1 pound) initially gains us a lot of guns (4), moving us to point B. The next 2 pounds of butter we give up gain us slightly fewer guns (point C). If we continue to trade butter for guns, we find that at point D we gain very few guns from giving up a pound of butter. The opportunity cost of choosing guns over butter increases as we increase the production of guns.

Comparative Advantage

The reason the opportunity cost of guns increases as we produce more guns is that some resources are relatively better suited to producing guns, while others are relatively better

---

FIGURE 2-2 (A AND B)   A Production Possibility Table and Curve

The table in (**a**) contains information on the trade-off between the production of guns and butter. This information has been plotted on the graph in (**b**). Notice in (**b**) that as we move along the production possibility curve from A to F, trading butter for guns, we get fewer and fewer guns for each pound of butter given up. That is, the opportunity cost of choosing guns over butter increases as we increase the production of guns. This concept is called the principle of increasing marginal opportunity cost. The phenomenon occurs because some resources are better suited for the production of butter than for the production of guns, and we use the better ones first.

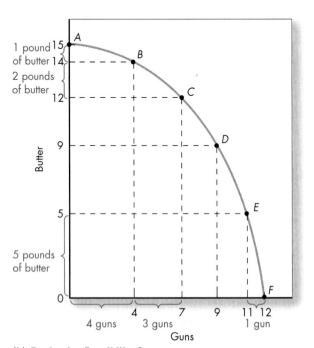

% of Resources Devoted to Production of Guns	Number of Guns	% of Resources Devoted to Production of Butter	Pounds of Butter	Row
0	0	100	15	A
20	4	80	14	B
40	7	60	12	C
60	9	40	9	D
80	11	20	5	E
100	12	0	0	F

(a) Production Possibility Table

(b) Production Possibility Curve

Production Possibility Curves

Definition	Shape	Shifts	Points In, Out, and On
The production possibility curve is a curve that measures the maximum combination of outputs that can be obtained with a given number of inputs.	Most are outward bowed because of increasing marginal opportunity cost; if opportunity cost doesn't change, the production possibility curve is a straight line.	Increases in inputs or increases in the productivity of inputs shift the production possibility curve out. Decreases have the opposite effect; the production possibility curve shifts along the axis whose input is changing.	Points inside the production possibility curve are points of inefficiency; points on the production possibility curve are points of efficiency; points outside the production possibility curve are not obtainable.

suited to producing butter. Put in economists' terminology, some resources have a **comparative advantage** over other resources—*the ability to be better suited to the production of one good than to the production of another good.* In this example, some resources have a comparative advantage over other resources in the production of butter, while other resources have a comparative advantage in the production of guns.

When making small amounts of guns and large amounts of butter, we first use the resources whose comparative advantage is in the production of guns to produce guns. All other resources are devoted to producing butter. Because the resources used in producing guns aren't good at producing butter, we're not giving up much butter to get those guns. As we produce more and more of a good, we must use resources whose comparative advantage is in the production of the other good—in this case, more suitable for producing butter than for producing guns. As we remove resources from the production of butter to get the same additional amount of guns, we must give up increasing amounts of butter. An alternative way of saying this is that the opportunity cost of producing guns becomes greater as the production of guns increases. As we continue to increase the production of guns, the opportunity cost of more guns becomes very high because we're using resources to produce guns that have a strong comparative advantage for producing butter.

Let's consider two more examples. Say the United States suddenly decides it needs more wheat. To get additional wheat, we must devote additional land to growing it. This land is less fertile than the land we're already using, so our additional output of wheat per acre of land devoted to wheat will be less. Alternatively, consider the use of relief pitchers in a baseball game. If only one relief pitcher is needed, the manager sends in the best; if he must send in a second one, then a third, and even a fourth, the likelihood of winning the game decreases.

Efficiency

We would like, if possible, to get as much output as possible from a given amount of inputs or resources. That's **productive efficiency**—*achieving as much output as possible from a given amount of inputs or resources.* We would like to be efficient. The production possibility curve helps us see what is meant by productive efficiency. Consider point A

Q-2 If no resource had a comparative advantage in the production of any good, what would the shape of the production possibility curve be? Why?

Comparative Advantage

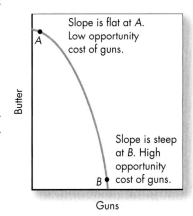

Slope is flat at A. Low opportunity cost of guns.

Slope is steep at B. High opportunity cost of guns.

Butter

Guns

Efficiency

Choices in Context

The production possibility curve presents choices without regard to time and therefore makes opportunity costs clear-cut; there are two choices, one with a higher cost and one with a lower cost. The reality is that most choices are dependent on other choices; they are made sequentially. With sequential choices, you cannot simply reverse your decision. Once you have started on a path, to take another path you have to return to the beginning. Thus, following one path often lowers the costs of options along that path, but it raises the costs of options along another path.

Such sequential decisions can best be seen within the framework of a decision tree—a visual description of sequential choices. A decision tree is shown in the accompanying figure.

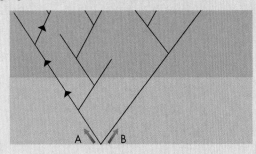

Once you make the initial decision to go on path A, the costs of path B options become higher; they include the

costs of retracing your path and starting over. The decision trees of life have thousands of branches; each decision you make rules out other paths, or at least increases their costs significantly. (Remember that day you decided to blow off your homework? That decision may have changed your future life.)

Another way of putting this same point is that *all decisions are made in context*: What makes sense in one context may not make sense in another. For example, say you're answering the question "Would society be better off if students were taught literature or if they were taught agriculture?" The answer depends on the institutional context. In a developing country whose goal is large increases in material output, teaching agriculture may make sense. In a developed country, where growth in material output is less important, teaching literature may make sense.

Recognizing the contextual nature of decisions is important when interpreting the production possibility curve. Because decisions are contextual, what the production possibility curve for a particular decision looks like depends on the existing institutions, and the analysis can be applied only in institutional and historical context. The production possibility curve is not a purely technical phenomenon. The curve is an engine of analysis to make contextual choices, not a definitive tool to decide what one should do in all cases.

Q-3 Identify the point(s) of inefficiency and efficiency. What point(s) are unattainable?

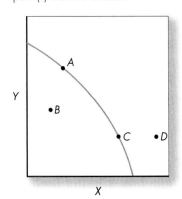

in Figure 2-3(a), which is inside the production possibility curve. If we are producing at point A, we are using all our resources to produce 6 guns and 4 pounds of butter. Point A represents **inefficiency**—*getting less output from inputs that, if devoted to some other activity, would produce more output.* That's because with the same inputs we could be getting either 8 guns and 4 pounds of butter (point B) or 6 pounds of butter and 6 guns (point C). As long as we prefer more to less, both points B and C represent **efficiency**—*achieving a goal using as few inputs as possible.* We always want to move our production out to a point on the production possibility curve.

Why not move out farther, to point D? If we could, we would, but by definition the production possibility curve represents the most output we can get from a certain combination of inputs. So point D is unattainable, given our resources and technology.

When technology improves, when more resources are discovered, or when the economic institutions get better at fulfilling our wants, we can get more output with the same inputs. What this means is that when technology or an economic institution improves, the entire production possibility curve shifts outward from *AB* to *CD* in Figure 2-3(b). How the production possibility curve shifts outward depends on how the technology improves. For example, say we become more efficient at producing butter,

FIGURE 2-3 (A, B, AND C)   **Efficiency, Inefficiency, and Technological Change**

The production possibility curve helps us see what is meant by efficiency. At point A, in (**a**), all inputs are used to make 4 pounds of butter and 6 guns. This is inefficient since there is a way to obtain more of one without giving up any of the other, that is, to obtain 6 pounds of butter and 6 guns (point C) or 8 guns and 4 pounds of butter (point B). All points inside the production possibility curve are inefficient. With existing inputs and technology, we cannot go beyond the production possibility curve. For example, point D is unattainable.

A technological change that improves production techniques will shift the production possibility curve outward, as shown in both (**b**) and (**c**). How the curve shifts outward depends on how technology improves. For example, if we become more efficient in the production of both guns and butter, the curve will shift out as in (**b**). If we become more efficient in producing butter, but not in producing guns, then the curve will shift as in (**c**).

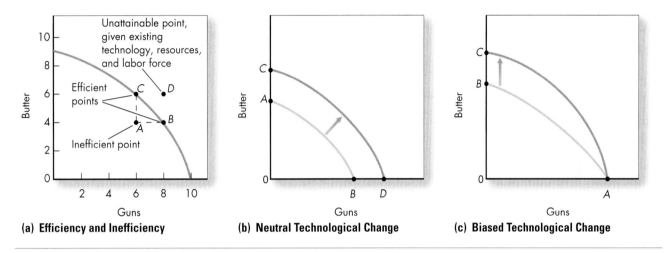

(a) Efficiency and Inefficiency   **(b) Neutral Technological Change**   **(c) Biased Technological Change**

but not more efficient at producing guns. Then the production possibility curve shifts outward to AC in Figure 2-3(c).

Distribution and Productive Efficiency

In discussing the production possibility curve for a society, I avoided questions of distribution: Who gets what? But such questions cannot be ignored in real-world situations. Specifically, if the method of production is tied to a particular income distribution and choosing one method will help some people but hurt others, we can't say that one method of production is efficient and the other inefficient, even if one method produces more total output than the other. As I stated above, the term *efficiency* involves achieving a goal as cheaply as possible. The term has meaning only in regard to a specified goal. Say, for example, that we have a society of ascetics who believe that consumption above some minimum is immoral. For such a society, producing more for less (productive efficiency) would not be efficient since consumption is not its goal. Or say that we have a society that cares that what is produced is fairly distributed. An increase in output that goes to only one person and not to anyone else would not necessarily be efficient.

In our society, however, most people prefer more to less, and many policies have relatively small distributional consequences. On the basis of the assumption that more is better than less, economists use their own kind of shorthand for such policies and talk about efficiency as identical to productive efficiency—increasing total output. But it's important to remember the assumption under which that shorthand is used: that the distributional effects that accompany the policy are acceptable, and that we, as a society, prefer more output.

Q-4 Your firm is establishing a trucking business in Saudi Arabia. The managers have noticed that women are generally paid much less than men in Saudi Arabia, and they suggest that hiring women would be more efficient than hiring men. What should you respond?

FIGURE 2-4 (A, B, C, AND D)   **Examples of Shifts in Production Possibility Curves**

Each of these curves reflects a different type of shift. (The axes are left unlabeled on purpose. Manufactured and agricultural goods may be placed on either axis.) Your assignment is to match these shifts with the situations given in the text.

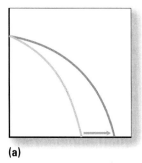

(a)

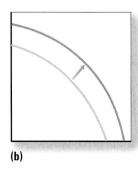

(b)

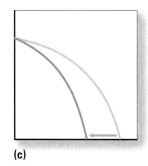

(c)

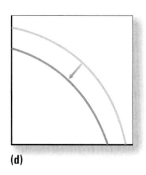

(d)

Examples of Shifts in the PPC

To see whether you understand the production possibility curve, let us now consider some situations that can be shown with it. Below, I list four situations. To test your understanding of the curve, match each situation to one of the curves in Figure 2-4.

Q-5 When a natural disaster hits the midwestern United States, where most of the U.S. butter is produced, what happens to the U.S. production possibility curve for guns and butter?

1. A meteor hits the world and destroys half the earth's natural resources.
2. Nanotechnology is perfected that lowers the cost of manufactured goods.
3. A new technology is discovered that doubles the speed at which all goods can be produced.
4. Global warming increases the cost of producing agricultural goods.

The correct answers are: 1–d; 2–a; 3–b; 4–c.

If you got them all right, you are well on your way to understanding the production possibility curve.

Trade and Comparative Advantage

Now that we have gone through the basics of the production possibility curve, let's dig a little deeper. From the above discussion, you know that production possibility curves are generally bowed outward and that the reason for this is comparative advantage. To remind you of the argument, consider Figure 2-5, which is the guns and butter production possibility example I presented earlier.

At point A, all resources are being used to produce butter. As more guns are produced, we take resources away from producing butter that had a comparative advantage in producing guns, so we gain a lot of guns for little butter (the opportunity cost of additional guns is low). As we continue down the curve, the comparative advantage of the resources we use changes, and as we approach B, we use almost all resources to produce guns, so we are using resources that aren't very good at producing guns. Thus, around point B we gain few guns for a lot of butter (the opportunity cost of additional guns is high).

A society wants to be on the frontier of its production possibility curve. This requires that individuals produce those goods for which they have a comparative advantage. The question for society, then, is how to direct individuals toward those activities. For a firm, the answer is easy. A manager can allocate the firm's resources to their best use. For example, he or she can assign an employee with good people skills to the human

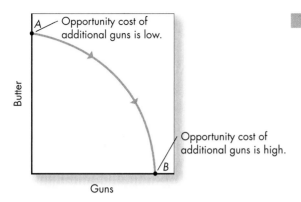

FIGURE 2-5 **Comparative Advantage and the Production Possibility Curve**

As we move down along the production possibility curve from point A to point B, the opportunity cost of producing guns is increasing since we are using resources less suited for gun production.

resources department and another with good research skills to research and development. But our economy has millions of individuals, and no manager directing everyone what to do. How do we know that these individuals will be directed to do those things for which they have a comparative advantage? It was this question that was central to the British moral philosopher Adam Smith when he wrote his most famous book, *The Wealth of Nations* (1776). In it he argued that it was humankind's proclivity to trade that leads to individuals using their comparative advantage. He writes:

> This division of labour, from which so many advantages are derived, is not originally the effect of any human wisdom, which foresees and intends that general opulence to which it gives occasion. It is the necessary, though very slow and gradual consequence of a certain propensity in human nature which has in view no such extensive utility; the propensity to truck, barter, and exchange one thing for another… [This propensity] is common to all men, and to be found in no other race of animals, which seem to know neither this nor any other species of contracts… Nobody ever saw a dog make a fair and deliberate exchange of one bone for another with another dog. Nobody ever saw one animal by its gestures and natural cries signify to another, this is mine, that yours; I am willing to give this for that.

As long as people trade, Smith argues, the market will guide people, like an invisible hand, to gravitate toward those activities for which they have a comparative advantage. By specializing in the production of goods in which they have a comparative advantage, they will produce the most goods they can. They can then trade with other people who specialize in the production of other goods. For Smith, what was especially neat about this process was that it could take place without enormous amounts of government intervention. Smith writes:

> Man has almost constant occasion for the help of his brethren, and it is in vain for him to expect it from their benevolence only. He will be more likely to prevail, if he can interest their self-love in his favour, and show them that it is for their own advantage to do for him what he requires of them. Whoever offers to another a bargain of any kind proposes to do this. Give me that which I want, and you shall have that which you want, is the meaning of every such offer; and it is in this manner that we obtain from one another the far greater part of those good offices which we stand in need of. It is not from the benevolence of the butcher, the brewer, or the baker, that we expect our dinner, but from their regard to their own interest. We address ourselves, not to their humanity but to their self-love, and never talk to them of our own necessities but of their advantages.

Adam Smith argued that it is humankind's proclivity to trade that leads to individuals using their comparative advantage.

It is not from the benevolence of the butcher, the brewer, or the baker that we expect our dinner, but from their regard to their own interest.

FIGURE 2-6   **Growth in the Past Two Millennia**

For 1,700 years the world economy grew very slowly. Then, since the end of the 18th century with the introduction of markets and the spread of democracy, the world economy has grown at increasing rates.

Source: Angus Maddison, *Monitoring the World Economy*, OECD, 1995; Angus Maddison, "Poor until 1820," *The Wall Street Journal*, January 11, 1999; and author extrapolations.

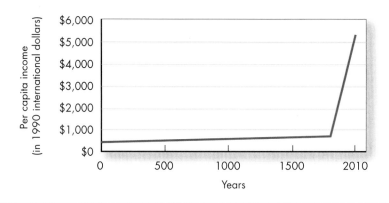

Markets, Specialization, and Growth

We can see the effect of trade on our well-being empirically by considering the growth of economies. As you can see from Figure 2-6, for 1,700 years the world economy grew very slowly. Then, at the end of the 18th century, the world economy started to grow, and it has grown at a high rate since then.

What changed? The introduction of markets that facilitate trade and the spread of democracy. There's something about markets that leads to economic growth. Markets allow specialization and encourage trade. The bowing out of the production possibilities from trade is part of the story, but a minor part. As individuals compete and specialize, they learn by doing, becoming even better at what they do. Markets also foster competition, which pushes individuals to find better ways of doing things. They devise new technologies that further the growth process.

The new millennium is offering new ways for individuals to specialize and compete. More and more businesses are trading on the Internet. For example, colleges such as the University of Phoenix are providing online competition for traditional colleges. Similarly, online bookstores and drugstores are proliferating. As Internet technology becomes built into our economy, we can expect more specialization, more division of labor, and the economic growth that follows.

Markets can be very simple or very complicated.

The Benefits of Trade

The reasons why markets can direct people to use their comparative advantages follows from a very simple argument: When people freely enter into a trade, both parties can be expected to benefit from the trade; otherwise, why would they have traded in the first place? So when the butcher sells you meat, he's better off with the money you give him, and you're better off with the meat he gives you.

Web Note 2.1
Wine and Cloth

When there is competition in trading, such that individuals are able to pick the best trades available to them, each individual drives the best bargain he or she can. The end result is that both individuals in the trade benefit as much as they possibly can, given what others are willing to trade. This argument for the benefits from trade underlies the general policy of **laissez-faire**—*an economic policy of leaving coordination of individuals' actions to the market.* (*Laissez-faire*, a French term, means "Let events take their course; leave things alone.")

Laissez-faire is an economic policy of leaving coordination of individuals' actions to the market.

Let's consider a numerical example of the gains that accrue to two countries when they trade, and show how that trade increases the production possibilities, creating the bowed shape of the production possibility curve. I use an international trade

FIGURE 2-7 (A AND B)   **The Gains from Trade**

Trade makes those involved in the trade better off. If each country specializes and takes advantage of its comparative advantage, the combined production possibility curve becomes bowed outward. In (a), the gains from trade are represented by the movements of the countries from points A and B to point C. In (b), you can see how the combined PPC reflects the "lowest cost rules" principle.

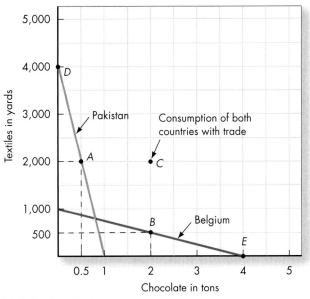

(a) Gains from Trade

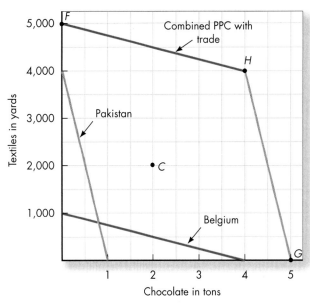

(b) Combined PPC

	Textiles	Chocolate
Pakistan	2,000 yards	0.5 ton
Belgium	500 yards	2 tons
Total	2,500 yards	2.5 tons

example so that you can see that the argument holds for international trade as well as domestic trade.

Let's say that the two countries are Pakistan and Belgium, and that Pakistan has a comparative advantage in producing textiles, while Belgium has a comparative advantage in producing chocolate. Specifically, Pakistan can produce 4,000 yards of textiles a day, or 1 ton of chocolate a day, or any proportional combination in between. (Pakistan's opportunity cost of 1 ton of chocolate is 4,000 yards of textiles.) Pakistan's production possibility curve is shown by the orange line in Figure 2-7(a). In a given day, Belgium can produce either 1,000 yards of textiles, 4 tons of chocolate, or any proportion in between. (Belgium's opportunity cost of 1 ton of chocolate is 250 yards of textiles.) Its production possibility curve is shown by the green line in Figure 2-7(a).

In the absence of trade, the most each country can consume is some combination along its production possibility curve. Say Pakistan has chosen to produce and consume 2,000 yards of textiles and 0.5 ton of chocolate (point A), while Belgium has chosen to produce and consume 500 yards of textiles and 2 tons of chocolate (point B).

Q-6 What argument underlies the general laissez-faire policy argument?

Let's now consider what would happen if each specialized, doing what it does best, and then traded with the other for the goods it wants. This separates the production and consumption decisions. Because Pakistan has the lower opportunity cost, it makes sense for Pakistan to specialize in textiles, producing 4,000 yards. Similarly, it makes sense for Belgium to specialize in chocolate, producing 4 tons. By specializing, the countries together produce 4 tons of chocolate and 4,000 yards of textiles. If the countries divide production so that each country gets 2,000 yards of fabric and 2 tons of chocolate, both countries will be consuming at point *C*, even as they are producing at points *D* and *E*, respectively. Point *C* is beyond both countries' production possibility curves. This tells us an important principle about trade:

Trade lets countries consume beyond their production possibility curve.

It is primarily these gains that lead to economists' support of free trade and their opposition to barriers to trade.

Comparative Advantage and the Combined PPC

Constructing a production possibility curve that shows the combination of goods these two countries can produce is a useful exercise. I do so in Figure 2-7(b) by first asking how much of each good can be produced if both countries produce the same good. If both countries produce only textiles, 5,000 yards of textiles are made (point *F*). Alternatively, if they produce only chocolate, 5 tons of chocolate are produced (point *G*). A third possibility is that Pakistan specializes in the good in which it has a comparative advantage—textiles—and produces 4,000 yards, while Belgium specializes in the good in which it has a comparative advantage—chocolate—producing 4 tons. This combination is shown by point *H*. Since other combinations of goods are possible, connecting points *F*, *H*, and *G* gives us the combined production possibility curve.

Notice that this combined production possibility curve has the same slope as Belgium's from *F* to *H*, and the same slope as Pakistan's from *H* to *G*. That is because, when trade is allowed, *the slope of the combined production possibility curve is determined by the country with the lowest opportunity cost*. It is by producing where costs are lowest that countries can achieve gains from trade. This principle—*lowest cost rules*—gives us a sense of what happens when we expand the production possibility curve analysis to include many countries rather than just two: The production possibility curve becomes smoother as each country's comparative advantage governs a smaller portion of the shape. Eventually, as the number of countries that trade gets large, it becomes the smooth bowed curve we drew above for guns and butter.

U.S. Textile Production and Trade

When each country follows its comparative advantage, production becomes more efficient and the consumption possibilities for both countries increase. Because of these benefits, most economists support free markets and free trade. The market system gives individual firms an incentive to search for comparative advantages and to produce with lowest-cost methods at lowest-cost locations. This pressures other producers to lower their costs or get out of the business.

The pressure to find comparative advantages is never ending, in part because comparative advantage can change. Two hundred years ago, the United States had a comparative advantage in producing textiles. It was rich in natural resources and labor, and it had a low-cost source of power (water). As the cost of U.S. labor went up, and as trade opportunities widened, that comparative advantage disappeared. As it did, the United States moved out of the textile industry. Countries with cheaper labor, such as Bangladesh, today have the comparative advantage in textiles. As firms have relocated

---

Specialization and trade create gains that make all better off.

Trade lets countries consume beyond their production possibility curve.

Q‑7   Steve can bake either 4 loaves of bread or 8 dozen cookies a day. Sarah can bake either 4 loaves of bread or 4 dozen cookies a day. Show, using production possibility curves, that Steve and Sarah would be better off specializing in their baking activities and then trading, rather than baking only for themselves.

Q‑8   True or false? Two countries can achieve the greatest gains from trade by each producing the goods for which the opportunity costs are greatest and then trading those goods.

The pressure to find comparative advantages is never ending.

textile production to Bangladesh, total costs have fallen. The gains from trade show up as higher pay for Bangladeshi workers and lower-priced cloth for U.S. consumers. Of course, trade is a two-way street. In return for Bangladesh's textiles, the United States sends computer software and airplanes, products that would be highly expensive, indeed almost impossible, for Bangladesh to produce on its own. So Bangladeshi consumers, on average, are also made better off by the trade.

Web Note 2.2
Wage Comparison

Outsourcing, Trade, and Comparative Advantage

There is much more to be said about both trade and the gains from trade, and later chapters will explore trade in much more detail. But let me briefly discuss the relationship of the theory of comparative advantage to two terms that you often read about in the newspaper—*outsourcing* and *globalization*. In this book, we will use the newspaper definition of **outsourcing**—*the relocation of production once done in the United States to foreign countries*.

Let's begin with outsourcing.

Outsourcing is the relocation of production once done in the United States to foreign countries.

Outsourcing   At one time, the term *outsourcing* was used in a broader context and referred to subcontracting a portion of a firm's production to another firm either within or outside the United States. However, recently, it has been used in this more narrow sense, and that is how I will use the term here. One service being outsourced today is customer support. More and more, customer support calls are routed to call centers in India, rather than in the United States. By outsourcing call services, the United States imports the service "assistance." Before recent developments in telecommunications, support call services could not be imported.

To put outsourcing in its proper perspective, you should think of it in relation to *insourcing*—the relocation of production done abroad to the United States. Outsourcing only becomes an important policy issue to the degree that it significantly exceeds insourcing. While the actual numbers on both are difficult to collect and interpret, there is a general sense that in recent years not only has outsourcing been increasing, insourcing has been decreasing, and hence insourcing is being overwhelmed by outsourcing.

Outsourcing scares many people in the United States because, with wages so much lower in many developing countries than in the United States, they wonder whether all jobs will move offshore: Will the United States be left producing anything? Economists' answer is: Of course it will. Comparative advantage, by definition, means that if one country has a comparative advantage in producing one set of goods, the other country has to have a comparative advantage in the other set of goods. The real questions are: In what goods will the United States have comparative advantages? and: How will those comparative advantages come about?

One reason people have a hard time thinking of goods in which the United States has a comparative advantage is that they are thinking in terms of labor costs. They ask: Since wages are lower in China, isn't it cheaper to produce all goods in China? The answer is no; production requires many more inputs than just "labor." Technology, institutional structure, specialized types of knowledge, and entrepreneurial know-how are also needed to produce goods, and the United States has significant advantages in these other factors. It is these advantages that result in higher U.S. wages compared to other countries.

Q.9 Is it likely that all U.S. jobs will one day be outsourced? Why or why not?

Globalization   The term globalization is broader than outsourcing. **Globalization** *is the increasing integration of economies, cultures, and institutions across the world*. In a globalized economy, firms think of production and sales at a global level. They produce where

Made in China?

Barbie and her companion Ken are as American as apple pie, and considering their origins gives us some insight into the modern U.S. economy and its interconnection with other countries. Barbie and Ken are not produced in the United States; they never were. When Barbie first came out in 1959, she was produced in Japan. Today, it is unclear where Barbie and Ken are produced. If you look at the box they come in, it says "Made in China," but looking deeper we find that Barbie and Ken are actually made in five different countries, each focusing on an aspect of production that reflects its comparative advantage. Japan produces the nylon hair. China provides much of what is normally considered manufacturing—factory spaces, labor, and energy for assembly—but it imports many of the components. The oil for the plastic comes from Saudi Arabia, which is refined into plastic pellets in Taiwan. The United States even provides some of the raw materials that go into the manufacturing process—it provides the cardboard, packing, paint pigments, and the mold.

The diversification of parts that go into the manufacturing of Barbie and Ken is typical of many goods today.

As the world economy has become more integrated, the process of supplying components of manufacturing has become more and more spread out, as firms have divided up the manufacturing process in search of the least-cost location for each component.

But the global diversity in manufacturing and supply of components is only half the story of modern production. The other half is the shrinking of the relative importance of that manufacturing, and it is this other half that explains how the United States maintains its position in the world when so much of the manufacturing takes place elsewhere. It does so by maintaining its control over the distribution and marketing of the goods. In fact, of the $15 retail cost of a Barbie or Ken, $12 can be accounted for by activities not associated with manufacturing—design, transportation, merchandising, and advertising. And, luckily for the United States, many of these activities are still done in the United States, allowing the country to maintain its high living standard even as manufacturing spreads around the globe.

---

costs are lowest, and sell across the world at the highest price they can get. A globalized world is a world in which economies of the world are highly integrated. Globalization has two effects on firms. The first is positive; because the world economy is so much larger than the domestic economy, the rewards for winning globally are much larger than the rewards for winning domestically. The second effect is negative; it is much harder to win, or even to stay in business, competing in a global market. A company may be the low-cost producer in a particular country yet may face foreign competitors that can undersell it. The global economy increases the number of competitors for the firm. Consider the automobile industry. Three companies are headquartered in the United States, but more than 20 automobile companies operate worldwide. U.S. automakers face stiff competition from foreign automakers; unless they meet that competition, they will not survive.

These two effects are, of course, related. When you compete in a larger market, you have to be better to survive, but if you do survive the rewards are greater.

Globalization increases competition by allowing greater specialization and division of labor, which, as Adam Smith first observed in *The Wealth of Nations*, increases growth and improves the standard of living for everyone. Thus, in many ways globalization is

The global economy increases the number of competitors for the firm.

Insourcing into the United States

In a global economy, a company will locate its operations to wherever it makes most sense to produce. Generally, this means that it will locate where the costs are lowest, or where the company can get some unique benefit. When you think of costs, you should think of all costs, not just labor costs. The same with benefits. Doing so, you can see why companies insource production into the United States—as well as outsource production out of the United States.

Consider Novartis, a global pharmaceutical company, which recently moved its global research headquarters from Switzerland to Cambridge, Massachusetts. It chose the United States because Cambridge had a strong concentration of academic biomedical research facilities, making it a great place for collaborations. In this case, the United States' primary cost advantage was that it had some unique benefits that couldn't be duplicated elsewhere.

Another example of insourcing is Toyota's moving of portions of their car production from Japan to the United States. It did so to reduce transportation costs and reduce the political pressure by the U.S. Congress to institute tariffs on cars produced by foreign-owned companies. Relocating also reduced overall costs relative to Japan since Japanese workers are more expensive than the U.S. workers Toyota hires, although not relative to China, where it also has production facilities.

Even Indian and Chinese firms are establishing branches here in the United States, which is a type of insourcing. For example, Lenovo, the Chinese computer maker, acquired IBM's personal computer division and established sales offices in the United States. Other non-U.S.-based global companies are establishing research and marketing divisions in the United States to take advantage of the creative workforce, and to establish a presence in the United States.

simply another name for increased specialization. Globalization allows (indeed, forces) companies to move operations to countries with a comparative advantage. As they do so, they lower costs of production. Globalization leads to companies specializing in smaller portions of the production process because the potential market is not just one country but the world. Such specialization can lead to increased productivity as firms learn from doing.

 **Q.10** How does globalization reduce the costs of production?

U.S. Comparative Advantage Today and Tomorrow   The United States has excelled particularly in goods that require creativity and innovation. The United States has remained the leader of the world economy and has kept a comparative advantage in many goods even with its high relative wages, in part because of continual innovation. For example, the Internet started in the United States, which is why the United States is the location of so many information technology firms. The United States also has led the way in biotechnology innovation. Similarly, the creative industries, such as film, art, and advertising, have flourished in the United States. These industries are dynamic, high-profit, high-wage industries. (One of the reasons insourcing occurs is that the United States has such a great comparative advantage in these other aspects of production.) As long as U.S. production maintains a comparative advantage in innovation, the United States will be able to specialize in goods that allow firms to pay higher wages.

The real concern about outsourcing involves what happens in the evolution and development of industries. The natural progression is that, as an industry matures, its technology and specialized knowledge spread, which allows more and more of that industry's production to be outsourced. This means that slowly over time the United States can be expected to lose its comparative advantage in currently "new" industries, such as information technology, just as has happened with other industries in the past.

The Developing Country's Perspective on Outsourcing

This book is written from a U.S. point of view. From that perspective, the relevant question is: Can the United States maintain its high wages relative to the low wages in China, India, and other developing countries? I suspect that most U.S. readers hope that it can. From a developing country's perspective, I suspect that the hope is that it cannot; their hope is that their wage rates catch up with U.S. wage rates. Judged from a developing country's perspective, the question is: Is it fair that U.S. workers don't work as hard as we do but earn much more?

The market does not directly take fairness into account. The market is interested only in who can produce a good or service at the lowest cost. This means that in a competitive economy, the United States can maintain its high wages only to the degree that it can produce sufficient goods and services cheaper than low-wage countries can at the market exchange rate. It must keep the trade balance roughly equal.

Developing countries recognize that, in the past, the United States has had a comparative advantage in creativity and innovation, and they are doing everything they can to compete on these levels as well as on basic production levels. They are actively trying to develop such skills in their population and to compete with the United States not only in manufacturing and low-tech jobs but also in research, development, finance, organizational activities, artistic activities, and high-tech jobs. Right now companies in China and India are working to challenge U.S. dominance in all high-tech and creativity fields. (For example, they too are working on nanotechnology.) To do this, they are trying to entice top scientists and engineers to stay in their country, or to return home if they have been studying or working in the United States. Since more than 50 percent of all PhD's given in science, engineering, and economics go to non-U.S. citizens (in economics, it is more than 70 percent), many observers believe that the United States cannot assume its past dominance in the innovative and high-tech fields will continue forever. The competitive front that will determine whether the United States can maintain much higher wages than developing countries is not the competition in current industries, but competition in industries of the future.

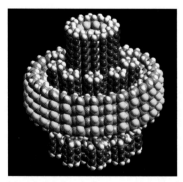

Nanotechnology—dynamic industry of the future?

However, as long as the United States remains as creative and innovative as it has in the past, the outsourcing of maturing industries can be replaced with industries that don't even exist today, just as information technology replaced many areas of manufacturing in the 1990s. One industry that some economists believe the United States is on the edge of developing is nanotechnology (machining at a subatomic level). The point is that with sufficient creativity and innovation, the U.S. economic future can be quite bright.

Exchange Rates and Comparative Advantage   There is, however, reason to be concerned. If innovation and creativity don't develop new industries in which the United States has a comparative advantage fast enough, as the current dynamic industries mature and move to low-wage areas, *at current exchange rates* (the value of a currency relative to the value of foreign currencies), the United States will not maintain comparative advantages in sufficient industries to warrant the relative wage differentials that exist today. In that case, U.S. demand for foreign goods and services will be higher than foreign demand for U.S. goods and services. To bring them into equilibrium, the U.S. wage premium will have to decline to regain our comparative advantages. Since nominal wages (the wages that you see in your paycheck) in the United States are unlikely to fall, this will most likely occur through a decline in the U.S. exchange rate, large increases in foreign wages, or both. Either of these will make foreign products imported into the United States more expensive and U.S. products cheaper for foreigners, and eventually will balance the comparative advantages.

Law of One Price   Many Americans do not like the "exchange rate answer," but in terms of policy, it is probably the best the United States can hope for. If the United States tries to prevent outsourcing with trade restrictions, U.S.-based companies will find that they can no longer compete internationally, and the United States will be in worse shape than if it had allowed outsourcing. The reality is that competition, combined with transferable technology and similar institutions, drives wages and prices of similar factors and goods toward equality. This reality often goes by the name of the **law of one price**—*the wages of workers in one country will not differ significantly from the wages of (equal) workers in another institutionally similar country.* As we will discuss in a later chapter, the debate is about what an "equal" worker is and what an equivalent institutional structure is.

The law of one price states that wages of workers in one country will not differ significantly from the wages of (equal) workers in another institutionally similar country.

Because of a variety of historical circumstances, the United States has been able to avoid the law of one price in wages since World War I. One factor has been the desire of foreigners to increase their holding of U.S. financial assets by trillions of dollars, which has let the United States consume more goods than it produces. Another is that the United States' institutional structure, technology, entrepreneurial labor force, and nonlabor inputs have given the United States sufficiently strong comparative advantages to offset the higher U.S. wage rates. The passage of time and modern technological changes have been eroding the United States' comparative advantages based on institutional structure and technology. To the degree that this continues to happen, to maintain a balance in the comparative advantages of various countries, the wages of workers in other countries such as India and China will have to move closer to the wages of U.S. workers.

Globalization and the Timing of Benefits of Trade   One final comment about outsourcing, globalization, and the U.S. economy is in order. None of the above discussion contradicts the proposition that trade makes both countries better off. Thus, the discussion does not support the position taken by some opponents to trade and globalization that outsourcing is hurting the United States and that the United States can be made better off by limiting outsourcing. Instead the discussion is about the timing of the benefits of trade. Many of the benefits of trade already have been consumed by the United States during the years that the United States has been running trade deficits (importing more than it is exporting). The reality is that the United States has been living better than it could have otherwise precisely because of trade and outsourcing. It also has been living much better than it otherwise could because it is paying for some of its imports with IOUs promising payment in the future instead of with exports. But there is no free lunch, and when these IOUs are presented for payment, the United States will have to pay for some of the benefits that it already has consumed.

The reality is that the United States has been living better than it could have otherwise precisely because of trade and outsourcing.

Conclusion

While the production possibility curve model does not give unambiguous answers as to what government's role should be in regulating trade, it does serve a very important purpose. It is a geometric tool that summarizes a number of ideas in economics: opportunity cost, comparative advantage, efficiency, and how trade leads to efficiency. These ideas are all essential to economists' conversations. They provide the framework within which those conversations take place. Thinking of the production possibility curve (and picturing the economy as being on it) directs you to think of the trade-offs involved in every decision.

Look at questions such as: Should we save the spotted owl or should we allow logging in the western forests? Should we expand the government health care system or should we strengthen our national defense system? Should we emphasize policies that

The production possibility curve represents the tough choices society must make.

allow more consumption now or should we emphasize policies that allow more consumption in the future? Such choices involve difficult trade-offs that can be pictured by the production possibility curve.

Not everyone recognizes these trade-offs. For example, politicians often talk as if the production possibility curve were nonexistent. They promise voters the world, telling them, "If you elect me, you can have more of everything." When they say that, they obscure the hard choices and increase their probability of getting elected.

Economists do the opposite. They promise little except that life is tough, and they continually point out that seemingly free lunches often involve significant hidden costs. Alas, political candidates who exhibit such reasonableness seldom get elected. Economists' reasonableness has earned economics the nickname *the dismal science*.

Economists continually point out that seemingly free lunches often involve significant hidden costs.

Summary

- The production possibility curve measures the maximum combination of outputs that can be obtained from a given number of inputs. It embodies the opportunity cost concept.

- In general, in order to get more and more of something, we must give up ever-increasing quantities of something else. This is the principle of increasing marginal opportunity cost.

- Trade allows people to use their comparative advantage and shift out society's production possibility curve.

- The rise of markets coincided with significant increases in output. Specialization, trade, and competition have all contributed to the increase.

- Points inside the production possibility curve are inefficient, points along the production possibility curve are efficient, and points outside are unattainable.

- By specializing in producing those goods for which one has a comparative advantage (lowest opportunity cost), one can produce the greatest amount of goods with which to trade. Doing so, countries can increase

consumption. The effects of specialization and trade also can be shown by a shift of the production possibility curve out.

- The typical outward bow of the production possibility curve is the result of comparative advantage and trade.

- Because many goods are cheaper to produce in countries such as China and India, production that formerly took place in the United States is being outsourced to foreign countries.

- If the United States can maintain its strong comparative advantage in goods using new technologies and innovation, the jobs lost by outsourcing can be replaced with other high-paying jobs. If it does not, then some adjustments in relative wage rates or exchange rates must occur.

- Outsourcing is a product of the law of one price, which reflects business's tendency to shift production to countries where it is cheapest to produce.

- Globalization is the increasing integration of economies, cultures, and institutions across the world.

Key Terms

comparative
   advantage (27)
efficiency (28)
globalization (35)
inefficiency (28)

input (24)
laissez-faire (32)
law of one price (39)
output (24)
outsourcing (35)

principle of increasing
   marginal opportunity
   cost (26)
production possibility
   curve (24)

production possibility
   table (23)
productive efficiency (27)

Questions for Thought and Review

1. Design a grade production possibility table and curve that embody the principle of increasing marginal opportunity cost.   LO2

2. What would the production possibility curve look like if there were decreasing marginal opportunity costs? Explain. What is an example of decreasing marginal opportunity costs? (Difficult)   LO2

3. Show how a production possibility curve would shift if a society became more productive in its output of widgets but less productive in its output of wadgets.   LO1

4. Show how a production possibility curve would shift if a society became more productive in the output of both widgets and wadgets.   LO1

5. How does the theory of comparative advantage relate to production possibility curves?   LO3

6. When all people use economic reasoning, inefficiency is impossible, because if the benefit of reducing that inefficiency were greater than the cost, the inefficiency would be eliminated. Thus, if people use economic reasoning, it's impossible to be on the interior of a production possibility curve. Is this statement true or false? Why? (Difficult)   LO1

7. If neither of two countries has a comparative advantage in either of two goods, what are the gains from trade?   LO4

8. If income distribution is tied to a particular production technique, how might that change one's view of alternative production techniques? (Difficult)   LO1

9. Does the fact that the production possibilities model tells us that trade is good mean that in the real world free trade is necessarily the best policy? Explain.   LO4

10. What effect has globalization had on the ability of firms to specialize? How has this affected the competitive process?   LO5

11. If workers in China and India become as productive as U.S. workers, what adjustments will allow the United States to regain its competitiveness?   LO5

12. How can exchange rates change to reduce wage differences between countries?   LO5

13. How is outsourcing related to the law of one price?   LO5

Problems and Exercises

14. A country has the following production possibility table:

Resources Devoted to Clothing	Output of Clothing	Resources Devoted to Food	Output of Food
100%	20	0%	0
80	16	20	5
60	12	40	9
40	8	60	12
20	4	80	14
0	0	100	15

   a. Draw the country's production possibility curve.
   b. What's happening to marginal opportunity costs as output of food increases?
   c. Say the country gets better at the production of food. What will happen to the production possibility curve?
   d. Say the country gets equally better at producing both food and clothing. What will happen to the production possibility curve?   LO1, LO2

15. Research shows that after-school jobs are highly correlated with decreases in grade point averages. Those who work 1 to 10 hours get a 3.0 GPA and those who work 21 hours or more have a 2.7 GPA. Higher GPAs are, however, highly correlated with higher lifetime earnings. Assume that a person earns $8,000 per year for working part-time in college, and that the return to a 0.1 increase in GPA gives one a 10 percent increase in one's lifetime earnings with a present value of $80,000.
   a. What would be the argument for working rather than studying harder?
   b. Is the assumption that there is a trade-off between working and grades reasonable?   LO1

16. Suppose the United States and Japan have the following production possibility tables:

Japan		United States	
Bolts of Cloth	Tons of Wheat	Bolts of Cloth	Tons of Wheat
1,000	0	500	0
800	100	400	200
600	200	300	400
400	300	200	600
200	400	100	800
0	500	0	1,000

   a. Draw each country's production possibility curve.
   b. In what good does the United States have a comparative advantage?

c. Is there a possible trade that benefits both countries?

d. Draw their combined production possibility curve.   LO4

17. Assume the United States can produce Toyotas at the cost of $18,000 per car and Chevrolets at $16,000 per car. In Japan, Toyotas can be produced at 1,000,000 yen and Chevrolets at 500,000 yen.

a. In terms of Chevrolets, what is the opportunity cost of producing Toyotas in each country?

b. Who has the comparative advantage in producing Chevrolets?

c. Assume Americans purchase 500,000 Chevrolets and 300,000 Toyotas each year and that the Japanese purchase far fewer of each. Using productive efficiency as the guide, which country should produce Chevrolets and which should produce Toyotas?   LO4

18. Lawns produce no crops but occupy more land (25 million acres) in the United States than any single crop, such as corn. This means that the United States is operating inefficiently and hence is at a point inside the production possibility curve. Right? If not, what does it mean?   LO1

19. Groucho Marx is reported to have said, "The secret of success is honesty and fair dealing. If you can fake those, you've got it made." What would likely happen to society's production possibility curve if everyone could fake honesty? Why? (Hint: Remember that society's production possibility curve reflects more than just technical relationships.) (Difficult)   LO1

20. In 2006 the hourly cost to employers per German industrial worker was $33. The hourly cost to employers per U.S. industrial worker was $23.65, while the average cost per Taiwanese industrial worker was $6.38.

a. Give three reasons why firms produce in Germany rather than in a lower-wage country.

b. Germany has just entered into an agreement with other EU countries that allows people in any EU country, including Greece and Italy, which have lower wage rates, to travel and work in any EU country, including high-wage countries. Would you expect a significant movement of workers from Greece and Italy to Germany right away? Why or why not?

c. Workers in Thailand are paid significantly less than workers in Taiwan. If you were a company CEO, what other information would you want before you decided where to establish a new production facility?   LO5

Questions from Alternative Perspectives

1. Why might government be less capable than the market to do good? (Austrian)

2. The text makes it look as if maximizing output is the goal of society.

a. Is maximizing output the goal of society?

b. If the country is a Christian country, should it be?

c. If not, what should it be? (Religious)

3. It has been said that "capitalism robs us of our sexuality and sells it back to us."

a. Does sex sell?

b. Is sex used to sell goods from Land Rovers to tissue paper?

c. Who, if anyone, is exploited in the use of sex to sell commodities?

d. Are both men and women exploited in the same ways? (Feminist)

4. Thorstein Veblen, one economist to whom this book is dedicated, wrote that *vested interests* are those seeking "something for nothing." In this chapter, you learned how technological bias shapes the economy's production possibilities over time so that a country becomes increasingly good at producing a subset of goods.

a. In what ways have vested interests used their influence to bias the U.S. economy toward the production of military goods at the expense of consumer goods?

b. What are the short-term and long-term consequences of that bias for human welfare, in the United States and abroad? (Institutionalist)

5. Writing in 1776, Adam Smith was concerned not only with the profound effects of the division of labor on productivity (as your textbook notes) but also its stultifying effect on the human capacity. In *The Wealth of Nations*, Smith warned that performing a few simple operations over and over again could render any worker, no matter his or her native intelligence, "stupid and ignorant."

a. Does the division of labor in today's economy continue to have both these effects?

b. What are the policy implications? (Radical)

Web Questions

1. Select a foreign country and, using the CIA World Factbook (www.cia.gov/cia/publications/factbook), answer the following questions:

a. What goods does the country produce? Purchase from another country?

b. In what goods does it have a comparative advantage? Explain your answer.

c. Name one of its trading partners. Why do you think that country is a trading partner?

2. Go to the International Monetary Fund's (IMF) Web site (www.imf.org) and search for the article "Globalization: Threat or Opportunity?" Based on this article:
   a. Does the IMF support or oppose globalization?
   b. Does globalization increase or decrease the amount of inequality in the world?

c. What strategies does it suggest for the poorest countries to benefit from globalization?
d. Does globalization automatically lead to periodic crises?

Answers to Margin Questions

1. You must give up 2 units of good Y to produce 4 units of good X, so the opportunity cost of X is ½ Y. *(24)*

2. If no resource had a comparative advantage, the production possibility curve would be a straight line connecting the points of maximum production of each product as in the graph below.

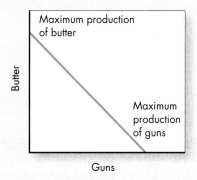

At all points along this curve, the opportunity cost of producing guns and butter is equal. *(27)*

3. Points A and C are along the production possibility curve, so they are points of efficiency. Point B is inside the production possibility curve, so it is a point of inefficiency. Point D is to the right of the production possibility curve, so it is unattainable. *(28)*

4. I remind them of the importance of cultural forces. In Saudi Arabia, women are not allowed to drive. *(29)*

5. The production possibility curve shifts in along the butter axis as in the graph below. *(30)*

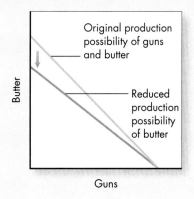

6. The argument that underlies the general laissez-faire policy argument is that when there is competition in trade, individuals are able to pick the best trades available to them and the end result is that both parties to the trade benefit as much as they possibly can. *(33)*

7. Steve's and Sarah's production possibility curves are shown in the figure below. If they specialize, they can, combined, produce 4 loaves of bread and 8 dozen cookies, which they can split up. Say that Steve gets 2 loaves of bread and 5 dozen cookies (point A). This puts him beyond his original production possibility curve, and thus is an improvement for him. That leaves 2 loaves of bread and 3 dozen cookies for Sarah (point B), which is beyond her original production possibility curve, which is an improvement for her. Both are better off than they would have been. *(34)*

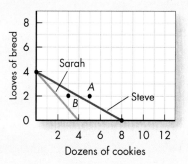

8. False. By producing the good for which it has a comparative advantage (lowest opportunity cost), a country will have the greatest amount of goods with which to trade and will reap the greatest gains from trade. *(34)*

9. No. By definition, if one country has a comparative advantage in producing one set of goods, the other country has a comparative advantage in the production in the other set. Jobs will be needed to support this production. Additionally, many jobs cannot be outsourced effectively because they require physical proximity to the point of sale. *(35)*

10. Globalization allows more trade and specialization. That specialization lowers costs of production since it allows the lowest cost producer to produce each good. *(37)*

Graphish: The Language of Graphs

A picture is worth 1,000 words. Economists, being efficient, like to present ideas in **graphs,** *pictures of points in a coordinate system in which points denote relationships between numbers.* But a graph is worth 1,000 words only if the person looking at the graph knows the graphical language: *Graphish,* we'll call it. (It's a bit like English.) Graphish is usually written on graph paper. If the person doesn't know Graphish, the picture isn't worth any words and Graphish can be babble.

I have enormous sympathy for students who don't understand Graphish. A number of my students get thrown for a loop by graphs. They understand the idea, but Graphish confuses them. This appendix is for them, and for those of you like them. It's a primer in Graphish.

Two Ways to Use Graphs

In this book I use graphs in two ways:

1. To present an economic model or theory visually, showing how two variables interrelate.
2. To present real-world data visually. To do this, I use primarily bar charts, line charts, and pie charts.

Actually, these two ways of using graphs are related. They are both ways of presenting visually the *relationship* between two things.

Graphs are built around a number line, or axis, like the one in Figure A2-1(a). The numbers are generally placed in order, equal distances from one another. That number line allows us to represent a number at an appro-

priate point on the line. For example, point A represents the number 4.

The number line in Figure A2-1(a) is drawn horizontally, but it doesn't have to be; it also can be drawn vertically, as in Figure A2-1(b).

How we divide our axes, or number lines, into intervals is up to us. In Figure A2-1(a), I called each interval 1; in Figure A2-1(b), I called each interval 10. Point A appears after 4 intervals of 1 (starting at 0 and reading from left to right), so it represents 4. In Figure A2-1(b), where each interval represents 10, to represent 5, I place point B halfway in the interval between 0 and 10.

So far, so good. Graphish developed when a vertical and a horizontal number line were combined, as in Figure A2-1(c). When the horizontal and vertical number lines are put together, they're called *axes.* (Each line is an axis. *Axes* is the plural of *axis.*) I now have a **coordinate system**—*a two-dimensional space in which one point represents two numbers.* For example, point A in Figure A2-1(c) represents the numbers (4, 5)—4 on the horizontal number line and 5 on the vertical number line. Point B represents the numbers (1, 20). (By convention, the horizontal numbers are written first.)

Being able to represent two numbers with one point is neat because it allows the relationships between two numbers to be presented visually instead of having to be expressed verbally, which is often cumbersome. For example, say the cost of producing 6 units of something is $4 per unit and the cost of producing 10 units is $3 per unit. By

---

FIGURE A2-1 (A, B, AND C)   **Horizontal and Vertical Number Lines and a Coordinate System**

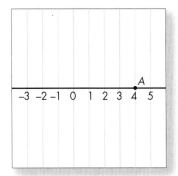

(a) Horizontal Number Line

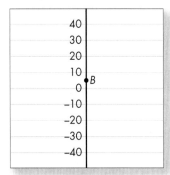

(b) Vertical Number Line

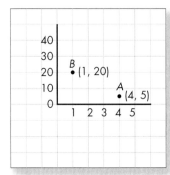

(c) Coordinate System

FIGURE A2-2 (A, B, C, AND D) A Table and Graphs Showing the Relationships between Price and Quantity

	Price per Pen	Quantity of Pens Bought per Day
A	$3.00	4
B	2.50	5
C	2.00	6
D	1.50	7
E	1.00	8

(a) Price Quantity Table

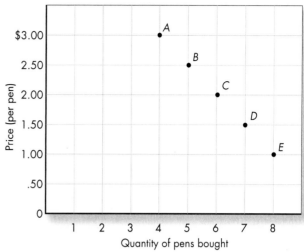

(b) From a Table to a Graph (1)

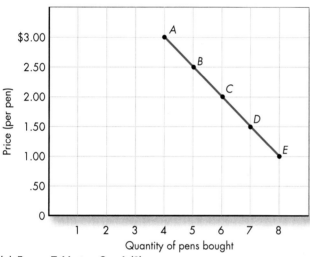

(c) From a Table to a Graph (2)

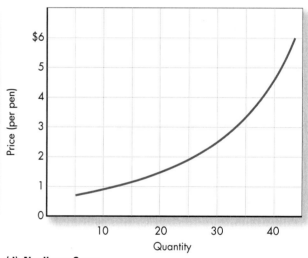

(d) Nonlinear Curve

putting both these points on a graph, we can visually see that producing 10 costs less per unit than does producing 6.

Another way to use graphs to present real-world data visually is to use the horizontal line to represent time. Say that we let each horizontal interval equal a year, and each vertical interval equal $100 in income. By graphing your income each year, you can obtain a visual representation of how your income has changed over time.

Using Graphs in Economic Modeling

I use graphs throughout the book as I present economic models, or simplifications of reality. A few terms are often used in describing these graphs, and we'll now go over them. Consider Figure A2-2(a), which lists the number of pens bought per day (column 2) at various prices (column 1).

We can present the table's information in a graph by combining the pairs of numbers in the two columns of the table and representing, or plotting, them on two axes. I do that in Figure A2-2(b).

By convention, when graphing a relationship between price and quantity, economists place price on the vertical axis and quantity on the horizontal axis.

I can now connect the points, producing a line like the one in Figure A2-2(c). With this line, I interpolate the numbers between the points (which makes for a nice visual presentation). That is, I make the **interpolation**

Inverse and Direct Relationships

Inverse relationship:
When *X* goes up, *Y* goes down.
When *X* goes down, *Y* goes up.

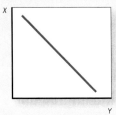

Direct relationship:
When *X* goes up, *Y* goes up.
When *X* goes down, *Y* goes down.

assumption—*the assumption that the relationship between variables is the same between points as it is at the points.* The interpolation assumption allows us to think of a line as a collection of points and therefore to connect the points into a line.

Even though the line in Figure A2-2(c) is straight, economists call any such line drawn on a graph a *curve.* Because it's straight, the curve in A2-2(c) is called a **linear curve**—*a curve that is drawn as a straight line.* Notice that this curve starts high on the left-hand side and goes down to the right. Economists say that any curve that looks like that is *downward-sloping.* They also say that a downward-sloping curve represents an **inverse relationship**—*a relationship between two variables in which when one goes up, the other goes down.* In this example, the line demonstrates an inverse relationship between price and quantity—that is, when the price of pens goes up, the quantity bought goes down.

Figure A2-2(d) presents a **nonlinear curve**—*a curve that is drawn as a curved line.* This curve, which really is curved, starts low on the left-hand side and goes up to the right. Economists say any curve that goes up to the right is *upward-sloping.* An upward-sloping curve represents a **direct relationship**—*a relationship in which when one variable goes up, the other goes up too.* The direct relationship I'm talking about here is the one between the two variables (what's measured on the horizontal and vertical lines). *Downward-sloping* and *upward-sloping* are terms you need to memorize if you want to read, write, and speak Graphish, keeping graphically in your mind the image of the relationships they represent.

46

Slope

One can, of course, be far more explicit about how much the curve is sloping upward or downward by defining it in terms of **slope**—*the change in the value on the vertical axis divided by the change in the value on the horizontal axis.* Sometimes the slope is presented as "rise over run":

$$\text{Slope} = \frac{\text{Rise}}{\text{Run}} = \frac{\text{Change in value on vertical axis}}{\text{Change in value on horizontal axis}}$$

Slopes of Linear Curves

In Figure A2-3, I present five linear curves and measure their slope. Let's go through an example to show how we can measure slope. To do so, we must pick two points. Let's use points *A* (6, 8) and *B* (7, 4) on curve *a.* Looking at these points, we see that as we move from 6 to 7 on the horizontal axis, we move from 8 to 4 on the vertical axis. So when the number on the vertical axis falls by 4, the number on the horizontal axis increases by 1. That means the slope is −4 divided by 1, or −4.

Notice that the inverse relationships represented by the two downward-sloping curves, *a* and *b*, have negative slopes, and that the direct relationships represented by the two upward-sloping curves, *c* and *d*, have positive slopes. Notice also that the flatter the curve, the smaller the numerical value of the slope; and the more vertical, or steeper, the curve, the larger the numerical value of the slope. There are two extreme cases:

1. When the curve is horizontal (flat), the slope is zero.
2. When the curve is vertical (straight up and down), the slope is infinite (larger than large).

Knowing the term *slope* and how it's measured lets us describe verbally the pictures we see visually. For example, if I say a curve has a slope of zero, you should picture in your mind a flat line; if I say "a curve with a slope of minus one," you should picture a falling line that makes a 45° angle with the horizontal and vertical axes. (It's the hypotenuse of an isosceles right triangle with the axes as the other two sides.)

Slopes of Nonlinear Curves

The preceding examples were of *linear (straight) curves.* With *nonlinear curves*—the ones that really do curve—the slope of the curve is constantly changing. As a result, we must talk about the slope of the curve at a particular point, rather than the slope of the whole curve. How can a point have a slope? Well, it can't really, but it can almost, and if that's good enough for mathematicians, it's good enough for us.

FIGURE A2-3   Slopes of Curves

The slope of a curve is determined by rise over run. The slope of curve *a* is shown in the graph. The rest are shown below:

	Rise	÷	Run	=	Slope
b	−1		+2		−.5
c	1		1		1
d	4		1		4
e	1		1		1

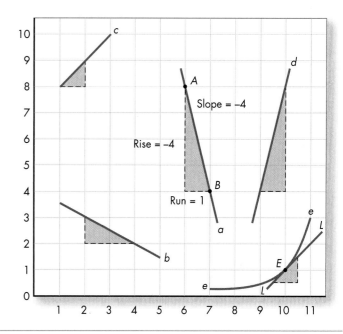

Defining the slope of a nonlinear curve is a bit more difficult. The slope at a given point on a nonlinear curve is determined by the slope of a linear (or straight) line that's tangent to that curve. (A line that's tangent to a curve is a line that just touches the curve, and touches it only at one point in the immediate vicinity of the given point.) In Figure A2-3, the line *LL* is tangent to the curve *ee* at point *E*. The slope of that line, and hence the slope of the curve at the one point where the line touches the curve, is +1.

Maximum and Minimum Points

Two points on a nonlinear curve deserve special mention. These points are the ones for which the slope of the curve is zero. I demonstrate those in Figure A2-4(a) and (b). At point *A* we're at the top of the curve, so it's at a maximum point; at point *B* we're at the bottom of the curve, so it's at a minimum point. These maximum and minimum points are often referred to by economists, and it's important to realize that the value of the slope of the curve at each of these points is zero.

There are, of course, many other types of curves, and much more can be said about the curves I've talked about. I won't do so because, for purposes of this course, we won't need to get into those refinements. I've presented as much Graphish as you need to know for this book.

FIGURE A2-4 (A AND B)   A Maximum and a Minimum Point

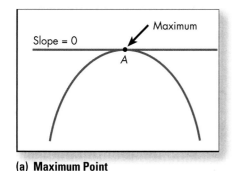

(a) Maximum Point

(b) Minimum Point

FIGURE A2-5 (A, B, AND C) A Shifting Curve versus a Movement along a Curve

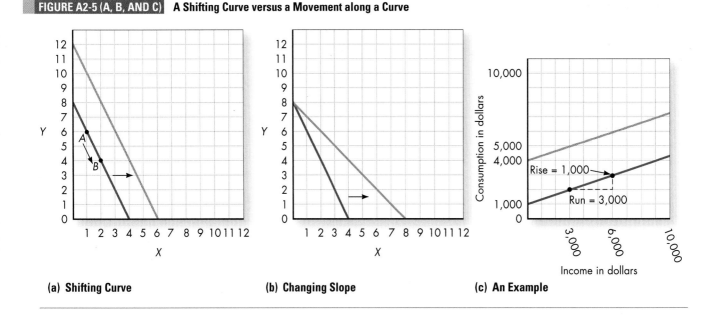

(a) Shifting Curve   (b) Changing Slope   (c) An Example

Equations and Graphs

Sometimes economists depict the relationships shown in graphs using equations. Since I present material algebraically in the appendixes to a few chapters, let me briefly discuss how to translate a linear curve into an equation. Linear curves are relatively easy to translate because all linear curves follow a particular mathematical form: $y = mx + b$, where y is the variable on the vertical axis, x is the variable on the horizontal axis, m is the slope of the line, and b is the vertical-axis intercept. To write the equation of a curve, look at that curve, plug in the values for the slope and vertical-axis intercept, and you've got the equation.

For example, consider the blue curve in Figure A2-5(a). The slope (rise over run) is -2 and the number where the curve intercepts the vertical axis is 8, so the equation that depicts this curve is $y = -2x + 8$. It's best to choose variables that correspond to what you're measuring on each axis, so if price is on the vertical axis and quantity is on the horizontal axis, the equation would be $p = -2q + 8$. This equation is true for any point along this line. Take point A (1, 6), for example. Substituting 1 for x and 6 for y into the equation, you see that $6 = -2(1) + 8$, or $6 = 6$. At point B, the equation is still true: $4 = -2(2) + 8$. A move from point A to point B is called a *movement along a curve*. A movement along a curve does not change the relationship of the variables; rather, it shows how a change in one variable affects the other.

Sometimes the relationship between variables will change. The curve will either shift, change slope, or both

shift and change slope. These changes are reflected in changes to the m and b variables in the equation. Suppose the vertical-axis intercept rises from 8 to 12, while the slope remains the same. The equation becomes $y = -2x + 12$; for every value of y, x has increased by 4. Plotting the new equation, we can see that the curve has *shifted* to the right, as shown by the orange line in Figure A2-5(a). If instead the slope changes from -2 to -1, while the vertical-axis intercept remains at 8, the equation becomes $y = -x + 8$. Figure A2-5(b) shows this change graphically. The original blue line stays anchored at 8 and rotates out along the horizontal axis to the new orange line.

Here's an example for you to try. The lines in Figure A2-5(c) show two relationships between consumption and income. Write the equation for the blue line.

The answer is $C = \frac{1}{3}Y + \$1,000$. Remember, to write the equation you need to know two things: the vertical-axis intercept (\$1,000) and the slope ($\frac{1}{3}$). If the intercept changes to \$4,000, the curve will shift up to the orange line as shown.

Presenting Real-World Data in Graphs

The previous discussion treated the Graphish terms that economists use in presenting models that focus on hypothetical relationships. Economists also use graphs in presenting actual economic data. Say, for example, that you want to show how exports have changed over time. Then you would place years on the horizontal axis (by convention) and exports on the vertical axis, as in Figure A2-6(a) and (b).

FIGURE A2-6 (A, B, AND C)   **Presenting Information Visually**

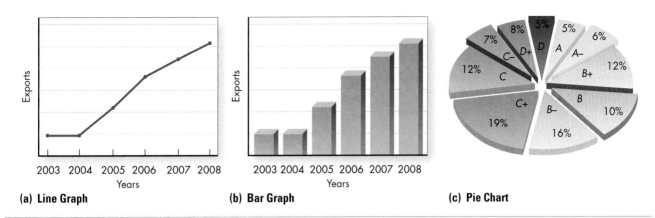

(a) Line Graph   (b) Bar Graph   (c) Pie Chart

Having done so, you have a couple of choices: you can draw a **line graph**—*a graph where the data are connected by a continuous line*; or you can make a **bar graph**—*a graph where the area under each point is filled in to look like a bar*. Figure A2-6(a) shows a line graph and Figure A2-6(b) shows a bar graph.

Another type of graph is a **pie chart**—*a circle divided into "pie pieces," where the undivided pie represents the total amount and the pie pieces reflect the percentage of the whole pie that the various components make up*. This type of graph is useful in visually presenting how a total amount is divided. Figure A2-6(c) shows a pie chart, which happens to represent the division of grades on a test I gave. Notice that 5 percent of the students got As.

There are other types of graphs, but they're all variations on line and bar graphs and pie charts. Once you understand these three basic types of graphs, you shouldn't have any trouble understanding the other types.

Interpreting Graphs about the Real World

Understanding Graphish is important because, if you don't, you can easily misinterpret the meaning of graphs. For example, consider the two graphs in Figure A2-7(a) and (b). Which graph demonstrates the larger rise in income? If you said (a), you're wrong. The intervals in the vertical axes differ, and if you look carefully you'll see that the curves in both graphs represent the same combination of points. So when considering graphs, always make sure you understand the markings on the axes. Only then can you interpret the graph.

FIGURE 2-7 (A AND B)   **The Importance of Scales**

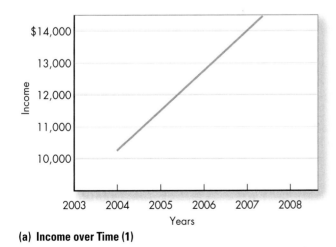

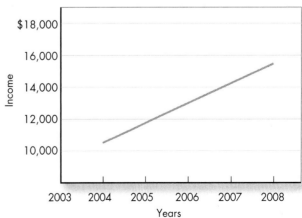

(a) Income over Time (1)   (b) Income over Time (2)

Quantitative Literacy: Avoiding Stupid Math Mistakes

The data of economics are often presented in graphs and tables. Numerical data are compared by the use of percentages, visual comparisons, and simple relationships based on quantitative differences. Economists who have studied the learning process of their students have found that some very bright students have some trouble with these presentations. Students sometimes mix up percentage changes with level changes, draw incorrect implications from visual comparisons, and calculate quantitative differences incorrectly. This is not necessarily a math problem—at least in the sense that most economists think of math. The mistakes are in relatively simple stuff—the kind of stuff learned in fifth, sixth, and seventh grades. Specifically, as reported in "Student Quantitative Literacy: Is the Glass Half-full or Half-empty?" (Robert Burns, Kim Marie McGoldrick, Jerry L. Petr, and Peter Schuhmann, 2002 University of North Carolina at Wilmington Working Paper), when the professors gave a test to students at a variety of schools, they found that a majority of students missed the following questions.

1. What is 25 percent of 400?
   a. 25   b. 50   c. 100
   d. 400   e. none of the above

2. Consider Figure A2-8 where U.S oil consumption and U.S. oil imports are plotted for 1990–2000. Fill in the blanks to construct a true statement: U.S. domestic oil consumption has been steady while imports have been _____ ; therefore U.S. domestic oil production has been

   _____.

   a. rising; rising   b. falling; falling
   c. rising; falling   d. falling; rising

3. Refer to the following table to select the true statement.

Economic Growth in Poland Percent Increase in GDP, 1990–1994				
1990	1991	1992	1993	1994
−11.7	−7.8	−1.5	4.0	3.5

   a. GDP in Poland was larger in 1992 than in 1991.
   b. GDP in Poland was larger in 1994 than in 1993.
   c. GDP in Poland was larger in 1991 than in 1992.
   d. GDP in Poland was larger in 1993 than in 1994.
   e. Both b and c are true.

FIGURE A2-8

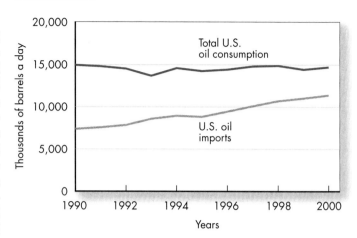

4. If U.S. production of corn was 60 million bushels in 2002 and 100 million bushels in 2003, what was the percentage change in corn production from 2002 to 2003?
   a. 40   b. 60   c. 66.67
   d. 100   e. 200

The reason students got these questions wrong is unknown. Many of them had had higher-level math courses, including calculus, so it is not that they weren't trained in math. I suspect that many students missed the questions because of carelessness: the students didn't think about the question carefully before they wrote down the answer.

Throughout this book we will be discussing issues assuming a quantitative literacy sufficient to answer these questions. Moreover, questions using similar reasoning will be on exams. So it is useful for you to see whether or not you fall in the majority. So please answer the four questions given above now if you haven't done so already.

Now that you've answered them, I give you the correct answers upside-down in the footnote at the bottom of the page.[1] If you got all four questions right, great! You can stop reading this appendix now. If you missed one or more, read the explanations of the correct answers carefully.

1. The correct answer is c. To calculate a percentage, you multiply the percentage times the number. Thus, 25 percent of 400 is 100.

2. The correct answer is c. To answer it you had to recognize that U.S. consumption of oil comes from U.S. imports and U.S. production. Thus, the distance between the two lines represents U.S. production, which is clearly getting smaller from 1990 to 2000.

1-c; 2-c; 3-e; 4-c.

3. The correct answer is e. The numbers given to you are percentage changes, and the question is about levels. If the percentage change is positive, as it is in 1993 and 1994, the level is increasing. Thus, 1994 is greater (by 3.5 percent) than 1993, even though the percentage change is smaller than in 1993. If the percentage change is negative, as it is in 1992, the level is falling. Because income fell in 1992, the level of income in 1991 is greater than the level of income in 1992.

4. The correct answer is c. To calculate percentage change, you first need to calculate the change, which in this case is $100 - 60$, or 40. So corn production started at a base of 60 and rose by 40. To calculate the percentage change that this represents, you divide the amount of the rise, 40, by the base, 60. Doing so gives us $40/60 = 2/3 = .6667$, which is 66.67 percent.

Now that I've given you the answers, I suspect that most of you will recognize that they are the right answers. If, after reading the explanations, you still don't follow the reasoning, you should look into getting some extra help in the course either from your teacher, from your TA, or from some program the college has. If, after reading the explanations, you follow them and believe that if you had really thought about them you would have gotten them right, then the next time you see a chart or a table of numbers being compared *really think about them*. Be a bit slower in drawing inferences since they are the building blocks of economic discussions. If you want to do well on exams, it probably makes sense to practice some similar questions to make sure that you have concepts down.

A Review

Let's now review what we've covered.

- A graph is a picture of points on a coordinate system in which the points denote relationships between numbers.
- A downward-sloping line represents an inverse relationship or a negative slope.
- An upward-sloping line represents a direct relationship or a positive slope.
- Slope is measured by rise over run, or a change of y (the number measured on the vertical axis) over a change in x (the number measured on the horizontal axis).
- The slope of a point on a nonlinear curve is measured by the rise over the run of a line tangent to that point.
- At the maximum and minimum points of a nonlinear curve, the value of the slope is zero.
- A linear curve has the form $y = mx + b$.
- A shift in a linear curve is reflected by a change in the b variable in the equation $y = mx + b$.
- A change in the slope of a linear curve is reflected by a change in the m variable in the equation $y = mx + b$.
- In reading graphs, one must be careful to understand what's being measured on the vertical and horizontal axes.

Key Terms

bar graph *(49)*
coordinate system *(44)*
direct relationship *(46)*

graph *(44)*
interpolation
    assumption *(45)*

inverse relationship *(46)*
line graph *(49)*
linear curve *(46)*

nonlinear curve *(46)*
pie chart *(49)*
slope *(46)*

Questions for Thought and Review

1. Create a coordinate space on graph paper and label the following points:
    a. (0, 5)
    b. (−5, −5)
    c. (2, −3)
    d. (−1, 1)

2. Graph the following costs per unit, and answer the questions that follow.

Horizontal Axis: Output	Vertical Axis: Cost per Unit
1	$30
2	20
3	12
4	6
5	2
6	6
7	12
8	20
9	30

a. Is the relationship between cost per unit and output linear or nonlinear? Why?
b. In what range in output is the relationship inverse? In what range in output is the relationship direct?
c. In what range in output is the slope negative? In what range in output is the slope positive?
d. What is the slope between 1 and 2 units?

3. Within a coordinate space, draw a line with
   a. Zero slope.   b. Infinite slope.
   c. Positive slope.   d. Negative slope.

4. Calculate the slope of lines *a* to *e* in the following coordinate system.

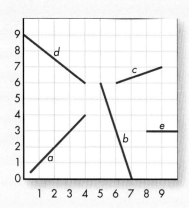

5. Given the following nonlinear curve, answer the following questions:

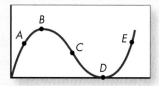

a. At what point(s) is the slope negative?
b. At what point(s) is the slope positive?
c. At what point(s) is the slope zero?
d. What point is the maximum? What point is the minimum?

6. Draw the graphs that correspond to the following equations:
   a. $y = 3x - 8$
   b. $y = 12 - x$
   c. $y = 4x + 2$

7. Using the equation $y = 3x + 1,000$, demonstrate the following:
   a. The slope of the curve changes to 5.
   b. The curve shifts up by 500.

8. State what type of graph or chart you might use to show the following real-world data:
   a. Interest rates from 1929 to 2005.
   b. Median income levels of various ethnic groups in the United States.
   c. Total federal expenditures by selected categories.
   d. Total costs of producing between 100 and 800 shoes.

Economic Institutions

3

Nobody can be a great economist who is only an economist—and I am even tempted to add that the economist who is only an economist is likely to become a nuisance if not a positive danger.

—F. Hayek

The powerful U.S. economy generates a high standard of living and sense of economic well-being (compared to most other countries) for almost all those living in the United States. The reason why is often attributed to its use of markets, and to the wonders of a market economy. To some degree, that's true, but simply saying markets are the reason for the strength of the U.S. economy obscures as much information as it conveys. First, it misses the point that other countries have markets too, but many of those have much lower standards of living. Second, it conveys a sense that markets exist independently of social and cultural institutions, and that's just not correct. Markets are highly developed social constructs that are part of a country's social and economic institutions. Markets are based on **institutions,** which Nobel Prize winning economist, Douglass North defines as *"the formal and informal rules that constrain human economic behavior."* Institutions include laws that protect ownership of property, and the legal system to enforce and interpret laws. They also include political institutions that develop those laws, the cultural traits of society that guide people's tastes and behaviors, and the many organizational structures, such as corporations, banks, and non-profit organizations, that make up our economy. To understand markets, you need to understand institutions. In a principles course, we don't have time to develop a full analysis of institutions, but what we can do is to provide an overview of U.S. economic institutions, and a brief discussion of why they are important. That's what we do in this chapter.

We begin by looking at the U.S. economic system in historical perspective, considering how it evolved and how it relates to other historical economic systems. Then we consider some of the central institutions of the modern U.S. economy and how they influence the way in which the economy works.

The U.S. Economy in Historical Perspective

A market economy is an economic system based on private property and the market. It gives private property rights to individuals and relies on market forces to coordinate economic activity.

The U.S. economy is a **market economy**—*an economic system based on private property and the market in which, in principle, individuals decide how, what, and for whom to produce.* In a market economy, individuals follow their own self-interest, while market forces of supply and demand are relied on to coordinate those individual pursuits. Businesses, guided by prices in the market, produce goods and services that they believe people want and that will earn a profit for the business. Prices in the market guide businesses in deciding what to produce. Distribution of goods is to each individual according to his or her ability, effort, inherited property, and luck.

Reliance on market forces doesn't mean that political, social, and historical forces play no role in coordinating economic decisions. These other forces do influence how the market works. For example, for a market to exist, government must allocate and defend **private property rights**—*the control a private individual or firm has over an asset.* The concept of private ownership must exist and must be accepted by individuals in society. When you say, "This car is mine," it means that it is unlawful for someone else to take it without your permission. If someone takes it without your permission, he or she is subject to punishment through the legal system.

Q-1 John, your study partner, is telling you that the best way to allocate property rights is through the market. How do you respond?

How Markets Work

Markets work through a system of rewards and payments. If you do something, you get paid for doing that something; if you take something, you pay for that something. How much you get is determined by how much you give. This relationship seems fair to most people. But there are instances when it doesn't seem fair. Say someone is unable to work. Should that person get nothing? How about Joe down the street, who was given $10 million by his parents? Is it fair that he gets lots of toys, like Corvettes and skiing trips to Aspen, and doesn't have to work, while the rest of us have to work 40 hours a week and maybe go to school at night?

I'll put those questions about fairness off at this point—they are very difficult questions. For now, all I want to present is the concept of fairness that underlies a market economy: "Them that works, gets; them that don't, starve."[1] In a market economy, individuals are encouraged to follow their own self-interest.

In market economies, individuals are free to do whatever they want as long as it's legal. The market is relied on to see that what people want to get, and want to do, is consistent with what's available. Price is the mechanism through which people's desires are coordinated and goods are rationed. If there's not enough of something to go around, its price goes up; if more of something needs to get done, the price given to individuals willing to do it goes up. If something isn't wanted or doesn't need to be done, its price goes down. In a market economy, fluctuations in prices play a central role in coordinating individuals' wants.

Fluctuations in prices play a central role in coordinating individuals' wants in a market economy.

---

[1] How come the professor gets to use rotten grammar but screams when he sees rotten grammar in your papers? Well, that's fairness for you. Actually, I should say a bit more about writing style. All writers are expected to know correct grammar; if they don't, they don't deserve to be called writers. Once you know grammar, you can individualize your writing style, breaking the rules of grammar where the meter and flow of the writing require it. In college you're still proving that you know grammar, so in papers handed in to your teacher, you shouldn't break the rules of grammar until you've proved to the teacher that you know them. Me, I've done lots of books, so my editors give me a bit more leeway than your teachers will give you.

What's Good about the Market?

Is the market a good way to coordinate individuals' activities? Much of this book will be devoted to answering that question. The answer that I, and most U.S. economists, come to is: Yes, it is a reasonable way. True, it has problems; the market can be unfair, mean, and arbitrary, and sometimes it is downright awful. Why then do economists support it? For the same reason that Oliver Wendell Holmes supported democracy—it is a lousy system, but, based on experience with alternatives, it is better than all the others we've thought of.

The primary debate among economists is not about using markets; it is about how markets should be structured, and whether they should be modified and adjusted by government regulation. Those are much harder questions, and on these questions, opinions differ enormously.

Capitalism and Socialism

The view that markets are a reasonable way to organize society has not always been shared by all economists. Throughout history strong philosophical and practical arguments have been made against markets. The philosophical argument against the market is that it brings out the worst in people—it glorifies greed. It encourages people to beat out others rather than to be cooperative. As an alternative some economists have supported socialism. In theory, **socialism** is *an economic system based on individuals' goodwill toward others, not on their own self-interest, and in which, in principle, society decides what, how, and for whom to produce.* The concept of socialism developed in the 1800s as a description of a hypothetical economic system to be contrasted with the predominant market-based economic system of the time, which was called capitalism. **Capitalism** is defined as *an economic system based on the market in which the ownership of the means of production resides with a small group of individuals called capitalists.*

You can best understand the idea behind theoretical socialism by thinking about how decisions are made in a family. In most families, benevolent parents decide who gets what, based on the needs of each member of the family. When Sabin gets a new coat and his sister Sally doesn't, it's because Sabin needs a coat while Sally already has two coats that fit her and are in good condition. Victor may be slow as molasses, but from his family he still gets as much as his superefficient brother Jerry gets. In fact, Victor may get more than Jerry because he needs extra help.

Markets have little role in most families. In my family, when food is placed on the table, we don't bid on what we want, with the highest bidder getting the food. In my family, every person can eat all he or she wants, although if one child eats more than a fair share, that child gets a lecture from me on the importance of sharing. "Be thoughtful; be considerate. Think of others first" are lessons that many families try to teach.

In theory, socialism was an economic system that tried to organize society in the same way as most families are organized, trying to see that individuals get what they need. Socialism tried to take other people's needs into account and adjust people's own wants in accordance with what's available. In socialist economies, individuals were urged to look out for the other person; if individuals' inherent goodness does not make them consider the general good, government would make them. In contrast, a capitalist economy expected people to be selfish; it relied on markets and competition to direct that selfishness to the general good.[2]

---

[2]As you probably surmised, the above distinction is too sharp. Even capitalist societies wanted people to be selfless, but not too selfless. Children in capitalist societies were generally taught to be selfless at least in dealing with friends and family. The difficulty parents and societies face is finding a balance between the two positions: selfless but not too selfless; selfish but not too selfish.

Web Note 3.1
What Are Markets?

The primary debate among economists is not about using markets but about how markets are structured.

Q.2 Which would be more likely to attempt to foster individualism: socialism or capitalism?

Q.3 Are there any activities in a family that you believe should be allocated by a market? What characteristics do those activities have?

Socialism is, in theory, an economic system that tries to organize society in the same way as most families are organized—all people contribute what they can and get what they need.

Tradition and Today's Economy

In a tradition-based society, the social and cultural forces create an inertia (a tendency to resist change) that predominates over economic and political forces.

"Why did you do it that way?"

"Because that's the way we've always done it."

Tradition-based societies had markets, but they were peripheral, not central, to economic life. In feudal times, what was produced, how it was produced, and for whom it was produced were primarily decided by tradition.

In today's U.S. economy, the market plays the central role in economic decisions. But that doesn't mean that tradition is dead. As I said in Chapter 1, tradition still plays a significant role in today's society, and, in many aspects of society, tradition still overwhelms the invisible hand. Consider the following:

1. The persistent view that women should be homemakers rather than factory workers, consumers rather than producers.

2. The raised eyebrows when a man is introduced as a nurse, secretary, homemaker, or member of any other profession conventionally identified as women's work.

3. Society's unwillingness to permit the sale of individuals or body organs.

4. Parents' willingness to care for their children without financial compensation.

Each of these tendencies reflects tradition's influence in Western society. Some are so deeply rooted that we see them as self-evident. Some of tradition's effects we like; others we don't—but we often take them for granted. Economic forces may work against these traditions, but the fact that they're still around indicates the continued strength of tradition in our market economy.

Q-4 What is the difference between socialism in theory and socialism in practice?

As I stated above, the term *socialism* originally developed as a description of a hypothetical, not an actual, economic system. Actual socialist economies came into being only in the early 1900s, and when they developed they differed enormously from the hypothetical socialist economies that writers had described earlier.

In practice socialist governments had to take a strong role in guiding the economy. Socialism became known as an economic system based on government ownership of the means of production, with economic activity governed by central planning. In a centrally planned socialist economy, sometimes called a command economy, government planning boards set society's goals and then directed individuals and firms as to how to achieve those goals.

For example, if government planning boards decided that whole-wheat bread was good for people, they directed firms to produce large quantities and priced it exceptionally low. Planners, not prices, coordinated people's actions. The results were often not quite what the planners desired. Bread prices were so low that pig farmers fed bread to their pigs even though pig feed would have been better for the pigs and bread was more costly to produce. At the low price, the quantity of bread demanded was so high that there were bread shortages; consumers had to stand in long lines to buy bread for their families.

As is often the case, over time the meaning of the word *socialism* expanded and evolved further. It was used to describe the market economies of Western Europe, which by the 1960s had evolved into economies that had major welfare support systems and governments that were very much involved in their market economies. For example, Sweden, even though it relied on markets as its central coordinating institution, was called a socialist economy because its taxes were high and it provided a cradle-to-grave welfare system.

When the Union of Soviet Socialist Republics (USSR) broke apart, Russia and the countries that evolved out of the USSR adopted a market economy as their organizing framework. China, which is ruled by the Communist Party, also adopted many market institutions. As they did, the terms *capitalism* and *socialism* fell out of favor. Since the 1990s, people have talked little about the differences in economic systems such as capitalism and socialism; instead they have talked about the differences in institutions. Most economies today are differentiated primarily by the degree to which their economies rely on markets, not whether they are a market, capitalist, or socialist economy.

The term *socialism*, however, still shows up in the news. China, for example, continues to call itself a socialist country, even though it is relying more and more heavily on markets to organize production, and is sometimes seen as more capitalistic than many Western economies. Another example of the interest in socialism can be found in the rhetoric of Venezuelan President Hugo Chavez who is attempting to transform Venezuela into what he calls "21st century socialism." He defines 21st century socialism as government ownership, or at least control, of major resources, and an economy dominated by business cooperatives owned and operated by workers supported by government loans and contracts. President Chavez argues that this "21st century socialism" will serve as a new economic model of egalitarianism for the entire world. To date, the Venezuelan economy has been growing, and the approach seems to be successful. But some of that success is due to the large oil revenues that the Venezuelan government began collecting after Chavez took over the oil companies. What will happen to the Venezuelan economy when that oil money ends is yet to be seen.

> Since the 1990s people have talked little about differences in economic systems; instead they have talked about differences in institutions.

Evolving Economic Systems[3]

An important lesson of the above discussion is that economic systems and the institutions that make them up are constantly evolving, and will likely continue to evolve. Let's consider that evolution briefly. What became known as capitalism came into widespread existence in the mid-1700s; socialism came into existence in the early 1900s. Before capitalism and socialism, other forms of economic systems existed, including **feudalism**—*an economic system in which traditions rule*. In feudalism if your parents were serfs (small farmers who lived on a manor), you would be a serf. Feudalism dominated the Western world from about the 8th century to the 15th century.

> Feudalism is an economic system in which traditions rule.

Throughout the feudalistic period, merchants and artisans (small manufacturers who produced goods by hand) grew in importance and wealth, and eventually their increased importance led to a change in the economic system from feudalism to **mercantilism**—*an economic system in which government determines the what, how, and for whom decisions by doling out the rights to undertake certain economic activities*.

Mercantilism remained the dominant economic system until the 1700s, when the **Industrial Revolution**—*a time when technology and machines rapidly modernized industrial production and mass-produced goods replaced handmade goods*—led to a decrease in power of small producers, an increase in power of capitalists, and eventually to a revolution instituting capitalism as the dominant economic system.

> Mercantilism is an economic system in which government doles out the rights to undertake economic activities.

I mention feudalism and mercantilism because aspects of both continue in economies today. For example, governments in Japan and Korea play significant roles in directing their economies. Their economic systems are sometimes referred to as *neomercantilist economies*.

---

[3]The appendix to this chapter traces the development of economic systems from feudalism to mercantilism to capitalism to socialism to modern-day forms of market economies in a bit more detail.

Revolutionary shifts that give rise to new economic systems are not the only way economic systems change. Systems also evolve internally, as I discussed above. For example, the U.S. economy is and has always been a market economy, but it has changed over the years, evolving with changes in social customs, political forces, and the strength of markets. In the 1930s, during the Great Depression, the U.S. economy integrated a number of what might be called socialist institutions into its existing institutions. Distribution of goods was no longer, even in theory, only according to ability; need also played a role. Governments began to play a larger role in the economy, taking control over some of the *how, what,* and *for whom* decisions. Since the 1980s, the process has been reversed. The United States became even more market oriented and the government tried to pull back its involvement in the market in favor of private enterprise. Whether that movement will continue remains to be seen, but we can expect institutions to continue to change.

The U.S. Economy

Q₅ Into what three sectors are market economies generally broken up?

Now that we have put the U.S. economic system in historical perspective, let's consider some of its main components. The U.S. economy can be divided up into three sectors: businesses, households, and government, as Figure 3-1 shows. Households supply labor and other factors of production to businesses and are paid by businesses for doing so. The market where this interaction takes place is called a *factor market*. Businesses produce goods and services and sell them to households and government. The market where this interaction takes place is called the *goods market*.

Each of the three sectors is interconnected; moreover, the entire U.S. economy is interconnected with the world economy. Notice also the arrows going out to and coming in from both business and households. Those arrows represent the connection of an economy to the world economy. It consists of interrelated flows of goods (exports

---

FIGURE 3-1   **Diagrammatic Representation of a Market Economy**

This circular-flow diagram of the economy is a good way to organize your thinking about the aggregate economy. As you can see, the three sectors—households, government, and business—interact in a variety of ways.

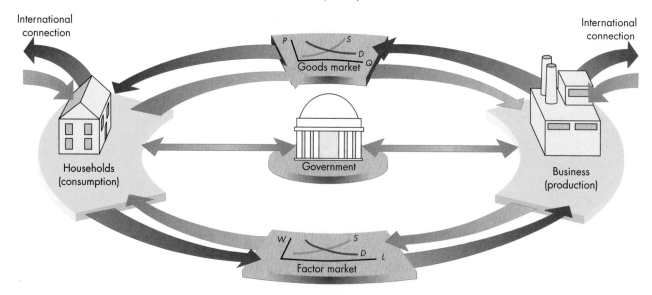

and imports) and money (capital flows). Finally, consider the arrows connecting government with households and business. Government taxes business and households. It buys goods and services from business and buys labor services from households. Then, with some of its tax revenue, it provides services (for example, roads, education) to both business and households and gives some of its tax revenue directly back to individuals. In doing so, it redistributes income. But government also serves a second function. It oversees the interaction of business and households in the goods and factor markets. Government, of course, is not independent. The United States, for instance, is a democracy, so households vote to determine who shall govern. Similarly, governments are limited not only by what voters want but also by their relationships with other countries. They are part of an international community of countries, and they must keep up relations with other countries in the world. For example, the United States is a member of many international organizations and has signed international treaties in which it has agreed to limit its domestic actions, such as its ability to tax imports.

Now let's look briefly at the individual components.

Business

President Calvin Coolidge once said, "The business of America is business." That's a bit of an overstatement, but business is responsible for over 80 percent of U.S. production. (Government is responsible for the other 20 percent.) In fact, anytime a household decides to produce something, it becomes a business. **Business** is simply the name given to *private producing units in our society.*

Businesses in the United States decide *what* to produce, *how* much to produce, and *for whom* to produce it. They make these central economic decisions on the basis of their own self-interest, which is influenced by market incentives. Anyone who wants to can start a business, provided he or she can come up with the required cash and meet the necessary regulatory requirements. Each year, about 700,000 businesses are started.

Don't think of business as something other than people. Businesses are ultimately made up of a group of people organized together to accomplish some end. Although corporations account for about 85 percent of all sales, in terms of numbers of businesses, most are one- or two-person operations. Home-based businesses are easy to start. All you have to do is say you're in business, and you are. However, some businesses require licenses, permits, and approvals from various government agencies. That's one reason why **entrepreneurship** (*the ability to organize and get something done*) is an important part of business.

What Do U.S. Firms Produce?   Producing physical goods is only one of society's economic tasks. Another task is to provide services (activities done for others). Services do not involve producing a physical good. When you get your hair cut, you buy a service, not a good. Much of the cost of the physical goods we buy actually is not a cost of producing the good, but is a cost of one of the most important services: distribution (getting the good to where the consumer is). After a good is produced, it has to get to the individuals who are going to consume it at the time they need it. If the distribution system gets botched up, it's as if the good had never been produced.

Let's consider an example. Take hot dogs at a baseball game. How many of us have been irked that a hot dog that costs 25¢ to fix at home costs $4 at a baseball game? But a hot dog at home isn't the same as a hot dog at a game. Distribution of the good is as important as production; you're paying the extra $3.75 for distribution, which is a central component of a service economy.

The importance of the service economy can be seen in modern technology companies. They provide information and methods of handling information, not physical goods. Computer operating systems such as Linux and Windows can be supplied over

Web Note 3.2
Starting a Business

Businesses in the United States decide *what* to produce, *how* much to produce, and *for whom* to produce it.

the Internet; no physical production is necessary. As the U.S. economy has evolved, the relative importance of services has increased. Today, services make up approximately 80 percent of the U.S. economy, compared to 20 percent in 1947, and services are likely to continue to rise in importance in the future.

Consumer Sovereignty and Business   To say that businesses decide what to produce isn't to say that **consumer sovereignty** (*the consumer's wishes determine what's produced*) doesn't reign in the United States. Businesses decide what to produce based on what they believe will sell. A key question a person in the United States generally asks about starting a business is: Can I make a profit from it? **Profit** is *what's left over from total revenues after all the appropriate costs have been subtracted.* Businesses that guess correctly what the consumer wants generally make a profit. Businesses that guess wrong generally operate at a loss.

People are free to start businesses for whatever purposes they want. No one asks them: "What's the social value of your term paper assistance business, your Twinkies business, your pornography business, or your textbook publishing business?" In the United States we rely on the market to channel individuals' desire to make a profit into the general good of society. That's the invisible hand at work. As long as the business violates no law and conforms to regulations, people in the United States are free to start whatever business they want, if they can get the money to finance it.

Forms of Business   The three primary forms of business are sole proprietorships, partnerships, and corporations. Of the 30 million businesses in the United States, approximately 72 percent are sole proprietorships, 8 percent are partnerships, and 20 percent are corporations, as we see in Figure 3-2(a). In terms of total receipts, however, we get a quite different picture, with corporations far surpassing all other business forms, as Figure 3-2(b) shows. In fact, the largest 1,000 corporations account for about 80 percent of the total receipts of all U.S. businesses.

Sole proprietorships—*businesses that have only one owner*—are the easiest to start and have the fewest bureaucratic hassles. **Partnerships**—*businesses with two or more owners*—create possibilities for sharing the burden, but they also create unlimited liability for

Although businesses decide what to produce, they are guided by consumer sovereignty.

Q-6 In the United States, the invisible hand ensures that only socially valuable businesses are started. True or false? Why?

Q-7 Are most businesses in the United States corporations? If not, what are most businesses?

FIGURE 3-2 (A AND B)   **Forms of Business**

The charts divide firms by the type of ownership. Approximately 72 percent of businesses in the United States are sole proprietorships (**a**). In terms of annual receipts, however, corporations surpass all other forms (**b**).

Source: *Statistics of Income*, IRS, Summer 2006 (www.irs.ustreas.gov).

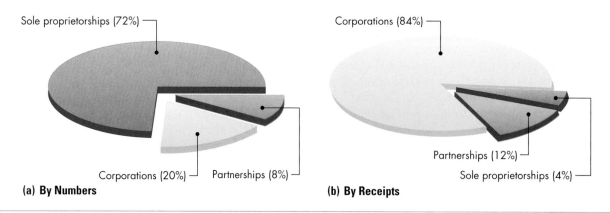

(a) **By Numbers**   (b) **By Receipts**

each of the partners. **Corporations**—*businesses that are treated as a person, and are legally owned by their stockholders, who are not liable for the actions of the corporate "person"*—are the largest form of business when measured in terms of receipts. In corporations, ownership is separated from control of the firm. When a corporation is formed, it issues **stock** (*certificates of ownership in a company*), which is sold or given to individuals. Proceeds from the sale of that stock make up what is called the *equity capital* of a company.

Corporations were initially developed as institutions to make it easier for company owners (i.e., stockholders) to be separated from company management, but today many corporations exist because they offer tax and legal advantages to their owners. A corporation provides the owners with **limited liability**—*the stockholder's liability is limited to the amount the stockholder has invested in the company*. With the other two forms of business, owners can lose everything they possess even if they have only a small amount invested in the company, but in a corporation the owners can lose only what they have invested in that corporation. If you've invested $100, you can lose only $100. In the other kinds of business, even if you've invested only $100, you could lose everything; the business's losses must be covered by the individual owners. Corporations' limited liability makes it easier for them to attract investment capital. Corporations pay taxes, but they also offer their individual owners ways of legally avoiding taxes.[4]

A corporation provides the owner with limited liability.

The advantages and disadvantages of each form of business are summarized in the following table:

Advantages and Disadvantages of Various Forms of For-Profit Businesses

	Sole Proprietorship	Partnership	Corporation
Advantages	1. Minimum bureaucratic hassle 2. Direct control by owner	1. Ability to share work and risks 2. Relatively easy to form	1. No personal liability 2. Increasing ability to get funds 3. Ability to avoid personal income taxes
Disadvantages	1. Limited ability to get funds 2. Unlimited personal liability	1. Unlimited personal liability (even for partner's blunder) 2. Limited ability to get funds	1. Legal hassle to organize 2. Possible double taxation of income 3. Monitoring problems

Finance and Business Much of what you hear in the news about business concerns financial assets—assets that acquire value from an obligation of someone else to pay. Stocks are one example of a financial asset; bonds are another. Financial assets are traded in markets such as the New York Stock Exchange. Trading in financial markets can make people rich (or poor) quickly. Stocks and bonds also can provide a means through which corporations can finance expansions and new investments.

Trading in financial markets can make people rich (or poor) quickly.

An important tool investors use to decide where to invest is the accounting statements firms provide. From these, individuals judge how profitable firms are, and how profitable they are likely to be in the future. In the early 2000s, investors' trust in firms

---

[4]As laws have evolved, the sharp distinctions among forms of businesses have blurred. Today there are many types of corporations and types of partnerships that have varying degrees of limited liabilities.

was shattered by a series of accounting frauds, which led government to increase the regulatory control of business accounting practices.

E-Commerce and the Digital Economy   Stocks were particularly important in the late 1990s to the development and expansion of new ".com" (read: dot-com) companies based on **e-commerce** (*buying and selling over the Internet*). E-commerce comes in a variety of forms, depending on who is buying and selling from whom. The following diagram provides the standard classifications. (The *B* refers to businesses and the *C* consumers.)

B2B (Business-to-Business)

Firms exchanging goods and services through online sales and auctions.

An example is a business that buys office supplies from Staples.com.

B2C (Business-to-Consumer)

Firms selling goods and services to consumers through online catalogs and shopping cart software.

An example is an individual buying a book from Amazon.com.

C2B (Consumer-to-Business)

An individual offering goods and services to firms online.

An example is a blogger who offers advertising space to businesses.

C2C (Consumer-to-Consumer)

Individuals buying and selling goods to one another online.

An example is an individual auctioning an item on eBay.

Notice that e-commerce includes business selling to business (B2B), business selling to consumers (B2C), consumers selling to business (C2B), and consumers selling to consumers (C2C). Although most of you see the influence of e-commerce in the B2C and C2C areas (Amazon.com and eBay are examples), B2B is the most important; it represents about 90 percent of e-commerce sales. With increasing frequency, companies are advertising specifications for needed parts and are accepting bids from a variety of new companies all over the world. The result is increased competition for existing suppliers, lower prices, and increased productivity—more output coming out of a given amount of inputs.

E-commerce is growing in importance in the other areas too. More and more individuals are buying cars, books, and prescription drugs on the Internet. Even when they don't buy on the Internet, they will often compare prices on the Internet before making a purchase. Traditional "brick-and-mortar" firms that don't adapt to this new reality will not stay competitive and will be forced out of business. Car dealers, for example, now face consumers who have researched dealer prices and dealer costs on the Internet. Similarly, local bookstores must compete with Amazon.com, which they do by both reducing their prices and providing services that can be provided only on-site, such as book groups and cafés to enhance the shopping experience. Other brick-and-mortar companies are starting their own Internet divisions, and will combine with Internet providers, becoming "bricks-and-clicks" firms. For example, Sears bought Lands' End, and the combined company offers goods in Sears stores, over the Internet, and by catalog.

The impact of e-commerce is just beginning. The government, in fact, began to collect data about e-commerce only in 1999. Although e-commerce is growing about 20 percent a year, just over 1 percent of purchases by consumers are made on the Internet.

E-commerce is growing in importance.

Sales among businesses on the Internet amount to over 15 percent of all business-to-business transactions, and are growing about 5 percent a year. The potential impact of e-commerce is enormous.

E-commerce brings people together at a low cost in a virtual marketplace where geographic location doesn't matter. By reducing the importance of location, e-commerce broadens the potential marketplace. No longer is Main Street, USA, or The Mall the market; the market can be as wide as the world.

For companies where location isn't important, e-commerce reduces the need for buildings, shelving, or a large retail staff, lowering the cost of starting up a new business and continuing to do business. Today, building a storefront can be as easy as registering a domain name and designing a home page. Because e-commerce creates a market without geographic boundaries, companies can search for the lowest-cost labor, hiring employees as far away as India, and sell goods to customers thousands of miles away.

Consumers can search for the lowest price from hundreds of virtual stores and, with a single click of a button, buy it. E-commerce allows small specialty firms to compete in niche markets, where previously they could not. For example, in my small Vermont town, a company exists that sells bow ties (Beau Ties Ltd.) all over the world, even though probably a total of five people in Middlebury wear bow ties. (I'm definitely not one of them.) By broadening the market and increasing the amount of information available, e-commerce places greater competitive pressure on firms. As e-commerce continues to evolve, existing firms will face greater pressure to lower their costs, lower their prices, and redefine their business models. E-commerce's long-run effect on the U.S. economy is uncertain, but what is not uncertain is that it will have an impact. To understand our economy is to understand that it has always been evolving and will continue to evolve in the future.

> E-commerce brings people together at a low cost in a virtual marketplace where geographic location doesn't matter.

Households

The second classification we'll consider in this overview of U.S. economic institutions is households. **Households** (*groups of individuals living together and making joint decisions*) are the most powerful economic institution. They ultimately control government and business, the other two economic institutions. Households' votes in the political arena determine government policy; their decisions about supplying labor and capital determine what businesses will have available to work with; and their spending decisions or expenditures (the "votes" they cast with their dollars) determine what business will be able to sell.

> In the economy, households vote with their dollars.

The Power of Households   While the ultimate power does in principle reside with the people and households, we, the people, have assigned much of that power to representatives. As I discussed above, corporations are only partially responsive to owners of their stocks, and much of that ownership is once-removed from individuals. Ownership of 1,000 shares in a company with a total of 2 million shares isn't going to get you any influence over the corporation's activities. As a stockholder, you simply accept what the corporation does.

A major decision that corporations make independently of their stockholders concerns what to produce. True, ultimately we, the people, decide whether we will buy what business produces, but business spends a lot of money telling us what services we want, what products make us "with it," what books we want to read, and the like. Most economists believe that consumer sovereignty reigns—that we are not fooled or controlled by advertising. Still, it is an open question in some economists' minds whether we, the people, control business or the business representatives control people.

> Consumer sovereignty reigns, but it works indirectly by influencing businesses.

Because of this assignment of power to other institutions, in many spheres of the economy households are not active producers of output but merely passive recipients of income, primarily in their role as suppliers of labor.

Suppliers of Labor   The largest source of household income is wages and salaries (the income households get from labor). Households supply the labor with which businesses produce and government governs. The total U.S. labor force is about 153 million people, about 4.5 percent (7 million) of whom were unemployed in 2006. The average U.S. workweek is 41.8 hours for males and 36.2 hours for females. The average pay in the United States was $743 per week for males and $600 for females, which translates to $17.18 per hour for males and $16.57 for females. Of course, that average represents enormous variability and depends on the occupation and region of the country where one is employed. For example, lawyers often earn $100,000 per year; physicians earn about $150,000 per year; and CEOs of large corporations often make $2 million per year or more. A beginning McDonald's employee generally makes about $12,000 per year.

The table below shows predicted growth rates of certain jobs. Notice that many of the fastest-growing jobs are in service industries; many of the fastest declining are in manufacturing and agriculture. This is not surprising, since the United States has become largely a service economy.

Fastest-Growing Jobs*	**Fastest-Declining Jobs***
Home health aides (56%)	Textile knitting and weaving (−56%)
Network systems and data communications analysts (52%)	Meter readers (−45%)
Medical assistants (50%)	Credit authorizers (−42%)
Physician assistants (50%)	Sewing machine operators (−37%)

*Projection for 2004–2014, based on moderate growth assumptions.

Source: *Employment and Earnings*, Bureau of Labor Statistics, and *Occupational Outlook Handbook, 2006–2007* (http://stats.bls.gov).

Government

The third major U.S. economic institution I'll consider is government. Government plays two general roles in the economy. It's both a referee (setting the rules that determine relations between business and households) and an actor (collecting money in taxes and spending that money on projects, such as defense and education). Let's first consider government's role as an actor.

Government as an Actor   The United States has a federal government system, which means we have various levels of government (federal, state, and local), each with its own powers. Together they consume about 20 percent of the country's total output and employ over 21 million individuals. The various levels of government also have a number of programs that redistribute income through taxation and social welfare and assistance programs designed to help specific groups.

State and local governments employ over 18 million people and spend nearly $2 trillion a year. As you can see in Figure 3-3(a), state and local governments get much of their income from taxes: property taxes, sales taxes, and state and local income taxes. They spend their tax revenues on public welfare, administration, education (education through high school is available free in U.S. public schools), and roads, as Figure 3-3(b) shows.

Web Note 3.3
Government Web Sites

FIGURE 3-3 (A AND B)   **Income and Expenditures of State and Local Governments**

The charts give you a sense of the importance of state and local governments—where they get **(a)** and where they spend **(b)** their revenues.

Source: *State and Local Government Finance Estimates,* Bureau of the Census (www.census.gov).

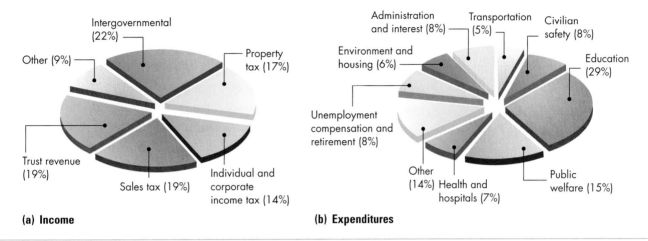

(a) Income   **(b) Expenditures**

Probably the best way to get an initial feel for the federal government and its size is to look at the various categories of its tax revenues and expenditures in Figure 3-4(a). Notice income taxes make up about 40 percent of the federal government's revenue, and Social Security taxes also make up about 40 percent. That's 80 percent of the federal government's revenues, most of which show up as a deduction from your paycheck. In Figure 3-4(b), notice that the federal government's two largest categories of spending are income security and health and education, with expenditures on national defense close behind.

Government as a Referee   Even if government spending made up only a small proportion of total expenditures, government would still be central to the study of

Q-8 The largest percentage of federal expenditures is in what general category?

FIGURE 3-4 (A AND B)   **Income and Expenditures of the Federal Government**

The pie charts show the sources and uses of federal government revenue. It is important to note that, when the government runs a deficit, expenditures exceed income and the difference is made up by borrowing, so the size of the income and expenditure pies may not be equal.

Source: *Survey of Current Business,* 2006, Bureau of Economic Analysis (www.bea.doc.gov).

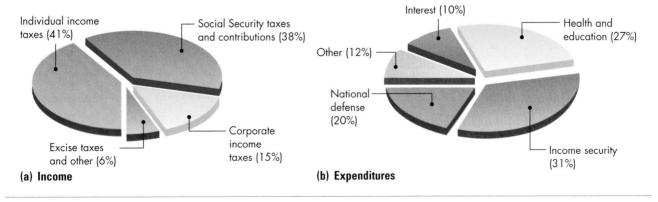

(a) Income   **(b) Expenditures**

economics. The reason is that, in a market economy, government sets the rules of interaction between households and businesses, and acts as a referee, changing the rules when it sees fit. Government decides whether economic forces will be allowed to operate freely.

Some examples of U.S. laws regulating the interaction between households and businesses today are

1. Businesses are not free to hire and fire whomever they want. They must comply with equal opportunity and labor laws. Even closing a plant requires 60 days' notice for many kinds of firms.

2. Many working conditions are subject to government regulation: safety rules, wage rules, overtime rules, hours-of-work rules, and the like.

3. Businesses cannot meet with other businesses to agree on prices they will charge.

4. In some businesses, workers must join a union to work at certain jobs.

Most of these laws evolved over time. Up until the 1930s, household members, in their roles as workers and consumers, had few rights. Businesses were free to hire and fire at will and, if they chose, to deceive and take advantage of consumers.

Over time, new laws to curb business abuses have been passed, and government agencies have been formed to enforce these laws. Many people think the pendulum has swung too far the other way. They believe businesses are saddled with too many regulatory burdens.

One big question that I'll address throughout this book is: What referee role should the government play in an economy? For example, should government use its taxing powers to redistribute income from the rich to the poor? Should it allow mergers between companies? Should it regulate air traffic? Should it regulate prices? Should it attempt to stabilize fluctuations of aggregate income?

In its role as both an actor and a referee, government plays a variety of specific roles in the economy. These include

1. Providing a stable set of institutions and rules.

2. Promoting effective and workable competition.

3. Correcting for externalities.

4. Ensuring economic stability and growth.

5. Providing public goods.

6. Adjusting for undesirable market results.

Provide a Stable Set of Institutions and Rules   A basic role of government is to provide a stable institutional framework that includes the set of laws specifying what can and cannot be done as well as a mechanism to enforce those laws. For example, if someone doesn't pay you, you can't go take what you are owed; you have to go through the government court system. The government restricts individuals from enforcing contracts; it retains that role for itself. Before people conduct business, they need to know the rules of the game and have a reasonable belief about what those rules will be in the future. These rules can initially develop spontaneously, but as society becomes more complex, the rules must be formalized into written laws within a legal system; enforcement mechanisms must be established. The modern market economy requires enforceable complex contractual arrangements among individuals. Where governments don't provide a stable institutional framework, as often happens in developing and transitional countries, economic activity is difficult; usually such economies are stagnant. Zimbabwe in the early 2000s is an example. As various groups fought for political control, the Zimbabwe economy stagnated.

Promote Effective and Workable Competition   In a market economy, the pressure to monopolize—for one firm to try to control the market—and competition are always in conflict, and the government must decide what role it is to play in protecting or promoting competition. Thus, when Microsoft gained a monopolistic control of the computer operating system market with Windows, the U.S. government took the company to court and challenged that monopoly.

Historically, U.S. sentiment runs against **monopoly power**—*the ability of individuals or firms currently in business to prevent other individuals or firms from entering the same kind of business*. Monopoly power gives existing firms and individuals the ability to raise their prices. Similarly, individuals' or firms' ability to enter freely into business activities is generally seen as good. Government's job is to promote competition and prevent excess monopoly power from limiting competition.

What makes this a difficult function for government is that most individuals and firms believe that competition is far better for the other guy than it is for themselves, that their own monopolies are necessary monopolies, and that competition facing them is unfair competition. For example, most farmers support competition, but these same farmers also support government farm subsidies (payments by government to producers based on production levels) and import restrictions. Likewise, most firms support competition, but these same firms also support tariffs, which protect them from foreign competition. Most professionals, such as architects and engineers, support competition, but they also support professional licensing, which limits the number of competitors who can enter their field. Now, as you will see when reading the newspapers, there are always arguments for limiting entry into fields. The job of the government is to determine whether these arguments are strong enough to overcome the negative effects those limitations have on competition.

Correct for Externalities   When two people freely enter into a trade or agreement, they both believe that they will benefit from the trade. But unless they're required to do so, traders are unlikely to take into account any effect that an action may have on a third party. Economists call *the effect of a decision on a third party not taken into account by the decision maker* an **externality**. An externality can be positive (in which case society as a whole benefits from the trade between the two parties) or negative (in which case society as a whole is harmed by the trade between the two parties).

An example of a positive externality is education. When someone educates herself or himself, all society benefits, since better-educated people usually make better citizens and are better equipped to figure out new approaches to solving problems— approaches that benefit society as a whole. An example of a negative externality is pollution. Air conditioners emit a small amount of chlorofluorocarbons into the earth's atmosphere and contribute to the destruction of the ozone layer. Since the ozone layer protects all living things by filtering some of the sun's harmful ultraviolet light rays, a thinner layer of ozone can contribute to cancer and other harmful or fatal conditions. Neither the firms that produce the air conditioners nor the consumers who buy them take those effects into account. This means that the destruction of the ozone layer is an externality—the result of an effect that is not taken into account by market participants.

When there are externalities, there is a potential role for government.

When there are externalities, there is a potential role for government to adjust the market result. If one's goal is to benefit society as much as possible, actions with positive externalities should be encouraged and actions with negative externalities should be discouraged. Governments can step in and change the rules so that the actors must take into account the effect of their actions on society as a whole. I emphasize that the role is a potential one for two reasons. The first is that government often has difficulty dealing with externalities in such a way that society gains. For example, even if the

U.S. government totally banned products that emit chlorofluorocarbons, other countries might not do the same and the ozone layer would continue to be destroyed. The second reason is that government is an institution that reflects, and is often guided by, politics and vested interests. It's not clear that, given the political realities, government intervention to correct externalities would improve the situation. In later chapters I'll have a lot more to say about government's role in correcting for externalities.

Ensure Economic Stability and Growth   In addition to providing general stability, government has the potential role of providing economic stability. Most people would agree that if it's possible, government should prevent large fluctuations in the level of economic activity, maintain a relatively constant price level, and provide an economic environment conducive to economic growth. These aims, which became the goals of the U.S. government in 1946 when the Employment Act was passed, are generally considered macroeconomic goals. They're justified as appropriate aims for government to pursue because they involve **macroeconomic externalities** (*externalities that affect the levels of unemployment, inflation, or growth in the economy as a whole*).

> A macroeconomic externality is the effect of an individual decision that affects the levels of unemployment, inflation, or growth in an economy as a whole but is not taken into account by the individual decision maker.

Here's how a macro externality could occur. When individuals decide how much to spend, they don't take into account the effects of their decision on others; thus, there may be too much or too little spending. Too little spending often leads to unemployment. But in making their spending decision, people don't take into account the fact that spending less might create unemployment. So their spending decisions can involve a macro externality. Similarly, when people raise their price and don't consider the effect on inflation, they too might be creating a macro externality.

Provide Public Goods   Another role for government is to supply public goods. A **public good** is *a good that if supplied to one person must be supplied to all and whose consumption by one individual does not prevent its consumption by another individual*. In contrast, a **private good** is *a good that, when consumed by one individual, cannot be consumed by another individual*. An example of a private good is an apple; once I eat that apple, no one else can consume it. An example of a public good is national defense, which, if supplied to one, will also protect others. In order to supply defense, governments must force people to pay for it with taxes, rather than leaving it to the market to supply it.

There are very few pure public goods, but many goods have public good aspects to them, and, in general, economists use the term *public good* to describe goods that are most efficiently provided collectively rather than privately. Parks, playgrounds, roads, and (as noted above) national defense are examples. Let's consider national defense more closely. For technological reasons, national defense must protect all individuals in an area; a missile system cannot protect some houses in an area without protecting others nearby.

Everyone agrees that national defense is needed, but not everyone takes part in it. If someone else defends the country, you're defended for free; you can be a **free rider**—*a person who gets a benefit but does not contribute to paying for the cost of that benefit*. Because self-interested people would like to enjoy the benefits of national defense while letting someone else pay for it, everyone has an incentive to be a free rider. But if everyone tries to be a free rider, there won't be any national defense. In such cases, government can step in and require that everyone pay part of the cost of national defense, reducing the free rider problem.

Adjust for Undesirable Market Results   A controversial role for government is to adjust the results of the market when those market results are seen as socially undesirable. Government redistributes income, taking it away from some individuals and giving it to others whom it sees as more deserving or more in need. In doing so, it attempts to see that the outcomes of trades are fair. Determining what's fair is a difficult philosophical question that economists can't answer. That question is for the people, through the government, to decide.

An example of this role involves having government decide what's best for people, independently of their desires. The market allows individuals to decide. But what if people don't know what's best for themselves? Or what if they do know but don't act on that knowledge? For example, people might know that addictive drugs are bad for them, but because of peer pressure, or because they just don't care, they may take drugs anyway. Government action prohibiting such activities through laws or high taxes may then be warranted. *Goods or activities that government believes are bad for people even though they choose to use the goods or engage in the activities* are called **demerit goods or activities**. Illegal drugs are a demerit good and using addictive drugs is a demerit activity.

Alternatively, there are some activities that government believes are good for people, even if people may not choose to engage in them. For example, government may believe that going to the opera or contributing to charity is a good activity. But in the United States only a small percentage of people go to the opera, and not everyone in the United States contributes to charity. Similarly, government may believe that whole-wheat bread is more nutritious than white bread. But many consumers prefer white bread. Goods like whole-wheat bread and activities like contributing to charity are known as **merit goods or activities**—*goods and activities that government believes are good for you even though you may not choose to engage in the activities or consume the goods*. Government sometimes provides support for them through subsidies or tax benefits.

> With merit and demerit goods, individuals are assumed to be doing what is not in their self-interest.

Market Failures and Government Failures   The reasons for government intervention are often summed up in the phrase *market failure*. **Market failures** are *situations in which the market does not lead to a desired result*. In the real world, market failures are pervasive—the market is always failing in one way or another. But the fact that there are market failures does not mean that government intervention will improve the situation. There are also **government failures**—*situations in which the government intervenes and makes things worse*. Government failures are pervasive in the government—the government is always failing in one way or another. So real-world policy makers usually end up choosing which failure—market failure or government failure—will be least problematic.

> Q₉ If there is an externality, does that mean that the government should intervene in the market to adjust for that externality?

Global Institutions

What we've done so far in this chapter is to put the U.S. economy in historical and institutional perspective. In this last section, we briefly put it into perspective relative to the world economy. By doing so, we gain a number of insights into the U.S. economy. The U.S. economy makes up 20 percent of world output and consumption, a percentage that is much larger than its relative size by geographic area (6 percent of the world's land mass) or by population (less than 5 percent of the world population). Second, it is becoming more integrated; it is impossible to talk about U.S. economic institutions without considering how those institutions integrate with the world economy.

Global Corporations

Consider corporations. Most large corporations today are not U.S., German, or Japanese corporations; they are **global corporations** (*corporations with substantial operations on both the production and sales sides in more than one country*). Just because a car has a Japanese or German name doesn't mean that it was produced abroad. Many Japanese and German companies now have manufacturing plants in the United States, and many U.S.

> Global corporations are corporations with substantial operations on both the production and sales sides in more than one country.

Our International Competitors

The world economy is often divided into three main areas or trading blocs: the Americas, Europe and Africa, and East Asia. These trading blocs are shown in the map below.

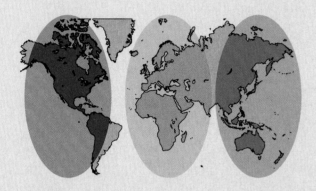

Each area has a major currency. In the Americas, it is the dollar; in Europe, it is the euro, a currency recently created by the European Union; and in East Asia, it is the Japanese yen. These areas are continually changing; the EU recently expanded to 27 countries, incorporating many of the countries of Eastern Europe. China's economy has been growing fast and, given the size of its population, is likely to overtake Japan as the key Asian economy in the coming decades.

The accompanying table gives you a sense of the similarities and differences in the economies of the United States, China, and the European Union.

	United States	China	European Union
Area (square miles)	3,537,438	3,705,407	1,535,286
Population	300 million	1.3 billion	457 million
GDP, 2006*	$13.2 trillion	$10 trillion	$12.8 trillion
Percentage of world output	20.3%	15.4%	19.6%
GDP per capita	$44,295	$7,690	$28,000
Natural resources	Coal, copper, lead, and others	Coal, iron ore	Coal, iron ore, natural gas, fish, and others
Exports as a percentage of GDP	8%	10%	10%
Imports as a percentage of GDP	14%	8%	11%
Currency value (as of March 2007)	Dollar ($1 = $1)	Yuan (7.75 Yuan = $1)	Euro (€0.76 = $1)

*Calculated using purchasing power parity.

Source: *Eurostat Yearbook 2006* (europa.eu.int/comm/eurostat); *CIA World Factbook 2006* (www.cia.gov); and current exchange rate tables. Currency changes can affect GDP figures. GDP updated by the author.

firms have manufacturing plants abroad. Others, such as Chrysler and Daimler Benz, merged and then split up again. When goods are produced by global corporations, corporate names don't always tell much about where a good is produced. As global corporations' importance has grown, most manufacturing decisions are made in reference to the international market, not the U.S. domestic market. This means that the consumer sovereignty that guides decisions of firms is becoming less and less U.S. consumer sovereignty, and more and more global consumer sovereignty.

Global corporations offer enormous benefits for countries. They create jobs; they bring new ideas and new technologies to a country; and they provide competition for domestic companies, keeping them on their toes. But global corporations also pose a number of problems for governments. One is their implication for domestic and international policy. A domestic corporation exists within a country and can be dealt with using policy measures within that country. A global corporation exists within many countries and there is no global government to regulate or control it. If it doesn't like the policies in one country—say taxes are too high or regulations too tight—it can shift its operations to other countries.

Coordinating Global Issues

Global economic issues differ from national economic issues because national economies have governments to referee disputes among players in the economy; global economies do not; no international government exists. Some argue that we need a global government to oversee global businesses. But, no such government exists. The closest institution there is to a world government is the United Nations (UN), which, according to critics, is simply a debating society. It has no ability to tax and no ability to impose its will separate from the political and military power of its members. When the United States opposes a UN mandate, it can, and often does, ignore it. Hence, international problems must be dealt with through negotiation, consensus, bullying, and concessions.

Governments, however, have developed a variety of international institutions to promote negotiations and coordinate economic relations among countries. Besides the United Nations, these include the World Bank, the World Court, and the International Monetary Fund (IMF). These organizations have a variety of goals. For example, the World Bank, a multinational, international financial institution, works with developing countries to secure low-interest loans, channeling such loans to them to foster economic growth. The International Monetary Fund (IMF), a multinational, international financial institution, is concerned primarily with monetary issues. It deals with international financial arrangements. When developing countries encountered financial problems in the 1980s and had large international debts that they could not pay, the IMF helped work on repayment plans.

Countries also have developed global and regional organizations whose job it is to coordinate trade among countries and reduce trade barriers. On the international level, the World Trade Organization (WTO) works to reduce trade barriers among countries. On the regional level, there are the European Union (EU), which is an organization of European countries that developed out of a trade association devoted to reducing trade barriers among member countries; the North American Free Trade Agreement (NAFTA), an organization devoted to reducing trade barriers between the United States, Mexico, and Canada; and Mercosur and the Free Trade Area of the Americas, organizations devoted to reducing trade barriers among North, Central, and South American countries.

In addition to these formal institutions, there are informal meetings of various countries. These include the Group of Five, which meets to promote negotiations and to coordinate economic relations among countries. The Five are Japan, Germany, Britain, France, and the United States. The Group of Eight also meets to promote negotiations and coordinate economic relations among countries. The Eight are the five countries just named plus Canada, Italy, and Russia.

Since governmental membership in international organizations is voluntary, their power is limited. When the United States doesn't like a World Court ruling, it simply states that it isn't going to follow the ruling. When the United States is unhappy with what the United Nations is doing, it withholds some of its dues. Other countries do the same from time to time. Other member countries complain but can do little to force compliance. It doesn't work that way domestically. If you decide you don't like U.S. policy and refuse to pay your taxes, you'll wind up in jail.

What keeps nations somewhat in line when it comes to international rules is a moral tradition: Countries want to (or at least want to look as if they want to) do what's "right." Countries will sometimes follow international rules to keep international opinion favorable to them. But perceived national self-interest often overrides international scruples.

Governments have developed international institutions to promote negotiations and coordinate economic relations among countries. Some are:

the UN
the World Bank
the World Court
the International Monetary Fund.

Countries have developed global and regional organizations to coordinate trade and reduce trade barriers. Some are:

the WTO
the EU
NAFTA.

Since governmental membership in international organizations is voluntary, their power is limited.

Q.10 If the United States chooses not to follow a World Court decision, what are the consequences?

Conclusion

This has been a whirlwind introduction to economic institutions and their role in the economy. Each of them—business, households, and government—is important, and to understand what happens in the economy, one must have a sense of how these institutions work and the role they play. In the remainder of the book we won't discuss institutions much as we concentrate on presenting economic analysis. I rely upon you to integrate the analysis with institutions, as you apply the economic analysis and reasoning that you learn to the real world.

Summary

- A market economy is an economic system based on private property and the market. It gives private property rights to individuals and relies on market forces to solve the *what*, *how*, and *for whom* problems.

- In a market economy, price is the mechanism through which people's desires are coordinated and goods are rationed. The U.S. economy today is a market economy.

- In principle, under socialism society solves the *what*, *how*, and *for whom* problems in the best interest of the individuals in society. It is based on individuals' goodwill toward one another.

- In practice, socialism is an economic system based on government ownership of the means of production, with economic activity governed by central planning. Socialism in practice is sometimes called a command economy.

- The predominant market-based system during the early 1900s was capitalism, an economic system based on the market in which the ownership of production resided with a small group of individuals called capitalists.

- In feudalism, tradition rules; in mercantilism, the government rules; in capitalism, the market rules.

- Economic systems are in a constant state of evolution.

- A diagram of the U.S. market economy shows the connections among businesses, households, and government. It also shows the U.S. economic connection to other countries.

- In the United States, businesses make the *what*, *how*, and *for whom* decisions.

- Although businesses decide what to produce, they succeed or fail depending on their ability to meet consumers' desires. That's consumer sovereignty.

- The three main forms of business are corporations, sole proprietorships, and partnerships. Each has its advantages and disadvantages.

- Although households are the most powerful economic institution, they have assigned much of their power to government and business. Economics focuses on households' role as the supplier of labor.

- Government plays two general roles in the economy: (1) as a referee and (2) as an actor.

- Six roles of government are to (1) provide a stable set of institutions and rules, (2) promote effective and workable competition, (3) correct for externalities, (4) ensure economic stability and growth, (5) provide public goods, and (6) adjust for undesirable market results.

- To understand the U.S. economy, one must understand its role in the world economy.

- Global corporations are corporations with significant operations in more than one country. They are increasing in importance.

- Global economic issues differ from national economic issues because national economies have governments. The global economy does not.

Key Terms

business *(59)*
capitalism *(55)*
consumer
   sovereignty *(60)*
corporation *(61)*
demerit good or
   activity *(69)*
e-commerce *(62)*
entrepreneurship *(59)*

externality *(67)*
feudalism *(57)*
free rider *(68)*
global corporation *(69)*
government failure *(69)*
households *(63)*
Industrial
   Revolution *(57)*
institutions *(53)*

limited liability *(61)*
macroeconomic
   externality *(68)*
market economy *(54)*
market failure *(69)*
mercantilism *(57)*
merit good or
   activity *(69)*
monopoly power *(67)*

partnership *(60)*
private good *(68)*
private property
   right *(54)*
profit *(60)*
public good *(68)*
socialism *(55)*
sole proprietorship *(60)*
stock *(61)*

Questions for Thought and Review

1. In a market economy, what is the central coordinating mechanism? LO1, LO2

2. In a centrally planned socialist economy, what is the central coordinating mechanism? LO2

3. How does a market economy solve the what, how, and for whom to produce problems? LO2

4. How does a centrally planned socialist economy solve the what, how, and for whom to produce problems? LO2

5. Is capitalism or socialism the better economic system? Why? LO2

6. What arguments can you give for supporting a socialist organization of a family and a market-based organization of the economy? LO2

7. True or false? As economic systems have evolved, there has been less need for planning. LO2

8. Why does an economy's strength ultimately reside in its people? LO3

9. A market system is often said to be based on consumer sovereignty—the consumer determines what's to be produced. Yet business decides what's to be produced. Can these two views be reconciled? How? If not, why? LO5

10. Why is entrepreneurship a central part of any business? LO4

11. You're starting a software company in which you plan to sell software to your fellow students. What form of business organization would you choose? Why? LO4

12. What are the two largest categories of federal government expenditures? LO6

13. A good measure of a country's importance to the world economy is its area and population. True or false? Why? LO7

14. What are the qualities of the Internet that have put competitive pressures on businesses? LO4

15. What are the six roles of government listed in the text? Which do you believe is the most controversial? Why? LO6

16. You've set up the rules for a game and started the game but now realize that the rules are unfair. Should you change the rules? LO6

17. Say the government establishes rights to pollute so that without a pollution permit you aren't allowed to emit pollutants into the air, water, or soil. Firms are allowed to buy and sell these rights. In what way will this correct for an externality? LO6

18. What are two organizations that countries can use to coordinate economic relations and reduce trade barriers? LO7

19. Why are international organizations limited in their effectiveness? LO7

Problems and Exercises

20. Tom Rollins heads a company called Teaching Co. He has taped lectures at the top universities, packaged the lectures on DVD and CD, and sells them for $90 and $150 per eight-hour series.
    a. Discuss whether such an idea could be expanded to include college courses that one could take at home.
    b. What are the technical, social, and economic issues involved?
    c. If it is technically possible and cost effective, will the new venture be a success? LO3, LO4

21. Economists Edward Lazear and Robert Michael have calculated that the average family spends two and a half times as much on each adult as they do on each child.
    a. Does this mean that children are deprived and that the distribution is unfair?

b. Do you think these percentages change with family income? If so, how?

c. Do you think that the allocation would be different in a family in a command economy than in a capitalist economy? Why?   LO2

22. One of the specific problems socialist economies had was keeping up with capitalist countries technologically. (Difficult)

a. Can you think of any reason inherent in a centrally planned economy that would make innovation difficult?

b. Can you think of any reason inherent in a capitalist country that would foster innovation?

c. Joseph Schumpeter, a famous Harvard economist of the 1930s, predicted that as firms in capitalist societies grew in size, they would innovate less. Can you suggest what his argument might have been?

d. Schumpeter's prediction did not come true. Modern capitalist economies have had enormous innovations. Can you provide explanations as to why?   LO2

23. Go to a store in your community.

a. Ask what limitations the owners faced in starting their business.

b. Were these limitations necessary?

c. Should there have been more or fewer limitations?

d. Under what heading of reasons for government intervention would you put each of the limitations?

e. Ask what kinds of taxes the business pays and what benefits it believes it gets for those taxes.

f. Is it satisfied with the existing situation? Why? What would it change?   LO4

24. Give an example of a merit good, a demerit good, a public good, and a good that involves an externality.

a. How might individuals disagree about the government's role in intervening in the market for each of the goods you listed?

b. Discuss the concepts of market failure and government failure in relation to the goods you listed.   LO6

25. In trade talks with Australia, the United States proposed that Australia cannot regulate the amount of foreign content on new media without first consulting the United States. Actress Bridie Carter of *McLeod's Daughters* argued against adopting the trade agreement, arguing the agreement trades away Australia's cultural identity. This highlights one of the effects of globalization: the loss of variety based on cultural differences. How important should such cultural identity issues be in trade negotiations?   LO7

Questions from Alternative Perspectives

1. Friedrich Hayek, the man quoted at the start of the chapter, is an Austrian economist who won a Nobel Prize in economics. He argued that government intervention is difficult to contain. Suppose central planners have decided to financially support all children with food vouchers, free day care, and public school.

a. What problems might this create?

b. How might this lead to further interference by central planners into family choices? (Austrian)

2. In his *The Social Contract*, Jean-Jacques Rousseau argued that "no State has ever been founded without a religious basis [but] the law of Christianity at bottom does more harm by weakening than good by strengthening the constitution of the State." What does he mean by that, and is he correct? (Religious)

3. In economics, a household is defined as a group of individuals making joint decisions as though acting as one person.

a. How do you think decisions are actually made about things like consumption and allocation of time within the household?

b. Does bargaining take place?

c. If so, what gives an individual power to bargain effectively for his or her preferences?

d. Do individuals act cooperatively within the family and competitively everywhere else?

e. Does this make sense? (Feminist)

4. This chapter emphasized the importance of the relationship between how the economic system is organized and value systems. Knowing that how I raise my child will greatly shape how he or she will ultimately fit into the social and economic process, should I raise my child to be selfless, compassionate, and dedicated to advancing the well-being of others, knowing she will probably be poor; or shall I raise her to be self-centered, uncaring, and greedy to increase her chances to acquire personal fortune? Which decision is just and why? (Institutionalist)

5. The text discusses consumer sovereignty and suggests that it guides the market choices.

a. Is consumer sovereignty a myth or reality in today's consumer culture?

b. Do consumers "direct" the economy as suggested by the text, or has invention become the mother of necessity, as Thorstein Veblen once quipped?

c. If the consumer is not sovereign, then who is and what does that imply for economics? (Radical)

Web Questions

1. Go to Levi Strauss's home page (www.levistrauss.com) and answer the following questions:
   a. Is Levi Strauss a sole proprietorship, partnership, or corporation? What reasons do you suspect it has chosen that form of business?
   b. Is Levi Strauss a global corporation? Explain your answer.
   c. Are the shares of Levi Strauss publicly traded?

2. The Social Security system is a program that is significant to the evolution of capitalism in the United States. Go to the Social Security Administration's home page (www.ssa.gov) and describe how changes in the Social Security system have moved the U.S. economy away from a market economy.
   a. What proposals are being discussed that will change the nature of Social Security?
   b. What does this say about the evolution of the U.S. economy?

Answers to Margin Questions

1. He is wrong. Property rights are required for a market to operate. Once property rights are allocated, the market will allocate goods, but the market cannot distribute the property rights that are required for the market to operate. (54)

2. Capitalism places much more emphasis on fostering individualism. Socialism tries to develop a system in which the individual's needs are placed second to society's needs. (55)

3. Most families allocate basic needs through control and command. The parents do (or try to do) the controlling and commanding. Generally parents are well-intentioned, trying to meet their perception of their children's needs. However, some family activities that are not basic needs might be allocated through the market. For example, if one child wants a go-cart and is willing to do extra work at home in order to get it, go-carts might be allocated through the market, with the child earning chits that can be used for such nonessentials. (55)

4. In theory, socialism is an economic system based upon individuals' goodwill. In practice, socialism followed the Soviet model and involved central planning and government ownership of the primary means of production. (56)

5. Market economies are generally broken up into businesses, households, and government. (58)

6. False. In the United States, individuals are free to start any type of business they want, provided it doesn't violate the law. The invisible hand sees to it that only those businesses that customers want earn a profit. The others lose money and eventually go out of business, so in that sense only businesses that customers want stay in business. (60)

7. As can be seen in Figure 3-2, most businesses in the United States are sole proprietorships, not corporations. Corporations, however, generate the most revenue. (60)

8. The largest percentage of federal expenditures is for income security. (65)

9. Not necessarily. The existence of an externality creates the possibility that government intervention might help. But there are also government failures in which the government intervenes and makes things worse. (69)

10. The World Court has no enforcement mechanism. Thus, when a country refuses to follow the court's decisions, the country cannot be directly punished except through indirect international pressures. (71)

APPENDIX A

The History of Economic Systems

In the text I made the distinction between market and economic forces: Economic forces have always existed—they operate in all aspects of our lives—but market forces have not always existed. Markets are social creations societies use to coordinate individuals' actions. Markets developed, sometimes spontaneously, sometimes by design, because they offered a better life for at least some—and usually a large majority of—individuals in a society.

To understand why markets developed, it is helpful to look briefly at the history of the economic systems from which our own system descended.

Feudal Society: Rule of Tradition

Let's go back in time to the year 1000 when Europe had no nation-states as we now know them. (Ideally, we would have gone back further and explained other economic systems, but, given the limited space, I had to draw the line somewhere—an example of a trade-off.) The predominant economic system at that time was feudalism. There was no coordinated central government, no unified system of law, no national patriotism, no national defense, although a strong religious institution simply called the Church fulfilled some of these roles. There were few towns; most individuals lived in walled manors, or "estates." These manors "belonged to" the "lord of the manor." (Occasionally the "lord" was a lady, but not often.) I say "belonged to" rather than "were owned by" because most of the empires or federations at that time were not formal nation-states that could organize, administer, and regulate ownership. No documents or deeds gave ownership of the land to an individual. Instead, tradition ruled, and in normal times nobody questioned the lord's right to the land. The land "belonged to" the lord because the land "belonged to" him—that's the way it was.

Without a central nation-state, the manor served many functions a nation-state would have served had it existed. The lord provided protection, often within a walled area surrounding the manor house or, if the manor was large enough, a castle. He provided administration and decided disputes. He also decided *what* would be done, *how* it would be done, and *who* would get what, but these decisions were limited. In the same way that the land belonged to the lord because that's the way it always had been, what people did and how they did it were determined by what they always had done. Tradition ruled the manor more than the lord did.

Problems of a Tradition-Based Society

Feudalism developed about the 8th and 9th centuries and lasted until about the 15th century, though in isolated countries such as Russia it continued well into the 19th century, and in all European countries its influence lingered for hundreds of years (as late as about 140 years ago in some parts of Germany). Such a long-lived system must have done some things right, and feudalism did: It solved the *what, how,* and *for whom* problems in an acceptable way.

But a tradition-based society has problems. In a traditional society, because someone's father was a baker, the son also must be a baker, and because a woman was a homemaker, she wouldn't be allowed to be anything but a homemaker. But what if Joe Blacksmith Jr., the son of Joe Blacksmith Sr., is a lousy blacksmith and longs to knead dough, while Joe Baker Jr. would be a superb blacksmith but hates making pastry? Tough. Tradition dictated who did what. In fact, tradition probably arranged things so that we will never know whether Joe Blacksmith Jr. would have made a superb baker.

As long as a society doesn't change too much, tradition operates reasonably well, although not especially efficiently, in holding the society together. However, when a society must undergo change, tradition does not work. Change means that the things that were done before no longer need to be done, while new things do need to get done. But if no one has traditionally done these new things, then they don't get done. If the change is important but a society can't figure out some way for the new things to get done, the society falls apart. That's what happened to feudal society. It didn't change when change was required.

The life of individuals living on the land, called *serfs,* was difficult, and feudalism was designed to benefit the lord. Some individuals in feudal society just couldn't take life on the manor, and they set off on their own. Because there was no organized police force, they were unlikely to be caught and forced to return to the manor. Going hungry, being killed, or both, however, were frequent fates of an escaped serf. One place to which serfs could safely escape, though, was a town or city—the remains of what in Roman times had been thriving and active cities. These cities, which had been decimated by plagues, plundering bands, and starvation in the preceding centuries, nevertheless remained an escape hatch for runaway serfs because they relied far less on tradition than did manors. City dwellers had to live by their wits; many became merchants who lived predominantly by trading. They were middlemen; they would buy from one group and sell to another.

Trading in towns was an alternative to the traditional feudal order because trading allowed people to have an income independent of the traditional social structure. Markets broke down tradition. Initially merchants traded using barter (exchange of one kind of good for another): silk and spices from the Orient for wheat, flour, and artisan products in Europe. But soon a generalized purchasing power (money) developed as a medium of exchange. Money greatly expanded the possibilities of trading because its use meant that goods no longer needed to be bartered. They could be sold for money, which could then be spent to buy other goods.

In the beginning, land was not traded, but soon the feudal lord who just had to have a silk robe but had no money was saying, "Why not? I'll sell you a small piece of land so I can buy a shipment of silk." Once land became tradable, the traditional base of the feudal society was undermined. Tradition that can be bought and sold is no longer tradition—it's just another commodity.

From Feudalism to Mercantilism

Toward the end of the Middle Ages (mid-15th century), markets went from being a sideshow, a fair that spiced up people's lives, to being the main event. Over time, some traders and merchants started to amass fortunes that dwarfed those of the feudal lords. Rich traders settled down; existing towns and cities expanded and new towns were formed. As towns grew and as fortunes shifted from feudal lords to merchants, power in society shifted to the towns. And with that shift came a change in society's political and economic structure.

As these traders became stronger politically and economically, they threw their support behind a king (the strongest lord) in the hope that the king would expand their ability to trade. In doing so, they made the king even stronger. Eventually, the king became so powerful that his will prevailed over the will of the other lords and even over the will of the Church. As the king consolidated his power, nation-states as we know them today evolved. *The government became an active influence on economic decision making.*

As markets grew, feudalism evolved into mercantilism. The evolution of feudal systems into mercantilism occurred in the following way: As cities and their markets grew in size and power relative to the feudal manors and the traditional economy, a whole new variety of possible economic activities developed. It was only natural that individuals began to look to a king to establish a new tradition that would determine who would do what. Individuals in particular occupations organized into groups called *guilds,* which were similar to strong labor unions today. These guilds, many of which had financed and supported the king, now expected the king and his government to protect their interests.

As new economic activities, such as trading companies, developed, individuals involved in these activities similarly depended on the king for the right to trade and for help in financing and organizing their activities. For example, in 1492, when Christopher Columbus had the wild idea that by sailing west he could get to the East Indies and trade for their riches, he went to Spain's Queen Isabella and King Ferdinand for financial support.

Since many traders had played and continued to play important roles in financing, establishing, and supporting the king, the king was usually happy to protect their interests. The government doled out the rights to undertake a variety of economic activities. By the late 1400s, western Europe had evolved from a feudal to a mercantilist economy.

The mercantilist period was marked by the increased role of government, which could be classified in two ways: by the way it encouraged growth and by the way it limited growth. Government legitimized and financed a variety of activities, thus encouraging growth. But government also limited economic activity in order to protect the monopolies of those it favored, thus limiting growth. So mercantilism allowed the market to operate, but it kept the market under its control. The market was not allowed to respond freely to the laws of supply and demand.

From Mercantilism to Capitalism

Mercantilism provided the source for major growth in western Europe, but mercantilism also unleashed new tensions within society. Like feudalism, mercantilism limited entry into economic activities. It used a different form of limitation—politics rather than social and cultural tradition—but individuals who were excluded still felt unfairly treated.

The most significant source of tension was the different roles played by craft guilds and owners of new businesses, who were called industrialists or capitalists (businesspeople who have acquired large amounts of money and use it to invest in businesses). Craft guild members were artists in their own crafts: pottery, shoemaking, and the like. New business owners destroyed the art of production by devising machines to replace hand production. Machines produced goods cheaper and faster than craftsmen.[1] The result was an increase in supply and a downward pressure on the price, which was set by the government. Craftsmen didn't want to be replaced by machines. They argued that machine-manufactured goods didn't have the same quality as hand-crafted goods, and that the new machines would disrupt the economic and social life of the community.

Industrialists were the outsiders with a vested interest in changing the existing system. They wanted the freedom to conduct business as they saw fit. Because of the enormous cost advantage of manufactured goods over crafted goods, a few industrialists overcame government opposition and succeeded within the mercantilist system. They earned their fortunes and became an independent political power.

Once again, the economic power base shifted, and two groups competed with each other for power—this time, the guilds and the industrialists. The government had to decide whether to support the industrialists (who wanted government to loosen its power over the country's economic affairs) or the craftsmen and guilds (who argued for strong government limitations and for maintaining

---

[1]Throughout this section I use *men* to emphasize that these societies were strongly male-dominated. There were almost no business women. In fact, a woman had to turn over her property to a man upon her marriage, and the marriage contract was written as if she were owned by her husband!

traditional values of workmanship). This struggle raged in the 1700s and 1800s. But during this time, governments themselves were changing. This was the Age of Revolutions, and the kings' powers were being limited by democratic reform movements—revolutions supported and financed in large part by the industrialists.

The Need for Coordination in an Economy

Craftsmen argued that coordination of the economy was necessary, and the government had to be involved. If government wasn't going to coordinate economic activity, who would? To answer that question, a British moral philosopher named Adam Smith developed the concept of the invisible hand, in his famous book *The Wealth of Nations* (1776), and used it to explain how markets could coordinate the economy without the active involvement of government.

As stated in Chapter 2, Smith argued that the market's invisible hand would guide suppliers' actions toward the general good. No government coordination was necessary.

With the help of economists such as Adam Smith, the industrialists' view won out. Government pulled back from its role in guiding the economy and adopted a laissez-faire policy.

The Industrial Revolution

The invisible hand worked; capitalism thrived. Beginning about 1750 and continuing through the late 1800s, machine production increased enormously, almost totally replacing hand production. This phenomenon has been given a name, the Industrial Revolution. The economy grew faster than ever before. Society was forever transformed. New inventions changed all aspects of life. James Watt's steam engine (1769) made manufacturing and travel easier. Eli Whitney's cotton gin (1793) changed the way cotton was processed. James Kay's flying shuttle (1733),[2] James Hargreaves' spinning jenny (1765), and Richard Arkwright's power loom (1769), combined with the steam engine, changed the way cloth was processed and the clothes people wore.

The need to mine vast amounts of coal to provide power to run the machines changed the economic and physical landscapes. The repeating rifle changed the nature of warfare. Modern economic institutions replaced guilds.

[2]The invention of the flying shuttle frustrated the textile industry because it enabled workers to weave so much cloth that the spinners of thread from which the cloth was woven couldn't keep up. This challenge to the textile industry was met by offering a prize to anyone who could invent something to increase the thread spinners' productivity. The prize was won when the spinning jenny was invented.

Stock markets, insurance companies, and corporations all became important. Trading was no longer financed by government; it was privately financed (although government policies, such as colonial policies giving certain companies monopoly trading rights with a country's colonies, helped in that trading). The Industrial Revolution, democracy, and capitalism all arose in the middle and late 1700s. By the 1800s, they were part of the institutional landscape of Western society. Capitalism had arrived.

Welfare Capitalism
From Capitalism to ~~Socialism~~

Capitalism was marked by significant economic growth in the Western world. But it was also marked by human abuses—18-hour workdays; low wages; children as young as five years old slaving long hours in dirty, dangerous factories and mines—to produce enormous wealth for an elite few. Such conditions and inequalities led to criticism of the capitalist or market economic system.

Marx's Analysis

The best-known critic of this system was Karl Marx, a German philosopher, economist, and sociologist who wrote in the 1800s and who developed an analysis of the dynamics of change in economic systems. Marx argued that economic systems are in a constant state of change, and that capitalism would not last. Workers would revolt, and capitalism would be replaced by a socialist economic system.

Marx saw an economy marked by tensions among economic classes. He saw capitalism as an economic system controlled by the capitalist class (businessmen). His class analysis was that capitalist society is divided into capitalist and worker classes. He said constant tension between these economic classes causes changes in the system. The capitalist class made large profits by exploiting the proletariat class—the working class—and extracting what he called surplus value from workers who, according to Marx's labor theory of value, produced all the value inherent in goods. Surplus value was the additional profit, rent, or interest that, according to Marx's normative views, capitalists added to the price of goods. What standard economic analysis sees as recognizing a need that society has and fulfilling it, Marx saw as exploitation.

Marx argued that this exploitation would increase as production facilities became larger and larger and as competition among capitalists decreased. At some point, he believed, exploitation would lead to a revolt by the proletariat, who would overthrow their capitalist exploiters.

By the late 1800s, some of what Marx predicted had occurred, although not in the way that he thought it would. Production moved from small to large factories.

Corporations developed, and classes became more distinct from one another. Workers were significantly differentiated from owners. Small firms merged and were organized into monopolies and trusts (large combinations of firms). The trusts developed ways to prevent competition among themselves and ways to limit entry of new competitors into the market. Marx was right in his predictions about these developments, but he was wrong in his prediction about society's response to them.

The Revolution That Did Not Occur

Western society's response to the problems of capitalism was not a revolt by the workers. Instead, governments stepped in to stop the worst abuses of capitalism. The hard edges of capitalism were softened.

Evolution, not revolution, was capitalism's destiny. The democratic state did not act, as Marx argued it would, as a mere representative of the capitalist class. Competing pressure groups developed; workers gained political power that offset the economic power of businesses.

In the late 1930s and the 1940s, workers dominated the political agenda. During this time, capitalist economies developed an economic safety net that included government-funded programs, such as public welfare and unemployment insurance, and established an extensive set of regulations affecting all aspects of the economy. Today, depressions are met with direct government policy. Antitrust laws, regulatory agencies, and social programs of government softened the hard edges of capitalism. Laws were passed prohibiting child labor, mandating a certain minimum wage, and limiting the hours of work. Capitalism became what is sometimes called welfare capitalism.

Due to these developments, government spending now accounts for about a fifth of all spending in the United States, and for more than half in some European countries. Were an economist from the late 1800s to return from the grave, he'd probably say socialism, not capitalism, exists in Western societies. Most modern-day economists wouldn't go that far, but they would agree that our economy today is better described as a welfare capitalist economy than as a capitalist, or even a market, economy. Because of these changes, the U.S. and Western European economies are a far cry from the competitive "capitalist" economy that Karl Marx criticized. Markets operate, but they are constrained by the government.

The concept *capitalism* developed to denote a market system controlled by one group in society, the capitalists. Looking at Western societies today, we see that domination by one group no longer characterizes Western economies. Although in theory capitalists control corporations through their ownership of shares of stock, in practice corporations are controlled in large part by managers. There remains an elite group who control business, but *capitalist* is not a good term to describe them. Managers, not capitalists, exercise primary control over business, and even their control is limited by laws or the fear of laws being passed by governments.

Governments, in turn, are controlled by a variety of pressure groups. Sometimes one group is in control; at other times, another. Government policies similarly fluctuate. Sometimes they are proworker, sometimes proindustrialist, sometimes progovernment, and sometimes prosociety.

From Feudalism to Socialism

You probably noticed that I crossed out *Socialism* in the previous section's heading and replaced it with *Welfare Capitalism*. That's because capitalism did not evolve to socialism as Karl Marx predicted it would. Instead, Marx's socialist ideas took root in feudalist Russia, a society that the Industrial Revolution had in large part bypassed. Since socialism arrived at a different place and a different time than Marx predicted it would, you shouldn't be surprised to read that socialism arrived in a different way than Marx predicted. The proletariat did not revolt to establish socialism. Instead, World War I, which the Russians were losing, crippled Russia's feudal economy and government. A small group of socialists overthrew the czar (Russia's king) and took over the government in 1917. They quickly pulled Russia out of the war, and then set out to organize a socialist society and economy.

Russian socialists tried to adhere to Marx's ideas, but they found that Marx had concentrated on how capitalist economies operate, not on how a socialist economy should be run. Thus, Russian socialists faced a huge task with little guidance. Their most immediate problem was how to increase production so that the economy could emerge from feudalism into the modern industrial world. In Marx's analysis, capitalism was a necessary stage in the evolution toward the ideal state for a very practical reason. The capitalists exploit the workers, but in doing so capitalists extract the necessary surplus—an amount of production in excess of what is consumed. That surplus had to be extracted in order to provide the factories and machinery upon which a socialist economic system would be built. But since capitalism did not exist in Russia, a true socialist state could not be established immediately. Instead, the socialists created *state socialism*—an economic system in which government sees to it that people work for the common good until they can be relied upon to do that on their own.

Socialists saw state socialism as a transition stage to pure socialism. This transition stage still exploited the workers; when Joseph Stalin took power in Russia in the late 1920s, he took the peasants' and small farmers' land and turned it into collective farms. The government then paid farmers low prices for their produce. When farmers balked at the low prices, millions of them were killed.

Simultaneously, Stalin created central planning agencies that directed individuals what to produce and how to produce it, and determined for whom things would be produced. During this period, *socialism* became synonymous with *central economic planning,* and Soviet-style socialism became the model of socialism in practice.

Also during this time, Russia took control of a number of neighboring states and established the Union of Soviet Socialist Republics (USSR), the formal name of the Soviet Union. The Soviet Union also installed Soviet-dominated governments in a number of Eastern European countries. In 1949 most of China, under the rule of Mao Zedong, adopted Soviet-style socialist principles.

Since the late 1980s, the Soviet socialist economic and political structure has fallen apart. The Soviet Union as a political state broke up, and its former republics became autonomous. Eastern European countries were released from Soviet control. Now they faced a new problem: transition from socialism to a market economy. Why did the Soviet socialist economy fall apart? Because workers lacked incentives to work; production was inefficient; consumer goods were either unavailable or of poor quality; and high Soviet officials were exploiting their positions, keeping the best jobs for themselves and moving themselves up in the waiting lists for consumer goods. In short, the parents of the socialist family (the Communist party) were no longer acting benevolently; they were taking many of the benefits for themselves.

These political and economic upheavals in Eastern Europe and the former Soviet Union suggest the kind of socialism these societies tried did not work. However, that failure does not mean that socialist goals are bad; nor does it mean that no type of socialism can ever work. The point is that all systems have problems, and it is likely that the political winds of change will lead to new forms of economic organization being tried as the problems of the existing system lead to political demands for change. Venezuela's recent attempt to establish a new form of socialism is an example. Given past experience with socialist systems, however, most economists believe that any future workable "new socialist" system will include important elements of market institutions.

Supply and Demand

4

Teach a parrot the terms supply *and* demand *and you've got an economist.*

— *Thomas Carlyle*

Supply and demand. Supply and demand. Roll the phrase around in your mouth; savor it like a good wine. *Supply* and *demand* are the most-used words in economics. And for good reason. They provide a good off-the-cuff answer for any economic question. Try it.

Why are bacon and oranges so expensive this winter? *Supply and demand.*

Why are interest rates falling? *Supply and demand.*

Why can't I find decent wool socks anymore? *Supply and demand.*

The importance of the interplay of supply and demand makes it only natural that, early in any economics course, you must learn about supply and demand. Let's start with demand.

Demand

People want lots of things; they "demand" much less than they want because demand means a willingness and ability to pay. Unless you are willing and able to pay for it, you may *want* it, but you don't *demand* it. For example, I want to own a Ferrari. But, I must admit, I'm not willing to do what's necessary to own one. If I really wanted one, I'd mortgage everything I own, increase my income by doubling the number of hours I work, not buy anything else, and get that car. But I don't do any of those things, so at the going price, $650,000, I do not demand a Ferrari. Sure, I'd buy one if it cost $30,000, but from my actions it's clear that, at $650,000, I don't demand it. This points to an important aspect of demand: The quantity you demand at a low price differs from the quantity you demand at a high price. Specifically, the quantity you demand varies inversely—in the opposite direction—with price.

Prices are the tool by which the market coordinates individuals' desires and limits how much people demand. When goods become scarce, the market reduces the quantity people demand; as their prices go up, people buy fewer goods.

AFTER READING THIS CHAPTER, YOU SHOULD BE ABLE TO:

1. State the law of demand and draw a demand curve from a demand table.
2. Explain the importance of substitution to the laws of supply and demand.
3. Distinguish shifts in demand from movements along a demand curve.
4. State the law of supply and draw a supply curve from a supply table.
5. Distinguish shifts in supply from movements along a supply curve.
6. Explain how the law of demand and the law of supply interact to bring about equilibrium.
7. Show the effect of a shift in demand and supply on equilibrium price and quantity.
8. State the limitations of demand and supply analysis.

As goods become abundant, their prices go down, and people buy more of them. The invisible hand—the price mechanism—sees to it that what people demand (do what's necessary to get) matches what's available.

The Law of Demand

The law of demand states that the quantity of a good demanded is inversely related to the good's price.

The ideas expressed above are the foundation of the **law of demand:**

> *Quantity demanded rises as price falls, other things constant.*

Or alternatively:

> *Quantity demanded falls as price rises, other things constant.*

This law is fundamental to the invisible hand's ability to coordinate individuals' desires: as prices change, people change how much they're willing to buy.

What accounts for the law of demand? If the price of something goes up, people will tend to buy less of it and buy something else instead. They will *substitute* other goods for goods whose relative price has gone up. If the price of MP3 files from the Internet rises, but the price of CDs stays the same, you're more likely to buy that new Snoop Dog recording on CD than to download it from the Internet.

Web Note 4.1
Markets without Money

To see that the law of demand makes intuitive sense, just think of something you'd really like but can't afford. If the price is cut in half, you—and other consumers— become more likely to buy it. Quantity demanded goes up as price goes down.

When price goes up, quantity demanded goes down. When price goes down, quantity demanded goes up.

Just to be sure you've got it, let's consider a real-world example: demand for vanity— specifically, vanity license plates. When the North Carolina state legislature increased the vanity plates' price from $30 to $40, the quantity demanded fell from 60,334 to 31,122. Assuming other things remained constant, that is the law of demand in action.

The Demand Curve

Q-1 Why does the demand curve slope downward?

A **demand curve** is *the graphic representation of the relationship between price and quantity demanded.* Figure 4-1 shows a demand curve.

As you can see, the demand curve slopes downward. That's because of the law of demand: as the price goes up, the quantity demanded goes down, other things constant. In other words, price and quantity demanded are inversely related.

FIGURE 4-1   **A Sample Demand Curve**

The law of demand states that the quantity demanded of a good is inversely related to the price of that good, other things constant. As the price of a good goes up, the quantity demanded goes down, so the demand curve is downward-sloping.

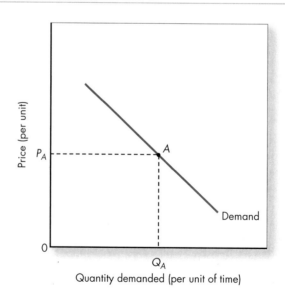

Notice that in stating the law of demand, I put in the qualification "other things constant." That's three extra words, and unless they were important I wouldn't have included them. But what does "other things constant" mean? Say that over two years, both the price of cars and the number of cars purchased rise. That seems to violate the law of demand, since the number of cars purchased should have fallen in response to the rise in price. Looking at the data more closely, however, we see that individuals' income has increased. Other things didn't remain the same.

The increase in price works as the law of demand states—it decreases the number of cars bought. But the rise in income increases the demand for cars at every price. That increase in demand outweighs the decrease in quantity demanded that results from a rise in price, so ultimately more cars are sold. If you want to study the effect of price alone—which is what the law of demand refers to—you must make adjustments to hold income constant. Because other things besides price affect demand, the qualifying phrase "other things constant" is an important part of the law of demand.

The other things that are held constant include individuals' tastes, prices of other goods, and even the weather. Those other factors must remain constant if you're to make a valid study of the effect of an increase in the price of a good on the quantity demanded. In practice, it's impossible to keep all other things constant, so you have to be careful when you say that when price goes up, quantity demanded goes down. It's likely to go down, but it's always possible that something besides price has changed.

"Other things constant" places a limitation on the application of the law of demand.

Shifts in Demand versus Movements along a Demand Curve

To distinguish between the effects of price and the effects of other factors on how much of a good is demanded, economists have developed the following precise terminology— terminology that inevitably shows up on exams. The first distinction is between demand and quantity demanded.

- **Demand** refers to *a schedule of quantities of a good that will be bought per unit of time at various prices, other things constant.*

- **Quantity demanded** refers to *a specific amount that will be demanded per unit of time at a specific price, other things constant.*

In graphical terms, the term *demand* refers to the entire demand curve. Demand tells us how much will be bought *at various prices. Quantity demanded* tells us how much will be bought at a specific price; it refers to a point on a demand curve, such as point A in Figure 4-1. This terminology allows us to distinguish between *changes in quantity demanded* and *shifts in demand.* A change in price changes the quantity demanded. It refers to a **movement along a demand curve**—*the graphical representation of the effect of a change in price on the quantity demanded.* A change in anything other than price that affects demand changes the entire demand curve. A shift factor of demand causes a **shift in demand,** *the graphical representation of the effect of anything other than price on demand.*

Shifts in Demand versus
Movements along a Demand Curve

Q₂ The uncertainty caused by the terrorist attacks of September 11, 2001, made consumers reluctant to spend on luxury items. This reduced _____. Should the missing words be *demand for luxury goods* or *quantity of luxury goods demanded?*

Shift Factors of Demand

Important shift factors of demand include

1. Society's income.
2. The prices of other goods.
3. Tastes.
4. Expectations.
5. Taxes on and subsidies to consumers.

Web Note 4.2
Income and Demand

Income   From our example above of the "other things constant" qualification, we saw that a rise in income increases the demand for goods. For most goods this is true. As individuals' income rises, they can afford more of the goods they want, such as steaks, computers, or clothing. These are normal goods. For other goods, called inferior goods, an increase in income reduces demand. An example is urban mass transit. A person whose income has risen tends to stop riding the bus to work because she can afford to buy a car and rent a parking space.

Price of Other Goods   Because people make their buying decisions based on the price of related goods, demand will be affected by the prices of other goods. Suppose the price of jeans rises from $25 to $35, but the price of khakis remains at $25. Next time you need pants, you're apt to try khakis instead of jeans. They are substitutes. When the price of a substitute rises, demand for the good whose price has remained the same will rise. Or consider another example. Suppose the price of movie tickets falls. What will happen to the demand for popcorn? You're likely to increase the number of times you go to the movies, so you'll also likely increase the amount of popcorn you purchase. The lower cost of a movie ticket increases the demand for popcorn because popcorn and movies are complements. When the price of a good declines, the demand for its complement rises.

Q.3 Explain the effect of each of the following on the demand for new computers:

1. The price of computers falls by 30 percent.
2. Total income in the economy rises.

Tastes   An old saying goes: "There's no accounting for taste." Of course, many advertisers believe otherwise. Changes in taste can affect the demand for a good without a change in price. As you become older, you may find that your taste for rock concerts has changed to a taste for an evening sitting at home watching TV.

Expectations   Expectations will also affect demand. Expectations can cover a lot. If you expect your income to rise in the future, you're bound to start spending some of it today. If you expect the price of computers to fall soon, you may put off buying one until later.

Taxes and Subsidies   Taxes levied on consumers increase the cost of goods to consumers and therefore reduce demand for those goods. Subsidies to consumers have the opposite effect. When states host tax-free weeks during August's back-to-school shopping season, consumers load up on products to avoid sales taxes. Demand for retail goods rises during the tax holiday.

These aren't the only shift factors. In fact anything—except the price of the good itself—that affects demand (and many things do) is a shift factor. While economists agree these shift factors are important, they believe that no shift factor influences how much of a good people buy as consistently as its price. That's why economists make the law of demand central to their analysis.

Change in price causes a movement along a demand curve; a change in a shift factor causes a shift in demand.

To make sure you understand the difference between a movement along a demand curve and a shift in demand, let's consider an example. Singapore has one of the world's highest number of cars per mile of road. This means that congestion is considerable. Singapore adopted two policies to reduce road use: It increased the fee charged to use roads and it provided an expanded public transportation system. Both policies reduced congestion. Figure 4-2(a) shows that increasing the toll charged to use roads from $1 to $2 per 50 miles of road reduces quantity demanded from 200 to 100 cars per mile every hour (a movement along the demand curve). Figure 4-2(b) shows that providing alternative methods of transportation such as buses and subways shifts the demand curve for roads in to the left so that at every price, demand drops by 25 cars per mile every hour.

FIGURE 4-2 (A AND B) **Shift in Demand versus a Change in Quantity Demanded**

A rise in a good's price results in a reduction in quantity demanded and is shown by a movement up along a demand curve from point A to point B in (**a**). A change in any other factor besides price that affects demand leads to a shift in the entire demand curve, as shown in (**b**).

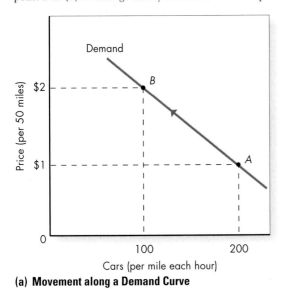

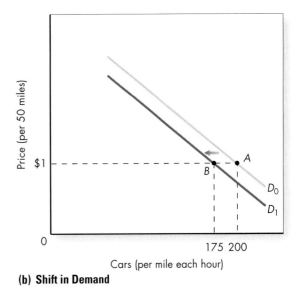

(a) Movement along a Demand Curve   **(b) Shift in Demand**

A Review

Let's test your understanding: What happens to your demand curve for CDs in the following examples: First, let's say you buy an MP3 player. Next, let's say that the price of CDs falls; and finally, say that you won $1 million in a lottery. What happens to the demand for CDs in each case? If you answered: It shifts in to the left; it remains unchanged; and it shifts out to the right—you've got it.

The Demand Table

As I emphasized in Chapter 2, introductory economics depends heavily on graphs and graphical analysis—translating ideas into graphs and back into words. So let's graph the demand curve.

Figure 4-3(a), a demand table, describes Alice's demand for renting DVDs. For example, at a price of $2, Alice will rent (buy the use of) 6 DVDs per week, and at a price of 50 cents she will rent 9.

Four points about the relationship between the number of DVDs Alice rents and the price of renting them are worth mentioning. First, the relationship follows the law of demand: As the rental price rises, quantity demanded decreases. Second, quantity demanded has a specific *time dimension* to it. In this example, demand refers to the number of DVD rentals per week. Without the time dimension, the table wouldn't provide us with any useful information. Nine DVD rentals per year is quite different from 9 DVD rentals per week. Third, the analysis assumes that Alice's DVD rentals are interchangeable—the 9th DVD rental doesn't significantly differ from the 1st, 3rd, or any other DVD rental. The fourth point is already familiar to you: The analysis assumes that everything else is held constant.

FIGURE 4-3 (A AND B)   **From a Demand Table to a Demand Curve**

The demand table in **(a)** is translated into a demand curve in **(b)**. Each combination of price and quantity in the table corresponds to a point on the curve. For example, point A on the graph represents row A in the table: Alice demands 9 DVD rentals at a price of 50 cents. A demand curve is constructed by plotting all points from the demand table and connecting the points with a line.

	Price per DVD	DVD Rentals Demanded per Week
A	$0.50	9
B	1.00	8
C	2.00	6
D	3.00	4
E	4.00	2

(a) A Demand Table

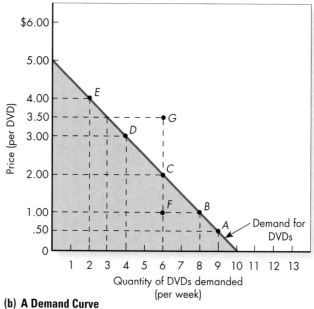

(b) A Demand Curve

From a Demand Table to a Demand Curve

Figure 4-3(b) translates the demand table in Figure 4-3(a) into a demand curve. Point A (quantity = 9, price = $.50) is graphed first at the (9, $.50) coordinates. Next we plot points B, C, D, and E in the same manner and connect the resulting dots with a solid line. The result is the demand curve, which graphically conveys the same information that's in the demand table. Notice that the demand curve is downward sloping, indicating that the law of demand holds.

> The demand curve represents the maximum price that an individual will pay.

The demand curve represents the *maximum price* that an individual will pay for various quantities of a good; the individual will happily pay less. For example, say Netflix offers Alice 6 DVD rentals at a price of $1 each (point F of Figure 4-3(b)). Will she accept? Sure; she'll pay any price within the shaded area to the left of the demand curve. But if Netflix offers her 6 rentals at $3.50 each (point G), she won't accept. At a price of $3.50 apiece, she's willing to rent only 3 DVDs.

Individual and Market Demand Curves

Normally, economists talk about market demand curves rather than individual demand curves. A **market demand curve** is *the horizontal sum of all individual demand curves*. Firms don't care whether individual A or individual B buys their goods; they only care that *someone* buys their goods.

It's a good graphical exercise to add individual demand curves together to create a market demand curve. I do that in Figure 4-4. In it I assume that the market consists of three buyers, Alice, Bruce, and Carmen, whose demand tables are given in Figure 4-4(a). Alice and Bruce have demand tables similar to the demand tables discussed previously. At a price of $3 each, Alice rents 4 DVDs; at a price of $2, she rents 6. Carmen is an all-or-nothing individual. She rents 1 DVD as long as the price is equal to or less than $1; otherwise she rents nothing. If you plot Carmen's demand curve, it's a vertical line. However, the law of demand still holds: As price increases, quantity demanded decreases.

Q-4 Derive a market demand curve from the following two individual demand curves:

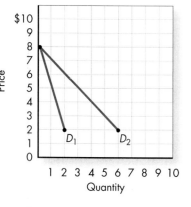

FIGURE 4-4 (A AND B) **From Individual Demands to a Market Demand Curve**

The table (**a**) shows the demand schedules for Alice, Bruce, and Carmen. Together they make up the market for DVD rentals. Their total quantity demanded (market demand) for DVD rentals at each price is given in column 5. As you can see in (**b**), Alice's, Bruce's, and Carmen's demand curves can be added together to get the total market demand curve. For example, at a price of $2, Carmen demands 0, Bruce demands 3, and Alice demands 6, for a market demand of 9 (point D).

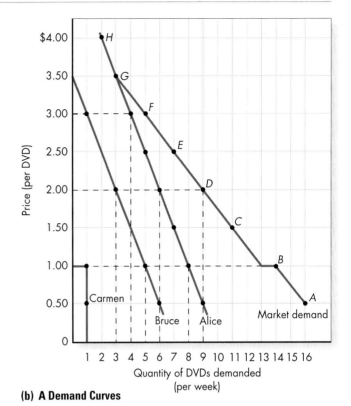

	(1) Price (per DVD)	(2) Alice's Demand	(3) Bruce's Demand	(4) Carmen's Demand	(5) Market Demand
A	$0.50	9	6	1	16
B	1.00	8	5	1	14
C	1.50	7	4	0	11
D	2.00	6	3	0	9
E	2.50	5	2	0	7
F	3.00	4	1	0	5
G	3.50	3	0	0	3
H	4.00	2	0	0	2

(a) A Demand Table

(b) A Demand Curves

The quantity demanded by each consumer is listed in columns 2, 3, and 4 of Figure 4-4(a). Column 5 shows total market demand; each entry is the horizontal sum of the entries in columns 2, 3, and 4. For example, at a price of $3 apiece (row F), Alice demands 4 DVD rentals, Bruce demands 1, and Carmen demands 0, for a total market demand of 5 DVD rentals.

Figure 4-4(b) shows three demand curves: one each for Alice, Bruce, and Carmen. The market, or total, demand curve is the horizontal sum of the individual demand curves. To see that this is the case, notice that if we take the quantity demanded at $1 by Alice (8), Bruce (5), and Carmen (1), they sum to 14, which is point B (14, $1) on the market demand curve. We can do that for each price. Alternatively, we can simply add the individual quantities demanded, given in the demand tables, prior to graphing (which we do in column 5 of Figure 4-4(a)), and graph that total in relation to price. Not surprisingly, we get the same total market demand curve.

In practice, of course, firms don't measure individual demand curves, so they don't sum them up in this fashion. Instead, they statistically estimate market demand. Still, summing up individual demand curves is a useful exercise because it shows you how the market demand curve is the sum (the horizontal sum, graphically speaking) of the individual demand curves, and it gives you a good sense of where market demand curves come from. It also shows you that, even if individuals don't respond to small changes in price, the market demand

Individual and Market Demand Curves

✓ A REMINDER

Six Things to Remember about a Demand Curve

- A demand curve follows the law of demand: When price rises, quantity demanded falls, and vice versa.
- The horizontal axis—quantity—has a time dimension.
- The quality of each unit is the same.
- The vertical axis—price—assumes all other prices remain the same.
- The curve assumes everything else is held constant.
- Effects of price changes are shown by movements along the demand curve. Effects of anything else on demand (shift factors) are shown by shifts of the entire demand curve.

For the market, the law of demand is based on two phenomena:
1. At lower prices, existing demanders buy more.
2. At lower prices, new demanders enter the market.

curve can still be smooth and downward sloping. That's because, for the market, the law of demand is based on two phenomena:

1. At lower prices, existing demanders buy more.
2. At lower prices, new demanders (some all-or-nothing demanders like Carmen) enter the market.

Supply

In one sense, supply is the mirror image of demand. Individuals control the factors of production—inputs, or resources, necessary to produce goods. Individuals' supply of these factors to the market mirrors other individuals' demand for those factors. For example, say you decide you want to rest rather than weed your garden. You hire someone to do the weeding; you demand labor. Someone else decides she would prefer more income instead of more rest; she supplies labor to you. You trade money for labor; she trades labor for money. Her supply is the mirror image of your demand.

For a large number of goods and services, however, the supply process is more complicated than demand. For many goods there's an intermediate step: individuals supply factors of production to firms.

Let's consider a simple example. Say you're a taco technician. You supply your labor to the factor market. The taco company demands your labor (hires you). The taco company combines your labor with other inputs such as meat, cheese, beans, and tables, and produces tacos (production), which it supplies to customers in the goods market. For produced goods, supply depends not only on individuals' decisions to supply factors of production but also on firms' ability to transform those factors of production into usable goods.

Supply of produced goods involves a much more complicated process than demand and is divided into analysis of factors of production and the transformation of those factors into goods.

The supply process of produced goods is generally complicated. Often there are many layers of firms—production firms, wholesale firms, distribution firms, and retailing firms—each of which passes on in-process goods to the next layer of firms. Real-world production and supply of produced goods is a multistage process.

The supply of nonproduced goods is more direct. Individuals supply their labor in the form of services directly to the goods market. For example, an independent contractor may repair your washing machine. That contractor supplies his labor directly to you.

Thus, the analysis of the supply of produced goods has two parts: an analysis of the supply of factors of production to households and to firms and an analysis of the process by which firms transform those factors of production into usable goods and services.

The Law of Supply

There's a law of supply that corresponds to the law of demand. The **law of supply** states:

Quantity supplied rises as price rises, other things constant.

Or alternatively:

Quantity supplied falls as price falls, other things constant.

Price determines quantity supplied just as it determines quantity demanded. Like the law of demand, the law of supply is fundamental to the invisible hand's (the market's) ability to coordinate individuals' actions.

The law of supply is based on substitution and the expectation of profits.

The law of supply is based on a firm's ability to switch from producing one good to another, that is, to substitute. When the price of a good a person or firm supplies rises, individuals and firms can rearrange their activities in order to supply more of that good to the market. They want to supply more because the opportunity cost of *not* supplying the good rises as its price rises. For example, if the price of corn rises and the price of soy beans has not changed, farmers will grow less soy beans and more corn, other things constant.

With firms, there's a second explanation of the law of supply. Assuming firms' costs are constant, a higher price means higher profits (the difference between a firm's

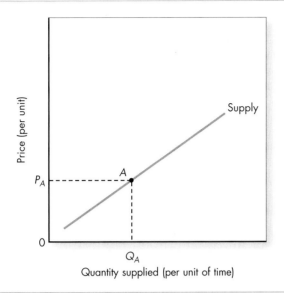

FIGURE 4-5 **A Sample Supply Curve**

The supply curve demonstrates graphically the law of supply, which states that the quantity supplied of a good is directly related to that good's price, other things constant. As the price of a good goes up, the quantity supplied also goes up, so the supply curve is upward sloping.

revenues and its costs). The expectation of those higher profits leads it to increase output as price rises, which is what the law of supply states.

The Supply Curve

A **supply curve** is *the graphical representation of the relationship between price and quantity supplied.* A supply curve is shown in Figure 4-5.

Notice how the supply curve slopes upward to the right. That upward slope captures the law of supply. It tells us that the quantity supplied varies *directly*—in the same direction—with the price.

As with the law of demand, the law of supply assumes other things are held constant. If the price of soy beans rises and quantity supplied falls, you'll look for something else that changed—for example, a drought might have caused a drop in supply. Your explanation would go as follows: Had there been no drought, the quantity supplied would have increased in response to the rise in price, but because there was a drought, the supply decreased, which caused prices to rise.

As with the law of demand, the law of supply represents economists' off-the-cuff response to the question "What happens to quantity supplied if price rises?" If the law seems to be violated, economists search for some other variable that has changed. As was the case with demand, these other variables that might change are called shift factors.

Shifts in Supply versus Movements along a Supply Curve

The same distinctions in terms made for demand apply to supply.

Supply refers to *a schedule of quantities a seller is willing to sell per unit of time at various prices, other things constant.*

Quantity supplied refers to *a specific amount that will be supplied at a specific price.*

In graphical terms, supply refers to the entire supply curve because a supply curve tells us how much will be offered for sale at various prices. "Quantity supplied" refers to a point on a supply curve, such as point A in Figure 4-5.

The second distinction that is important to make is between the effects of a change in price and the effects of shift factors on how much is supplied. Changes in price cause

Shifts in Supply versus Movements along a Supply Curve

 In the early 2000s the price of gasoline rose, causing the demand for hybrid cars to rise. As a result, the price of hybrid cars rose. This made _____ rise. Should the missing words be *the supply* or *the quantity supplied?*

changes in quantity supplied; such changes are represented by a **movement along a supply curve**—*the graphical representation of the effect of a change in price on the quantity supplied.* If the amount supplied is affected by anything other than price, that is, by a shift factor of supply, there will be a **shift in supply**—*the graphical representation of the effect of a change in a factor other than price on supply.*

Shift Factors of Supply

Other factors besides price that affect how much will be supplied include the price of inputs used in production, technology, expectations, and taxes and subsidies. Let's see how.

Price of Inputs   Firms produce to earn a profit. Since their profit is tied to costs, it's no surprise that costs will affect how much a firm is willing to supply. If costs rise, profits will decline, and a firm has less incentive to supply. Supply falls when the price of inputs rises. If costs rise substantially, a firm might even shut down.

Technology   Advances in technology change the production process, reducing the number of inputs needed to produce a good, and thereby reducing its cost of production. A reduction in the cost of production increases profits and leads suppliers to increase production. Advances in technology increase supply.

Expectations   Supplier expectations are an important factor in the production decision. If a supplier expects the price of her good to rise at some time in the future, she may store some of today's output in order to sell it later and reap higher profits, decreasing supply now and increasing it later.

Taxes and Subsidies   Taxes on suppliers increase the cost of production by requiring a firm to pay the government a portion of the income from products or services sold. Because taxes increase the cost of production, profit declines and suppliers will reduce supply. The opposite is true for subsidies. Subsidies to suppliers are payments by the government to produce goods; they reduce the cost of production. Subsidies increase supply. Taxes on suppliers reduce supply.

These aren't the only shift factors. As was the case with demand, a shift factor of supply is anything other than its price that affects supply.

A Shift in Supply versus a Movement along a Supply Curve

The same "movement along" and "shift of" distinction that we developed for demand exists for supply. To make that distinction clear, let's consider an example: the supply of oil. In September 2005, Hurricane Katrina hit the Gulf Coast region of the United States and disrupted oil supply lines and production in the United States. U.S. production of oil declined from 4.6 to 4.1 million barrels each day at a $50 price. This disruption reduced the amount of oil U.S. producers were offering for sale *at every price,* thereby shifting the supply of U.S. oil to the left from S_0 to S_1, and the quantity of oil supplied at the $50 price fell from point A to point B in Figure 4-6. But the price did not stay at $50. It rose to $80. In response to the higher price, other areas in the United States increased their quantity supplied (from point B to point C in Figure 4-6). That increase *due to the higher price* is called a movement along the supply curve. So if a change in quantity supplied occurs because of a higher price, it is called a *movement along the supply curve;* if a change in supply occurs because of one of the shift factors (i.e., for any reason other than a change in price), it is called a *shift in supply.*

Q-6 Explain the effect of each of the following on the supply of romance novels:

1. The price of paper rises by 20 percent.
2. Government increases the sales tax on producers of all books by 5 percentage points.

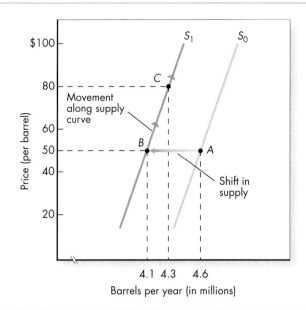

FIGURE 4-6 **Shifts in Supply versus Movement along a Supply Curve**

A *shift in supply* results when the shift is due to any cause other than a change in price. It is a shift in the entire supply curve (see the arrow from A to B). A *movement along a supply curve* is due to a change in price only (see the arrow from B to C). To differentiate the two, movements caused by changes in price are called *changes in the quantity supplied*, not changes in supply.

A Review

To be sure you understand shifts in supply, explain what is likely to happen to your supply curve for labor in the following cases: (1) You suddenly decide that you absolutely need a new car. (2) You win a million dollars in the lottery. And finally, (3) the wage you earn doubles. If you came up with the answers: shift out to the right, shift in to the left, and no change—you've got it down. If not, it's time for a review.

Do we see such shifts in the supply curve often? Yes. A good example is computers. For the past 30 years, technological changes have continually shifted the supply curve for computers out to the right.

The Supply Table

Remember Figure 4-4(a)'s demand table for DVD rentals? In Figure 4-7(a), we follow the same reasoning to construct a supply table for three hypothetical DVD suppliers. Each supplier follows the law of supply: When price rises, each supplies more, or at least as much as each did at a lower price.

From a Supply Table to a Supply Curve

Figure 4-7(b) takes the information in Figure 4-7(a)'s supply table and translates it into a graph of each supplier's supply curve. For instance, point C_A on Ann's supply curve corresponds to the information in columns 1 and 2, row C. Point C_A is at a price of $1 per DVD and a quantity of 2 DVDs per week. Notice that Ann's supply curve is upward sloping, meaning that price is positively related to quantity. Charlie's and Barry's supply curves are similarly derived.

The supply curve represents the set of *minimum* prices an individual seller will accept for various quantities of a good. The market's invisible hand stops suppliers from charging more than the market price. If suppliers could escape the market's invisible hand and charge a higher price, they would gladly do so. Unfortunately for them, and fortunately for consumers, a higher price encourages other suppliers to begin selling DVDs. Competing suppliers' entry into the market sets a limit on the price any supplier can charge.

FIGURE 4-7 (A AND B)   **From Individual Supplies to a Market Supply**

As with market demand, market supply is determined by adding all quantities supplied at a given price. Three suppliers—Ann, Barry, and Charlie—make up the market of DVD suppliers. The total market supply is the sum of their individual supplies at each price, shown in column 5 of (a).

Each of the individual supply curves and the market supply curve have been plotted in (b). Notice how the market supply curve is the horizontal sum of the individual supply curves.

Quantities Supplied	(1) Price (per DVD)	(2) Ann's Supply	(3) Barry's Supply	(4) Charlie's Supply	(5) Market Supply
A	$0.00	0	0	0	0
B	0.50	1	0	0	1
C	1.00	2	1	0	3
D	1.50	3	2	0	5
E	2.00	4	3	0	7
F	2.50	5	4	0	9
G	3.00	6	5	0	11
H	3.50	7	5	2	14
I	4.00	8	5	2	15

(a) A Supply Table

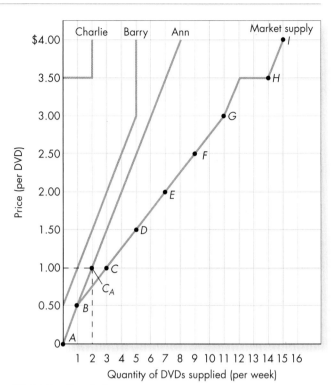

(b) Adding Supply Curves

Individual and Market Supply Curves

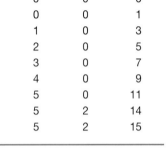

Individual and Market Supply Curves

The law of supply is based on two phenomena:

1. At higher prices, existing suppliers supply more.
2. At higher prices, new suppliers enter the market.

The market supply curve is derived from individual supply curves in precisely the same way that the market demand curve was. To emphasize the symmetry, I've made the three suppliers quite similar to the three demanders. Ann (column 2) will supply 2 at $1; if price goes up to $2, she increases her supply to 4. Barry (column 3) begins supplying at $1, and at $3 supplies 5, the most he'll supply regardless of how high price rises. Charlie (column 4) has only two units to supply. At a price of $3.50 he'll supply that quantity, but higher prices won't get him to supply any more.

The **market supply curve** is *the horizontal sum of all individual supply curves.* In Figure 4-7(a) (column 5), we add together Ann's, Barry's, and Charlie's supplies to arrive at the market supply curve, which is graphed in Figure 4-7(b). Notice that each point corresponds to the information in columns 1 and 5 for each row. For example, point *H* corresponds to a price of $3.50 and a quantity of 14.

The market supply curve's upward slope is determined by two different sources: as price rises, existing suppliers supply more and new suppliers enter the market. Sometimes existing suppliers may not be willing to increase their quantity supplied in response to an increase in prices, but a rise in price often brings brand-new suppliers into the market. For example, a rise in teachers' salaries will have little effect on the number of hours current teachers teach, but it will increase the number of people choosing to be teachers.

The Interaction of Supply and Demand

Thomas Carlyle, the English historian who dubbed economics "the dismal science," also wrote this chapter's introductory tidbit. "Teach a parrot the terms *supply* and *demand* and you've got an economist." In earlier chapters, I tried to convince you that economics is *not* dismal. In the rest of this chapter, I hope to convince you that, while supply and demand are important to economics, parrots don't make good economists. If students think that when they've learned the terms *supply* and *demand* they've learned economics, they're mistaken. Those terms are just labels for the ideas behind supply and demand, and it's the ideas that are important. What matters about supply and demand isn't the labels but how the concepts interact. For instance, what happens if a freeze kills the blossoms on the orange trees? If price doesn't change, the quantity of oranges supplied isn't expected to equal the quantity demanded. But in the real world, prices do change, often before the frost hits, as expectations of the frost lead people to adjust. It's in understanding the interaction of supply and demand that economics becomes interesting and relevant.

Equilibrium

When you have a market in which neither suppliers nor consumers collude and in which prices are free to move up and down, the forces of supply and demand interact to arrive at an equilibrium. The concept of equilibrium comes from physics—classical mechanics. **Equilibrium** is *a concept in which opposing dynamic forces cancel each other out.* For example, a hot-air balloon is in equilibrium when the upward force exerted by the hot air in the balloon equals the downward pressure exerted on the balloon by gravity. In supply/demand analysis, equilibrium means that the upward pressure on price is exactly offset by the downward pressure on price. **Equilibrium quantity** is *the amount bought and sold at the equilibrium price.* **Equilibrium price** is *the price toward which the invisible hand drives the market.* At the equilibrium price, quantity demanded equals quantity supplied.

What happens if the market is not in equilibrium—if quantity supplied doesn't equal quantity demanded? You get either excess supply or excess demand, and a tendency for prices to change.

Excess Supply   If there is **excess supply** (a surplus), *quantity supplied is greater than quantity demanded,* and some suppliers won't be able to sell all their goods. Each supplier will think: "Gee, if I offer to sell it for a bit less, I'll be the lucky one who sells my goods; someone else will be stuck with goods they can't sell." But because all suppliers with excess goods will be thinking the same thing, the price in the market will fall. As that happens, consumers will increase their quantity demanded. So the movement toward equilibrium caused by excess supply is on both the supply and demand sides.

Excess Demand   The reverse is also true. Say that instead of excess supply, there's **excess demand** (a shortage)—*quantity demanded is greater than quantity supplied.* There are more consumers who want the good than there are suppliers selling the good. Let's consider what's likely to go through demanders' minds. They'll likely call long-lost friends who just happen to be sellers of that good and tell them it's good to talk to them and, by the way, don't they want to sell that . . . ? Suppliers will be rather pleased that so many of their old friends have remembered them, but they'll also likely see the connection between excess demand and their friends' thoughtfulness. To stop their phones from ringing all the time, they'll likely raise their price. The reverse is true for excess

Six Things to Remember about a Supply Curve

- A supply curve follows the law of supply. When price rises, quantity supplied increases, and vice versa.
- The horizontal axis—quantity—has a time dimension.
- The quality of each unit is the same.
- The vertical axis—price—assumes all other prices remain constant.
- The curve assumes everything else is constant.
- Effects of price changes are shown by movements along the supply curve. Effects of nonprice determinants of supply are shown by shifts of the entire supply curve.

Bargain hunters can get a deal when there is excess supply.

supply. It's amazing how friendly suppliers become to potential consumers when there's excess supply.

Price Adjusts   This tendency for prices to rise when the quantity demanded exceeds the quantity supplied and for prices to fall when the quantity supplied exceeds the quantity demanded is a central element to understanding supply and demand. So remember:

When quantity demanded is greater than quantity supplied, prices tend to rise.

When quantity supplied is greater than quantity demanded, prices tend to fall.

Two other things to note about supply and demand are (1) the greater the difference between quantity supplied and quantity demanded, the more pressure there is for prices to rise or fall, and (2) when quantity demanded equals quantity supplied, the market is in equilibrium.

People's tendencies to change prices exist as long as quantity supplied and quantity demanded differ. But the change in price brings the laws of supply and demand into play. As price falls, quantity supplied decreases as some suppliers leave the business (the law of supply). And as some people who originally weren't really interested in buying the good think, "Well, at this low price, maybe I do want to buy," quantity demanded increases (the law of demand). Similarly, when price rises, quantity supplied will increase (the law of supply) and quantity demanded will decrease (the law of demand).

Whenever quantity supplied and quantity demanded are unequal, price tends to change. If, however, quantity supplied and quantity demanded are equal, price will stay the same because no one will have an incentive to change.

The Graphical Interaction of Supply and Demand   Figure 4-8 shows supply and demand curves for DVD rentals and demonstrates the force of the invisible hand. Let's consider what will happen to the price of DVDs in three cases:

1. When the price is $3.50 each.
2. When the price is $1.50 each.
3. When the price is $2.50 each.

1. When price is $3.50, quantity supplied is 7 and quantity demanded is only 3. Excess supply is 4. Individual consumers can get all they want, but most suppliers can't sell all they wish; they'll be stuck with DVDs that they'd like to rent. Suppliers will tend to offer their goods at a lower price and demanders, who see plenty of suppliers out there, will bargain harder for an even lower price. Both these forces will push the price as indicated by the down arrows in Figure 4-8.

Now let's start from the other side.

2. Say price is $1.50. The situation is now reversed. Quantity supplied is 3 and quantity demanded is 7. Excess demand is 4. Now it's consumers who can't get what they want and suppliers who are in the strong bargaining position. The pressures will be on price to rise in the direction of the up arrows in Figure 4-8.

3. At $2.50, price is at its equilibrium: quantity supplied equals quantity demanded. Suppliers offer to sell 5 and consumers want to buy 5, so there's no pressure on price to rise or fall. Price will tend to remain where it is (point *E* in Figure 4-8). Notice that the equilibrium price is where the supply and demand curves intersect.

What Equilibrium Isn't

It is important to remember two points about equilibrium. First, equilibrium isn't a state of the world. It's a characteristic of the model—the framework you use to look at the

Prices tend to rise when there is excess demand and fall when there is excess supply.

Price Adjustment and Equilibrium

FIGURE 4-8   The Interaction of Supply and Demand

Combining Ann's supply from Figure 4-7 and Alice's demand from Figure 4-4, let's see the force of the invisible hand. When there is excess demand, there is upward pressure on price. When there is excess supply, there is downward pressure on price. Understanding these pressures is essential to understanding how to apply economics to reality.

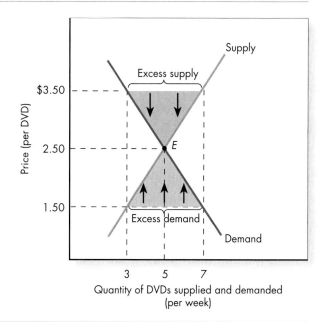

Price (per DVD)	Quantity Supplied	Quantity Demanded	Surplus (+)/ Shortage (−)
$3.50	7	3	+4
$2.50	5	5	0
$1.50	3	7	−4

world. The same situation could be seen as an equilibrium in one framework and as a disequilibrium in another. Say you're describing a car that's speeding along at 100 miles an hour. That car is changing position relative to objects on the ground. Its movement could be, and generally is, described as if it were in disequilibrium. However, if you consider this car relative to another car going 100 miles an hour, the cars could be modeled as being in equilibrium because their positions relative to each other aren't changing.

Second, equilibrium isn't inherently good or bad. It's simply a state in which dynamic pressures offset each other. Some equilibria are awful. Say two countries are engaged in a nuclear war against each other and both sides are blown away. An equilibrium will have been reached, but there's nothing good about it.

Equilibrium is not inherently good or bad.

Political and Social Forces and Equilibrium

Understanding that equilibrium is a characteristic of the model, not of the real world, is important in applying economic models to reality. For example, in the preceding description, I said equilibrium occurs where quantity supplied equals quantity demanded. In a model where economic forces were the only forces operating, that's true. In the real world, however, other forces—political and social forces—are operating. These will likely push price away from that supply/demand equilibrium. Were we to consider a model that included all these forces—political, social, and economic—equilibrium would be likely to exist where quantity supplied isn't equal to quantity demanded. For example:

- Farmers use political pressure to obtain prices that are higher than supply/demand equilibrium prices.
- Social pressures often offset economic pressures and prevent unemployed individuals from accepting work at lower wages than currently employed workers receive.
- Existing firms conspire to limit new competition by lobbying Congress to pass restrictive regulations and by devising pricing strategies to scare off new entrants.
- Renters often organize to pressure local government to set caps on the rental price of apartments.

FIGURE 4-9 (A AND B)   **Shifts In Supply and Demand**

If demand increases from D_0 to D_1, as shown in **(a)**, the quantity of DVD rentals that was demanded at a price of $2.25, 8, increases to 10, but the quantity supplied remains at 8. This excess demand tends to cause prices to rise. Eventually, a new equilibrium is reached at the price of $2.50, where the quantity supplied and the quantity demanded are 9 (point B).

If supply of DVD rentals decreases, then the entire supply curve shifts inward to the left, as shown in **(b)**, from S_0 to S_1. At the price of $2.25, the quantity supplied has now decreased to 6 DVDs, but the quantity demanded has remained at 8 DVDs. The excess demand tends to force the price upward. Eventually, an equilibrium is reached at the price of $2.50 and quantity 7 (point C).

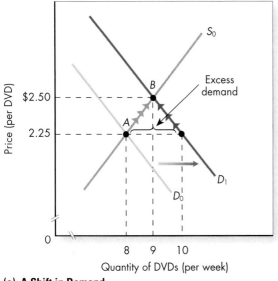

(a) A Shift in Demand

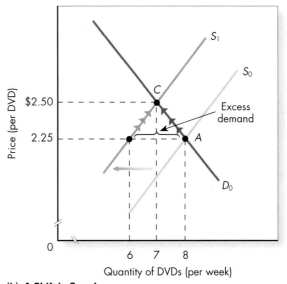

(b) A Shift in Supply

If social and political forces were included in the analysis, they'd provide a counter-pressure to the dynamic forces of supply and demand. The result would be an equilibrium with continual excess supply or excess demand if the market were considered only in reference to economic forces. Economic forces pushing toward a supply/demand equilibrium would be thwarted by social and political forces pushing in the other direction.

Shifts in Supply and Demand

Supply and demand are most useful when trying to figure out what will happen to equilibrium price and quantity if either supply or demand shifts. Figure 4-9(a) deals with an increase in demand. Figure 4-9(b) deals with a decrease in supply.

Q-7 Demonstrate graphically the effect of a heavy frost in Florida on the equilibrium quantity and price of oranges.

Let's consider again the supply and demand for DVD rentals. In Figure 4-9(a), the supply is S_0 and initial demand is D_0. They meet at an equilibrium price of $2.25 per DVD and an equilibrium quantity of 8 DVDs per week (point A). Now say that the demand for DVD rentals increases from D_0 to D_1. At a price of $2.25, the quantity of DVD rentals supplied will be 8 and the quantity demanded will be 10; excess demand of 2 exists.

The excess demand pushes prices upward in the direction of the small arrows, decreasing the quantity demanded and increasing the quantity supplied. As it does so, movement takes place along both the supply curve and the demand curve.

The upward push on price decreases the gap between the quantity supplied and the quantity demanded. As the gap decreases, the upward pressure decreases, but as long as that gap exists at all, price will be pushed upward until the new equilibrium price ($2.50) and new quantity (9) are reached (point B). At point B, quantity supplied equals quantity demanded. So the market is in equilibrium. Notice that

The Supply and Demand for Children

In Chapter 1, I distinguished between an economic force and a market force. Economic forces are operative in all aspects of our lives; market forces are economic forces that are allowed to be expressed through a market. My examples in this chapter are of market forces—of goods sold in a market—but supply and demand also can be used to analyze situations in which economic, but not market, forces operate. An economist who is adept at this is Gary Becker of the University of Chicago. He has applied supply and demand analysis to a wide range of issues, even the supply and demand for children.

Becker doesn't argue that children should be bought and sold. But he does argue that economic considerations play a large role in people's decisions on how many children

to have. In farming communities, children can be productive early in life; by age six or seven, they can work on a farm. In an advanced industrial community, children provide pleasure but generally don't contribute productively to family income. Even getting them to help around the house can be difficult.

Becker argues that since the price of having children is lower for a farming society than for an industrial society, farming societies will have more children per family. Quantity of children demanded will be larger. And that's what we find. Developing countries that rely primarily on farming often have three, four, or more children per family. Industrial societies average fewer than two children per family.

the adjustment is twofold: The higher price brings about equilibrium by both increasing the quantity supplied (from 8 to 9) and decreasing the quantity demanded (from 10 to 9).

Figure 4-9(b) begins with the same situation that we started with in Figure 4-9(a); the initial equilibrium quantity and price are 8 DVDs per week and $2.25 per DVD (point A). In this example, however, instead of demand increasing, let's assume supply decreases—say because some suppliers change what they like to do and decide they will no longer supply DVDs. That means that the entire supply curve shifts inward to the left (from S_0 to S_1). At the initial equilibrium price of $2.25, the quantity demanded is greater than the quantity supplied. Two more DVDs are demanded than are supplied. (Excess demand = 2.)

This excess demand exerts upward pressure on price. Price is pushed in the direction of the small arrows. As the price rises, the upward pressure on price is reduced but will still exist until the new equilibrium price, $2.50, and new quantity, 7, are reached. At $2.50, the quantity supplied equals the quantity demanded. The adjustment has involved a movement along the demand curve and the new supply curve. As price rises, quantity supplied is adjusted upward and quantity demanded is adjusted downward until quantity supplied equals quantity demanded where the new supply curve intersects the demand curve at point C, an equilibrium of 7 and $2.50.

Here is an exercise for you to try. Demonstrate graphically how the price of computers could have fallen dramatically in the past 10 years, even as demand increased. (Hint: Supply has increased even more, so even at lower prices, far more computers have been supplied than were being supplied 10 years ago.)

Q-8 Demonstrate graphically the likely effect of an increase in the price of gas on the equilibrium quantity and price of hybrid cars.

The Limitations of Supply/Demand Analysis

Supply and demand are tools, and, like most tools, they help us enormously when used appropriately. Used inappropriately, however, they can be misleading. Throughout the book I'll introduce you to the limitations of the tools, but let me discuss an important one here.

Q.9 When determining the effect of a shift factor on price and quantity, in which of the following markets could you likely assume that other things will remain constant?

1. Market for eggs.

2. Labor market.

3. World oil market.

4. Market for luxury boats.

The fallacy of composition is the false assumption that what is true for a part will also be true for the whole.

Q.10 Why is the fallacy of composition relevant for macroeconomic issues?

It is to account for interdependency between aggregate supply decisions and aggregate demand decisions that we have a separate micro analysis and a separate macro analysis.

In supply/demand analysis, other things are assumed constant. If other things change, then one cannot directly apply supply/demand analysis. Sometimes supply and demand are interconnected, making it impossible to hold other things constant. Let's take an example. Say we are considering the effect of a fall in the wage rate on unemployment. In supply/demand analysis, you would look at the effect that fall would have on workers' decisions to supply labor, and on business's decision to hire workers. But there are also other effects. For instance, the fall in the wage lowers people's income and thereby reduces demand. That reduction may feed back to firms and reduce the demand for their goods, which might reduce the firms' demand for workers. If these effects do occur, and are important enough to affect the result, they have to be added for the analysis to be complete. A complete analysis always includes the relevant feedback effects.

There is no single answer to the question of which ripples must be included, and much debate among economists involves which ripple effects to include. But there are some general rules. Supply/demand analysis, used without adjustment, is most appropriate for questions where the goods are a small percentage of the entire economy. That is when the other-things-constant assumption will most likely hold. As soon as one starts analyzing goods that are a large percentage of the entire economy, the other-things-constant assumption is likely not to hold true. The reason is found in the **fallacy of composition**—*the false assumption that what is true for a part will also be true for the whole*.

Consider a lone supplier who lowers the price of his or her good. People will substitute that good for other goods, and the quantity of the good demanded will increase. But what if all suppliers lower their prices? Since all prices have gone down, why should consumers switch? The substitution story can't be used in the aggregate. There are many such examples.

An understanding of the fallacy of composition is of central relevance to macroeconomics. In the aggregate, whenever firms produce (whenever they supply), they create income (demand for their goods). So in macro, when supply changes, demand changes. This interdependence is one of the primary reasons we have a separate macroeconomics. In macroeconomics, the other-things-constant assumption central to microeconomic supply/demand analysis cannot hold.

It is to account for these interdependencies that we separate macro analysis from micro analysis. In macro we use curves whose underlying foundations are much more complicated than the supply and demand curves we use in micro.

One final comment: The fact that supply and demand may be interdependent does not mean that you can't use supply/demand analysis; it simply means that you must modify its results with the interdependency that, if you've done the analysis correctly, you've kept in the back of your head. Using supply and demand analysis is generally a step in any good economic analysis, but you must remember that it may be only a step.

Conclusion

Throughout the book, I'll be presenting examples of supply and demand. So I'll end this chapter here because its intended purposes have been served. What were those intended purposes? First, I exposed you to enough economic terminology and economic thinking to allow you to proceed to my more complicated examples. Second, I have set your mind to work putting the events around you into a supply/demand framework. Doing that will give you new insights into the events that shape all our lives. Once you incorporate the supply/demand framework into your way of looking at the world, you will have made an important step toward thinking like an economist.

Summary

- The law of demand states that quantity demanded rises as price falls, other things constant.

- The law of supply states that quantity supplied rises as price rises, other things constant.

- Factors that affect supply and demand other than price are called shift factors. Shift factors of demand include income, prices of other goods, tastes, expectations, and taxes on and subsidies to consumers. Shift factors of supply include the price of inputs, technology, expectations, and taxes on and subsidies to producers.

- A change in quantity demanded (supplied) is a movement along the demand (supply) curve. A change in demand (supply) is a shift of the entire demand (supply) curve.

- The laws of supply and demand hold true because individuals can substitute.

- A market demand (supply) curve is the horizontal sum of all individual demand (supply) curves.

- When quantity supplied equals quantity demanded, prices have no tendency to change. This is equilibrium.

- When quantity demanded is greater than quantity supplied, prices tend to rise. When quantity supplied is greater than quantity demanded, prices tend to fall.

- When the demand curve shifts to the right (left), equilibrium price rises (declines) and equilibrium quantity rises (falls).

- When the supply curve shifts to the right (left), equilibrium price declines (rises) and equilibrium quantity rises (falls).

- In the real world, you must add political and social forces to the supply/demand model. When you do, equilibrium is likely not going to be where quantity demanded equals quantity supplied.

- In macro, small side effects that can be assumed away in micro are multiplied enormously and can significantly change the results. To ignore them is to fall into the fallacy of composition.

Key Terms

demand (83)
demand curve (82)
equilibrium (93)
equilibrium price (93)
equilibrium quantity (93)
excess demand (93)
excess supply (93)

fallacy of
   composition (98)
law of demand (82)
law of supply (88)
market demand
   curve (86)
market supply curve (92)

movement along a
   demand curve (83)
movement along a supply
   curve (90)
quantity demanded (83)
quantity supplied (89)

shift in demand (83)
shift in supply (90)
supply (89)
supply curve (89)

Questions for Thought and Review

1. State the law of demand. Why is price inversely related to quantity demanded?   LO1, LO2

2. State the law of supply. Why is price directly related to quantity supplied?   LO4

3. List four shift factors of demand and explain how each affects demand.   LO3

4. Distinguish the effect of a shift factor of demand on the demand curve from the effect of a change in price on the demand curve.   LO3

5. Mary has just stated that normally, as price rises, supply will increase. Her teacher grimaces. Why?   LO4

6. List four shift factors of supply and explain how each affects supply.   LO5

7. Derive the market supply curve from the following two individual supply curves.   LO4

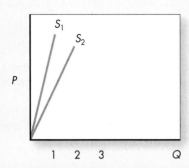

8. It has just been reported that eating red meat is bad for your health. Using supply and demand curves, demonstrate the report's likely effect on the equilibrium price and quantity of steak sold in the market.   LO7

9. Why does the price of airline tickets rise during the summer months? Demonstrate your answer graphically.   LO7

10. Why does sales volume rise during weeks when states suspend taxes on sales by retailers? Demonstrate your answer graphically.   LO7

11. What is the expected impact of increased security measures imposed by the federal government on airlines on fares and volume of travel? Demonstrate your answer graphically. (Difficult)   LO7

12. Explain what a sudden popularity of "Economics Professor" brand casual wear would likely do to prices of that brand.   LO7

13. In a flood, usable water supplies ironically tend to decline because the pumps and water lines are damaged. What will a flood likely do to prices of bottled water?   LO7

14. The price of gas shot up significantly in 2005 to over $2.50 a gallon. What effect did this likely have on the demand for diesel cars that get better mileage than the typical car?   LO7

15. In June 2004, OPEC announced it would increase oil production by 11 percent. What was the effect on the price of oil? Demonstrate your answer graphically.   LO7

16. Oftentimes, to be considered for a job, you have to know someone in the firm. What does this observation tell you about the wage paid for that job? (Difficult)   LO6

17. In most developing countries, there are long lines of taxis at airports, and these taxis often wait two or three hours. What does this tell you about the price in that market? Demonstrate with supply and demand analysis.   LO7

18. Define the fallacy of composition. How does it affect the supply/demand model?   LO8

19. Why is a supply/demand analysis that includes only economic forces likely to be incomplete?   LO8

20. In which of the following three markets are there likely to be the greatest feedback effects: market for housing, market for wheat, market for manufactured goods?   LO8

Problems and Exercises

21. You're given the following individual demand tables for comic books.

Price	John	Liz	Alex
$ 2	4	36	24
4	4	32	20
6	0	28	16
8	0	24	12
10	0	20	8
12	0	16	4
14	0	12	0
16	0	8	0

a. Determine the market demand table.
b. Graph the individual and market demand curves.
c. If the current market price is $4, what's total market demand? What happens to total market demand if price rises to $8?
d. Say that an advertising campaign increases demand by 50 percent. Illustrate graphically what will happen to the individual and market demand curves.   LO1

22. You're given the following demand and supply tables:

	Demand		
P	D₁	D₂	D₃
$37	20	4	8
47	15	2	7
57	10	0	6
67	5	0	5

	Supply		
P	S₁	S₂	S₃
$37	0	4	14
47	0	8	16
57	10	12	18
67	10	16	20

a. Draw the market demand and market supply curves.
b. What is excess supply/demand at price $37? Price $67?
c. Label equilibrium price and quantity.   LO1, LO2, LO6

23. Draw hypothetical supply and demand curves for tea. Show how the equilibrium price and quantity will be affected by each of the following occurrences:
    a. Bad weather wreaks havoc with the tea crop.
    b. A medical report implying tea is bad for your health is published.
    c. A technological innovation lowers the cost of producing tea.
    d. Consumers' income falls. (Assume tea is a normal good.) LO7

24. You're a commodity trader and you've just heard a report that the winter wheat harvest will be 2.09 billion bushels, a 44 percent jump, rather than an expected 35 percent jump to 1.96 billion bushels. (Difficult)
    a. What would you expect would happen to wheat prices?
    b. Demonstrate graphically the effect you suggested in *a*. LO7

25. In the United States, say gasoline costs consumers about $2.50 per gallon. In Italy, say it costs consumers about $6 per gallon. What effect does this price differential likely have on:
    a. The size of cars in the United States and in Italy?
    b. The use of public transportation in the United States and in Italy?
    c. The fuel efficiency of cars in the United States and in Italy? What would be the effect of raising the price of gasoline in the United States to $4 per gallon? LO7

26. In 2004, Argentina imposed a 20 percent tax on natural gas exports.
    a. Demonstrate the likely effect of that tax on gas exports using supply and demand curves.
    b. What did it likely do to the price of natural gas in Argentina?
    c. What did it likely do to the price of natural gas outside of Argentina? LO7

27. In the early 2000s, the demand for housing increased substantially as low interest rates increased the number of people who could afford homes.
    a. What was the likely effect of this on housing prices? Demonstrate graphically.
    b. In 2005, mortgage rates began increasing. What was the likely effect of this increase on housing prices? Demonstrate graphically.
    c. In a period of increasing demand for housing, would you expect housing prices to rise more in Miami suburbs, which had room for expansion and fairly loose laws about subdivisions, or in a city such as San Francisco, which had limited land and tight subdivision restrictions? LO7

28. In 1994, the U.S. postal service put a picture of rodeo rider Ben Pickett, not the rodeo star, Bill Pickett, whom it meant to honor, on a stamp. It printed 150,000 sheets. Recognizing its error, it recalled the stamp, but it found that 183 sheets had already been sold. (Difficult)
    a. What would the recall likely do to the price of the 183 sheets that were sold?
    b. When the government recognized that it could not recall all the stamps, it decided to issue the remaining ones. What would that decision likely do?
    c. What would the holders of the misprinted sheet likely do when they heard of the government's decision? LO7

29. What would be the effect of a 75 percent tax on lawsuit punitive awards that was proposed by California Governor Arnold Schwarzenegger in 2004 on: (Difficult)
    a. The number of punitive awards. Demonstrate your answer using supply and demand curves.
    b. The number of pre-trial settlements. LO7

30. State whether supply/demand analysis used without significant modification is suitable to assess the following:
    a. The impact of an increase in the demand for pencils on the price of pencils.
    b. The impact of an increase in the supply of labor on the quantity of labor demanded.
    c. The impact of an increase in aggregate savings on aggregate expenditures.
    d. The impact of a new method of producing CDs on the price of CDs. LO8

Questions from Alternative Perspectives

1. In a centrally planned economy, how might central planners estimate supply or demand? (Austrian)

2. In the late 19th century, Washington Gladden said, "He who battles for the Christianization of society, will find their strongest foe in the field of economics. Economics is indeed the dismal science because of the selfishness of its maxims and the inhumanity of its conclusions."
   a. Evaluate this statement.
   b. Is there a conflict between the ideology of capitalism and the precepts of Christianity?

   c. Would a society that emphasized a capitalist mode of production benefit by a moral framework that emphasized selflessness rather than selfishness? (Religious)

3. Economics is often referred to as the study of choice.
   a. In U.S. history, have men and women been equally free to choose the amount of education they receive even within the same family?
   b. What other areas can you see where men and women have not been equally free to choose?

c. If you agree that men and women have not had equal rights to choose, what implications does that have about the objectivity of economic analysis? (Feminist)

4. Knowledge is derived from a tautology when something is true because you assume it is true. In this chapter, you have learned the conditions under which supply and demand explain outcomes. Yet, as your text author cautions, these conditions may not hold. How can you be sure if they ever hold? (Institutionalist)

5. Do you think consumers make purchasing decisions based on general rules of thumb instead of price?
   a. Why would consumers do this?

b. What implication might this have for the conclusions drawn about markets? (Post-Keynesian)

6. Some economists believe that imposing international labor standards would cost jobs. In support of this argument, one economist said, "Either you believe labor demand curves are downward sloping, or you don't." Of course, not to believe that demand curves are negatively sloped would be tantamount to declaring yourself an economic illiterate. What else about the nature of labor demand curves might help a policy maker design policies that could counteract the negative effects of labor standards employment? (Radical)

Web Questions

1. Go to the U.S. Census Bureau's home page (www.census.gov) and navigate to the population pyramids for 2000, for 2025, and for 2050. What is projected to happen to the age distribution in the United States? Other things constant, what do you expect will happen in the next 50 years to the relative demand and supply for each of the following, being careful to distinguish between shifts of and a movement along a curve:
   a. Nursing homes.
   b. Prescription medication.
   c. Baby high chairs.
   d. College education.

2. Go to the Energy Information Administration's home page (www.eia.doe.gov) and look up its most recent "Short-Term Energy Outlook" and answer the following questions:
   a. List the factors that are expected to affect demand and supply for energy in the near term. How will each affect demand? Supply?

   b. What is the EIA's forecast for world oil prices? Show graphically how the factors listed in your answer to *a* are consistent with the EIA's forecast. Label all shifts in demand and supply.
   c. Describe and explain EIA's forecast for the price of gasoline, heating oil, and natural gas. Be sure to mention the factors that are affecting the forecast.

3. Go to the Tax Administration home page (www.taxadmin.org) and look up sales tax rates for the 50 U.S. states.
   a. Which states have no sales tax? Which state has the highest sales tax?
   b. Show graphically the effect of sales tax on supply, demand, equilibrium quantity, and equilibrium price.
   c. Name two neighboring states that have significantly different sales tax rates. How does that affect the supply or demand for goods in those states?

Answers to Margin Questions

1. The demand curve slopes downward because price and quantity demanded are inversely related. As the price of a good rises, people switch to purchasing other goods whose prices have not risen by as much. *(82)*

2. *Demand for luxury goods.* The other possibility, *quantity of luxury goods demanded,* is used to refer to movements along (not shifts of) the demand curve. *(83)*

3. (1) The decline in price will increase the quantity of computers demanded (movement down along the demand curve); (2) With more income, demand for computers will rise (shift of the demand curve out to the right). *(84)*

4. When adding two demand curves, you sum them horizontally, as in the accompanying diagram. *(86)*

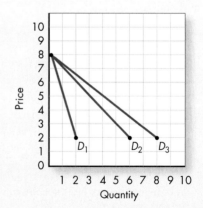

5. *The quantity supplied* rose because there was a movement along the supply curve. The supply curve itself remained unchanged. *(89)*

6. (1) The supply of romance novels declines since paper is an input to production (supply shifts in to the left); (2) the supply of romance novels declines since the tax increases the cost to the producer (supply shifts in to the left). *(90)*

7. A heavy frost in Florida will decrease the supply of oranges, increasing the price and decreasing the quantity demanded, as in the accompanying graph. *(96)*

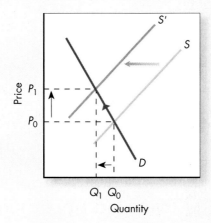

8. An increase in the price of gas will likely increase the demand for hybrid cars, increasing their price and increasing the quantity supplied, as in the accompanying graph. *(97)*

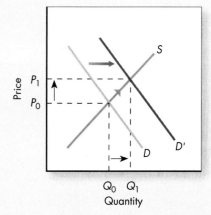

9. Other things are most likely to remain constant in the egg and luxury boat markets because each is a small percentage of the whole economy. Factors that affect the world oil market and the labor market will have ripple effects that must be taken into account in any analysis. *(98)*

10. The fallacy of composition is relevant for macroeconomic issues because it reminds us that, in the aggregate, small effects that are immaterial for micro issues can add up and be material. *(98)*

5 Using Supply and Demand

It is by invisible hands that we are bent and tortured worst.

—*Nietzsche*

Supply and demand give you a lens through which to view the economy. That lens brings into focus issues that would otherwise seem like a muddle. In this chapter, we use the supply/demand lens to consider real-world events.

Real-World Supply and Demand Applications

Let's begin by giving you an opportunity to apply supply/demand analysis to real-world events. Below are three events. After reading each, try your hand at explaining what happened, using supply and demand curves. To help you in the process Figure 5-1 provides some diagrams. *Before* reading my explanation, try to match the shifts to the examples. In each, be careful to explain which curve, or curves, shifted and how those shifts affected equilibrium price and quantity.

1. In the spring of 2006, Cyclone Larry tore through key growing regions of Australia with 180-miles-per-hour winds wiping out 80 percent of Australia's banana crop. Banana prices rose overnight from $1.00 to $2.00 a pound, where they were expected to remain for some time. Market: Bananas in Australia.

2. Now that it can cost as much as $100 to fill a tank of gas, Americans are switching from SUVs to more fuel-efficient cars. The number of people shopping for used SUVs fell over 30 percent in 2006 and the price of used SUVs fell an average of 10 percent. Market: Used SUVs in the United States.

3. Due to the entry of new coffee-growers (such as Vietnam) in the market, improved growing techniques, and favorable growing weather, the price of raw coffee beans fell from about $2.00 a pound in 1997 to less than $0.50 a pound in 2002. Some growers have proposed a marketing campaign to boost demand to match the increase in supply. While it's unlikely to be successful, for this analysis, let's assume it is. Market: Raw coffee beans.

Now that you've matched them, let's see if your analysis matches mine.

FIGURE 5-1 (A, B, AND C)

In this exhibit, three shifts of supply and demand are shown. Your task is to match them with the events listed in the text.

Answers: 1–b; 2–a; 3–c.

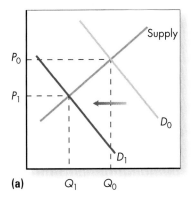

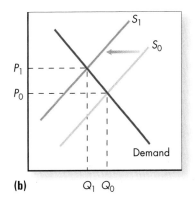

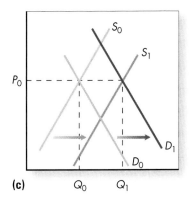

(a)   (b)   (c)

Cyclone Larry   Weather is a shift factor of supply. The cyclone shifted the supply curve for bananas from Australia to the left, as shown in Figure 5-1(b). At the original price, $1 a pound (shown by P_0), quantity demanded exceeded quantity supplied and the invisible hand of the market pressured the price to rise until quantity demanded equaled quantity supplied at $2 a pound (shown by P_1).

Sales of SUVs   Gas is a significant cost of driving a car. To reduce their automotive gas bills, Americans reduced their demand for gas-guzzling SUVs, both new and used. Figure 5-1(a) shows that the demand curve for SUVs in the used-car market shifted from D_0 to D_1. At the original price P_0, sellers were unable to sell the SUVs they wanted to sell and began to lower their price. Buyers of used SUVs were able to purchase them at a 10 percent lower price, shown by P_1.

Coffee Beans   Increased rainfall in Brazil, as well as more efficient farm machinery, has increased the coffee bean yield per acre. The entry of Vietnam into the coffee market has added more coffee beans on the market. This increase in supply is represented by a shift of the supply curve out to the right, as Figure 5-1(c) shows. Equilibrium price declined from $2.00 to $0.50 per pound in just two years and equilibrium quantity rose (where D_0 and S_1 intersect). Let's now consider the Coffee Growers' Federation recommendation to market coffee so that increases in demand would match increases in consumption. If successful, this would shift the demand curve out to the right sufficiently to raise the price of coffee back to $2.00 a pound and to raise equilibrium quantity even further. So in this case both supply and demand shift out.

Now that we've been through some straightforward examples, let's get more adventurous and apply supply/demand analysis to a case where you really have to be careful about what price you are talking about—the demand and supply for euros, the common currency in Europe.

Q_{-1} True or false? If supply rises, price will rise.

Web Note 5.1
Fair Trade Coffee

The Price of a Foreign Currency

The market for foreign currencies is called the foreign exchange (forex) market. It is this market that determines the **exchange rates**—*the price of one country's currency in terms of another's currency*—that newspapers report daily in tables such as the table on

Supply and Demand in Action

Sorting out the effects of the shifts of supply or demand or both can be confusing. Here are some helpful hints to keep things straight:

- Draw the initial demand and supply curves and label them. The equilibrium price and quantity is where these curves intersect. Label them.

- If only price has changed, no curves will shift and a shortage or surplus will result.

- If a nonprice factor affects demand, determine the direction demand has shifted and add the new demand curve. Do the same for supply.

- Equilibrium price and quantity is where the new demand and supply curves intersect. Label them.

- Compare the initial equilibrium price and quantity to the new equilibrium price and quantity.

See if you can describe what happened in the three graphs below.

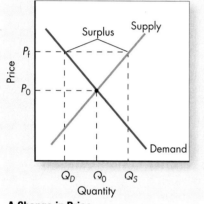

A Change in Price

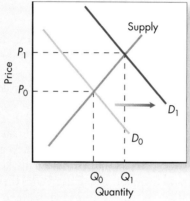

A Shift in Demand

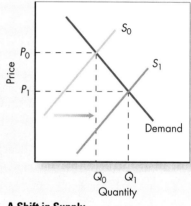

A Shift in Supply

the next page that shows the cost of various currencies in terms of dollars and dollars in terms of other currencies. From it you can see that on March 6, 2007, one riyal cost about 27 cents and one rand cost 14 cents. (If you are wondering which countries have riyals and rands for currencies, look at the table.)

Unless you collect currencies, the reason you want the currency of another country is that you want to buy something that country produces or an existing asset of that country. Say you want to buy a Hyundai car that costs 12.793 million South Korean won. Looking at the table, you see that 1 won costs $0.0010553. This means that 12.793 million won will cost you $13,500.45. So before you can buy the Hyundai, somebody must go to a forex market with $13,500.45 and exchange those dollars for 12.793 million won. Only then can the car be bought in the United States. Most final buyers don't do this; the importer does it for them. But whenever a foreign good is bought, someone must trade currencies.

To see what determines exchange rates, let's consider the price of the **euro**—*the currency used by 13 of the members of the European Union*. In 2001, one euro sold for $0.85. It rose to $1.30 in the early 2000s. What caused this rise? Supply and demand. Once you recognize that a currency is just another good, what may appear to be a hard subject (the determination of exchange rates) becomes an easy subject (what determines a good's price). All you have to do is to replace the good I used in Chapter 4 (DVDs) with euros, and apply the same reasoning process we've used so far to determine the equilibrium price of the euro.

People demand currencies of other countries to buy those countries' goods and assets.

The determination of exchange rates is the same as the determination of price. A currency is just another good.

Currencies

March 6, 2007

U.S.-dollar foreign-exchange rates in late New York trading

Country/currency	Tues in US$	Tues per US$	US$ vs, YTD chg (%)	Country/currency	Tues in US$	Tues per US$	US$ vs, YTD chg (%)
Americas				**Europe**			
Argentina peso*	.3225	3.1008	1.4	**Czech Rep.** koruna**	.04662	21.450	3.0
Brazil real	.4723	2.1173	−0.9	**Denmark** krone	.1762	5.6754	0.5
Canada dollar	.8500	1.1765	0.9	**Euro area** euro	1.3123	.7620	0.6
1-mos forward	.8508	1.1754	0.9	**Hungary** forint	.005186	192.83	1.3
2-mos forward	.8523	1.1733	0.9	**Malta** lira	3.0556	.3273	0.6
6-mos forward	.8544	1.1704	0.9	**Norway** krone	.1609	6.2150	−0.3
Chile peso	.001860	537.63	1.0	**Poland** zloty	.3365	2.9718	2.3
Colombia peso	.0004505	2219.76	−0.8	**Russia** ruble‡	.03812	26.233	−0.3
Ecuador US dollar	1	1	...	**Slovak Rep** koruna	.03821	26.171	0.2
Mexico peso*	.0898	11.1408	3.1	**Sweden** krona	.1417	7.0572	3.1
Peru new sol	.3137	3.188	−0.3	**Switzerland** franc	.8170	1.2240	0.4
Uruguay peso†	.04120	24.27	−0.5	1-mos forward	.819	1.2206	0.4
Venezuela bolivar	.000466	2145.92	unch	3-mos forward	.8234	1.2145	0.4
				6-mos forward	.8294	1.2057	0.5
Asia-Pacific				**Turkey** lira**	.6978	1.4330	1.2
Australian dollar	.7748	1.2907	1.9	**UK pound**	1.9314	.5178	1.4
China yuan	.1292	7.7416	−0.8	1-mos forward	1.9313	.5178	1.4
Hong Kong dollar	.1280	7.8155	0.5	3-mos forward	1.9308	.5179	1.4
India rupee	.02263	44.189	0.2	6-mos forward	1.9288	.5185	1.5
Indonesia rupiah	.0001085	9217	2.5				
Japan yen	.008575	116.62	−2.0	**Middle East/Africa**			
1-mos forward	.00861	116.14	−2.0	**Bahrain** dollar	2.6524	.3770	unch
3-mos forward	.00868	115.26	−2.0	**Egypt** pound*	.1755	5.6990	−0.2
6-mos forward	.00878	113.93	−2.0	**Israel** shekel	.2369	4.2212	0.1
Malaysia ringgits§	.2846	3.5137	−0.5	**Jordan** dinar	1.4114	.7085	−0.1
New Zealand dollar	.6829	1.4643	3.2	**Kuwait** dinar	3.4577	.2892	unch
Pakistan rupee	.01647	60.717	−0.1	**Lebanon** pound	.0006616	1511.49	unch
Phillipines peso	.0205	48.828	−0.4	**Saudia Arabia** riyal	.2667	3.7495	unch
Singapore dollar	.6543	1.5284	−0.3	**South Africa** rand	.1354	7.3855	5.6
South Korea won	.0010553	947.60	1.9	**UAE** dirham	.2723	3.6724	unch
Taiwan dollar	.03033	32.971	1.2				
Thailand baht	.03040	32.895	−7.2	**SDR††**	1.5019	.6658	0.2

* Floating rate †Financial §Government rate ‡Russian Central Bank rate ** Rebased as of Jan 1, 2005
††Special Drawing Rights (SDR); from the International Monetary Fund; based on exchange rates for
U.S., British and Japanese currencies.
Note: Based on trading among banks of $1 million and more, as quoted at 4p.m. ET by Reuters.

Source: Reprinted by permission of *The Wall Street Journal* © 2007, Dow Jones & Company, Inc. All rights reserved worldwide.

Q-2 You are going to Chile and plan to exchange $100. According to the foreign exchange rate table in the text, how many Chilean pesos will you receive?

Figure 5-2 shows supply and demand curves for the euro. As with any good, the supply of euros represents those people who are selling euros and the demand for the euro represents those people who are buying euros. Sellers of euros are Europeans who want to buy U.S. goods and assets. Buyers of euros are U.S. citizens who want to buy European goods and assets. (For simplicity, we assume that the only countries that exist are the United States and European countries that use the euro as their currency.)

The rise in the value of the euro in the early 2000s occurred for a number of reasons. The one we will focus on here is the recession and falling interest rates in the United States. We begin with demand D_0 and supply S_0 for euros, resulting in an equilibrium price of $0.85 in 2001. Because the U.S. economy entered a recession, and because U.S. interest rates fell, Europeans bought fewer U.S. financial assets such as stocks and bonds. That meant they supplied fewer euros because they needed to buy fewer U.S. dollars. The supply of euros fell from S_0 to S_1. At the same time, Americans also decided to buy more European stocks and bonds because European interest rates were relatively higher. In addition, the Chinese and Japanese governments increased their demand for European assets. Because they needed to pay for these European assets with euros, the demand for euros rose from D_0 to D_1. Combined, the two shifts led to a rise in the price of the euro as shown in Figure 5-2, increasing the price to $1.30 in 2005, where it remained into 2007.

There is more to the determination of exchange rates than this, but as is often the case, supply/demand analysis gives you a good first entry into what is otherwise a potentially confusing issue.

Foreign Exchange

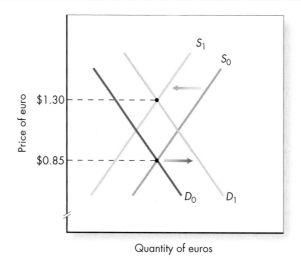

FIGURE 5-2 **The Market for Euros**

The price of the euro increased as American investors increased their demand for euros to buy European goods and invest in the European stock market, while Europeans bought fewer U.S. goods and fewer American stocks, decreasing Americans' supply of euros. The combined effect was a rise in the dollar price of euros.

A Review

Anything other than price that affects demand or supply will shift the curves.

Now that we've been through some examples, let's review. Remember: Anything that affects demand and supply other than price of the good will shift the curves. Changes in the price of the good result in movements along the curves. Another thing to recognize is that when both curves are shifting, you can get a change in price but little change in quantity, or a change in quantity but little change in price.

Q.3 Say a hormone has been discovered that increases cows' milk production by 20 percent. Demonstrate graphically what effect this discovery would have on the price and quantity of milk sold in a market.

To test your understanding Table 5-1 gives you six generic results from the interaction of supply and demand. Your job is to decide what shifts produced those results. This exercise is a variation of the one with which I began the chapter. It goes over the same issues, but this time without the graphs. On the left-hand side of Table 5-1, I list combinations of movements of observed prices and quantities, labeling them 1–6. On the right I give six shifts in supply and demand, labeling them a–f.

If you don't confuse your "shifts of" with your "movements along," supply and demand provide good off-the-cuff answers for any economic questions.

TABLE 5-1

Price and Quantity Changes			Shifts in Supply and Demand
1.	P↑	Q↑	a. Supply shifts in. No change in demand.
2.	P↑	Q↓	b. Demand shifts out. Supply shifts in.
3.	P↑	Q?	c. Demand shifts in. No change in supply.
4.	P↓	Q?	d. Demand shifts out. Supply shifts out.
5.	P?	Q↑	e. Demand shifts out. No change in supply.
6.	P↓	Q↓	f. Demand shifts in. Supply shifts out.

You are to match the shifts with the price and quantity movements that best fit each described shift, using each shift and movement only once. My recommendation to you is to draw the graphs that are described in a–f, decide what happens to price and quantity, and then find the match in 1–6.

Q.4 If both demand and supply shift in to the left, what happens to price and quantity?

Now that you've worked them, let me give you the answers I came up with. They are: 1–e; 2–a; 3–b; 4–f; 5–d; 6–c. How did I come up with the answers? I did what I suggested you do—took each of the scenarios on the right and predicted what happens to price and quantity. For case a, supply shifts in to the left and there is a movement up along the

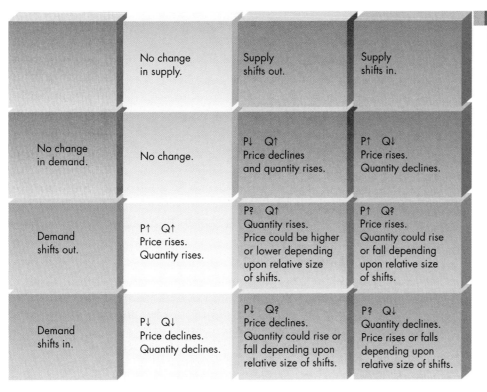

	No change in supply.	Supply shifts out.	Supply shifts in.
No change in demand.	No change.	P↓ Q↑ Price declines and quantity rises.	P↑ Q↓ Price rises. Quantity declines.
Demand shifts out.	P↑ Q↑ Price rises. Quantity rises.	P? Q↑ Quantity rises. Price could be higher or lower depending upon relative size of shifts.	P↑ Q? Price rises. Quantity could rise or fall depending upon relative size of shifts.
Demand shifts in.	P↓ Q↓ Price declines. Quantity declines.	P↓ Q? Price declines. Quantity could rise or fall depending upon relative size of shifts.	P? Q↓ Quantity declines. Price rises or falls depending upon relative size of shifts.

TABLE 5-2 **Diagram of Effects of Shifts of Demand and Supply on Price and Quantity**

This table provides a summary of the effects of shifts in supply and demand on equilibrium price and equilibrium quantity. Notice that when both curves shift, the effect on either price or quantity depends on the relative size of the shifts.

demand curve. Since the demand curve is downward-sloping, the price rises and quantity declines. This matches number *2* on the left. For case *b*, demand shifts out to the right. Along the original supply curve, price and quantity would rise. But supply shifts in to the left, leading to even higher prices but lower quantity. What happens to quantity is unclear, so the match must be number *3*. For case *c*, demand shifts in to the left. There is movement down along the supply curve with lower price and lower quantity. This matches number *6*. For case *d*, demand shifts out and supply shifts out. As demand shifts out, we move along the supply curve to the right and price and quantity rise. But supply shifts out too, and we move out along the new demand curve. Price declines, erasing the previous rise, and the quantity rises even more. This matches number *5*.

I'll leave it up to you to confirm my answers to *e* and *f*. Notice that when supply and demand both shift, the change in either price or quantity is uncertain—it depends on the relative size of the shifts. As a summary, I present a diagrammatic of the combinations in Table 5-2.

Q-5 If price and quantity both fell, what would you say was the most likely cause?

Government Intervention in the Market

People don't always like the market-determined price. If the invisible hand were the only factor that determined prices, people would have to accept it. But it isn't; social and political forces also determine price. For example, when prices fall, sellers look to government for ways to hold prices up; when prices rise, buyers look to government for ways to hold prices down. Let's now consider the effect of such actions. Let's start with an example of the price being held down.

Price Ceilings

When government wants to hold prices down, it imposes a **price ceiling**—*a government-imposed limit on how high a price can be charged.* That limit is generally below the equilibrium

FIGURE 5-3 **Rent Control in Paris**

A price ceiling imposed on housing rent in Paris during World War II created a shortage of housing when World War II ended and veterans returned home. The shortage would have been eliminated if rents had been allowed to rise to $17 per month.

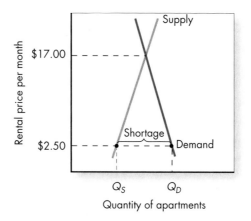

Web Note 5.2
Rent Control

Price Ceilings

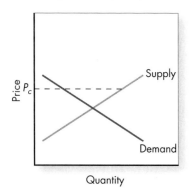
Q-6 What is the effect of the price ceiling, P_c, shown in the graph below on price and quantity?

price. (A price ceiling that is above the equilibrium price will not have any effect at all.) From Chapter 4, you already know the effect of a price that is below the equilibrium price—quantity demanded will exceed quantity supplied and there will be excess demand. Let's now look at an example of **rent control**—*a price ceiling on rents, set by government*—and see how that excess demand shows up in the real world.

Rent controls exist today in a number of American cities as well as other cities throughout the world. Many of the laws governing rent were first instituted during the two world wars in the first half of the 20th century. Consider Paris, for example. In World War II, the Paris government froze rent to ease the financial burden of those families whose wage earners were sent to fight in the war. When the soldiers returned at the end of the war, the rent control was continued; removing it would have resulted in an increase in rents from $2.50 to $17 a month, and that was felt to be an unfair burden for veterans.

Figure 5-3 shows this situation. The below-market rent set by government created an enormous shortage of apartments. Initially this shortage didn't bother those renting apartments, since they got low-cost apartments. But it created severe hardships for those who didn't have apartments. Many families moved in with friends or extended families. Others couldn't find housing at all and lived on the streets. Eventually the rent controls started to cause problems even for those who did have apartments. The reason why is that owners of buildings cut back on maintenance. More than 80 percent of Parisians had no private bathrooms and 20 percent had no running water. Since rental properties weren't profitable, no new buildings were being constructed and existing buildings weren't kept in repair. It was even harder for those who didn't have apartments.

Since the market price was not allowed to ration apartments, alternative methods of rationing developed. People paid landlords bribes to get an apartment, or watched the obituaries and then simply moved in their furniture before anyone else did. Eventually the situation got so bad that rent controls were lifted.

The system of rent controls is not only of historical interest. Below I list some phenomena that existed in New York City recently.

1. A couple paid $350 a month for a two-bedroom Park Avenue apartment with a solarium and two terraces, while another individual paid $1,200 a month for a studio apartment shared with two roommates.

2. The vacancy rate for apartments in New York City was 3.5 percent. Anything under 5 percent is considered a housing emergency.

3. The actress Mia Farrow paid $2,900 a month (a fraction of the market-clearing rent) for 10 rooms on Central Park West. It was an apartment her mother first leased 60 years ago.

4. Would-be tenants made payments, called key money, to current tenants or landlords to get apartments.

Your assignment is to explain how these phenomena might have come about, and to demonstrate, with supply and demand, the situation that likely caused them. (Hint: New York City had rent control.)

Now that you have done your assignment (you have, haven't you?), let me give you my answers so that you can check them with your answers.

The situation is identical with that presented above in Figure 5-3. Take the first item. The couple lived in a rent-controlled apartment while the individual with room-mates did not. If rent control were eliminated, rent on the Park Avenue apartment would rise and rent on the studio would most likely decline. Item 2: The housing emergency was a result of rent control. Below-market rent resulted in excess demand and little vacancy. Item 3: That Mia Farrow rents a rent-controlled apartment was the result of nonprice rationing. Instead of being rationed by price, other methods of rationing arose. These other methods of rationing scarce resources are called nonprice rationing. In New York City, strict rules determined the handing down of rent-controlled apartments from family member to family member. Item 4: New residents searched for a long time to find apartments to rent, and many discovered that illegal payments to landlords were the only way to obtain a rent-controlled apartment. Key money is a black market payment for a rent-controlled apartment. Because of the limited supply of apartments, individuals were willing to pay far more than the controlled price. Landlords used other methods of rationing the limited supply of apartments—instituting first-come, first-served policies, and, in practice, selecting tenants based on gender, race, or other personal characteristics, even though such discriminatory selection was illegal.

If rent controls had only the bad effects described above, no community would institute them. They are, however, implemented with good intentions—to cope with sudden increases in demand for housing that would otherwise cause rents to explode and force many poor people out of their apartments. The negative effects occur over time as buildings begin to deteriorate and the number of people looking to rent and unable to find apartments increases. As this happens, people focus less on the original renters and more on new renters excluded from the market and on the inefficiencies of price ceilings. Since politicians tend to focus on the short run, we can expect rent control to continue to be used when demand for housing suddenly increases.

Price Floors

Sometimes political forces favor suppliers, sometimes consumers. So let us now go briefly through a case when the government is trying to favor suppliers by attempting to prevent the price from falling below a certain level. **Price floors**—*government-imposed limits on how low a price can be charged*—do just this. The price floor is generally above the existing price. (A price floor below equilibrium price would have no effect.) When there is an effective price floor, quantity supplied exceeds quantity demanded and the result is excess supply.

An example of a price floor is the minimum wage. Both individual states and the federal government impose **minimum wage laws**—*laws specifying the lowest wage a firm can legally pay an employee.* The U.S. federal government first instituted a minimum wage of 25 cents per hour in 1938 as part of the Fair Labor Standards Act. It has been raised many times since, and in the early 2000s the federal government voted to raise it to over $7.00 an hour. (With inflation, that's a much smaller increase than it looks.)

With price ceilings, existing goods are no longer rationed entirely by price. Other methods of rationing existing goods arise called nonprice rationing.

Q-7 What is the effect of the price floor, P_f, shown in the graph below, on price and quantity?

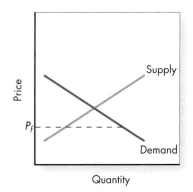

FIGURE 5-4   A Minimum Wage

A minimum wage, W_{min}, above equilibrium wage, W_e, helps those who are able to find work, shown by Q_2, but hurts those who would have been employed at the equilibrium wage but can no longer find employment, shown by $Q_e - Q_2$. A minimum wage also hurts producers who have higher costs of production and consumers who may face higher product prices.

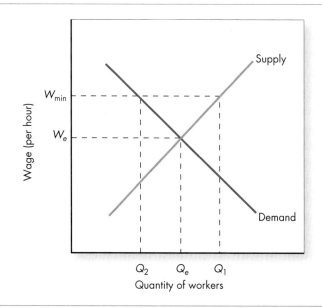

Web Note 5.3
Minimum Wage

Price Floors

The minimum wage helps some people and hurts others.

In 2007 about 1.7 million hourly wage earners received the minimum wage, or about 2.2 percent of hourly paid workers, most of whom are unskilled. The market-determined equilibrium wage for skilled workers is generally above the minimum wage.

The effect of a minimum wage on the unskilled labor market is shown in Figure 5-4. The government-set minimum wage is above equilibrium, as shown by W_{min}. At the market-determined equilibrium wage W_e, the quantity of labor supplied and demanded equals Q_e. At the higher minimum wage, the quantity of labor supplied rises to Q_1 and the quantity of labor demanded declines to Q_2. There is an excess supply of workers (a shortage of jobs) represented by the difference $Q_1 - Q_2$. This represents people who are looking for work but cannot find it.

Who wins and who loses from a minimum wage? The minimum wage improves the wages of the Q_2 workers who are able to find work. Without the minimum wage, they would have earned W_e per hour. The minimum wage hurts those, however, who cannot find work at the minimum wage but who are willing to work, and would have been hired, at the market-determined wage. These workers are represented by the distance $Q_e - Q_2$ in Figure 5-4. The minimum wage also hurts firms that now must pay their workers more, increasing the cost of production, and consumers to the extent that firms are able to pass that increase in production cost on in the form of higher product prices.

All economists agree that the above analysis is logical and correct. But they disagree about whether governments should have minimum wage laws. One reason is that the empirical effects of minimum wage laws are relatively small; in fact, some studies have found them to be negligible. (There is, however, much debate about these estimates, since "other things" never remain constant.) A second reason is that some real-world labor markets are not sufficiently competitive to fit the supply/demand model. A third reason is that the minimum wage affects the economy in ways that some economists see as desirable and others see as undesirable. I point this out to remind you that the supply/demand framework is a tool to be used to analyze issues. It does not provide final answers about policy. (In microeconomics, economists explore the policy issues of interferences in markets much more carefully.)

Because the federal minimum wage is low, and not binding for most workers, a movement called the living-wage movement has begun. The living-wage movement focuses on local governments, calling on them to establish a minimum wage at a *living wage*—a wage necessary to support a family at or above the federally determined poverty line. By 2007, over 70 local governments had passed living-wage laws, with minimum wages ranging between $6.25 an hour in Milwaukee and $12.00 in Santa Cruz. The analysis of these living-wage laws is the same as that for minimum wages.

Excise Taxes

Let's now consider an example of a tax on goods. An **excise tax** is *a tax that is levied on a specific good*. The luxury tax on expensive cars that the United States imposed in 1991 is an example. A **tariff** is *an excise tax on an imported good*. What effect will excise taxes and tariffs have on the price and quantity in a market?

To lend some sense of reality, let's take the example from the early 1990s, when the United States taxed the suppliers of expensive boats. Say the price of a boat before the luxury tax was $60,000, and 600 boats were sold at that price. Now the government taxes suppliers $10,000 for every luxury boat sold. What will the new price of the boat be, and how many will be sold?

If you were about to answer "$70,000," be careful. Ask yourself whether I would have given you that question if the answer were that easy. By looking at supply and demand curves in Figure 5-5, you can see why $70,000 is the wrong answer.

To sell 600 boats, suppliers must be fully compensated for the tax. So the tax of $10,000 on the supplier shifts the supply curve up from S_0 to S_1. However, at $70,000, consumers are not willing to purchase 600 boats. They are willing to purchase only 420 boats. Quantity supplied exceeds quantity demanded at $70,000. Suppliers lower their prices until quantity supplied equals quantity demanded at $65,000, the new equilibrium price.

The new equilibrium price is $65,000, not $70,000. The reason is that at the higher price, the quantity of boats people demand is less. Some people choose not to buy boats and others find substitute vehicles or purchase their boats outside the United States. This is a movement up along a demand curve to the left. Excise taxes reduce the quantity of goods demanded. That's why boat manufacturers were up in arms after the tax was imposed and why the revenue generated from the tax was less than expected. Instead of collecting $10,000 × 600 ($6 million), revenue collected was only $10,000 × 510 ($5.1 million). (The tax was repealed in 1993.)

A tariff has the same effect on the equilibrium price and quantity as an excise tax. The difference is that only foreign producers sending goods into the United States pay

A tax on suppliers shifts the supply curve up by the amount of the tax.

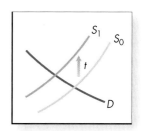

 Q-8 Your study partner, Umar, has just stated that a tax on demanders of $2 per unit will raise the equilibrium price from $4 to $6. How do you respond?

Excise Taxes

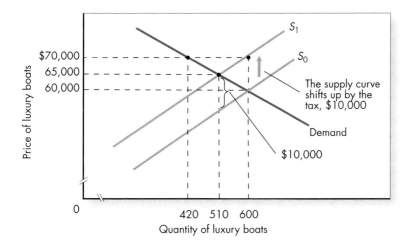

FIGURE 5-5 **The Effect of an Excise Tax**

An excise tax on suppliers shifts the entire supply curve up by the amount of the tax. Since at a price equal to the original price plus the tax there is excess supply, the price of the good rises by less than the tax.

the tax. An example is the 30 percent tariff imposed on steel imported into the United States in 2002. The government instituted the tariffs because U.S. steelmakers were having difficulty competing with lower-cost foreign steel. The tariff increased the price of imported steel, making U.S. steel more competitive to domestic buyers. As expected, the price of imported steel rose by over 15 percent, to about $230 a ton, and the quantity imported declined. Tariffs don't hurt just the foreign producer. Tariffs increase the cost of imported products to domestic consumers. In the case of steel, manufacturing companies such as automakers faced higher production costs. The increase in the cost of steel lowered production in those industries and increased the cost of a variety of goods to U.S. consumers.

Quantity Restrictions

Another way in which governments often interfere with, or regulate, markets is with licenses, which limit entry into a market. For example, to be a doctor you need a license; to be a vet you need a license; and in some places to be an electrician, a financial planner, or a cosmetologist, or to fish, you need a license. There are many reasons for licenses, and we will not consider them here. Instead, we will simply consider what effect licenses have on the price and quantity of the activity being licensed. Specifically, we'll look at a case where the government issues a specific number of licenses and holds that number constant. The example we'll take is licenses to drive a taxi. In New York City, these are called taxi medallions because the license is an aluminum plate attached to the hood of a taxi. Taxi medallions were established in 1937 as a way to increase the wages of licensed taxi drivers. Wages of taxi drivers had fallen from $26 a week in 1929 to $15 a week in 1933. As wages fell, the number of taxi drivers fell from 19,000 to about 12,000. The remaining 12,000 taxi drivers successfully lobbied New York City to grant drivers with current licenses who met certain requirements permanent rights to drive taxis—medallions. (It wasn't until the early 2000s that the number of medallions was increased slightly.) The restriction had the desired effect. As the economy grew, demand for taxis grew (the demand for taxis shifted out) and because the supply of taxis remained at about 12,000, the wages of the taxi drivers owning medallions increased, as is shown in Figure 5-6(a).

Issuing taxi medallions had a secondary effect. Because New York City also granted medallion owners the right to sell their medallions, a market in medallions developed. Those fortunate enough to have been granted a medallion by the city found that they had a valuable asset. A person wanting to drive a taxi, and earn those high wages, had to buy a medallion from an existing driver. This meant that while new taxi drivers would

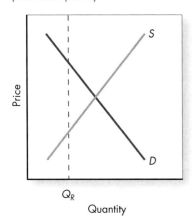

Q.9 What is the effect of the quantity restrictions, Q_R, shown in the graph below, on equilibrium price and quantity?

FIGURE 5-6 (A AND B) **Quantity Restrictions in the Market for Taxi Licenses**

In 1937, New York City limited the number of taxi licenses to 12,000 as a way to increase the wages of taxi drivers. It had the intended effect, as (**a**) shows. Because taxi medallions were limited in supply, as demand for taxi services rose, so did the demand for medallions. Their price rose significantly, as (**b**) shows.

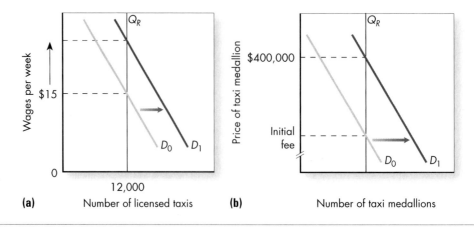

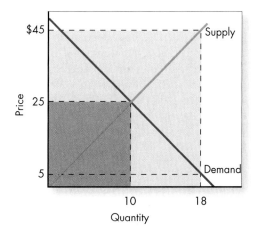

FIGURE 5-7 **Third-Party-Payer Markets**

In a third-party-payer system, the person who chooses the product doesn't pay the entire cost. Here, with a co-payment of $5, consumers demand 18 units. Sellers require $45 per unit for that quantity. Total expenditures, shown by the entire shaded region, are much greater compared to when the consumer pays the entire cost, shown by just the dark shaded region.

earn a higher wage once they had bought a license, their wage after taking into account the cost of the license would be much lower.

As the demand for taxis rose, the medallions became more and more valuable. The effect on the price of medallions is shown in Figure 5-6(b). The quantity restriction, Q_R, means that any increases in demand lead only to price increases. Although the initial license fee was minimal, increases in demand for taxis quickly led to higher and higher medallion prices.

Quantity restrictions tend to increase price.

The demand for taxi medallions continues to increase each year as the New York City population grows more than the supply is increased. The result is that the price of a taxi medallion continues to rise. Even with the slight increase in the number of medallions, today taxi medallions cost about $400,000, giving anyone who has bought that license a strong reason to oppose an expansion in the number of licenses being issued.[1]

Third-Party-Payer Markets

As a final example for this chapter, let's consider third-party-payer markets. In **third-party-payer markets,** *the person who receives the good differs from the person paying for the good.* An example is the health care market where many individuals have insurance. They generally pay a co-payment for health care services and an HMO or other insurer pays the remainder. Medicare and Medicaid are both third-party payers. Figure 5-7 shows what happens in the supply/demand model when there is a third-party-payer market and a small co-payment. In the normal case, when the individual demander pays for the good, equilibrium quantity is where quantity demanded equals quantity supplied—in this case at an equilibrium price of $25 and an equilibrium quantity of 10.

Under a third-party-payer system, the person who chooses how much to purchase doesn't pay the entire cost. Because the co-payment faced by the consumer is much lower, quantity demanded is much greater. In this example with a co-payment of $5, the consumer demands 18. Given an upward-sloping supply curve, the seller requires a higher price, in this case $45 for each unit supplied to provide that quantity. Assuming the co-payment is for each unit, the consumers pay $5 of that price for a total out-of-pocket cost of $90 ($5 times 18). The third-party payer pays the remainder, $40, for a cost of $720

---

[1]As is usually the case, the analysis is more complicated in real life. In New York there are both individual and corporate licenses. But the general reasoning carries through: Effective quantity restrictions increase the value of a license.

In third-party-payer markets, equilibrium quantity and total spending are much higher.

($40 times 18). Total spending is $810. This compares to total spending of only $250 (25 times 10) if the consumer had to pay the entire price. Notice that with a third-party-payer system, total spending, represented by the large shaded rectangle, is much higher than total spending if the consumer paid, represented by the small darker rectangle.

The third-party-payer system describes much of the health care system in the United States today. Typically, a person with health insurance makes a fixed co-payment of $5 to $10 for an office visit, regardless of procedures and tests provided. Given this payment system, the insured patient has little incentive to limit the procedures offered by the doctor. The doctor charges the insurance company, and the insurance company pays. The rise in health care costs over the past decades can be attributed in part to the third-party-payer system.

Q-10 If the cost of textbooks were included in tuition, what would likely happen to their prices? Why?

A classic example of how third-party-payer systems can affect choices is a case where a 70-year-old man spent weeks in a hospital recovering from surgery to address abdominal bleeding. The bill, to be paid by Medicare, was nearing $275,000 and the patient wasn't recovering as quickly as expected. The doctor finally figured out that the patient's condition wasn't improving because ill-fitting dentures didn't allow him to eat properly. The doctor ordered the hospital dentist to fix the dentures, but the patient refused the treatment. Why? The patient explained: "Seventy-five dollars is a lot of money." The $75 procedure wasn't covered by Medicare.

Third-party-payer systems are not limited to health care. (Are your parents or the government paying for part of your college? If you were paying the full amount, would you be demanding as much college as you currently are?) Anytime a third-party-payer system exists, the quantity demanded will be higher than it otherwise would be. Market forces will not hold down costs as much as they would otherwise because the person using the service doesn't have an incentive to hold down costs. Of course, that doesn't mean that there are no pressures. The third-party payers—parents, employers, and government—will respond to this by trying to limit both the quantity of the good individuals consume and the amount they pay for it. For example, parents will put pressure on their kids to get through school quickly rather than lingering for five or six years, and government will place limitations on what procedures Medicare and Medicaid patients can use. The goods will be rationed through social and political means. Such effects are not unexpected; they are just another example of supply and demand in action.

Conclusion

I began this chapter by pointing out that supply and demand are the lens through which economists look at reality. It takes practice to use that lens, and this chapter gave you some practice. Focusing the lens on a number of issues highlighted certain aspects of those issues. The analysis was simple but powerful and should, if you followed it, provide you with a good foundation for understanding the economist's way of thinking about policy issues.

Summary

- By minding your *P*s and *Q*s—the shifts of and movements along curves—you can describe almost all events in terms of supply and demand.

- The determination of prices of currencies—foreign exchange rates—can be analyzed with the supply and demand model in the same way as any other good can be.

- A price ceiling is a government-imposed limit on how high a price can be charged. Price ceilings below market price create shortages.

- A price floor is a government-imposed limit on how low a price can be charged. Price floors above market price create surpluses.

- Taxes and tariffs paid by suppliers shift the supply curve up by the amount of the tax or tariff. They raise the equilibrium price (inclusive of tax) and decrease the equilibrium quantity.

- Quantity restrictions increase equilibrium price and reduce equilibrium quantity.

- In a third-party-payer market, the consumer and the one who pays the cost differ. Quantity demanded, price, and total spending are greater when a third party pays than when the consumer pays.

Key Terms

euro (106)
exchange rate (105)
excise tax (113)

minimum wage
    law (111)
price ceiling (109)

price floor (111)
rent control (110)
tariff (113)

third-party-payer
    market (115)

Questions for Thought and Review

1. Say that the equilibrium price and quantity both rose. What would you say was the most likely cause?   LO1

2. Say that equilibrium price fell and quantity remained constant. What would you say was the most likely cause?   LO1

3. The dollar price of the South African rand fell from 29 cents to 22 cents in 1996, the same year the country was rocked by political turmoil. Using supply/demand analysis, explain why the turmoil led to a decline in the price of the rand.   LO2

4. Demonstrate graphically the effect of a price ceiling.   LO3

5. Demonstrate graphically why rent controls might increase the total payment that new renters pay for an apartment.   LO3

6. Demonstrate graphically the effect of a price floor.   LO3

7. Graphically show the effects of a minimum wage on the number of unemployed.   LO3

8. Demonstrate graphically the effect of a tax of $4 per unit on equilibrium price and quantity.   LO4

9. Quotas, like medallions, are quantity restrictions on imported goods. Demonstrate the effect of a quota on the price of imported goods.   LO4

10. Supply/demand analysis states that equilibrium occurs where quantity supplied equals quantity demanded, but in U.S. agricultural markets quantity supplied almost always exceeds quantity demanded. How can this be?   LO4

11. Nobel Prize–winning economist Bill Vickrey has suggested that automobile insurance should be paid as a tax on gas, rather than as a fixed fee per year per car. How would that change likely affect the number of automobiles that individuals own? (Difficult)   LO4

12. In early 2004, following the toppling of President Aristide, the price of a 110-pound sack of rice in Haiti doubled from $22.50 to $45 because of disruptions at Haitian ports. (Eighty percent of Haiti's rice is imported.) Demonstrate graphically the effect of the import disruptions on the equilibrium price and quantity of rice purchased in Haiti.   LO2

13. The U.S. imposes substantial taxes on cigarettes but not on loose tobacco. When the tax went into effect, what effect did it likely have for cigarette rolling machines? (Difficult)   LO4

14. In what ways is the market for public post-secondary education an example of a third-party-payer market? What's the impact of this on total educational expenditures?   LO5

15. What reasons might governments have to support third-party-payer markets? (Difficult)   LO5

Problems and Exercises

16. Since 1981, the U.S. government has supported the price of sugar produced by U.S. sugar producers by limiting import of sugar into the United States. Restricting imports is effective because the United States consumes more sugar than it produces.
    a. Using supply/demand analysis, demonstrate how import restrictions increase the price of domestic sugar.
    b. What other import policy could the government implement to have the same effect as the import restriction?   LO1

c. Under the Uruguay Round of the General Agreement on Tariffs and Trade in 1997, the United States agreed to permit at least 1.25 million tons of sugar to be imported into the United States. How does this affect the U.S. sugar price support program?

17. In some states and localities "scalping" is against the law, although enforcement of these laws is spotty. (Difficult)
    a. Using supply/demand analysis and words, demonstrate what a weakly enforced antiscalping law would likely do to the price of tickets.
    b. Using supply/demand analysis and words, demonstrate what a strongly enforced antiscalping law would likely do to the price of tickets.   LO1

18. Apartments in New York City are often hard to find. One of the major reasons is rent control. (Difficult)
    a. Demonstrate graphically how rent controls could make apartments hard to find.
    b. Often one can get an apartment if one makes a side payment to the current tenant. Can you explain why?
    c. What would be the likely effect of eliminating rent controls?
    d. What is the political appeal of rent controls?   LO1, LO3

19. Until recently, angora goat wool (mohair) has been designated as a strategic commodity (it used to be utilized in some military clothing). Because of that, in 1992 for every dollar's worth of mohair sold to manufacturers, ranchers received $3.60. (Difficult)
    a. Demonstrate graphically the effect of the elimination of this designation and subsidy.
    b. Explain why the program was likely kept in existence for so long.
    c. Say that a politician has suggested that the government should pass a law that requires all consumers to pay a price for angora goat wool high enough so that the sellers of that wool would receive $3.60 more than the market price. Demonstrate the effect of the law graphically. Would consumers support it? How about suppliers?   LO4

20. The technology is now developing so that road use can be priced by computer. A computer in the surface of the road picks up a signal from your car and automatically charges you for the use of the road.
    a. How could this technological change contribute to ending bottlenecks and rush hour congestion?
    b. What are some of the problems that might develop with such a system?
    c. How would your transportation habits likely change if you had to pay to use roads?   LO1

21. In 1938 Congress created a Board of Cosmetology in Washington, D.C., to license beauticians. To obtain a license, people had to attend a cosmetology school. In 1992 this law was used by the board to close down a hair braiding salon specializing in cornrows and braids oper-

ated by unlicensed Mr. Uqdah, even though little was then taught in cosmetology schools about braiding and cornrows. (Difficult)
    a. What possible reason can you give for why this board exists?
    b. What options might you propose to change the system?
    c. What will be the political difficulties of implementing those options?   LO1

22. In the Oregon health care plan for rationing Medicaid expenditures, therapy to slow the progression of AIDS and treatment for brain cancer were covered, while liver transplants and treatment for infectious mononucleosis were not covered. (Difficult)
    a. What criteria do you think were used to determine what was covered and what was not covered?
    b. Should an economist oppose the Oregon plan because it involves rationing?
    c. How does the rationing that occurs in the market differ from the rationing that occurs in the Oregon plan?   LO1

23. Airlines and hotels have many frequent flyer and frequent visitor programs in which individuals who fly the airline or stay at the hotel receive bonuses that are the equivalent to discounts.
    a. Give two reasons why these companies have such programs rather than simply offering lower prices.
    b. Can you give other examples of such programs?
    c. What is a likely reason why firms whose employees receive these benefits do not require their employees to give the benefits to the firm?   LO1

24. You're given the following supply and demand tables:

Demand		Supply	
P	Q	P	Q
$ 0	1,200	$ 0	0
2	900	2	0
4	600	4	150
6	300	6	300
8	0	8	600
10	0	10	600
12	0	12	750
14	0	14	900

    a. What is equilibrium price and quantity in a market system with no interferences?
    b. If this were a third-party-payer market where the consumer pays $2, what is the quantity demanded? What is the price charged by the seller?
    c. What is total spending in the two situations described in a and b?   LO5

25. Demonstrate the effect on price and quantity of each of the following events:
    a. In a recent popularity test, Elmo topped Cookie Monster in popularity (this represents a trend in children's tastes). Market: cookies.
    b. The Atkins Diet that limits carbohydrates was reported to be very effective. Market: bread.   LO1

26. In 1996, the television networks were given $70 billion worth of space on public airways for broadcasting high definition television rather than auction it off. (Difficult)
    a. Why do airways have value?
    b. After the airway had been given to the network, would you expect that the broadcaster would produce high definition television?   LO1

27. In 2004, oil facilities in Iraq were attacked and strong economies in the United States and China boosted the demand for oil.
    a. Demonstrate graphically how these events led to oil prices in excess of $40 a barrel in June 2004. What was the effect on the equilibrium quantity of oil bought and sold?
    b. As a result of political pressure, OPEC agreed to increase the daily quota by 2 million barrels a day. What was the likely effect on equilibrium oil price and quantity? Demonstrate your answer graphically.   LO1

28. About 10,000 tickets for the 2005 Men's Final Four college basketball games at the St. Louis Edward Jones Dome were to be sold in a lottery system for between $110 and $130 apiece. Typically applications exceed available tickets by 100,000. A year before the game, scalpers were already offering to sell tickets for between $200 and $2,000 depending on seat location, even though the practice is illegal. (Difficult)
    a. Demonstrate the supply and demand for Final Four tickets. How do you know that there is an excess demand for tickets at $130?
    b. Demonstrate the scalped price of between $200 and $2,000.
    c. What would be the effect of legalizing scalping on the resale value of Final Four tickets?   LO1

29. In the early 2000s, Whole Foods Market Inc. switched to a medical care plan that had a high deductible, which meant that employees were responsible for the first $1,500 of care, whereas after that they received 80 percent coverage. The firm also put about $800 in an account for each employee to use for medical care. If they did not use this money, they could carry it over to the next year.
    a. What do you expect happened to medical claim costs?
    b. What do you believe happened to hospital admissions?
    c. Demonstrate graphically the reasons for your answers in a and b.   LO5

30. In Japan, doctors prescribe drugs and supply the drugs to the patient, receiving a 25 percent markup. In the United States, doctors prescribe drugs, but, generally, they do not sell them. (Difficult)
    a. Which country prescribes the most drugs? Why?
    b. How would a plan to limit the price of old drugs, but not new drugs to allow for innovation, likely affect the drug industry?
    c. How might a drug company in the United States encourage a doctor in the United States, where doctors receive nothing for drugs, to prescribe more drugs?   LO5

31. Kennesaw University Professor Frank A. Adams III and Auburn University Professors A. H. Barnett and David L. Kaserman recently estimated the effect of legalizing the sale of cadaverous organs, which currently are in shortage at zero price. Demonstrating with supply and demand curves, what are the effects of the following two possibilities on the equilibrium price and quantity of transplanted organs if their sale were to be legalized?
    a. Many of those currently willing to donate the organs of a deceased relative at zero price are offended that organs can be bought and sold.
    b. People are willing to provide significantly more organs as price offered rises only marginally.   LO1

Questions from Alternative Perspectives

1. Some economists believe minimum wages create distortions in the labor market. If you are an employer and unable to hire the one willing and able to work for the lowest wage, how else might you choose a worker? Is this fair? Why or why not? (Austrian)

2. The book gives the example of a man who treated Medicare payments as different from his out-of-pocket payments. If you could save Medicare $100,000 by spending $20 of your own, should you? (Religious)

3. On average, women are paid less than men. What are the likely reasons for that? Should the government intervene with a law that requires firms to pay equal wages to those with comparable skills? (Feminist)

4. Biological evolution occurs very slowly; cultural evolution occurs less slowly, but still slowly compared to institutional and market evolution.
    a. Give some examples of these observations about the different speeds of adjustment.
    b. Explain the relevance of these observations to economic reasoning. (Institutionalist)

5. Most religions argue that individuals should not fully exploit market positions. For example, the text makes it sound as if

allowing prices to rise to whatever level clears the market is the best policy to follow. That means that if, for example, someone were stranded in the desert and were willing to pay half his or her future income for life for a drink of water, that it would be appropriate to charge him or her that price. Is it appropriate? Why or why not? (Religious)

6. Rent control today looks far different than the rent freeze New York City enacted after World War II. Most rent controls today simply restrict annual rent increases and guarantee landlords a "fair return" in return for maintaining their properties.

a. How would the economic effects of today's rent controls differ from the rent control programs depicted in your textbook?

b. Do you consider them an appropriate mechanism to address the disproportionate power that landlords hold over tenants?

c. If not, what policies would you recommend to address that inequity and the lack of affordable housing in U.S. cities? (Radical)

Web Questions

1. Go to the Cato Institute's home page (www.cato.org) and search for the article "How Rent Control Drives Out Affordable Housing" by William Tucker. After reading the article, answer the following questions:
   a. What is a shadow market, and why does one develop when there is rent control?
   b. Why is housing a particularly easy good to hoard? How does this affect newcomers to a city?
   c. How do vacancy rates compare among cities with and without rent control? Does this make sense within the supply/demand framework?

2. Go to the Economic Policy Institute's home page (www.epinet.org) and search for the article "Minimum Wage Issue Guide: Facts at a Glance." Using that article, answer the following questions:
   a. What has happened to the minimum wage adjusted for inflation since the 1970s? Within the standard supply/demand framework, how does this affect unemployment resulting from the minimum wage?
   b. Who is affected by the minimum wage?
   c. Do the authors believe jobs will be lost if the minimum wage is raised? Why or why not?

Answers to Margin Questions

1. False. When supply rises, supply shifts out to the right. Price falls because demand slopes downward. (105)

2. You will receive 53,763 pesos. One U.S. dollar = 537.63 Chilean pesos. So multiplying 537.63 by 100 gives you 53,763 pesos. (107)

3. A discovery of a hormone that will increase cows' milk production by 20 percent will increase the supply of milk, pushing the price down and increasing the quantity demanded, as in the accompanying graph. (108)

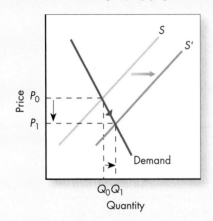

4. Quantity decreases but it is unclear what happens to price. (108)

5. It is likely demand shifted in and supply remained constant. (109)

6. Since the price ceiling is above the equilibrium price, it will have no effect on the market-determined equilibrium price and quantity. (110)

7. Since the price floor is below the equilibrium price, it will have no effect on the market-determined equilibrium price and quantity. (111)

8. I state that the tax will most likely raise the price by less than $2 since the tax will cause the quantity demanded to decrease. This will decrease quantity supplied, and hence decrease the price the suppliers receive. In the diagram below, Q falls from Q_0 to Q_1 and the price the supplier receives falls from $4 to $3, making the final price $5, not $6. (113)

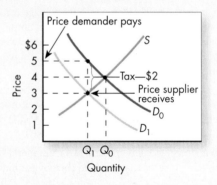

9. Given the quantity restriction, equilibrium quantity will be Q_R and equilibrium price will be P_0, which is higher than the market equilibrium price of P_e. *(114)*

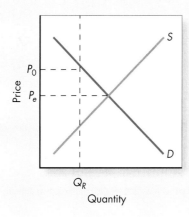

10. Universities would probably charge the high tuition they do now, but they would likely negotiate with publishers for lower textbook prices, because they are both demanding and paying for the textbook. *(116)*

APPENDIX A

Algebraic Representation of Supply, Demand, and Equilibrium

In this chapter and Chapter 4, I discussed demand, supply, and the determination of equilibrium price and quantity in words and graphs. These concepts can also be presented in equations. In this appendix I do so, using straight-line supply and demand curves.

The Laws of Supply and Demand in Equations

Since the law of supply states that quantity supplied is positively related to price, the slope of an equation specifying a supply curve is positive. (The quantity intercept term is generally less than zero since suppliers are generally unwilling to supply a good at a price less than zero.) An example of a supply equation is

$$Q_S = -5 + 2P$$

where Q_S is units supplied and P is the price of each unit in dollars per unit. The law of demand states that as price rises, quantity demanded declines. Price and quantity are negatively related, so a demand curve has a negative slope. An example of a demand equation is

$$Q_D = 10 - P$$

where Q_D is units demanded and P is the price of each unit in dollars per unit.

Determination of Equilibrium

The equilibrium price and quantity can be determined in three steps using these two equations. To find the equilibrium price and quantity for these particular demand and supply curves, you must find the quantity and price that solve both equations simultaneously.

Step 1: Set the quantity demanded equal to quantity supplied:

$$Q_S = Q_D \boxtimes -5 + 2P = 10 - P$$

Step 2: Solve for the price by rearranging terms. Doing so gives:

$$3P = 15$$
$$P = \$5$$

Thus, equilibrium price is $5.

Step 3: To find equilibrium quantity, you can substitute $5 for P in either the demand or supply equation. Let's do it for supply: $Q_S = -5 + (2 \times 5) = 5$ units. I'll leave it to you to confirm that the quantity you obtain by substituting $P = \$5$ in the demand equation is also 5 units.

The answer could also be found graphically. The supply and demand curves specified by these equations are depicted in Figure A5-1. As you can see, demand and supply intersect; quantity demanded equals quantity supplied at a quantity of 5 units and a price of $5.

The algebra in this appendix leads to the same results as the geometry in the chapter. Equilibrium occurs where quantity supplied equals quantity demanded.

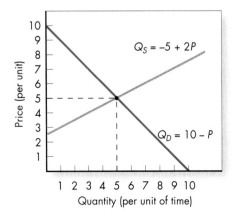

Movements along a Demand and Supply Curve

The demand and supply curves above represent schedules of quantities demanded and supplied at various prices. Movements along each can be represented by selecting various prices and solving for quantity demanded and supplied. Let's create a supply and demand table using the above equations—supply: $Q_S = -5 + 2P$; demand: $Q_D = 10 - P$.

P	$Q_S = -5 + 2P$	$Q_D = 10 - P$
$0	−5	10
1	−3	9
2	−1	8
3	1	7
4	3	6
5	5	5
6	7	4
7	9	3
8	11	2
9	13	1
10	15	0

As you move down the rows, you are moving up along the supply schedule, as shown by increasing quantity supplied, and moving down along the demand schedule, as shown by decreasing quantity demanded. Just to confirm your equilibrium quantity and price calculations, notice that at a price of $5, quantity demanded equals quantity supplied.

Shifts of a Demand and Supply Schedule

What would happen if suppliers changed their expectations so that they would be willing to sell more goods at every price? This shift factor of supply would shift the entire supply curve out to the right. Let's say that at every price, quantity supplied increases by 3. Mathematically the new equation would be $Q_S = -2 + 2P$. The quantity intercept increases by 3. What would you expect to happen to equilibrium price and quantity? Let's solve the equations mathematically first.

Step 1: To determine equilibrium price, set the new quantity supplied equal to quantity demanded:

$$10 - P = -2 + 2P$$

Step 2: Solve for the equilibrium price:

$$12 = 3P$$
$$P = \$4$$

Step 3: To determine equilibrium quantity, substitute P in either the demand or supply equation:

$$Q_D = 10 - (1 \times 4) = 6 \text{ units}$$
$$Q_S = -2 + (2 \times 4) = 6 \text{ units}$$

Equilibrium price declined to $4 and equilibrium quantity rose to 6, just as you would expect with a rightward shift in a supply curve.

Now let's suppose that demand shifts out to the right. Here we would expect both equilibrium price and equilibrium quantity to rise. We begin with our original supply and demand curves—supply: $Q_S = -5 + 2P$; demand: $Q_D = 10 - P$. Let's say at every price, the quantity demanded rises by 3. The new equation for demand would be $Q_D = 13 - P$. You may want to solve this equation for various prices to confirm that at every price, quantity demanded rises by 3. Let's solve the equations for equilibrium price and quantity.

Step 1: Set the quantities equal to one another:

$$13 - P = -5 + 2P$$

Step 2: Solve for equilibrium price:

$$18 = 3P$$
$$P = \$6$$

Step 3: Substitute P in either the demand or supply equation:

$$Q_D = 13 - (1 \times 6) = 7 \text{ units}$$
$$Q_S = -5 + (2 \times 6) = 7 \text{ units}$$

Equilibrium price rose to $6 and equilibrium quantity rose to 7 units, just as you would expect with a rightward shift in a demand curve.

Just to make sure you've got it, I will do two more examples. First, suppose the demand and supply equations for wheat per year in the United States can be specified as follows (notice that the slope is negative for the demand curve and positive for the supply curve):

$$Q_D = 500 - 2P$$
$$Q_S = -100 + 4P$$

P is the price in dollars per thousand bushels and Q is the quantity of wheat in thousands of bushels. Remember that the units must always be stated. What are the equilibrium price and quantity?

Step 1: Set the quantities equal to one another:

$$500 - 2P = -100 + 4P$$

Step 2: Solve for equilibrium price:

$$600 = 6P$$
$$P = \$100$$

Step 3: Substitute P in either the demand or supply equation:

$$Q_D = 500 - (2 \times 100) = 300$$
$$Q_S = -100 + (4 \times 100) = 300$$

Equilibrium quantity is 300 thousand bushels.

As my final example, take a look at Alice's demand curve depicted in Figure 4-4(b) in Chapter 4. Can you write an equation that represents the demand curve in that figure? It is $Q_D = 10 - 2P$. At a price of zero, the quantity of DVD rentals Alice demands is 10, and for every increase in price of \$1, the quantity she demands falls by 2. Now look at Ann's supply curve shown in Figure 4-7(b) in Chapter 4. Ann's supply curve mathematically is $Q_S = 2P$. At a zero price, the quantity Ann supplies is zero, and for every \$1 increase in price, the quantity she supplies rises by 2. What are the equilibrium price and quantity?

Step 1: Set the quantities equal to one another:

$$10 - 2P = 2P$$

Step 2: Solve for equilibrium price:

$$4P = 10$$
$$P = \$2.5$$

Step 3: Substitute P in either the demand or supply equation:

$$Q_D = 10 - (2 \times 2.5) = 5, \text{ or}$$
$$Q_S = 2 \times 2.5 = 5 \text{ DVDs per week}$$

Ann is willing to supply 5 DVDs per week at \$2.50 per rental and Alice demands 5 DVDs at \$2.50 per DVD rental. Remember that in Figure 4-8 in Chapter 4, I showed you graphically the equilibrium quantity and price of Alice's demand curve and Ann's supply curve. I'll leave it up to you to check that the graphic solution in Figure 4-8 is the same as the mathematical solution we came up with here.

Price Ceilings and Price Floors

Let's now consider a price ceiling and price floor. We start with the supply and demand curves:

$$Q_S = -5 + 2P$$
$$Q_D = 10 + P$$

This gave us the solution:

$$P = 5$$
$$Q = 5$$

Now, say that a price ceiling of \$4 is imposed. Would you expect a shortage or a surplus? If you said "shortage," you're doing well. If not, review the chapter before continuing with this appendix. To find out how much the shortage is, we must find out how much will be supplied and how much will be demanded at the price ceiling. Substituting \$4 for price in both equations lets us see that $Q_S = 3$ units and $Q_D = 6$ units. There will be a shortage of 3 units. Next, let's consider a price floor of \$6. To determine the surplus, we follow the same exercise. Substituting \$6 into the two equations gives a quantity supplied of 7 units and a quantity demanded of 4 units, so there is a surplus of 3 units.

Taxes and Subsidies

Next, let's consider the effect of a tax of \$1 placed on the supplier. That tax would decrease the price received by suppliers by \$1. In other words:

$$Q_S = -5 + 2(P - 1)$$

Multiplying the terms in parentheses by 2 and collecting terms results in

$$Q_S = -7 + 2P$$

This supply equation has the same slope as in the previous case, but a new intercept term—just what you'd expect. To determine the new equilibrium price and quantity, follow steps 1 to 3 discussed earlier. Setting this new equation equal to demand and solving for price gives

$$P = 5\tfrac{2}{3}$$

Substituting this price into the demand and supply equations tells us equilibrium quantity:

$$Q_S = Q_D = 4\tfrac{1}{3} \text{ units}$$

Of that price, the supplier must pay $1 in tax, so the price the supplier receives net of tax is $4⅔.

Next, let's say that the tax were put on the demander rather than on the supplier. In that case, the tax increases the price for demanders by $1 and the demand equation becomes

$$Q_D = 10 - (P + 1), \text{ or}$$
$$Q_D = 9 - P$$

Again solving for equilibrium price and quantity requires setting the demand and supply equations equal to one another and solving for price. I leave the steps to you. The result is

$$P = 4⅔$$

This is the price the supplier receives. The price demanders pay is $5⅔. The equilibrium quantity will be 4⅓ units.

These are the same results we got in the previous cases showing that, given the assumptions, it doesn't matter who actually pays the tax: The effect on equilibrium price and quantity is identical no matter who pays it.

Quotas

Finally, let's consider the effect of a quota of 4⅓ placed on the market. Since a quota limits the quantity supplied, as long as the quota is less than the market equilibrium quantity, the supply equation becomes

$$Q_S = 4⅓$$

where Q_S is the actual amount supplied. The price that the market will arrive at for this quantity is determined by the demand curve. To find that price, substitute the quantity 4⅓ into the demand equation ($Q_D = 10 - P$):

$$4⅓ = 10 - P$$

and solve for P:

$$P = 5⅔$$

Since consumers are willing to pay $5⅔, this is what suppliers will receive. The price that suppliers would have been willing to accept for a quantity of 4⅓ is $4⅔. This can be found by substituting the amount of the quota in the supply equation:

$$4⅓ = -5 + 2P$$

and solving for P:

$$2P = 9⅓$$
$$P = 4⅔$$

Notice that this result is very similar to the tax. For demanders it is identical; they pay $5⅔ and receive 4⅓ units. For suppliers, however, the situation is much preferable; instead of receiving a price of $4⅔, the amount they received with the tax, they receive 5⅔. With a quota, suppliers receive the "implicit tax revenue" that results from the higher price.

Questions for Thought and Review

1. Suppose the demand and supply for milk are described by the following equations: $Q_D = 600 - 100P$; $Q_S = -150 + 150P$, where P is price in dollars, Q_D is quantity demanded in millions of gallons per year, and Q_S is quantity supplied in millions of gallons per year.
   a. Create demand and supply tables corresponding to these equations.
   b. Graph supply and demand and determine equilibrium price and quantity.
   c. Confirm your answer to b by solving the equations mathematically.

2. Beginning with the equations in question 1, suppose a growth hormone is introduced that allows dairy farmers to offer 125 million more gallons of milk per year at each price.
   a. Construct new demand and supply curves reflecting this change. Describe with words what happened to the supply curve and to the demand curve.
   b. Graph the new curves and determine equilibrium price and quantity.
   c. Determine equilibrium price and quantity by solving the equations mathematically.
   d. Suppose the government set the price of milk at $3 a gallon. Demonstrate the effect of this regulation on the market for milk. What is quantity demanded? What is quantity supplied?

3. Write demand and supply equations that represent demand, D_0, and supply, S_0, in Figure A5-1 in this appendix.
   a. Solve for equilibrium price and quantity mathematically. Show your work.
   b. Rewrite the demand equation to reflect an increase in demand of 3 units. What happens to equilibrium price and quantity?
   c. Rewrite the supply equation to reflect a decrease in supply of 3 units at every price level. What happens to equilibrium price and quantity using the demand curve from b?

4. a. How is a shift in demand reflected in a demand equation?
   b. How is a shift in supply reflected in a supply equation?
   c. How is a movement along a demand (supply) curve reflected in a demand (supply) equation?

5. Suppose the demand and supply for wheat are described by the following equations: $Q_D = 10 - P$; $Q_S = 2 + P$, where P is the price in dollars, Q_D is quantity demanded in millions of bushels per year, and Q_S is quantity supplied in millions of bushels per year.
   a. Solve for equilibrium price and quantity of wheat.
   b. Would a government-set price of $5 create a surplus or a shortage of wheat? How much? Is $5 a price ceiling or a price floor?

6. Suppose the U.S. government imposes a $1 per gallon of milk tax on dairy farmers. Using the demand and supply equations from question 1:
   a. What is the effect of the tax on the supply equation? The demand equation?
   b. What are the new equilibrium price and quantity?
   c. How much do dairy farmers receive per gallon of milk after the tax? How much do demanders pay?

7. Repeat question 6 assuming the tax is placed on the buyers of milk. Does it matter who pays the tax?

8. Repeat question 6 assuming the government pays a subsidy of $1 per gallon of milk to farmers.

9. Suppose the demand for DVDs is represented by $Q_D = 15 - 4P$, and the supply of DVDs is represented by $Q_S = 4P - 1$. Determine if each of the following is a price floor, price ceiling, or neither. In each case, determine the shortage or surplus.
   a. $P = \$3$
   b. $P = \$1.50$
   c. $P = \$2.25$
   d. $P = \$2.50$

PART II

Macroeconomics

The specific focus of macroeconomics is the study of unemployment, business cycles (fluctuations in the economy), growth, and inflation. While the macroeconomic theories studied have changed considerably over the past 65 years, the focus of macroeconomics on those problems has remained. Thus, we'll define macroeconomics as the study of the economy in the aggregate with specific focus on unemployment, inflation, business cycles, and growth.

The following chapters provide you with the background necessary to discuss the modern debate about these issues. Let's begin with a little history.

Macroeconomics emerged as a separate subject within economics in the 1930s, when the U.S. economy fell into the Great Depression. Businesses collapsed and unemployment rose until 25 percent of the workforce—millions of people—were out of work.

The Depression changed the way economics was taught and the way in which economic problems were conceived. Before the 1930s, economics was microeconomics (the study of partial-equilibrium supply and demand). After the 1930s, the study of the core of economic thinking was broken into two discrete areas: microeconomics, as before, and macroeconomics (the study of the economy in the aggregate).

Macroeconomic policy debates have centered on a struggle between two groups: Keynesian (pronounced KAIN-sian) economists and Classical economists. Should the government run a budget deficit or surplus? Should the government increase the money supply when a recession threatens? Should it decrease the money supply when inflation threatens? Can government prevent recessions? Keynesians generally answer one way; Classicals, another.

Classical economists generally oppose government intervention in the economy; they favor a laissez-faire policy.[1] Keynesians are more likely to favor government intervention in the economy. They feel a laissez-faire policy can sometimes lead to disaster. Both views represent reasonable economic positions. The differences between them are often subtle and result from their taking slightly different views of what government can do and slightly different perspectives on the economy.

In the last 20 years, the differences between Keynesians and Classicals have shrunk so that now, at the turn of the century, there seems to be a consensus view of macro that captures the views held by the majority of the profession. It is that consensus view that all introductory textbooks, including this one, present. Even so, it is helpful to keep the traditional policy differences between Keynesians and Classicals in mind, because the differences often do flare up in debates about current policy. So while I will emphasize the presentation of a consensus view, I will from time to time discuss differences and difficulties in holding the consensus together.

The structure of Part II, Macroeconomics, is as follows: Section I, Macroeconomic Problems (Chapters 6 and 7), introduces the macroeconomic problems, terminology, and statistics used in tracking the economy's macroeconomic performance. Section II, The Macroeconomic Framework (Chapters 8–10), provides the long-run and short-run frameworks economists use when they discuss policy questions and presents the models for those frameworks. Section III, Money, Inflation, and Monetary Policy (Chapters 11–13), looks at how money and the financial system fit into the macro model and discusses monetary policy—the most used policy in macro today. Section IV, Taxes, Budget, and Fiscal Policy (Chapters 14 and 15), looks at the issues in fiscal policy and tax policy. Section V, International Policy Issues (Chapters 16–19), discusses policy within an international context.

---

[1]*Laissez-faire* (introduced to you in Chapter 2) is a French expression meaning "Leave things alone; let them go on without interference."

6 Economic Growth, Business Cycles, Unemployment, and Inflation

AFTER READING THIS CHAPTER, YOU SHOULD BE ABLE TO:

1. Explain the difference between the long-run framework and the short-run framework.
2. Summarize some relevant statistics about growth, business cycles, unemployment, and inflation.
3. List four phases of the business cycle.
4. Explain how unemployment is measured and state some microeconomic categories of unemployment.
5. Relate the target rate of unemployment to potential income.
6. Define inflation and distinguish a real concept from a nominal concept.
7. State two important costs of inflation.

Lagging Behind

Wages have risen, but not as fast as inflation in the last two years.

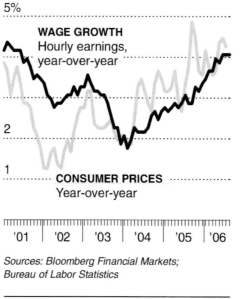

Sources: Bloomberg Financial Markets; Bureau of Labor Statistics

The New York Times

Open the pages of any major newspaper, or log onto CNN.com or a major network news source any day of the week, and you'll read about the economy: "Gas prices rose for the 10th straight week." "Consumer prices tumbled." "U.S. industrial output fell."

Like people, the economy has moods. Sometimes it's in wonderful shape—it's expansive; at other times, it's depressed. Like people whose moods are often associated with specific problems (headaches, sore back, itchy skin), the economy's moods are associated with various problems.

Macroeconomics is the study of the aggregate moods of the economy, with specific focus on issues associated with those moods—growth, business cycles, unemployment, and inflation. The macroeconomic theory we'll consider is designed to explain how supply and demand forces in the aggregate interact to create business cycles, unemployment, and inflation, and how they affect the level of growth in a country. The macroeconomic policy controversies we'll consider concern these four issues. So it's only appropriate that in this first macro chapter we consider an overview of these issues, their causes, their consequences, and the debate over what to do about them.[1]

Two Frameworks: The Long Run and the Short Run

In analyzing macroeconomic issues, economists generally use two frameworks: a short-run and a long-run framework. Issues of growth are generally considered in

---

[1]As I stated in the introduction to this part of the text, I present a consensus view of macroeconomics, although sometimes I distinguish between Keynesian and Classical approaches. I do so to keep the presentation at a level appropriate for a principles book. In reality, there is not always consensus among economists and many more distinctions can be made among economic viewpoints.

The Power of Compounding

A difference in growth rates of one percentage point may not seem like much, but over a number of years, the power of compounding can turn these small differences in growth rates into large differences in income levels. Consider Eastern European countries compared to Western European countries. In 1950, average per capita income was about $3,000 in Eastern European countries and about $6,000 in Western European countries. Over the next 50 years, income grew 1 percent a year in Eastern European countries and 1.5 percent a year in Western European countries. One-half percentage point may be small, but it meant that in those 50 years, income in Western European countries more than tripled, rising to $20,000, while income in Eastern European countries only doubled to about $6,000.

The reason small differences in growth rates can mean huge differences in income levels is *compounding.* Compounding means that growth is based not only on the original level of income but also on the accumulation of previous-year increases in income. For example, say your income starts at $100 and grows at a rate of 10 percent each year; the first year your income grows by $10, to $110. The second year the same growth rate increases income by $11, to $121. The third year income grows by $12.10, which is still 10 percent but a larger dollar increase. After 50 years, that same 10 percent annual increase means income will be growing by over $1,000 a year.

---

a long-run framework. Business cycles are generally considered in a short-run framework. Inflation and unemployment fall within both frameworks. Economists use these two frameworks because the long-run forces that affect growth and the short-run forces that cause business cycles are different. Having two different frameworks allows us to consider these forces separately, making life easier for you.

What is the difference between the two frameworks? The long-run growth framework focuses on incentives for supply; that's why sometimes it is called *supply-side economics.* In the long run, policies that affect production or supply—such as incentives that promote work, capital accumulation, and technological change—are key. The short-run business cycle framework focuses on demand. That is why short-run macro analysis is sometimes called *demand-side economics.* Much of the policy discussion of short-run business cycles focuses on ways to increase or decrease components of aggregate expenditures, such as policies to get consumers and businesses to increase their spending.[2]

As an introduction to the central issues in macroeconomics, let's look briefly at growth, business cycles, unemployment, and inflation.

Q-1 From 2001 to 2002, employment in the United States declined by 122,500. The decline was in part due to a recession and in part due to U.S. firms outsourcing jobs to foreign countries. Is the decline in employment an issue best studied in the long-run framework or the short-run framework?

Growth

Generally the U.S. economy is growing or expanding. Economists measure growth with changes in **real gross domestic product (real GDP)**—*the market value of final goods and services produced in an economy, stated in the prices of a given year.* When people produce and sell their goods, they earn income, so when an economy is growing, both total output and total income are increasing. Such growth gives most people more income this year than they had last year. Since most of us prefer more to less, growth is easy to take.

The U.S. Department of Commerce traced U.S. economic growth in output since about 1890 and discovered that, on average, output of goods and services grew about

Real GDP is GDP adjusted for price changes.

---

[2]A short-run/long-run distinction helps make complicated issues somewhat clearer, but it obscures other issues such as: How long is the short run, and how do we move from the short run to the long run? Some economists argue that in the long run we are only in another short run, while others argue that since our actions are forward-looking, we are always in the long run.

U.S. economic output has grown at an annual 2.5 to 3.5 percent rate.

Q₂ Output in the United States in 2007 was about $14 trillion, and there were about 300 million people living in the United States. What was per capita output?

3.5 percent per year. In the 1970s and 1980s, the growth was more like 2.5 percent. In the late 1990s and early 2000s, it was again 3.5 percent. This 2.5 to 3.5 percent growth rate is sometimes called the *secular growth trend*. The rate at which the actual output grows in any one year fluctuates, but on average the U.S. economy has been growing at that long-term trend. Since population has also been growing, per capita economic growth (growth per person) has been less than 2.5 to 3.5 percent.

This brings us to another measure of growth—changes in per capita real output. **Per capita real output** is *real GDP divided by the total population*. Output per person is an important measure of growth because, even if total output is increasing, the population may be growing even faster, so per capita real output would be falling.

Global Experiences with Growth

Table 6-1 shows per capita growth for various areas of the world from 1820 to 2007. It tells us a number of important facts about growth:

1. Growth rates today are high by historical standards. For 130 years beginning in 1820, world output grew by only 0.9 percent per year. At that rate it took 82 years for world income to double. From 1950 until today, the world economy has grown at a much faster rate, approximately 1.9 percent per year, cutting the number of years it has taken income to double from 80 to 40.

2. The range in growth rates among countries is wide. From 1820 to 1950, North America led, with 1.6 percent annual growth. From 1950 to 2007, however, Japan and Western Europe were among the fastest growing, partially due to the opportunities for growth lost during World War II and the replacement of productive capital destroyed in the war. Japan's growth acceleration is the most pronounced. Japan turned from investing in military might before World War II to investing in capital destroyed by the war. This acceleration meant that these countries were catching up to other high-growth areas of the world. Japan's average income in 1950 was around one-fifth of the average income in North America. By 1990 it had grown close to equal, although recently its economy slowed and it lost ground in the early 2000s. Another country that has been catching up is China. While income in China was actually lower in 1950 than in 1820, beginning in

TABLE 6-1   Average Annual per Capita Income, Various Regions: 1820 to 2007

	Growth Rates			Income Levels (1990 international dollars)		
	1820–1950	1950–2007*	1820–2007*	1820	1950	2007*
The world	0.9	2.0	1.2	$ 675	$2,108	$ 6,600
Western Europe	1.1	2.2	1.6	1,269	6,546	23,000
North America	1.6	2.1	1.7	1,233	9,463	31,000
Japan	0.8	4.2	1.8	675	1,927	21,000
Eastern Europe	1.1	1.7	1.2	803	3,162	7,700
Latin America	1.0	2.0	1.3	671	2,478	7,600
China	−0.2	4.9	1.2	600	439	6,000
Other Asia	0.3	3.4	1.1	560	848	5,300
Africa	0.6	0.4	0.7	400	1,307	1,700

*Author estimated updates.

Source: Angus Maddison, *Monitoring the World Economy* (1995) and *Chinese Economic Performance in the Long Run* (1998), OECD Development Center, Paris.

the last part of the 20th century and continuing into the 21st century, China's income has been one of the fastest growing in the world.

3. African countries have consistently grown below the average for the world. In 1820, Africa's per capita income was 40 percent less than the world average. The gap widened to 60 percent in 1950, and to 75 percent by 2007.

This 187-year perspective of growth is useful, but by historical standards even 187 years is relatively short. Looking back even further shows us how high our current growth rates are. Before 1820 world income per capita grew about 0.03 percent a year. The growth trend that we now take for granted started only at the end of the 18th century, about the time that markets and democracies became the primary organizing structures of the economy and society. Thus, growth seems to be associated with the development of markets and democracy. Significant growth took off only as the market system developed, and it increased as markets increased in importance.

The growth trend we now take for granted started only at the end of the 18th century.

The Prospect for Future U.S. Growth

Past data are not necessarily a good predictor of future events, and while predictions are always dangerous, it is worthwhile asking: How may the future differ from the past, and what do those differences suggest about future U.S. economic growth? One big difference is the current economic development of the Indian and Chinese economies, which is similar to the growth experienced by other Asian countries, such as Korea and, Thailand, in the 1980s. What's different about China and India is their size; combined, they have a population of 2.5 billion. As they develop into highly industrialized countries, the world economic landscape will change tremendously. Specifically, their development will likely place pressures on U.S. firms in both services and manufacturing industries either to become more competitive (by holding down wage increases or by developing more efficient production methods) or to move their production facilities abroad. It will also be accompanied by greater demand for natural resources. Some economists believe that China's and India's rise may be accompanied by slower growth in the United States, Western Europe, and other highly industrialized nations, as the growth dynamic gravitates to these Asian countries.

The Benefits and Costs of Growth

Economic growth (per capita) allows everyone in society, on average, to have more. Thus, it isn't surprising that most governments are generally searching for policies that will allow their economies to grow. Indeed, one reason market economies have been so successful is that they have consistently channeled individual efforts toward production and growth. Individuals feel a sense of accomplishment in making things grow and, if sufficient economic incentives and resources exist, individuals' actions can lead to a continually growing economy.

Politically, growth (or predictions of growth) allows governments to avoid hard distributional questions of who should get what part of our existing output: With growth there is more to go around for everyone. A growing economy generates jobs, so politicians who want to claim that their policies will create jobs generally predict those policies will create growth.

Politically, growth (or predictions of growth) allows governments to avoid hard questions.

Of course, material growth comes with costs: pollution, resource exhaustion, and destruction of natural habitat. These costs lead some people to believe that we would be better off in a society that deemphasized material growth. (That doesn't mean we shouldn't grow emotionally, spiritually, and intellectually; it simply means we should grow out of our material goods fetish.) Many people believe these environmental costs are important, and the result is often an environmental-economic growth stalemate.

To reconcile the two goals, some have argued that spending on the environment can create growth and jobs, so the two need not be incompatible. Unfortunately, this argument has a problem. It confuses growth and jobs with increased material consumption—what most people are worried about. As more material goods made available by growth are used for pollution control equipment, less is available for the growth of an average individual's personal consumption, since the added material goods created by growth have already been used. What society gets, at best, from these expenditures is a better physical environment, not more of everything. Getting more of everything would violate the TANSTAAFL law.

This reasoning has implications for the debate about what policies to introduce to deal with global warming. Reducing global warming requires reducing carbon emissions, which means changing production methods away from methods that use carbon fuel. We can do it, but doing it will cost resources, and those resources will not be available for consumption goods. Of course, as economist Nicholas Stern argues, there is also a cost of not doing anything; he calculates that, if we do nothing, growth will be 20 percent less than it otherwise would be. If he is correct, there is a large cost of not doing anything. There is much debate about these issues and the relationship between global warming and economic growth is likely to be a hot topic of discussion over the coming years.

Business Cycles

While the secular, or long-term, trend is a 2.5 to 3.5 percent increase in GDP, there are numerous fluctuations around that trend. Sometimes real GDP grows above the trend; at other times GDP falls below the trend. This phenomenon has given rise to the term *business cycle*. A **business cycle** is *the upward or downward movement of economic activity, or real GDP, that occurs around the growth trend.* Figure 6-1 graphs the fluctuations in GDP for the U.S. economy since 1860.

A business cycle is the upward or downward movement of economic activity that occurs around the growth trend.

FIGURE 6-1   U.S. Business Cycles

Business cycles have always been a part of the U.S. economic scene. This figure suggests that fluctuations in economic output have become less severe since 1945, although some economists dispute the data.
Source: *Historical Statistics of the United States, Colonial Times to 1970*, and U.S. Department of Commerce (www.doc.gov).

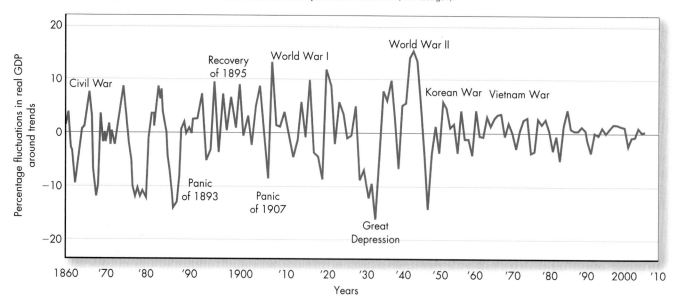

NBER Dating of the Business Cycle

In November 2001, the six members of the NBER Business Cycle Dating Committee issued this statement:

> The NBER's Business Cycle Dating Committee has determined that a peak in business activity occurred in the U.S. economy in March 2001. A peak marks the end of an expansion and the beginning of a recession. The determination of a peak date in March is thus a determination that the expansion that began in March 1991 ended in March 2001 and a recession began. The expansion lasted exactly 10 years, the longest in the NBER's chronology.

Technically, an economy is in a recession only after it has been declared to be in a recession by a group of economists appointed by the National Bureau of Economic Research (NBER). Because real output is reported only quarterly and

NBER

National Bureau of Economic Research

is sometimes revised substantially, the NBER Dating Committee looks at monthly data such as industrial production, employment, real income, sales, and sometimes even people's perceptions of what is happening in the economy to determine whether a recession has occurred. In 2001, for example, in the statement quoted above, the committee announced that a recession had begun in March even though, according to preliminary GDP figures, real output did not fall for two consecutive quarters. (Revised figures, which came out more than six months later, showed that GDP had actually started falling earlier and fell for three quarters.) The fact (1) that the NBER economists include many factors when determining a recession and (2) that they base their decision on preliminary data makes it difficult to provide an unambiguous definition of recession.

Until the late 1930s, economists took such cycles as facts of life. They had no convincing theory to explain why business cycles occurred, nor did they have policy suggestions to smooth them out. In fact, they felt that any attempt to smooth them through government intervention would make the situation worse.

Since the 1940s, however, many economists have not taken business cycles as facts of life. They have hotly debated the nature and causes of business cycles and of the underlying growth. In this book I distinguish two groups of macroeconomists: **Keynesians** (who *generally favor activist government policy*) and **Classicals** (who *generally favor laissez-faire or nonactivist policies*). Classical economists argue that fluctuations in economic activity are to be expected in a market economy. Indeed, they say, it would be strange if fluctuations did not occur when individuals are free to decide what they want to do. We should simply accept these fluctuations as we do the seasons of the year. Keynesian economists argue that fluctuations can and should be controlled. They argue that *expansions* (the part of the business cycle above the long-term trend) and *contractions* (the part of the cycle below the long-term trend) are symptoms of underlying problems of the economy, which should be dealt with by government actions. Classical economists respond that individuals will anticipate government's reaction, thereby undermining government's attempts to control cycles. Which of these two views is correct is still a matter of debate.

Keynesians generally favor activist government policy; Classicals generally favor laissez-faire policies.

The Phases of the Business Cycle

Much research has gone into measuring business cycles and setting official reference dates for the beginnings and ends of contractions and expansions. As a result of this research, business cycles have been divided into phases, and an explicit terminology has been developed. The National Bureau of Economic Research announces the government's official dates of contractions and expansions. In the postwar era (since mid-1945), the average business

FIGURE 6-2 **Business Cycle Phases**

Economists have many terms that describe the position of the economy on the business cycle. Some of them are given in this graph.

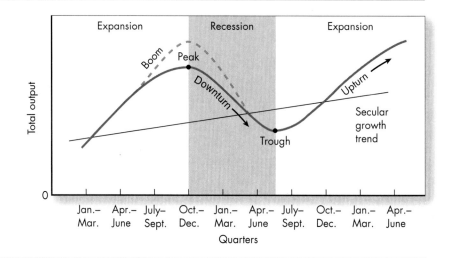

expansion has lasted about 57 months. A major expansion occurred from 1982 until mid-1990, when the U.S. economy fell into a recession. In mid-1991 it slowly came out of the recession, and began the longest expansion in U.S. history, which ended in March 2001. The recession ended in November 2001 and the economy has been expanding since.

Business cycles have varying durations and intensities, but economists have developed a terminology to describe all business cycles and just about any place within a given business cycle. Since the press often uses this terminology, it is helpful to go over it. I do so in reference to Figure 6-2, which gives a visual representation of a business cycle.

Let's start at the top. The top of a cycle is called the *peak*. A *boom* is a very high peak, representing a big jump in output. (That's when the economy is doing great. Most everyone who wants a job has one.) Eventually an expansion peaks. (At least, in the past, they always have.) A *downturn* describes the phenomenon of economic activity starting to fall from a peak. In a recession the economy isn't doing so great and many people are unemployed. A **recession** is generally considered to be *a decline in real output that persists for more than two consecutive quarters of a year.* The actual definition of a recession is more ambiguous than this generally accepted definition as the box "NBER Dating of the Business Cycle" on the previous page points out.

A **depression** is *a large recession.* There is no formal line indicating when a recession becomes a depression. In general, a depression is much longer and more severe than a recession. This ambiguity allows some economists to joke, "When your neighbor is unemployed, it's a recession; when you're unemployed, it's a depression." If pushed for something more specific, I'd say that if unemployment exceeds 12 percent for more than a year, the economy is in a depression. The last time the United States was in a depression was in the 1930s.

The bottom of a recession or depression is called the *trough*. As total output begins to expand, the economy comes out of the trough; economists say it's in an *upturn*, which may turn into an **expansion**—*an upturn that lasts at least two consecutive quarters of a year.* An expansion leads us back up to the peak. And so it goes.

This terminology is important because if you're going to talk about the state of the economy, you need the words to do it. Why are businesses so interested in the state of the economy? They want to be able to predict whether it's going into a contraction or an expansion. Making the right prediction can determine whether the business will be profitable or not. That's why economists spend a lot of time trying to predict the future course of the economy.

The four phases of the business cycle are

1. The peak.
2. The downturn.
3. The trough.
4. The upturn.

Web Note 6.1
Depression Images

Why Do Business Cycles Occur?

Why do business cycles occur? Are they simply random events, a bit like static on a radio, or do they have some fundamental causes that make them predictable? And if they have causes, are those causes on the supply side or demand side of the economy? These questions will be addressed in the short-run chapters on business cycles. What we will see is that most economists believe that fluctuations of output around the growth trend are caused by changes in the demand for goods and services in the economy. We will also see that economists disagree whether these economic fluctuations can and should be reduced.

There is far less policy debate about depressions. The general view that something must and could be done to offset depressions emerged as the consensus during the Great Depression when, from 1929 to 1933, production of goods and services fell by 30 percent. The new consensus led to changes in the U.S. economy's structure, which included a more active role for government in reducing the severity of cyclical fluctuations. Both the financial structure and the government taxing and spending structure were changed, giving the government a more important role in stabilizing the economy.

Look back at Figure 6-1 and compare the periods before and after World War II. (World War II began in 1941 and ended in 1945.) Notice that the downturns since 1945 have generally been less severe.

This change in the nature of business cycles can be better seen in the table below.

If prolonged contractions are a type of cold the economy catches, the Great Depression of the 1930s was double pneumonia.

Business Cycles	Duration (in months)	
	Pre–World War II (1854–1945)	Post–World War II (1945–2006)
Number	22	10
Average duration (trough to trough)	50	67
Length of longest cycle	99 (1870–79)	128 (1991–2001)
Length of shortest cycle	28 (1919–21)	28 (1980–82)
Average length of expansions	29	57
Length of shortest expansion	10 (1919–20)	12 (1980–81)
Length of longest expansion	80 (1938–45)	120 (1991–2001)
Average length of recessions	21	10
Length of shortest recession	7 (1918–19)	6 (1980)
Length of longest recession	65 (1873–79)	16 (1981–82)

Web Note 6.2
Dating Business Cycles

Source: National Bureau of Economic Research (http://nber.org) and *Survey of Current Business* (www.bea.doc.gov).

Notice also that since the late 1940s cycle duration has increased but, more important, the average length of expansions has increased while the average length of contractions has decreased.

How to interpret this reduction is the subject of much controversy, as is the case with much economic evidence. Some economists argue that a large part of the reduction in the fluctuations' severity is statistical illusion. Others argue that the stronger government policy in trying to offset recessions has played a big role. If the severity of the fluctuations has been reduced (which most economists believe has happened), one reason is that changes in institutional structure were made as a result of the Great Depression.

Leading Indicators

List three leading indicators.

Economists have developed a set of signs that indicate when a recession is about to occur and when the economy is in one. These signs are called *leading indicators*—indicators that tell us what's likely to happen 12 to 15 months from now, much as a barometer gives us a clue about tomorrow's weather. They include

1. Average workweek for production workers in manufacturing.
2. Average weekly claims for unemployment insurance.
3. Manufacturers' new orders for consumer goods and materials.
4. Vendor performance, measured as a percentage of companies reporting slower deliveries from suppliers.
5. Index of consumer expectations.
6. New orders for nondefense capital goods.
7. Number of new building permits issued for private housing units.
8. Stock prices—500 common stocks.
9. Interest rate spread—10-year government bond less federal funds rate.
10. Money supply, M2.

These leading indicators are followed carefully by economic reporters and form the grist of many newspaper articles suggesting that the economy is moving one way or another. There is even an index of leading economic indicators that combines all these measures into a single number. (You can find the most recent index at www.conferenceboard.org, the home page of The Conference Board.) Economists use leading indicators in making forecasts about the economy.

Notice that these measures are called *indicators*, not *predictors*. That's because they provide only rough approximations of what's likely to happen in the future. Take building permits (item 7) as an example. Building a house creates demand for goods and services and boosts output. Before building a house, you must apply for a building permit. Usually this occurs six to nine months before the actual start of construction. By looking at the number of building permits that have been issued, you can predict how much building is likely to begin in six months or so. But the prediction might be wrong, since getting a building permit does not require someone to actually build. Economists also have *coincident indicators* that suggest what is currently happening in the economy and *lagging indicators* that suggest what has happened. Business economists—who spend much of their time and effort delving deeper into these indicators trying to see what they are really telling us, as opposed to what they seem to be telling us—joke that the leading indicators have predicted six of the past two recessions.

Unemployment

Both business cycles and growth are directly related to unemployment in the U.S. economy. Unemployment occurs when people are looking for a job and cannot find one. The **unemployment rate** is *the percentage of people in the economy who are willing and able to work but who are not working.* When an economy is growing and is in an expansion, unemployment is usually falling; when an economy is in a recession, unemployment is usually rising, although often with a lag.

The relationship between the business cycle and unemployment is obvious to most people, but often the seemingly obvious hides important insights. Just why are the business cycle and growth related to unemployment? True, aggregate income must fall in a recession, but, logically, unemployment need not result. A different possibility is that unemployment doesn't rise, but that all people, on average, work less.

The unemployment rate is the percentage of people in the economy who are willing and able to work but who are not working.

Unemployment has not always been a problem associated with business cycles. In preindustrial societies, households—from farms to cottage craftspeople—produced goods and services. The entire family contributed to farming, weaving, or blacksmithing. When times were good, the family enjoyed a higher level of income. When times weren't so good, they still worked, but accepted less income for the goods they produced. When economic activity fell, people's income earned per hour (wage) fell. Low income was a problem; but since people didn't become unemployed, **cyclical unemployment** (*unemployment resulting from fluctuations in economic activity*) was not a problem.

While cyclical unemployment did not exist in preindustrial society, **structural unemployment** (*unemployment caused by the institutional structure of an economy or by economic restructuring making some skills obsolete*) did. For example, scribes in Europe had less work after the invention of the printing press in the 1400s. Some unemployment would likely result; that unemployment would be called *structural unemployment*. But structural unemployment wasn't much of a problem for government, or at least people did not consider it government's problem. The reason is that those in the family, or community, with income would share it with unemployed family members.

Q4 True or false? In a recession, structural unemployment is expected to rise.

Unemployment as a Social Problem

The Industrial Revolution changed the nature of work and introduced unemployment as a problem for society. This is because the Industrial Revolution was accompanied by a shift to wage labor and to a division of responsibilities. Some individuals (capitalists) took on ownership of the means of production and *hired* others to work for them, paying them a wage per hour. This change in the nature of production marked a significant change in the nature of the unemployment problem.

First, it created the possibility of cyclical unemployment. With wages set at a certain level, when economic activity fell, workers' income per hour did not fall. Instead, factories would lay off or fire some workers. That isn't what happened on the farm; when a slack period occurred on the farm, the income per hour of all workers fell and few were laid off.

Second, the Industrial Revolution was accompanied by a change in how families dealt with unemployment. Whereas in preindustrial economies individuals or families took responsibility for their own slack periods, in a capitalist industrial society factory owners didn't take responsibility for their workers in slack periods. The pink slip (a common name for the notice workers get telling them they are laid off) and the problem of unemployment were born in the Industrial Revolution.

Without wage income, unemployed workers were in a pickle. They couldn't pay their rent, they couldn't eat, they couldn't put clothes on their backs. What was previously a family problem became a social problem. Not surprisingly, it was at that time—the late 1700s—that economists began paying more attention to the problem of unemployment.

When they initially recognized unemployment as a problem, economists and society still did not view it as a social problem. It was the individual's problem. If people were unemployed, it was their own fault; hunger, or at least the fear of hunger, and people's desire to maintain their lifestyle would drive them to find other jobs relatively quickly. Early capitalism had an unemployment solution: the fear of hunger.

Unemployment as Government's Problem

As capitalism evolved, the fear-of-hunger solution to unemployment became less acceptable. The government developed social welfare programs such as unemployment insurance and assistance to the poor. In the Employment Act of 1946, the U.S. government specifically took responsibility for unemployment. The act assigned

As capitalism evolved, capitalist societies no longer saw the fear of hunger as an acceptable answer to unemployment.

From Full Employment to the Target Rate of Unemployment

As I emphasized in Chapter 1, good economists attempt to remain neutral and objective. It isn't always easy, especially since the language we use is often biased.

This problem has proved to be a difficult one for economists in their attempt to find an alternative to the concept of full employment. An early contender was the natural rate of unemployment. Economists have often used the word *natural* to describe economic concepts. For example, they've talked about "natural" rights and a "natural" rate of interest. The problem with this usage is that what's natural to one person isn't necessarily natural to another. The word *natural* often conveys a sense of "that's the way it should be." However, in describing as "natural" the rate of unemployment that an economy can achieve, economists weren't making any value judgments about whether 4.5–5 percent unemployment is what should, or

should not, be. They simply were saying that, given the institutions in the economy, that is what is achievable. So a number of economists objected to the use of the word *natural*.

As an alternative, a number of economists started to use the term *nonaccelerating inflation rate of unemployment (NAIRU)*, but even they agreed it was a horrendous term. And so many avoided its use and shifted to the relatively neutral term *target rate of unemployment*.

The target rate of unemployment is the rate that one believes is attainable without causing accelerating inflation. It is not determined theoretically; it is determined empirically. Economists look at what seems to be achievable and is historically normal, adjust that for structural and demographic changes they believe are occurring, and come up with the target rate of unemployment.

The target rate of unemployment is the lowest sustainable rate of unemployment that policy makers believe is achievable under existing conditions.

government the responsibility of creating *full employment*, an economic climate in which just about everyone who wants a job can have one. Government was responsible for offsetting cyclical fluctuations and thereby preventing cyclical unemployment, and somehow dealing with structural unemployment.

Initially government regarded 2 percent unemployment as a condition of full employment. The 2 percent was made up of **frictional unemployment** (*unemployment caused by people entering the job market and people quitting a job just long enough to look for and find another one*) and of a few "unemployables," such as alcoholics and drug addicts, along with a certain amount of necessary structural and seasonal unemployment resulting when the structure of the economy changed. Any unemployment higher than 2 percent was considered either unnecessary structural or cyclical unemployment and was now government's responsibility; frictional and necessary structural unemployment were still the individual's problem.

By the 1950s, government had given up its view that 2 percent unemployment was consistent with full employment. It raised its definition of full employment to 3 percent, then to 4 percent, then to 5 percent unemployment. In the 1970s and early 1980s, government raised it further, to 6.5 percent unemployment. At that point the term *full employment* fell out of favor (it's hard to call 6.5 percent unemployment "full employment"), and the terminology changed. The term I will use in this book is *target rate of unemployment*, although you should note that it is also sometimes called the *natural rate of unemployment* or the *NAIRU* (the nonaccelerating inflation rate of unemployment). As discussed in the accompanying box, these terms are interchangeable. The **target rate of unemployment** is *the lowest sustainable rate of unemployment that policy makers believe is achievable given existing demographics and the economy's institutional structure*. Since the late 1980s the appropriate target rate of unemployment has been a matter of debate, but most economists place it at somewhere around 5 percent unemployment.

Categories of Unemployment

A good sense of the differing types of unemployment and the differing social views that unemployment embodies can be conveyed through three examples of unemployed individuals. As you read the following stories, ask yourself which category of unemployment each individual falls into.

Example 1

Joe has lost his steady job and collects unemployment insurance. He's had various jobs in the past and was laid off from his last one. He spent a few weeks on household projects, believing he would be called back by his most recent employer—but he wasn't. He's grown to like being on his own schedule. He's living on his unemployment insurance (while it lasts, which usually isn't more than six months), his savings, and money he picks up by being paid cash under the table working a few hours now and then at construction sites.

The Unemployment Compensation Office requires him to make at least an attempt to find work, and he's turned up a few prospects. However, some were back-breaking laboring jobs and one would have required him to move to a distant city, so he's avoiding accepting regular work. Joe knows the unemployment payments won't last forever. When they're used up, he plans to increase his under-the-table activity. Then, when he gets good and ready, he'll really look for a job.

Example 2

Flo is a middle-aged, small-town housewife. She worked before her marriage, but when she and her husband started their family she quit her job to be a full-time housewife and mother. She never questioned her family values of hard work, independence, belief in free enterprise, and scorn of government handouts. When her youngest child left the nest, she decided to finish the college education she'd only just started when she married.

After getting her degree, she looked for a job, but found the market for middle-aged women with no recent experience to be depressed—and depressing. The state employment office where she sought listings recognized her abilities and gave her a temporary job in that very office.

Because she was a "temp," however, she was the first to be laid off when the state legislature cut the local office budget—but she'd worked long enough to be eligible for unemployment insurance.

She hesitated about applying, since handouts were against her principles. But while working there she'd seen plenty of people, including her friends, applying for benefits after work histories even slimmer than hers. She decided to take the benefits. While they lasted, she found family finances on almost as sound a footing as when she was working. Although she was bringing in less money, net family income didn't suffer much since she didn't have Social Security withheld nor did she have the commuting and clothing expenses of going to a daily job.

Example 3

Tom had a good job at a manufacturing plant where he'd worked up to a wage of $800 a week. Occasionally he was laid off, but only for a few weeks, and then he'd be called back. But then the work at the plant was outsourced. Tom, an older worker with comparatively high wages, was "let go."

Tom had a wife, three children, a car payment, and a mortgage. He looked for other work but couldn't find anything paying close to what he'd been getting. Tom used up his unemployment insurance and his savings. He sold the house and moved his family into a trailer. Finally he heard that there were a lot of jobs in Massachusetts, 800 miles away. He moved there, found a job, and began sending money home every week. Then the Massachusetts economy faltered. Tom was laid off again, and his unemployment insurance ran out again. He became depressed and, relying on his $300,000 life insurance policy, he figured he was worth more to his family dead than alive, so he killed himself.

As these three examples suggest, unemployment encompasses a wide range of cases. Unemployment is anything but a one-dimensional problem, so it's not surprising that people's views of how to deal with it differ.

Why the Target Rate of Unemployment Changed

Why has the target rate of unemployment changed over time? One reason is that, in the 1970s and early 1980s, a low inflation rate, which also was a government goal, seemed to be incompatible with a low unemployment rate. I'll talk about this incompatibility later when I discuss the problem of simultaneous inflation and unemployment. A second reason is demographics: Different age groups have different unemployment rates, and as the population's age structure changes, so does the target rate of unemployment.

A third reason is our economy's changing social and institutional structure. These social and institutional changes affected the nature of the unemployment problem. For example, women's role in the workforce has changed significantly in the past 50 years. In the 1950s, the traditional view was that "a woman's place is in the home." Usually only one family member—the man—had a job. If he lost his job, the family had no income. Since the 1970s, more and more women have entered the workforce so that today, in over 70 percent of all married-couple families, both husband and wife work. In a two-earner family, if one person loses a job, the family doesn't face immediate starvation. The other person's income carries the family over, allowing the one who lost a job to spend more time looking for another.

Government institutions also changed. As programs like unemployment insurance and public welfare were created to reduce suffering associated with unemployment, people's responses to unemployment changed. People today are more picky about what jobs they take than they were in the 1920s and 1930s. People don't just want any job; they want a *fulfilling* job with a decent wage. As people have become choosier about jobs, a debate has raged over the extent of government's responsibility for unemployment.

Whose Responsibility Is Unemployment?

Whether you consider someone unemployed depends on your sense of individual and societal responsibility. Classical economists generally believe individuals are responsible for finding jobs. They emphasize that an individual can always find *some* job at *some* wage, even if it's only selling apples on the street for 40 cents apiece. Given this view of individual responsibility, unemployment is impossible. If a person isn't working, that's his or her choice; the person simply isn't looking hard enough for a job. For an economist with this view, almost all unemployment is actually frictional unemployment.

Keynesian economists tend to say society owes people jobs commensurate with their training or past job experience. They further argue that the jobs should be close enough to home so people don't have to move. Given this view, frictional unemployment is only a small part of total unemployment. Structural and cyclical unemployment are far more common.

In the 1960s the average rate of unemployment in Europe was considerably below the average rate of unemployment in the United States. In the 1990s and early 2000s that reversed and the average unemployment rate in Europe has now significantly exceeded that in the United States. One of the reasons for this reversal is that Europe tried to create high-paying jobs, and it left a variety of taxes and social programs in place that discouraged the creation of low-paying jobs.

The United States, in contrast, actively promoted the creation of jobs of any type. The result has been a large growth of jobs in the United States, many of which are low-paying jobs. For example, an unemployed engineer in the United States might become a restaurant manager; in Europe, he would likely stay unemployed.

Q₅ How are Keynesians and Classicals likely to differ in their views about what to do about outsourcing?

FIGURE 6-3 **Unemployment Rate since 1900**

The unemployment rate has always fluctuated, with the average around 5 or 6 percent. Since the 1930s, fluctuations have decreased. In the mid-1940s, the U.S. government started focusing on the unemployment rate as a goal. Initially, it chose 2 percent, but gradually that increased to somewhere around 5 percent.

Source: U.S. Bureau of Labor Statistics (www.bls.gov).

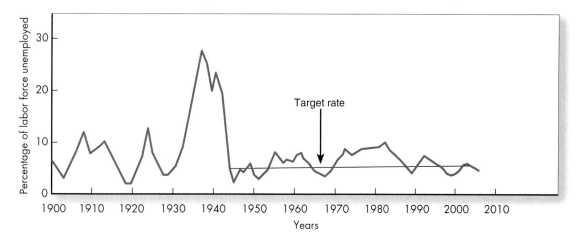

How Is Unemployment Measured?

When there's debate about what the unemployment problem is, it isn't surprising that there's also a debate about how to measure it. When talking about unemployment, economists usually refer to the "unemployment rate" published by the U.S. Department of Labor's Bureau of Labor Statistics. Fluctuations in the official unemployment rate since 1900 appear in Figure 6-3. In it you can see that during World War II (1941–45) unemployment fell from the high rates of the 1930s Depression to an extremely low rate, only 1.2 percent. You also can see that while the rate started back up in the 1950s, reaching 4 or 5 percent, it remained low until the 1970s, when the rate began gradually to rise again, peaking at 10.8 percent in 1983. In the 1990s and early 2000s, the unemployment rate has fluctuated from a high of 7.8 percent during the 1991 recession to a low of 3.8 percent in 2000. In 2007, the unemployment rate was about 4.6 percent.

Calculating the Unemployment Rate The U.S. unemployment rate is determined by dividing the number of people who are unemployed by the number of people in the **labor force**—*those people in an economy who are willing and able to work*—and multiplying by 100. For example, if the total unemployed stands at 7 million and the labor force stands at 150 million, the unemployment rate is

$$\frac{7 \text{ million}}{150 \text{ million}} = 0.046 \times 100 = 4.6\%$$

To calculate the unemployment rate, we must measure both the labor force and the number of unemployed. To determine the labor force, start with the total civilian population and subtract all persons unavailable for work, such as inmates of institutions and people under 16 years of age. From that figure subtract the number of people not in the labor force, including homemakers, students, retirees, the voluntarily idle, and the disabled. The result is the potential workforce, which is about 150 million people, or

The unemployment rate is measured by dividing the number of unemployed individuals by the number of people in the civilian labor force and multiplying by 100.

FIGURE 6-4   **Unemployment/Employment Figures (in millions)**

This exhibit shows you how the unemployment rate is calculated. Notice that the labor force is not the entire population.
Source: *Employment and Earnings 2006.* Bureau of Labor Statistics (www.bls.gov). Data may not add up due to rounding.

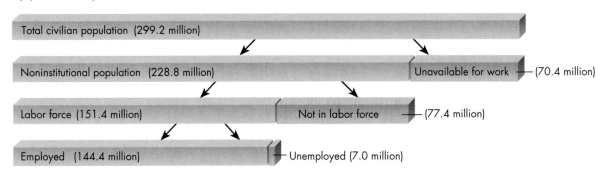

Q.6 During some months, the unemployment rate declines, but the number of unemployed rises. How can this happen?

about 50 percent of the civilian population (see Figure 6-4). (The civilian population excludes about 2 million individuals who are in the armed forces.)

The number of unemployed can be calculated by subtracting the number of employed from the labor force. The Bureau of Labor Statistics (BLS) defines people as *employed* if they work at a paid job (including part-time jobs) or if they are unpaid workers in an enterprise operated by a family member. The BLS's definition of *employed* includes all those who were temporarily absent from their jobs the week of the BLS survey because of illness, bad weather, vacation, labor-management dispute, or personal reasons, whether or not they were paid by their employers for the time off.

In 2006 the number of unemployed individuals was about 7.0 million. Dividing this number by the labor force (151.4 million) gives us an unemployment rate of 4.6 percent.

Web Note 6.3
Defining Unemployment

How Accurate Is the Official Unemployment Rate?   The BLS measures unemployment using a number of assumptions that have been the source of debate. For example, should *discouraged workers*—people who do not look for a job because they feel they don't have a chance of finding one—be counted as unemployed? Some Keynesian economists believe these individuals should be considered unemployed. Moreover they question whether part-time workers who would prefer full-time work, the *underemployed,* should be classified as employed.

The Keynesian argument is that there is such a lack of decent jobs and of affordable transportation to get to the jobs that do exist that many people become very discouraged and have simply stopped looking for work. Because BLS statisticians define these people as voluntarily idle, and do not count them as unemployed, Keynesians argue that the BLS undercounts unemployment significantly.

Q.7 In what way is the very concept of unemployment dependent on the value judgments made by the individual?

The Classical argument about unemployment is that being without a job often is voluntary. People may say they are looking for a job when they're not really looking. Many are working "off the books"; others are simply vacationing. Some Classicals contend that the way the BLS measures unemployment exaggerates the number of those who are truly unemployed. They argue that many so-called unemployed are not actively seeking work.

To help overcome these problems, economists use supplemental measures to give them insight into the state of the labor market. These include the **labor force participation rate,** which *measures the labor force as a percentage of the total population at least 16 years old,* and the **employment-population ratio**—*the number of people who are working as a percentage of people available to work.*

TABLE 6-2	Unemployment and Capacity Utilization Rates for Selected Countries (percentages)

	Capacity Utilization			Unemployment			Annual Growth in Real Output 1975–2006
	1975	1985	2006**	1975	1985	2006	
United States	74.6	79.8	81.8	8.5	7.2	4.6	3.2
Japan	81.4	82.5	74.6	1.9	2.6	4.2	2.7
Germany***	76.9	79.6	84.1	3.4	8.2	8.0	1.6
United Kingdom	81.9	81.1	81.8	4.6	11.2	5.5	2.4
Canada	83.1	82.5	84.0	6.9	10.5	6.4	2.9
Mexico	85.0	92.0	85.7	*	*	3.4	3.2
Republic of Korea	86.4	74.6	83.3	*	10.9	3.4	6.9

*Unavailable.
**Capacity utilization rates are for most recent year available.
***For unified Germany: from 1989 to 2006.
Source: Organization for Economic Cooperation and Development (www.oecd.org).

Despite problems, the unemployment rate statistic still gives us useful information about changes in the economy. The measurement problems themselves change little from year to year, so you can ignore them when comparing unemployment from one year to another. Keynesian and Classical economists agree that a changing unemployment rate generally tells us something about the economy, especially if interpreted in the light of other statistics. That's why the unemployment rate is used as a measure of the state of the economy.

Unemployment and Potential Output

The unemployment rate gives a good indication of how much labor is available to increase production and thus provides a good idea of how fast the economy could grow. Capital is the second major input to production. Thus, the *capacity utilization rate*—the rate at which factories and machines are operating compared to the maximum sustainable rate at which they could be used—indicates how much capital is available for economic growth.

Table 6-2 shows the unemployment rates and the capacity utilization rates for selected countries over the last 30 years. Generally U.S. economists today feel that unemployment rates of about 4.5-5 percent and capacity utilization rates between 80 and 85 percent are about as much as we should expect from this economy. To push the economy beyond that would be like driving your car 110 miles an hour. True, the marks on your speedometer might go up to 130, but 90 is a more realistic top speed. Beyond 120 (assuming that's where your car is red-lined), the engine is likely to blow up (unless you have a Maserati).

These expectations differ among countries. For example, in the early 2000s, Germany tended to have a higher achievable capacity utilization rate than the United States (85 percent for Germany; 80 percent for the United States) but its achievable unemployment rate was higher (closer to 8 percent unemployment compared to 4.5 to 5.0 percent unemployment in the United States) due to more restrictive labor market rules. Thus, as is the case with cars, maximum speeds differ among economies.

Economists translate the target unemployment rate and target capacity utilization rate into the target level of potential output, or simply potential output (or *potential*

Despite problems, the unemployment rate statistic still gives us useful information about changes in the economy.

Potential output is defined as the output that will be achieved at the target rate of unemployment and the target level of capacity utilization.

income, because output creates income). **Potential output** is *the output that would materialize at the target rate of unemployment and the target rate of capacity utilization.* It is the rate of output beyond which prices would rise at ever-increasing rates; that is, the economy would experience accelerating inflation. Potential output grows at the secular (long-term) trend rate of 2.5 to 3.5 percent per year. When the economy is in a downturn or recession, actual output is below potential output. As you will see throughout the rest of the book, there is much debate about what are the appropriate target rates of unemployment, capacity utilization, and potential output.

To determine how changes in the unemployment rate are related to changes in output, we use **Okun's rule of thumb,** which states that *a 1 percentage point change in the unemployment rate will be associated with a 2 percent change in output in the opposite direction.*[3]

Okun's rule of thumb states that a 1 percentage point change in the unemployment rate will be associated with a 2 percent change in output in the opposite direction.

+1 percentage point change in unemployment → −2 percent change in output

For example, if unemployment rises from 5 percent to 6 percent, total output of $14 trillion will fall by 2 percent, or $280 billion, to $13.7 trillion. In terms of number of workers, a 1 percentage point increase in the unemployment rate means about 1.5 million additional people are out of work.

These figures are rough, but they give you a sense of the implications of a change. For example, say unemployment falls 0.2 percentage point, from 4.5 to 4.3 percent. That means about 300,000 more people have jobs and that output will be $56 billion higher than it otherwise would have been, if the increase holds for the entire year.

Notice I said "will be $56 billion higher than it otherwise would have been" rather than simply saying "will increase by $56 billion." That's because generally the economy is growing as a result of increases in productivity or increases in the number of people choosing to work. Changes in either of these can cause output and employment to grow, even if the unemployment rate doesn't change. We must point this out because in the 1980s the number of people choosing to work increased substantially, significantly increasing the labor participation rate. Then, in the early 2000s, as many large firms structurally adjusted their production methods to increase their productivity, unemployment sometimes rose even as output rose. Thus, when the labor participation rate and productivity change, an increase in unemployment doesn't necessarily mean a decrease in employment or a decrease in output.

Microeconomic Categories of Unemployment

In the decades after World War II, unemployment was seen primarily as cyclical unemployment, and the focus of macroeconomic policy was on how to eliminate that unemployment through a specific set of macroeconomic policies. Understanding those macroeconomic policies is important, but today it's not enough. Unemployment has many dimensions, so different types of unemployment are susceptible to different types of policies.

Today's view is that you don't use a sledgehammer to pound in finishing nails, and you don't use macro policies to deal with certain types of unemployment; instead you use micro policies. To determine where microeconomic policies are appropriate as a supplement to macroeconomic policies, economists break unemployment down into a number of categories and analyze each category separately. These categories include how people become unemployed, demographic characteristics, duration of unemployment, and industry (see Figure 6-5).

Some microeconomic categories of unemployment are: how people become unemployed, demographic unemployment, duration of unemployment, and unemployment by industry.

[3]The precise specification of Okun's rule of thumb has changed over time. Earlier estimates placed it at a 1 to 2.5 ratio.

FIGURE 6-5 **Unemployment by Microeconomic Subcategories, 2006**

Unemployment isn't all the same. This figure gives you a sense of some of the subcategories of unemployment.

Source: *Employment and Earnings 2007*, Bureau of Labor Statistics (www.bls.gov).

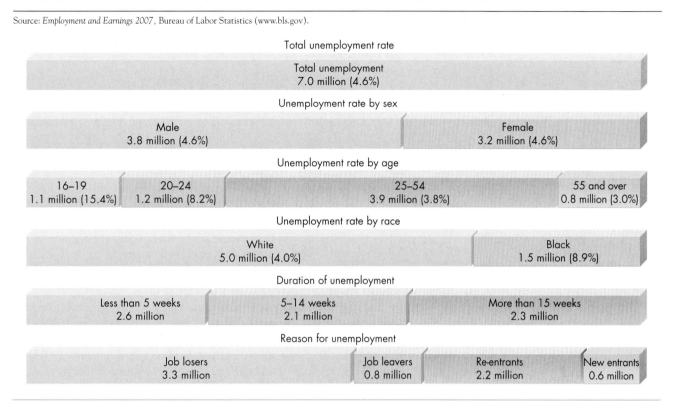

Inflation

Inflation is *a continual rise in the price level*. The price level is an index of all prices in the economy. Even when inflation itself isn't a problem, the fear of inflation guides macroeconomic policy. Fear of inflation prevents governments from expanding the economy and reducing unemployment. It prevents governments from using macroeconomic policies to lower interest rates. It gets some political parties booted out of office and others elected.

A one-time rise in the price level is not inflation. Unfortunately, it's often hard to tell if a one-time rise in the price level is going to stop, so the distinction blurs in practice, but we must understand the distinction. If the price level goes up 10 percent in a month, but then remains constant, the economy doesn't have an inflation problem. Inflation is an *ongoing rise* in the price level.

From 1800 until World War II, the U.S. inflation rate and price level fluctuated; sometimes the price level would rise, and sometimes the price level would fall—there would be deflation. Since World War II, the price level has continually risen, which means the inflation rate (the measure of the change in prices over time) has been positive, as can be seen in Figure 6-6. The rate fluctuates, but the movement of the price level has been consistently upward.

It is also possible to have **deflation**—*a continual fall in the price level*. Historically, we have seldom seen long periods of deflation, although in the late 1990s and early 2000s some countries, such as Japan, had deflation. It is important to note, however, that

Inflation is a continual rise in the price level.

Deflation is a continual fall in the price level.

FIGURE 6-6 **Inflation since 1900**

Until 1940, rises in the price level were
followed by falls in the price level, keeping
the price level relatively constant. Since the
1940s, inflation has generally been positive,
which means that the price level has been
continually rising.

Source: U.S. Department of Commerce (www.doc.gov).

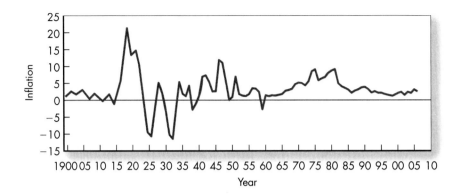

much of the concern about deflation is about asset deflation—a continual fall in the
prices of assets such as houses and stocks—not goods and services deflation, which the
standard price indices measure.

Measurement of Inflation

Since inflation is a sustained rise in the general price level, we must first determine what
the general price level was at a given time by creating a **price index,** *a number that summa-*
rizes what happens to a weighted composite of prices of a selection of goods (often called a market
basket of goods) over time. An index converts prices relative to base year prices. Price indexes are important. Many people lament the high cost of goods and services today. They
complain, for example, that an automobile that costs $15,000 today cost only $3,000 in
the "good old days." But that comparison is meaningless, because most prices have risen.
Today, the average wage is more than five times what it was when cars cost only $3,000.
To relate the two prices, we need a price index. There are a number of different measures
of the price level. The most often used are the producer price index, the GDP deflator, and
the consumer price index. Each has certain advantages and disadvantages.

Creating a Price Index   Before introducing the official price indexes, let's work
through the creation of a fictitious price index—the Colander price index—and calculate
the associated inflation. I'll do so for 2007 and 2008, using 2007 as the base year. A price
index is calculated by dividing the current price of a basket of goods by the base price of a
basket of goods. The table below lists a market basket of goods I consume in a base year and
their associated prices in 2007 and 2008. The market basket of goods is listed in column 1
and represents the quantity of each item purchased in the base year.

(1)	(2)	(3)	(4)	(5)
	Prices		**Expenditures**	
Basket of Goods	**2007**	**2008**	**2007**	**2008**
10 pairs jeans	$20.00/pr.	$25.00/pr.	$200	$250
12 flannel shirts	15.00/shirt	20.00/shirt	180	240
100 lbs. apples	0.80/lb.	1.05/lb.	80	105
80 lbs. oranges	1.00/lb.	1.00/lb.	80	80
Total expenditures			$540	$675

The price of the market basket in each year is the sum of the expenditures on each item—the quantity of each good purchased times its market price. The market basket remains the same in each year; only the prices change. The price of the market basket in 2007 is $540 and in 2008 is $675. To calculate the Colander price index, divide the 2008 price of the market basket by the price of the market basket in the base year and multiply it by 100. In this case 2007 is the base year, so the price index in 2008 is

$$\$675/\$540 \times 100 = 125$$

To make sure you are following this example, calculate the Colander price index in 2007.

The answer is 100. The base year index is always 100 since you are dividing base years by the base year prices and multiplying by 100.

Inflation in 2008, then, is the percent change in the price index. This is calculated in 2008 as the difference between the price indices in the two years ($125 - 100 = 25$) divided by the base index, 100, times 100.

$$\left(\frac{125 - 100}{100}\right) \times 100 = 25\%$$

But enough on price indexes in general. Let's now discuss the price indexes most commonly used when talking about inflation.

Real-World Price Indexes   The total output deflator, or **GDP deflator** (gross domestic product deflator), is *an index of the price level of aggregate output, or the average price of the components in total output (or GDP), relative to a base year.* (Recently, another price index, the chain-type price index for GDP, has become more popular; it is a GDP deflator with a constantly moving base year.) GDP is a measure of the total market value of aggregate production of goods and services produced in an economy in a year. (We'll discuss the calculation of GDP in more detail in the next chapter.) A deflator is an adjustment for "too much air." In this context, it is an adjustment for inflation—so that we know how much total output would have risen if there were no inflation.

The GDP deflator is the inflation index economists generally favor because it includes the widest number of goods, and because the base period is adjusted yearly. Unfortunately, since it's difficult to compute, it's published only quarterly with a fairly substantial lag. That is, by the time the figures come out, the period the figures measure has been over for quite a while.

Published monthly, the **consumer price index (CPI)** *measures the prices of a fixed basket of consumer goods, weighted according to each component's share of an average consumer's expenditures.* It measures the price of a fixed basket of goods rather than measuring the prices of all goods. It is the index of inflation most often used in news reports about the economy and is the index most relevant to consumers. Since different groups of consumers have different expenditures, there are different CPIs for different groups. One often-cited measure is the CPI for all urban consumers (the urban CPI)—about 87 percent of the U.S. population. The numbers that compose the urban CPI are collected at 87 urban areas and include prices from over 50,000 landlords or tenants and 23,000 business establishments.

Figure 6-7 shows the relative percentages of the basket's components. As you see, housing, transportation, and food make up the largest percentages of the CPI. To give you an idea of what effect the rise in price of a component of the CPI will have on the CPI as a whole, let's say food prices rise 10 percent in a year and all other prices remain constant. Since food is about 15 percent of the total, the CPI will rise 15% × 10% = 1.5%. The CPI and GDP deflator indexes roughly equal each other when averaged over an entire year. (For more information on the CPI, go to www.bls.gov/cpi/cpifaq.htm.)

The GDP deflator is an index of the price level of aggregate output or the average price of the components in GDP relative to a base year.

The consumer price index (CPI) is an index of inflation measuring prices of a fixed basket of consumer goods, weighted according to each component's share of an average consumer's expenditures.

Q-8   Say that health care costs make up 15 percent of total expenditures. Say they rise by 10 percent, while the other components of the price index remain constant. By how much does the price index rise?

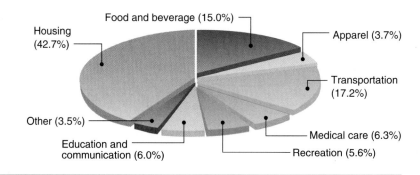

FIGURE 6-7 **Composition of CPI**

The consumer price index is determined by looking at the prices of goods in the categories listed in this exhibit. These categories represent the rough percentages of people's expenditures.
Source: *CPI Detailed Reports*, Bureau of Labor Statistics (www.bls.gov).

The personal consumption expenditure (PCE) deflator allows yearly changes in the basket of goods.

CPI vs. PCE

In the mid-1990s, many economists believed that the CPI overstated inflation by about 1 percentage point a year, and the Bureau of Labor Statistics implemented a number of changes that address some of those problems. In order to avoid some of the problems with the CPI, some policy makers have recently been focusing on another measure of consumer prices—the **personal consumption expenditure (PCE) deflator.** The PCE deflator is *a measure of prices of goods that consumers buy that allows yearly changes in the basket of goods that reflect actual consumer purchasing habits.* The measure smoothes out some of the problems associated with the CPI. Why are there different measures for consumer price changes? Indexes are simply composite measures; they cannot be perfect. (See the box "Measurement Problems with Price Indexes.")

The **producer price index (PPI)** *is an index of prices that measures average change in the selling prices received by domestic producers of goods and services over time.* This index measures price change from the perspective of the sellers, which may differ from the purchaser's price because of subsidies, taxes, and distribution costs and includes many goods that most consumers do not purchase. There are actually three different producer price indexes for goods at various stages of production—crude materials, intermediate goods, and finished goods. Even though the PPI doesn't directly measure the prices consumers pay, because it includes intermediate goods at early stages of production, it serves as an early predictor of consumer inflation since when costs go up, firms often raise their prices. (For more on the PPI, go to www.bls.gov/ppi/ppifaq.htm.)

Real and Nominal Concepts

One important way in which inflation indexes are used is to separate changes in real output from changes in nominal output. Economists use the term *real* when talking about concepts that are adjusted for inflation. **Real output** is *the total amount of goods and services produced, adjusted for price-level changes.* It is the measure of output that would exist if the price level had remained constant. **Nominal output** is *the total amount of goods and services produced measured at current prices.* For example, say total output rises from $8 trillion to $10 trillion. Nominal output has risen by

$$\frac{\$10 \text{ trillion} - \$8 \text{ trillion}}{\$8 \text{ trillion}} = \frac{\$2 \text{ trillion}}{\$8 \text{ trillion}} \times 100 = 25\%$$

Q₉ Nominal output has increased from $10 trillion to $12 trillion. The GDP deflator has risen by 15 percent. By how much has real output risen?

Let's say, however, the price level has risen 20 percent, from 100 percent to 120 percent. The price index is 120. Because the price index has increased, real output (nominal output adjusted for inflation) hasn't risen by 25 percent; it has risen by less than the increase in nominal output. To determine how much less, we use a formula to adjust the nominal figures to account for inflation. This is called *deflating* the nominal figures.

Measurement Problems with Price Indexes

You may have wondered about the fixed basket of goods used to calculate our fictitious price index and the CPI. The basket of goods was fixed in the base year. But buying habits change. The further in time that fixed basket is from the current basket, the worse any fixed-basket price index is at measuring inflation because of a substitution bias and measurement biases.

- **Substitution bias.** Changes in prices change consumption patterns. In our fictitious price index example, the price of apples rose, but the price of oranges did not. It is likely that the basket of goods in 2008 included more oranges and fewer apples than in the base year basket, in which case total expenditures in 2008 would have been less and measured inflation would have been less. Any fixed-basket price index has a substitution bias because it does not take into account the fact that when the price of one good rises, consumers substitute a cheaper item.

- **Measurement biases**

  - **Quality bias.** A good today is seldom identical to a good yesterday. For example, a car in 1998 is assumed to be the same as a car in 2008. But by 2008, cars had much improved corrosion protection, and plastics were replacing metals. Adjustments must be made for these changes and they are seldom perfect. This makes it difficult to compare prices over time since the good is changing.

  - **New product bias.** A fixed basket of goods leaves no room for the introduction of new products. This would not be a problem if the prices of new products changed at about the same rate as prices of other goods in the basket, but in the 1970s this was not true. For years, the CPI did not include the price of computers, whose prices were declining at a 17 percent annual rate!

  - **Store measurement bias.** Ever since World War II, consumers have shifted consumption toward discount purchases. The Bureau of Labor Statistics, however, treats a product sold at a discount store as different from products sold at retail stores. Products sold at discount stores are assumed to be of lower quality. To the extent that they are not different, however, changes in the CPI overstate true inflation.

- **Nonmarket transaction measurement bias.** The cost of housing is included in GDP. For nearly one-third of Americans, this cost is their monthly rent. But what about the remaining two-thirds of Americans who own their own homes? What is the cost of their housing? Remember opportunity costs from Chapter 1? The cost of living in one's own home is the rent you could have gotten for renting it to someone else. So, economists use market rental rates as an implicit rental rate for home ownership (called "owner's equivalent rent"). In recent years, as housing prices have risen, some people began buying two or three houses in the hopes of selling them for more in the future. That significantly increased the number of houses available for rent and held rents down. So although housing prices were soaring, the "owner's equivalent rent" was not, and that was holding measured inflation down. Then, in 2006 and 2007 housing prices fell and rental prices rose, pushing measured inflation up.

These and other problems arise because of the choices with no "correct" answer that must be made when constructing a price index. The reality is that price indices are far from perfect measures and, depending on the choices made, various indices can differ by as much as 3 or 4 percentage points a year. These and other problems arise because of the choices we must make when constructing a price index.

To deflate we divide the most recent nominal figure, $10 trillion, by the price index of 120 percent and multiply by 100:

$$\text{Real output} = \frac{\text{Nominal output}}{120} \times 100 = \frac{\$10 \text{ trillion}}{1.2} = \$8.3 \text{ trillion}$$

That $8.3 trillion is the measure of output that would have existed if the price level had not changed, that is, the measure of real output. Real output has increased from $8 trillion to $8.3 trillion, or by $300 billion.

A way of finding out the percentage rise in real output without actually calculating real output is to use the formula:

$$\text{\% change in real output} = \text{\% change in nominal output} - \text{Inflation}$$

> **% change in real output = % change in nominal output − Inflation**

In this example, the nominal output rose 25 percent and inflation rose 20 percent, so real output rose 5 percent.

When you consider price indexes, you mustn't lose sight of the forest for the trees. Keep in mind the general distinction between real and nominal output. The concepts *real* and *nominal* and the process of adjusting from nominal to real by dividing the nominal amount by a price index will come up again and again. So whenever you see the word *real*, remember:

> **The "real" amount is the nominal amount divided by the price index. It is the nominal amount adjusted for inflation.**

The "real" amount is the nominal amount divided by the price index. It is the nominal amount adjusted for inflation.

Economists' distinction between real and nominal concepts extends to other concepts besides output. They also distinguish real and nominal interest rates. A nominal interest rate is the interest rate you pay or receive. Say you have a student loan on which you pay 5 percent interest. That means the nominal interest rate is 5 percent. The real interest rate is the nominal interest rate adjusted for inflation. In the case of interest rates, to get the real interest rate, all we have to do is subtract the inflation rate from the nominal interest rate.

> **Real interest rate = Nominal interest − Inflation**

Thus, if the nominal interest rate is 5 percent and the inflation rate is 3 percent, the real interest rate is $5 - 3 = 2$ percent. The real interest rate is the amount that the loan is actually costing you, because you will be paying it off with inflated dollars. To see this, let's consider an example. Say the nominal interest rate is 5 percent and the inflation rate is 5 percent. Your income is increasing at the same rate as the balance on your loan, including interest. The real interest rate is 0 percent; it is equivalent to getting an interest-free loan if there were no inflation since in terms of real spending power, you will be paying back precisely what you borrowed.

Expected and Unexpected Inflation

When an individual sets a price (for goods or labor), he or she is actually setting a relative price—relative to other prices in the economy. The money price is the good's nominal price. The laws of supply and demand affect relative prices, not nominal prices.

Now let's say that everyone suddenly expects the price level to rise 10 percent. Let's also say that all individual sellers want a ½ percent increase in their relative price. They're not greedy; they just want a little bit more than what they're currently getting. The relative price increase people want must be tacked onto the inflation they expect. In this case, they have to raise their money price by 10½ percent—10 percent to keep up and ½ percent to get ahead. Ten percent of the inflation is caused by expectations of inflation; ½ percent of the inflation is caused by pressures from suppliers wanting to increase profits. Thus, whether or not inflation is expected makes a big difference in individuals' behavior. That is why we make a distinction between expected and unexpected inflation. **Expected inflation** is *inflation people expect to occur*. **Unexpected inflation** is *inflation that surprises people*.

Since prices and wages are often set for periods of two months to three years ahead, whether inflation is expected can play an important role in the inflation process. In the early 1970s people didn't expect the high inflation rates that did occur. When inflation

Real vs. Nominal

hit, people just tried to keep up with it. By the end of the 1970s, people expected more inflation than actually occurred and raised their prices—and, in doing so, caused the inflation rate to increase.

Expectations of inflation play an important role in any ongoing inflation. They can snowball a small inflationary pressure into an accelerating large inflation. Individuals keep raising their prices because they expect inflation, and inflation keeps on growing because individuals keep raising their prices. That's why expectations of inflation are of central concern to economic policy makers.

Costs of Inflation

Inflation has costs, but not the costs that most people associate with it. Specifically, inflation doesn't make the nation poorer. True, whenever prices go up somebody (the person paying the higher price) is worse off, but the person to whom the higher price is paid is better off. The two offset each other. So inflation does not make society on average any poorer. Inflation does, however, redistribute income from people who cannot or do not raise their prices to people who can and do raise their prices. Thus, inflation can have significant distributional or equity effects, which often creates feelings of injustice about the economic system.

A second cost of inflation is its effect on the information that prices convey to people. Consider an individual who laments the high cost of housing, pointing out that it has doubled in 10 years. But if inflation averaged 7 percent a year over the past 10 years, a doubling of housing prices should be expected. In fact, with 7 percent inflation, on average *all* prices double every 10 years. That means the individual's wages have probably also doubled, so he or she is no better off and no worse off than 10 years ago. The price of housing relative to other goods, which is the relevant price for making decisions, hasn't changed. When there's inflation, it's hard for people to know what is and what isn't a relative price change. People's minds aren't computers, so inflation reduces the amount of information that prices can convey and causes people to make choices that do not reflect relative prices.

Despite these costs, inflation is usually accepted by governments as long as it stays low, which for the United States currently means under 2½ to 3 percent. What scares economists is inflationary pressures above and beyond expectations of inflation. In that case, expectations of higher inflation can cause inflation to build up and compound itself. A 3 percent inflation becomes a 6 percent inflation, which in turn becomes a 12 percent inflation. Once inflation hits 5 percent or 6 percent, it's definitely no longer a little thing. Inflation of 10 percent or more is significant. While there is no precise definition, we may reasonably say that inflation has become **hyperinflation** *when inflation hits triple digits—100 percent or more per year.*

The United States has been either relatively lucky or wise because it has not experienced hyperinflation since the Civil War (1861–65). Other countries, such as Brazil, Israel, and Argentina, have not been so lucky (or have not followed the same policies the United States has). These countries have frequently had hyperinflation. But even with inflation at these levels, economies have continued to operate and, in some cases, continued to do well.

In hyperinflation people try to spend their money quickly, but they still use the money. Let's say the U.S. price level is increasing 1 percent a day, which is a yearly inflation rate of over 3,000 percent.[4] Is an expected decrease in value of 1 percent per

---

While inflation may not make the nation poorer, it does cause income to be redistributed, and it can reduce the amount of information that prices are supposed to convey.

Q.10 True or false? Inflation makes everyone in an economy worse off because everyone is paying higher prices.

Hyperinflation is exceptionally high inflation of, say, 100 percent or more per year.

Web Note 6.4
Living with Hyperinflation

---

[4]Why over 3,000 percent and not 365 percent? Because of compounding. In the second day the increase is on the initial price level *and* the 1 percent rise in price level that occurred the first day. When you carry out this compounding for all 365 days, you get over 3,000 percent.

day going to cause you to stop using dollars? Probably not, unless you have a good alternative. You will, however, avoid putting your money into a savings account unless that savings account somehow compensates you for the expected inflation (the expected fall in the value of the dollar), and you will try to ensure that your wage is adjusted for inflation. In hyperinflation, wages, the prices firms receive, and individual savings are all in some way adjusted for inflation. Hyperinflation leads to economic institutions with built-in expectations of inflation. For example, usually in a hyperinflation the government issues indexed bonds whose value keeps pace with inflation.

Once these adjustments have been made, substantial inflation will not destroy an economy, but it certainly is not good for it. Such inflation tends to break down confidence in the monetary system, the economy, and the government.

Conclusion

This chapter has talked about growth, unemployment, and inflation. The interrelationship among these three concepts centers on trade-offs between inflation on the one hand and growth and unemployment on the other. If the government could attack inflation without worrying about unemployment or growth, it probably would have solved the problem of inflation by now. Unfortunately, when the government tries to stop inflation, it often causes a recession—increasing unemployment and slowing growth. Similarly, reducing unemployment by stimulating growth tends to increase inflation. To the degree that inflation and unemployment are opposite sides of the coin, the opportunity cost of reducing unemployment is inflation. The government must make a trade-off between low unemployment and slow growth on the one hand and inflation on the other. Opportunity costs must be faced in macro as well as in micro. The models you will learn in later chapters will help clarify the choices policy makers face.

Summary

- Economists use two frameworks to analyze macro-economic problems. The long-run growth framework focuses on supply, while the short-run business-cycle framework focuses on demand.

- Growth is measured by the change in real gross domestic product (real GDP) and by the change in per capita real GDP. Per capita real GDP is real GDP divided by the total population.

- The secular trend growth rate of the economy is 2.5 to 3.5 percent. Fluctuations of real output around the secular trend growth rate are called *business cycles*.

- Phases of the business cycle include peak, trough, upturn, and downturn.

- Unemployment is calculated as the number of unemployed individuals divided by the labor force. Unemployment rises during a recession and falls during an expansion.

- The target rate of unemployment is the lowest sustainable rate of unemployment possible under existing institutions. It's associated with an economy's potential output. The lower the target rate of unemployment, the higher an economy's potential output.

- The microeconomic approach to unemployment subdivides unemployment into categories and looks at those individual components.

- A real concept is a nominal concept adjusted for inflation. Real output equals nominal output divided by the price index.

- Inflation is a continual rise in the price level. The CPI, the PPI, and the GDP deflator are all price indexes used to measure inflation.

- The GDP deflator is the broadest price index. It measures inflation of all goods produced in an economy.

The CPI measures inflation faced by consumers. The PPI measures inflation faced by producers.

- Expectations of inflation can provide pressure for an inflation to continue even when other causes don't exist.

- Inflation redistributes income from people who do not raise their prices to people who do raise their prices. Inflation also reduces the information that prices convey.

Key Terms

business cycle (132)
Classicals (133)
consumer price index (CPI) (147)
cyclical unemployment (137)
deflation (145)
depression (134)
employment-population ratio (142)
expansion (134)
expected inflation (150)

frictional unemployment (138)
GDP deflator (147)
hyperinflation (151)
inflation (145)
Keynesians (133)
labor force (141)
labor force participation rate (142)
nominal output (148)
Okun's rule of thumb (144)

per capita real output (130)
personal consumption expenditure (PCE) deflator (148)
potential output (144)
price index (146)
producer price index (PPI) (148)
real gross domestic product (real GDP) (129)

real output (148)
recession (134)
structural unemployment (137)
target rate of unemployment (138)
unemployment rate (136)
unexpected inflation (150)

Questions for Thought and Review

1. What are two ways in which long-term economic growth is measured? LO1

2. How does the U.S. per capita growth rate of 1.5 to 2 percent a year since 1950 compare to growth rates in other areas around the world? LO2

3. What is the difference between real output and potential output? LO2

4. Draw a representative business cycle, and label each of the four phases. LO3

5. The index of leading indicators has predicted all past recessions. Nonetheless it's not especially useful for predicting recessions. Explain. LO3

6. If unemployment fell to 1.2 percent in World War II, why couldn't it be reduced to 1.2 percent today? (Difficult) LO4

7. Distinguish between structural unemployment and cyclical unemployment. LO4

8. What type of unemployment is best studied within the long-run framework? What type is best studied under the short-run framework? LO4

9. Does the unemployment rate underestimate or overestimate the unemployment problem? Explain. LO4

10. If unemployment rises by 2 percentage points, what will likely happen to output in the United States? LO5

11. If nominal output is $250 and the price index is 150, what is real output? LO6

12. If nominal output rose 15 percent and the price index rose 2 percent, how much did real output increase? LO6

13. Why are expectations central to understanding inflation? LO7

14. Inflation, on average, makes people neither richer nor poorer. Therefore it has no cost. True or false? Explain. LO7

15. Would you expect that inflation would generally be associated with low unemployment? Why? LO7

Problems and Exercises

16. The Bureau of Labor Statistics reported that in May 2007 the total labor force was 152,762,000 of a possible 231,480,000 working-age adults. The total number of unemployed was 6,819,000. From this information, calculate the following for May 2007:
    a. Labor force participation rate.
    b. Unemployment rate.
    c. Employment-population ratio.   LO2

17. In H. G. Wells's *Time Machine*, a late-Victorian time traveler arrives in England some time in the future to find a new race of people, the Eloi, in their idleness. Their idleness is, however, supported by another race, the Morlocks, underground slaves who produce the output. If technology were such that the Elois' lifestyle could be sustained by machines, not slaves, is it a lifestyle that would be desirable? What implications does the above discussion have for unemployment? (Difficult)   LO2

18. In 1991, Japanese workers' average tenure with a firm was 10.9 years; in 1991 in the United States the average tenure of workers was 6.7 years.
    a. What are two possible explanations for these differences?
    b. Which system is better?

    c. In the mid-1990s, Japan experienced a recession while the United States economy grew. What effect did this likely have on these ratios? (Difficult)   LO4, LO5

19. Answer the following questions about real output, nominal output, and inflation:
    a. The price level of a basket of goods in 2006 was $64. The price level of that same basket of goods in 2007 was $68. If 2006 is the base year, what was the price index in 2007?
    b. If nominal output is $300 billion and the price index is 115, what is real output?
    c. Inflation is 5 percent; real output rises 2 percent. What would you expect to happen to nominal output?
    d. Real output rose 3 percent and nominal output rose 7 percent. What happened to inflation?   LO6

20. Assume that nominal output rises from $13.5 billion in 2007 to $14 billion in 2008. Assume also that the GDP deflator rises from 100 to 105.
    a. What is the percentage increase in nominal output?
    b. What is the percentage increase in the price index?
    c. How much has real output increased?
    d. What is the percentage increase in real output?
    e. By how much would the price index have had to rise for real income to remain constant?   LO6

Questions from Alternative Perspectives

1. It is unfair, but true, that bad things happen. Unfortunately, to attempt to prevent unavoidable bad things can actually make things worse, not better. How might the above ideas be relevant to how society deals with business cycles? (Austrian)

2. Wesley Mitchell, a founder of Institutional economics, said that to understand the business cycle, a distinction must be made between making goods and making money. All societies make goods. In the modern money economy, those who control the production and distribution of goods will only allow economic activity to occur if they can "make money." He used this line of reasoning to conclude that what drives the business cycle are business expectations; production, and thus increased employment today, will only be allowed if business expects to sell those goods at a profit tomorrow. Is his proposition reasonable? Explain. (Institutionalist)

3. Since the Great Depression, the United States has been able to avoid severe economic downturns.
   a. What macroeconomic policies do you think have allowed us to avoid another Great Depression?
   b. Would you classify those policies as being Classical or Keynesian?
   c. Are such policies still relevant today? (Post-Keynesian)

4. The text presents the target rate of unemployment as being about 5 percent. William Vickrey, a Nobel Prize-winning economist, argued that the target unemployment rate should be seen as being between 1 percent and 2 percent. Only an unemployment rate that low, he argued, would produce genuine full employment that guaranteed job openings for all those looking for work. Achieving a low unemployment rate would, according to Vickrey, bring about "a major reduction in the illness of poverty, homelessness, sickness, and crime."
   a. What is the appropriate target unemployment rate?
   b. Explain your position.
   c. What policies would you recommend to counteract the human tragedy of unemployment? (Radical)

5. Studies have shown that women tend to pay more than men for things such as auto repairs, haircuts, and dry cleaning.
   a. Why do you think this is?
   b. How does this fact affect the usefulness of aggregate statistics such as the consumer price index (CPI)? (Feminist)

Web Questions

1. Use the Bureau of Labor Statistics' home page (www.bls.gov) and the Philadelphia Federal Reserve Bank's Livingston Survey (www.phil.frb.org/econ/liv) to answer the following questions:
   a. What are the current unemployment rate and inflation rate?
   b. What do forecasters predict for these variables according to the Livingston Survey?
   c. Are these predictions consistent with your predictions?

2. Go to Economagic.com to answer the following:
   a. Graph quarterly real GDP since 1989. Mark a peak and a trough of a business cycle.
   b. What phase of the business cycle is the economy currently in?
   c. For how many quarters has the economy been in this phase?
   d. How long ago was the last recession?

Answers to Margin Questions

1. The change in employment is both a long-run and a short-run issue. It is a short-run issue because when the U.S. economy is in a recession, employment tends to decline. It is a long-run issue because outsourcing is the result of changes in the institutional structure of the global economy caused by reduced trade barriers and reduced communications costs. (129)

2. To calculate per capita output, divide real output ($14 trillion) by the total population (300 million). This equals $46,667. (130)

3. Three leading indicators are the average workweek, the layoff rate, and changes in the money supply. There are others. (136)

4. False. Structural unemployment is determined by the institutional structure of an economy, not fluctuations in economic activity. (137)

5. Keynesians are more likely to see outsourcing as a government problem and look for a government solution. Classicals are more likely to see it as an individual problem, part of the normal workings of the economy, and something that we must just accept. (140)

6. The unemployment rate is the number of unemployed divided by the labor force. The unemployment rate can fall while the number of unemployed rises if the labor force rises by a proportionately greater amount than the rise in the number of unemployed. (142)

7. Since people can always sell apples on the street, one can always get a job. So the value judgment is what type of job and at what wage society owes individuals jobs. (142)

8. The price index will rise by $0.15 \times 0.1 = 0.015 = 1.5\%$. (147)

9. Real output equals the nominal amount divided by the price index. Since the price index has risen by 15 percent, real output has risen to $10.435 trillion ($12 trillion divided by 1.15). Real output has risen by $435 billion. (148)

10. False. Inflation does not make everyone worse off because, although some people are paying higher prices, others are receiving higher prices. (151)

7 Measuring the Aggregate Economy

The government is very keen on amassing statistics . . . They collect them, add them, raise them to the nth power, take the cube root and prepare wonderful diagrams. But you must never forget that every one of these figures comes in the first instance from the village watchman, who just puts down what he damn pleases.

—*Sir Josiah Stamp (head of Britain's revenue department in the late 19th century)*

AFTER READING THIS CHAPTER, YOU SHOULD BE ABLE TO:

1. Define GDP and list the four expenditure components of aggregate output.
2. Calculate GDP in a simple example, avoiding double counting.
3. Distinguish between "net" and "gross" and between "national" and "domestic."
4. List the four components of aggregate income.
5. Explain how profit is the key to the equality between aggregate income and aggregate production.
6. Distinguish between real GDP and nominal GDP.
7. Describe the shortcomings of using GDP.

Before you can talk about macroeconomics in depth, you need to be introduced to some terminology used in macroeconomics. That terminology can be divided into two parts. The first part deals with the macroeconomic statistics you are likely to see in the newspaper—GDP and its components. The second part discusses problems of using GDP figures. Among other things, it distinguishes between real and nominal (or money) concepts, which are used to differentiate and compare goods and services over time. These concepts play a central role in interpreting the movement in components of the national income accounts.

Aggregate Accounting

In the 1930s, it was impossible for macroeconomics to exist in the form we know it today because many concepts we now take for granted either had not yet been formulated or were so poorly formulated that it was useless to talk rigorously about them. This lack of terminology to describe the economy as a whole was consistent with the Classical economists' lack of interest in studying the aggregate economy in the 1930s; they preferred to focus on microeconomics.

With the advent of Keynesian macroeconomics in the mid-1930s, development of a terminology to describe the macroeconomy became crucial. Measurement is a necessary step toward rigor. A group of Keynesian economists set out to develop a terminology and to measure the concepts they defined so that people would have concrete terms to use when talking about macroeconomic problems. Their work (for which two of them, Simon Kuznets and Richard Stone, received the Nobel Prize) set up an *aggregate* accounting system—a set of rules and definitions for measuring economic activity in the economy as a whole. That aggregate accounting system often goes by the name *national income accounting*.

Aggregate accounting provides a way of measuring aggregate production and aggregate income. Both aggregate production and aggregate income can be broken down into subaggregates; aggregate accounting defines the relationship among these subaggregates.

Calculating GDP

The previous chapter introduced economists' primary measure of domestic output: real gross domestic product (real GDP). **Gross domestic product (GDP)** is *the total market value of all final goods and services produced in an economy in a one-year period.* GDP is probably the single most-used economic measure. When economists, journalists, and other analysts talk about the economy, they continually discuss GDP, how much it has increased or decreased, and what it's likely to do.

Aggregate final output (GDP) consists of millions of different services and products: apples, oranges, computers, haircuts, financial advice, and so on. To arrive at total output, somehow we've got to add them all together into a composite measure. Say we produced 7 oranges plus 6 apples plus 12 computers. We have not produced 25 comapplorgs. You can't add apples and oranges and computers. You can only add like things (things that are measured in the same units). For example, 2 apples + 4 apples = 6 apples. If we want to add unlike things, we must convert them into like things. We do that by multiplying each good by its *price*. Economists call this *weighting the importance of each good by its price*. For example, if you have 4 pigs and 4 horses and you price pigs at $200 each and horses at $400 each, the horses are weighted as being twice as important as the pigs.

Multiplying the quantity of each good by its market price changes the terms in which we discuss each good from a quantity of a specific product to a *value* measure of that good. For example, when we multiply 6 apples by their price, 25 cents each, we get $1.50; $1.50 is a value measure. Once all goods are expressed in that value measure, they can be added together.

Take the example of 7 oranges and 6 apples. (For simplicity let's forget the computers, haircuts, and financial advice.) If the oranges cost 50 cents each, their total value is $3.50; if the apples cost 25 cents each, their total value is $1.50. Their values are expressed in identical measures, so we can add them together. When we do so, we don't get 13 orples; we get $5 worth of apples and oranges.

If we follow that same procedure with all the final goods and services produced in the economy in the entire year, multiplying the quantity produced by the market price per unit, we have all the goods and services an economy has produced expressed in units of value. If we then add up all these units of value, we have that year's gross domestic product.

The Components of GDP

GDP is usually divided into four categories depending on who buys the output, or by what are called *expenditure categories*. The four expenditure categories that comprise GDP are consumption, investment, government spending, and net exports.

Consumption   **Consumption** is *spending by households on goods and services.* Consumption includes such things as food, shampoo, televisions, furniture, and the services of doctors and lawyers. This is the production in the economy that consumers buy. When you buy a DVD, you are contributing to consumption expenditures.

Investment   **Investment** is *spending for the purpose of additional production.* Investment includes business spending on factories and equipment for production, the change

This 17th-century engraving, "The Money Lender," shows that careful bookkeeping and accounting have been around for a long time.

Gross domestic product (GDP) is the aggregate final output of residents and businesses in an economy in a one-year period.

Once all goods are expressed in a value measure, they can be added together.

in business inventories, and purchases by households of new owner-occupied houses. Investment is output that is used to produce goods and services in the future. You should take note that when economists speak of investment as they discuss aggregate accounting, they don't mean the kind of activity taking place when individuals buy stocks rather than consuming—economists call such activity *saving*. So in economists' terminology when you buy a bond or stock rather than consuming, you are saving. When that savings is borrowed by businesses to buy factories, tractors, computers, or other goods or services that will increase their output, they are *investing*. The amount they spend on goods that will increase future output is what in aggregate accounting is called *investment*.

You might have been surprised to see the change in inventories and residential construction included in investment. Inventories are goods that have been produced, so they must be counted if one is going to include all produced goods, which is what GDP is designed to include, but they have not yet been purchased; inventories represent goods to be sold in the future. This means that they will increase future output, so they are counted as investment. Residential construction is part of investment because most of the housing services from a new house will be provided in the future, not the present.

Government Spending

Government spending is *goods and services that government buys*. Although government generally does not sell its "production" but provides it free, aggregate accounting rules count government production at the government's cost of providing that output. Thus, when the government buys the services of an analyst, or buys equipment for its space program, it is undertaking economic activity. These activities are classified as government expenditures.

In thinking about government expenditures, you should note that they include expenditures that involve production. Many government payments do not involve production, however, so the government's budget is much larger than government spending included in GDP. The most important category of government spending that is not included in GDP is **transfer payments**—*payments to individuals that do not involve production by those individuals*. Transfer payments include Social Security payments and unemployment insurance among others. These payments are not part of GDP since there is no production associated with them.

Net Exports

Net exports—*spending on goods and services produced in the United States that foreigners buy (exports) minus goods and services produced abroad that U.S. citizens buy (imports)*. (In economics and business, the word "net" is used to distinguish two offsetting flows: exports, which represent a spending flow into the country, and imports, which represent a spending flow out of the country.) The reason we have to use the "net concept" for exports is that GDP measures production *within* the geographic borders of a country. Because exports represent spending by foreigners for goods and services produced within the United States, exports are added. But because imports represent spending on goods and services produced outside the United States, they are subtracted. Our interest is in spending on only those goods and services produced in the geographic confines of the United States.

Summarizing: GDP measures aggregate final production taking place in a country. This production can be subdivided into expenditure categories, and all production must fit into one of the four categories. A shorthand way of expressing this division of GDP into expenditure categories is

$$GDP = \text{Consumption} + \text{Investment} + \text{Government spending} + \text{Net exports, or}$$
$$GDP = C + I + G + (X - M)$$

Q-1 Calculate GDP with the information below:
  Consumption = 60
  Investment = 20
  Government spending = 20
  Exports = 10
  Imports = 15

TABLE 7-1	Expenditure Breakdown of GDP for Selected Countries, 2005

Country	GDP (U.S. $ in billions)	= Consumption (% of GDP)	+ Investment (% of GDP)	+ Government Spending (% of GDP)	+ Exports (% of GDP)	− Imports (−% of GDP)
United States	$13,247	$9,269	$2,213	$2,528	$1,466	−$2,229
		70%	17%	19%	11%	−17%
Belgium	365	53	21	23	87	−84
Czech Republic	122	50	26	22	72	−70
Germany	2,782	59	18	18	45	−40
Japan	4,506	57	23	18	14	−13
Mexico	768	68	22	12	30	−32
Poland	299	62	20	18	41	−41

Note: Percentages may not sum to 100 due to rounding. Data for United States are for 2006.

Source: *World Development Report*, 2006, The World Bank (www.worldbank.org), and *Survey of Current Business*, Bureau of Economic Analysis.

Since all production is categorized into one or another of these four divisions, by adding up these four categories, we get total production of U.S. goods and services. Table 7-1 gives the breakdown of GDP by expenditure category for selected countries. Notice that, in all countries, consumption expenditures is the largest component of production.

Two Things to Remember about GDP

In thinking about GDP, it is important to remember that (1) GDP represents a flow (an amount per year), not a stock (an amount at a particular moment of time); and (2) GDP refers to the market value of *final* output. Let's consider these statements separately.

GDP Is a Flow Concept   Say a student just out of college tells you she earns $8,000. You'd probably think, "Wow! She's got a low-paying job!" That's because you implicitly assume she means $8,000 per year. If you later learned that she earns $8,000 per week, you'd quickly change your mind. The confusion occurred because how much you earn is a flow concept; it has meaning only when a time period is associated with it: so much per week, per month, per year. A stock concept is an amount at a given point in time. No time interval is associated with it. Your weight is a stock concept. You weigh 150 pounds; you don't weigh 150 pounds per week.

GDP is a flow concept, the amount of total final output a country produces per year. The *per year* is often left unstated, but is essential. GDP is usually reported quarterly (every three months), but it is reported on an *annualized basis*, meaning the U.S. Department of Commerce, which compiles GDP figures, uses quarterly figures to estimate total output for the whole year.

The store of wealth, in contrast, is a stock concept. The stock equivalent to national income accounts is the **wealth accounts**—*a balance sheet of an economy's stock of assets and liabilities*. Table 7-2 shows a summary account of U.S. net worth from the wealth accounts for the United States in 2006. These are stock measures; they exist at a moment of time. For example, on December 31, 2006, the accounting date for these accounts, U.S. private net worth was $55.6 trillion.

GDP Measures Final Output   As a student in my first economics class, I was asked how to calculate GDP. I said, "Add up the value of the goods and services produced

Two important aspects to remember about GDP are

1. GDP represents a flow.
2. GDP represents the market value of final output.

Q-2   How do wealth accounts differ from national income accounts?

TABLE 7-2   U.S. National Wealth Accounts in 2006 (net worth)

	Dollars (in trillions)			Percentage of Component
Private net worth	$55.6			114%
Tangible wealth		$26.8		
Owner-occupied real estate			$22.6	46
Consumer durables			3.9	8
Other			0.3	0
Financial wealth		28.8		
Corporate equities			10.4	21
Noncorporate equities			7.4	15
Other (pension reserves, life insurance, etc.)			11	23
Government net financial assets	−6.9			−14
Federal		−4.9		−10
State and local		−2.0		−4
Total net worth	48.7			100

Source: *Flow of Funds Accounts*, Board of Governors, Federal Reserve (www.federalreserve.gov). The value of the government's financial liabilities is greater than the value of its financial assets, which is why it shows up as a negative percentage.

by all the companies in the United States to arrive at GDP." I was wrong (which is why I remember it). Many goods produced by one firm are sold to other firms, which use those goods to make other goods. GDP doesn't measure total transactions in an economy; it measures **final output**—*goods and services purchased for their final use*. When one firm sells products to another firm for use in production of yet another good, the first firm's products aren't considered final output. They're **intermediate products**—*products used as input in the production of some other product*. To count intermediate goods as well as final goods as part of GDP would be to double count them. An example of an intermediate good would be wheat sold to a cereal company. If we counted both the wheat (the intermediate good) and the cereal (the final good) made from that wheat, the wheat would be double counted. Double counting would significantly overestimate final output.

If we did not eliminate intermediate goods, a change in organization would look like a change in output. Say a firm that produced steel merged with a firm that produced cars. Together they produce exactly what each did separately before the merger. Final output hasn't changed, nor has intermediate output. The only difference is that the intermediate output of steel is now internal to the firm. Using only each firm's sales of goods to final consumers (and not sales to other firms) as the measure of GDP means that changes in organization do not affect the measure of output.

Two Ways of Eliminating Intermediate Goods   There are two ways to eliminate intermediate goods from the measure of GDP. One way is to calculate the final sales that make up GDP directly, either by measuring the expenditures on the products by final users or by measuring the production done specifically for final users. A second way to eliminate double counting is to follow the value added approach. **Value added** is *the increase in value that a firm contributes to a product or service*. It is calculated by subtracting intermediate goods (the cost of materials that a firm uses to produce a good or service) from the value of its sales. For instance, if a firm buys $100 worth of thread and $10,000 worth of cloth and uses them in making a thousand pairs of jeans that are sold for $20,000, the firm's value added is not $20,000; it is $9,900 ($20,000 in sales minus the $10,100 in intermediate goods that the firm bought).

To avoid double counting, you must eliminate intermediate goods, either by calculating only final output (expenditures approach) or by using the value added approach.

The table below provides another example.

Participants	I Cost of Materials	II Value of Sales	III Value Added	Row
Farmer	$ 0	$ 100	$100	1
Cone factory and ice cream maker	100	250	150	2
Middleperson (final sales)	250	400	150	3
Vendor	400	500	100	4
Totals	$750	$1,250	$500	5

It gives the cost of materials (intermediate goods) and the value of sales in the following scenario: Say we want to measure the contribution to GDP made by ice cream production of 200 ice cream cones at $2.50 each for total sales of $500. The vendor bought his cones and ice cream at a cost of $400 from a middleperson, who in turn paid the cone factory and ice cream maker a total of $250. The farmer who sold the cream to the factory got $100. Adding up all these transactions, we get $1,250, but that includes intermediate goods. Either by counting only the final value of the vendor's sales, $500, or by adding the value added at each stage of production (column III), we eliminate intermediate sales and arrive at the contribution of ice cream production to GDP of $500.

Value added is calculated by subtracting the cost of materials from the value of sales at each stage of production. The aggregate value added at each stage of production is, by definition, precisely equal to the value of final sales, since it excludes all intermediate products. In the table illustrating our example, the equality of the value added approach and the final sales approach can be seen by comparing the vendor's final sales of $500 (row 4, column II) with the $500 value added (row 5, column III).

Calculating GDP: Some Examples

To make sure you understand what value added is and what makes up GDP, let's consider some sample transactions and determine what value they add and whether they should be included in GDP. Let's first consider secondhand sales: When you sell your two-year-old car, how much value has been added? The answer is none. The sale involves no current output, so there's no value added. If, however, you sold the car to a used-car dealer for $2,000 and he or she resold it for $2,500, $500 of value has been added—the used-car dealer's efforts transferred the car from someone who didn't want it to someone who did. I point this out to remind you that GDP is not only a measure of the production of goods; it is a measure of the production of goods *and services*.

Now let's consider a financial transaction. Say you sell a bond (with a face value of $1,000) that you bought last year. You sell it for $1,250 and pay $100 commission to the dealer through whom you sell it. What value is added to final output? You might be tempted to say that $250 of value has been added, since the value of the bond has increased by $250. GDP, however, refers only to value that is added as the result of production or services, not to changes in the values of financial assets. Therefore, the price at which you buy or sell the bond is irrelevant to the question at hand. The only value that is added by the sale is the transfer of that bond from someone who doesn't want it to someone who does. Thus, the only value added as a result of economic activity is the dealer's commission, $100. The remaining $1,150 (the $1,250 you got from the bond minus the $100 commission you paid) is a transfer of an asset from one individual

Q-3 If a used-car dealer buys a car for $2,000 and resells it for $2,500, how much has been added to GDP?

Is GDP Biased against Women?

Although in the example in the book the housespouse is a man, the reality is that most housespouses are women. The fact that GDP doesn't include the work of housespouses is seen, by some, as a type of discrimination against women who work without pay at home since their work is not counted as part of the domestic product. One answer for why it is not counted is that housework does not involve a market transaction and hence could not be measured. That makes some sense, but it does not explain why the services houses provide to homeowners are estimated and included in GDP. Why can't housework also be estimated?

The answer is that it can be estimated, and my suspicion is that not including housespouses' services in GDP does represent the latent discrimination against women that was built into the culture in the 1930s when national income accounting was first developed. That latent discrimination

against women was so deep that it wasn't even noticed. Anyone who has seen the movie *Rosie the Riveter,* which shows government programs to get women out from wartime employment and back into their role in the home, will have a good sense of the cultural views of people in the mid-1900s and earlier.

In thinking about whether GDP is biased against women, it is important to remember that the concepts we use are culturally determined and, over time, as cultural views change, the concepts no longer match our changed views. There is no escaping the fact that language is value-loaded. But so, too, is our attempt to point out the values in language. There are many other ways in which GDP reflects arbitrary choices and discrimination against groups. The major discussion of the fact that latent discrimination against women is embodied in GDP accounting itself reflects our current values, just as not including housespouses' work reflected earlier values.

Q-4 How can the federal government have a $2.7 trillion budget but only have $900 billion of that included in GDP?

to another, but such transfers do not enter into GDP calculations. Only production of goods and services enters into GDP.

Let's consider a different type of financial transaction: The federal government pays an individual Social Security benefits. What value is added? Clearly no production has taken place, but money has been transferred. As in the case of the bond, only the cost of transferring it—not the amount that gets transferred—is included in GDP. This is accomplished by including in GDP government expenditures on goods and services, but not the value of government transfer payments. Thus, Social Security payments, welfare payments, and veterans' benefits do not enter into calculations of GDP. That's why the government can have a $2.7 trillion budget but only $900 billion ($2.7 trillion minus $1,800 billion of transfer payments) is included in GDP.

Finally, let's consider the work of a housespouse. (See the box "Is GDP Biased against Women?" for further discussion of this issue.) How much value does it add to economic activity in a year? Clearly if the housespouse is any good at what he or she does, a lot of value is added. Taking care of the house and children is hard work. Estimates of the yearly value of a housespouse's services range from $35,000 to $130,000, and some estimate that including housework in the national accounts would raise GDP more than 50 percent. Even though much value is added and hence, in principle, housespouse services should be part of GDP, by convention a housespouse contributes nothing to GDP. GDP measures only *market activities;* since housespouses are not paid, their value added is not included in GDP. This leads to some problems in measurement. For example, suppose a woman divorces her housespouse and then hires him to continue cleaning her house for $20,000 per year. That $20,000 value added, since it is now a market transaction, is included in GDP.

The housespouse example shows one of the problems with GDP. It also has other problems, but these are best left for intermediate courses. What's important for an introductory economics student to remember is that numerous decisions about how to handle various types of transactions had to be made to get a workable measure.

Some Complications

The above presentation of aggregate accounting makes it look as if aggregate accounting is quite simple—just measure consumption, investment, government spending, and net exports; add them together; and you have GDP. Conceptually, it is that simple, but, in practice, complicated conceptual decisions and accounting adjustments have to be made to ensure that all final production is included and that no double counting takes place. This leads to complicated accounting rules and alternative measures to account for different methods of measuring different concepts. Let me briefly introduce you to two of them.

Gross and Net Concepts   Notice that we use the term *gross* domestic product or GDP. Gross does not mean outrageous; it is a technical accounting term that distinguishes a concept that has not been adjusted for an offsetting flow. (Remember we used the term "net" in our discussion of the export component of GDP to distinguish a concept that is adjusted for an offsetting flow.) The complication is that during the production process, the machines and equipment wear out or simply become technologically obsolete. Economists call this wearing out process **depreciation**—*the decrease in an asset's value.* Depreciation is part of the cost of producing a good; it is the amount by which plants and equipment decrease in value as they grow older. Much of each year's investment involves expenditures to replace assets that have worn out. For example, as you drive your car, it wears out. A car with 80,000 miles on it is worth less than the same type of car with only 1,000 miles on it. The difference in value is attributed to depreciation.

Because some production is used to replace worn-out plant and equipment (depreciation), this production is not available for purchase for consumption, investment, or government spending. To account for this, economists have created another aggregate term that adjusts for depreciation. That term is *net domestic product.* **Net domestic product (NDP)** is *GDP less depreciation.*

$$NDP = GDP - Depreciation$$

NDP = GDP − Depreciation

Because depreciation affects capital available for production, depreciation shows up in the investment category of expenditures. Specifically, investment we have talked about so far is gross investment; **net investment** is *gross investment less depreciation.*

NDP takes depreciation into account. Since we want to measure output available for purchase, NDP is actually preferable to GDP as the expression of a country's domestic output. However, measuring true depreciation (the actual decrease in an asset's value) is difficult because asset values fluctuate. In fact, it's so difficult that, in the real world, accountants don't try to measure true depreciation, but instead use a number of conventional rules of thumb. In recognition of this reality, economists call the adjustment made to GDP to arrive at NDP the *capital consumption allowance* rather than *depreciation.* Since estimating depreciation is difficult, GDP rather than NDP is generally used in discussions of aggregate output.

National and Domestic Concepts

A second complication of measuring aggregate output is whether the aggregate output that one is referring to is output produced within the borders of the country, or by the citizens and firms of the country.

Until 1992, the United States (unlike the rest of the world) used an accounting measure that focused on output produced by its firms and citizens. This was called *gross national product*. As economic issues have become internationalized, aggregate accounting has been affected. In 1992, the United States followed the rest of the world and switched to gross domestic product as its primary measure of aggregate output.

Whereas gross domestic product measures the economic activity that occurs within the geographic borders of a country, the economic activity of the citizens and businesses of a country is measured by **gross national product (GNP)**—*the aggregate final output of citizens and businesses of an economy in a one-year period.* So the economic activity of U.S. citizens working abroad is counted in U.S. GNP but isn't counted in U.S. GDP. Similarly for the foreign economic activity of U.S. companies. However, the production of a Mexican or German person or business working in the United States isn't counted in U.S. GNP but is counted in U.S. GDP. Thus, GDP describes the economic output within the physical borders of a country while GNP describes the economic output produced by the citizens of a country. To move from GDP to GNP we must add *net foreign factor income* to GDP. (That income reflects output of equal value.) **Net foreign factor income** is defined as *the income from foreign domestic factor sources minus foreign factor income earned domestically.* Put another way, we must add the foreign income of our citizens and subtract the income of residents who are not citizens.

$$\text{GNP} = \text{GDP} + \text{Net foreign factor income}$$

For many countries there's a significant difference between GNP and GDP. For example, consider Kuwait. Its citizens and companies have significant foreign income—income that far exceeds the income of the foreigners in Kuwait. This means that Kuwait's GNP (the output of its citizens) far exceeds its GDP (the output produced in Kuwait). For the United States, however, foreign output of U.S. businesses and people for the most part offsets the output of foreign businesses and people within the United States. Kuwait's net foreign factor income has been large and positive, while that of the United States has been minimal. Most discussions today focus on GDP since it is the primary measure presented in government statistics, but it is important to know GNP since aggregate income is normally measured on a national basis.

Calculating Aggregate Income

Aggregate accounting also calculates the aggregate income—the total income earned by citizens and firms of a country. This aggregate income is divided into the following four categories:

Compensation of Employees   Employee compensation (the largest component of national income) consists of wages and salaries paid to individuals, along with fringe benefits and government taxes for Social Security and unemployment insurance.

Rents   Rents are the income from property received by households. Rents received by firms are not included because a firm's rents are simply another source of income to the firm and hence are classified as profits. In most years, the rent component of national income is small, since the depreciation owners take on buildings is close to the income they earn from those buildings.

Interest   Interest is the income private businesses pay to households that have lent the businesses money, generally by purchasing bonds issued by the businesses. (Interest received by firms doesn't show up in this category for the same reason that rents received by firms don't show up in the *rent* category.) Interest payments by government

GDP is output produced within a country's borders; GNP is output produced by a country's citizens.

Q.5 Which is higher: Kuwait's GDP or its GNP? Why?

TABLE 7-3 **Aggregate Income Breakdown for Selected Countries, 2005**

(1) Country	(2) Aggregate Income (billions of $)	=	(3) Employee Compensation (% of total)	+	(4) Rents (% of total)	+	(5) Interest (% of total)	+	(6) Profits (% of total)
United States	$13,623		70%		1%		5%		24%
Japan	4,549		73		2		2		23
Germany	2,897		73		2		6		19
United Kingdom	2,374		62		4		3		30
Canada	1,132		68		8		6		18
Sweden	384		64		4		13		19

Note: Aggregate income in this table does not equal GDP in Table 7-1 because of statistical and conceptual adjustments. Percentages may not sum to 100 due to rounding. Data for the United States are for 2006.

Source: National Accounts, OECD and individual country home pages.

and households aren't included in national income since by convention they're assumed not to flow from the production of goods and services.

Profits   Profits are the amount that is left after compensation to employees, rents, and interest have been paid out. (The national income accounts use accounting profits that must be distinguished from economic profits, which are calculated on the basis of opportunity costs.)

Table 7-3 shows these components for the United States and selected countries. It lists the aggregate income of countries and the components in absolute amounts and in percentages for the United States and in percentages for the remaining countries. As you can see, in all countries compensation of employees is the largest component of national income followed by profits. (One final word of caution: In each country statistics are collected using slightly different methods. This makes international comparison difficult.)

Q-6 Calculate aggregate income with the information below:

Employee compensation = 140
Rents = 4
Interest = 12
Profits = 42

Equality of Aggregate Income and Aggregate Production

By definition, whenever a good or service is produced (output), somebody receives an income for producing it. This means that aggregate income equals aggregate production, which can be expressed in the following identity:

$$\text{Aggregate income} \equiv \text{Aggregate production}[1]$$

In establishing this identity, many accounting decisions need to be made to ensure complete equality. For example, since production figures are collected on a domestic basis (it measures what is produced in the geographic confines of the United States) while income figures are collected on a national basis (it measures what citizens and firms of the United States earn), it is necessary to make adjustments to equalize these. Similarly, taxes placed on corporations have to be accounted for to ensure that they are treated in a way that will maintain the equality. There are many more decisions, but at this introductory level, they are best left alone, so that the main point—that aggregate income—the

[1]An *identity* is a statement of equality that's true by definition. In algebra, an identity is sometimes written as a triple equal sign ($\equiv$). It is more equal than simply equal. How something can be more equal than equal is beyond me, too, but I'm no mathematician.

Profit is a residual that makes the income side equal the expenditure side.

value of the employee compensation, rents, interest, and profits—equals aggregate production—the value of goods produced—doesn't get lost in the complications.[2]

How are these values kept exactly equal? The definition of profit is the key to the equality. Recall that *profit* is defined as what remains after all the firm's other income (employee compensation, rent, and interest) is paid out. For example, say a firm has a total output of $800 and that it paid $400 in wages, $200 in rent, and $100 in interest. The firm's profit is total output less these payments. Profit equals $800 − $700 = $100.

The accounting identity works even if a firm incurs a loss. Say that instead of paying $400 in wages, the firm paid $700, along with its other payments of $200 in rent and $100 in interest. Total output is still $800, but total payments are $1,000. Profits, still defined as total output minus payments, are negative: $800 − $1,000 = (−$200). There's a loss of $200. Adding that loss to other income [$1,000 + (−$200)] gives total income of $800—which is identical to the firm's total output of $800. It is no surprise that total output and total income, defined in this way, are equal.

The aggregate accounting identity (Total output = Total income) allows us to calculate GDP either by adding up all values of final outputs or by adding up the values of all earnings or income.

Using GDP Figures

The most important use of GDP figures is to compare one country's production with another country's and one year's production with another year's.

Web Note 7.1
The Human
Development Index

Comparing GDP among Countries

Most countries use somewhat similar measures to calculate GDP. Thus, we can compare various countries' GDP levels and get a sense of their economic size and power.

Per capita GDP is another measure often used to compare various nations' income. To arrive at per capita GDP, we divide GDP by the country's total population. Doing so gives us a sense of the relative standards of living of the people in various countries.

Some of the comparisons of these measures should give you cause to wonder. For example, at existing exchange rates Bangladesh has per capita GDP of about $270, compared to U.S. per capita GDP of about $45,000. How do people in Bangladesh live? In answering that question, remember that GDP measures market transactions. In poor countries, individuals often grow their own food (subsistence farming), build their own shelter, and make their own clothes. None of those activities are market activities, and while they're sometimes estimated and included in GDP, they often aren't estimated accurately. They certainly aren't estimated at the value of what these activities would cost in the United States. Also, remember that GDP is an aggregate measure that values activities at the market price in a society. The relative prices of the products and services a consumer buys often differ substantially among countries. In New York City, $2,000 a month gets you only a small studio apartment. In Haiti, $2,000 a month might get you a mansion with four servants. Thus, GDP can be a poor measure of the relative living standards.

Q-7 Why are GDP statistics not especially good for discussing the income of developing countries?

---

[2]In my previous classes, and in previous editions of this book, I've presented a number of these complications to my students in the belief that a bit of accounting suffering was good for their souls, and useful to know. (Besides, I had to learn them, so why shouldn't my students?) My students, along with some reviewers of the book, argued forcefully that the distinctions weren't central for students in introductory economics. Upon reflection, I agreed, so I eliminated them from the book. So you can thank my students for my not presenting them, and consult an intermediate macroeconomics text (mine preferably) if you want to go deeper into aggregate accounting issues.

To avoid this problem in comparing per capita GDP, economists often calculate a different concept, *purchasing power parity*, which adjusts for the different relative prices among countries before making comparisons.

Just how much of a difference the two approaches can make can be seen in the case of China. In 1992, the International Monetary Fund (IMF) changed from calculating China's GDP using the exchange rate approach to calculating it using the purchasing power parity approach. Upon doing so, the IMF calculated that China's GDP grew over 400 percent in one year. Per capita income rose from about $300 to well over $1,000. When methods of calculation can make that much difference, one must use statistics very carefully.

Economic Welfare over Time

A second way in which the GDP concept is used is to compare one year with another. Using GDP figures to compare the economy's performance over time is much better than relying merely on our perceptions. Most of us have heard the phrase *the good old days*. Generally we hear it from our parents or grandparents, who are lamenting the state of the nation or economy. In comparing today to yesterday, they always seem to picture the past with greener grass, an easier life, and happier times. Compared to the good old days, today always comes out a poor second.

> Using GDP figures to compare the economy's performance over time is much better than relying merely on our perceptions.

Our parents and grandparents may be right when they look back at particular events in their own lives, but if society were to follow such reasoning, it would conclude that all of history has been just one long downhill slide, worsening every year. In actuality, perceptions of the good old days are likely to be biased. It's easy to remember the nice things of yesterday while forgetting its harsh realities. Relying on past perception is not an especially helpful way of making accurate comparisons.

A preferable way is to rely on data that are not affected by emotion or other subjective perceptions. Looking at GDP over time provides a way of using data to make comparisons over time. For example, say we compare U.S. GDP in 1932 ($58 billion) to GDP in 2006 ($13.2 trillion). Would it be correct to conclude the economy had grown 228 times larger? No. As I discussed earlier, GDP figures aren't affected by emotions, but they are affected by inflation. To make comparisons over time, we can't confine ourselves to a simple look at what has happened to GDP. We must also look at what happened to prices.

Suppose prices of all goods and hence the price level go up 25 percent in one year, but outputs of all goods remain constant. GDP will have risen 25 percent, but will society be any better off? No. To compare GDP over time, you must distinguish between increases in GDP due to inflation and increases in GDP that represent real increases in production and income.

> A real concept is a nominal concept adjusted for inflation.

Real and Nominal GDP

As stated earlier, to separate increases in GDP caused by inflation from increases in GDP that represent real increases in production and income, economists distinguish between **nominal GDP** (*GDP calculated at existing prices*) and **real GDP** (*nominal GDP adjusted for inflation*). This distinction is sufficiently important to warrant repetition in this chapter. To calculate real GDP, we create a price index (a measure of how much the price level has risen from one year to the next), divide nominal GDP by that price index, and multiply by 100. That price index is the GDP deflator, introduced in the previous chapter.[3] Thus, we have

> Real GDP is nominal GDP adjusted for inflation.

$$\text{Real GDP} = \frac{\text{Nominal GDP}}{\text{GDP deflator}} \times 100$$

---

[3]Now you know why the total output deflator is called the *GDP deflator*. It is an index of the rise in prices of the goods and services that make up GDP.

Rearranging terms, we can provide a formula for calculating the GDP deflator if you know both nominal GDP and real GDP:

$$\text{GDP deflator} = \frac{\text{Nominal GDP}}{\text{Real GDP}} \times 100$$

To see how these formulas can be used, say the price level rises 10 percent (from a GDP deflator of 100 to a GDP deflator of 110) and nominal GDP rises from $10 trillion to $12 trillion. Part of that rise in nominal GDP represents the 10 percent rise in the price level. If you divide nominal GDP, $12 trillion, by the new GDP deflator, 110, and multiply by 100, you get $10.9 trillion (the amount GDP would have been if the price level had not risen).

$$\text{Real GDP} = \frac{\$12}{110} \times 100 = \$10.9$$

That $10.9 trillion is called real GDP. To decide whether production has increased or decreased over time, we simply compare the real incomes. In this example, real income has risen from $10 trillion to $10.9 trillion, so we can conclude that the real economy has grown by .9/10, or 9 percent.

To move from GDP deflators to the rate of inflation, you calculate the change in the deflator from one year to another, divide that change by the initial year's deflator, and multiply by 100. For example, if the initial deflator is 101 and the current deflator is 103, you can calculate the rate of inflation by dividing the difference, 2, by the initial deflator, 101, and multiplying by 100. Doing so gives an inflation rate of 1.98. For numbers close to 100, simply subtracting the two deflators (103 − 101 = 2) provides a reasonably good approximation to the rate of inflation.

The percentage change, or growth rate, of nominal and real GDP can be calculated by the same method; you calculate the difference between the figures for the two years, divide that difference by the initial year figure, and multiply by 100. For example, if nominal GDP rises from 12,455.8 in 2005 to 13,246.6 in 2006, the difference is 790.8. Dividing that difference by the initial year's GDP, 12,455.8, and multiplying by 100 gives 6.34, which rounds off to a growth rate of 6.3 percent.

As I discussed in the last chapter, the growth rates of real GDP, nominal GDP, and inflation are related: Specifically:

% change in real GDP = % change in nominal GDP − inflation.

Doing that subtraction is what economists mean when they say that real GDP is equal to nominal GDP adjusted for inflation. We can see these relationships in the table below, which lists nominal GDP, the GDP deflator, and real GDP (base year 2000) for recent years and their percent changes from the previous year.

	Nominal GDP	GDP Deflator	Real GDP
2004 level in billions	$11,712.5	109.4	$10,703.5
2005 level in billions	$12,455.8	112.7	$11,048.6
% change from '04 to '05	6.3	3.03	3.22
2006 level in billions	$13,246.6	116.0	$11,415.3
% change from '05 to '06	6.3	2.98	3.32

Notice that you can arrive at the growth rate in real GDP by subtracting inflation from the percent change in nominal GDP. For example, in 2006 real GDP rose by 3.32 percent, which equals the growth of nominal GDP, 6.3% minus inflation of 2.98%.

Q-8 If real income has risen from $4 trillion to $4.2 trillion and the price level went up by 10 percent, by how much has nominal income risen?

Real GDP is what is important to a society because it measures what is *really* produced. Considering nominal GDP instead of real GDP can distort what's really happening. Let's say the U.S. price level doubled tomorrow. Nominal GDP would also double, but would the United States be better off? No.

We'll use the distinction between real and nominal continually in this course, so to firm up the concepts in your mind, let's go through another example. Consider Venezuela in 2004 and 2005, when nominal GDP rose from $105.3 billion to $127.8 billion while the GDP deflator rose from 100 to 129. Dividing nominal GDP in 2005 by the GDP deflator and multiplying by 100, we see that *real GDP* fell by 6 percent. So not only did Venezuela's economy not grow; it actually shrank.

Some Limitations of Aggregate Accounting

The quotation at this chapter's start pointed out that statistics can be misleading. I want to reiterate that here. Before you can work with statistics, you need to know how they are collected and the problems they have. If you don't, the results can be disastrous.

Here's a possible scenario: A student who isn't careful looks at the data and discovers an almost perfect relationship between imports and investment in a Latin American country. Whenever capital goods imports go up, investment of capital goods goes up by an equal proportion. The student develops a thesis based on that insight, only to learn after submitting the thesis that no data on investment are available for that country. Instead of gathering actual data, the foreign country's statisticians estimate investment by assuming it to be a constant percentage of imports. Since many investment goods are imported, this is reasonable, but the estimate is not a reasonable basis for an economic policy. It would be back to the drawing board for the student.

If you ever work in business as an economist, statistics will be your life's blood. Much of what economists do is based on knowing, interpreting, and drawing inferences from statistics. Statistics must be treated carefully. They don't always measure what they seem to measure. Though U.S. national income accounting statistics are among the most accurate in the world, they still have serious limitations.

> Limitations of aggregate accounting include the following:
>
> 1. Measurement problems exist.
> 2. GDP measures economic activity, not welfare.
> 3. Subcategories are often interdependent.

GDP Measures Market Activity, Not Welfare

The first, and most important, limitation to remember is that GDP measures neither happiness nor economic welfare. GDP measures economic (market) activity. Real GDP could rise and economic welfare could fall. For example, say some Martians came down and let loose a million Martian burglars in the United States just to see what would happen. GDP would be likely to rise as individuals bought guns and locks and spent millions of dollars on protecting their property and replacing stolen items. At the same time, however, welfare would fall.

Welfare is a complicated concept. The economy's goal should not be to increase output for the sake of increasing output, but to make people better off or at least happier. But a pure happiness measure is impossible. Economists have struggled with the concept of welfare and most have decided that the best they can do is to concentrate their analysis on economic activity, leaving others to consider how economic activity relates to happiness. I should warn you, however, that there is no neat correlation between increases in GDP and increases in happiness.

Measurement Errors

GDP figures are supposed to measure all market economic activity, but they do not. Illegal drug sales, under-the-counter sales of goods to avoid income and sales taxes, work performed and paid for in cash to avoid income tax, nonreported sales, and

Q.9 How can measurement errors occur in adjusting GDP figures for inflation?

The Underground Economy and Illegal Immigration

In the text, we mentioned how the national income accounts fail to measure the underground economy and gave some examples of underground activities. One underground activity that has become increasingly important involves illegal immigration. Currently about 12 million people in the United States are undocumented workers, although the precise number isn't known since illegal immigrants aren't especially forthcoming when the government comes around to do a census study.

Most people in the United States are affected by this group. You can see them throughout the country in a variety of lower-level jobs such as maids, day laborers, construction workers, truckers, and farm laborers, among others. Many of these jobs are "on the books," which means that the undocumented workers have acquired a forged identity, with a Social Security number. They end up paying taxes and contributing to measured output

even though they are illegal. Others work "off the books" and, like the many U.S. citizens who work off the books, their contribution to output does not show up in the national income accounts. Such "off the books" transactions occur when restaurants don't ring up cash sales or when waiters forget to declare tips on their tax returns—they reduce their tax payments and make it look as if they have less income and as if the economy has less production than actually exists.

How important is illegal immigration to the underground economy? While the standard measure is that there are about 12 million undocumented workers in the United States and that the underground economy is about 10 percent the size of the U.S. economy, some economists have estimated that the true number of undocumented workers is closer to 18 to 20 million, and that the underground economy is much larger than that 10 percent.

Web Note 7.2
The Underground
Economy

Measurements of inflation can involve significant measurement errors.

prostitution are all market activities, yet none of them is included in GDP figures. Estimates of the underground, nonmeasured economy range from 1.5 to 20 percent of GDP in the United States and as high as 70 percent in Nigeria. That is, if measured U.S. GDP is $14 trillion, including the underground, nonmeasured activity would raise it to between $14.2 trillion and $16.8 trillion. If we were able to halt underground activity and direct those efforts to the above-ground economy, GDP would rise significantly. For instance, if we legalized prostitution and marijuana sales and quadrupled tax-collection mechanisms, GDP would rise. But that rise in GDP wouldn't necessarily make us better off. See the box "The Underground Economy and Illegal Immigration" for further discussion.

A second type of measurement error occurs in adjusting GDP figures for inflation. Earlier I discussed problems using indexes. Measurement of inflation involves numerous arbitrary decisions including what base year to use, how to weight various prices, and how to adjust for changes in the quality of products. Let's take, for example, changes in the quality of products. If the price of a Toyota went up 5 percent from 2007 ($20,000) to 2008 ($21,000), that's certainly a 5 percent rise in price. But what if the 2008 Toyota had a "new, improved" 16-valve engine? Can you say that the price of cars rose 5 percent, or should you adjust for the improvement in quality? And if you adjust, how do you adjust? The people who keep track of the price indexes used to measure inflation will be the first to tell you these questions have no one right answer. How that question, and a million other similar questions involved in measuring inflation, is answered can lead to significant differences in estimates of inflation and hence in estimates of real GDP growth.

One study for Canada argued inflation could be either 5.4 or 15 percent, depending on how the inflation index was calculated. Which inflation figure you chose would make a big difference in your estimate of how the economy was doing.

Misinterpretation of Subcategories

A third limitation of aggregate accounting concerns possible misinterpretation of the components. In setting up the accounts, a large number of arbitrary decisions had to be made: What to include in "investment"? What to include in "consumption"? How to treat government expenditures? The decisions made were, for the most part, reasonable, but they weren't the only ones that could have been made. Once made, however, they influence our interpretations of events. For example, when we see that investment rises, we normally think that our future productive capacity is rising, but remember that investment includes housing investment, which does not increase our future productive capacity. In fact, some types of consumption (say, purchases of personal computers by people who will become computer-literate and use their knowledge and skills to be more productive than they were before they owned computers) increase our productive capacity more than some types of investment.

Q-10 How can some types of consumption increase our productive capacity by more than some types of investment?

Genuine Progress Indicator

The problems of aggregate accounting have led to a variety of measures of economic activity. One of the most interesting of these is the *genuine progress indicator (GPI)*, developed by Redefining Progress (www.redefiningprogress.org), which makes a variety of adjustments to GDP to better measure the progress of society rather than simply economic activity. The GPI makes adjustments to GDP for changes in other social goals. For example, if pollution worsens, the GPI falls even though the GDP remains constant. Each of these adjustments requires someone to value these other social goals, and there is significant debate about how social goals should be valued. Advocates of the GPI agree that such valuations are difficult, but they argue that avoiding any such valuation, as is done with the GDP, implicitly values other social goals, such as having no pollution, at zero. Since some index will be used as an indicator of the progress of the economy, it is better to have an index that includes all social goals rather than an index of only economic activity.

Web Note 7.3
Measuring Welfare

By pointing out these problems, economists are not suggesting that aggregate accounting statistics should be thrown out. Far from it; measurement is necessary, and the GDP measurements and categories have made it possible to think and talk about the aggregate economy. I wouldn't have devoted an entire chapter of this book to aggregate accounting if I didn't believe it was important. I am simply arguing that aggregate accounting concepts should be used with sophistication, that is, with an awareness of their weaknesses as well as their strengths.

Measurement is necessary, and the GDP measurements and categories have made it possible to think and talk about the aggregate economy.

Conclusion

Used with that awareness, aggregate accounting is a powerful tool; you wouldn't want to be an economist without it. For those of you who aren't planning to be economists, it's still a good idea for you to understand the concepts of national income accounting. If you do, the business section of the newspaper will seem less like Greek to you. You'll be a more informed citizen and will be better able to make up your own mind about macroeconomic debates.

Summary

- Aggregate accounting is a set of rules and definitions for measuring activity in the aggregate economy.

- GDP is the total market value of all final goods produced in an economy in one year. It's a flow, not a stock, measure of market activity.

- GDP is divided up into four types of expenditures:

  GDP = Consumption + Investment + Government spending + Net exports

- Intermediate goods can be eliminated from GDP in two ways:

  1. By measuring only final sales.
  2. By measuring only value added.

- Net domestic product is GDP less depreciation. NDP represents output available for purchase because production used to replace worn out plant and equipment (depreciation) has been subtracted.

- GDP describes the economic output produced within the physical borders of an economy, while GNP describes the economic output produced by the citizens of a country.

- Aggregate income = Compensation to employees + Rent + Interest + Profit.

- Aggregate income equals aggregate production because whenever a good is produced somebody receives income for producing it. Profit is key to that equality.

- Because GDP measures only market activities, GDP can be a poor measure of relative living standards among countries.

- To compare income over time, we must adjust for price-level changes. After adjusting for inflation, nominal measures are changed to "real" measures.

  % change in real GDP =
  % change in nominal GDP − Inflation

- $\text{Real GDP} = \dfrac{\text{Nominal GDP}}{\text{GDP deflator}} \times 100$

- GDP has its problems: GDP does not measure economic welfare; it does not include transactions in the underground economy; the price index used to calculate real GDP is problematic; subcategories of GDP are often interdependent.

Key Terms

consumption (*157*)
depreciation (*163*)
final output (*160*)
government
   spending (*158*)
gross domestic product
   (GDP) (*157*)

gross national product
   (GNP) (*164*)
intermediate
   products (*160*)
investment (*157*)
net domestic product
   (NDP) (*163*)

net exports (*158*)
net foreign factor
   income (*164*)
net investment (*163*)
nominal GDP (*167*)

real GDP (*167*)
transfer payments (*158*)
value added (*160*)
wealth accounts (*159*)

Questions for Thought and Review

1. What expenditure category of production is largest for most countries? LO1

2. What's the relationship between a stock concept and a flow concept? Give an example that hasn't already been given in this chapter. LO1

3. If you add up all the transactions in an economy, do you arrive at GDP, GNP, or something else? LO2

4. The United States is considering introducing a value-added tax. What tax rate on value added is needed to get the same revenue as is gotten from an income tax rate of 15 percent? Why? LO2

5. Economists normally talk about GDP even though they know NDP is a better measure of economic activity. Why? LO3

6. Which will be larger, gross domestic product or gross national product? LO3

7. What is the largest component of aggregate income for most countries? LO4

8. If the government increases transfer payments, what happens to aggregate output? LO2

9. Why are aggregate output and aggregate income essentially the same? LO5

10. What makes it difficult to compare GDP over time? How is the problem addressed?   LO6

11. If the United States introduces universal child care, what will likely happen to GDP? What are the welfare implications of that rise?   LO7

12. If society's goal is to make people happier, and higher GDP isn't closely associated with being happier, why do economists even talk about GDP? (Difficult)   LO7

Problems and Exercises

13. State whether the following actions will increase or decrease GDP:
    a. The United States legalizes gay marriages.
    b. An individual sells her house on her own.
    c. An individual sells his house through a broker.
    d. Government increases Social Security payments.
    e. Stock prices rise by 20 percent.
    f. An unemployed worker gets a job.   LO1

14. Find consumption expenditures (as a percent of GDP) for the following countries. (Requires research.)
    a. Mexico
    b. Thailand
    c. Poland
    d. Nigeria
    e. Kuwait   LO1

15. There are three firms in an economy: A, B, and C. Firm A buys $250 worth of goods from firm B and $200 worth of goods from firm C, and produces 200 units of output, which it sells at $5 per unit. Firm B buys $100 worth of goods from firm A and $150 worth of goods from firm C, and produces 300 units of output, which it sells at $7 per unit. Firm C buys $50 worth of goods from firm A and nothing from firm B. It produces output worth $1,000. All other products are sold to consumers.
    a. Calculate GDP.
    b. If a value-added tax (a tax on the total value added of each firm) of 10 percent is introduced, how much revenue will the government get?
    c. How much would government get if it introduced a 10 percent income tax?
    d. How much would government get if it introduced a 10 percent sales tax on final output?   LO2

16. You've been given the following data:

Net exports	$ 4
Net foreign factor income	2
Investment	185
Government spending	195
Consumption	500
Depreciation	59

From this data, calculate GDP, GNP and NDP.   LO3

17. Given the following data about the economy:

Profits	$ 628
Consumption	700
Investment	500
Government spending	300
Net exports	275
Rents	25
Depreciation	25
Net foreign factor income	−3
Interest	150
Employee compensation	1,329

   a. Calculate aggregate output (GDP) and aggregate income.
   b. Compare the two calculations in *a*. Why are they not precisely equal?
   c. Calculate GNP.
   d. Calculate NDP.   LO1, LO3, LO4

18. You have been hired as a research assistant and are given the following data.

Employee compensation	$329
Consumption	370
Exports	55
Net foreign factor income	3
Government spending	43
Investment	80
Imports	63
Interest	49
Profits	96
Rents	14
Net Investment	72

   a. Calculate GNP, GDP, and aggregate income.
   b. What is depreciation in this year?
   c. What is NDP?   LO1, LO3, LO4

19. Below are nominal GDP and GDP deflators for four years.

Year	Nominal GDP	GDP Deflator
2003	$ 10,961	106.4
2004	11,713	109.4
2005	12,456	112.7
2006	13,247	116.0

   a. Calculate real GDP in each year.
   b. Did the percentage change in nominal GDP exceed the percentage change in real GDP in any of the last three years listed?
   c. In which year did society's welfare increase the most?   LO6

Questions from Alternative Perspectives

1. Your textbook points out that GDP fails to recognize much of the work done in the home, largely by women. Most estimates assign that work great economic value. For instance, one measure, developed by the UN's International Training and Research Institute, calculates that counting unpaid household production would add 30–60 percent to the GDP of industrialized countries and far more for developing countries.
   a. Why do you think that work done at home is left out, but housing services are not?
   b. Does it make any difference to how women are treated and thought about that work done at home is not counted in GDP?
   c. If you were valuing the services of a housespouse, how would you go about measuring the value of those services? (Feminist)

2. In "Christianity and Economics: A Review of the Recent Literature," economist John Tiemstra states, "taking good to mean self-perceived happiness derived from economic consumption adopts an ethic that is foreign to biblical Christianity." Your textbook cautions that GDP is not the same as welfare.
   a. What would you include in an index to measure the welfare of a society that takes into account Christian ethics?
   b. What would you purposefully not include in that index? (Religious)

3. Explain the sense in which GDP accounting is an institution (see the *Oxford Dictionary of the English Language* for a precise definition of an institution).
   a. How does GDP as an institution shape our understanding of the economic system?

   b. Who benefits from using GDP accounting as a measure of welfare? (Institutionalist)

4. In the expenditure approach of GDP, should G (government purchases) be taken into account within the calculation the same way C (consumption) and I (investment) are measured? If not, is there something inherently different about the nature of private and public expenditures? (Austrian)

5. The government spends far too much money collecting and organizing statistics. If those statistics were necessary, the private market would collect them.
   a. Explain the sense in which the above statement is true.
   b. Who do you think is the major supporter of government collection of data? (Austrian)

6. Unlike GDP, the "Genuine Progress Indicator" measures the costs as well as the benefits of economic growth by accounting for how production and consumption create social ills such as inequality and create environmental problems that threaten future generations, such as global warming and the depletion of natural resources. GPI adjusts GDP downward to account for these costs, along with underemployment and the loss of leisure time. The result: the GPI rose from the 1950s through the early 1970s but has fallen since and today is still below its level in 1973.
   a. In your opinion, does gross national product per capita or the Genuine Progress Indicator provide a better measure of economic progress?
   b. Why? (Radical)

Web Questions

1. Find GDP for the most recent quarter from the home page of the Bureau of Economic Analysis at www.bea.gov.
   a. What were consumption, investment, government consumption and investment, and net exports?
   b. What was nominal GDP? Real GDP?
   c. By how much did GDP increase? How much of the increase was due to an increase in the aggregate price level?
   d. Which of the components listed in *a* contributed the most to the change in GDP? Did any of the components move in opposite directions?

2. Some economists have proposed that we use the genuine progress indicator (GPI) rather than GDP as an indication of economic well-being. Using the information you find at the home page of Redefining Progress at www.redefiningprogress.org, answer the following questions:
   a. What is one category included in the GPI that suggests that GDP understates economic well-being?

   b. Name four categories included in the GPI that suggest that GDP overstates economic well-being. What is the largest of these categories?
   c. Has the GPI gone up or down during the most recent year for which there are data? What happened to GDP during that year?

3. One can get some idea about outsourcing and insourcing from the national income accounts. You can find the national income and product accounts online at www.bea.gov. (Look specifically at Table 4.2.6 of the NIPAs.)
   a. What specific expenditures component of the NIPA accounts is most relevant to outsourcing?
   b. What is the annual percent change in this component over the past five years?
   c. Answer *a* and *b* for insourcing.
   d. Compare what you have found about insourcing and outsourcing.

Answers to Margin Questions

1. GDP is the sum of consumption, investment, and government spending plus the total of exports minus imports, in this case 95. (158)

2. Wealth accounts measure stocks—a country's assets and liabilities at a point in time. Income accounts measure flows—a country's income and expenditures over a period of time. (159)

3. Only the value added by the sale would be added to GDP. In this case, the value added is the difference between the purchase price and the sale price, or $500. (161)

4. The government budget includes transfer payments, which are not included in GDP. Only those government expenditures that are for goods and services are included in GDP. (162)

5. GDP measures the output of the residents of a country—the output within its geographical borders. GNP measures the output of the citizens and businesses of a country. Kuwait is a very rich country whose residents have a high income, much of it from investments overseas. Thus, their GNP will be high. However, Kuwait also has large numbers of foreign workers who are not citizens and whose incomes would be included in GDP but not in GNP. In reality, Kuwait citizens' and businesses' foreign income exceeds foreign workers' and foreign companies' income within Kuwait, so Kuwait's GNP is greater than its GDP. (164)

6. Aggregate income is the sum of employee compensation, rents, interest, and profits, in this case 198. (165)

7. In developing countries, individuals often grow their own food and take part in many activities that are not measured by the GDP statistics. The income figures that one gets from the GDP statistics of developing countries do not include such activities and, thus, can be quite misleading. (167)

8. Nominal income must have risen $400 billion to slightly over $4.6 trillion so that, when it is adjusted for inflation, the real income will have risen to $4.2 trillion. (168)

9. Measurement errors occur in adjusting GDP figures for inflation because measuring inflation involves numerous arbitrary decisions such as choosing a base year, adjusting for quality changes in products, and weighting prices. (169)

10. Dividing goods into consumption and investment does not always capture the effect of the spending on productive capacity. For example, housing "investment" does little to expand the productive capacity. However, "consumption" of computers or books could expand the productive capacity significantly. (171)

8 Growth, Productivity, and the Wealth of Nations

Queen Elizabeth owned silk stockings. The capitalist achievement does not typically consist in providing more silk stockings for queens but in bringing them within the reach of factory girls in return for steadily decreasing amounts of effort.

—*Joseph Schumpeter*

AFTER READING THIS CHAPTER, YOU SHOULD BE ABLE TO:

1. Define growth and relate it to living standards.
2. List five important sources of growth.
3. Distinguish diminishing marginal productivity from decreasing returns to scale.
4. Explain the convergence hypothesis and list four reasons why it has not taken place.
5. Distinguish Classical growth theory from new growth theory.

Growth matters. In the long run, growth matters a lot. For example, if current growth rates continue, in 50 years China's economy will be larger than the U.S. economy. Given the importance of growth, it is not surprising that modern economics began with a study of growth. In *The Wealth of Nations*, Adam Smith noted that what was good about market economies was that they raised society's standard of living. He argued that people's natural tendency to exchange and specialize was the driving force behind growth. Specialization and trade, and the investment and capital that made these possible, were responsible for the wealth of nations.

As we discussed in an earlier chapter, through the 1920s, long-run growth remained an important focus of economics. Then, in the 1930s, the world economy fell into a serious depression. It was at that time that modern macroeconomics developed as a separate subject with a significant focus on short-run business cycles. It asked the questions "What causes depressions?" and "How does an economy get out of one?" Short-run macroeconomics became known as Keynesian economics, and remained the standard macroeconomics through the 1960s. Keynesian economics focuses on fluctuations around the growth trend and on whether those fluctuations influence that trend.

In the 1970s, as the memories of the Great Depression faded, the pendulum started to swing back again towards a focus on long-run growth and now, at the start of the 21st century, macroeconomists are taking a more balanced position that includes both long-run growth and short-run business cycles as the core content of macro. In this chapter I consider long-run growth, and in later chapters, I examine business cycles and policies to deal with them.

General Observations about Growth

Let's begin our consideration with some general observations about growth.

Growth and the Economy's Potential Output

Long-run growth occurs when the economy produces more goods and services from existing production processes and resources. The study of growth is the study of why that increase comes about. In discussing growth economists use the term **potential output**—*the highest amount of output an economy can produce from existing production processes and resources.* Potential output conveys a sense of the growth that is possible. (Recall that *potential output* can also be called *potential income* because, in the aggregate, income and output are identical.) One way to think about growth and potential output is to relate them to the production possibility curve, presented in Chapter 2. That curve gave us a picture of the choices an economy faces given available resources. When an economy is at its potential output, it is operating on its production possibility curve. When an economy is below its potential output, it is operating inside its production possibility curve. The analysis of growth focuses on the forces that increase potential output; in other words, that shift out the production possibility curve.

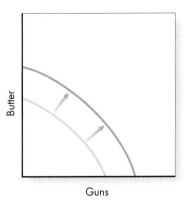

The analysis of growth focuses on forces that shift out the production possibility curve.

Why do we use potential output in macro rather than the production possibility curve? Because macro focuses on aggregate output—GDP—and does not focus on the choices of dividing up GDP among alternative products as does micro and the production possibility curve. But the concept is the same. Potential output is a barrier beyond which an economy cannot expand without either increasing available factors of production or increasing **productivity** (*output per unit of input*).

Long-run growth analysis focuses on supply; it assumes demand is sufficient to buy whatever is supplied. That assumption is called **Say's law** (*supply creates its own demand*), named after a French economist, Jean Baptiste Say, who first pointed it out. The reasoning behind Say's law is as follows: People work and supply goods to the market because they want other goods. The very fact that they supply goods means that they demand goods of equal value. According to Say's law, aggregate demand will always equal aggregate supply.

Q₁ How does long-run growth analysis justify its focus on supply?

In the short run, economists consider potential output fixed; they focus on how to get the economy operating at its potential if, for some reason, it is not. In the long run, economists consider an economy's potential output changeable. Growth analysis is a consideration of why an economy's potential shifts out, and growth policy is aimed at increasing an economy's potential output.

The Importance of Growth for Living Standards

In 2004, Nobel Prize winner Robert Lucas wrote, "Of the tendencies that are harmful to sound economics, the most seductive, and in my opinion most poisonous, is to focus on questions of distribution . . . The potential for improving the lives of poor people by finding different ways of distributing current production is *nothing* [his italics] compared to the apparently limitless potential of increasing production." For Lucas, and many other economists, growth, not distribution or business cycles, is the most important macroeconomic issue.

Growth in income improves lives by fulfilling basic needs and making more goods available to more people.

All economists agree that growth makes an enormous difference for living standards. Take France and Argentina as examples. In the 1950s, per capita income was about $5,000 in each country, but their growth rates differed. From 1950 to 2006, France's income grew at an average rate of 3 percent per year while Argentina's grew at an average rate of 1.6 percent per year. Because of the differences in growth rates, France's per capita income is now about $30,100 and Argentina's per capita income is about $15,000. The difference in income levels translates into very real differences in the quality of life. For example, in France 100 percent of the people have access to safe

Is Growth Good?

The discussion in the chapter emphasizes the generally held view among economists that growth is inherently good. It increases our incomes, thereby improving our standard of living. But that does not mean that all economists support unlimited growth. Growth has costs, and economics requires us to look at both costs and benefits. For example, growth may contribute to increased pollution—reducing the quality of the air we breathe and the water we drink, and endangering the variety of species in the world. In short, the wrong type of growth may produce undesirable side effects including global warming and polluted rivers, land, and air.

New technology, upon which growth depends, also raises serious moral questions: Do we want to replace sexual reproduction with cloning? Will a brain implant be an improvement over 12 years of education? Will selecting your baby's genetic makeup be better than relying on nature? Just because growth *can* continue does not mean that it *should* continue. Moral judgments can be made against growth. For example, some argue that growth changes traditional cultures with beautiful handiwork, music, and dance into cultures of gadgets where people have lost touch with what is important. They argue that we have enough gadgets cluttering our lives and that it is time to start focusing on noneconomic priorities.

This moral argument against growth carries the most weight in highly developed countries—countries with per capita incomes of at least $20,000 a year. For developing countries, where per capita income can be as low as $150 per year, the reality is the choice between growth or poverty or even between growth or starvation. In these countries it is difficult to argue against growth.

One final comment: The benefits of growth do not have to be just higher incomes and more gadgets. They could also include more leisure activities and improved working conditions. In the 19th century, a 12-hour workday was common. Today the workday is eight hours, but had we been content with a lower income, the workday could now be two hours, with the remainder left for free time. We'd have less growth in GDP, but we'd have a lot more time to play.

water; in Argentina 90 percent have such access. France has 414 computers per 1,000 people; Argentina has 94 computers per 1,000 people.

Other examples are South Korea and the Congo. In the 1950s, their incomes were also nearly identical, at $150 per person. Because of differing growth rates, Korea's per capita income has multiplied about 80 times, to about $12,000, while the Congo's per capita income is still $150. Why? Because the Congo has a zero growth rate while Korea has averaged an 8 percent annual growth rate. The moral of these stories: In the long run, growth rates matter a lot.

Small differences in growth rates can mean huge differences in income levels because of *compounding*. Compounding means that growth is based not only on the original level of income but also on the accumulation of previous-year increases in income. For example, say you start with $10,000. At a 7 percent interest rate that $10,000 after 10 years will be more than $20,000; after 20 years it will be more than $40,000; after 30 years it will be more than $80,000; and after 50 years it will be more than $320,000. So if you are worried about your retirement, it pays to start saving early at as high an interest rate as you can get. The longer you save, and the higher the interest rate you receive, the more you end up with.

Another way to see the effects of the difference in growth rates is to see how long it would take income to double at different growth rates. The Rule of 72 tells you that. The **Rule of 72** states: *The number of years it takes for a certain amount to double in value is equal to 72 divided by its annual rate of increase.* For example, if Argentina's income grows at a 1 percent annual rate, it will double in 72 years (72/1). If France's income grows at a 3 percent annual rate, it will double in only 24 years (72/3).

Q.2 If an economy is growing at 4 percent a year, how long will it take for its income to double?

$$\frac{72}{(\text{Rate of Growth})} = \text{number of years to double}$$

Let's conclude our discussion by applying the Rule of 72 to the future growth of China and the United States and the comparison with which we started the chapter. Let's say that the current U.S. per capita income is $40,000 and that U.S. per capita income grows 1 percent per year; that means its per capita income will double every 72 years, so in 72 years its income will be $80,000 per capita. Let's say that China's income is $2,000 per capita, but that it grows at 9 percent per year, which means that it doubles every 8 years. If that actually happens, within 40 years per capita income in China will surpass that in the United States and after 8 more years will be significantly higher at $128,000 per capita. While such extrapolations are precarious, and it is highly unlikely that such different growth rates will continue, even a partial movement in that direction will involve significant changes in the world economic and political structure. That's why differential growth rates are so important.

Markets, Specialization, and Growth

Growth began when markets developed, and then, as markets expanded, growth accelerated. Why are markets so important to growth? To answer that question, let's go back to Adam Smith's argument for markets. Smith argued that markets allow **specialization** (*the concentration of individuals on certain aspects of production*) and **division of labor** (*the splitting up of a task to allow for specialization of production*). According to Smith, markets create an interdependent economy in which individuals can take advantage of the benefits of specialization and trade for their other needs. In doing so, markets increase productivity—and, in turn, improve the standard of living.

> Specialization and the division of labor that accompany markets increase productivity and growth.

You saw in Chapter 2 how comparative advantage and specialization increase productivity. If individuals concentrate on the production of goods for which their skills and other resources are suited, and trade for those goods for which they do not have a comparative advantage, everyone can end up with more of all goods. To see this even more clearly, consider what your life would be like without markets, trade, and specialization. You would have to grow all your food, build your own living space, and provide all your own transportation. Simply to exist under these conditions, you'd need a lot of skills, and it is unlikely that you'd become sufficiently adept in any one of them to provide yourself with anything other than the basics. You'd have all you can do to keep up.

Now consider your life today with specialization. Someone who specializes in dairy farming produces the milk you need. You don't need to know how it is produced, just where to buy it. How about transportation? You buy, not build, your car. It runs somehow—you're not quite sure how—but if it breaks down, you take it to a garage. And consider your education: Are you learning how to grow food or build a house? No, you are probably learning a specific skill that has little relevance to the production of most goods. But you'll most likely provide some good or service that will benefit the dairy farmer and auto mechanic. You get the picture—for most of the things you consume, you don't have the faintest idea who makes them or how they are made, nor do you need to know.

Economic Growth, Distribution, and Markets

Markets and growth are often seen as unfair with regard to the distribution of income. Is it fair that markets give some individuals so much (billions to Bill Gates), and others so little ($7.00 an hour to Joe Wall, who has a minimum wage job and two kids)? Such questions are legitimate and need to be asked. But in answering them we should

FIGURE 8-1   **Cost of Goods in Hours of Work**

Growth in the U.S. economy in the past century has reduced the number of hours the average person needs to work to buy consumer goods.

Source: Federal Reserve Bank of Dallas, *Time Well Spent* (1997 annual report). Updated by author.

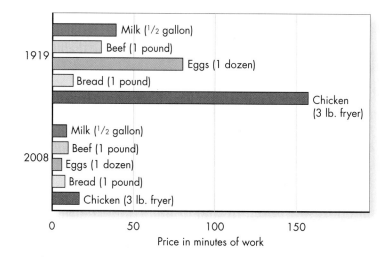

Even though growth isn't evenly distributed, it generally raises the incomes of the poor.

also remember the quotation from Joseph Schumpeter that opened this chapter: Even if markets and growth do not provide equality, they tend to make everyone, even the poor, better off. The relevant question is: Would the poor be better off with or without markets and growth?

There are strong arguments, based on historical evidence, that people are better off with markets. Consider the number of hours an average person must work to buy certain goods at various periods in U.S. history. A century ago it took a worker 1 hour and 41 minutes to earn enough to buy a pair of stockings; today it takes only 18 minutes of work. Figure 8-1 gives a number of other examples. As you can see from the figure, growth has made average workers significantly better off; to get the same amount, they have to work far less now than they did in the past. Growth also has made new products available. For example, before 1952 air conditioners were not available at any price.

The reality is that, judged from an *absolute* standard, the poor benefit enormously from the growth that markets foster. Markets, through competition, make the factors of production more productive and lower the cost of goods so that more goods are available to everyone. Today, the U.S. poverty level for a family of four is about $20,000. If we go back 100 years in U.S. history, and adjust for inflation, that $20,000 income would put a family in the upper middle class. Markets and growth have made that possible.

Just because the poor benefit from growth does not mean they might not be better off if income were distributed more in their favor.

The above argument does not mean that the poor always benefit from growth; many of us judge our well-being by relative, not absolute, standards. Growth often reduces the share of income earned by the poorest proportion of society, making the poor *relatively* worse off. So, if one uses relative standards, one could say that the poor have become worse off over certain periods. Moreover, it is not at all clear that markets require the large differentials in pay that have accompanied growth in market economies. If such large differentials did not exist, and growth had been at the same rate, the poor would be even better off than they are.

Per Capita Growth

When thinking about growth, it is important to distinguish between increases in total output and increases in per capita output, or total output divided by the total population. If there is **per capita growth,** the country is *producing more goods and* *services per person.* For example, say the real output of the economy is $4 billion and there are 1 million people. Each person, on average, has $4,000 to spend. Now say that output increases by 50 percent but that population also increases by 50 percent. In this case *output* has grown but *per capita output* has not; each person still has only $4,000 to spend. A number of countries have found themselves in such situations. Of the approximately 130 countries whose economies grew from 1990 to 2007, in about 10, the population grew even faster so that their per capita incomes fell. Take Kenya as an example. Its economy grew at an annual rate of 2.2 percent, but its population grew at a higher 2.5 percent annual rate, meaning that per capita income fell an average 0.3 percent each year over 14 years. Over this same time period, the U.S. economy grew an average 3.5 percent a year, but its population grew only 1.2 percent a year so that, on average, per capita income grew 2.3 percent a year.

If you know the percentage change in output and percentage change in population, you can approximate per capita growth:

Per capita growth = % change in output − % change in population

Let's consider two examples. In 2005, the French economy grew 1.4 percent but the population grew 0.4 percent. Per capita growth equaled 1 percent (1.4 − .4). In that same year in Guinea, output rose 2.0 percent and the population rose 2.4 percent. Per capita growth fell 0.4 percent (2.0 − 2.4).

Here are some additional examples showing per capita growth, real growth, and population growth for various countries in 2006:

Q.3 Which country has experienced higher growth per capita: country A, whose economy is growing at a 4 percent rate and whose population is growing at a 3 percent rate, or country B, whose economy is growing at a 3 percent rate and whose population is growing at a 1 percent rate?

Country	Per capita GDP growth	=	Real GDP growth	−	Population growth
Canada	1.9		2.8		0.9
Denmark	2.7		3.0		0.3
Russia	7.0		6.6		−0.4
Thailand	4.1		4.8		0.7
Sudan	7.0		9.6		2.6
Venezuela	7.4		8.8		1.4

Source: *CIA World Factbook*, 2007.

Some economists have argued that per capita income is not what we should be focusing on; they suggest that it would be better to look at median income. (Remember, income and output are the same.) Per capita income measures the average, or *mean*, income. The *median* income, in contrast, is the income level that divides the population in equal halves. Half the people earn more and half the people earn less than the median income. In 2005, median income per household in the United States was $46,326. Half of all households earned less than $46,326, and half earned more.

Why focus on median income? Because it partially takes into account how income is distributed. If the growth in income goes to a small minority of individuals who already receive the majority of income, the mean will rise but the median will not. Let's consider an example where there is a large difference between the two measures. Say that the incomes of five people in a five-person economy are $20,000; $20,000; $30,000; $120,000; and $450,000. The median income is $30,000 (the middle income with two above and two below); the mean income is $128,000. Now say that the economy grows but that the two richest people get all the benefits, raising their incomes to $150,000 and $500,000, respectively. The median income remains $30,000; the mean income

Q.4 How would increases in income have to be distributed for the median to remain constant and the mean income to rise?

rises to $144,000. Unfortunately, statistics on median income are often not collected, so I will follow convention and focus on the mean, or per capita, income.

Whether you're looking at per capita or median income, growth provides more goods and services for the people in an economy, allowing society to sidestep the more difficult issues of how those goods are distributed. That's why policy makers are interested in knowing what makes an economy grow.

The Sources of Growth

Economists generally single out five important sources of growth:

1. Growth-compatible institutions.
2. Capital accumulation—investment in productive capacity.
3. Available resources.
4. Technological development.
5. Entrepreneurship.

Let's consider each in turn.

Growth-Compatible Institutions

Throughout this book I have emphasized the importance of economic institutions and that having the right institutions is vitally necessary for growth. Consider China. Up until 1980 it grew at an average annual rate of 3 percent. After 1980, when it changed its institutional structure from a command-and-control to a more market-oriented economy, it started its rapid growth of 8.5 percent per year. Growth-compatible institutions—institutions that foster growth—must have incentives built into them that lead people to put forth effort and discourage people from spending a lot of their time in leisure pursuits or creating impediments for others to gain income for themselves.

When individuals get much of the gains of growth themselves, they have incentives to work harder. That's why markets and private ownership of property play an important role in growth. In the former Soviet Union, individuals didn't gain much from their own initiative and, hence, often spent their time in pursuits other than those that would foster measured economic growth. Another growth-compatible institution is the corporation, a legal institution that gives owners limited liability and thereby encourages large enterprises (because people are more willing to invest their savings when their potential losses are limited).

Some developing countries follow a type of mercantilist policy in which government must approve any new economic activity. Some government officials get a large portion of their income from bribes offered to them by individuals who want to undertake economic activity. Such policies inhibit economic growth. Many regulations, even reasonable ones, also tend to inhibit economic growth because they inhibit entrepreneurial activities.

Peruvian economist Hernando DeSoto has given some vivid examples of how the lack of formal property rights limits development. He points out that because of regulations it takes an average of 500 working days to legalize a bakery in Cairo. He has many similar examples. Excessive regulations combined with bribery and corruption are important reasons why people don't legalize their businesses. In some ways, whether a business is legal or not is not of concern: both legal and illegal businesses provide goods. But legality impacts growth; illegal or semi-legal businesses must stay small to remain below the government's radar, and because the owners have no property rights, they do not have access to business loans to grow. Similarly, squatters only informally own their residence; their lack of formal ownership is a barrier to getting loans to improve their

Q5 Why is private property a source of growth?

Informal property rights limit borrowing of the poor, and hence limit growth.

living space, which keeps them in the vicious cycle of poverty. DeSoto points out that the poor have informal control of trillions of dollars of assets but can't get loans on those assets to advance their economic futures in the normal market economy. The lack of property rights and the regulations doom the poor to remain in poverty.

The above argument is not an argument against all regulation; some regulation is necessary to ensure that growth is of a socially desirable type. The policy problem is in deciding between necessary and unnecessary regulation.

Investment and Accumulated Capital

A second important source of growth is capital and investment. In *Nickled and Dimed: On (Not) Getting By in America*, Barbara Ehrenreich explores how minimum wage workers manage to scrape by. What they don't have time or income for is saving—putting together a nest egg to invest. Lacking savings, they often remained mired in poverty, just scraping by. The same argument holds for society as a whole; societies that can't afford to save will not grow either. Investment is absolutely necessary for growth. Somehow, the society as a whole has to manage to save (forgo consumption) if it wants to grow.

Some economists even argue that it is the savers, not the "givers," who are the beneficent people. University of Rochester economist Steven Landsbury makes the argument most explicitly. He argues that misers—the people who could deplete the world's resources but choose not to—are the true philanthropists. He writes that "nobody is more generous than the miser" and that when Scrooge gave up his miserly ways, the world was worse off, not better off. (As with all such provocative statements, the issues are complicated, and there is a deeper question about the justness of the institutional structure and whether that institutional structure could be changed to channel more income to the "nickled and dimed" while maintaining the level of saving. But those issues quickly go beyond the principles levels.)

Actually, it isn't saving that is important for growth; it's investment, and, for saving to be helpful, some method of translating saving into investment must exist in the society. Financial markets provide a method, which is why financial markets are an important aspect of macro. The role of financial markets in transferring savings into investment is captured in the loanable funds market shown in Figure 8-2.

FIGURE 8-2 (A AND B)   The Loanable Funds Market

Savings is the supply of loanable funds; it is an upward sloping curve. Investment is the demand for loanable funds; it is a downward sloping curve. The interest rate equilibrates the supply and demand for loanable funds. When the supply of loanable funds (savings) increases as shown in **(b)** the interest rate falls from i_0 to i_1, and the quantity of loanable funds demanded (investment) increases from I_0 to I_1.

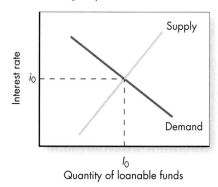
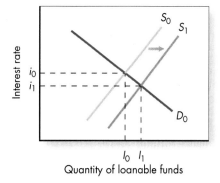

Q.6 If the demand for loanable funds increases, what will likely happen to the interest rate?

Savings is the supply of loanable funds; it is an upward-sloping curve because, as the interest rate rises, more people are willing to save more. Investment is the demand for loanable funds; it is a downward-sloping curve because, as the interest rate falls, it pays businesses to borrow more and invest more. Notice in this market that the interest rate—the rate paid to borrow savings—is key; it equilibrates the supply and demand for loanable funds. When the supply of loanable funds (savings) increases, as shown in Figure 8-2(b), the interest rate falls from i_0 to i_1, and the quantity of loanable funds demanded (investment) increases from I_0 to I_1. Thus, societies interested in growth look carefully at the interest rate in the economy. (The interest rate that is important to this market is the real interest rate—the nominal interest rate minus the rate of inflation. This distinction will be discussed in depth below.)

Fifty years ago, capital accumulation (where capital was thought of as just *physical capital*) and investment were seen as the key elements in growth. Physical capital includes both private capital—buildings and machines available for production—and public capital—infrastructure such as highways and water supply. The *flow* of investment leads to the growth of the *stock* of capital. While physical capital is still considered a key element in growth, it is now generally recognized that the growth recipe is far more complicated. One of the reasons physical capital accumulation has been de-emphasized is that empirical evidence has suggested that capital accumulation doesn't necessarily lead to growth. For instance, the former Soviet Union invested a lot and accumulated lots of capital goods, but its economy didn't grow much because its capital was often internationally obsolete. Another reason is that products change, and buildings and machines useful in one time period may be useless in another (e.g., a six-year-old computer often is worthless). The value of the capital stock depends on its future expected earnings, which are very uncertain. Capital's role in growth is extraordinarily difficult to measure with accuracy.

A third reason for this de-emphasis on capital accumulation is that it has become clear that capital includes much more than machines. In addition to physical capital, modern economics includes **human capital** (*the skills that are embodied in workers through experience, education, and on-the-job training, or, more simply, people's knowledge*) and **social capital** (*the habitual way of doing things that guides people in how they approach production*) as types of capital. The importance of human capital is obvious: A skilled labor force is far more productive than an unskilled labor force. Social capital is embodied in institutions such as the government, the legal system, and the fabric of society. In a way, anything that contributes to growth can be called a type of capital, and anything that slows growth can be called a destroyer of capital. With the concept of capital including such a wide range of things, it is difficult to say what is not capital, which makes the concept of capital less useful.

Despite this modern de-emphasis on investment and physical capital, all economists agree that the right kind of investment at the right time is a central element of growth. If an economy is to grow, it must invest. The debate is about what kinds and what times are the right ones.

There are three types of capital:
1. Physical capital.
2. Social capital.
3. Human capital.

Available Resources

If an economy is to grow, it will need resources. England grew in the late 1700s because it had iron and coal; the United States grew in the 20th century because it had a major supply of many natural resources, and it imported people, a resource it needed.

Of course, you have to be careful in thinking about what is considered a resource. A resource in one time period may not be a resource in another. For example, at one time oil was simply black gooey stuff that made land unusable. When people learned that the black gooey stuff could be burned as fuel, oil became a resource. What's considered a resource depends on technology. If solar technology is ever perfected, oil will go back to being black gooey stuff. So creativity can replace resources, and if you develop new technology fast enough, you can overcome almost any lack of existing resources. Even if a country doesn't have the physical resources it needs for growth, it can import them—as did Japan following World War II.

The enormous growth of China has involved an increase in the demand for physical resources such as oil, iron ore, and copper—throughout the world. This has led both the United States and China to work toward securing continued access to sufficient physical resources in the future. China, in particular, is making deals with Latin American and African countries to lend them money with the proviso that they provide natural resources to China in the future.

Greater participation in the market is another means by which to increase available resources. In China at the end of the 20th century, for example, many individuals migrated into the southern provinces, which have free trade sectors. Before they migrated they were only marginally involved in the market economy. After they migrated they became employed in the market economy. This increased the labor available to the market, helping push up China's growth rate. In the United States beginning in the 1950s, the percentage of women entering the workforce increased, contributing to economic growth.

Increasing the labor force participation rate is not a totally costless way of increasing growth. We lose whatever people were doing before they joined the labor force (which was, presumably, something of value to society). Our aggregate income accounting figures, which are measures of market activity, simply do not measure such losses.

> What is a resource depends on the production processes of an economy and technology.

Technological Development

Advances in technology shift the production possibility curve out by making workers more productive. Technological advances increase their ability to produce more of the things they already produce but also allow them to produce new and different products. While in some ways growth involves more of the same, a much larger aspect of growth involves changes in **technology**—*the way we make goods and supply services*—and changes in the goods and services we buy. Think of what this generation buys—music downloads, cell phones, cars, computers, fast food—and compare that to what the preceding generation bought—LP records, cars that would now be considered obsolete, and tube and transistor radios. (When I was 11, I saved $30—the equivalent of over $100 now—so I could afford a six-transistor Motorola radio; personal computers didn't exist.)

Contrast today's goods with the goods the next generation might have available: video brain implants (little gadgets in your head to receive sound and full-vision broadcasts—you simply close your eyes and tune in whatever you want, if you've paid your cellular fee for that month); fuel-cell-powered cars (gas cars will be considered quaint but polluting); and instant food (little pills that fulfill all your nutritional needs, letting your video brain implant supply all the ambiance). Just imagine! You probably can get the picture, even without a video brain implant.

How does society get people to work on developments that may change the very nature of what we do and how we think? One way is through economic incentives; another is with institutions that foster creativity and bold thinking—such as this book; a third is through institutions that foster hard work. There are, of course, trade-offs. For example, the Japanese educational system, which fosters hard work and discipline, doesn't do as good a job at fostering creativity as the U.S. educational system, and vice versa.

Important advances in biotechnology, computers, and communications initially developed in the United States, and those developments helped fuel U.S. growth. Those new industries were much slower to develop in another important U.S. competitor, the

> Growth isn't just getting more of the same thing. It's also getting some things that are different.

> Five sources of growth are
> 1. Growth-compatible institutions.
> 2. Capital accumulation.
> 3. Available resources.
> 4. Technological development.
> 5. Entrepreneurship.

Growth and Terrorism

When talking about the costs of terrorism, many focus on the short-term effects—the tremendous cost in destruction of property and loss of life. But, according to a study by the Organization for Economic Coordination and Development, there are also long-term effects on growth, which may be less dramatic but even more costly. The study points out that the reaction to the terrorist attack of September 11, 2001,

9/11

- Caused significant increases in insurance premiums, increasing costs and making firms less likely to undertake new projects.

- Made it impossible to get insurance for a number of projects, stopping these projects altogether.

- Increased transportation costs because of increased security.

- Slowed international trade because of security, making it impossible to get goods when they were needed, forcing firms to hold more inventory and increasing costs.

- Caused firms to spend more on security, lowering productivity.

Each of these effects contributed to slower growth by reducing the sources of growth. The terrorist attacks acted like sand in the wheels of trade, reduced expenditures on capital, lowered productivity, and reduced start-ups by entrepreneurs. The end result was hundreds of billions of dollars of lost output. The cost will be especially great for many Islamic countries, making it difficult for these countries to tie into the global economy.

European Union, which is one important reason why EU countries have grown far more slowly than has the United States in recent years.

Entrepreneurship

Entrepreneurship is the ability to get things done. That ability involves creativity, vision, willingness to accept risk, and a talent for translating that vision into reality. Entrepreneurs have been central to growth in the United States. They have created large companies, produced new products, and transformed the landscape of the economy. Examples of entrepreneurs include Thomas Edison, who revolutionized the generation and use of electricity in the late 1800s; Henry Ford, who revolutionized transportation in the early 1900s; and Bill Gates, who led Microsoft as it transformed and dominated the computer industry. When a country's population demonstrates entrepreneurship, it can overcome deficiencies in other ingredients that contribute to growth.

Turning the Sources of Growth into Growth

The five sources of growth cannot be taken as givens. Even if a country has all five ingredients, it may not have them in the right proportions. For instance, when Nicolas Appert discovered canning (storing food in a sealed container in such a way that it wouldn't spoil) in the early 19th century, the economic possibilities of society expanded enormously. But if, when the technological developments occurred, the savings at the time were not sufficient to finance the investment, the result would not have been growth. It is finding the right combination of the sources of growth that plays a central role in the growth of any economy.

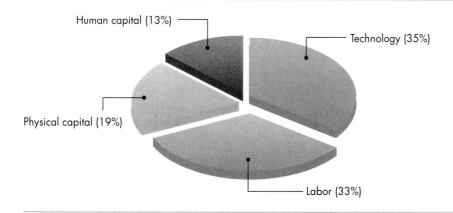

FIGURE 8-3 **Sources of Real U.S. GDP Growth**

Technology accounts for the majority of growth in the United States, followed closely by increases in labor.

Source: Edward E. Denison, *Trends in Economic Growth, 1928–82* (Washington, DC: The Brookings Institution, 1985), and author estimates.

Empirical Estimates of Factor Contribution to Growth

To determine the relative importance of the various causes of growth, economist Edward Denison empirically estimated the importance of each of the sources of growth for many countries, including the United States. These estimates, shown in Figure 8-3, suggest that increases in labor account for 33 percent, increases in physical capital account for 19 percent, increases in human capital account for 13 percent, and advances in technology account for the remaining 35 percent of growth. (Land does not appear in Denison's estimates; countries are assumed to be endowed with a given amount of land and natural resources.) While the specific percentages are at best rough, the importance of technology to growth is not. It is for that reason that modern economic thinking about growth has focused more and more on technology.

The Production Function and Theories of Growth

To try to get a better handle on the sources of growth, economists have developed a number of theories of growth. These have centered around the **production function,** an abstraction that shows *the relationship between the quantity of inputs used in production and the quantity of output resulting from production.* The production function we shall use is the following:

$$\text{Output} = A \cdot f(\text{Labor, Capital, Land})$$

This production function has land, labor, and capital as factors of production, and an adjustment factor A to capture the effect of changes in technology. The adjustment factor is outside the production function since it can affect the production of all factors. (The *f* stands for "function of.") The production function emphasizes the sources of growth: entrepreneurship is captured by labor, available resources by land, capital accumulation by capital, and technology and institutions by the production function itself and the adjustment factor, A.

Describing Production Functions

In talking about production functions, economists use a couple of important terms. The first describes what happens when all inputs increase equally—this is called *scale economies*. Scale economies describe what happens to output if all inputs increase by the same percentage. Say the amount of labor, land, and capital is doubled. What happens to output? If output also doubles, economists say that the production function exhibits

The production function shows the relationship between the quantity of inputs used in production and the quantity of output resulting from production.

Q-7 True or false? If you can increase production 10 percent by increasing all inputs 20 percent, the production process exhibits diminishing marginal productivity.

constant returns to scale, which means that *output will rise by the same proportionate increase as all inputs.* With constant returns to scale, if all inputs rise by, say, 10 percent, output also will rise by 10 percent. When *output rises by a greater proportionate increase than all inputs,* there are **increasing returns to scale;** and when *output rises by a smaller proportionate increase than all inputs,* there are **decreasing returns to scale.**

The second term describes what happens *when more of one input is added without increasing any other inputs.* This case follows the **law of diminishing marginal productivity** (*increasing one input, keeping all others constant, will lead to smaller and smaller gains in output*). The difference between decreasing returns to scale and diminishing marginal productivity is that decreasing returns to scale refers to what happens to output when *all* inputs increase by the same proportion. Diminishing marginal productivity refers to what happens to output when some inputs are increased, but the others are held constant. Generally, it is capital that is assumed fixed, and labor that is assumed variable. Returns to scale is a long-run concept—diminishing marginal productivity is a short-run concept.

The law of diminishing marginal productivity applies to increases in any input, holding the others constant. As you put more and more laborers on a fixed plot of land, the increase in output contributed by each additional worker falls; eventually workers will get in each other's way and not only will the output per worker decline, but so too will total output. The same goes for capital. The first computer will help a secretary prepare documents more quickly. A second might help, too, but less so than the first. A third would clutter the office.

The Standard Theory of Growth—the Classical Growth Model

Classical economists recognized that all the above factors contributed to growth, but (as mentioned earlier in this chapter) their models of growth focused on capital accumulation. The **Classical growth model** is *a model of growth that focuses on the role of capital accumulation in the growth process.* The Classical economists' major policy conclusion was: The more capital an economy has, the faster it will grow. This focus on capital is what caused market economies to be called *capitalist economies.*

Since investment leads to the increase in capital, Classical economists focused their analysis, and their policy advice, on how to increase investment. The way to do that was for people to save:

Saving, investment, and capital are central to the Classical growth model.

Saving → Investment → Increase in capital → Growth

According to the Classical growth model, if society wants its economy to grow, it has to save; the more saving, the better. Saving was good for both private individuals and governments. Thus, Classical economists objected to government deficits, which occur when government spends more than it collects in taxes. (This view of deficits and saving was directly challenged by Keynes in the 1930s, as we will see in the next chapter.)

Focus on Diminishing Marginal Productivity of Labor   The early economists also focused on the law of diminishing marginal productivity. In the 1800s, when farming was the major activity of the economy, economists such as Thomas Malthus emphasized the limitations land placed on growth. They predicted that since land was relatively fixed, as the population grew, diminishing marginal productivity would set in. Figure 8-4 shows a production function exhibiting diminishing marginal productivity.

Demand, Keynesian Economics, and Growth

The presentation in this chapter is the generally accepted analysis of growth. It focuses on the supply-side sources of growth. But because empirical relationships in growth are so difficult to discern, groups of economists raise a variety of different issues. One such group, which has its origins in Keynesian ideas, argues that demand and supply are so interrelated in macro that demand has to be considered as a source of growth. The argument goes as follows: Firms produce only if they expect there to be demand for their product. If they expect demand to be growing, they will try new projects and in the process will learn by doing and develop new technology. Both of these activities shift the production function out and thereby create growth. So while it looks like a supply-side issue, it is the demand side that leads the supply side: By increasing demand, one can increase long-run supply.

True, they argue, increasing aggregate demand is only a short-run phenomenon, but since the long run is simply a set of successive short runs, the short run influences the long-run path that the economy follows. They are not separable, and, under the right conditions, demand-side policies should be considered as one way to increase supply. As Abba Lerner, one of the early Keynesian advocates of this view, has put it, *"In the long run we are simply in another short run."*

Since each additional worker adds less output to production than the individual before, the production function is bowed downward. Output rises as the number of laborers increases, but it does not keep pace with increases in labor. Because of diminishing marginal productivity, per capita income declines as the labor supply increases. As output per person declines, at some point output available is no longer sufficient to feed everyone.

In Figure 8-4, the straight line, labeled *subsistence level of output*, shows the minimum amount of output necessary to feed the labor force L. For example, at L_1 output is Q_2 and the minimum level of income for subsistence is Q_1. There is a surplus of $Q_2 - Q_1$. At L^* output is at its subsistence level. There is no surplus. Beyond L^* income falls below subsistence. If the population grows beyond L^*, some people would starve to death and the population would decline. Classical economists argued that the economy would be driven to point L^* in the long run, because whenever there was a surplus of output, workers would have more children, increasing the labor supply. This belief, called the *iron law of wages*, combined with the diminishing marginal productivity led to

Q-8 If individuals suddenly needed less food to subsist, what would happen to labor and output, according to the Classical growth model?

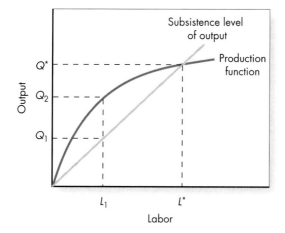

FIGURE 8-4 **Classical Growth Theory**

The classical theory of growth focused on diminishing marginal productivity of labor. Because of diminishing marginal productivity, per capita income declines as the labor supply increases, other inputs held constant. As output per person declines, at some point output available per person is no longer sufficient to feed the population.

the conclusion that in the long run there was no surplus and no growth. They called the long run the *stationary state*.

Focus on Diminishing Marginal Productivity of Capital   The Classical economists' predictions were wrong. Per capita output did not stagnate; it grew because of technological progress and increases in capital. Increases in technology and capital overwhelmed the law of diminishing marginal productivity and eventually economists no longer saw land as a constraint. Modern economists, such as Robert Solow, then changed the focus of the law of diminishing marginal productivity from land to capital. They argued that as capital grew faster than labor, capital would become less productive and lead to slower and slower growth; eventually the per capita growth of our economy would stagnate. The economy could still grow if labor increased at the same rate as capital, but output would not grow any faster than the growth of the population. That is, per capita income would not grow.

The Convergence Debate

The Classical growth model also has strong implications about the future growth of the U.S. economy. It leads to the **convergence hypothesis**—*the hypothesis that per capita income in countries with similar institutional structures will gravitate toward the same level of income per person.* As countries get more capital and become richer, their growth rates would slow down. Thus, poorer countries with little capital (such as the Latin American countries) should grow faster than richer countries with lots of capital (such as the United States). Why? Because diminishing marginal productivity would be stronger for richer countries with lots of capital than for poorer countries with little capital. Eventually per capita incomes among countries should converge.

The convergence hypothesis suggests that because the United States currently has a higher per capita income, its economy should grow more slowly than the economies of developing countries with similar institutional structures. That's because the marginal product of capital is higher in the developing countries (which hence have lower costs of production), which leads to capital investment flows out of the United States and into developing countries. The argument for convergence is based on the law of one price introduced in Chapter 2: There will be pressure for equivalent factors of production, using equivalent capital and technology and operating in similar institutional structures, to be paid equally. If they are not, production will gravitate toward those countries with lower factor prices. The outsourcing of production to countries such as China and India is an example of the forces generated by the law of one price. If the convergence hypothesis is correct, these countries will continue growing faster than will the United States over the coming decades.

These predictions of convergence have not come true as of the early 2000s for many countries. As we saw in an earlier chapter, growth rates have increased, not decreased, in the United States, and relative income levels of rich and poor countries have in many cases diverged, not converged. This difference between the observed reality and the predictions of the model caused economists to study the growth process empirically. Why doesn't the theory match the reality?

Economists have a number of explanations why convergence has not taken place, including lack of mobility of the factors of production, differing institutional structure, incomparable factors of production, and what are called technological agglomeration effects. Let's briefly consider each.

Lack of Factor Mobility   The speed of convergence depends on factor and technological mobility. It is the transfer of capital and technology that causes convergence.

Technological progress and increases in capital have overwhelmed diminishing marginal productivity of labor.

The convergence hypothesis states that per capita income in countries with similar institutional structures will gravitate toward the same level of income per person.

Q₉ Why would an economist likely predict that India and China will grow faster than the United States in the next decade?

These transfers occur because firms have an incentive to shift production of goods—say toys—to lower-cost countries such as China. As production facilities move, capital and technological know-how will shift from the United States to China. If, however, there are either perceived or real barriers to factor mobility—say China limits foreign ownership of domestically based firms—convergence will be slowed down.

Differing Institutional Structure   The convergence hypothesis is relevant to countries with similar institutional structures. The more similar the institutional structures, the more likely it is that convergence will take place because firms are likely to move production to countries whose institutions are well-suited for the businesses' practices and culture. That's why Europe and Japan caught up quickly with the United States after World War II; they all had democratic governments, market-based economies, and stable political structures. These general institutional characteristics that are compatible sometimes go under the name *social capital*.

Web Note 8.1
Social Capital

The debate about whether the economies of China and the United States are likely to converge is in large part due to the ambiguity about what are similar or equivalent institutional structures. China has recently adopted market-based institutions, but these are still new, and the political structure in China is not democratic; it remains under Communist party control. Is the Chinese institutional structure sufficiently similar to ours to fit the convergence hypothesis? Views on this differ, and hence views on how much convergence we can expect also differ.

Incomparable Factors of Production   On the surface, the terms in the production function seem relatively straightforward, but in reality they involve enormous ambiguity. I will focus on one important ambiguity—precisely what we mean by *labor*. As an input in production, labor may seem rather simple—it is the number of hours worked. As a first approximation, that is what economists use as their measure of labor input. But labor is much more than that. The measure of labor needs to be adjusted to capture the skills, education, experience, and effort that laborers bring to production. These adjustments make measuring labor, and comparing the measurements among different countries, difficult.

Here's an example of the type of problem that develops: About the same number of people live in Bangladesh as in Japan, but the average worker in Japan has more education than the average worker in Bangladesh. Do we increase the labor measured in Japan to account for this difference? Generally, economists do so by separating labor into two components: standard labor (the actual number of workers or hours worked) and human capital (the skills that are embodied in workers through experience, education, and on-the-job training). Human capital gives us a measure for comparing the relative productivity of different workers. Thus, for example, when a society's workers become more educated, the country's human capital increases, even though labor hours may not increase.

Notice how modifying the definition of *labor* to emphasize human capital provides a possible answer for the Classical growth model's incorrect predictions. If labor skills can be continually increasing, there is no need for physical capital to exhibit diminishing marginal productivity. The labor force might be growing at 5 percent, and capital at 7 percent, but the human capital measure of labor also may be increasing at 2 percent, so no diminishing marginal productivity should be expected and per capita output will rise. A variation of this argument can be used to explain why incomes between poor and rich countries have not converged. If skills in rich countries are increasing at a faster rate than skills in poor countries, incomes would not be expected to converge.

Increases in human capital have allowed labor to keep pace with capital, allowing economies to avoid the diminishing productivity of capital.

Technological Agglomeration Effects   An additional explanation for the failure of the Classical growth model to accurately predict our growth experience and the lack

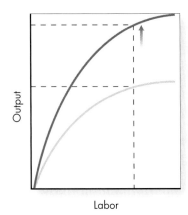

Technological growth shifts the production function up and the production possibility curve out.

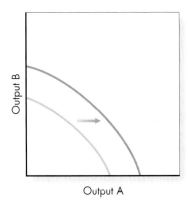

New growth theory emphasizes technology as the primary source of growth.

Web Note 8.2
A New Growth Theorist

of convergence is **technological agglomeration**—*the geographic concentration of technological advances caused by the tendency of innovations to lead to further innovations in that industry and other industries.* Technology has developed, and is growing, faster in rich countries than in poor countries. If technology grows, it increases the productivity of all inputs and allows growth to continue. In terms of the production function, technology shifts the production function up, as shown in the margin, so that more can be produced at every quantity of labor. If technology grows faster than the diminishing marginal productivity of new capital, and grows faster over time, growth for all practical purposes has no limit. Technology overwhelms diminishing marginal productivity and growth rates increase over time: the economy gets richer and richer. Although the Classical model acknowledged the role of technology in growth, it took technology as given—determined outside the model. It did not explain what causes technology to grow.

If technology increased equally in both developed and less-developed countries, these advances in technology would not affect the convergence hypothesis since it would shift both countries' production functions up. But it does not; technology tends to agglomerate, accelerating the advance of technology in developed countries, and only later spreading to less-developed countries. That's why the information technology revolution pushed up the U.S. growth rate over the past decade, slowing and even offsetting convergence.

As long as new technological advances occur faster in the rich developed countries than older technologies' diffuse into less-developed countries, then convergence need not take place. So how well the United States does in the future depends in a significant part on how good we are at developing technologies for industries that do not yet exist. For example, if information technology jobs that are outsourced to India are replaced with even higher-paying fuel cell, nanotechnology, and biotechnical jobs in the United States, the U.S. future is pleasant. The U.S. growth rate could exceed rates in developing countries, even as we lose jobs through outsourcing.

What's of concern for the United States is that the pressures for convergence are also occurring in research and development. Developing countries are themselves trying to take the lead in developing new technologies. Should that occur, and the fuel cell, nanotechnology, and biotechnology jobs develop in India and China rather than in the United States, the positive agglomeration effects will occur there, and the speed of convergence would increase significantly.

New Growth Theory

Modern growth theory goes under the name *new growth theory.* Because technology is now recognized as an important ingredient in growth, modern growth theorists have made technology central to their analysis. They look for what makes technology grow. Thus, **new growth theory** is *a theory that emphasizes the role of technology rather than capital in the growth process.* Increases in technology shift the production possibility curve out, and thus make the choices an economy faces a bit easier to make—they allow the society to get more of everything. Unlike Classical growth theory, which left technology outside of economic analysis, new growth theory focuses its analysis on technology. For new growth theorists the focus isn't on savings and capital; it is on technology:

Technological advance → Investment → Further technological advance → Growth

Technology   New growth theory's central argument is that increases in technology do not just happen. Technological advance is the result of what the economy does—it invests in research and development (e.g., drug companies researching new ways to fight disease); makes advances in pure science (e.g., the human genome project); and

Is the 21st Century the Age of Technology or One of Many Ages of Technology?

Sometimes newspapers write as if the importance of technology to the economy in the 21st century is a new phenomenon. It is not. Technology has been changing our society for the last two centuries, and it is not at all clear that the technological changes we are currently experiencing are any more revolutionary than those experienced by other generations in the last 200 years. For example, in terms of its impact on people's lives and communications in general, the Internet is small potatoes compared to the phone system.

One economist who recognized the importance of technology was Joseph Schumpeter. Schumpeter emphasized the role of the entrepreneur. He argued that entrepreneurs create major technological changes that drive the economy forward.

According to Schumpeter, the economy's growth depends on these entrepreneurs, and the industries they are in will be the leading industries, pulling the rest of the economy along after them. The accompanying figure lists five waves of technological innovation that have driven our economy. As you can see, in the late 1700, steam power and iron manufacturing were the driving forces. In the 1860s, railroads were the dynamic industry. Later, electronics, automobiles, and chemicals drove our economy. In the 1980s through the early 21st century, computers and biotechnology have been the leading industries.

First wave 1785–1835	Second wave 1835–1885	Third wave 1885–1935	Fourth wave 1935–1985	Fifth wave 1985–?
Steam power Iron manufacturing	Railroad construction Mobile steam power Steam shipping	Chemicals Electricity Telegraph Telephone Automobiles	Electronics Drugs Oil Air transport Nuclear power	Genetic engineering Telecommunications Biotechnology Computers

Time

works out new ways to organize production (e.g., just-in-time inventory techniques). Thus, in a sense, investment in technology increases the technological stock of an economy just as investment in capital increases the capital stock of an economy. Investment in technology is called research and development; firms hire researchers to explore options. Some of those options pay off and others do not, but the net return of that investment in technology is an increase in technology.

If investment in technology is similar to investment in capital, why does new growth theory separate the two? The reason is twofold. First, increases in technology are not as directly linked to investment as capital is. Increases in investment require increases in saving, that is, building the capital. Increases in technology can occur with little investment and saving if the proverbial light bulb goes off in someone's head and that person sees a new way of doing something.

Second, increases in technology often have enormous *positive spillover effects*, especially if the new technology involves common knowledge and is freely available to all. A technological gain in one sector of production gives people in other sectors of production new ideas on how to change what they are doing, which gives other people new ideas. Ideas spread like pool balls after the break. One hits another, and soon all the nearby balls have moved. Put in technical economic terms, technological

The common knowledge aspect of technology creates positive externalities, which new growth theory sees as the key to growth.

change often has significant **positive externalities**—*positive effects on others not taken into account by the decision maker.* Through those externalities, what is called general purpose technological change can have a much larger effect on growth than can an increase in capital.

The positive externalities result from the *common knowledge* aspect of technology because the idea behind the technology can often be used by others without payment to the developer. Using the same assembly line for different car models is just one example of a technological advance that has become incorporated into common knowledge. Any car manufacturer can use it.

Basic research is not always freely available; it is often protected by **patents**—*legal protection of a technological innovation that gives the owner of the patent sole rights to its use and distribution for a limited time.* (If the development is an idea rather than a good, it can be copyrighted rather than patented, but the general concept is the same.) Patents turn innovations into private property. The Windows operating system is an example of a technology that is owned, and hence is not common knowledge. The ideas in technologies that are covered by patents, however, often have common knowledge elements. Once people have seen the new technology, they figure out sufficiently different ways of achieving the same end while avoiding violating the patent.

Learning by Doing   As the new growth theory has analyzed technology, it has focused economic thinking on another aspect of economic processes—an individual's tendency to **learn by doing,** or to *improve the methods of production through experience.* As people do something, they become better and better at it, sometimes because of new technologies, and sometimes simply because they learned better ways to do it just from practice. Thus, as production increases, costs of production tend to decrease over time. The introduction of new technology is sometimes the result of learning by doing.

Learning by doing overcomes the law of diminishing marginal productivity because learning by doing increases the productivity of workers.

Learning by doing changes the laws of economics enormously. It suggests that production has positive externalities in learning. If these positive externalities overwhelm diminishing marginal productivity, as new growth theory suggests they do, the predictions about growth change. In the Classical theory, growth is limited by diminishing marginal productivity; in the new theory, growth potential is unlimited and can accelerate over time. It's a whole new world out there—one in which, holding wants constant, scarcity decreases over time.

We can see in Figure 8-5 new growth theory's predictions for future growth. All inputs are on the horizontal axis, and the production function exhibits increasing

FIGURE 8-5   New Growth Theory

New growth theory focuses on increasing returns to scale. With increasing returns, increases in inputs lead to proportionately greater increases in output. For example, the initial increase of inputs from 0 to 10 results in a 5-unit increase in output. An increase in inputs from 10 to 20 results in a higher 10-unit increase in output. With increasing returns, output per person can rise forever.

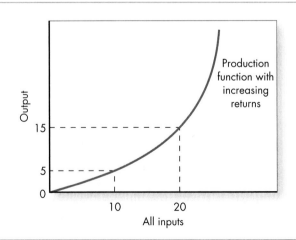

returns to scale. (As more of all inputs are added, the additional output per combination of inputs increases.) With this curve, per capita income can grow forever and the dismal science of economics becomes the optimistic science.

Technological Lock-In   One of the questions new growth theory raises is: Does the economy always use the "best" technology available? Some say no and point to examples of technologies that have become entrenched in the market, or locked in to new products despite the availability of more efficient technologies. This is known as *technological lock-in.*

One proposed example of technological lock-in goes under the name QWERTY, which is the upper-left five keys on the standard computer keyboard. Economist Paul David argues that the design of this keyboard was chosen to slow people's typing down so that the keys in old-style mechanical typewriters would not lock up. He further argues that developments in word processing have since eliminated the problem the QWERTY keyboard was designed to solve (we don't use mechanical typewriters any more). But once people started choosing this keyboard, it was too costly for them to develop another.

This interpretation of history has been disputed by other economists, who argue that the QWERTY keyboard is not significantly less efficient than other keyboard arrangements and that, if it were, competition would have eliminated it. Sometimes this counter-argument almost seems to state that the very fact that a technology exists means that it is the most efficient. Most economists do not go that far; they argue that even if the QWERTY keyboard is not a highly inefficient technology, other examples of lock-in exist: beta format videos were preferable to VHS, the Windows operating system is inferior to many alternatives, the English language doesn't compare to Esperanto, and English measurement systems are quite inefficient compared to metric.

One reason for technological lock-in is the existence of *network externalities*—an externality in which the use of a good by one individual makes that technology more valuable to other people. Telephones exhibit network externalities. A single telephone is pretty useless. Whom would you call? Two telephones are more useful, but as more and more people get telephones, the possible interactions (and the benefits of telephones) increase exponentially. Network externalities can make switching to a superior technology expensive or nearly impossible. The Windows operating system is another example of a product that exhibits network externalities, and makes it difficult for other operating systems to develop.

Q-10 In what way does the Internet demonstrate network externalities?

Growth Policies

Exactly what these theories mean for growth and growth policies is the subject of much debate among economists. But there is some agreement about general policies that are good for growth. These include

- Encouraging saving and investment.
- Formalizing property rights and reducing bureaucracy and corruption.
- Providing more of the right kind of education.
- Promoting policies that encourage technological innovation.
- Promoting policies that allow taking advantage of specialization.

Most economists would agree that each of these is good for growth. Unfortunately, the devil is in the details, and the policy problem is translating these general policies into specific politically acceptable policies.

Micro Credit

In 2006 the Nobel Peace Prize went to Mohammed Yunus, a U.S.-trained economist. He won the prize for developing a financial institution in one of the poorest countries of the world—Bangladesh—called the Grameen Bank that makes loans to poor village women at market interest rates. Even though the bank loaned to individuals with little or no collateral, the bank has had excellent payback ratios, far exceeding what most people thought possible.[1]

How did he do it? Most banks in developing countries tend to focus on loans to well-off people with resources to serve as collateral. This leaves the traditional part of many developing countries' economies without an effective way to translate saving into investment, stranding many entrepreneurial individuals without ways to develop their ideas. Yunus reconsidered the fundamental role of banking in an economy: to make it possible for people with good ideas to develop those ideas by providing them with funds—and to devise a structure that allowed such lending to take place.

He saw that Western banking institutions did not fulfill that role for Bangladesh. By basing their lending decisions on the amount of collateral a borrower had, they essentially made it impossible for most people in Bangladesh to get loans. But Yunus also recognized that collateral served a useful purpose: It forced people to make the difficult decision about whether they really needed the loans, and to work hard to see that they could pay the loans back, even if the going got tough. If you eliminate collateral, something else must replace it.

With a loan from the Grameen Bank (www.grameen-info.org), these women purchased the raw materials to weave baskets whose sale will provide a source of income.

Yunus's ingenious solution was the *borrowing circle*—a credit system that replaces traditional collateral with guarantees by friends of the borrower. Recognizing that social pressures were extremely strong in Bangladesh, Yunus offered to make loans to any woman who could find four friends who would agree to help her pay the loan back if necessary. If the borrower defaulted, the others could not borrow until the loan was repaid.

This simple concept worked. Today the Grameen Bank has more than 6.6 million borrowers and lends $60 million every month. The loans are taken out to buy such things as a cow or material to make a fishing net—not large items, but items to use in activities that generate bottom-up growth. Other microcredit banks—banks that make small loans to poor people using alternative forms of collateral—have developed similar plans.

Other countries have also replicated the microcredit approach pioneered by Grameen Bank and today there are more than 90 Grameen replicas across Asia, Africa, Latin America, Europe, and the United States. In the United States, microcredit banks focus on helping low-income people who are generally excluded from formal credit markets develop home-based businesses. Today, the idea of microfinance has spread to the Internet, making it possible for you to make a loan to, say, a baker in Afghanistan. Go to kiva.org to explore how.

While the concept of microfinance is extraordinarily simple, it made use of economic insights that simultaneously reflected an understanding of the cultural and social dimensions of the economy.

---

[1] Recently some observers have questioned whether the bank has overstated the payback ratios, but even if they are lower than reported, they are still higher than most people thought possible before the bank was created.

Conclusion

Growth happens, or at least it generally has happened, in market economies. But that doesn't mean it happens on its own. While saying precisely why growth happens is beyond economists at this point, economists have identified important sources of growth. These include capital accumulation, available resources, growth-compatible institutions, technological development, and entrepreneurship. What economists haven't been able to determine yet is how they all fit together to bring about growth, and the general feeling is that there is no single way of putting them together—what works likely changes over time. This makes developing an actual growth policy prescription difficult, though no less important.

Summary

- Growth is an increase in the amount of goods and services an economy can produce when both labor and capital are fully employed.

- Growth increases potential output and shifts the production possibility curve out, allowing an economy to produce more goods.

- Per capita growth means producing more goods and services per person. It can be calculated by subtracting the percentage change in the population from the percentage change in output.

- Five sources of growth are (1) growth-compatible institutions, (2) capital accumulation, (3) available resources, (4) technological development, and (5) entrepreneurship.

- The loanable funds market translates savings into investment that is necessary for growth. The interest rate equilibrates saving and investment.

- The production function shows the relationship between the quantity of labor, capital, and land used in production and the quantity of output resulting from production.

- The law of diminishing marginal productivity states that increasing one input, keeping all others constant, will lead to smaller and smaller gains in output.

- Returns to scale describes what happens to output when all inputs increase proportionately.

- The convergence hypothesis is that per capita income in countries with similar institutional structures will converge.

- Convergence has not taken place because of the lack of factor mobility, differing institutional structures, incomparable factors of production, and technological agglomeration.

- The Classical growth model focuses on the role of capital accumulation in the growth process. The law of diminishing productivity limits growth of per capita income.

- New growth theory emphasizes the role of technology in the growth process. Increasing returns to scale means output per person can rise forever.

- Advances in technology, which account for 35 percent of growth, have overwhelmed the effects of diminishing returns.

Key Terms

Classical growth
   model (188)
constant returns to
   scale (188)
convergence
   hypothesis (190)
decreasing returns
   to scale (188)

division of labor (179)
human capital (184)
increasing returns to
   scale (188)
law of diminishing
   marginal
   productivity (188)
learn by doing (194)

new growth
   theory (192)
patent (194)
per capita growth (180)
positive externality (194)
potential output (177)
production
   function (187)

productivity (177)
Rule of 72 (178)
Say's law (177)
social capital (184)
specialization (179)
technological
   agglomeration (192)
technology (185)

Questions for Thought and Review

1. a. If you suddenly found yourself living as a poor person in a developing country, what are some things that you now do that you would no longer be able to do? What new things would you have to do?
   b. Answer the questions again assuming that you are living in the United States 100 years ago.   LO1

2. Who most likely worked longer to buy a dozen eggs: a person living in 2007 or a person living in 1910? Why?   LO1

3. Have the poor benefited more or less from economic growth than the rich?   LO1

4. What roles do specialization and division of labor play in economists' support of free trade?   LO2

5. How can an increase in the U.S. saving rate lead to higher living standards? What problem would a politician face when promoting policies to encourage saving?   LO2

6. De Paul University Professor Ludovic Comeau Jr. hypothesizes that the length of time that a country has had a democratic political structure contributes positively to growth. In what way can a political structure be capital?   LO2

7. Demonstrate graphically how the loanable funds market translates savings into investment. What equilibrates saving and investment?   LO2

8. Name three types of capital and explain the differences among them.   LO2

9. In what ways do informal property rights limit growth?   LO2

10. Name two ways in which growth through technology differs from growth through the accumulation of physical capital.   LO2

11. *Credentialism* occurs when a person's academic degrees become more important than his or her actual knowledge. How can credentialism hurt economic growth?   LO2

12. On what law of production did Thomas Malthus base his prediction that population growth would exceed growth in goods and services? Why hasn't his prediction come true?   LO3

13. If individuals suddenly needed more food to subsist, what would the Classical growth model predict would happen to labor and output? Demonstrate graphically.   LO5

14. According to the convergence hypothesis, which country will grow faster—the United States or Bangladesh? Why?   LO4

15. List four reasons why convergence might not occur.   LO4

16. How does new growth theory explain the lack of convergence?   LO5

17. What are network externalities and how do they lead to growth?   LO5

Problems and Exercises

18. Say that income in the EU grows an average of 2 percent per year and in India it grows at 6 percent per year. Say also that EU income is $32,000 and Indian income is $2,000 annually.
    a. In how many years will Indian income catch up with EU income?
    b. How would your answer differ if India grows at 12 percent per year?   LO1

19. Per capita income is growing at different rates in the following countries: Nepal, 1.1 percent; Kenya, 1.7 percent; Singapore, 7.2 percent; Egypt, 3.9 percent. How long will it take for each country to double its income per person?   LO1

20. Calculate real growth per capita from 1994 to 2003 in the following countries:
    a. Democratic Republic of Congo: population growth = 3.0 percent; real output growth = −1.8 percent.
    b. Estonia: population growth = −0.4 percent; real output growth = 4.2 percent.

c. India: population growth = 2.0 percent; real output growth = 6 percent.
d. United States: population growth = 0.5 percent; real output growth = 2.5 percent.   LO1

21. Using the demand and supply of loanable funds, demonstrate the effect of the following on the interest rate. As a result, what would you expect to be the impact of the change on growth?
    a. Government increases spending.
    b. Businesses become more productive.
    c. The people as a whole save more.   LO2

22. Could the borrowing circle concept be easily adapted for use in the United States?
    a. Why or why not?
    b. What modifications would you suggest if it were to be adopted?
    c. Minorities in the United States often do not use banks. In what ways are U.S. minorities' problems similar to those of people in developing countries? (Requires reading "Real-World Application: Micro Credit" on page 572.)   LO2

23. If output increases by 20 percent when one of two inputs increases by 20 percent, are there constant returns to scale? Why or why not?   LO3

24. The graph below shows a production function and the subsistence level of output.
    a. Does the production function exhibit increasing or decreasing marginal productivity?
    b. Label a level of population at which the population is expected to grow. What is the surplus output at that population level?
    c. Label a level of population at which the population is expected to decline. Why is the population declining at this point?
    d. Label the population at which the economy is in long-run equilibrium. Why is this a long-run equilibrium?   LO5

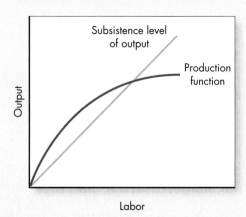

25. Explain how each of the following is expected to affect growth:
    a. Increase in technology.   d. Learning by doing.
    b. Positive externalities.   e. Technological lock-
    c. Patents.   in.   LO5

Questions from Alternative Perspectives

1. Capitalism was a derogatory term coined by Karl Marx to deride the riches of those who accumulated capital. He said that the accumulation of capital helps the rich get richer while simultaneously making the poor get poorer.
   a. Have the poor become poorer under capitalism?
   b. Based on the growth model presented in the text, what would you expect to happen to poor people's income when society accumulates capital? (Austrian)

2. Ecological economists believe that economic possibilities are constrained by natural laws (for example, the laws of thermodynamics, biological assimilation, and the limiting factor). Unlimited material growth from a finite resource base—spaceship earth—is therefore impossible. How many "earths" would it take for everyone to live like U.S. citizens? (To help answer this question you might visit and take the test at http://redefiningprogress.org/footprint. (Institutionalist)

3. Many Keynesians believe the best way to deal with growth is to have government promote an industrial policy that focuses on the development of technological change using tax credits, government research funding, and the transfer of technological knowledge from the military to the civilian sector.
   a. Would such a policy be consistent with the new growth theory?

   b. Would those believing in the Classical growth model support such a policy? (Post-Keynesian)

4. There is a furious debate among economists about the relationship between equality (or inequality) and economic growth. Based on the observation that developing countries often experience increasing inequality during their initial periods of rapid growth, some economists emphasize the role of inequality in establishing incentives to work, save, and invest. The experience of the East Asian economies that grew rapidly after reducing their levels of inequality (through land reform and other means) led other economists to argue that greater equality leads to faster economic growth. The reasons they cite are numerous: more political stability, greater access to credit, higher levels of spending on education, and wider land ownership.
   a. How do these arguments about the positive link between equality and economic growth fit with your textbook's list of the sources of economic growth?
   b. What do you think is the relationship between equality (or inequality) and economic growth? (Radical)

5. Christians believe that everything ultimately belongs to God. Is that belief consistent with economists' belief that property rights are necessary for growth? (Religious)

Web Questions

1. Go to the World Bank's home page (www.worldbank.org) and look up the World Development Report for 2007.
   a. According to Box 1 in the report, how many years will it take Kenya to recouperate loss of human capital due to AIDS?
   b. According to Figure 1.2a, what level of schooling has the highest return in Latin America?
   c. According to Box 2.5, do girls or boys have a greater say in their future in Pakistan? How does this matter to growth?

2. The Heritage Foundation and *The Wall Street Journal* co-publish an Index of Economic Freedom designed to measure the extent to which markets are allowed to operate freely in a country. Go to the home page of the Heritage

Foundation (www.index.heritage.org) and look up the index for two of the top-rated countries and two of the bottom-rated countries.
   a. What are the reasons for their ratings?
   b. Compare the recent per capita growth rates of each country. Is economic freedom related to growth? If so, how?

3. Go to the U.S. patent office Web site (www.uspto.gov) and find out for how long patents are granted in the United States.
   a. What are the advantages of shortening the length of patents?
   b. What are the disadvantages of shortening the length of patents?

Answers to Margin Questions

1. The long-run growth analysis justifies its focus on supply by assuming that aggregate supply will create an equal level of aggregate demand. This is known as Say's law. *(177)*

2. Using the Rule of 72 (divide 72 by the growth rate of income), we can calculate that it will take 18 years for

income to double when its growth rate is 4 percent a year. *(178)*

3. Country B is experiencing the higher growth in income per capita. To calculate this, subtract the population growth rates from the income growth rates for each

country. Country A's per capita growth rate is 1 percent (4 − 3) and country B's per capita growth rate is 2 percent (3 − 1) *(181)*

4. The increases would have to be distributed so that no one whose income is below the median receives enough to bring his or her income above the median. *(181)*

5. Private property provides an incentive for people to produce by creating the possibility of benefiting from their efforts. *(182)*

6. With the demand for loanable funds shifting out, the interest rate will likely rise. *(184)*

7. False. A 20 percent increase in production that results from a 10 percent increase in all inputs means the production process exhibits decreasing *returns to scale*. A key part of the statement is that all inputs are changing. If one input were being kept fixed, the production function would be exhibiting diminishing marginal productivity. *(188)*

8. If individuals suddenly needed less food, the subsistence level line would rotate down. The number of laborers the economy could sustain would rise, and output would rise as well. *(189)*

9. An economist would likely predict that India and China will likely grow faster than the United States in the next decade because of the law of one price, which states that, assuming similar institutional structures, equivalent factors will be paid the same wage; until that happens, firms will have an incentive to transfer production to the lower-wage countries, leading to higher growth in those countries. *(190)*

10. The Internet connects hundreds of millions of people around the globe and reduces communication costs. The benefit of one person using the Internet is virtually nonexistent. The benefit of the Internet rises as more people use it, because the higher usage increases the amount of information available on the Internet and increases the ability of each user to communicate. *(195)*

The Aggregate Demand/Aggregate Supply Model

The Theory of Economics . . . is a method rather than a doctrine, an apparatus of the mind, a technique of thinking which helps its possessor to draw correct conclusions.

—J. M. Keynes

The previous chapter's discussion of growth and markets focused on the positive side of markets: markets unleash individual incentives, increase supply, and bring about growth. But markets can run into serious problems—markets can create recessions, inflation, and unemployment. The United States in 2001 is a good example. After the longest expansion ever recorded, the U.S. economy slowed, and the terrorist attacks on the World Trade Center and Pentagon in September 2001 threatened to slow the economy further. Faced with a likely recession, the U.S. government turned its attention away from concern about inflation, growth, and supply-side policies to recession and demand-side policies—both monetary and fiscal policy—that would keep the economy from going into a deep recession. It worked, at least temporarily, and the recession that followed the attacks was the shortest on record.

The tools that government has to deal with recessions, unemployment, and inflation—i.e., monetary and fiscal policies (policies that we will discuss in depth below)—affect the aggregate demand side of the economy. Thus, whereas the last chapter's policy focus was on production (the supply side) and individual incentives, this chapter and the next focus on expenditures (the demand side). As you will see, economists debate the effectiveness of monetary and fiscal policy. Some favor intervention; some don't. While the problems of a recession are serious, so too are the problems with government policies. The debate among economists is about whether the cure (intervention) is worse than the disease.

Even if the noninterventionist economists were to convince all other economists that government should not intervene with monetary and fiscal policy, the odds are that government would still intervene. As I've said before, the reality is that politicians make policy; they listen to economists only when they want to. And whenever the economy faces the threat of a recession, politicians' focus inevitably changes from long-run supply issues and growth to short-run demand issues and stabilization.

AFTER READING THIS CHAPTER, YOU SHOULD BE ABLE TO:

1. Discuss the historical development of modern macroeconomics.
2. Explain the shape of the aggregate demand curve and what factors shift the curve.
3. Explain the shape of the short-run aggregate supply curve and what factors shift the curve.
4. Explain the shape of the long-run aggregate supply curve.
5. Show the effects of shifts of the aggregate demand and aggregate supply curves on the price level and output in both the short run and long run.
6. Discuss the limitations of the macro policy model.

Web Note 9.1
The Great Depression

During the Depression, unemployment lines were enormously long.

Q.1 Distinguish a Classical economist from a Keynesian economist.

Classical economists support laissez-faire policies.

The Historical Development of Modern Macro

An important reason for politicians' initial interest in short-run demand policies is the Great Depression of the 1930s, a deep recession that lasted for 10 years. Most of you think of the Great Depression only as something your grandparents and great-grandparents experienced. But it was a defining event that undermined people's faith in markets and was the beginning of modern macro's focus on the demand side of the economy. It is also where our story of modern macroeconomics begins.

During the Depression, output fell by 30 percent and unemployment rose to 25 percent. Not only was the deadbeat up the street unemployed but so were your brother, your mother, your uncle—the hardworking backbone of the country. These people wanted to work; if the market wasn't creating jobs for them, it was the market system that was at fault.

From Classical to Keynesian Economics   As I discussed in an earlier chapter, economists before the Depression focused on the long run and the problem of growth. Their policy recommendations were designed to lead to long-run growth, and they avoided discussing policies that would affect the economy in the short run. In the 1930s, macroeconomists started focusing their discussion of macroeconomic policy on short-run issues. To distinguish the two types of economics, the earlier economists who focused on long-run issues such as growth were called *Classical economists* and economists who focused on the short run were called *Keynesian economists*. Keynesian economists were named because a leading advocate of the short-run focus was John Maynard Keynes, the author of *The General Theory of Employment, Interest and Money*, and the originator of modern macroeconomics.

Classical Economists

Classical economists believed in the market's ability to be self-regulating through the invisible hand (the pricing mechanism of the market). Short-run problems were seen as temporary glitches; the Classical framework said that the economy would always return to its potential output and its target (or natural) rate of unemployment in the long run. Thus, the essence of Classical economists' approach to problems was laissez-faire (leave the market alone).

As long as the economy was operating relatively smoothly, the Classical analysis of the aggregate economy met no serious opposition. But when the Great Depression hit and unemployment became a serious problem, most Classical economists avoided the issue (as most people tend to do when they don't have a good answer). When pushed by curious students to explain how the invisible hand, if it was so wonderful, could have allowed the Depression, Classical economists used microeconomic supply and demand arguments. They argued that labor unions and government policies kept prices and wages from falling. The problem, they said, was that the invisible hand was not being allowed to coordinate economic activity.

Their laissez-faire policy prescription followed from their analysis: Eliminate labor unions and change government policies that held wages too high. If government did so, the wage rate would fall, unemployment would be eliminated, and the Depression would end.

The Layperson's Explanation for Unemployment

Laypeople (average citizens) weren't pleased with this argument. (Remember, economists don't try to present pleasing arguments—only arguments they believe are correct.) But laypeople couldn't point to anything wrong with it. It made sense, but it wasn't satisfying. People thought, "Gee, Uncle Joe, who's unemployed, would take a job at half the going wage. But he can't find one—there just aren't enough jobs to go around at any wage." So most laypeople developed different explanations. One popular explanation of the Depression was that an oversupply of goods had glutted the market. All that was needed to eliminate unemployment was for government to hire the unemployed, even if only to dig ditches and fill them back up. The people who got the new jobs would spend their money, creating even more jobs. Pretty soon, the United States would be out of the Depression.

Classical economists argued against this lay view. They felt that money to hire people would have to be borrowed. Such borrowing would use money that would have financed private economic activity and jobs, and would thus reduce private economic activity even further. The net effect would be essentially zero. Their advice was simply to have faith in markets.

The Essence of Keynesian Economics

As the Depression deepened, the Classical "have-faith" solution lost its support. Everyone was interested in the short run, not the long run. John Maynard Keynes put the concern most eloquently: "In the long run, we're all dead."

Keynes stopped asking whether the economy would eventually get out of the Depression on its own and started asking what short-run forces were causing the Depression and what society could do to counteract them. By taking this approach, he created the macroeconomic framework that focuses on short-run issues such as business cycles and how to stabilize output fluctuations.

While Keynes's ideas had many dimensions, the essence was that as wages and the price level adjusted to sudden changes in expenditures (such as an unexpected decrease in investment demand), the economy could get stuck in a rut.

If, for some reason, people stopped buying—decreased their demand in the aggregate—firms would decrease production, causing people to be laid off; these people would, in turn, buy less—causing other firms to further decrease production, which would cause more workers to be laid off, and so on. Firms' supply decisions would be affected by consumers' buying decisions, and the economy would end up in a cumulative cycle of declining production that would end with the economy stuck at a low level of income. In developing this line of reasoning, Keynes provided the theoretical foundation for the view that unemployment could be caused by too little spending. The issue was not whether a more desirable equilibrium existed; it was whether a market economy, once it had fallen into a depression, and was caught in a cumulative cycle, could get out of it on its own in an acceptable period of time.

In making his argument, Keynes carefully distinguished the adjustment process for a single market (a micro issue) from the adjustment process for the aggregate economy (a macro issue), arguing that the effects differ significantly when everyone does something versus when only one person does it. You were introduced to this problem in Chapter 4 under the name *fallacy of composition*.

The problem is neatly seen by considering an analogy to a football game. If everyone is standing, and you sit down, you can't see. Everyone is better off standing. No one has an incentive to sit down. However, if somehow all individuals could be enticed to sit down, all individuals would be even better off. Sitting down is a public good—a good that benefits others but one that nobody on his or her own will do. Keynesians argued that, in times of recession, spending is a public good because it benefits everyone, so government should spend or find ways of inducing private individuals to spend. This difference between individual and economywide reactions to spending decisions creates a possibility for government to exercise control over aggregate expenditures and

Keynes focused on the short run, not the long run.

Web Note 9.2
John Maynard Keynes

Keynesians argued that, in times of recession, spending is a public good that benefits everyone.

In the Long Run, We're All Dead

When Keynes said, "In the long run, we're all dead," he didn't mean that we can forget the long run. What he meant was that if the long run is so long that short-run forces do not let it come about, then for all practical purposes there is no long run. In that case, the short-run problem must be focused on.

Keynes believed that voters would not be satisfied waiting for market forces to bring about full employment. If something were not done in the short run to alleviate unemployment, he felt, voters would opt for fascism (as had the Germans) or communism (as had the Russians). He saw both alternatives as undesirable. For him, what would happen in the long run was academic.

Classicals, in contrast, argued that the short-run problems were not as bad as Keynes made them out to be and therefore should not be focused on to the exclusion of long-run problems.

Modern-day Classicals argue that while Keynes is dead, we are not, and the result of his short-run focus was long-run problems—specifically an inflationary bias in the economy. It is only by giving up Keynesian policies that we eliminated that bias.

---

thereby over aggregate output and income. *Government's attempt to control the aggregate level of spending in the economy* is called **aggregate demand management.**

The key idea in Keynesian economics is that equilibrium income fluctuates and can differ from potential income.

Equilibrium Income Fluctuates   The key idea of the Keynesian model is that, in the short run, equilibrium income is not fixed at the economy's long-run potential income; it fluctuates. Thus, for Keynes, there was a difference between **equilibrium income** (*the level of income toward which the economy gravitates in the short run because of the cumulative cycles of declining or increasing production*) and **potential income** (*the level of income that the economy technically is capable of producing without generating accelerating inflation*). Keynes believed that at certain times the economy needed some help in reaching its potential income.

He argued that market forces that are supposed to bring the economy back to long-run potential income don't work fast, and at times will not be strong enough to get the economy out of a recession; the economy could get stuck in a low-income, high-unemployment rut. As the economy adjusts to fluctuations of supply and demand in the aggregate, the equilibrium income toward which the economy would gravitate would change. The economy would not naturally gravitate to potential income in the short run.

Keynesian economists advocated an activist demand management policy.

The Paradox of Thrift   Let's say that a large portion of the people in the economy suddenly decide to save more and consume less. Expenditures would decrease and saving would increase. If that saving is not immediately transferred into investment, and hence back into expenditures (as the Classicals assumed it would be), investment demand will not increase by enough to offset the fall in consumption demand, and total demand will fall. There will be excess supply. Faced with this excess supply, firms will likely cut back production, which will decrease income. People will be laid off. As people's incomes fall, both their consumption and saving will decrease. (When you're laid off, you don't save.) Eventually income will fall far enough so that once again saving and investment will be in equilibrium, but then the economy could be at an almost permanent recession, with ongoing unemployment. Keynesians believed that in this case the economy would need government's help to hold up aggregate expenditures. That is the essence of macro demand-side expansionary policy.

Notice that the Keynesian framework gives a quite different view of saving than did the growth framework in the last chapter. There, saving was seen as something good; more saving leads to more investment, which leads to more growth. In the Keynesian framework, there is a *paradox of thrift*—an increase in saving can lead to a decrease in expenditures, decreasing output and causing a recession.

By the 1950s, Keynesian economics had been accepted by most of the profession. It was taught almost everywhere in the United States. The terminology of aggregate accounting developed, which is closely tied to Keynesian concepts. The model that eventually developed from these early debates is called the *aggregate supply/aggregate demand (AS/AD) model*. Aggregate supply captures production and pricing decisions by firms, and aggregate demand captures aggregate spending decisions. Even though economists still debate how business cycles in an economy arise, this model, which focuses on aggregate expenditures as the primary determinant of short-run income, is used by most real-world economists to discuss short-run fluctuations in output and unemployment.

How does the short-run view of saving differ from the long-run view?

The *AS/AD* Model

The *AS/AD* model consists of three curves. The curve describing the supply side of the aggregate economy in the short run is the short-run aggregate supply (*SAS*) curve, the curve describing the demand side of the economy is the aggregate demand curve, and the curve describing the highest sustainable level of output is the long-run aggregate supply (*LAS*) curve.

The first thing to note about the *AS/AD* model is that it is fundamentally different from the microeconomic supply/demand model. In microeconomics the price of a single good is on the vertical axis and the quantity of a single good on the horizontal axis. The reasoning for the shapes of the micro supply and demand curves is based on the concepts of substitution and opportunity cost. In the macro *AS/AD* model, the price level of all goods, not just the price of one good, is on the vertical axis and aggregate output, not a single good, is on the horizontal axis. The shapes of the curves have nothing to do with opportunity cost or substitution.

Knowing the difference between microeconomic supply and demand curves and macroeconomic aggregate demand and supply curves is very important.

The second thing to note about the *AS/AD* model is that it is a *historical model*. A historical model is a model that starts at a point in time and says what will likely happen when changes affect the economy. It does not try to explain how the economy got to its starting point; the macroeconomy is too complicated for that. Instead, the model starts from historically given price and output levels and, given the institutional structure of the economy, considers how changes in the economy are likely to affect those levels. What this means is that much of the discussion in this chapter is based on the economy's institutional realities and observed empirical regularities.

Let's now consider the three central components of the *AS/AD* model: the aggregate demand (*AD*) curve, the short-run aggregate supply (*SAS*) curve, and the long-run aggregate supply (*LAS*) curve.

The Aggregate Demand Curve

The **aggregate demand (AD) curve** is *a curve that shows how a change in the price level will change aggregate expenditures on all goods and services in an economy.* (Aggregate expenditures is the sum of consumption, investment, government expenditures, and net exports.) A standard *AD* curve is shown in Figure 9-1. Although the curve is called an aggregate demand curve, let me repeat that it is not the same as a microeconomic

Take the time to draw an *AD* curve, making sure to label the axes correctly.

FIGURE 9-1 **The Aggregate De-mand Curve**

The *AD* curve is a downward-sloping curve that looks like a typical demand curve, but it is important to remember that it is quite a different curve. The reason it slopes downward is not the substitution effect, but instead the wealth effect, the interest rate effect, and the international effect. The multiplier effect strengthens each of these effects.

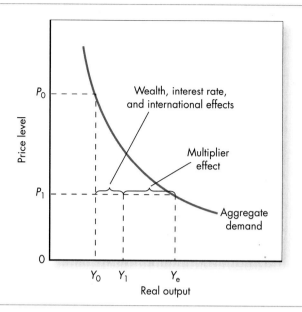

Aggregate Demand

demand curve. The *AD* curve is more an equilibrium curve.[1] It shows the level of aggregate expenditures at every price level, taking into account interactions among all producers and consumers in an economy.

The Slope of the *AD* Curve

As you can see, the *AD* curve is downward-sloping. A good place to begin understanding why it is downward-sloping is to remember the composition of aggregate demand. As I discussed in the chapter on aggregate accounting, aggregate expenditures (demand) is the sum of consumption, investment, government spending, and net exports. The slope of the *AD* curve depends on how these components respond to changes in the price level. In particular, expenditures on consumption, investment, and net exports rise when the price level falls. A number of explanations have been suggested for why a falling price level increases aggregate expenditures. I'll discuss three of them: the wealth effect, the interest-rate effect, and the international effect.

The Wealth Effect   Let's start at price P_0 and output Y_0 in Figure 9-1. (Remember, as I said above, in a historical model we start at a given price and output and determine what would happen if the price level rises or falls from that level.) Now, say that the price level falls to P_1. How will this affect the total amount of goods and services that people demand? Let's first consider what is called the **wealth effect** (sometimes called the *real balance effect*), which tells us that *a fall in the price level will make the holders of money and of other financial assets richer, so they buy more*. In other words, if the price level falls, the dollar bill in your pocket will buy more than before because the purchasing power of the dollar rises. You are, in effect, richer and as you get richer, you will buy more goods and services. Since consumption expenditures are a component of aggregate

---

[1]In a number of articles and in previous editions, I tried to change the terminology so that students would not be misled into thinking that the *AD* curve was a normal demand curve. But my changes did not catch on.

demand, aggregate expenditures will increase, which is shown graphically by a movement along the *AD* curve. (To differentiate such movements along the *AD* curve from a shift in the *AD* curve, I call movements due to changes in the price level "changes in the quantity of aggregate demand.") Most economists do not see the wealth effect as strong; they do, however, accept the logic of the argument.

The Interest Rate Effect   A second explanation for why the aggregate demand curve slopes downward is called the **interest rate effect**—*the effect that a lower price level has on investment expenditures through the effect that a change in the price level has on interest rates*. The interest rate effect works as follows: a decrease in the price level will increase real cash on hand (called *money balances*), as in the wealth effect. But the path of the interest rate effect is not through making holders of cash richer. The interest rate effect focuses on the effect that changes in real money balances have on interest rates. Because the decline in the price level increases the purchasing power of the money in people's pockets, they will find they're holding more money than they need. So, they deposit the extra money at banks in some form, giving banks more money to loan out. As banks make more loans, interest rates will fall, which, in turn, will increase investment expenditures. Why? Because at lower interest rates businesses will undertake more investment projects. Since investment is one component of aggregate demand, the quantity of aggregate demand will increase when the price level falls.

The International Effect   A third reason why aggregate quantity demanded increases with a fall in the price level is the **international effect,** which tells us that *as the price level falls (assuming the exchange rate does not change), net exports will rise*. As the price level in the United States falls, the price of U.S. goods relative to foreign goods goes down and U.S. goods become more competitive than foreign goods; thus, U.S. exports increase and U.S. imports decrease. Let's consider an example. In the mid-1990s, the Bulgarian currency was fixed to the German mark. Bulgaria's price level rose enormously, increasing the demand for German imports and reducing the quantity of aggregate demand in Bulgaria.

So, in Figure 9-1 when we include the international effect, the interest rate effect, and the wealth effect, a fall in the price level from P_0 to P_1 causes the quantity of aggregate demand to increase to Y_1.

The Multiplier Effect   The wealth effect, the interest rate effect, and the international effect tell us that the quantity of aggregate demand will increase with a fall in the price level, and will decrease with an increase in the price level. But the story about the slope of the aggregate demand curve doesn't end there. It also takes into account the **multiplier effect**—*the amplification of initial changes in expenditures*. It is important to recognize that when considering the demand curve in micro, we can reasonably assume that other things remain constant; in macro, other things change. Whereas the demand curve in micro includes only the initial change, the aggregate demand curve includes the repercussions that these initial changes have throughout the economy. What I mean by *repercussions* is that the initial changes in expenditures set in motion a process in the economy that amplifies these initial effects.

To see how these repercussions will likely work in the real world, imagine that the price level in the United States rises. U.S. citizens will reduce their purchases of U.S. goods and increase their purchases of foreign goods. (That's the international effect.) U.S. firms will see the demand for their goods and services fall and will decrease their output. Profits will fall and people will be laid off. Both these effects will cause income to fall, and as income falls, people will demand still fewer goods and services. (If you're unemployed, you cut back your purchases.) Again production and income fall, which again leads to a drop in

The slope of the *AD* curve is determined by the wealth effect, the interest rate effect, the international effect, and the multiplier effect.

In micro other things can be assumed to remain constant, whereas in macro other things change.

expenditures. This secondary cutback is an example of a repercussion. These repercussions *multiply* the initial effect that a change in the price level has on expenditures.

The multiplier effect amplifies the initial wealth, interest rate, and international effects, thereby making the slope of the AD curve flatter than it would have been. You can see this in Figure 9-1. The three effects discussed above increase output from Y_0 to Y_1. The repercussions multiply that effect so that output increases to Y_e.

Economists have suggested other reasons why changes in the price level affect the quantity of aggregate demand, but these four should be sufficient to give you an initial understanding. Going through the same exercise that I did above for the wealth, interest rate, international, and multiplier effects for a fall (rather than a rise) in the price level is a useful exercise.

Let's conclude this section with an example that brings out the importance of the multiplier effect in determining the slope of the AD curve. Say that the multiplier effect amplifies the wealth, interest rate, and international effects by a factor of 2 and that the international, wealth, and interest rate effects reduce output by 4 when the price level rises from 100 to 110. What will be the slope of the AD curve? Since the multiplier effect is 2, the total decline in output will be $2 \times 4 = 8$, so the slope will be -1.25 or $(10/8)$.

How Steep Is the AD Curve?　While all economists agree about the logic of the wealth effect, the interest rate effect, and the international effect, most also agree that for small changes in the price level, the net effect is relatively small, so, even after the effect has been expanded by the multiplier, the AD curve has a very steep slope.[2] Unfortunately, statistically separating out the effects determining the slope of the AD curve from shifts in the AD curve is difficult because there is much noise—random unexplained movements—in the relationship between the price level and aggregate expenditures. It is that noise on the aggregate level that makes the economy so hard to predict, and accounts for the description of economic forecasting as "driving a car blindfolded while following directions given by a person who is looking out of the back window." In order to make the graphs easy to follow, they show a flatter AD curve than it probably has in reality.

Shifts in the AD Curve

Next, let's consider what causes the AD curve to shift. A shift in the AD curve means that at every price level, total expenditures have changed. Anything other than the price level that changes the components of aggregate demand (consumption, investment, government spending, and net exports) will shift the AD curve. Five important shift factors of aggregate demand are foreign income, exchange rate fluctuations, expectations, the distribution of income, and government policies.

Foreign Income　A country is not an island unto itself. U.S. economic output is closely tied to the income of its major world trading partners. When our trading partners go into a recession, the demand for U.S. goods, and hence U.S. exports, will fall, causing the U.S. AD curve to shift in to the left. Similarly, a rise in foreign income leads to an increase in U.S. exports and a rightward shift of the U.S. AD curve.

Exchange Rates　The currencies of various countries are connected through exchange rates. When a country's currency loses value relative to other currencies, its goods become more competitive compared to foreign goods. Foreign demand for

Q-3 True or false? As the price level falls from 110 to 100, the international effect increases output by 10. Therefore, the slope of the AD curve will be −1.

Q-4 If a country's exchange rate rises, what happens to its AD curve?

---

[2]Of the three, the international effect is probably the strongest, but its strength depends on whether fluctuations in the exchange rate offset it; exchange rate determination will be discussed in depth in a later chapter.

domestic goods increases and domestic demand for foreign goods decreases as individuals shift their spending to domestic goods at home. Both these effects increase net exports and shift the *AD* curve to the right. By the same reasoning, when a country's currency gains value, the *AD* curve shifts in the opposite direction. You can see these effects on the U.S.-Canadian border. In the early 1990s, the Canadian dollar had a high value relative to the U.S. dollar. This caused many Canadians near the border to make buying trips to the United States. When the Canadian dollar fell in value, those buying trips decreased, and the Canadian *AD* curve shifted right.

Expectations   Another important shift factor of aggregate demand is expectations. Many different types of expectations can affect the *AD* curve. To give you an idea of the role of expectations, let's consider two expectational shift factors: expectations of future output and future prices. When businesspeople expect demand to be high in the future, they will want to increase their productive capacity; their investment demand, a component of aggregate demand, will increase. Thus, positive expectations about future demand will shift the *AD* curve to the right.

Expectations of higher future income increase expenditures and shift the AD curve out.

Similarly, when consumers expect the economy to do well, they will be less worried about saving for the future, and they will spend more now—the *AD* curve will shift to the right. Alternatively, if consumers expect the future to be gloomy, they will likely try to save for the future and will decrease the consumption expenditures. The *AD* curve will shift to the left.

Another type of expectation that shifts the *AD* curve concerns expectations of future prices. If you expect the prices of goods to rise in the future, it pays to buy goods now that you might want in the future—before their prices rise. The current price level hasn't changed, but aggregate quantity demanded at that price level has increased, indicating a shift of the *AD* curve to the right.

Expectations of a rising price level in the future increase expenditures and shift the AD curve out to the right.

The effect of expectations of future price levels is seen more clearly in a hyperinflation. In most cases of hyperinflation, people rush out to spend their money quickly—to buy whatever they can to beat the price increase. So even though prices are rising, aggregate demand stays high because the rise in price creates an expectation of even higher prices, and thus the current high price is seen as a low price relative to the future. I said that an increase in expectations of inflation will "have a tendency to" rather than "definitely" shift the *AD* curve to the right because those expectations of inflation are interrelated with a variety of other expectations. For example, an expectation of a rise in the price of goods you buy could be accompanied by an expectation of a fall in income, and that fall in income would work in the opposite direction, decreasing aggregate demand.

This interrelation of various types of expectations makes it very difficult to specify precisely what effect certain types of expectations have on the *AD* curve. But it does not eliminate the importance of expectations as shift factors. It simply means that we often aren't sure what the net effect of a change in expectations on aggregate demand will be.

Distribution of Income   Some people save more than others, and everyone's spending habits differ. Thus, as income distribution changes, so too will aggregate demand. One of the most important distributional effects concerns the distribution of income between wages and profits. Workers receive wage income and are more likely to spend the income they receive; firms' profits are distributed to stockholders or are retained by the firm. Since stockholders in the United States tend to be wealthy, and the wealthy save a greater portion of their income than the poor do, a higher portion of income received as profits will likely be saved. Assuming all saving is not translated into investment, as the real wage decreases but total income remains constant, it is likely that consumption expenditures will fall and the aggregate demand curve will shift to the left. Similarly, as the real wage increases, it is likely that aggregate demand will shift to the right.

Five important shift factors of *AD* are

1. Foreign income.
2. Exchange rates.
3. Expectations.
4. The distribution of income.
5. Monetary and fiscal policies.

Deliberate shifting of the *AD* curve is what most policy makers mean by macro policy.

Q-5 If government spending increases by 20, by how much does the *AD* curve shift out?

The *AD* curve holds all shift factors constant, so the slope of the *AD* curve reflects only the effects of a change in the price level (including multiplier effects).

Monetary and Fiscal Policies   One of the most important reasons why the aggregate demand curve has been so important in macro policy analysis is that often macro policy makers think that they can control it, at least to some degree. For example, if the government spends lots of money without increasing taxes, it shifts the *AD* curve to the right; if the government raises taxes significantly and holds spending constant, consumers will have less disposable income and will reduce their expenditures, shifting the *AD* curve to the left. Similarly, when the Federal Reserve Bank, the U.S. economy's central bank, expands the money supply, it can often lower interest rates, making it easier for both consumers and investors to borrow, increasing their spending, and thereby shifting the *AD* curve to the right. This deliberate increase in aggregate demand to influence the level of income in the economy is what most policy makers mean by the term *macro policy*. Expansionary macro policy shifts the *AD* curve to the right; contractionary macro policy shifts it to the left.

Multiplier Effects of Shift Factors   As I emphasized when I introduced the *AD* curve, you cannot treat the *AD* curve like a micro demand curve. This comes out most clearly when considering shifts in the curve caused by shift factors. The aggregate demand curve may shift by more than the amount of the initial shift factor because of the multiplier effect. The explanation is the same as when I introduced the multiplier effect. When government increases its spending, firms increase production, which leads to higher income. A fraction of that increase in income is spent on more goods and services, shifting the *AD* curve even further to the right. This leads firms to increase production again; income and expenditures also rise. Each round, the increase gets smaller and smaller until the increase becomes negligible. In the end the *AD* curve will have shifted by a multiple of the initial shift. Just how large that multiple is depends on how much the change in income affects spending in each round. Thus, in Figure 9-2, when an initial shift factor of aggregate demand is 100 and the multiplier is 3, the *AD* curve will shift to the right by 300, three times the initial shift. The extra 200 shift is due to the multiplier effect.

To see that you are following the argument, consider the following two shifts: (1) a fall in the U.S. exchange rate, increasing net exports by 50, and (2) an increase

---

FIGURE 9-2   Effect of a Shift Factor on the *AD* Curve

The *AD* curve shifts out by more than the initial change in expenditures. In this example, exports increase by 100. The multiplier magnifies this shift, and the *AD* curve shifts to the right by a multiple of 100, in this case by 300.

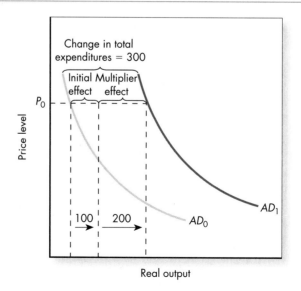

in government spending of 100. Explain how the *AD* curve will shift in each of these cases, and why that shift will be larger than the initial shift. If you are not sure about these explanations, review the multiplier effect discussion above.

The Short-Run Aggregate Supply Curve

The second component of the *AS/AD* model is the **short-run aggregate supply (SAS) curve**—*a curve that specifies how a shift in the aggregate demand curve affects the price level and real output in the short run, other things constant.* A standard *SAS* curve is shown in Figure 9-3.

The Slope of the SAS Curve

As you can see, the *SAS* curve is upward-sloping, which means that in the short run, other things constant, an increase in output is accompanied by a rise in the price level. That is, when aggregate demand increases, the price level—the composite of all prices—rises. The shape of the *SAS* curve reflects two different types of markets in our economy: auction markets (which are the markets represented by the supply/demand model) and posted-price markets (in which prices are set by the producers and change only infrequently).

In markets where prices are set by the interaction between buyers and sellers, none of whom have enough market power to set prices, there is little question why prices rise when demand increases as long as the supply curve for firms in the market is upward-sloping. But these auction markets make up only a small percentage of final goods markets. (They are much more common in markets for resources such as oil or farm products.) In most final goods markets, sellers set a price for their goods and buyers take these prices as given. These posted-price markets comprise 90 percent of the total final goods markets. In posted-price markets, firms set prices as a markup over costs. For example, if the markup is 40 percent and the cost of production is $10 per unit, the firm would set a price of $14.

Posted-price markets are often called **quantity-adjusting markets**—*markets in which firms respond to changes in demand primarily by changing production instead of changing their prices.* It would be wrong, however, to assume that prices in these markets are totally unresponsive to changes in demand. When demand increases, some firms will take the opportunity to raise their prices slightly, increasing their markup, and when demand falls, firms have a tendency to lower their prices slightly, decreasing their markup. This tendency to change markups as aggregate demand changes contributes to the upward slope of the *SAS* curve. So, the two reasons the *SAS* curve slopes upward are (1) upward-sloping supply curves in auction markets and (2) firms' tendency to increase their markup when demand increases.

One reason I did not give for the upward slope of the *SAS* curve is changes in cost of production. That's because along an *SAS* curve, all other things, including input prices, are assumed to remain constant. Increases in input prices shift the *SAS* curve.

Shifts in the SAS Curve

Notice that in the definition of the *SAS* curve, we have assumed that other things remain constant. As discussed above, this does not mean that other things *will* remain constant. It simply means that changes in other things, such as input prices, shift the *SAS* curve. For example, if input prices rise, the *SAS* curve shifts up; if input prices fall, the *SAS* curve shifts down. So a change in input prices, such as wages, is a shift factor of aggregate supply. An important reason why wages change is expectations of inflation. If workers expect prices to be rising by 2 percent, they are likely to ask for at least a 2 percent rise in wages

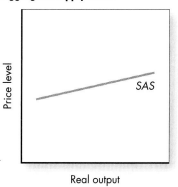

FIGURE 9-3 **The Short-Run Aggregate Supply Curve**

The two reasons the *SAS* curve slopes upward are (1) upward-sloping supply curves in auction markets and (2) firms' tendency to increase their markup when demand increases.

Changes in input prices cause a shift in the *SAS* curve.

Why Are Prices Inflexible?

Why do firms adjust production instead of price? A number of reasons have been put forward by economists, and recently a group of economists, led by Princeton economist Alan Blinder, surveyed firms to find out which reasons firms believed were most important. The survey choices included strategic pricing, cost-based pricing rules, and implicit contracts.

1. **Strategic pricing.** About 90 percent of final-goods markets in the United States are markets in which a few major firms compete, each taking each other's reactions into account in their decisions. Although, under U.S. law, firms cannot get together and decide on a pricing strategy for the industry, they can informally coordinate their pricing procedures. If all firms can implicitly agree to hold their prices up when faced with decreased demand, they are not violating the law and will be better off than they would be if they acted in an uncoordinated fashion.

    They also won't increase prices when they experience an increase in demand because they fear that doing so will undermine the coordinated pricing strategy with other firms or they will lose market share when other firms don't raise prices.

    This is not to say that the U.S. economy is not competitive. Ask any businessperson and he or she will tell you that it is highly competitive. But firms now often compete on fronts other than price.

2. **Cost-based pricing rules.** Strategic pricing is maintained by firms' tendency to use cost-based pricing rules. In a cost-plus-markup pricing procedure, firms set prices based on the costs of production. For a majority of firms, the most important costs are labor costs, which tend to be fixed by long-term wage contracts between workers and employers. (Unions, for example, typically negotiate wage contracts for three-year periods.) Thus, costs do not change with changes in demand, and, following a cost-plus-markup strategy, neither do prices.

3. **Implicit contracts.** Most firms have ongoing relationships with their customers. That means that they don't want to antagonize them. They have found that one way to avoid antagonizing customers is not to take advantage of them even when they could. In the Blinder survey, firms felt that they had implicit contracts with their customers to raise prices only when their costs changed, or when market conditions changed substantially.

The combination of these reasons leads to a large segment of the economy in which the prices do not significantly change as demand changes. For that reason, we generally don't see big changes in the overall price level. Of course, if costs, especially labor costs, start rising significantly, then prices will rise too. To the degree that demand changes affect costs, prices will respond, but, as a first approximation, it is generally acceptable to say that the price level does not significantly move in response to demand. That's why the short-run aggregate supply curve is not very steep.

---

simply to keep up with inflation and maintain their real wage. If they expect the price level to fall by 2 percent, they are far more likely to be happy with their current wage. So the expectation of inflation is a shift factor that works through wages.

Another shift factor of aggregate supply is a change in the productivity of the factors of production such as labor. An increase in productivity, by reducing the amount of inputs required for a given amount of output, reduces input costs per unit of output and shifts the SAS curve down. A fall in productivity shifts the SAS curve up.

Two other shift factors are changes in import prices of final goods, and changes in excise and sales taxes. Import prices are a shift factor because they are a component of an economy's price level. When import prices rise, the SAS curve shifts up; when import prices fall, the SAS curve shifts down. By raising the cost of goods, higher sales taxes shift the SAS curve up, and lower sales taxes shift the SAS curve down.

In summary, anything that changes factor costs will be a shift factor of supply. Such factors include

- Changes in input prices.
- Productivity.
- Import prices.
- Excise and sales taxes.

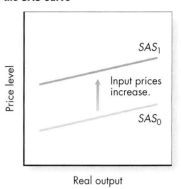

FIGURE 9-4 **Input Price Rise and the *SAS* Curve**

Economists spend a lot of time tracking these shift factors because they are central to whether the economy will have an inflation problem. Two of these—the wage component of input prices and labor productivity—are followed with special care because labor costs make up about two-thirds of total production costs.

The rule of thumb economists use when estimating how much the *SAS* curve will shift is that it will shift by the percentage change in wages and other factor prices minus changes in productivity. For example, if productivity rises by 3 percent and wages rise by 7 percent, we can expect the price level to rise by 4 percent for a given level of output. I show a shift up in the *SAS* curve in Figure 9-4. If wages and productivity rise by equal percentages, the price level would remain constant. If wages and other factor prices rise by less than the increase in productivity, the price level can fall, as recently happened in Japan. The relationship can be written as follows:

% change in the price level = % change in wages − % change in productivity

In the real world, we see shifts in the *SAS* curve in many areas. In the 1970s, for example, oil prices shot up enormously. That led to a sharp rise in the producer price index and a significant rise in factor prices, causing the *SAS* curve to shift up. Another example occurred in Argentina in early 2002 when the value of its currency, the peso, fell drastically. That caused the price of imports measured in pesos to increase substantially, which shifted its *SAS* curve up. In the early 2000s in the United States, we saw contrasting forces; oil prices rose substantially, pushing the *SAS* curve up, but labor productivity also rose in large part offsetting the upward push of oil prices and keeping inflation low.

The Long-Run Aggregate Supply Curve

The final curve that makes up the *AS/AD* model is the **long-run aggregate supply (LAS) curve**—*a curve that shows the long-run relationship between output and the price level*. Whereas the *SAS* curve holds input prices constant, no prices are assumed held constant on the *LAS* curve. The position of the *LAS* curve is determined by potential output—the amount of goods and services an economy can produce when both labor and capital are fully employed. Figure 9-5(a) shows an *LAS* curve.

The SAS curve holds input prices constant; no prices are assumed held constant on the LAS curve.

Notice that the *LAS* curve is vertical. Since at potential output all resources are being fully utilized, a rise in the price level means that the price of goods and factors of production, including wages, rise. Consider it this way: If all prices doubled, including your wage, your real income would not change. Since potential output is unaffected by the price level, the *LAS* curve is vertical.

A Range for Potential Output and the *LAS* Curve

The position of the *LAS* curve is determined by potential output. Because our estimates of potential output are inexact, precisely where to draw the *LAS* curve is generally somewhat in debate. To understand policy debates, it is helpful to consider potential

FIGURE 9-5 (A AND B)　**The Long-Run Aggregate Supply Curve**

The long-run aggregate supply curve shows the output that an economy can produce when both labor and capital are fully employed. It is vertical because at potential output a rise in the price level means that all prices, including input prices, rise. Available resources do not rise and thus neither does potential output.

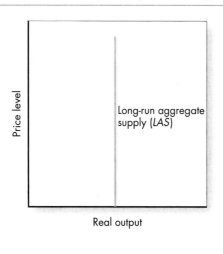

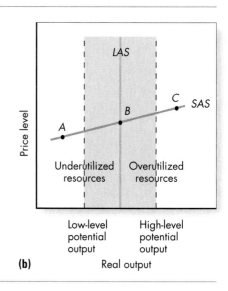

(a)

(b)

Short-Run Aggregate Supply vs. Long-Run Aggregate Supply

output to be a range of values. This range is bounded by a high level of potential output and a low level of potential output, as Figure 9-5(b) shows. The *LAS* curve can be thought of as being in the middle of that range.

This range is important because how close actual output (the position of the economy on the *SAS* curve) is to potential output is a key determinant of whether the *SAS* curve is expected to shift up or down. At points on the *SAS* curve to the left of the *LAS* curve (such as point A), resources are likely to be underutilized and we would expect factor prices to fall and, other things equal, the *SAS* curve to shift down. At points to the right of the *LAS* curve (such as point C), we would expect factor prices to be bid up and, other things equal, the *SAS* curve to shift up. Moreover, the further actual output is from potential output, the greater the pressure we would expect on factor prices to rise or fall. At the point of intersection between the *SAS* curve and the *LAS* curve (point B), other things equal, factor prices have no pressure to rise or fall.

In reality, whether factor prices will rise or fall in response to a change in demand is often in debate. That debate reflects the different estimates of potential output. Given the uncertainty of measured potential output, we would expect there to be a debate about whether the *SAS* curve will be shifting up or down. We will discuss these issues later. For now, all I want you to remember is that the *LAS* curve is an abstraction that reduces what is actually a range of potential output into a single value.

Shifts in the *LAS* Curve

Because the position of the *LAS* curve is determined by potential output, it shifts for the same reasons that potential output shifts. As discussed in the chapter about growth, those reasons are changes in capital, available resources, growth-compatible institutions, technology, and entrepreneurship. Increases in any of these increase potential output and shift the *LAS* curve out to the right. Decreases in any of these reduce potential output and shift the *LAS* curve in to the left. The position of the *LAS* curve plays an important role in determining long-run equilibrium and in determining whether policy should focus on long-run or short-run issues.

A Review of the *AS/AD* Model

	What Shape Is It?	What Determines Its Shape?	What Shifts the Curve?
Aggregate demand	Downward-sloping: As the price level declines expenditures rise.	The wealth effect, the interest rate effect, the international effect, and the multiplier effect.	Sudden changes in C, I, (X– M), or G caused by changes in foreign income, expectations about future income or prices, exchange rates, monetary policy, fiscal policy.
Short-run aggregate supply	Upward-sloping: The price level increases as output increases.	Firm behavior. Most firms change production instead of price when demand changes. Some firms will raise prices when output increases.	Increases in input prices shift the *SAS* curve up. Decreases in input prices shift the *SAS* curve down.
Long-run aggregate supply	Vertical: Changes in the price level have no effect on output.	Potential output is output that the economy can produce when labor and capital are fully utilized. It is not affected by prices.	Anything that increases potential output, such as increases in available resources and technological innovation.

Equilibrium in the Aggregate Economy

Now that we have introduced the *SAS*, *AD*, and *LAS* curves, we'll consider short-run and long-run equilibrium and how changes in the curves affect those equilibria. I start with the short run.

In the short run, equilibrium in the economy is where the short-run aggregate supply curve and the aggregate demand curve intersect. Thus, short-run equilibrium is shown by point *E* in Figure 9-6(a). If the *AD* curve shifts to the right, from AD_0 to AD_1, equilibrium will shift from point *E* to point *F*. The price level will rise to P_1 and output will increase to Y_1. A decrease in aggregate demand will shift output and the price level down.

Figure 9-6(b) shows the effect on equilibrium of a shift up in the *SAS* curve. Initially equilibrium is at point *E*. An upward shift in the *SAS* curve from SAS_0 to SAS_1 increases the price level from P_0 to P_2 and reduces equilibrium output from Y_0 to Y_2.

Long-run equilibrium is determined by the intersection of the *AD* curve and the *LAS* curve, as shown by point *E* in Figure 9-7(a). Since in the long run output is determined by the position of the *LAS* curve, which is at potential output Y_p, the aggregate demand curve can determine only the price level; it does not affect the level of real output. Thus, as shown in Figure 9-7(a), when aggregate demand increases from AD_0 to AD_1, the price level rises (from P_0 to P_1) but output does not change. When aggregate demand decreases, the price level falls and output remains at potential. In the long run, output is

Macroeconomic Equilibrium

Long-run equilibrium is determined by the intersection of the *AD* curve and the *LAS* curve.

215

FIGURE 9-6 (A AND B) **Equilibrium in the *AS/AD* Model**

Short-run equilibrium is where the short-run aggregate supply and aggregate demand curves intersect. Point *E* in **(a)** is equilibrium; **(a)** also shows how a shift in the aggregate demand curve to the right changes equilibrium from *E* to *F*, increasing output from Y_0 to Y_1 and increasing price level from P_0 to P_1. In **(b)** a shift up in the short-run aggregate supply curve changes equilibrium from *E* to *G*.

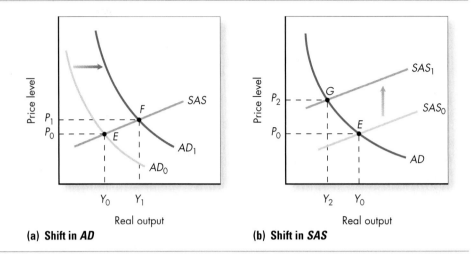

(a) **Shift in *AD***   (b) **Shift in *SAS***

fixed and the price level is variable, so aggregate output is determined not by aggregate demand but by potential output. Aggregate demand determines the price level.

Integrating the Short-Run and Long-Run Frameworks

To complete our analysis, we have to relate the long run and short run. We start with the economy in both long-run and short-run equilibrium. As you can see in Figure 9-7(b), at

FIGURE 9-7 (A AND B) **Long-Run Equilibrium**

Long-run equilibrium is where the *LAS* and *AD* curves intersect. Point *E* is long-run equilibrium. In **(a)** you can see how a shift in the aggregate demand curve changes equilibrium from *E* to *H*, increasing the price level from P_0 to P_1 but leaving output unchanged. The economy is in both short-run and long-run equilibrium when all three curves intersect in the same location. In **(b)** you can see the adjustment from recessionary and inflationary gaps to long-run equilibrium.

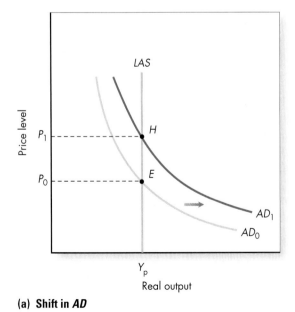
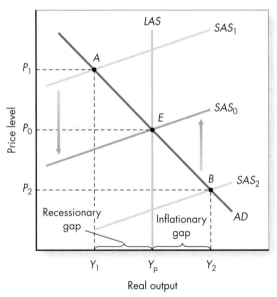

(a) **Shift in *AD***   (b) **Movement to Long-Run Equilibrium**

point E, with output Y_p, and price level P_0, the economy is in both a long-run equilibrium and a short-run equilibrium, since at point E the AD curve and SAS curve intersect at the economy's LAS curve. That is the situation economists hope for—that aggregate demand grows at just the same rate as potential output, so that growth and unemployment are at their target rates, with no, or minimal, inflation. In the late 1990s, the U.S. economy was in just such a position—potential output was increasing at the same rate that aggregate demand was increasing; unemployment was low, as was inflation.

The Recessionary Gap Alas, the economy is not always at that point E. An economy at point A in Figure 9-7(b) is in a situation where the quantity of aggregate demand is below potential output and not all the resources in the economy are being fully used. The distance $Y_p - Y_1$ shows the amount of output that is not being produced but could be. This distance is often referred to as a **recessionary gap,** *the amount by which equilibrium output is below potential output*.

If the economy remains at this level of output for a long time, costs and wages would tend to fall because there would be an excess supply of factors of production. As costs and wages fall, the price level also falls. The short-run aggregate supply curve would shift down (from SAS_1 to SAS_0) until eventually the long-run and short-run equilibrium would be reached at point E. But generally in our economy that does not happen.[3] Long before that happens, either the economy picks up on its own or the government introduces policies to expand output. That's why we seldom see declines in the price level. If the government expands aggregate demand, or some other shift factor expands aggregate demand, the AD curve shifts to the right, eliminating the recessionary gap and keeping the price level constant.

The Inflationary Gap An economy at point B in Figure 9-7(b) demonstrates a case where the short-run equilibrium is at a higher income than the economy's potential output. In this case, economists say that the economy has an **inflationary gap** shown by $Y_2 - Y_p$—*aggregate expenditures above potential output that exist at the current price level*. Output cannot remain at Y_2 for long because the economy's resources are being used beyond their potential. Factor prices will rise and the SAS curve will shift up from SAS_2 to SAS_0 the new equilibrium is at point E.

The Economy beyond Potential How can resources be used beyond their potential? By overutilizing them. Consider the resources you put into classwork. Suppose that your potential is a B+. If you stay up all night studying and cram in extra reading during mealtimes, you could earn an A. You can't keep up that effort for long. Eventually you'll get tired. The same is true for production. Extra shifts can be added and machinery can be run longer periods, but eventually the workers will become exhausted and the machinery will wear out. Output will have to return to its potential.

The result of this inflationary gap will be a bidding up of factor prices and a rise in costs for firms. When an economy is below potential, firms can hire additional factors of production without increasing production costs. Once the economy reaches its potential output, however, that is no longer possible. If a firm is to increase its factors of production, it must lure resources away from other firms. It will do so by offering higher wages and prices. But the firm facing a loss of its resources will likely respond by increasing its wages and other prices it pays to its employees and to other suppliers.

Q-6 If the *SAS*, *AD*, and *LAS* curves intersect at the same point and wages are constant, what is likely to happen to output and the price level?

Q-7 Demonstrate graphically both the short-run and long-run *AS/AD* equilibrium with a recessionary gap.

When income exceeds potential output, there is an inflationary gap.

If aggregate expenditures are above potential output, then increased demand for labor would put upward pressure on wages and subsequently on the overall level of prices.

---

[3]If, as happened in the Great Depression in the 1930s and in Japan in the early 2000s, the economy stays below its potential output long enough, we would likely see the price level fall.

As firms compete for resources, their costs rise beyond increases in productivity, shifting up the *SAS* curve. This means that once an economy's potential output is reached, the price level tends to rise. In fact, economists sometimes look to see whether the price level has begun to rise before deciding where potential output is. Thus, in the late 1990s, economists kept increasing their estimates of potential output because the price level did not rise even as the economy approached, and exceeded, what they previously thought was its potential output.

If the economy is operating above potential, the *SAS* curve will shift up until the inflationary gap is eliminated. That, however, is usually not what happens. Either the economy slows down on its own or the government introduces aggregate demand policy to contract output and eliminate the inflationary gap.

Aggregate Demand Policy

A primary reason for government policy makers' interest in the *AS/AD* model is their ability to shift the *AD* curve with policy. As I mentioned above, they can do this with monetary or fiscal policy. Monetary policy involves the Federal Reserve Bank changing the money supply and interest rates: understanding the process requires a knowledge of the financial sector. (This will be discussed at length in later chapters.) In this chapter I'll concentrate on **fiscal policy**—*the deliberate change in either government spending or taxes to stimulate or slow down the economy.* Fiscal policy is often discussed in terms of the government budget deficit (government expenditures less government revenue). If aggregate income is too low (actual income is below potential income), the appropriate fiscal policy is expansionary fiscal policy: increase the deficit by decreasing taxes or increasing government spending. Expansionary fiscal policy shifts the *AD* curve out to the right. If aggregate income is too high (actual income is above potential income), the appropriate fiscal policy is contractionary fiscal policy: decrease the deficit by increasing taxes or decreasing government spending. Contractionary fiscal policy shifts the *AD* curve to the left.

Let's go through a couple of examples. Say the economy is in a recessionary gap at point A in Figure 9-8(a). To eliminate the recessionary gap, government needs to implement expansionary fiscal policy. The appropriate fiscal policy would be to cut taxes or increase government spending, letting the multiplier augment those effects

Fiscal policy is the deliberate change in either government spending or taxes to stimulate or slow down the economy.

Q.8 If politicians suddenly raise government expenditures, and the economy is well below potential output, what will happen to prices and real income?

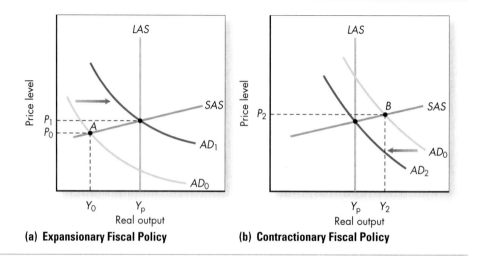

FIGURE 9-8 (A AND B)
Fiscal Policy

Expansionary fiscal policy can bring an economy out of a recessionary gap, as shown in (**a**). If an economy is in an inflationary gap, contractionary fiscal policy can reduce real output to prevent inflation, as shown in (**b**).

(a) Expansionary Fiscal Policy

(b) Contractionary Fiscal Policy

so that the *AD* curve shifts out to *AD*$_1$. This would raise the price level slightly but would eliminate the recessionary gap. Alternatively, say the economy is in an inflationary gap at point *B* in Figure 9-8(b). To prevent the inflation caused by the upward shift of the *SAS* curve, the appropriate fiscal policy is to increase taxes or cut government spending. Either of these actions will shift the *AD* curve in to *AD*$_2$. This lowers the price level slightly and eliminates the inflationary gap. So the best way to picture fiscal policy is as a policy designed to shift the *AD* curve to keep output at potential.

Some Additional Policy Examples

Now that we've been through the model, let's give you some practice with it by making you an adviser to the president. He comes to you for some advice. Unemployment is 12 percent and there is no inflation. History suggests that the economy is well below its potential output, so there is no need to worry about increasing factor prices. What policy would you recommend?

Pause for answer

The answer I hope you gave was expansionary fiscal policy, shifting the *AD* curve out to its potential income, as in Figure 9-9(a).

Now let's try a different scenario. Unemployment is 5 percent and it is believed that that 5 percent is the *target rate of unemployment*—the rate of unemployment that is consistent with potential output. But measures of consumer optimism suggest that a large rise in consumer expenditures is likely. What policy would you recommend?

Pause for answer

The answer I hope you gave is contractionary fiscal policy to counteract the expected rise in the *AD* curve before it occurs and prevent the economy from creating an inflationary gap. What would happen without that fiscal policy is shown in Figure 9-9(b). The economy is initially at point *C*, where the price level is *P*$_0$ and output is *Y*$_p$. In the absence of offsetting policy, the increase in expenditures along with the multiplier would move the economy to point *D* at a level of output (*Y*$_1$) above potential, creating an inflationary gap. If left alone, factor prices will rise, shifting the *SAS* curve up until it reaches *SAS*$_1$. The price level would rise to *P*$_1$ and the real output would return to *Y*$_p$,

Aggregate Demand Policy

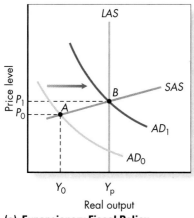

(a) Expansionary Fiscal Policy

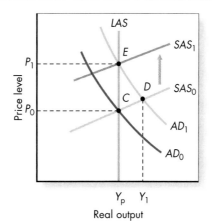

(b) Economy above Potential

FIGURE 9-9 (A AND B) **Shifting *AD* and *SAS* Curves**

In **(a)** you can see what happens when the economy is below potential and aggregate demand increases just enough to bring output to its potential. In **(b)** you can see what happens when the economy begins at potential and aggregate expenditures rise. Since the economy rises to above potential, input prices begin to rise and the *SAS* curve shifts up.

point E. But of course that didn't happen, because you recommended a policy of cutting government spending or raising taxes so that the AD curve shifts back to AD_0, making the equilibrium at point C, not point E, and avoiding any rise in prices. The economy remains at potential output at a constant price level, P_0.

To give you an idea of how fiscal policy has worked in the real world, we'll look at two examples: the effect of wartime spending in the 1940s and the prolonged expansion of the mid-1990s to early 2000s.

Fiscal Policy in World War II   In the 1940s the focus of U.S. policy switched from the Depression to fighting World War II. Fighting a war requires transferring civilian production to war production, so economists' attention turned to how to do so. Taxes went up enormously, but government expenditures rose far more. The result can be seen in Figure 9-10(a), which tabulates GDP, the deficit (government expenditures less taxes), and unemployment data for the wartime time span 1937–1946. As you can see, the deficit increased greatly and real GDP rose by more than the increase in the deficit. Figure 9-10(b) shows the effect in the AS/AD model. The AD curve shifts to the right by more than the increase in the deficit. As predicted, the U.S. economy expanded enormously in response to the expansionary fiscal policy that accompanied the war. One thing should bother you about this episode: If the economy exceeded its potential output, shouldn't the short-run aggregate supply curve have started to shift up, causing a serious inflation problem? It didn't because the wartime expansion was accompanied by wage and price controls, which prevented significant price-level increases, and by rationing.

Web Note 9.3
War Bonds

During the war, economic output expanded as far as anyone dared hope it could. This expansion was also accompanied by an expansionary monetary policy, so we

---

FIGURE 9-10 (A AND B)   **War Finance: Expansionary Fiscal Policy**

During wars, government budget deficits have risen significantly. As they have, unemployment has fallen and GDP has risen enormously. You can see the effect in the table in (a), which presents the U.S. government budget deficit and unemployment rate during World War II. The graph in (b) shows that this is what would be predicted in the AS/AD model.

Source: *Historical Statistics of the United States: Colonial Times to 1970.*

Year	GDP (billions of 1958 dollars)	Deficit (billions of dollars)	Unemployment rate
1937	$ 90	$ −2.8	14.3%
1938	84	−1.0	19.0
1939	90	−2.9	17.2
1940	99	−2.7	14.6
1941	124	−4.8	9.9
1942	157	−19.4	4.7
1943	191	−53.8	1.9
1944	210	−46.1	1.2
1945	211	−45.0	1.9
1946	208	−18.2	3.9

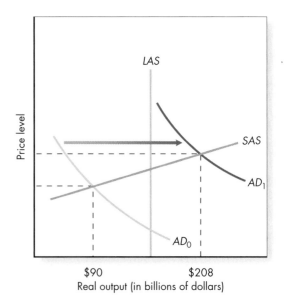

(a) U.S. GDP, Budget Deficits, and Unemployment Rates

(b) Prediction of *AS/AD* Model

must be careful about drawing too strong an inference about the effect of fiscal policy from the episode. (The importance of monetary policy will be discussed in a later chapter.)

It might seem from the example of World War II, when the U.S. economy expanded sharply, that wars are good for the economy. They certainly do bring about expansionary policy, increase GDP, and decrease unemployment. But remember, GDP is *not* welfare and a decrease in unemployment is not necessarily good. In World War II people went without many goods; production of guns and bombs increased, but production of butter decreased. Many people were killed or permanently disabled, which decreases unemployment but can hardly be called a good way to expand the economy.

U.S. Economic Expansion   As a second example, let's consider the government budget picture in the early 2000s. In the late 1990s and early 2000s, the budget went from a large deficit to a large surplus, so it would seem as if government fiscal policy was slowing the economy down. But the economy was booming. There are two explanations for this seeming paradox. The first is that, yes, the surplus was slowing the economy, but the contractionary effect of the surplus was offset by significant increases in consumer and investment spending. The private saving rate actually fell to zero at times and consumption increased enormously. Had the government budget not been in surplus, the economy would have likely exceeded potential output and inflation would have accelerated.

The second explanation for the paradox is that much of the surplus was the result of the booming economy, not contractionary fiscal policy. In fact, much of the deficit reduction, and movement into budget surplus, resulted from unexpected increases in income. When an economy is booming, as income rises, tax revenues rise and expenditures on income-support programs decline automatically. Much of the unexpected decline in the deficit was a result of tax revenue surprises.

Despite pressures in 2000 and 2001 by most economists to maintain the budget surplus (when tax revenues exceed expenditures), political pressures led to decreasing it, both by increasing government spending and by decreasing taxes. Then in mid-2001, the economy started to slow down. That slowdown was exacerbated by the terrorist attacks of September 11, following which investment and consumption fell, throwing the economy into a recession. Because of the recession, government had far less reason to run a surplus to slow the economy. In fact, the tax cut came at just the right time, keeping the recession very mild by helping hold up consumer spending. So here we have a case of expansionary fiscal policy working to prevent a recession. However, it is important to remember that the tax cuts were not proposed for their expansionary fiscal policy effects. Sometimes dumb luck is an important part of good economic policy.

Why Macro Policy Is More Complicated Than the *AS/AD* Model Makes It Look

The *AS/AD* model makes the analysis of the aggregate economy look easy. All you do is determine where the economy is relative to its potential output and, based on that, choose the appropriate policy to shift the *AD* curve. Alas, it's much harder than that.

First, implementing fiscal policy—changing government spending and taxes—is a slow legislative process. Government spending and taxing decisions are generally made

Policy is more complicated than the AS/AD model makes it seem.

Q.9 Why is it so important for policy makers to know what potential output is?

Web Note 9.4
Unemployed Machines

Q.10 If politicians suddenly raise government expenditures and the economy is above potential income, what will happen to prices and real income?

A countercyclical fiscal policy designed to keep the economy always at its target or potential level of income is called fine-tuning.

Almost all economists agree the government is not up to fine-tuning the economy.

for political, not economic, reasons. Thus, there is no guarantee that government will do what economists say is necessary. And even if it does, the changes often cannot be completed in a timely fashion.

A second problem is that we have no way of measuring potential output, so when we increase aggregate demand, we can't determine whether or not the *SAS* curve will be shifting up. Thus, the key to applying the policy is to know the location of the *LAS* curve, which is vertical at the economy's potential output. Unfortunately, we have no way of knowing that with certainty. Fortunately, we do have ways to get a rough idea of where it is.

Because inflation accelerates when an economy is operating above potential, one way of estimating potential output is to estimate the rate of unemployment below which inflation has begun to accelerate in the past. This is the target rate of unemployment. We can then estimate potential output by calculating output at the target rate of unemployment and adjusting for productivity growth. Unfortunately the target rate of unemployment fluctuates and is difficult to predict.

In summary, there are two ways to think about the effectiveness of fiscal policy: in the model and in reality. Models are great, and simple models, such as the one I've presented in this book, that you can understand intuitively are even greater. Put in the numbers and out comes the answer. Questions based on such models make great exam questions. But don't think that policies that work in a model will necessarily work in the real world.

The effectiveness of fiscal policy in reality depends on the government's ability to perceive a problem and to react appropriately to it. The essence of fiscal policy is government changing its taxes and its spending to offset any fluctuation that would occur in other autonomous expenditures, thereby keeping the economy at its potential level of income. If the model is a correct description of the economy, and if the government can act fast enough and change its taxes and spending in a *countercyclical* way, recessions can be prevented. This type of management of the economy is called **countercyclical fiscal policy**—*fiscal policy in which the government offsets any change in aggregate expenditures that would create a business cycle.* The term **fine-tuning** is used to describe such *fiscal policy designed to keep the economy always at its target or potential level of income.* With fine-tuning, the government responds to problems before they happen, and the aggregate economy runs smoothly.

As I will discuss below, today almost all economists agree the government is not up to fine-tuning the economy. The modern debate is whether it is up to any tuning of the economy at all. The reason is that the dynamic adjustment in the economy is extraordinarily complicated and that, once you take into account reasonable expectations of future policy, the formal model (called the dynamic stochastic general equilibrium model) becomes hopelessly complex. Graduate students in economics get Ph.D.s for worrying about such hopeless complexities. At the introductory level, all we require is that you (1) know this simple *AS/AD* model and (2) remember that, in the real world, it cannot be used in a mechanistic manner; it must be used with judgment.

Conclusion

Let's conclude the chapter with a brief summary. In the 1930s modern macroeconomics developed as Classical economists' interest in growth and supply-side issues shifted to Keynesian economists' interest in business cycles and demand-side issues. To capture the issues about the effect of aggregate demand on the economy, economists developed the *AS/AD* model.

The *AS/AD* model summarizes the expected effects that shifts in aggregate supply and aggregate demand have on output and the price level. In the short run, outward shifts in the *AD* curve cause real output and the price level to rise. Inward shifts cause the opposite. If the economy is beyond potential output and the *LAS* curve, the *SAS* curve will shift up, causing the price level to increase and real output to decrease, until real output falls back to potential. The equilibrium is where aggregate demand intersects the *LAS* curve. In the model, the government can, through fiscal policy, shift the *AD* curve in or out, thereby achieving the desired level of real output, as long as that desired level does not exceed potential output.

Unfortunately, potential output is hard to estimate, and implementing fiscal policy in a timely fashion is difficult, making macroeconomic policy more an art than a science.

Macro policy is more an art than a science.

Summary

- The Depression marked a significant change in U.S. economic institutions. Keynesian economics developed.

- Classical economists focus on the long run and use a laissez-faire approach.

- Keynesian economists focus on short-run fluctuations and use an activist government approach.

- The *AS/AD* model consists of the aggregate demand curve, the short-run aggregate supply curve, and the long-run aggregate supply curve.

- The aggregate demand curve slopes downward because of the wealth effect, the interest rate effect, the international effect, and the multiplier effect.

- The short-run aggregate supply (*SAS*) curve is upward-sloping because, while for the most part firms in the United States adjust production to meet demand instead of changing price, some firms will raise prices when demand increases.

- The long-run aggregate supply (*LAS*) curve is vertical at potential output.

- The *LAS* curve shifts out when available resources, capital, labor, technology, and/or growth-compatible institutions increase.

- Short-run equilibrium is where the *SAS* and *AD* curves intersect. Long-run equilibrium is where the *AD* and *LAS* curves intersect.

- When the economy is in a short-run equilibrium but not long-run equilibrium, the *SAS* curve will shift up or down to bring the economy back to long-run equilibrium unless government policy shifts the *AD* curve first.

- When output exceeds potential, there is an inflationary gap and the *SAS* curve will shift up to eliminate the gap. When output is below potential, there is a recessionary gap and the *SAS* curve will shift down to eliminate the gap.

- Aggregate demand management policy attempts to influence the level of output in the economy by influencing aggregate demand and relying on the multiplier to expand any policy-induced change in aggregate demand.

- Fiscal policy—the change in government spending or taxes—works by providing a deliberate countershock to offset unexpected shocks to the economy.

- Macroeconomic policy is difficult to conduct because implementing fiscal policy is a slow process and we don't really know where potential output is.

- We must estimate potential output by looking at past levels of potential output and by looking at where the price level begins to rise.

Key Terms

aggregate demand (*AD*) curve (*205*)

aggregate demand management (*204*)

countercyclical fiscal policy (*222*)

equilibrium income (*204*)

fine-tuning (*222*)

fiscal policy (*218*)

inflationary gap (*217*)

interest rate effect (*207*)

international effect (*207*)

long-run aggregate supply (*LAS*) curve (*213*)

multiplier effect (*207*)

potential income (*204*)

quantity-adjusting markets (*211*)

recessionary gap (*217*)

short-run aggregate supply (*SAS*) curve (*211*)

wealth effect (*206*)

Questions for Thought and Review

1. Distinguish between a laissez-faire economist and an activist economist.   LO1

2. Classicals saw the Depression as a political problem, not an economic problem. Why?   LO1

3. What are five factors that cause the *AD* curve to shift?   LO2

4. Use the wealth, interest rate, international, and multiplier effects to explain how a rise in the price level affects aggregate quantity demanded.   LO2

5. What are two factors that cause the *SAS* curve to shift?   LO3

6. Why is the *LAS* curve vertical?   LO4

7. If an economy is in short-run equilibrium that is below potential, what forces will bring the economy to long-run equilibrium?   LO5

8. Moore's law states that every 18 months, the computing speed of a microchip doubles. What effect does this likely have on the economy? Explain your answer using the *AS/AD* model.   LO5

9. If the economy were close to high potential output, would policy makers present their policy prescriptions to increase real output any differently than if the economy were far from potential output? Why?   LO5

10. Why is countercyclical fiscal policy difficult to implement?   LO6

11. Why is knowing the level of potential output important to designing appropriate fiscal policy?   LO6

12. In the late 1990s, a growing number of economists argued that world policy makers were focusing too much on fighting inflation. The economists also argued that the technical level of potential output had risen. Show their argument using the *AS/AD* model.   LO6

13. Explain why macro policy is more difficult than the simple model suggests.   LO6

Problems and Exercises

14. The opening quotation of the chapter refers to Keynes's view of theory.
    a. What do you think he meant by it?
    b. How does it relate to the emphasis on the "other things constant" assumption?
    c. Do you think Keynes's interest was mainly in positive economics, the art of economics, or normative economics? Why?   LO1

15. Explain what will likely happen to the slope or position of the *AD* curve in the following circumstances:
    a. The exchange rate changes from fixed to flexible.
    b. A fall in the price level doesn't make people feel richer.
    c. A fall in the price level creates expectations of a further-falling price level.
    d. Income is redistributed from rich people to poor people.
    e. Autonomous exports increase by 20.
    f. Government spending decreases by 10.   LO2

16. Explain what will likely happen to the *SAS* curve in each of the following instances:
    a. Productivity rises 3 percent; wages rise 4 percent.
    b. Productivity rises 3 percent; wages rise 1 percent.
    c. Productivity declines 1 percent; wages rise 1 percent.
    d. Productivity rises 2 percent; wages rise 2 percent.   LO3

17. Explain what will happen to the position of the *SAS* curve and/or *LAS* curve in the following circumstances:
    a. Available factors of production increase.
    b. A civil war occurs.
    c. The price of oil quadruples.
    d. Wages that were fixed become flexible, and aggregate demand increases.   LO3, LO4

18. Congratulations! You have been appointed an economic policy adviser to the United States. You are told that the economy is significantly below its potential output and that the following will happen

next year: World income will fall significantly and the price of oil will rise significantly. (The United States is an oil importer.)
a. What will happen to the price level and output? Using the *AS/AD* model, demonstrate your predictions graphically.
b. What policy might you suggest to the government?   LO5

19. What fiscal policy actions would you recommend in the following instances?
a. The economy begins at potential output, but foreign economies slow dramatically.
b. The economy has been operating above potential output and inflationary pressures rise.
c. A new technology is invented that significantly raises potential output.   LO5

Questions from Alternative Perspectives

1. Austrian economist Murray Rothbard has argued that government intervention during 1929 made what could have been a 1-year recession set off by the stock market crash into a 12-year depression. He believed that by creating confusing signals, government intervention kept investors from gaining knowledge of what investments to avoid.
a. Is Rothbard's explanation of the Depression consistent with the *AS/AD* model?
b. If one agrees with Rothbard, how would one's proposed policies to deal with recessions differ from those presented in the book? (Austrian)

2. In the 1950s, Michael Hubert King, an oil geologist, mathematically determined that when 50 percent of oil reserves have been extracted, annual oil output would inexorably decline. He looked at the rate of oil discovery in the United States and predicted that domestic oil production would peak in 1969. The peak occurred in 1970! Today global oil production is nearly at maximum production capacity, and it is likely that in the very near future the inexorable decline will begin globally.
a. Use the *AS/AD* model and the production possibility curve to describe what will happen when oil production declines.

b. What will this do to the question of "distribution," both within and between nations? (Institutionalist)

3. Consider the following economic principles held by Classical economists: (1) Short-run problems are temporary glitches that are solved by the market; (2) The economy always returns to its potential in the long run; and (3) Unemployment is the result of institutional barriers to the market.
a. What are Keynes's criticisms of these economic principles?
b. Why did he believe that they were wrong? (Post-Keynesian)

4. Draw an *AS/AD* diagram from the Keynesian viewpoint. Assume the initial equilibrium in your diagram is just at the level of potential output. Then reduce the level of aggregate demand in your diagram. Now stare at this diagram.
a. Can you identify the excess capacity or depression in the diagram and what caused it?
b. What should be done to return the economy to a full employment level of output?
c. What does this exercise suggest about the distinction between economic theorizing (or positive economics) and policy recommendations (normative economics)?
d. Is one more value laden than the other? (Radical)

Web Questions

1. Go to the Bureau of Labor Statistics' home page (www.bls.gov) and look up the recent changes in the consumer price index. Using that information, answer the following:
a. Where do you think the economy is relative to potential?
b. How does your answer to *a* determine what policy you would suggest the government should follow?

2. Go to the Council of Economic Advisers' home page (www.whitehouse.gov/cea) and look in the *Economic Report of the President*.
a. Find the U.S. price level and the level of output (GDP) over the last 10 years.

b. Graph the data with price level on the vertical axis and the level of GDP on the horizontal axis.
c. Is the curve you have drawn a supply curve, a demand curve, or neither? Why?

3. Go to the Conference Board's home page (www.conference-board.org) and read the press release of the consumer confidence index. Based on this release, what do you think will happen to the *AD* curve? How will this affect the price level and equilibrium output? Demonstrate your answer graphically.

Answers to Margin Questions

1. A Classical economist takes a laissez-faire approach, and believes the economy is self-regulating. A Keynesian economist takes an interventionist approach, and believes that equilibrium output can remain below potential output. (*202*)

2. In the short run, saving can lead to a decrease in expenditures and reduce equilibrium output. In the long run, saving leads to the accumulation of capital and an increase in potential output. In the long run, saving increases equilibrium output. (*205*)

3. False. The multiplier magnifies the initial effect. The rise in expenditures will be greater than 10, making the *AD* curve flatter than a slope of −1. (*208*)

4. A rise in a country's exchange rate will make domestic goods more expensive to foreigners and foreign goods less expensive to domestic residents. It will shift the *AD* curve in to the left because net exports will fall. (*208*)

5. The *AD* curve will shift out by more than 20 because of the multiplier. (*210*)

6. If the *AD*, *SAS*, and *LAS* curves intersect at the same point, the economy is in both long-run and short-run equilibrium. Nothing will happen to the price level and output. (*217*)

7. If there is a recessionary gap, the *SAS* and *AD* curves intersect to the left of potential output at a point such as A in the figure in the next column. At that level of output there will be pressure for factor prices to fall, pushing the *SAS* curve down. Unless the *AD* curve shifts out (as it usually does), the *SAS* curve will shift down and output

will rise until output equals potential output and the economy is in both long-run and short-run equilibrium at a point such as B. (*217*)

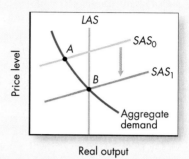

8. If the economy is well below potential, I would predict that output will rise and the price level will rise only slightly. (*218*)

9. Where the economy is relative to potential will determine whether the price level will rise (inflationary gap) or fall (recessionary gap) and determine the type of fiscal policy needed. (*222*)

10. If the economy is above potential output, I would predict that factor prices will rise, shifting the *SAS* curve up. The expansion in government expenditures will shift the *AD* curve out further, putting even more pressure on factor prices to rise. My answer, therefore, is that the price level will rise very quickly and real output will fall until it equals potential output. (*222*)

The Multiplier Model

Keynes stirred the stale economic frog pond to its depth.

—*Gottfried Haberler*

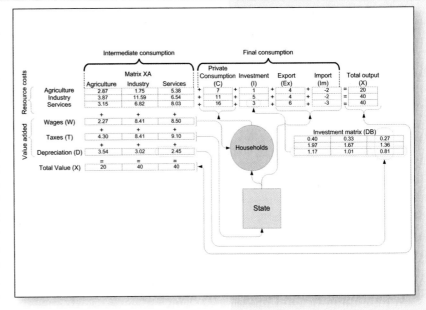

Policy makers want numbers. Exactly how much can we expect GDP to rise if we cut taxes by $100 billion? How much should we lower interest rates—¼ point or ½ point? The *AS/AD* model of the last chapter didn't give them numbers; it talked about the multiplier and about how an initial shift in aggregate expenditures (other things equal) would have a multiplied effect on income. In this chapter I present a model—the multiplier model—that provides numbers. Even though it is a highly simplified model, it forms an important element of most modern econometric models (computer models that economists use to make forecasts about the economy). Policy makers at the Fed, the Congressional Budget Office, and the White House use such models to guide their decisions.

The Multiplier Model

The multiplier model explores what happens when aggregate expenditures expand by a certain number, say, 20. In terms of the *AS/AD* model, the question it explores (shown in Figure 10-1) is: When a shift factor of aggregate demand increases by, say, 20, how much will the *AD* curve shift out? Notice in Figure 10-1 that the *SAS* curve is horizontal. That's because the multiplier model assumes that the price level remains constant. (Factor prices are assumed not to change.) This assumption means that we don't have to differentiate between real and nominal income in our discussion. Whereas the *AS/AD* model gives us insights into the general *qualitative* effects of these shifts, the multiplier model tells us about their *quantitative* effects. For example, say that the economists at the Federal Reserve Bank (the Fed) have determined that the multiplier effect of an increase in expenditures will be 2. Their research department informs them that investment and consumption have suddenly fallen by 1 percent of GDP because a stock market bubble has burst. The Fed economists would then predict that output would fall by 2 percent.

It was just such a precipitous fall in income that the multiplier model was initially designed to explain. As I discussed in the last chapter, in the 1930s income

AFTER READING THIS CHAPTER, YOU SHOULD BE ABLE TO:

1. Explain the difference between induced and autonomous expenditures.
2. Show how the level of income is graphically determined in the multiplier model.
3. Use the multiplier equation to determine equilibrium income.
4. Explain how the multiplier process amplifies shifts in autonomous expenditures.
5. Demonstrate how fiscal policy can eliminate recessionary and inflationary gaps.
6. List six reasons why the multiplier model might be misleading.

ADDED DIMENSION

Econometric Models

U.S. government agencies and virtually every major corporation in the United States subscribe to, or generate their own, forecasts of the economy. Such forecasts about interest rates, prices, investment, consumption, and government policy actions are essential to corporate decisions from whether to open a new factory to how much to pay its employees. They are also essential to government decisions that impact the economy. If some day you work in government or in a firm, you will likely come across a report that forecasts the economy.

Economists forecast the future of the economy using *econometric* models, models that forecast a variety of *measures* of the economy. (The word "metric" means measure.) The models presented in this chapter are a major simplification of econometric models. Two well-known econometric models are the Fed (Federal Reserve Bank) econometric model and the DRI–WEFA

model. In econometric models, economists find standard relationships among aspects of the macroeconomy and use those relationships to predict what will happen to inflation, unemployment, and growth under certain conditions. For example, when President Bush wanted to know the effect his proposed tax cut would have on the economy, he went to economists who entered the tax cut into their econometric models and estimated the effect. He went back to them when he wanted to know how the Iraq War spending would affect the economy. Using their econometric models, they estimated the effect.

While econometric models are much more complicated than the models presented here, they have the same structure: a short-run aggregate supply component with essentially fixed prices, an aggregate demand component, and a potential output component.

decreased enormously and the economy fell into a depression. The multiplier model was designed to show how an initial drop in investment could have led to such a large drop in income.

We'll start our discussion of the multiplier model by looking separately at production decisions and expenditure decisions.

FIGURE 10-1 The *AS/AD* Model When Prices Are Fixed

The multiplier model was designed to explain how an initial shift in expenditures changes equilibrium output when the price level is fixed. It is designed to fill in the question mark in this figure. An increase in expenditures of 20 causes additional induced effects. These shifts are called multiplier effects.

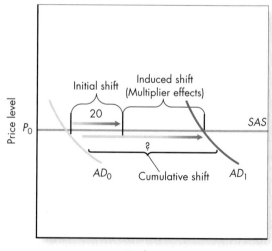

228

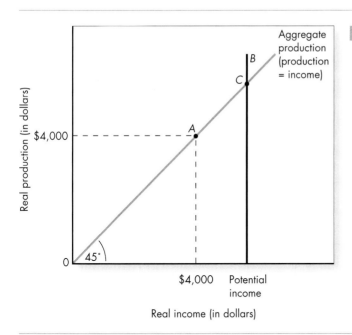

FIGURE 10-2 **The Aggregate Production Curve**

Since, by definition, real output equals real income, on each point of the aggregate production curve, income must equal production. This equality holds true only on the 45° line.

Aggregate Production

Aggregate production is *the total amount of final goods and services produced in every industry in an economy*. It is at the center of the multiplier model. As I noted in the chapter on national income accounting, production creates an equal amount of income, so actual income and actual production are always equal; the terms can be used interchangeably.

Graphically, aggregate production in the multiplier model is represented by a 45° line on a graph, with real income in dollars measured on the horizontal axis and real production measured in dollars on the vertical axis, as in Figure 10-2. Given the definition of the axes, connecting all the points at which real production equals real income produces a 45° line through the origin. Since, by definition, production creates an amount of income equal to the amount of production or output, this 45° line can be thought of as an *aggregate production curve*, or, alternatively, the *aggregate income curve*. At all points on the aggregate production curve, income equals production. For example, consider point A in Figure 10-2, where real income (measured on the horizontal axis) is $4,000 and real production (measured on the vertical axis) is also $4,000. That identity between real production and real income is true only on the 45° line. Output and income, however, cannot expand without limit. The model is most relevant when output is below its potential. Once production expands to the capacity constraint of the existing institutional structure—to potential income (line B)—any increase beyond that can only be temporary.

Graphically, aggregate production in the multiplier model is represented by a 45° line through the origin.

What is true about the relationship between income and production on the aggregate production curve?

Aggregate Expenditures

The term **aggregate expenditures** refers to *the total amount of spending on final goods and services in the economy*. This amount consists of four main expenditure classifications: consumption (spending by consumers), investment (spending by business), spending by government, and net exports (the difference between U.S. exports and U.S. imports). These four components were presented in our earlier discussion of aggregate accounting, which isn't surprising since the aggregate accounts were designed around the multiplier

Aggregate expenditures in an economy (AE) equal C + I + G + (X − M).

model. In the multiplier model, we focus on the four components' relationship to income. The multiplier model asks the question "How does each of these change as income changes?" To keep the exposition as simple but as general as possible, we focus in this chapter on the aggregate relationship between all expenditure components combined and income, that is, on the relationship between aggregate expenditures and income. (In Appendix A at the end of this chapter, we present a disaggregated discussion.)

Autonomous and Induced Expenditures

For purposes of the multiplier model, all forms of expenditures are classified as either autonomous or induced. **Autonomous expenditures** are *expenditures that do not systematically vary with income*. **Induced expenditures** are *expenditures that change as income changes*. Say that each time income rises by 100, expenditures increase by 60. The induced expenditures would be 60.

This assumed empirical relationship between income and aggregate expenditures can be represented graphically with the aggregate expenditure (*AE*) curve. To keep the analysis simple, the *AE* curve is usually estimated to be a linear relationship (a straight line) for incomes near current income. To make the graphical exposition easier, we will also assume that the linear relationship continues for all levels of income. This allows us to draw a linear aggregate expenditures curve such as the one shown in Figure 10-3.

Notice that when income is $6,000, aggregate expenditures are also $6,000; but when income rises by $1,000 to $7,000, aggregate expenditures rise by $500 to $6,500. The reason is that only induced expenditures change as income changes. When income falls to $5,000, expenditures fall to $5,500. Along this *AE* curve, induced expenditures fall by $500 when income falls by $1,000.

To figure out autonomous expenditures, we have to extend the *AE* curve to the left, to the point where income is zero (where the *AE* curve intersects the vertical axis). Doing so, you can see that when income is zero, aggregate expenditures are $3,000. So, autonomous expenditures are $3,000. Consumption, investment, government spending, and net exports each has an autonomous component. Autonomous expenditures

Autonomous expenditures are expenditures that do not systematically vary with income.

Autonomous vs. Induced Expenditures

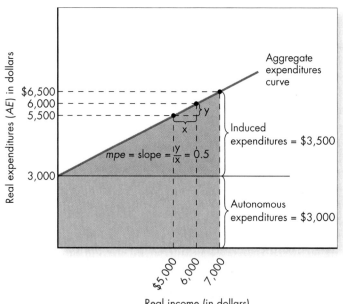

FIGURE 10-3 Aggregate Expenditures Curve

The *AE* curve depicted here has a slope of .5, the *mpe*, and an intercept of $3,000, the level of autonomous expenditures. The brown shaded area represents induced expenditures. Aggregate expenditures are the sum of these two components.

are the sum of all of them. It is the level of expenditures that would exist at zero income, assuming the *AE* curve is linear. (Again, it is important to recognize that this linear extension is just for expositional purposes. In reality, income is not expected to fall to zero, and the model is used to describe changes around the existing level of income.) The point to remember about autonomous expenditures is that they remain constant at all levels of income; therefore, a graph of autonomous expenditures is a straight, horizontal line as shown in Figure 10-3.

To summarize, aggregate expenditures are comprised of two components: autonomous expenditures that do not vary with income and induced expenditures that vary with income. The gray shaded region in Figure 10-3 represents autonomous expenditures; the brown shaded region represents induced expenditures. So, at income $7,000, aggregate expenditures of $6,500 are comprised of $3,000 of autonomous expenditures and $3,500 of induced expenditures.

The Marginal Propensity to Expend The slope of an aggregate expenditures curve is equal to the **marginal propensity to expend (*mpe*)**—*the ratio of the change in aggregate expenditures to a change in income*. (Remember, slope is the change in the value on the vertical axis divided by the change in the value on the horizontal axis, or rise over run.) The expenditures function I have drawn has a slope of .5, which means that for every $1,000 increase in income, aggregate expenditures rise by $500. If the *mpe* were .4, the slope of the *AE* curve would be .4 and aggregate expenditures would rise by $400 for every $1,000 increase in income.

The marginal propensity to expend is assumed to be greater than 0 and less than 1. Therefore, the aggregate expenditures curve will have a slope that is less than the 45-degree *AP* curve and greater than a horizontal line (such as autonomous expenditures). Economists estimate the slope of the *AE* curve by looking at how much aggregate expenditures have changed with a change in income around past income and then use that information to estimate the relationship for current levels of income.

The marginal propensity to expend is an aggregation of the various relationships between each component of aggregate expenditures (consumption, investment, government spending, exports, and imports) and aggregate income. There is a marginal propensity to consume, a marginal propensity to import, and, in more complicated models, a variety of other marginal propensities. (Appendix A at the end of the chapter provides a disaggregated presentation of these components.) But it is the aggregate of these—the *mpe*—that is the key to the multiplier model.

While the presentation will focus on the aggregate *mpe*, let me briefly discuss its components. The most important determinant of the marginal propensity to expend is the marginal propensity to consume (*mpc*)—the change in consumption that occurs with a change in income.[1] It is less than 1 because individuals tend to save a portion of their income, so when income goes up by 100 their spending will go up by, say, only 80. In that case the marginal propensity to consume would be .8. If induced consumption were the only component, the marginal propensity to expend would be .8.

While the marginal propensity to consume is important to expenditures, other important, policy-relevant factors also affect how expenditures change with income. One of these factors is the income tax. As income rises, people pay higher income tax, which

Autonomous expenditures are unrelated to income; induced expenditures are directly related to income.

Q-2 What is the difference between induced expenditures and autonomous expenditures?

$$mpe = \frac{\text{Change in expenditures}}{\text{Change in income}}$$

Q-3 If expenditures change by $60 when income changes by $100, what is the *mpe*?

The marginal propensity to consume (*mpc*) is the most important component of the *mpe*.

---

[1]The importance of this component has led some to concentrate the multiplier model presented in principles books on consumption and the marginal propensity to consume. However, to keep the analysis simple, this focus generally requires them to assume that the other components do not vary with income. I focus on a broader concept—marginal propensity to expend—because it is more inclusive, requires less algebraic manipulation, and incorporates two other primary reasons why income may not get translated into expenditures. This allows us to talk more about policy and less about the model.

History of the Multiplier Model

Policy fights in economics occur on many levels. Keynes fought on most of them. But it wasn't Keynes who convinced U.S. policy makers to accept his ideas. (Indeed, President Franklin D. Roosevelt met Keynes only once and thought he was a pompous academic.) Instead, it was Alvin Hansen, a textbook writer and policy adviser to government who was hired away from the University of Wisconsin by Harvard in the mid-1930s, who played the key role in getting Keynesian economic policies introduced into the United States.

The story of how Hansen converted to Keynes's ideas is somewhat mysterious. At the time, almost all economists were Classicals, and Hansen was no exception. (Otherwise it's doubtful Harvard would have recruited him.) But, somehow, on the train trip from Wisconsin to Massachusetts, Hansen metamorphosed from a Classical to a Keynesian. His graduate seminar at Harvard in the late 1930s and the 1940s became the U.S. breeding ground for Keynesian economics.

What made Hansen and other economists switch from Classical to Keynesian economics? It was the Depression; the Keynesian story explained it much better than did the Classical story, which centered on the real wage being too high.

Hansen quickly realized that talking about interdependencies of supply and demand decisions didn't work for policy makers and businesspeople. They wanted numbers—specifics—and Keynes's work had no specifics. So Alvin Hansen and his students, especially Paul Samuelson, set about to develop specifics. They developed what is now called the textbook model of Keynesian economics.

lowers how much additional income people have at their disposal to spend, which lowers the increase in their expenditures. Thinking back to the national income classifications, remember that disposable income is less than GDP. So taxes reduce the size of the marginal propensity to expend from what it would have been if all income were available to households to spend. In the United States, taxes that vary with income are approximately 20 percent of total income. Another important determinant of the marginal propensity to expend is the marginal propensity to import   the change in imports that occurs with a change in income. With increasing globalization, individuals are spending a larger portion of their income on imports. That portion is not part of aggregate expenditures on domestic goods. Instead, it is part of the aggregate expenditures of other countries, so the fact that imports increase as income increases also reduces the size of the marginal propensity to expend. Americans spend about 15 percent of increases of their income on imports. In some countries, such as the Netherlands, that fraction can be as high as 50 or 60 percent.

The Aggregate Expenditures Function   The relationship between aggregate expenditures and income that is depicted by the *AE* curve can be written mathematically as follows:

$$AE = \underbrace{AE_0}_{\text{autonomous}} + \underbrace{mpeY}_{\text{induced}}$$

It consists of the same two components that make up the *AE* curve: autonomous expenditures (the AE_0—the subscript zero tells you it is autonomous) and induced expenditures (the *mpeY*). The aggregate expenditures function depicted by the *AE* curve we've discussed so far and shown in Figure 10-3 is $AE = \$3,000 + .5Y$. Autonomous expenditures are \$3,000 and the *mpe* is .5. Just like the *AE* curve, the aggregate expenditures function takes into account all components of aggregate spending. Therefore, autonomous expenditures are the sum of the autonomous components of expenditures [$AE_0 = C_0 + I_0 + G_0 + (X_0 - M_0)$] and induced expenditures are the sum of the

$AE_0 = C_0 + I_0 + G_0 + (X_0 - M_0)$

FIGURE 10-4 (A, B, AND C)   Three Aggregate Expenditure Functions

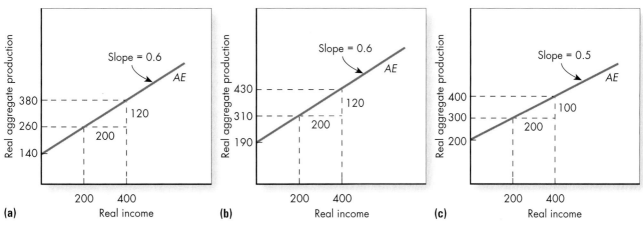

induced components of expenditures. These induced expenditures are determined by the marginal propensity to consume, the marginal propensity to import, and taxes that vary with income.

In Figure 10-4, I graph three expenditures functions. A good exercise is to determine which of the AE curves (*a*, *b*, or *c*) is associated with which expenditures function described by the following situations:

- *Situation 1*. Autonomous consumption is 100; autonomous investment is 40; autonomous net exports are 30; autonomous spending by government is 20; and the marginal propensity to expend is .6.

- *Situation 2*. Autonomous consumption is 100; autonomous investment is 40; autonomous net exports are 30; autonomous spending by government is 30; and the marginal propensity to expend is .5.

- *Situation 3*. Autonomous expenditures are 140 and the marginal propensity to expend is .6.

The answers are 1-*b*, 2-*c*, and 3-*a*. There are a number of ways you could have associated each of these situations with the graphs. Since the marginal propensity to expend in Situation 2 was .5, its slope had to be .5. Thus, only graph *c* is consistent with it. Situations 1 and 3 have the same marginal propensity to expend, so we have to differentiate them by their autonomous expenditures component. Adding up autonomous expenditures in Situation 1 gives us 190, so the intercept (the level of expenditures at zero income) must be 190. That is the case for *b*. Checking, graph *a* has an intercept of 140, and a slope of .6, which means that it is consistent with Situation 3.

The aggregate expenditures function is important because once you have estimated an expenditures function for the economy, you can predict expenditures at any income. Say you have estimated an aggregate expenditures function to be AE = 240 + .4Y. If income is $500, you would estimate aggregate expenditures to be $440 [240 + .4(500)]. Estimating aggregate expenditures is fundamental to predicting whether the economy will grow or fall into a recession.

Shifts in the Expenditures Function   A key element of the expenditures function for our purposes concerns changes in autonomous expenditures. These changes are usually classified by which of the four subcomponents of autonomous expenditures changed—autonomous consumption, autonomous investment, autonomous government spending, or autonomous net exports. All of these can change suddenly, and, when one or more do, the AE curve shifts up or down. For example, if autonomous consumption rises by $200, and autonomous investment falls by $80, autonomous expenditures will rise by $120 ($200 − $80).

Economists keep close tabs on these autonomous components as they develop their forecasts of the economy. For example, imagine that consumer confidence suddenly decreases, perhaps because of a terrorist threat. Consumers figure they had better save more to prepare themselves for the upcoming recession, so they cut back expenditures; autonomous consumption falls and the expenditures function shifts down. Alternatively, imagine that businesses come to believe that the economy will grow faster than they expected. To prepare, they will increase investment, increasing autonomous investment and shifting the aggregate expenditures curve up.

Web Note 10.1
Keynes on Investment

I'll let you work these final two examples by yourself. The first is that the government enters into a major war, and the second is that the country's exchange rate suddenly falls, causing the price of the country's exports to fall and the price of imports to rise. If you answered that they both shift the expenditures function up, you've got the reasoning down.

The multiplier model is a historical model most useful for analyzing shifts in autonomous expenditures.

The reason it is important to focus on shifts is that the multiplier model is a historical model. It can be used to analyze shifts in aggregate expenditures from a historically given income level, but not to determine income independent of the economy's historical position. Notice how I discussed the model in the examples—some shift in autonomous expenditures occurred and that shift led to a change in income from its existing level.

As I mentioned above, while economists speak of what expenditures would be at zero income, or while we say the *mpe* is constant over all ranges of income, that is done simply to make the geometric portrayal of the model easier. What is actually assumed is that within the relevant range around existing income—say a 5 percent increase or decrease—the *mpe* remains constant, and the autonomous portion of the expenditures is the intercept that would occur if we extended the expenditures function.

Determining the Equilibrium Level of Aggregate Income

Now that we've developed the graphical framework for the multiplier model, we can put the aggregate production and aggregate expenditures together and see how the level of aggregate income is determined. We begin by considering the relationship between the aggregate expenditures curve and the aggregate production curve more carefully. We do so in Figure 10-5.

The aggregate production (AP) curve is a 45° line up until the economy reaches potential income. Its slope is 1, so at all points on the AP curve, aggregate expenditures equal aggregate income. It tells you the level of aggregate production and also the level of aggregate income since, by definition, real income equals real production when the price level does not change. Expenditures are shown by the AE curve. Planned expenditures (expenditures as calculated using the expenditures function) do not necessarily equal production or income. In equilibrium, however, planned expenditures must equal production.

To determine income graphically in the multiplier model, you find the income level at which aggregate expenditures equal planned aggregate production.

To see why that's the case, let's first say that production, and hence income, is $14,000. As you can see, at income of $14,000, planned expenditures are $12,000. Aggregate production exceeds planned aggregate expenditures. Firms are producing more goods than are bought, and inventories are rising by more than firms want. This is true for any income level above $10,000. Similarly, at all income levels below $10,000,

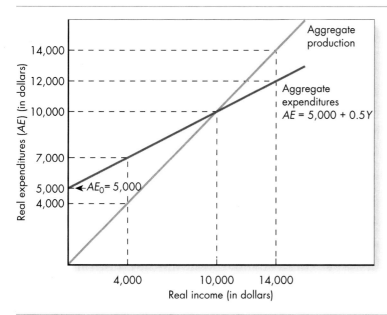

FIGURE 10-5 **Comparing *AE* to *AP* and Solving for Equilibrium Graphically**

Equilibrium in the multiplier model is determined where the *AE* and *AP* curves intersect. That equilibrium is at $10,000. At income levels higher or lower than that, planned production will not equal planned expenditures.

Real Income	Planned Expenditures	Aggregate Production	Inventories
$ 0	$ 5,000	$ 0	−$5,000
4,000	7,000	4,000	−3,000
10,000	**10,000**	**10,000**	**0**
14,000	12,000	14,000	+2,000

aggregate production is less than planned aggregate expenditures and inventories are falling below levels desired by firms. For example, at a production level of $4,000, planned aggregate expenditures are $7,000. Inventories are falling by $3,000.

The only income level at which aggregate production equals planned aggregate expenditures is $10,000. Since we know that, in equilibrium, planned aggregate expenditures must equal planned aggregate production, $10,000 is the equilibrium level of income in the economy. It is the level of income at which neither producers nor consumers have any reason to change what they are doing. At any other level of income, since there is either a shortage or a surplus of goods, or firms' inventory is greater than or less than desired, there will be incentive to change production. Thus, you can use the aggregate production curve and the aggregate expenditures curve to determine the level of income at which the economy will be in equilibrium.

The Keynesian Model

The Multiplier Equation

Another useful way to determine the level of income in the multiplier model is through the **multiplier equation,** *an equation that tells us that income equals the multiplier times autonomous expenditures.*[2]

$$Y = \text{Multiplier} \times \text{Autonomous expenditures}$$

The **expenditures multiplier** is *a number that tells us how much income will change in response to a change in autonomous expenditures.* To calculate the expenditures multiplier, you divide 1 by (1 minus the marginal propensity to expend). Thus:

$$\text{Multiplier} = \frac{1}{(1 - mpe)}$$

The multiplier equation is an equation showing the relationship between autonomous expenditures and the equilibrium level of income: $Y = \text{Multiplier} \times \text{Autonomous expenditures}$.

The expenditures multiplier is a number that tells us how much income will change in response to a change in autonomous expenditures: $[1/(1 - mpe)]$.

---

[2]The multiplier equation does not come out of thin air. It comes from combining the set of equations underlying the graphical presentation of the multiplier model into the two brackets. The multiplier equation is derived in the box, "Solving for Equilibrium Income Algebraically."

Once you know the value of the marginal propensity to expend, you can calculate the expenditures multiplier by reducing $[1/(1- mpe)]$ to a simple number. For example, if $mpe = .8$, the multiplier is

$$\frac{1}{(1-.8)} = \frac{1}{.2} = 5$$

Since the expenditures multiplier tells you the relationship between autonomous expenditures and income, once you know the multiplier and the level of autonomous expenditures, calculating the equilibrium level of income is easy. All you do is multiply autonomous expenditures by the multiplier. For example, using the autonomous expenditures of \$5,000 and a multiplier of 2, from Figure 10-5, we can calculate equilibrium income in the economy to be \$10,000. This is the same equilibrium income we got from the graphical exercise.

Let's see how the equation works by considering another example. Say the mpe is .4. Subtracting .4 from 1 gives .6. Dividing 1 by .6 gives approximately 1.7. Say, also, that autonomous expenditures (AE_0) are \$750. The multiplier equation tells us to calculate income, multiply autonomous expenditures, \$750, by 1.7. Doing so gives $1.7 \times \$750 = \$1,275$.

The multiplier equation gives you a simple way to determine equilibrium income in the multiplier model. Five different marginal propensities to expend and the multiplier associated with each (I round off to the nearest 10th) are shown in the table below.

mpe	Multiplier = $1/(1 - mpe)$
.3	1.4
.4	1.7
.5	2
.75	4
.8	5

Notice as mpe increases, the multiplier increases. The reason is that as the mpe gets larger, the induced effects of any initial shift in income also get larger. Knowing the multiplier associated with each marginal propensity to expend gives you an easy way to determine equilibrium income in the economy.

Let's look at one more example of the multiplier. Say that the mpe is .4 and that autonomous expenditures rise by \$250 so they are \$1,000 instead of \$750. What is the level of equilibrium income? Multiplying autonomous expenditures, \$1,000, by 1.7 tells us that equilibrium income is \$1,700. With a multiplier of 1.7, income rises by \$425 (250×1.7) because of the \$250 increase in autonomous expenditures.

The Multiplier Process

Let's now look more carefully at the forces that are pushing the economy toward equilibrium. What happens when the macroeconomy is in disequilibrium—when the amount being injected into the economy does not equal the amount leaking from the economy? Put another way, what happens when aggregate production does not equal aggregate expenditures? Figure 10-6 shows us.

Let's first consider the economy at income level A, where aggregate production equals \$7,000 and planned aggregate expenditures equal \$5,500. Since production exceeds planned expenditures by \$1,500 at income level A, firms can't sell all they produce; inventories pile up. In response, firms make an adjustment. They decrease aggregate production and hence income. As businesses slow production, the economy moves

---

To determine equilibrium income using the multiplier equation, you determine the expenditures multiplier and multiply it by the level of autonomous expenditures.

mpe and the Multiplier

Q₄ If the $mpe = .5$, what is the expenditures multiplier?

Q₅ If autonomous expenditures are \$2,000 and the $mpe = .4$, what is the level of equilibrium income in the economy?

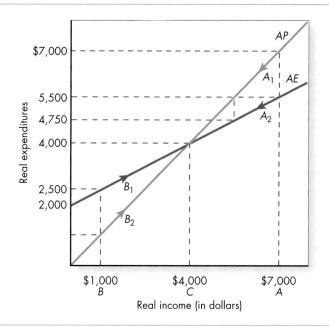

FIGURE 10-6 **The Multiplier Process**

At income levels A and B, the economy is in disequilibrium. Depending on which direction the disequilibrium goes, it generates increases or decreases in planned production and expenditures until the economy reaches income level C, where planned aggregate expenditures equal aggregate production.

inward along the aggregate production curve, as shown by arrow A_1. As income falls, people's expenditures fall, and the gap between aggregate production and aggregate expenditures decreases. For example, say businesses decrease aggregate production to $5,500. Aggregate income also falls to $5,500, which causes aggregate expenditures to fall, as indicated by arrow A_2, to $4,750. Production still exceeds planned expenditures, but the gap has been reduced by $750, from $1,500 to $750.

Since a gap still remains, production and income keep falling. A good exercise is to go through two more steps. With each step, the economy moves closer to equilibrium.

Now let's consider the economy at income level B ($1,000) and expenditures level $2,500. Here production is *less* than planned expenditures. Firms find their inventory is running down. (Their investment in inventory is far less than they'd planned.) In response, they increase aggregate production and hence income. The economy starts to expand as aggregate production moves along arrow B_2 and aggregate expenditures move along arrow B_1. As individuals' income increases, their expenditures also increase, but by less than the increase in income, so the gap between aggregate expenditures and aggregate production decreases. But as long as expenditures exceed production, production and hence income keep rising.

Finally, let's consider the economy at income level C, $4,000. At point C, production is $4,000 and planned expenditures are $4,000. Firms are selling all they produce, so they have no reason to change their production levels. The aggregate economy is in equilibrium. This discussion should give you insight into what's behind the arithmetic of those earlier models.

The Circular Flow Model and the Intuition behind the Multiplier Process

Now let's think about the intuition behind the multiplier. You know from the circular flow diagram that when all individuals spend all their income (which they derive from production), the aggregate economy is in equilibrium. The circular flow diagram shown in the margin expresses the national income identity: aggregate income equals

Q-6 When inventories fall below planned inventories, what is likely happening to the economy?

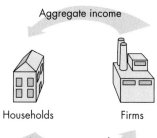

Circular flow diagram.

Solving for Equilibrium Income Algebraically

For those of you who are mathematically inclined, the multiplier equation can be derived by combining the equations presented in the text algebraically to arrive at the equation for income. Rewriting the expenditures relationship, we have

$$AE = AE_0 + mpeY$$

Aggregate production, by definition, equals aggregate income (Y) and, in equilibrium, aggregate income must equal the four components of aggregate expenditures. Beginning with the equilibrium condition, we have

$$Y = AE$$

Substituting the terms from the first equation, we have

$$Y = AE_0 + mpeY$$

We want to solve this equation for Y, so first we subtract $mpeY$ from both sides,

$$Y - mpeY = AE_0$$

We then factor out Y:

$$Y(1 - mpe) = AE_0$$

and finally we solve for Y by dividing both sides by $(1 - mpe)$:

$$Y = \left[\frac{1}{(1 - mpe)} \right] \times \left[AE_0 \right]$$

This is the multiplier equation and $\left[\dfrac{1}{(1 - mpe)} \right]$ is the multiplier.

---

aggregate output. The flow of expenditures equals the flow of income (production). How, if not all income is spent (the *mpe* is less than 1), can expenditures equal income? The answer is that the withdrawals (income that is not spent on domestic goods) are offset by injections of autonomous expenditures.

When thinking about the multiplier process, I picture a leaking bathtub. Withdrawals are leaks out of the bathtub. Injections are people dumping buckets of water into the tub. When the water leaking out of the bathtub just equals the water being poured in, the level of water in the tub will remain constant; the bathtub will be in equilibrium. If the amount being poured in is either more or less than the amount leaking out, the level of the water in the bathtub will be either increasing or decreasing. Thus, equilibrium in the economy requires the withdrawals from the spending stream to equal injections into the spending stream. If they don't, the economy will not be in equilibrium and will be either expanding or contracting.

Web Note 10.2
Local Multipliers

To see this, let's consider what happens if injections and withdrawals are not equal. Say that withdrawals exceed injections (more water is leaking out than is being poured in). In that case, the income in the economy (the level of water in the bathtub) will be declining. As income declines, so will withdrawals. Income will continue to decline until the autonomous injections flowing in (the buckets of water) just equal the withdrawals flowing out (the water leaks).

The Multiplier Model in Action

Determining the equilibrium level of income using the multiplier is an important first step in understanding the multiplier analysis. The second step is to modify that analysis to answer a question that is of much more interest to policy makers: How much would a change in autonomous expenditures change the equilibrium level of income? This second step is important since it is precisely those sudden changes in autonomous expenditures that can cause a recession. That is why we discussed shifts in autonomous expenditures above.

It is because autonomous expenditures are subject to sudden shifts that I was careful to point out *autonomous* means "determined outside the model and not affected by income." Autonomous expenditures can, and do, shift for a variety of reasons. When they do, the multiplier process is continually being called into play.

Autonomous means "determined outside the model."

The Steps of the Multiplier Process

Any initial change in autonomous aggregate expenditures is amplified in the multiplier process. Let's see how this works in the example in Figure 10-7, which will also serve as a review. Assume that trade negotiations between the United States and other countries have fallen apart and U.S. exports decrease by $100. This is shown in the AE curve's downward shift from AE_0 to AE_1.

How far must income fall until equilibrium is reached? To answer that question, we need to know the initial change, $\Delta AE = -\$100$, and the size of the multiplier, $[1/(1 - mpe)]$. In this example, $mpe = .5$, so the multiplier is 2. That means the final decrease in income that brings about equilibrium is $200 (two times as large as the initial shift of $100).

Figure 10-7(b), a blowup of the circled area in Figure 10-7(a), shows the detailed steps of the multiplier process so you can see how it works. Initially, autonomous expenditures fall by $100 (length A), causing firms to decrease production by $100 (length B). But that decrease in income causes expenditures to decrease by another $50 (.5 × $100) (length C). Again firms respond by cutting production, this time by $50 (length D). Again

Q-7 If exports fall by $30 and the $mpe = .9$, what happens to equilibrium income?

FIGURE 10-7 (A AND B)   **Shifts in the Aggregate Expenditures Curve**

Graph (**a**) shows the effect of a shift of the aggregate expenditures curve. When autonomous expenditures decrease by $100, the aggregate expenditures curve shifts downward from AE_1 to AE_2. In response, income falls by a multiple of the shift, in this case by $200.

Graph (**b**) shows the multiplier process under a microscope. In it the adjustment process is broken into discrete steps. For example, when income falls by $100 (length B), expenditures fall by $50 (length C). In response to that fall of expenditures, producers reduce output by $50, which decreases income by $50 (length D). The lower income causes expenditures to fall further (length E) and the process continues.

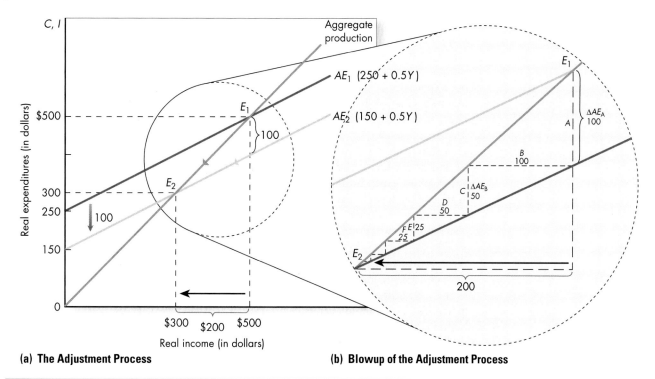

(a) The Adjustment Process   (b) Blowup of the Adjustment Process

FIGURE 10-8   **The First Five Steps of Four Multipliers**

The larger the marginal propensity to expend, the more steps are required before the shifts become small.

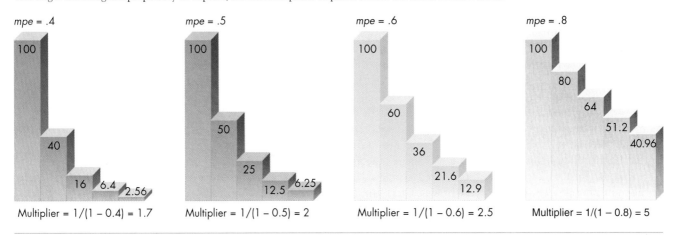

mpe = .4

100

40

16 6.4 2.56

Multiplier = 1/(1 − 0.4) = 1.7

mpe = .5

100

50

25

12.5 6.25

Multiplier = 1/(1 − 0.5) = 2

mpe = .6

100

60

36

21.6

12.9

Multiplier = 1/(1 − 0.6) = 2.5

mpe = .8

100

80

64

51.2

40.96

Multiplier = 1/(1 − 0.8) = 5

income falls (length *E*), causing production to fall (length *F*). The process continues again and again (the remaining steps) until equilibrium income falls by $200, two times the amount of the initial change. The *mpe* tells how much closer at each step aggregate expenditures will be to aggregate production. You can see this adjustment process in Figure 10-8, which shows the first steps with multipliers of various sizes.

Examples of the Effect of Shifts in Aggregate Expenditures

There are many reasons for shifts in autonomous expenditures that can affect the economy: natural disasters, changes in investment caused by technological developments, shifts in government expenditures, large changes in the exchange rate, and so on. As I discussed above, in order to focus on these shift factors, autonomous expenditures are often broken up into their component parts: autonomous consumption (C_0), autonomous investment (I_0), autonomous government spending (G_0), and autonomous net exports ($X_0 - M_0$) (the difference between autonomous exports and autonomous imports). Changes in consumer sentiment affect C_0; major technological breakthroughs affect I_0; changes in government's spending decisions affect G_0; and changes in foreign income and exchange rates affect ($X_0 - M_0$).

Learning to work with the multiplier model requires practice, so in Figure 10-9 (a and b) I present two different expenditures functions and two different shifts in autonomous expenditures. Below each model is the equation representing how much aggregate income changes in terms of the multiplier and autonomous expenditures. As you see, the multiplier equation calculates the shift, while the graph determines it in a visual way. Now let's turn to some real-world examples.

The United States at the Turn of the Millennium   In the United States in the late 1990s, consumer confidence rose substantially, causing autonomous consumption expenditures to increase by about $200 billion more than economists had predicted. Assuming a multiplier of 2, that increase meant that income rose $400 billion higher than expected. Economists had expected the economy to grow slowly; instead it boomed. In 2001 business confidence started falling and the boom slowed. Then in September 2001, following the terrorist attacks, both consumer spending and investment fell, sending the economy into a recession. By 2002 autonomous consumption

FIGURE 10-9 (A AND B)   **Two Different Expenditures Functions and Two Different Shifts in Autonomous Expenditures**

The steeper the slope of the AE curve, the greater the effect of a shift in the AE curve on equilibrium income. In (**a**) the slope of the AE curve is .75 and a shift of $30 of autonomous expenditures causes an increase in income of $120. In (**b**), the slope of the AE curve is .66 and a shift of $30 of autonomous expenditures causes a decrease in income of $90.

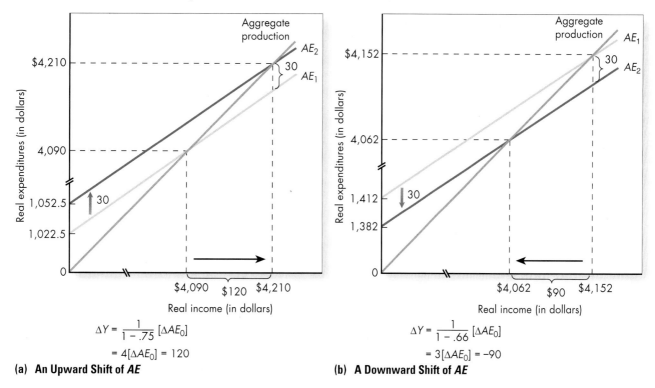

$$\Delta Y = \frac{1}{1 - .75} [\Delta AE_0]$$
$$= 4[\Delta AE_0] = 120$$

(a) An Upward Shift of AE

$$\Delta Y = \frac{1}{1 - .66} [\Delta AE_0]$$
$$= 3[\Delta AE_0] = -90$$

(b) A Downward Shift of AE

expenditures had increased sufficiently so that the U.S. economy came out of the recession and started expanding slowly. It continued expanding slowly through 2007.

Japan in the 1990s   A dramatic appreciation of the Japanese exchange rate in 1995 cut Japanese exports, decreasing aggregate expenditures so that aggregate production was greater than planned aggregate expenditures. Then, simultaneously, consumers became worried and autonomous consumption fell. Suppliers could not sell all that they produced. Their reaction was to lay off workers and decrease output. That response would have solved the problem if only one firm had been affected. But since all firms (or at least a large majority) were affected, the fallacy of composition came into play. As all producers responded in this fashion, aggregate income, and hence aggregate expenditures, also fell. The suppliers' cutback started what is sometimes called a vicious cycle. Aggregate expenditures and production spiraled downward, which is what the multiplier process explains.

Fiscal Policy in the Multiplier Model

The multiplier model is of such interest to policy makers not only because it allows them to predict the effects of shifts in autonomous expenditures but also because they believe that it allows them to control it with countershifts of their own. By implementing policies affecting autonomous spending, governments can shift the AE curve up or down and, in the model at least, achieve the desired level of output.

Fighting Recession: Expansionary Fiscal Policy

To see how this is done, let's consider how government policy can get an economy out of a recession with fiscal policy. I consider this case in both the *AS/AD* model with a fixed price level and the multiplier model in Figure 10-10(a). The top panel shows fiscal policy in the multiplier model. The bottom part shows fiscal policy in the *AS/AD* model. Initially the economy is at equilibrium at income level $1,000, which is below potential income ($1,180). The economy is in a recessionary gap. This is what ideally

---

FIGURE 10-10 (A AND B)   **Fiscal Policy**

In (**a**) if the economy is below its potential income level, the government can increase government spending to stimulate the economy. Doing so shifts the *AD* curve to the right and the *AE* curve shifts up. Income expands by a multiple of that increase. In (**b**) we see appropriate government policy for an inflationary gap. In the absence of any policy, shortages and accelerating inflation will occur. To prevent this, government must use contractionary fiscal policy, shifting the *AE* curve downward from AE_1 to AE_2 to reduce equilibrium income from $5,000 to $4,000. The bottom part of (**b**) shows this policy in the *AS/AD* model.

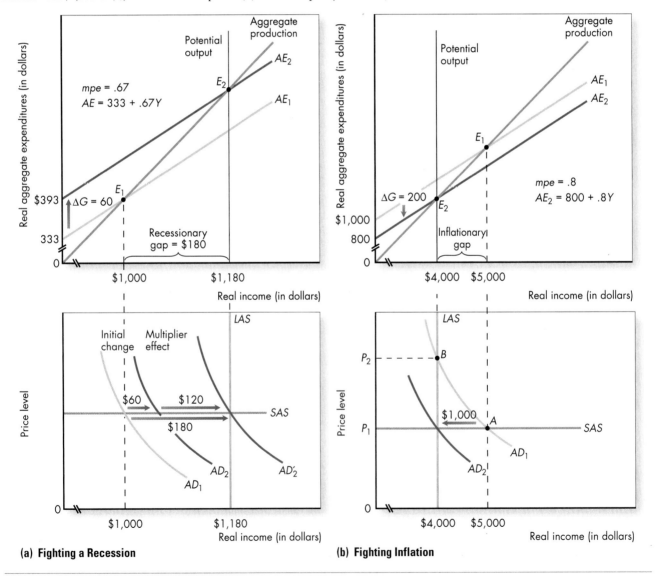

(a) Fighting a Recession   **(b) Fighting Inflation**

happens: The government recognizes this recessionary gap in aggregate income of, say, $180 and responds with expansionary fiscal policy by increasing government expenditures by $60.

Assuming the price level is constant (the SAS curve is flat), the increased government spending shifts the AE curve from AE_1 upward to AE_2. Businesses that receive government contracts hire the workers who have been laid off by other firms and open new plants; output increases by the initial expenditure of $60. But the process doesn't stop there. At this point, the multiplier process sets in. As the newly employed workers spend more, other businesses find that their demand increases. They hire more workers, who spend an additional $40 (since their *mpe* = .67). This increases income further. The same process occurs again and again. By the time the process has ended, income has risen by $180 to $1,180, the potential level of income.

The effects are shown in the AS/AD model in the bottom part of Figure 10-10(a). The AD curve shifts to the right by three times the increase in government expenditures, or by $180. The initial shock shifts the AD curve to the right by $60; the $120 shift is due to the multiplier effects that the initial shift brings about.

How did the government economists know to increase spending by $60? By backward induction. They empirically estimated that the *mpe*—the slope of the aggregate expenditures curve—was .67, which meant that the multiplier was $1/(1 - .67) = 1/.33 = 3$. They divided the multiplier, 3, into the recessionary gap, $180, and determined that if they increased spending by $60, income would increase by $180.

If the SAS curve had been upward-sloping, and the price level had not remained constant, predicting the precise level of increase in real income would have been harder because the increase would have been split between a change in real income and a change in nominal income. The increase in real income would have been less than it was with a flat SAS curve. The precise amount would depend on the degree of upward slope of the SAS curve.[3] The steeper the slope of the SAS curve, the less real income would have changed.

The Moniac was an analog computer that used flows of colored water to simulate income and expenditures. It was used as a teaching tool.

Fighting Inflation: Contractionary Fiscal Policy

Fiscal policy can also work in reverse, decreasing expenditures that are too high. Expenditures are "too high" when the economy temporarily exceeds its potential output. An economy operating above potential will generate accelerating inflation.

Figure 10-10(b) shows contractionary fiscal policy in the multiplier and AS/AD models. Potential income is $4,000, but the equilibrium level of income is $5,000. The difference between the two, $1,000, is the inflationary gap. This inflationary gap causes upward pressure on wages and prices with no additional lasting increase in output. If the government wants to avoid inflation, it can use contractionary policy. By how much should government reduce government expenditures? To determine that, it has to calculate the multiplier. In this example, the marginal propensity to expend is assumed to be .8, which means that the multiplier would be 5. So a cut in autonomous expenditures of $200 would shift the AE curve down by $200 and decrease equilibrium income by $1,000.

Q-8 Demonstrate graphically the effect of contractionary fiscal policy.

Q-9 The marginal propensity to expend is .33, and there is an inflationary gap of $100. What fiscal policy would you recommend?

---

[3]You can determine the approximate percentage reduction in the multiplier effect on real income by writing the slope of the SAS curve as a fraction and then placing the numerator of that fraction over the sum of the numerator and the denominator. The result is the approximate decrease in the size of the multiplier effect on real income. For example, if the slope of the SAS curve is 1/10, the multiplier effect on real income will be reduced by about $[1/(1 + 10)]$, or 1/11, from what it would have been had the SAS curve been horizontal.

Keynes and Fiscal Policy

One of the themes of this book is that economic thought and policy are more complicated than an introductory book must necessarily make them seem. Fiscal policy is a good case in point. In the early 1930s, before Keynes wrote *The General Theory*, he was advocating public works programs and deficits (government spending in excess of tax revenues) as a way to get the British economy out of the Depression. He came upon what we now call the *Keynesian theory* as he tried to explain to Classical economists why he supported deficits. After arriving at his new theory, however, he spent little time advocating fiscal policy and, in fact, never mentions fiscal policy in *The General Theory*. The book's primary policy recommendation is the need to socialize investments—for the government to take over the investment decisions from private individuals. When one of his followers, Abba Lerner, advocated expansionary fiscal policy at a seminar Keynes attended, Keynes strongly objected, leading Evsey Domar, another Keynesian follower, to whisper to a friend, "Keynes should read *The General Theory*."

What's going on here? There are many interpretations, but the one I find most convincing is the one presented by historian Peter Clarke. He argues that, while working on *The General Theory*, Keynes turned his interest from a policy revolution to a theoretical revolution. He believed he had found a serious flaw in Classical economic theory. The Classicals assumed that an economy in equilibrium was at full employment, but they did not show how the economy could move to that equilibrium from a disequilibrium. That's when Keynes's interest changed from a policy to a theoretical revolution.

His followers, such as Lerner, carried out the policy implications of his theory. Why did Keynes sometimes oppose these policy implications? Because he was also a student of politics and he recognized that economic theory can often lead to politically unacceptable policies. In a letter to a friend, he later said Lerner was right in his logic, but he hoped the opposition didn't discover what Lerner was saying. Keynes was more than an economist; he was a politician as well.

The bottom part of Figure 10-10(b) shows the effects of a $200 cut in government expenditures in the *AS/AD* model. With a multiplier of 5, the *AD* curve shifts to the left by $1,000. Because the *SAS* curve is flat, equilibrium output declines to $4,000.

Using Taxes Rather Than Expenditures as the Tool of Fiscal Policy

A change in taxes affects initial expenditures differently than a direct change in expenditures.

As a brain teaser, you might try to figure out what you would have advised the government to do if it had wanted to increase taxes rather than decrease expenditures to get the economy out of the inflationary gap in Figure 10-10(b). By how much should it increase taxes? If you said by $200 since the multiplier is 5, you're on the right wavelength, but not quite right. True, the multiplier, $1/(1 - mpe)$, is 5, but a change in taxes affects initial expenditures in a slightly different way than does a direct change in expenditures. Specifically, expenditures will not decrease by the full amount of the tax increase. The reason why is that people will likely reduce their saving in order to hold up their expenditures. Expenditures will initially fall by that portion of the decrease in their disposable income that consumers spend on U.S. goods, which, as I stated earlier, is measured by consumer's marginal propensity to consume (*mpc*). For simplicity, let's assume that the marginal propensity to consume equals the marginal propensity to expend. Then, initially, the decrease in expenditures from the tax increase will be (.8 × $200) = $160, rather than $200. To get the initial shift of $200 from increasing taxes, the government must increase taxes by $200/.8, or $250. Then when people reduce spending by .8 of that, their expenditures will fall by $200.

Limitations of the Multiplier Model

On the surface, the multiplier model makes a lot of intuitive sense. However, surface sense can often be misleading. Some of the model's limitations are discussed below.

The Multiplier Model Is Not a Complete Model of the Economy

The multiplier model provides a technical method of determining equilibrium income. But in reality the model doesn't do what it purports to do—determine equilibrium income from scratch. Why? Because it doesn't tell us where those autonomous expenditures come from or how we would go about measuring them.

At best, what we can measure, or at least estimate, are directions and rough sizes of autonomous demand shifts, and we can determine the direction and possible overadjustment the economy might make in response to those changes. If you think back to our initial discussion of the multiplier model, this is how I introduced it—as an explanation of forces affecting the adjustment process, not as a determinant of the final equilibrium independent of where the economy started. It is a historical, not an analytical, model. Without some additional information about where the economy started from, or what is the desired level of output, the multiplier model is incomplete.

> At best, what we can estimate are directions and rough sizes of autonomous demand or supply shifts.

Shifts Are Not as Great as Intuition Suggests

A second problem with the multiplier model is that it leads people to overemphasize the shifts that would occur in aggregate expenditures in response to a shift in autonomous expenditures. Say people decide to save some more. You might think that it would lead to a fall in expenditures. But wait, that saving will go into the financial sector and be translated back into the expenditures sector as loans to other consumers or as loans to businesses funding investment. So if you take a broad view of aggregate expenditures, many of the shifts in expenditures are simply rearrangements from one group of expenditures to another.

The Price Level Will Often Change in Response to Shifts in Demand

One of the assumptions of the multiplier model is that the price level is fixed—that makes aggregate production a 45° line. But in reality the price level can change as aggregate demand changes because price markups and labor market conditions change. These changes in the price level reduce the effect of the multiplier on real income. Some adjustment must be made for changes in the price level when the price level changes in response to changes in aggregate demand. That adjustment is usually made by shifting the *AE* curve up (in the case of a falling price level) or down (in the case of a rising price level). The quantitative amount of that shift is uncertain, making the quantitative effect of policy on real income uncertain when the price level changes. (These adjustments are discussed in Appendix B.)

People's Forward-Looking Expectations Make the Adjustment Process Much More Complicated

People's forward-looking expectations make the adjustment process much more complicated. The multiplier model presented here assumes that people respond to current changes in income. Most people, however, act on the basis of expectations of the future.

Consider the assumed response of businesses to changes in expenditures. They lay off workers and cut production at the slightest fall in demand. In reality, their response is far more complicated. They may well see the fall as a temporary blip. They will allow their inventory to rise in the expectation that the next month another temporary blip will offset the previous fall. Business decisions about production are forward looking, and do not respond simply to current changes. As a contrast to the simple multiplier model, some modern economists have put forward a **rational expectations model** of the macroeconomy in which *all decisions are based on the expected equilibrium in the economy.* Some economists go so far as to argue that since people rationally expect the economy to achieve its potential income, it will do so.

Shifts in Expenditures Might Reflect Desired Shifts in Supply and Demand

There is an implicit assumption in the multiplier model that shifts in demand are not reflections of shifts in desired production or supply. Reality is much more complicated. Shifts can occur for many reasons, and many shifts can reflect desired shifts in aggregate production, which are accompanied by shifts in aggregate expenditures. An example of such a change occurred in Japan in the 1990s as Japan's industries lost their competitive edge to Korean, Chinese, and Taiwanese industries. The Japanese economy faltered, but the problem was not simply a fall in aggregate demand, and therefore the solution to it was not simply to increase aggregate demand. There was a simultaneous shift in aggregate supply that had to be dealt with.

Suppliers operate in the future—shifting supply, not to existing demand, but to expected demand, making the relationship between aggregate production and current demand far more complicated than it seems in the multiplier model. Expansion of this line of thought has led some economists, called *real-business-cycle economists*, to develop the **real-business-cycle theory** of the economy: *the theory that fluctuations in the economy reflect real phenomena—simultaneous shifts in supply and demand, not simply supply responses to demand shifts.* Supply drives the economy. Let's consider an example—the expansion of the U.S. economy in the late 1990s. The AS/AD model would attribute that to a shift of the AD curve to the right, combined with a relatively fixed SAS curve that did not shift up as output expanded. The real-business-cycle theory would attribute that shift in income to businesses' decision to increase supply due to technological developments, and a subsequent increase in demand via Say's law.

Real-business-cycle theory suggests that fluctuations in the economy reflect real phenomena.

Expenditures Depend on Much More Than Current Income

Let's say your income goes down 10 percent. The multiplier model says that your expenditures will go down by some specific percentage of that. But will they? If you are rational, it seems reasonable to base your consumption on more than one year's income—say, instead, on your permanent or lifetime income. What happens to your income in a particular year has little effect on your lifetime income. If it is true that people base their spending primarily on lifetime income, not yearly income, the marginal propensity to consume out of changes in current income could be very low, approaching zero. In that case, the expenditures function would essentially be a flat line, and the multiplier would be 1. There would be no secondary effects of an initial shift in expenditures. This set of arguments is called the **permanent income hypothesis**—*the hypothesis that expenditures are determined by permanent or lifetime income.* It undermines the reasoning of much of the specific results of the simple multiplier model.

Q-10 What effect would expenditures being dependent on permanent income have on the size of the multiplier?

Conclusion

While each of the above criticisms has some validity, most macro policy makers still use some variation of the multiplier model as the basis for their policy decisions. They don't see it as a *mechanistic model*—a model that pictures the economy as representable by a mechanically determined, timeless model with a determinant equilibrium. Modern economists have come to the conclusion that there is no simple way to understand the aggregate economy. Any mechanistic interpretation of an aggregate model is doomed to fail. The hope of economists to have a model that would give them a specific numeric guide to policy has not been fulfilled.

The model is still useful if it is seen as an interpretive model or an aid in understanding complicated disequilibrium dynamics. The specific results of the multiplier model are a guide to common sense, enabling us to emphasize a particular important dynamic interdependency while keeping others in mind. With that addendum—that it is not meant to be taken literally but only as an aid to intuition—the simple multiplier model deals with the issues that concern today's highest-level macro theorists.

Summary

- The multiplier model focuses on the induced effect that a change in production has on expenditures, which affects production, and so on.

- The multiplier model is made up of the aggregate production and aggregate expenditures curves. In equilibrium, aggregate production must equal planned aggregate expenditures.

- The aggregate production curve is a line along which real income equals real production. It is a 45° line.

- Aggregate expenditures (AE) are made up of consumption, investment, government spending, and net exports:

  $AE = C + I + G + (X - M)$

- Expenditures depend on the level of income; the marginal propensity to expend (mpe) tells us the change in expenditures that occurs with a change in income.

- The AE curve shows aggregate expenditures graphically. Its slope is the mpe and its y-intercept equals autonomous expenditures.

- Equilibrium output, or income, is where the AP and AE curves intersect.

- Equilibrium output can be calculated using the multiplier equation:

  $Y = \text{Multiplier} \times \text{Autonomous expenditures}$

- The multiplier tells us how much a change in autonomous expenditures will change equilibrium income. The multiplier equals $1/(1 - mpe)$.

- When an economy is in equilibrium, withdrawals from the spending stream equal injections into the spending stream (autonomous expenditures).

- Shifts in autonomous expenditures can be the initial change that begins the multiplier process. The multiplier process expands that initial shift to a much larger decrease or increase in production and income.

- Expansionary fiscal policy, increasing government expenditures or decreasing taxes, is represented graphically as an upward shift of the aggregate expenditures curve or a rightward shift in the AD curve.

- Contractionary fiscal policy, decreasing government expenditures or increasing taxes, is represented graphically as a downward shift of the aggregate expenditures curve or a leftward shift in the AD curve.

- The multiplier model has limitations: (1) it is incomplete without information about where the economy started and what is the desired level of output, (2) it overemphasizes shifts that occur in aggregate expenditures, (3) it assumes that the price level is fixed when in reality it isn't, (4) it doesn't take expectations into account, (5) it ignores the possibility that shifts in expenditures are desired, and (6) it ignores the possibility that consumption is based on lifetime income, not annual income.

- Macroeconomic models cannot be applied mechanistically; they are only guides to common sense.

Key Terms

aggregate
  expenditures (229)
aggregate
  production (229)
autonomous
  expenditures (230)

expenditures
  multiplier (235)
induced
  expenditures (230)
marginal propensity to
  expend (mpe) (231)

multiplier equation (235)
permanent income
  hypothesis (246)
rational expectations
  model (246)

real-business-cycle
  theory (246)

Questions for Thought and Review

1. What are induced and autonomous expenditures at point A in the graph below?   LO1

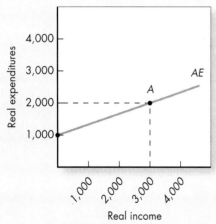

2. If planned expenditures are below actual production, what will happen to income? Explain the process by which this happens.   LO2

3. Are inventories building up at levels of output above or below equilibrium output? Explain your answer.   LO2

4. What happens to the aggregate expenditures curve when autonomous expenditures fall?   LO2

5. What happens to equilibrium income when the marginal propensity to expend rises?   LO2

6. What is equilibrium income if the aggregate expenditures function is AE = 300 + .4Y?   LO3

7. If saving were instantaneously translated into investment, what would be the multiplier's size? What would be the level of autonomous expenditures?   LO4

8. Name some forces that might cause shocks to aggregate expenditures.   LO5

9. What is the current state of U.S. fiscal policy? Would you advise the United States to change its fiscal policy? Why?   LO5

10. The marginal propensity to expend is .5 and there is a recessionary gap of $200. What fiscal policy would you recommend?   LO5

11. Why does cutting taxes by $100 have a smaller effect on GDP than increasing expenditures by $100?   LO5

12. Mr. Whammo has just invented a magic pill. Take it and it transports you anywhere. Explain his invention's effects on the economy.   LO5

13. Why is the circular flow diagram of the economy an only partially correct conception of the multiplier model?   LO6

14. How do mechanistic models differ from interpretive models?   LO6

15. Charlie Black, a GOP strategist, was once quoted as stating, "I can't tell you why this happens, but there's a lag time (before people tune into good economic news)." What is the effect of this delay in the adjustment of expectations by consumers on the dynamics of the multiplier model?   LO6

Problems and Exercises

16. The marginal propensity to expend is .8. Autonomous expenditures are $4,200. What is the level of equilibrium income in the economy? Demonstrate graphically.   LO3

17. The marginal propensity to expend is .66 and autonomous expenditures have just fallen by $20.
    a. What will likely happen to equilibrium income?
    b. Demonstrate graphically.   LO3

18. Congratulations. You've been appointed economic adviser to Happyland. Your research assistant says the country's mpe is .8 and autonomous expenditures have just risen by $20.
    a. What will happen to income?
    b. Your research assistant comes in and says he's sorry but the mpe wasn't .8; it was .5. How does your answer change?

c. He runs in again and says exports have fallen by $10 and investment has risen by $10. How does your answer change?

d. You now have to present your analysis to the president, who wants to see it all graphically. Naturally you oblige.   LO2, LO3, LO4

19. Congratulations again. You've just been appointed economic adviser to Examland. The *mpe* is .6; autonomous investment is $1,000; autonomous government spending is $8,000; autonomous consumption is $10,000; and autonomous net exports are $1,000.

a. What is the level of income in the country?

b. Autonomous net exports increase by $2,000. What will happen to income?

c. What will happen to unemployment? (Remember Okun's rule of thumb.)

d. You've just learned the *mpe* changed from .6 to .5. How will this information change your answers in *a*, *b*, and *c*?   LO2, LO3, LO4

20. In 1992, as President George H. W. Bush was running (unsuccessfully) for reelection, the economy slowed down; then in late 1993, after President Bill Clinton's election, the economy picked up steam.

a. Demonstrate graphically with the multiplier model a shift in the *AE* curve that would have caused the slowdown. Which component of aggregate expenditures was the likely culprit?

b. Demonstrate graphically with the multiplier model a shift in the *AE* curve that would have caused the improvement. Which component of aggregate expenditures was likely responsible?

c. What policies do you think President Bush could have used to stop the slowdown?

d. What policies do you think President Clinton used to try to speed up the economy?   LO4, LO5

21. Congratulations yet again. You've just been appointed chairman to the Council of Economic Advisers in Textland. You must rely on your research assistant for the specific numbers. He says income is $50,000, *mpe* is .75, and the president wants to lower unemployment from 8 to 6 percent. (Remember Okun's rule of thumb.)

a. Advise him.

b. Your research assistant comes in and says "Sorry, I meant that the *mpe* is .67." You redo your calculations.

c. You're just about to see the president when your research assistant comes running, saying, "Sorry, sorry, I meant that the *mpe* is .5." Redo your calculations.   LO4, LO5

22. State what fiscal policy you would recommend to eliminate the inflationary or recessionary gap in the following scenarios:

a. Recessionary gap of $800; *mpe* = .5.

b. Inflationary gap of $1,500; *mpe* = .8.

c. Real GDP = $10,200; potential GDP = $9,000; *mpe* = .2.

d. Real GDP = $40,500; potential GDP = $42,000; *mpe* = .7.   LO5

23. Congratulations one more time. You have been appointed chair of Economic Advisers in Fantasyland. Income is currently $600,000, unemployment is 5 percent, and there are signs of coming inflation. You rely on your research assistant for specific numbers. He tells you that potential income is $564,000 and the *mpe* is .5.

a. The government wants to eliminate the inflationary gap by changing expenditures. What policy do you suggest?

b. By how much will unemployment change after your policy has taken effect?

c. Your research assistant comes in and says "Sorry, I meant that the *mpe* is .8." Redo your calculations for parts *a* and *b*.   LO5

Questions from Alternative Perspectives

1. Traffic engineer Hans Monderman has shown that traffic flows can be made safer and flow better if the number of road signs is reduced and, in many types of intersections, eliminated altogether. What relevance do his insights about traffic flows have for macroeconomic policy? (Austrian)

2. During the Great Depression, Norman Cousins made the following remark: "There are approximately 10,000,000 people out of work in the U.S. today. There are also 10,000,000 or more women married and single who are job holders. Simply fire the women, who should not be working anyway, and hire the men. Presto! No unemployment. No relief. No depression." How would you evaluate this statement? Is work a human right or a gender-based privilege? Do you think that men would have taken jobs that were traditionally considered "women's work" in the 1930s even if they were unemployed? (Feminist)

3. When the federal government uses expenditures to stimulate the economy, it changes not only the present but the future as well. Use the *AS/AD* model and the production possibility curve to explore the probable near-term and long-term consequences of three alternative stimulus options: medical care for all Americans; an increased military presence across the Middle East to promote U.S. domestic tranquility; the development of oil-saving and climate-friendly energy alternatives. In your analysis be sure to include the effect of increased deficits on investment. (Institutionalist)

4. One remarkable thing about U.S. households is how little they save. The U.S. personal savings rate through the first five months of 2007 was negative. This negative savings rate seems to be the product of increased borrowing by poorer households, reduced savings by richer households, and the proliferation of low-wage jobs (which provide incomes too low from which to save). The flip side of the savings rate is the marginal propensity to consume. Rough estimates suggest that the *mpc* for the U.S. economy averaged about 90 percent between 1946 and 1990. But between 1991 and 2000, the *mpc* was 105 percent, and has been even higher since then. People are, on balance, consuming all their income and then some, and are up to their eyeballs in consumer debt.
   a. What do these data imply for a multiplier model?
   b. What do they say about who has powered the U.S. economy recovery that began back in November 2001 and the sustainability of that recovery? (Radical)

5. Coaxing spending out of the private sector, especially investment spending, has never been an easy matter. What persuades investors to part with their money? Economist Stephen Fazzari provided one answer to that question in his study of 5,000 U.S. manufacturing firms. Fazzari found that interest rates exerted far less influence on investment decisions than either sales growth or a firm's available funds or financial conditions. What do Fazzari's findings suggest about the importance of Classical cost-side factors and Keynesian spending-side factors in the investment decisions of manufacturing firms? Also, what do Fazzari's findings suggest about what public policies might effectively promote investment? (Post-Keynesian)

Web Questions

1. The Conference Board publishes a report detailing consumer attitudes and buying plans and compiles the consumer confidence index. It also reports on business executives' expectations. Go to the Conference Board's home page (www.conference-board.org) and read the most recent reports on consumer confidence and CEO confidence to answer the following questions:
   a. What has happened to the consumer confidence index in the past few months?
   b. Using the multiplier model, show the likely effect of the change in consumer confidence on equilibrium output.
   c. What has happened to CEO confidence over the past few quarters?
   d. Do the consumer confidence and CEO confidence match? If not, what do you expect to happen to inventories in the coming months?

2. The U.S. Census Bureau collects data about the economy. Go to the Bureau's home page (www.census.gov) and look under "Latest Economic Indicators" to answer the following questions:
   a. What has happened to manufacturing inventories during the past twelve months?
   b. What does the change in inventories suggest about the direction of the economy in the coming months? Explain your answer using the multiplier model.

Answers to Margin Questions

1. Income equals production on the aggregate production curve. (*229*)

2. Induced expenditures change as income changes. Autonomous expenditures are independent of income. (*231*)

3. The *mpe* is .6. (*231*)

4. The multiplier is 2 when the *mpe* = .5. (*236*)

5. The level of income is $3,333. (*236*)

6. When inventories fall below planned inventories, the economy is probably expanding; firms will likely increase production, which will cause expenditures to increase, which will further draw down inventories. (*237*)

7. Equilibrium income falls by $300. (*239*)

8. As you can see in the accompanying graph, contractionary fiscal policy shifts the *AD* curve to the left. The multiplier then takes over to shift the *AD* curve to the left by a multiple of the initial decline in aggregate expenditures.

Assuming a flat *SAS* curve, income falls by a multiple of the initial shift. In the multiplier model, the *AE* curve shifts down and equilibrium income falls by a multiple of the decline in government expenditures. (*243*)

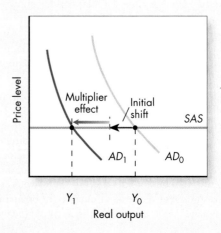

9. Since there is an inflationary gap, I would recommend contractionary fiscal policy. Since the multiplier is 1.5 (given the marginal propensity to expend of .33), I would recommend decreasing government spending by $66. *(243)*

10. If expenditures are dependent on permanent income, not current income, expenditures would not change as much with a change in current income and the multiplier would get smaller. *(246)*

APPENDIX A

An Algebraic Presentation of the Expanded Multiplier Model

In the chapter, I developed the basic multiplier model, focusing on the *mpe*. In this appendix, I briefly outline a fuller presentation in which consumption, taxes, and imports are related to income. That means that instead of having a single expenditures curve, we have a separate curve for each component of aggregate expenditures: consumption, investment, government spending, and net exports.

The Consumption Function Model

I begin with a model in which only consumption varies with income. The table below shows the components of the model as they are usually presented at the introductory level; Figure A10-1 graphs them.

(1) C	(2) + I	(3) + G	(4) + X−M	(5) = AE	(6) Y	(7) ΔAE	(8) ΔY	ROW
1,000	1,000	1,000	1,000	4,000	0			A
1,500	1,000	1,000	1,000	4,500	1,000	500	1,000	B
2,000	1,000	1,000	1,000	5,000	2,000	500	1,000	C
2,500	1,000	1,000	1,000	5,500	3,000	500	1,000	D
3,000	1,000	1,000	1,000	6,000	4,000	500	1,000	E
3,500	1,000	1,000	1,000	6,500	5,000	500	1,000	F
4,000	1,000	1,000	1,000	7,000	6,000	500	1,000	G
4,500	1,000	1,000	1,000	7,500	7,000	500	1,000	H
5,000	1,000	1,000	1,000	8,000	8,000	500	1,000	I
5,500	1,000	1,000	1,000	8,500	9,000	500	1,000	J
6,000	1,000	1,000	1,000	9,000	10,000	500	1,000	K
6,500	1,000	1,000	1,000	9,500	11,000	500	1,000	L
7,000	1,000	1,000	1,000	10,000	12,000	500	1,000	M

Notice that the only expenditure that is assumed to vary with income is consumption, which varies linearly with income and has a slope equal to the marginal propensity to consume (*mpc*)—the additional consumption that results from additional income. In this case, the *mpc* is assumed to be .5, so the slope of the consumption function is .5. All other

expenditures are assumed to be autonomous. The summation of expenditures, aggregate expenditures, is in column 5.

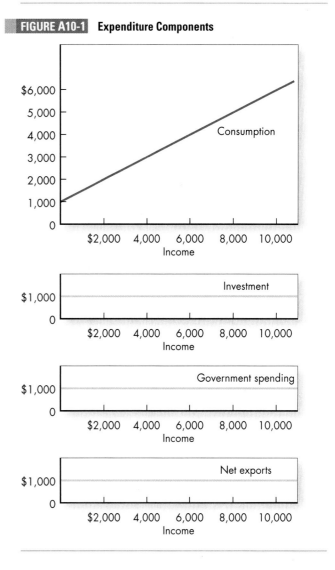

FIGURE A10-1 **Expenditure Components**

FIGURE A10-2 (A AND B) **Summation of Aggregate Expenditures**

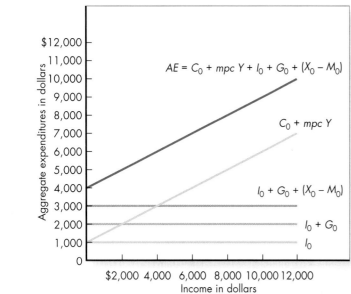

$$AE = C_0 + mpc\ Y + I_0 + G_0 + (X_0 - M_0)$$

$C_0 + mpc\ Y$

$I_0 + G_0 + (X_0 - M_0)$

$I_0 + G_0$

I_0

(a) Components of Aggregate Expenditures

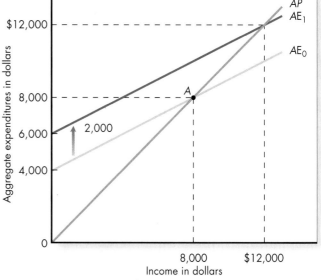

(b) Increased Investment of $2,000

To arrive at an aggregate expenditures function, we add up the curves vertically. I do this in Figure A10-2(a). Because we have assumed that consumption is the only expenditure that varies with income, the aggregate expenditures curve has the same slope as the consumption function. Notice that the aggregate expenditures curve crosses the vertical axis at a point that's the sum of all four autonomous expenditures: $C_0 + I_0 + G_0 + (X_0 - M_0) =$ $4,000. A good exercise to help you visualize the relationships involved is to compare the data in the columns with points on the graph to see how they correspond.

As was discussed in the text, aggregate equilibrium is where the aggregate expenditures function intersects the aggregate production curve—at point A in Figure A10-2(b). If any of the autonomous expenditures increase, the aggregate equilibrium will change. Say that autonomous investment increased by 2,000. That shifts up the AE curve by 2,000 and, as you can see, increases the equilibrium income by 4,000. Why by 4,000? Because of the multiplier discussed in the chapter. With only consumption varying with income, the marginal propensity to expend is determined by the marginal propensity to consume. Since in this case $mpe = mpc$, the multiplier is $1/(1 - mpc)$.

A More Complete Model

More generally, the various components of aggregate expenditures will depend on income in varying degrees, which will mean that the components each will have some

slope—they will have both an induced and an autonomous component. The slope of the aggregate expenditures curve will be the composite of all these slopes. Presenting that case geometrically becomes quite messy, so we will switch to an algebraic presentation.

In this fuller presentation, we break up the *mpe* into its component parts so that there is an *mpc*, specified as *c* in the equations; a marginal propensity to import, specified as *m* in the equations; and a marginal tax rate, specified as *t* in the equations.

This more complete multiplier model consists of the following equations:

(1) $C = C_0 = cY_d$
(2) $Y_d = Y - T + R$
(3) $I = I_0$
(4) $G = G_0$
(5) $R = R_0$
(6) $T = T_0 + tY$
(7) $X = X_0$
(8) $M = M_0 + mY$
(9) $C + I + G + (X - M) = Y$

Equation (1) is the consumption function: C_0 is autonomous consumption; *c* is the marginal propensity to consume; cY_d is the *mpc* multiplied by disposable income.

Equation (2) defines disposable income as a function of income minus taxes plus government transfers, R.

Equation (3) is the investment function. I_0 is autonomous investment.

Equation (4) is the government expenditures function. G_0 is autonomous spending.

Equation (5) is the government transfer function. R_0 is autonomous transfer payments.

Equation (6) is the tax function. Taxes are composed of two parts. The autonomous component, T_0, is unaffected by income. The induced portion of taxes is tY. The tax rate is represented by t.

Equation (7) is the exogenous export function.

Equation (8) is the import function. Imports are composed of two parts. M_0 is the autonomous portion. The induced portion is mY. The marginal propensity to import is represented by m.

Equation (9) is the national income accounting identity: Total expenditures = income

To use this model meaningfully, we must combine all these equations into a single equation, called a *reduced-form equation*, which will neatly show the effect of various shifts on the equilibrium level of income. To do so we first substitute Equation (2) into Equation (1), giving us

(1a) $C = C_0 + c(Y - T + R)$

We then substitute (1a), (3), (4), (5), (6), (7), and (8) into Equation (9), giving

$$C_0 + c[Y - (T_0 + tY) + R_0] + I_0 + G_0 \\ + [X_0 - (M_0 + mY)] = Y$$

Removing the parentheses:

$$C_0 + cY - cT_0 - ctY + cR_0 + I_0 + G_0 \\ + X_0 - M_0 - mY = Y$$

Moving all of the Y terms to the right side:

$$C_0 - cT_0 + cR_0 + I_0 + G_0 + X_0 - M_0 \\ = Y - cY + ctY + mY$$

Factoring out Y on the right side:

$$C_0 - cT_0 - cR_0 + I_0 + G_0 + X_0 - M_0 \\ = Y(1 - c + ct + m)$$

Dividing by $(1 - c + ct + m)$ gives

$$[C_0 - cT_0 - cR_0 + I_0 + G_0 + X_0 - M_0]$$

$$\left[\frac{1}{(1 - c + ct + m)} \right] = Y$$

$1/(1 - c + ct + m)$ is the multiplier for a simple multiplier model with endogenous taxes and endogenous imports.

We can relate this multiplier to the multiplier presented in the text $[1/(1 - mpe)]$ by recognizing that the marginal propensity to expend is

- Composed of the marginal propensity to consume, the marginal propensity to consume times the tax rate, and the marginal propensity to import and

- Equal to $c - ct - m$

Thus, $mpe = c - ct - m$. We can see that the two are the same by collecting terms and rewriting the multiplier as $1/[1 - (c - ct - m)]$. We can then replace the $c - ct - m$ with mpe. In the geometric case presented initially, the income tax, t, and the marginal propensity to import, m, were assumed to be zero, which reduces the multiplier to $1/(1 - c)$.

To see whether you follow the math, let's try a numerical example. Say you want to increase income (Y) by 100. Assume $c = .8$, $t = .2$, and $m = .14$. Substituting in these numbers, you find that the multiplier is 2. (The approximate multiplier for the United States is usually around 2.) Having calculated the multiplier, we can now determine how much to change autonomous expenditures to affect income. For example, to increase income by 100, we must increase autonomous expenditures by $(100/2) = 50$.

Questions for Thought and Review

1. You have just been made our nation's adviser. The president wants output to increase by 400 by decreasing taxes. Your research assistant tells you that the *mpc* is .8, and all other components of aggregate expenditures are determined outside the model. What policy would you suggest?

2. The president returns to you and tells you that instead of changing taxes, he wants to achieve the same result by increasing government expenditures. What policy would you recommend?

3. Your research assistant has a worried look on her face. "What's the problem?" you ask. "I goofed," she confesses. "I thought taxes were exogenous when actually there's a marginal tax rate of .1." Before she can utter another word, you say, "No problem. I'll simply recalculate my answers to questions 1 and 2 and change them before I send them in." What are your corrected answers?

4. She still has a pained expression. "What's wrong?" you ask. "You didn't let me finish," she says. "Not only was there a marginal tax rate of .1; there's also a marginal propensity to import of .2." Again you interrupt to make

sure she doesn't feel guilty. Again you say, "No problem. I'll simply recalculate my answers to questions 1 and 2 to account for the new information." What are your new answers?

5. Explain, using the words *expenditures* and *leakages*, why making taxes and imports endogenous reduces the multiplier.

6. Suppose imports were a function of disposable income instead of income. What would be the new multiplier? How does it compare with the multiplier when imports were a function of income?

APPENDIX B

The Multiplier Model and the *AS/AD* Model

In the last chapter, I emphasized that the *AD* curve was quite different from a micro demand curve; it was an equilibrium curve—a curve that told us the relationship between different price levels and different equilibria in the goods market. It has traditionally been derived from the multiplier model, and thus it has implicitly accepted the dynamics of that model. To see how it is derived from the multiplier model, we must first recall how the *AE* curve shifts as the price level rises and falls.

In Figure B10-1(a) I draw three *AE* curves—one for each of the price levels P_1, P_2, and P_3, where $P_1 > P_2 > P_3$. How a change in the price level affects the *AE* curve can be explained by the wealth, interest rate, and international effects. A rise in the price level will shift the *AE* curve down. Similarly, a fall in the price level will shift the *AE* curve up. (A much more detailed discussion of the relationship between the price level and expenditures can be found in the last chapter.)

The initial equilibrium is at point A. Notice that as the price level falls, aggregate expenditures rise. This initial increase causes induced expenditures to change. Production shifts because of these induced effects, increasing output further than the initial shift in aggregate expenditures and the initial increase in output to Y_1'. The new equilibrium output at P_2 is Y_2 (point B), and at P_3 the new equilibrium output is Y_3 (point C).

In Figure B10-1(b) I show the equilibrium price levels and outputs on a graph, with price level on the vertical axis and real output on the horizontal axis. That gives us points A, B, and C, which correspond to points A, B, and C in Figure B10-1(a). Drawing a line through these points gives us the aggregate demand curve: a curve that shows how a change in the price level will affect quantity of aggregate demand. Notice that the slope of the

AD curve includes both the effect of the initial shift in aggregate expenditures from a change in the price level and the multiplier effects as production and expenditures move to equilibrium. The initial shift in aggregate expenditures is shown by point B′. If there were no multiplier effects, the *AD* curve would go through points A and B′.

The first thing to note when considering the two models is that the multiplier model assumes that the price level is constant, so it assumes that the aggregate supply curve is flat. This means that the multiplier model tells us precisely how much the *AD* curve will shift when autonomous expenditures shift by a specified amount. The difference between the shift in autonomous expenditures and the *AD* curve shift is due to the multiplier.

The relationship between a shift in autonomous expenditures in the *AS/AD* model and the multiplier model can be seen in Figure B10-1(c) and (d). These consider a fall in autonomous expenditures of $20 when the multiplier is 2. In Figure B10-1(c) you can see that, in the multiplier model, a fall in expenditures of $20 will cause income to fall by $40, from $4,052 to $4,012.

Figure B10-1(d) shows that same adjustment in the *AS/AD* model. Initially expenditures fall by $20, but the *AD* curve shifts back not by $20, but by $40—the initial shift multiplied by the multiplier. That's because the *AD* curves take into account the interdependent shifts between supply and demand decisions that are set in motion by the initial shift. Thus, we need the multiplier model, or some alternative model of induced effects, before we can draw an *AD* curve. (I make the qualification "or some other model" to emphasize that the interdependent shifts assumed in the multiplier model are not the only interdependent shifts that could occur. Had we assumed a different dynamic adjustment process, we would have had a different *AD* curve.)

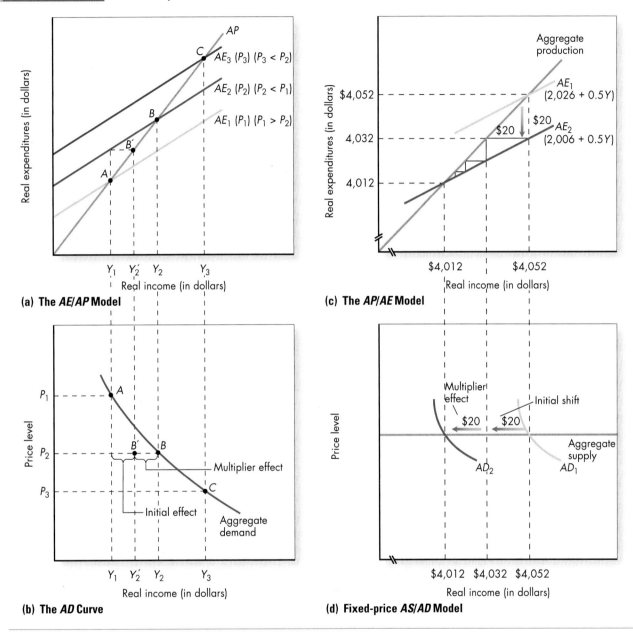

FIGURE B10-1 (A–D)   Relationship between the *AS/AD* Model and the *AP/AE* Model

(a) The *AE/AP* Model

(b) The *AD* Curve

(c) The *AP/AE* Model

(d) Fixed-price *AS/AD* Model

A good test of your understanding here is to ask yourself what happens in the long run if the economy is operating above its potential where prices are perfectly flexible. (In that case, the rise in aggregate demand is fully offset by a rise in the price level, and the *AE* curve shifts right back where it started.)

Much of the modern debate in macro concerns the dynamic adjustment process that the multiplier model is meant to describe. We won't go into that debate here since it quickly becomes very complicated, but I do want to point out to you that the multiplier model is not the end of the analysis; it is simply the beginning—one of the simplest cases of dynamic adjustment. The real-world dynamic adjustment is more complicated, which is one of the reasons why there is so much debate about macro- economic issues.

Questions for Thought and Review

1. Demonstrate graphically the effect of an increase in autonomous expenditures when the $mpe = .5$ and the SAS curve is flat:
   a. In the multiplier model.
   b. In the AS/AD model.
   c. Do the same thing as in a and b, only this time assume that the SAS curve is upward-sloping.

2. State how the following information changes the slope of the AD curve.

   a. The effect of price level changes on autonomous expenditures is reduced.
   b. The size of the multiplier increases.
   c. Autonomous expenditures increase by $20.
   d. Falls in the price level disrupt financial markets, which offset the normally assumed effects of a change in the price level.

The Financial Sector and the Demand for Money

The process by which banks create money is so simple that the mind is repelled.

—*John Kenneth Galbraith*

The financial sector is exciting (as suggested in this famous painting, "The Bulls and the Bears in the Market"); it is also central to almost all macroeconomic debates. This central role is often not immediately obvious to students. In thinking about the economy, students often focus on the *real sector*—the market for the production and exchange of goods and services. In the real sector, real goods or services such as shoes, operas, automobiles, and textbooks are exchanged. That's an incomplete view of the economy. The *financial sector*—the market for the creation and exchange of financial assets such as money, stocks, and bonds—plays a central role in organizing and coordinating our economy; it makes modern economic society possible. A car won't run without oil; a modern economy won't operate without a financial sector.

As I've noted throughout this book, markets make specialization and trade possible and thereby make the economy far more efficient than it otherwise would be. But the efficient use of markets requires a financial sector that facilitates and lubricates those trades. Let's consider an example of how the financial sector facilitates trade. Say you walk into a store and buy a CD. You shell out a 20-dollar bill and the salesperson hands you the CD. Easy, right? Right—but why did the salesperson give you a CD for a little piece of paper? The answer to that question is: Because the economy has a financial system that has convinced him that that piece of paper has value. To convince him (and you) of that requires an enormous structural system, called the financial sector, underlying the CD transaction and all other transactions. That financial system makes the transaction possible; without it the economy as we know it would not exist.

Why Is the Financial Sector Important to Macro?

In thinking about the financial sector's role, remember the following insight: *For every real transaction, there is a financial transaction that mirrors it.* For example, when you buy an apple, the person selling the apple is buying 50 cents from you

AFTER READING THIS CHAPTER, YOU SHOULD BE ABLE TO:

1. Explain why the financial sector is central to almost all macroeconomic debates.
2. Demonstrate graphically how the long-term interest rate is determined.
3. Explain what money is.
4. Enumerate the three functions of money.
5. State the alternative measures of money and their primary components.
6. Explain how banks create money.
7. Calculate both the simple money multiplier and the money multiplier.
8. Explain why people hold money and how the short-term interest rate is determined in the money market.

FIGURE 11-1   **The Financial Sector as a Conduit for Savings**

Financial institutions channel saving—outflows from the spending stream from various entities (government, households, and corporations)—back into the spending stream as loans to various entities (government, households, and corporations). To emphasize the fact that savings take many forms, a breakdown of the type of savings for one entity, households, is shown on the left. The same is done for loans on the right, but for corporations. Each of these loans can itself be broken down again and again until each particular loan is identified individually. The lending process is an individualistic process, and each loan is different in some way from each other loan.

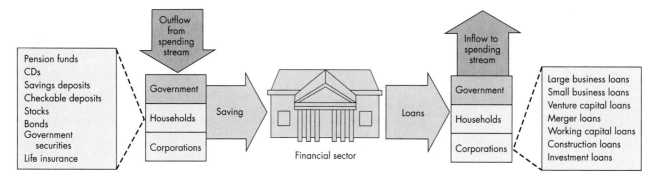

The financial sector is central to almost all macroeconomic debates because behind every real transaction, there is a financial transaction that mirrors it.

Q-1 Joe, your study partner, says that since goods and services are produced only in the real sector, the financial sector is not important to the macroeconomy. How do you respond?

The financial sector channels saving back into spending.

For every financial asset, there is a financial liability.

by spending his apple. The financial transaction is the transfer of 50 cents; the real transaction is the transfer of the apple.

As long as the financial system is operating smoothly, you hardly know it's there; but should that system break down, the entire economy would be disrupted and would either stagnate or go into a recession. That's why it is necessary to give you an overview of the financial sector as part of your foundation of macroeconomics. Thus, although in this book I don't have a separate section on the steel sector or even the computer sector of the economy, I do have a separate section on money, banking, and the financial sector of the economy.

The financial sector—financial markets and institutions—transfers saving— outflows from the spending stream in hundreds of different forms—back into spending. Think of the financial sector as a gigantic channeling device, something like that shown in Figure 11-1. If the financial sector expands the spending flow too much, you get inflationary pressures. If it contracts the spending flow too much, you get a recession. And if it transfers just the right amount, you get a smoothly running economy.

Flow from the spending stream is channeled into the financial sector as saving when individuals buy **financial assets**—*assets such as stocks or bonds, whose benefit to the owner depends on the issuer of the asset meeting certain obligations*. These obligations by the issuer of the financial asset are called financial liabilities. For every financial asset, there is a corresponding financial liability. (Financial assets and liabilities are discussed in detail in Appendix A to this chapter.)

The Role of Interest Rates in the Financial Sector

Web Note 11.1
Interest Rates

Interest rates—*the prices paid for the use of a financial asset*—are key variables in the financial sector. While there are many interest rates in the economy—mortgage interest rates, interest rates on credit cards, interest rates on government bills, interest rates on corporate bonds, and many more—for simplicity I will talk about interest rates as if there were just two: a short-term interest rate and a long-term interest rate.

The long-term interest rate is the price paid for the use of financial assets with long repayment periods. Examples are mortgages and government bonds. The market for

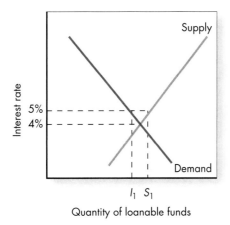

FIGURE 11-2 **Market for Loanable Funds**

The quantity of loanable funds supplied (savings) is equal to the quantity of loanable funds demanded (investment) at an interest rate of 4 percent. If the interest rate for some reason does not equal the 4 percent, say it is 5 percent, the quantity of savings (in this example S_1) will exceed the quantity of investment (in this case I_1), and all savings will not be channeled back into investment. The circular flow will be broken.

these long-term financial assets is called the *loanable funds market*. The short-term interest rate is the price paid for the use of financial assets with shorter repayment periods such as savings deposits and checking accounts. These short-term financial assets are called *money*. So, the long-term interest rate is determined in the loanable funds market and the short-term interest rate is determined in the money market.

The long-term interest rate is determined in the market for loanable funds as shown in Figure 11-2. In it you can see that the quantity of loanable funds supplied (savings) is equal to the quantity of loanable funds demanded (investment) at an interest rate of 4 percent. If the interest rate for some reason does not equal 4 percent, say it is 5 percent, the quantity of savings (in this case S_1) will exceed the quantity of investment (in this case I_1), and all savings will not be channeled back into investment. The circular flow will be broken, and macroeconomic problems can develop.

To get at the problems that can develop, macroeconomics simplifies the flow of saving into two types of financial assets. One type works its way back into the system: bonds, loans, and stocks. These are translated back into investment by financial intermediaries. It is these financial assets to which the loanable funds market refers.[1] The other type of financial asset, when held by individuals, is not necessarily assumed to work its way back into the flow—we'll call this financial asset "money." Savings held as money are assumed not to work their way back into the loanable funds market and hence those savings do not get translated into investment. This means that some savings escape the circular flow. Compared to the complicated maze of interconnected flows that exists in reality, this is an enormous simplification, but it captures a potentially serious problem and possible cause of fluctuations in the economy.

The Definition and Functions of Money

Let's now turn our attention to money.

At this point you're probably saying, "I know what money is; it's currency—the dollar bills I carry around." In one sense you're right: currency is money. But in another sense you're wrong; currency is just one example of money. In fact, a number of

Q-2 Why are interest rates important to the economy?

---

[1]With a different interest rate for each different type of financial asset, you may be wondering which interest rate we are talking about. The answer is that we are talking about an average of the many different interest rates. Since that average interest rate is generally not easily calculable, often the interest rate on 10-year bonds is used as a proxy for the interest rate on all loanable funds.

Money is a financial asset that makes the real economy function smoothly by serving as a medium of exchange, a unit of account, and a store of wealth.

short-term financial assets are included as money. To see why, let's consider the definition of money: **Money** is *a highly liquid financial asset that's generally accepted in exchange for other goods, is used as a reference in valuing other goods, and can be stored as wealth.*

To be *liquid* means to be easily changeable into another asset or good. When you buy something with money, you are exchanging money for another asset. So any of your assets that are easily spendable are money. Social customs and standard practices are central to the liquidity of money. The reason you are willing to hold money is that you know someone else will accept it in trade for something else. Its value is determined by its general acceptability to others. If you don't believe that, try spending yuan (Chinese money) in the United States. If you try to buy dinner with 100 yuan, you will be told, "No way—give me money."

The U.S. Central Bank: The Fed

So is there any characteristic other than general acceptability that gives value to money? Consider the dollar bill that you know is money. Look at it. It states right on the bill that it is a Federal Reserve note, which means that it is an IOU (a liability) of the **Federal Reserve Bank (the Fed)**—*the U.S. central bank whose liabilities (Federal Reserve notes) serve as cash in the United States.* Individuals are willing to accept the Fed's IOUs in return for real goods and services, which means that Fed notes are money.

What, you ask, is a central bank? To answer that question, we had better first consider what a bank is. A **bank** is *a financial institution whose primary function is accepting deposits for, and lending money to, individuals and firms.* (There are more complicated definitions and many types of banks, but that will do for now; the issues are discussed more fully in Appendix A to this chapter.) If you have more currency than you want, you take it to the bank and it will "hold" the extra for you, giving you a piece of paper (or a computer entry) that says you have that much currency held here ("hold" is in quotation marks because the bank does not actually hold the currency). What the bank used to give you was a bank note, and what you used to bring in to the bank was gold, but those days are gone forever. These days what you bring is that Federal Reserve note described above, and what you get is a paper receipt and a computer entry in your checking or savings account. Individuals' deposits in these accounts serve the same purpose as does currency and are also considered money.

Which brings us back to the Federal Reserve Bank, the U.S. central bank. It is a bank that has the right to issue notes (IOUs). By law these Federal Reserve Bank notes are acceptable payment for people's taxes, and by convention these notes are acceptable payment to all people in the United States, and to many people outside the United States. IOUs of the Fed are what most of you think of as cash.

To understand why money is more than just cash, it is helpful to consider the functions of money in more detail. Having done so, we will consider which financial assets are included in various measures of money.

Functions of Money

Q₃ What are the three functions of money?

As I stated above, money is an asset that can be quickly exchanged for any other asset or good. Money serves three functions:

1. It serves as a medium of exchange.
2. It serves as a unit of account.
3. It serves as a store of wealth.

To get a better understanding of what money is, let's consider each of its functions in turn.

Money as a Medium of Exchange   The easiest way to understand money's medium-of-exchange use is to imagine what an economy would be like without money. Say you want something to eat at a restaurant. Without money you'd have to barter with the restaurant owner for your meal. *Barter* is a direct exchange of goods and/or services. You might suggest bartering one of your papers or the shirt in the sack that you'd be forced to carry with you to trade for things you want. Not liking to carry big sacks around, you'd probably decide to fix your own meal and forgo eating out. Bartering is simply too difficult. Money makes many more trades possible because it does not require a double coincidence of wants by two individuals, as simple barter does.

The use of money as a medium of exchange makes it possible to trade real goods and services without bartering. Instead of carrying around a sack full of diverse goods, all you need to carry around is a billfold full of money. You go into the restaurant and pay for your meal with money; the restaurant owner can spend (trade) that money for anything she wants.

Money doesn't have to have any inherent value to function as a medium of exchange. All that's necessary is that everyone believes that other people will accept it in exchange for their goods. This neat social convention makes the economy function more smoothly.

Money doesn't have to have any inherent value to function as a medium of exchange.

Money as a Unit of Account   A second use of money is as a unit of account, that is, a measure of value. Money prices are actually relative prices. A money price, say 25 cents, for a pencil conveys the information of a relative price—1 pencil = ¼ of 1 dollar—because money is both our unit of account and our medium of exchange. When you think of 25 cents, you think of ¼ of a dollar and of what a dollar will buy. The 25 cents a pencil costs only has meaning relative to the information you've stored in your mind about what money can buy. If a hamburger costs $1.50, you can compare hamburgers and pencils (1 pencil = ⅙ of a hamburger) without making the relative price calculations explicitly.

Having a unit of account makes life much easier. For example, say we had no unit of account and you had to remember the relative prices of all goods. For instance, with three goods you'd have to memorize that an airplane ticket to Miami costs 6 lobster dinners in Boston or 4 pairs of running shoes, which makes a pair of shoes worth 1½ lobster dinners.

Memorizing even a few relationships is hard enough, so it isn't surprising that societies began using a single unit of account. If you don't have a single unit of account, all combinations of 100 goods will require that you remember thousands of relative prices. If you have a single unit of account, you need know only 100 prices. A single unit of account saves our limited memories and helps us make reasonable decisions based on relative prices.

Money is used as a unit of account at a point in time, and it's also a unit of account *over time*. For example, money is a standard of deferred payments such as on college loans that many of you will be making after graduation. The value of those loan payments depends on how the money prices of all other goods change over time.

Money is a useful unit of account only as long as its value relative to the average of all other prices doesn't change too quickly. For example, in hyperinflation all prices rise so much that our frame of reference for making relative price comparisons is lost. Is 25 cents for a pencil high or low? If the price level increased 33,000 percent (as it did in 1988 in Nicaragua) or over 100,000 percent (as it did in the early 2000s in Zimbabwe), 25 cents for a pencil would definitely be low, but would $100 be low? Without a lot of calculations we can't answer that question. A relatively stable unit of account makes it easy to answer.

Money is a useful unit of account only as long as its value relative to other prices doesn't change too quickly.

In hyperinflation, all prices rise so much that our frame of reference is lost.

Given the advantages to society of having a unit of account, it's not surprising that a monetary unit of account develops even in societies with no central bank or government. For example, in a prisoner of war camp during World War II, prisoners had no money, so they used cigarettes as their unit of account. Everything traded was given a price in cigarettes. The exchange rates on December 1, 1944, were

1 bar of soap: 2 cigarettes

1 candy bar: 4 cigarettes

1 razor blade: 6 cigarettes

1 can of fruit: 8 cigarettes

1 can of cookies: 20 cigarettes

As you can see, all prices were in cigarettes. If candy bars rose to 6 cigarettes and the normal price was 4 cigarettes, you'd know the price of candy bars was high.

Money as a Store of Wealth   When you save, you forgo consumption now so that you can consume in the future. To bridge the gap between now and the future, you must acquire a financial asset. This is true even if you squirrel away currency under the mattress. In that case, the financial asset you've acquired is simply the currency itself. Money is a financial asset. (It's simply a bond that pays no interest.) So a third use of money is as a store of wealth. As long as money is serving as a medium of exchange, it automatically also serves as a store of wealth. The restaurant owner can accept your money and hold it for as long as she wants before she spends it. (But had you paid her in fish, she'd be wise not to hold it more than a few hours.)

You might wonder why people would hold money that pays no interest. Put another way: Why do people hold a government bond that pays no interest? The reason is that money, by definition, is highly liquid—it is more easily translated into other goods than are other financial assets. Since money is also the medium of exchange, it can be spent instantaneously (as long as there's a shop open nearby). Our ability to spend money for goods makes money worthwhile to hold even if it doesn't pay interest.

Alternative Measures of Money

According to the definition of *money*, what people believe is money and what people will accept as money are determining factors in deciding whether a financial asset is money. Consequently, it's difficult to measure *money* unambiguously. A number of different financial assets serve some of the functions of money and thus have claims to being called *money*. To handle this ambiguity, economists have developed different measures of money and have called them M_1 and M_2. Each is a reasonable concept of money. Let's consider their components.

M_1

M_1 consists of *currency in the hands of the public, checking account balances, and traveler's checks*. Clearly, currency in the hands of the public (the dollar bills and coins you carry around with you) are money, but how about your checking account deposits? The reason they're included in this measure of money is that just about anything you can do with currency, you can do with a check. You can store your wealth in your checking account; you can use a check as a medium of exchange (indeed, for some transactions you have no choice but to use a check), and your checking account balance is denominated in the same unit of account (dollars) as is currency. If it looks like money, acts like money, and functions as money, it's a good bet it's money. Indeed, checking account deposits are included in all measures of money.

The same arguments can be made about traveler's checks. (Some advertisements even claim that traveler's checks are better than money because you can get them

As long as money is serving as a medium of exchange, it automatically also serves as a store of wealth.

Q-4 Why do people hold money rather than bonds when bonds pay higher interest than money?

M_1 is the component of the money supply that consists of currency in the hands of the public plus checking accounts and traveler's checks.

FIGURE 11-3 Components of M₂ and M₁

The two most-used measures of the money supply are M_1 and M_2. The two primary components of M_1 are currency in the hands of the public and checking accounts. M_2 includes all of M_1, plus savings deposits, time deposits, and money market mutual funds.
Source: *H.6 Money Stock Measures, 2007* (www.federalreserve.gov).

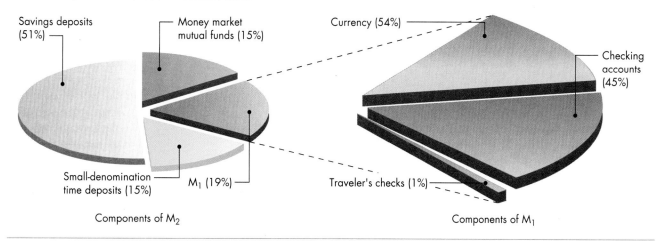

Savings deposits (51%)

Money market mutual funds (15%)

Currency (54%)

Checking accounts (45%)

Small-denomination time deposits (15%)

M₁ (19%)

Traveler's checks (1%)

Components of M₂

Components of M₁

replaced.) Currency, checking account deposits, and traveler's checks make up the components of M_1, the narrowest measure of money. Figure 11-3 presents the relative sizes of M_1's components.

M₂

M_2 is made up of M_1 *plus savings deposits, small-denomination time deposits, and money market mutual fund shares.* The relative sizes of the components of M_2 are given in Figure 11-3.

The money in savings accounts (savings deposits) is counted as money because it is readily spendable—all you need do is go to the bank and draw it out. Small-denomination time deposits are also called *certificates of deposit* (CDs).

M_2's components include more financial assets than M_1. All its components are highly liquid and play an important role in providing reserves and lending capacity for commercial banks. What makes the M_2 measure important is that economic research has shown that M_2 is the measure of money often most closely correlated with the price level and economic activity.

M_2 is the component of the money supply that consists of M_1 plus other relatively liquid assets.

Q.5 Which would be a larger number, M_1 or M_2? Why?

Distinguishing between Money and Credit

You might have thought that credit cards would be included in one of the measures of *money.* But I didn't include them. In fact, credit cards are nowhere to be seen in a list of the components of money. Credit cards are not money. Credit cards aren't a financial liability of the bank that issues them. Instead, credit cards create a liability for their users (money owed to the company or bank that issued the card) and the banks have a financial asset as a result.

Let's consider how a credit card works. You go into a store and buy something with your credit card. You have a real asset—the item you bought. The store has a financial asset—an account receivable. The store sells that financial asset at a slight discount to the bank and gets cash in return. Either the bank collects cash when you pay off your financial liability or, if you don't pay it off, the bank earns interest on its financial asset

Credit cards are not money.

Characteristics of a Good Money

The characteristics of a good money are that its supply be relatively constant, that it be limited in supply (sand wouldn't make good money), that it be difficult to counterfeit, that it be divisible (have you ever tried to spend half a horse?), that it be durable (raspberries wouldn't make good money), and that it be relatively small and light compared to its value (watermelon wouldn't make good money either). All these characteristics were reasonably (but not perfectly) embodied in gold. Many other goods have served as units of account (shells, wampum, rocks, cattle, horses, silver), but gold historically became the most important money, and in the 17th and 18th centuries gold was synonymous with money.

But gold has flaws as money. It's relatively heavy, easy to counterfeit with coins made only partly of gold, and, when new gold fields are discovered, subject to fluctuations in supply. These flaws led to gold's replacement by paper currency backed only by trust that the government would keep its commitment to limit its supply.

Paper money can be a good money if somehow people can trust the government to limit its supply and guarantee that its supply will be limited in the future. That trust has not always been well placed.

Most societies today supplement paper money such as dollar bills with electronic money that exists as debits and credit entries recorded on the computer. Both electronic money and paper money are vulnerable to fraud. Electronic money can be created by criminals who electronically change debit and credit entries, which is why banks spend billions of dollars on computer security and encryption technology each year. Paper money can be counterfeited. For example, in World War II, Germany planned to counterfeit a significant amount of British pounds and drop them in Britain to disrupt the British economy. It didn't succeed; by the time they had printed the notes, they didn't have the aircraft to fly them over and drop them in Britain.

Counterfeiting continues today. For example, you may have noticed that some of the higher-denomination-dollar bills you carry have changed their look in recent years. That's because counterfeiters with new technology could create almost perfect counterfeit copies of the older designs. In 1989, authorities found some counterfeit U.S. $100 bills that had the right mix of cotton and linen and that had been manufactured on the very expensive Intaglio press, the same kind of press used to print real dollar bills. They called these counterfeit notes "supernotes." To stop the counterfeiters of the supernotes, the United States redesigned the U.S currency, adding additional security measures such as color-shifting ink, watermarks, a security thread, an ultraviolet glow, and microprinting. Counterfeiters will copy these newly designed bills, which means that it is likely that U.S. authorities will have to redesign U.S. paper currency about every 10 years in order to keep ahead of counterfeiters.

So far, counterfeiting is still relatively unimportant in the United States. But in some developing countries, merchants and even banks are hesitant to accept large-denomination U.S. currency, which means that counterfeiting in those countries, is undermining the usefulness of the dollar as money.

(often at a high rate, from 12 to 18 percent per year). Credit cards are essentially prearranged loans.

This distinction between credit and money should be kept in mind. Money is a financial asset of individuals and a financial liability of banks. Credit is savings made available to be borrowed. Credit is not an asset of the borrowing public.

Q.6 Are credit cards money?

Credit cards and credit impact the amount of money people hold. When preapproved loan credit is instantly available (as it is with a credit card), there's less need to hold money. (If you didn't have a credit card, you'd carry a lot more currency.) With credit immediately available, liquidity is less valuable to people. So credit and credit cards do make a difference in how much money people hold, but because they are not financial liabilities of banks, they are not money.

Money Laundering

The U.S. government has issued over $820 billion worth of cash. That's about $2,700 for every man, woman, and child. Now ask yourself how much cash you're carrying on you. Add to that the amounts banks and businesses keep, and divide that by the number of people in the United States. The number economists get when they do that calculation is way below the total amount of cash the United States has issued. So what happens to the extra cash?

Let's switch for a minute to a Miami safehouse being raided by drug enforcement officers. They find $50 million in cash. That's what most economists believe happens to much of the extra cash that remains in the United States. It goes underground. An underground economy lurks below the real economy. The underground economy consists of two components: (1) the production and distribution of illegal goods and services and (2) the nonreporting of legal economic activity.

Illegal activity, such as selling illegal drugs and prostitution, generates huge amounts of cash. (Most people who buy an illegal good or service would prefer not to have the transaction appear on their monthly credit card statements.) This presents a problem for a big-time illegal business. It must explain to the Internal Revenue Service (IRS) where all that money came from. That's where money laundering comes in. Money laundering is simply making illegally gained income look as if it came from a legal business. Any business through which lots of cash moves is a good front for money laundering. Laundromats move lots of cash, which is where the term money laundering came from. The mob bought laundromats and claimed a much higher income from the laundromats than it actually received. The mob thus "laundered" the excess money. Today money laundering is much more sophisticated. It involves billions of dollars and international transactions in three or four different countries, but the purpose is the same: making illegally earned money look legal.

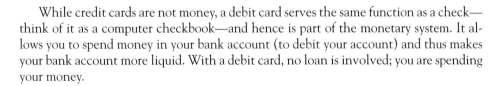

While credit cards are not money, a debit card serves the same function as a check—think of it as a computer checkbook—and hence is part of the monetary system. It allows you to spend money in your bank account (to debit your account) and thus makes your bank account more liquid. With a debit card, no loan is involved; you are spending your money.

Banks and the Creation of Money

Banks are financial institutions that borrow from people (take in deposits) and use the money they borrow to make loans to other individuals. Banks make a profit by charging a higher interest on the money they lend out than they pay for the money they borrow. Individuals keep their money in banks, accepting lower interest rates, because doing so is safer and more convenient than the alternatives.

Banking is generally analyzed from the perspective of **asset management** (*how a bank handles its loans and other assets*) and **liability management** (*how a bank attracts deposits and what it pays for them*). When banks offer people "free checking" and special money market accounts paying 4 percent, they do so after carefully considering the costs of those liabilities to them.

To think of banks as borrowers as well as lenders may seem a bit unusual, but borrowing is what they do. When you own a savings account or a checking account, the bank is borrowing from you, paying you a zero (or low) interest rate. It then lends your money to other people at a higher interest rate.

The Creation of Money

It is important to think of banks as both borrowers and lenders.

How Banks Create Money

Banks are centrally important to macroeconomics because they create money. How do banks create money? As John Kenneth Galbraith's epigram at the start of this chapter suggests, the process is simple—so simple it seems almost magical to many.

Banks "create" money because a bank's liabilities are defined as money. So when a bank incurs liabilities, it creates money.

The key to understanding how banks create money is to remember the nature of financial assets: Financial assets can be created from nothing as long as an offsetting financial liability is simultaneously created. Since money is any financial asset that can be used as a medium of exchange, unit of account, and store of value, money can be created rather easily. The asset just needs to serve the functions of money. Seeing how dollar bills are created is the easiest way to begin examining the process. Whenever the Fed issues an IOU, it creates money.[2] Similarly, other banks create money by creating financial assets that serve the functions of money. As we saw when we considered the measures of money, bank checking accounts serve those functions, so they are money, just as currency is money. When a bank places the proceeds of a loan it makes to you in your checking account, it is creating money. You have a financial asset that did not previously exist.

The First Step in the Creation of Money   To see how banks create money, let's consider what would happen if you were given a freshly printed $100 bill. Remember, the Fed created that $100 bill simply by printing it. The $100 bill is a $100 financial asset of yours and a financial liability of the Fed, which issued it.

If the process of creating money stopped there, it wouldn't be particularly mysterious. But it doesn't stop there. Let's consider what happens next as you use that money.

About 95 percent of all bills printed each year replace worn-out notes. The remaining 5 percent represent new currency in circulation.

The Second Step in the Creation of Money   The second step in the creation of money involves the transfer of money from one form to another—from currency to a bank deposit. Say you decide to put the $100 bill in your checking account. To make the analysis easier, let's assume that your bank is a branch of the country's only bank, Big Bank. All money deposited in branch banks goes into Big Bank. After you make your deposit, Big Bank is holding $100 in currency for you, and you have $100 more in your checking account. You can spend it whenever you want simply by writing a check. So Big Bank is performing a service for you (holding your money and keeping track of your expenditures) for free. Neat, huh? Big Bank must be run by a bunch of nice people.

But wait. You and I know that bankers, while they may be nice, aren't as nice as all that. There ain't no such thing as a free lunch. Let's see why the bank is being so nice.

Web Note 11.2
Gold

Banking and Goldsmiths   To see why banks are so nice, let's go way back in history to when banks first developed.[3] At that time, gold was used for money and people carried around gold to make their payments. But because gold is rather heavy, it was difficult to use for big purchases. Moreover, carrying around a lot of gold left people vulnerable to being robbed by the likes of Robin Hood. So they looked for a place to store their gold until they needed some of it.

From Gold to Gold Receipts   The natural place to store gold was the goldsmith shop, which already had a vault. For a small fee, the goldsmith shop would hold your gold, giving you a receipt for it. Whenever you needed your gold, you'd go to the goldsmith and exchange the receipt for gold.

Pretty soon most people kept their gold at the goldsmith's, and they began to wonder: Why go through the bother of getting my gold out to buy something when all that

---

[2]As we'll see when we discuss the Fed in more detail, dollar bills aren't the Fed's only IOUs.
[3]The banking history reported here is, according to historians, apocryphal (more myth than reality). But it so nicely makes the point that I repeat it anyhow.

happens is that the seller takes the gold I pay and puts it right back into the goldsmith's vault? That's two extra trips.

Consequently, people began using the receipts the goldsmith gave them to certify that they had deposited $100 worth (or whatever) of gold in his vault. At that point, gold was no longer the only money—gold receipts were also money since they were accepted in exchange for goods. However, as long as the total amount in the gold receipts directly represented the total amount of gold, it was still reasonable to say, since the receipts were 100 percent backed by gold, that gold was the money supply.

Gold Receipts Become Money Once this process of using the receipts rather than the gold became generally accepted, the goldsmith found that he had substantial amounts of gold in his vault. All that gold, just sitting there! On a normal day, only 1 percent of the gold was claimed by "depositors" and had to be given out. Usually on the same day an amount at least equal to that 1 percent came in from other depositors. What a waste! Gold sitting around doing nothing! So when a good friend came in, needing a loan, the goldsmith said, "Sure, I'll lend you some gold receipts as long as you pay me some interest." When the goldsmith made this loan, he created more gold receipts than he had covered in gold in his vault. He created money.

Pretty soon the goldsmith realized he could earn more from the interest he received on loans than he could earn from goldsmithing. So he stopped goldsmithing and went full-time into making loans of gold receipts. At that point, the number of gold receipts outstanding significantly exceeded the amount of gold in the goldsmith's vaults. But not to worry; since everyone was willing to accept gold receipts rather than gold, the goldsmith had plenty of gold for those few who wanted actual gold.

It was, however, no longer accurate to say that gold was the country's money or currency. Gold receipts were also money. They met the definition of *money*. These gold receipts were backed partially by gold and partially by people's trust that the goldsmiths would pay off their deposits on demand. The goldsmith shops had become banks.

Banking Is Profitable The banking business was very profitable for goldsmiths. Soon other people started competing with them, offering to hold gold for free. After all, if they could store gold, they could make a profit on the loans to other people (with the first people's money). Some even offered to pay people to store their gold.

The goldsmith story is directly relevant to banks. People store their currency in banks and the banks issue receipts—checking accounts—that become a second form of money. When people place their currency in banks and use their receipts from the bank as money, those receipts also become money because they meet the definition of *money*: They serve as a medium of exchange, a unit of account, and a store of wealth. So money includes both currency that people hold and their deposits in the bank.

Which brings us back to why banks hold your currency for free. They do it not because they're nice, but because when you deposit currency in the bank, your deposit allows banks to make profitable loans they otherwise couldn't make.

The Money Multiplier

With that background, let's go back to your $100, which the bank is now holding for you. You have a checking account balance of $100 and the bank has $100 currency. As long as other people are willing to accept your check in payment for $100 worth of goods, your check is as good as money. In fact, it is money in the same way gold receipts were money. But when you deposit $100, no additional money has been created yet. The form of the money has simply been changed from currency to a checking account or demand deposit.

Now let's say Big Bank lends out 90 percent of the currency you deposit, keeping only 10 percent as **reserves**—*currency and deposits a bank keeps on hand or at the Fed or*

Q.7 Most banks prefer to have many depositors rather than one big depositor. Why?

Money is whatever meets the definition of money.

The reserve ratio is the ratio of currency (or deposits at the central bank) to deposits a bank keeps as a reserve against currency withdrawals.

central bank, *to manage the normal cash inflows and outflows.* This 10 percent is the **reserve ratio** (*the ratio of reserves to total deposits*). Banks are required by the Fed to hold a percentage of deposits; that percentage is called the required reserve ratio. Banks may also choose to hold an additional percentage, called the *excess reserve ratio.* The reserve ratio is the sum of the required reserve ratio and the excess reserve ratio. Thus, the reserve ratio is at least as large as the required reserve ratio, but it can be larger.

So, like the goldsmith, Big Bank lends out $90 to someone who qualifies for a loan. That person the bank loaned the money to now has $90 currency and you have $100 in a demand deposit, so now there's $190 of money, rather than just $100 of money. The $10 in currency the bank holds in reserve isn't counted as money since the bank must keep it as reserves and may not use it as long as it's backing loans. Only currency held by the public, not currency held by banks, is counted as money. By making the loan, the bank has created $90 in money.

Of course, no one borrows money just to hold it. The borrower spends the money, say on a new sweater, and the sweater store owner now has the $90 in currency. The store owner doesn't want to hold it either. She'll deposit it back into the bank. Since there's only one bank, Big Bank discovers that the $90 it has loaned out is once again in its coffers. The money operates like a boomerang: Big Bank loans $90 out and gets the $90 back again.

The same process occurs again. The bank doesn't earn interest income by holding $90, so if the bank can find additional credible borrowers, it lends out $81, keeping $9 (10 percent of $90) in reserve. The story repeats and repeats itself, with a slightly smaller amount coming back to the bank each time. At each step in the process, money (in the form of checking account deposits) is being created.

Determining How Many Demand Deposits Will Be Created   What's the total amount of demand deposits that will ultimately be created from your $100 when individuals hold no currency? To answer that question, we continue the process over and over: 100 + 90 + 81 + 72.9 + 65.6 + 59 + 53.1 + 47.8 + 43.0 + 38.7 + 34.9. Adding up these numbers gives us $686. Adding up $686 plus the numbers from the next 20 rounds gives us $961.08.

As you can see, that's a lot of adding. Luckily there's an easier way. Economists have shown that you can determine the amount of money that will eventually be created by such a process by multiplying the initial $100 in money that was printed by the Fed and deposited by $1/r$, where r is the reserve ratio (the percentage banks keep out of each round). In this case the reserve ratio is 10 percent.

Dividing,

$$\frac{1}{r} = \frac{1}{.10} = 10$$

so the amount of demand deposits that will ultimately exist at the end of the process is

$$(10 \times \$100) = \$1,000$$

The $1,000 is in the form of checking account deposits (demand deposits). The entire $100 in currency that you were given, and that started the whole process, is in the bank as reserves, which means that $900 ($1,000 − $100) of money has been created by the process.

The simple money multiplier is the measure of the amount of money ultimately created per dollar deposited by the banking system. When people hold no currency, it equals $1/r$.

Calculating the Money Multiplier   We will call the ratio $1/r$ the **simple money multiplier**—*the measure of the amount of money ultimately created per dollar deposited in the banking system, when people hold no currency.* It tells us how much money will ultimately be created by the banking system from an initial inflow of money. In our example, $1/.10 = 10$. Had the bank kept out 20 percent each time, the money multiplier would have been $1/.20 = 5$. If the reserve ratio were 5 percent, the money multiplier would

TABLE 11-1 **The Money-Creating Process**

In the money-creating process, the currency keeps coming back to the banking system like a boomerang. With a 20 percent reserve requirement, ultimately $(1/.2) \times \$10,000 = \$50,000$ will be created. In this example, you can see that after 5 rounds, much of the creation of deposits will have taken place. As you carry out the analysis further, the money creation will approach the $50,000 shown in the last line.

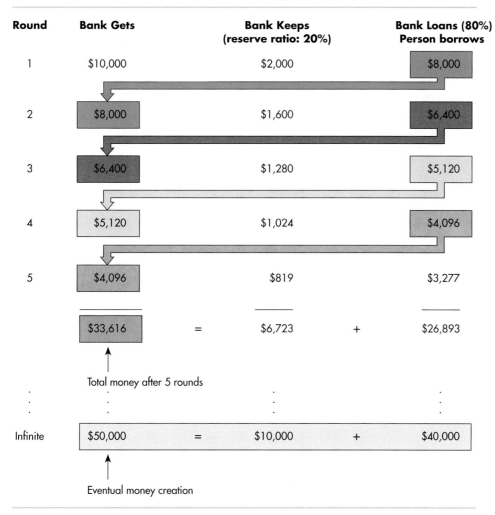

Round	Bank Gets		Bank Keeps (reserve ratio: 20%)		Bank Loans (80%) Person borrows
1	$10,000		$2,000		$8,000
2	$8,000		$1,600		$6,400
3	$6,400		$1,280		$5,120
4	$5,120		$1,024		$4,096
5	$4,096		$819		$3,277
	$33,616	=	$6,723	+	$26,893

Total money after 5 rounds

Infinite	$50,000	=	$10,000	+	$40,000

Eventual money creation

have been $1/.05 = 20$. The higher the reserve ratio, the smaller the money multiplier, and the less money will be created.

An Example of the Creation of Money[4]   To make sure you understand the process, let's consider an example. Say that the reserve ratio is 20 percent and that John Finder finds $10,000 in currency, which he deposits in the bank. Thus, he has $10,000 in his checking account and the bank has $8,000 ($10,000 − $2,000 in reserves) to lend out. Once it lends that money to Fred Baker, there is $8,000 of additional money in the economy. Fred Baker uses the money to buy a new oven from Mary Builder, who, in turn, deposits the money back into the banking system. Big Bank lends out $6,400 ($8,000 − $1,600 in reserves).

Now the process occurs again. Table 11-1 shows the effects of the process for 5 rounds, starting with the initial $10,000. Each time it lends the money out, the money

The higher the reserve ratio, the smaller the money multiplier.

___

[4]The first three rounds of this example are shown in Appendix B to this chapter, using T-accounts.

returns like a boomerang and serves as reserves for more loans. After 5 rounds we reach a point where total demand deposits are $33,616, and the bank has $6,723 in reserves. This is approaching the $50,000 we'd arrive at using the money multiplier:

$$\frac{1}{r}\,(\$10{,}000) = \frac{1}{.2}\,(\$10{,}000) = 5(\$10{,}000) = \$50{,}000$$

If we carried it out for more rounds, we'd actually reach what the formula predicted.

Note that the process ends only when the bank holds all the currency in the economy, and the only money held by the public is in the form of demand deposits. Notice also that the total amount of money created depends on the amount banks hold in reserve. Specifically, an economy can support a supply of money equal to reserves times the money multiplier.

To see that you understand the process, say that banks suddenly get concerned about the safety of their loans, and they decide to keep **excess reserves**—*reserves held by banks in excess of what banks are required to hold.* What will happen to the money multiplier? If you answered that it will decrease, you've got it. Excess reserves decrease the money multiplier as much as required reserves do. I mention this example because this is precisely what happened to the banking system in the early 1990s. Banks became concerned about the safety of their loans; they held large excess reserves, and the money multiplier decreased.

In summary, the process of money creation isn't difficult to understand as long as you remember that money is simply a bank's financial liability held by the public. Whenever banks create financial liabilities for themselves, they create financial assets for individuals, and those financial assets are money.

Calculating the Money Multiplier   In the example, I assumed that only banks hold currency. The simple money multiplier reflects that assumption. In reality, banks are not the only holders of currency. Firms and individuals hold currency too, so in each round we must also make an adjustment in the multiplier for what people and firms hold. When firms and individuals hold currency, the **money multiplier** in the economy is:

$$\frac{(1 + c)}{(r + c)}$$

where r is *the percentage of deposits banks hold in reserve* and c is *the ratio of money people hold in currency to the money they hold as deposits.*[5] Let's consider an example. Say the banks keep 10 percent in reserve and the ratio of individuals' currency holdings to their deposits is 25 percent. This means the money multiplier will be:

$$\frac{1 + 0.25}{(0.1 + 0.25)} = \frac{1.25}{0.35} = 3.43$$

The more cash people hold, the smaller the money multiplier.

Faith as the Backing of Our Money Supply

The creation of money and the money multiplier are easy to understand if you remember that money held in the form of a checking account (the financial asset created) is offset by an equal amount of financial liabilities of the bank. The bank owes its depositors the amount in their checking accounts. Its financial liabilities to depositors, in

----

[5]Notice that this becomes the simple money multiplier when $c = 0$; that is, when people do not hold currency.

Margin notes

When people hold currency, the money multiplier is $(1 + c)/(r + c)$.

Q-8   If banks hold 20 percent of their deposits as reserves, and the ratio of money people hold as currency to deposits is 20 percent, what is the money multiplier?

Q-9   If people suddenly decide to hold more currency, what happens to the size of the money multiplier?

Web Note 11.3
Paper Money

The Real-World Money Multiplier and Recent Banking Reforms

Life keeps getting tougher. In the old days, economics students only had to learn the simple money multiplier. Recent reforms in the U.S. banking system have made that impossible. The Depository Institutions Deregulation Act of 1980 extended the reserve requirement to a wide variety of financial institutions besides banks, but it also lowered the reserve requirement for most deposits. In the early 2000s, the average reserve requirement for all types of bank deposits was under 2 percent and banks held very few excess reserves. (The U.S. reserve requirement on checking accounts is between 3 and 10 percent. Great Britain has no reserve requirements.)

If you insert that low average ratio into the simple money multiplier, you get a multiplier of 50! The real-world

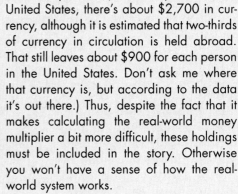

money multiplier is much lower than that because of people's holding of currency; the ratio of money people hold as currency is over 50 percent. (For each person in the United States, there's about $2,700 in currency, although it is estimated that two-thirds of currency in circulation is held abroad. That still leaves about $900 for each person in the United States. Don't ask me where that currency is, but according to the data it's out there.) Thus, despite the fact that it makes calculating the real-world money multiplier a bit more difficult, these holdings must be included in the story. Otherwise you won't have a sense of how the real-world system works.

turn, are secured by the loans (the bank's financial assets) and by the financial liabilities of people to whom the loans were made. Promises to pay underlie any modern financial system.

The initial money in the story about the goldsmiths was gold, but it quickly became apparent that it was far more reasonable to use gold certificates as money. Therefore, gold certificates backed by gold soon replaced gold itself as the money supply. Then, as goldsmiths made more loans than they had gold, the gold certificates were no longer backed by gold. They were backed by promises to get gold if the person wanted gold in exchange for the gold certificate. Eventually the percentage of gold supposedly backing the money became so small that it was clear to everyone that the promises, not the gold, underlay the money supply.

The same holds true with banks. Initially, currency (Federal Reserve IOUs) was backed by gold, and banks' demand deposits were in turn backed by Federal Reserve IOUs. But by the 1930s the percentage of gold backing money grew so small that even the illusion of the money being backed by anything but promises was removed. All that backs the modern money supply are bank customers' promises to repay loans and the guarantee of the government to see that the banks' liabilities to individuals will be met.

All that backs the modern money supply are bank customers' promises to repay loans and government guarantees of banks' liabilities to individuals.

The Demand for Money and the Role of the Interest Rate

Now that we've discussed the nature of money, let's consider how money fits in with the financial flows discussed at the beginning of the chapter, and the potential problems that may develop in the macro economy as people shift their holdings between financial assets and money. To do that, we must first ask: Why do people hold money? This is a relevant question because, by assumption, money doesn't pay any interest, whereas other financial assets do pay interest, so to hold money people are forgoing interest payments.[6]

Why People Hold Money

The only reason people would be willing to hold money is if they get some benefit from doing so, so we need to examine that benefit. The first benefit is easy: money allows you to buy things. You can *spend* money; you can't spend bonds. You can change a financial asset into spendable money, but that takes time and effort. *The need to hold money for spending* is called the **transactions motive.** Second, you hold money for emergencies. For example, if your car breaks down, you'll need cash to get it towed. Knowing that there will always be unforeseen needs, you might carry $20 cash in addition to what you would otherwise carry. *Holding money for unexpected expenses and impulse buying* is called the **precautionary motive** for holding money. The third reason for holding money is called the speculative motive. The **speculative motive** is *holding cash to avoid holding financial assets whose prices are falling.* It comes about because the price of financial assets such as bonds varies in value as the interest rate fluctuates. For example, if you expect the price of a bond (or any financial asset) to fall, that bond is not something you would want to be holding, because you will be losing money by holding it; you'd rather be holding money. Your money holdings might not be earning any interest, but at least their value isn't falling like the price of the asset. In a sense, you are speculating on what the future value of the bond will be. That's why it's called the speculative motive for holding money. You hold money rather than longer-term financial assets so you don't lose if asset prices fall. (Of course, if asset prices are expected to rise, then you want to reduce your holdings of money and increase your asset holdings.)

This 18th-century etching by Robert Goez, The Speculator, captures a popular view of financial activities. It shows a man reduced to rags by bad speculation.

Let's consider an example of bond price fluctuations. (Remember, bonds are often used as the reference asset for all financial assets when people provide loanable funds.) Say you have a one-year $1,000 bond that pays an interest rate of 4 percent a year, and that 4 percent is the interest rate in the economy. The bond sells for $1,000 and will provide $40 interest for the year. You're happy earning that 4 percent (that's the best you can do) so you buy the bond for $1,000. Now say that the day after you buy the bond, the interest rate in the economy rises to 6 percent. Because the price of the bond is inversely related to the interest rate in the economy, the price of that 4 percent $1,000 bond that you bought for $1,000 will fall, in this case to $981.13. (See the box "Interest Rates and the Price of Bonds" for a further explanation.) In one day, your bond has fallen in value by $18.87, an amount that far exceeds the interest you earned on the bond for that day. In this case, you would have preferred to have held cash instead of the bond because the cash would not have fallen in value. Holding cash in the expectation of falling bond prices is the speculative demand for money.

Most professional bond speculators, who often carry portfolios of millions and even billions of dollars of bonds, make their money on changes in the prices of bonds, not on the interest payments of bonds. The reason is that although the changes in

---

[6]As discussed above, in today's economy, many components of money pay interest, but they pay a lower interest than do other financial assets. The analysis I present here applies to the differential rate of interest paid between money and longer-term financial assets; we assume zero interest on money simply to keep the presentation as simple as possible.

Interest Rates and the Price of Bonds

In the example in the text, you may have thought that if the interest rate in the economy rose from 4 percent to 6 percent, and you had bought the bond paying 4 percent, that you would just sell it and buy the 6 percent bond. Would that you could, but that's not the way the bond market works. You only get your $1,000 back when the bond matures. If you wanted your money before that time, you would have to sell it to someone else, but the price of the 4 percent bond would have fallen as soon as the interest rate in the economy rose. More generally, we have the following relationship:

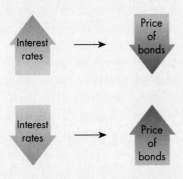

As an example, say that you buy a $1,000, one-year bond with a coupon rate (the fixed rate of interest paid on the bond) of 4 percent when the economy's interest rate

is 4 percent. The price of that bond is determined by the formula:

$$P = \frac{(1000 + 40)}{1 + r}$$

where r is the interest rate in the economy and the numerator is the face value of the bond and the interest it pays. Since the bond's interest rate is the same as the interest rate for other savings instruments, you pay $1,000 for that bond. Now say that the economy's interest rate falls to 2 percent so that all new bonds being offered pay only 2 percent. That makes your bond especially desirable since it pays a higher interest rate. The price of the bond rises:

$$P = \frac{1040}{1.02} = 1,019.61$$

People would be willing to pay up to $1,019.61. Alternatively, if the economy's interest rate rises to 6 percent, as it did in the example in the text, your bond will be less desirable and people would be willing to pay only $981.13. In summary, when the interest rate falls, the price of existing bonds rises, and when the interest rate rises, the price of existing bonds falls.

The longer the length of the bond to maturity, the more the price varies with the change in the interest rate. (For a further discussion of this inverse relationship, see the present value discussion in Appendix A to this chapter.)

annualized interest rates on any particular day are generally small—so small that they are measured in basis points, each of which is one one-hundredth of a percentage point—even those small changes in interest rates swamp the income made on the interest rate payments for the day.

In the real world, interest rates fluctuate all the time, and bond investors are continually looking for clues about whether the interest rates are going to rise or fall. When they expect bond prices to rise, they get rid of their cash and buy bonds; when they expect bond prices to fall, they get out of bonds and into cash.

Taking all three of these motives—transactions, precautionary, and speculative—into account, you can see that it makes sense to hold some money even though it is costing you something in forgone interest to do so—and the lower the interest rate, the greater the quantity of money demanded.

Equilibrium in the Money Market

We can capture this demand for money relationship in the graph in Figure 11-4, which has the interest rate on the vertical axis and the quantity of money you want to hold on the horizontal axis.

Interest Rates and the
Price of Bonds

FIGURE 11-4 **The Money Market**

The demand and supply for money determine the short-term interest rate, as shown in the graph. The demand for money is downward-sloping because, as the interest rate falls, the cost of holding money falls, so it makes more sense to hold more money. The supply of money is fixed; that is, the supply of money is independent of the interest rate.

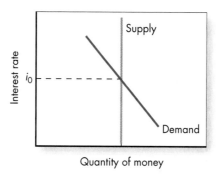

Notice that the demand for money is downward-sloping. That's because, as the interest rate falls, the cost of holding money falls (that is, the interest you don't earn by holding money falls), so it makes sense to hold more money. When interest rates rise, bonds and other financial assets that pay that high interest rate become more attractive, so you hold more financial assets and less money.

To complete our analysis of the financial sector, we need to add a supply of money to Figure 11-4. For simplicity, at this point, we assume the supply of money is set at some fixed level regardless of the interest rate. That is, we assume that the supply curve of money is vertical. (We will discuss the supply of money in much more detail in the next chapter.) The equilibrium interest rate will be where the demand for, and supply of, money intersect—in this case, at i_0. As we discussed in the beginning of the chapter, the interest rate determined in this market (the money market) is the short-term interest rate.

The Many Interest Rates in the Economy

As I stated at the beginning, the economy doesn't have just a single interest rate; it has many, just as there are many types of financial assets. (With recent developments in financial markets, the variety of financial assets grows every year.) Each of these financial assets will have an implicit interest rate associated with it (the implicit interest rate of an asset that pays no interest is the expected percentage change in the price of that asset, so if the asset price is expected to rise by 10 percent, its implicit interest rate is 10 percent). In such a multiple-asset market, which is what we have in the real world, the potential for the interest rate in the loanable funds market (which can be thought of as a composite market for all these varied financial assets) to differ from the interest rate in the market for a particular asset is large. The result can be what is sometimes called a financial asset market bubble.

Let's take an example: the housing market in the early 2000s. During that period, housing prices were rising 10–15 percent per year (more than 50 percent in some areas) and were expected to continue to rise. That meant that the implicit rate of interest paid by houses was 10–15 percent (minus the costs of buying and selling the house). The interest rate that one could borrow at—the mortgage rate—was about 5.5 percent, which meant that it made sense to borrow as much as one possibly could and buy as many houses as one could. And that's what many people did. As they did, housing prices rose, and the expectations were confirmed, which led to more and more people buying houses for speculative purposes. The strong housing market, because it led to additional construction and expenditures related to house buying, pulled the real economy along and helped the real economy expand. As long as one expected the housing prices to rise

The Housing Bust of 2007

Throughout history, market economies have experienced financial panics, which result when what are called financial bubbles burst. There is debate in economics about what a financial bubble is, and whether a seeming financial bubble actually is one, but the general agreement is that if a rise in asset prices is "unsustainable," then it should be considered a bubble. Let's consider as an example of what is meant by "unsustainable" the recent housing price increase, where houses in some areas increased by more than 30 percent a year for four or five years. The beginning of the rise was grounded in supply and demand forces—demand was increasing, and since supply was relatively inelastic, prices rose. The people who were buying could afford to pay the mortgages and were buying to live in the houses. The price rise concerned some people who didn't yet own houses, and they didn't want to get left out. So they bought more expensive houses that they might not easily afford, but that they could continue to make payments on in a pinch. Had credit been limited to standard mortgages, the price rise in housing would have likely stopped there. But the financial industry began to give out *teaser mortgages*—mortgages that have low payments in the first couple of years, but which become much more expensive after that. Many people took out these mortgages in the belief that they would either be able to refinance when the higher-rate mortgage kicked in or sell the house at a profit, and pay back the loan. So housing prices rose more, and the houses sold.

These price increases were potentially sustainable as long as the mortgages were only given to people who could pay them off with other assets, should housing prices not continue to rise. But then, a new type of mortgage—the subprime

mortgage—developed, which granted mortgages to people who did not have the financial assets or earnings to pay off the loan unless housing prices rose. (They were sometimes called "liar loans" because to get them the mortgage broker and the borrower often had to lie about the borrower's income.) That development introduced some unsustainability into the situation. The reason is that if prices stopped rising, these buyers would have to sell their houses to meet their mortgage commitments. That meant that there could be a sudden large increase in the supply of houses to the market, which would depress prices. That's what happened in 2007.

At that point, there was concern that the housing market troubles could spread to other financial markets and to the real economy. How could it spread? If people had to sell other assets to cover their losses in the housing market, the supply of assets in those markets could increase, which would put downward pressure on prices in those markets as well. If all asset prices fell, then people would be forced to reduce their spending on goods, which would shift the aggregate demand curve in to the left and lead to a recession. That recession could feed back on the asset market, further increasing the number of people who couldn't meet their mortgages. The result would be a vicious cycle and a sustained recession.

Most economists felt that the housing bust of 2007 would be contained to the housing market. But they agreed that, since credit and trust underlie all financial markets, the possibility existed for the housing bust to spread to other sectors, and that the large increase in the indebtedness of the U.S. consumer increased the possibility for broader "financial market adjustment" in the next decade.

at a higher rate than the interest rate at which one could borrow, the strategy of buying as many houses as one could made good sense.

In 2006, people lowered their expectations of housing price appreciation; some even expected housing prices to fall. So, many of those who had purchased houses with the intention of selling them at a higher price began to sell their houses more aggressively so that they could return to holding their financial assets in cash before housing prices really fell. The demand for housing decreased substantially, and the equilibrium price of housing available for sale fell. Other asset markets continued to boom, and economists are taking a careful look at whether these markets follow a similar path, and what repercussions, if any, such booms and busts have on the real economy. As of 2007, the U.S. economy seemed to weather the housing market bust reasonably well, but there were concerns about it spreading into a broader financial panic. (See the box "The Housing Bust of 2007.")

Conclusion

We'll stop our consideration of money and the financial sector there. As you can see, money is central to the operation of the macroeconomy. If money functions smoothly, it keeps the outflow from the expenditure stream (saving) and the flow back into the expenditure stream at a level that reflects people's desires. Money can be treated simply as a mirror of people's real desires.

When money doesn't function smoothly, it can influence the flows, sometimes creating too large a flow back into the expenditures stream, causing inflationary pressures, and other times creating too small a flow back in, causing a recession.

Summary

- The financial sector is the market where financial assets are created and exchanged. It channels flows out of the circular flow and back into the circular flow.

- Every financial asset has a corresponding financial liability.

- The economy has many interest rates. The long-term interest rate is determined in the market for loanable funds, while the short-term interest rate is determined in the money market.

- Money is a highly liquid financial asset that serves as a unit of account, a medium of exchange, and a store of wealth.

- There are various measures of money: M_1 and M_2. M_1 consists of currency in the hands of the public, checking account balances, and traveler's checks. M_2 is M_1 plus savings deposits, small-denomination time deposits, and money market mutual fund shares.

- Since money is what people believe money to be, creating money out of thin air is easy. How banks create money out of thin air is easily understood if you remember that money is simply a financial liability of a bank. Banks create money by loaning out deposits.

- The simple money multiplier is $1/r$. It tells you the amount of money ultimately created per dollar deposited in the banking system.

- The money multiplier when people hold cash is $(1 + c)/(r + c)$.

- There are three reasons people hold money, referred to as (1) the transactions motive, (2) the precautionary motive, and (3) the speculative motive. The demand for money is inversely related to the interest rate paid on money.

- Financial asset market bubbles can cause problems for an economy.

Key Terms

asset management (265)
bank (260)
excess reserves (270)
Federal Reserve Bank (the Fed) (260)
financial assets (258)

interest rate (258)
liability management (265)
M_1 (262)
M_2 (263)
money (260)

money multiplier (270)
precautionary motive (272)
reserve ratio (268)
reserves (267)
simple money multiplier (268)

speculative motive (272)
transactions motive (272)

Questions for Thought and Review

1. If financial institutions don't produce any tangible real assets, why are they considered a vital part of the U.S. economy?   LO1

2. What are loanable funds?   LO2

3. In what market are long-term interest rates determined? Short-term interest rates?   LO2

4. Will there be too much or too little investment in the economy if the interest rate is higher than the rate that would equilibrate the supply and demand for loanable funds?   LO2

5. Money is to the economy as oil is to an engine. Explain.   LO3

6. If dollar bills (Federal Reserve notes) are backed by nothing but promises and are in real terms worthless, why do people accept them?   LO3

7. About 30 U.S. localities circulate their own currency with names like "Ithaca Hours" and "Dillo Hours." Doing so is perfectly legal (although by law they are subject to a 10 percent federal tax, which currently the government is not collecting). These currencies are used as payment for rent, wages, goods, and so on. Are these currencies money? Explain.   LO3

8. What function is money serving when people compare the price of chicken to the price of beef?   LO4

9. How does inflation affect money's function as a store of wealth?   LO4

10. What are two components of M_2 that are not components of M_1?   LO5

11. Why was character George Bailey in the film *It's a Wonderful Life* right when he stated on the day of a bank run that depositors could not withdraw all their money from the bank?   LO6

12. Write the equations for the simple money multiplier and the money multiplier. Which multiplier is most likely to be larger?   LO7

13. If the U.S. government were to raise the reserve requirement to 100 percent, what would likely happen to the interest rate banks pay on deposits? Why?   LO7

14. If people expect interest rates to rise in the future, how will they change the quantity of money they demand? Explain your answer.   LO8

15. Do interest rates and prices of bonds vary inversely or directly with one another? Explain your answer.   LO8

16. Why is the demand for money downward-sloping?   LO8

17. If the interest rate equilibrates the loanable funds market, but is too high to equilibrate the money market, what will happen to the price of financial assets?   LO8

Problems and Exercises

18. Explain the effect of the following events on the interest rate in the loanable funds market. Demonstrate your answer graphically.
    a. Tax revenue is lower than expected and people expect cities to default on municipal bonds. They sell their bonds and hold cash instead.
    b. A significant number of people begin to use online banking services, allowing them to lower the average balance on their checking account.
    c. Economists begin to expect economic growth to pick up. In response, firms increase the amount they spend on capital goods.   LO2

19. For each of the following, state whether it is considered money in the United States. Explain why or why not.
    a. A check you write against deposits you have at Bank USA.
    b. Brazilian reals.
    c. The available credit you have on your MasterCard.
    d. Reserves held by banks at the Federal Reserve Bank.
    e. Federal Reserve notes in your wallet.
    f. Gold bullion.
    g. Grocery store coupons.   LO3

20. Economist Michael Bryan reports that on the island of Palau, the Yapese used stone disks as their currency. The number of stones in front of a person's house denoted how rich he or she was.
    a. Would you expect these stones to be used for small transactions?
    b. An Irish-American trader, David O'Keefe, was shipwrecked on the island, and thereafter returned to the island with a boatload of stones. If they were identical to the existing stones, what would that do to the value of the stones?
    c. If O'Keefe's stones could be distinguished from the existing stones, how would that change your answer to *b*?
    d. An anthropologist described the stones as "a memory of contributions"—the more stones a person has, the more that person has contributed to the community. Could the same description be used to describe our money?   LO3

21. State whether the following is an example of the transactions, precautionary, or speculative motive for holding money:
    a. I like to have the flexibility of buying a few things for myself, such as a latte or a snack, every day, so I generally carry $10 in my pocket.
    b. You never know when your car will break down, so I always keep $50 in my pocket.
    c. When the stock market is falling, money managers generally hold more in cash than when the stock market is rising.
    d. Any household has bills that are due every month.   LO4

22. Categorize the following as components of M_1, M_2, both, or neither.
    a. State and local government bonds.
    b. Checking accounts.
    c. Money market mutual funds.
    d. Currency.
    e. Stocks.
    f. Corporate bonds.
    g. Traveler's checks.   LO5

23. State the immediate effect of each of the following actions on M_1 and M_2:
    a. Barry writes his plumber a check for $200. The plumber takes the check to the bank, keeps $50 in cash, and deposits the remainder in his savings account.
    b. Maureen deposits the $1,000 from her CD in a money market mutual fund.
    c. Sylvia withdraws $50 in cash from her savings account.
    d. Paulo cashes a $100 traveler's check that was issued in his Ohio bank at a New York bank.   LO5

24. While Jon is walking to school one morning, a helicopter flying overhead drops a $100 bill. Not knowing how to return it, Jon keeps the money and deposits it in his bank. (No one in this economy holds currency.) If the bank keeps 5 percent of its money in reserves:
    a. How much money can the bank now lend out?
    b. After this initial transaction, by how much is the money in the economy changed?

    c. What's the money multiplier?
    d. How much money will eventually be created by the banking system from Jon's $100?   LO6, LO7

25. U.S. paper currency is made with several features that are difficult to counterfeit including a security thread, color-shifting ink, microprinting, a portrait, a watermark, and a fine-line printing pattern. As duplication technology, however, continually improves and more and more counterfeits are circulated, what will happen to the following?
    a. The value of money circulated.
    b. The volume of cashless transactions.
    c. The amount of money the U.S. Treasury spends to introduce additional security measures.   LO6

26. Calculate the money multipliers below:
    a. Assuming individuals hold no currency, calculate the simple money multiplier for each of the following: 5%, 10%, 20%, 25%, 50%, 75%, 100%.
    b. Assuming the currency to deposit ratio is 20 percent, recalculate the money multipliers in *a*.   LO7

27. Explain the effect of the following events on the interest rate in the money market. Demonstrate your answer graphically.
    a. The supply of money increases.
    b. A significant number of people begin to use credit cards for daily transactions, reducing the amount of money they hold.
    c. Bond traders expect bond prices to rise, and therefore reduce their cash holdings.   LO8

Questions from Alternative Perspectives

1. The U.S. government has a monopoly on U.S. dollars.
   a. Could money be supplied privately?
   b. Has money ever been supplied privately? If so, how do you suppose people knew its value? (Austrian)

2. The Federal Reserve's Board of Governors is arguably the most powerful policy-making body in the United States.
   a. Since its inception, how many women have served on the Board of Governors?
   b. What do all of the current members of the Board of Governors have in common? www.federalreserve.gov/bios/boardmembership.htm (Feminist)

3. In Institutional economists' view, money not only serves as a medium of exchange, a unit of account, and a store of wealth, it also operates as an idea that shapes human understanding and interaction. Construct a list of examples during a day's interactions where money operates as an idea whereby people interact or attempt to understand a situation. For example, a friend might say, "Sherry is dating Herbert; she can do better than that!" (Institutionalist)

4. The chapter talks about the role that depositors and banks play in the "creation" of money.
   a. Do you think this role is consistent with the view that the money supply is only determined exogenously by the central bank?
   b. How could depositors and banks endogenously determine the money supply? (Post-Keynesian)

5. While *sharia* (interest) is banned in Islam, profit-sharing is not. An Islamically sound banking practice could be a system in which depositors deposited money under a principle of profit-sharing and the bank provided funds on the same principle with a mark-up as payment for their financial services.
   a. How does this system differ from a system based on interest?
   b. How might the system of interest be exploitative and a system based on profit-sharing not be exploitative? (Religious)

Web Questions

1. Evocash is advertised as the Web's currency. But is it money? Go to www.evocash.com and check it out.
   a. What is evocash? How do you acquire it and how do you spend it?
   b. Does evocash fulfill the three functions of money? Explain your answer.
   c. Are evos money?

2. The Federal Reserve publishes a number of pamphlets describing its activities and the financial market. Go to the New York Fed's home page to read Fed Point #1 at www.newyorkfed.org/aboutthefed/fedpoint/fed01.html, and answer the following questions:

   a. How much currency is in circulation today? How much is that per person?
   b. What days during the week is there more cash in circulation?
   c. What's the life expectancy of a $1 bill?
   d. What collateral does the Fed put up when accepting currency from the Treasury?
   e. Which agency pays for the printing of Federal Reserve notes?

Answers to Margin Questions

1. I would respond by saying that the financial sector is central to the macroeconomy. It facilitates the trades that occur in the real sector. (258)

2. Savings that escape the circular flow can cause fluctuations in the economy. Interest rates help translate the flow of saving into investment, which make their way back into the spending stream. (259)

3. The three functions of money are (1) medium of exchange, (2) unit of account, and (3) store of wealth. (260)

4. Money provides liquidity and ease of payment. People hold money rather than bonds to get this liquidity and hold down transaction costs. (262)

5. M_2 would be the larger number, since it includes all of the components of M_1 plus additional components. (263)

6. Credit cards are not money. Credit cards are a method by which people borrow. (264)

7. Banks operate on the fact that they will have some money flowing in and some money flowing out at all

times. When the number of withdrawals and deposits is large, on average, they will offset one another, allowing banks to make loans on the "float," the average amount that they are holding. If there is one big depositor at a bank, this is less likely to happen, and the bank must hold larger reserves in case that big depositor withdraws that money. (267)

8. The money multiplier is $(1 + c)/(r + c)$, which is equal to $1.2/0.4 = 3$. (270)

9. The real-world money multiplier would decrease since individuals holding cash make the denominator of the money multiplier larger. (270)

10. People hold money to spend (transactions motive), for unexpected expenses and impulse buying (precautionary motive), and to avoid holding financial assets whose prices are falling (speculative motive). (272)

APPENDIX A

A Closer Look at Financial Assets and Liabilities

Financial Assets and Financial Liabilities

To understand the financial sector and its relation to the real sector, you must understand how financial assets and liabilities work and how they affect the real economy.

An *asset* is something that provides its owner with expected future benefits. There are two types of assets: real assets and financial assets. Real assets are assets whose

services provide direct benefits to their owners, either now or in the future. A house is a real asset—you can live in it. A machine is a real asset—you can produce goods with it.

Financial assets are *assets, such as stocks or bonds, whose benefit to the owner depends on the issuer of the asset meeting certain obligations.* **Financial liabilities** are *liabilities incurred by the issuer of a financial asset to stand behind the issued asset.*

It's important to remember that *every financial asset has a corresponding financial liability*; it's that financial liability that gives the financial asset its value. In the case of bonds, for example, a company's agreement to pay interest and repay the principal gives bonds their value. If the company goes bankrupt and reneges on its liability to pay interest and repay the principal, the asset becomes worthless. The corresponding liability gives the financial asset its value.

For example, a **stock** is *a financial asset that conveys ownership rights in a corporation*. It is a liability of the firm; it gives the holder ownership rights that are spelled out in the financial asset. An equity liability such as a stock usually conveys a general right to dividends, but only if the company's board of directors decides to pay them.

A debt liability conveys no ownership right. It's a type of loan. An example of a debt liability is a bond that a firm issues. A **bond** is *a promise to pay a certain amount of money plus interest in the future*. A bond is a liability of the firm but an asset of the individual who holds the bond. A debt liability such as a bond usually conveys legal rights to interest payments and repayment of principal.

Real assets are created by real economic activity. For example, a house or a machine must be built. Financial assets are created whenever somebody takes on a financial liability or establishes an ownership claim. For example, say I promise to pay you $1 billion in the future. You now have a financial asset and I have a financial liability. Understanding that financial assets can be created by a simple agreement of two people is fundamentally important to understanding how the financial sector works.

Valuing Stocks and Bonds

A financial asset's worth comes from the stream of income it will pay in the future. With financial assets such as bonds, that stream of income can be calculated rather precisely. With stocks, where the stream of income is a percentage of the firm's profits, which fluctuate significantly, the stream of future income is uncertain and valuations depend significantly on expectations.

Let's start by considering some generally held beliefs among economists and financial experts. The first is that an average share of stock in a company in a mature industry sells for somewhere between 15 and 20 times its normal profits. The second is that bond prices rise as market interest rates fall, and fall as market interest rates rise. The first step in understanding where the beliefs come from is to recognize that $1 today is not equal to $1 next year. Why? Because if I have $1 today, I can invest it and earn interest (say 10 percent per year), and next year I will have $1.10, not $1. So if the annual interest rate is 10 percent, $1.10 next year is worth $1 today; alternatively, $1 next year is

worth roughly 91 cents today. A dollar two years in the future is worth even less today, and dollars 30 years in the future are worth very little today.

Present value is *a method of translating a flow of future income or savings into its current worth*. For example, say a smooth-talking, high-pressure salesperson is wining and dining you. "Isn't that amazing?" the salesman says. "My company will pay $10 a year not only to you, but also to your great-great-great-grandchildren, and more, for 500 years—thousands of dollars in all. And I will sell this annuity—this promise to pay money at periodic intervals in the future—to you for a payment to me now of only $800, but you must act fast. After tonight the price will rise to $2,000."

Do you buy it? My rhetoric suggests that the answer should be no—but can you explain why? And what price *would* you be willing to pay?

To decide how much an annuity is worth, you need some way of valuing that $10 per year. *You can't simply add up the $10 five hundred times*. Doing so is wrong. Instead you must *discount* all future dollars by the interest rate in the economy. Discounting is required because a dollar in the future is not worth a dollar now.

If you have $1 now, you can take that dollar, put it in the bank, and in a year you will have that dollar plus interest. If the interest rate you can get from the bank is 5 percent, that dollar will grow to $1.05 a year from now. That means also that if the interest rate in the economy is 5 percent, if you have 95 cents now, in a year it will be worth $0.9975 (5% × $0.95 = $0.0475). Reversing the reasoning, $1 one year in the future is worth 95 cents today. So the present value of $1 one year in the future at a 5 percent interest rate is 95 cents.

A dollar *two* years from now is worth even less today. Carry out that same reasoning and you'll find that if the interest rate is 5 percent, $1 two years from now is worth approximately 90 cents today. Why? Because you could take 90 cents now, put it in the bank at 5 percent interest, and in two years have $1.

The Present Value Formula

Carrying out such reasoning for every case would be a real pain. But luckily, there's a formula and a table that can be used to determine the present value (PV) of future income. The formula is

$$PV = A_1/(1 + i) + A_2/(1 + i)^2 + \cdots + A_n/(1 + i)^n$$

where

A_n = the amount of money received n periods in the future

i = the interest rate in the economy (assumed constant)

TABLE A11-1 (A AND B)   Sample Present Value and Annuity Tables

Year	Interest Rate 3%	4%	6%	9%	12%	15%	18%
1	$0.97	$0.96	$0.94	$0.92	$0.89	$0.87	$0.85
2	0.94	0.92	0.89	0.84	0.80	0.76	0.72
3	0.92	0.89	0.84	0.77	0.71	0.66	0.61
4	0.89	0.85	0.79	0.71	0.64	0.57	0.52
5	0.86	0.82	0.75	0.65	0.57	0.50	0.44
6	0.84	0.79	0.70	0.60	0.51	0.43	0.37
7	0.81	0.76	0.67	0.55	0.45	0.38	0.31
8	0.79	0.73	0.63	0.50	0.40	0.33	0.27
9	0.77	0.70	0.59	0.46	0.36	0.28	0.23
10	0.74	0.68	0.56	0.42	0.32	0.25	0.19
15	0.64	0.56	0.42	0.27	0.18	0.12	0.08
20	0.55	0.46	0.31	0.18	0.10	0.06	0.04
30	0.41	0.31	0.17	0.08	0.03	0.02	0.01
40	0.31	0.21	0.10	0.03	0.01	0.00	0.00
50	0.23	0.14	0.05	0.01	0.00	0.00	0.00

Number of Years	Interest Rate 3%	4%	6%	9%	12%	15%	18%
1	$ 0.97	$ 0.96	$ 0.94	$ 0.92	$0.89	$0.87	$0.85
2	1.91	1.89	1.83	1.76	1.69	1.63	1.57
3	2.83	2.78	2.67	2.53	2.40	2.28	2.17
4	3.72	3.63	3.47	3.24	3.04	2.85	2.69
5	4.58	4.45	4.21	3.89	3.60	3.35	3.13
6	5.42	5.24	4.92	4.49	4.11	3.78	3.50
7	6.23	6.00	5.58	5.03	4.56	4.16	3.81
8	7.02	6.73	6.21	5.53	4.97	4.49	4.08
9	7.79	7.44	6.80	6.00	5.33	4.77	4.30
10	8.53	8.11	7.36	6.42	5.65	5.02	4.49
15	11.94	11.12	9.71	8.06	6.81	5.85	5.09
20	14.88	13.59	11.47	9.13	7.47	6.26	5.35
30	19.60	17.29	13.76	10.27	8.06	6.57	5.52
40	23.11	19.79	15.05	10.76	8.24	6.64	5.55
50	25.73	21.48	15.76	10.96	8.30	6.66	5.55

(a) Present Value Table (value now of $1 to be received *x* years in the future)

The present value table converts a future amount into a present amount.

(b) Annuity Table (value now of $1 per year to be received for *x* years)

The annuity table converts a known stream of income into a present amount.

Solving this formula for any time period longer than one or two years is complicated. To deal with it, people either use a business calculator or a present value table such as the one in Table A11-1.

Table A11-1(a) gives the present value of a single dollar at some time in the future at various interest rates. Notice a couple of things about the chart. First, the further into the future one goes, the lower the present value. Second, the higher the interest rate, the lower the present value. At a 12 percent interest rate, $1 fifty years from now has a present value of essentially zero.

Table A11-1(b) is an annuity table; it tells us how much a constant stream of income for a specific number of years is worth. Notice that as the interest rate rises, the value of an annuity falls. At an 18 percent interest rate, $1 per year for 50 years has a present value of $5.55. To get the value of amounts other than $1, simply multiply the entry in the table by the amount. For example, $10 per year for 50 years at 18 percent interest is 10 × $5.55 or $55.50.

As you can see, the interest rate in the economy is a key to present value. *You must know the interest rate to know the value of money over time.* The higher the current (and assumed constant) interest rate, the more a given amount of money in the present will be worth in the future. Or, alternatively, the higher the current interest rate, the less

a given amount of money in the future will be worth in the present.

Some Rules of Thumb for Determining Present Value

Sometimes you don't have a present value table or a business calculator handy. For those times, there are a few rules of thumb and simplified formulas for which you don't need either a present value table or a calculator. Let's consider two of them: the infinite annuity rule and the Rule of 72.

The Annuity Rule   To find the present value of an annuity that will pay $1 for an infinite number of years in the future when the interest rate is 5 percent, we simply divide $1 by 5 percent (.05). Doing so gives us $20. So at 5 percent, $1 a year paid to you forever has a present value of $20. The **annuity rule** is that *the present value of any annuity is the annual income it yields divided by the interest rate.* Our general annuity rule for any annuity is expressed as

$$PV = X/i$$

That is, the present value of an infinite flow in income, X, is that income divided by the interest rate, *i*.

The Press and Present Value

The failure to understand the concept of present value often shows up in the popular press. Here are three examples.

Headline: **COURT SETTLEMENT IS $40,000,000.**

Inside story: The money will be paid out over a 40-year period.

Actual value: $11,925,000 (8 percent interest rate).

Headline: **DISABLED WIDOW WINS $25 MILLION LOTTERY**

Inside story: The money will be paid over 20 years.

Actual value: $13,254,499 (8 percent interest rate).

Headline: **BOND ISSUE TO COST TAXPAYERS $68 MILLION**

Inside story: The $68 million is the total of interest and principal payments. The interest is paid yearly; the principal won't be paid back to the bond purchasers until 30 years from now.

Actual value: $20,000,000 (8 percent interest rate).

Such stories are common. Be on the lookout for them as you read the newspaper or watch the evening news.

Most of the time, people don't offer to sell you annuities for the infinite future. A typical annuity runs for 30, 40, or 50 years. However, the annuity rule is still useful. As you can see from the present value table, in 30 years at a 9 percent interest rate, the present value of $1 isn't much (it's 8 cents), so we can use this infinite flow formula as an approximation of long-lasting, but less than infinite, flows of future income. We simply subtract a little bit from what we get with our formula. The longer the time period, the less we subtract. For example, say you are wondering what $200 a year for 40 years is worth when the interest rate is 8 percent. Dividing $200 by .08 gives $2,500, so we know the annuity must be worth a bit less than $2,500. (It's actually worth $2,411.)

The annuity rule allows us to answer the question posed at the beginning of this section: How much is $10 a year for 500 years worth right now? The answer is that it depends on the interest rate you could earn on a specified amount of money now. If the interest rate is 10 percent, the maximum you should be willing to pay for that 500-year $10 annuity is $100:

$$\$10/.10 = \$100$$

If the interest rate is 5 percent, the most you should pay is $200 ($10/.05 = $200). So now you know why you should have said no to that supersalesman who offered it to you for $800.

The Rule of 72   A second rule of thumb for determining present values of shorter time periods is the **Rule of 72,** which states:

The number of years it takes for a certain amount to double in value is equal to 72 divided by the rate of interest.

Say, for example, that the interest rate is 4 percent. How long will it take for your $100 to become $200? Dividing 72 by 4 gives 18, so the answer is 18 years. Conversely, the present value of $200 at a 4 percent interest rate 18 years in the future is about $100. (Actually it's $102.67.)

Alternatively, say that you will receive $1,000 in 10 years. Is it worth paying $500 for that amount now if the interest rate is 9 percent? Using the rule of 72, we know that at a 9 percent interest rate it will take about eight years for $500 to double:

$$72/9 = 8$$

so the future value of $500 in 10 years is more than $1,000. It's probably about $1,200. (Actually it's $1,184.) So if the interest rate in the economy is 9 percent, it's not worth paying $500 now in order to get that $1,000 in 10 years. By investing that same $500 today at 9 percent, you can have $1,184 in 10 years.

The Importance of Present Value

Many business decisions require such present value calculations. In almost any business, you'll be looking at flows of income in the future and comparing them to present costs or to other flows of money in the future.

Generally, however, when most people calculate present value, they don't use any of the formulas. They pull out a handy business calculator, press in the numbers to calculate the present value, and watch while the calculator graphically displays the results.

Let's now use our knowledge of present value to explain the two observations at the beginning of this section: (1) an average share of stock sells for between 15 and 20 times its normal profits and (2) bond prices and interest rates are inversely related. Since all financial assets can be broken down into promises to pay certain amounts at certain times in the future, we can determine their value with the present value formula. If the asset is a bond, it consists of a stream of income payments over a number of years and the repayment of the face value of the bond. Each year's interest payment and the eventual repayment of the face value must be calculated separately, and then the results must be added together.

If the financial asset is a share of stock, the valuation is a bit less clear since a stock does not guarantee the payment of anything definite—just a share of the profits. No profits, no payment. So, with stocks, expectations of profits are of central importance. Let's consider an example: Say a share of stock is earning $1 per share per year and is expected to continue to earn that long into the future. Using the annuity rule and an interest rate of 6.5 percent, the present value of that future stream of expected earnings is about $1/.065$, or a bit more than $15. Assuming profits are expected to grow slightly, that would mean that the stock should sell for somewhere around $20, or 20 times its profit per share, which is the explanation to economists' view that an average stock sells for about 15 times normal profits.

To see the answer to the second—bond prices and interest rates are inversely related—say the interest rate rises to 10 percent. Then the value of the stock or bond that is earning a fixed amount—in this case $1 per share—will go down to $10. Interest rate up, value of stock or bond down. This is the explanation of the second observation.

There is nothing immutable in the above reasoning. For example, if promises to pay aren't trustworthy, you don't put the amount that's promised into your calculation; you put in the amount you actually expect to receive. That's why when a company or a country looks as if it's going to default on loans or stop paying dividends, the value of its bonds and stock will fall considerably. For example, in the early 2000s, many people thought Argentina would default on its bonds. That expectation caused the price of Argentinean bonds to fall and interest rates to rise more than 30 percentage points.

Of course, the expectations could go in the opposite direction. Say that the interest rate is 10 percent, and that you expect a company's annual profit, which is now $1 per share, to grow by 10 percent per year. In that case, since expected profit growth is as high as the interest rate, the current value of the stock is infinite. It is such expectations of future profit growth that fueled the Internet stock craze and caused the valuation of firms with no current profits (indeed, many were experiencing significant losses) at multiples of sales of 300 or more. Financial valuations based on such optimistic expectations are the reason most economists considered the stock market in Internet stocks to be significantly overvalued in the late 1990s and correctly predicted the fall in prices that occurred in 2001 and 2002.

Financial Institutions

A **financial institution** is *a business whose primary activity is buying, selling, or holding financial assets.* For example, some financial institutions (depository institutions and investment intermediaries) sell promises to pay in the future. These promises can be their own promises or someone else's promises. When you open a savings account at a bank, the bank is selling you its own promise that you can withdraw your money, plus interest, at some unspecified time in the future. Such a bank is a **depository institution**—*a financial institution whose primary financial liability is deposits in checking or savings accounts.* When you buy a newly issued government bond or security from a securities firm, it's also selling you a promise to pay in the future. But in this case, it's a third party's promise. So a securities firm is a financial broker that sells third parties' promises to pay. It's a type of marketing firm for financial IOUs.

As financial institutions sell financial assets, they channel saving from savers (individuals who give other people money now in return for promises to pay it back with interest later) to borrowers (investors or consumers who get the money now in return for their promise to pay it and the interest later).

As economists use the term, when economists buy a financial asset they are saving not investing. To invest (in economic terminology) is to buy real, not financial, assets that you hope will yield a return in the future.[1] How do you get funds to invest if you don't already have them? You borrow them. That means you create a financial asset that you sell to someone else who saves.

Some financial institutions serve several purposes and their various functions may have various names. For example, a depository institution such as a commercial bank may also serve as a **contractual intermediary**—*a financial institution that holds and stores individuals' financial assets.* Contractual intermediaries intermediate (serve as a

---

[1] This terminology isn't the terminology most laypeople use. When a person buys a stock, in economic terms that person is saving, though most laypeople call that *investing*.

Do Financial Assets Make Society Richer?

Financial assets are neat. You can call them into existence simply by getting someone to accept your IOU. *Remember, every financial asset has a corresponding financial liability equal to it.* So when you say a country has $1 trillion of financial assets, you're also saying that the country has $1 trillion of financial liabilities. An optimist would say a country is rich. A pessimist would say it's poor. An economist would say that financial assets and financial liabilities are simply opposite sides of the ledger and don't indicate whether a country is rich or poor.

To find out whether a country is rich or poor, you must look at its *real assets.* If financial assets increase the economy's efficiency and thereby increase the amount of real assets, they make society better off. This is most economists' view of financial assets. If, however, they decrease the efficiency of the economy (as some economists have suggested some financial assets do because they focus productive effort on financial gamesmanship), financial assets make society worse off.

The same correspondence between a financial asset and its liability exists when a financial asset's value changes. Say stock prices fall significantly. Is society poorer? The answer is: It depends on the reason for the change. Let's say there is no known reason. Then, while the people who own the stock are poorer, the people who might want to buy stock in the future are richer since the price of assets has fallen. So in a pure accounting sense, society is neither richer nor poorer when the prices of stocks rise or fall for no reason.

But there are ways in which changes in the value of financial assets might signify that society is richer or poorer. For example, the changes in the values of financial assets might *reflect* (rather than cause) real changes. If suddenly a company finds a cure for cancer, its stock prices will rise and society will be richer. But the rise in the price of the stock doesn't cause society to be richer. It reflects the discovery that made society richer. Society would be richer because of the discovery even if the stock's price didn't rise.

There's significant debate about how well the stock market reflects real changes in the economy. Classical economists believe it closely reflects real changes; Keynesian economists believe it doesn't. But both sides agree that the changes in the real economy, not the changes in the price of financial assets, underlie what makes an economy richer or poorer.

go-between) between savers and investors. For example, a pension fund is a financial institution that takes in individuals' savings, relends those savings, and ultimately pays back those savings plus interest after the individuals retire. It uses individuals' savings to buy financial assets from people and firms who want to borrow. Similarly, a commercial bank is a financial institution that relends an individual's checking account deposits. A checking deposit is a financial asset of an individual and a financial liability of the bank.

Leading You Through Two Financial Transactions

To give you an idea of how financial markets work, let's follow two transactions you'll likely make in your lifetime and see how they work their way through the financial system.

Insuring Your Car

You want to drive. The law requires you to have insurance, so you go to two or three insurance companies, get quotes of their rates, and choose the one offering the lowest rate. Say it costs you $800 for the year. You write a check for $800 and hand the check to the insurance agent, who keeps a commission (let's say $80) and then sends her check for $720 to the insurance company. The insurance company has $720 more sitting in the bank than it had before you paid your insurance premium.

The insurance company earns income in two ways: (1) in the difference between the money it receives in payments and the claims it pays out and (2) in the interest it makes on its financial assets. What does the company use to buy these financial assets? It has payments from its customers (your $720, for example) available because payments come in long before claims are paid out.

Because earnings on financial assets are an important source of an insurance company's income, your $720 doesn't stay in the insurance company's bank for long. The insurance company has a financial assets division that chooses financial assets it believes have the highest returns for the risk involved. Bond salespeople telephone the financial assets division offering to sell bonds. Similarly, developers who want to build shopping malls or ski resorts go to the financial assets division, offering an opportunity to participate (really asking to borrow money).

The financial assets division might decide to lend your $720 (along with $10 million more) to a mall developer who builds in suburban locations. The division transfers the $720 to the mall developer and receives a four-year, 12 percent promissory note (a promise to pay the $720 back in four years along with $86.40 per year in interest payments). The promissory note is a financial asset of the insurance company and a financial liability of the developer. When the developer spends the money, the $720 leaves the financial sector and reenters the spending stream in the real economy. At that point, it becomes investment in the economic sense.

Buying a House

Most people, when they buy a house, don't go out and pay the thousands of dollars it costs in cash. Instead, they go to a bank or similar financial institution and borrow a large portion of the sales price, taking out a mortgage on the house. A **mortgage** is simply *a special name for a secured loan on real estate*. By mortgaging a house, you are creating a financial liability for yourself and a financial asset for someone else. This financial asset is secured by the house. If you default on the loan, the mortgage holder (who, as you will see, may or may not be the bank) can foreclose on the mortgage and take title to the house.

The funds available in banks come primarily from depositors who keep their savings in the bank in the form of savings accounts or checking accounts. Balances in these accounts are often small, but with lots of depositors they add up and provide banks with money to lend out. If you're planning to buy a house, you'll most likely go to a bank.

The bank's loan officer will have you fill in a lengthy form, and the bank will send an appraiser out to the house to assess its value. The appraiser asks questions about the house: Does it meet the electrical code? What kind of pipes does it have? What kind of windows does it have? All this information about you and the house is transferred onto a master form that the loan officer uses to decide whether to make the loan. (Contrary to what many laypeople believe, in normal times a loan officer wants to make the loan. Remember, a bank's profits are the difference between what it pays in interest and what it receives in interest; it needs to make loans to make profits. So the loan officer often looks at hazy answers on the form and puts an interpretation on them that's favorable to granting the loan.)

In a month or so, depending on how busy the bank is, you hear back that the loan is approved for, say, $180,000 at 6 percent interest and two points. A point is 1 percent of the loan; it is a charge the bank makes for the loan. So two points means the bank is charging you $3,600 for making you a loan of $180,000 at 6 percent interest. (And you wondered why the bank was anxious to make you a loan!) The bank credits your account with $176,400, which allows you to write a check to the seller of the house at a meeting called the *closing*.

The bank gets a lot of money in deposits, but generally it doesn't have anywhere near enough deposits to cover all the mortgages it would like to make. So the process doesn't stop there. Instead, the bank generally sells your mortgage on the secondary market to the Federal National Mortgage Association (FNMA or, popularly, Fannie Mae) or the Government National Mortgage Association (GNMA, or Ginnie Mae), which pay, say, $180,400 for the $180,000 mortgage. They're buying your mortgage (which you paid $3,600 in points to be allowed to get) for $400 more than its amount. The bank makes money both ways: when it makes the loan and when it sells the loan.

Fannie Mae and Ginnie Mae are companies organized by the government to encourage home ownership. They do this by easing the flow of savings into mortgages. They take your mortgage and a number of similar ones from different areas and make them into a bond package: a $100 million bond fund secured by a group of mortgages. (Remember the long forms and the questions the appraiser asked? Those forms and answers allow Fannie Mae and Ginnie Mae to classify the mortgage and put it in a group with similar mortgages.) They then sell shares in that bond fund to some other institution that gives Fannie Mae and Ginnie Mae money in return. The Maes use that money to buy more mortgages, thereby channeling more savings into financing home ownership.

Who buys Fannie Mae and Ginnie Mae bonds? Let's go back and consider our insurance company. If the insurance company hadn't made the loan to the developer, the company might have decided that Ginnie Mae bonds were the best investment it could make. So who knows? Your insurance company may hold the mortgage to your house.

You, of course, don't know any of this. You simply keep making your mortgage payment to the bank, which, for a fee, forwards it to Ginnie Mae, which uses it to pay the interest on the bond it sold to the insurance company.

Summary

We could go through other transactions, but these two should give you a sense of how real-world financial transactions work their way through financial institutions. Financial institutions make money by the fees and commissions they charge for buying and selling loans, and on the difference between the interest they pay to get the money and the interest they receive when they lend the money out.

Key Terms

annuity rule *(281)*

bond *(280)*

contractual
  intermediary *(283)*

depository
  institution *(283)*

financial assets *(279)*

financial institution *(283)*

financial liabilities *(279)*

mortgage *(285)*

present value *(280)*

Rule of 72 *(282)*

stock *(280)*

Questions for Thought and Review

1. If the government prints new $1,000 bills and gives them to all introductory students who are using the Colander text, who incurs a financial liability and who gains a financial asset?

2. Is the currency in your pocketbook or wallet a real or a financial asset? Why?

3. Joe, your study partner, has just said that, in economic terminology, when he buys a bond he is investing. Is he correct? Why?

4. Joan, your study partner, has just made the following statement: "A loan is a loan and therefore cannot be an asset." Is she correct? Why or why not?

5. How much is $50 to be received 50 years from now worth if the interest rate is 6 percent? (Use Table A11-1.)

6. How much is $50 to be received 50 years from now worth if the interest rate is 9 percent? (Use Table A11-1.)

7. Your employer offers you a choice of two bonus packages: $1,400 today or $2,000 five years from now. Assuming a 6 percent rate of interest, which is the better value? Assuming an interest rate of 10 percent, which is the better value?

8. Suppose the price of a one-year 10 percent coupon bond with a $100 face value is $98.
   a. Are market interest rates likely to be above or below 10 percent? Explain.
   b. What is the bond's yield or return?
   c. If market interest rates fell, what would happen to the price of the bond?

9. Explain in words why the present value of $100 to be received in 10 years would decline as the interest rate rises.

10. A 6 percent bond will pay you $1,060 one year from now. The interest rate in the economy is 10 percent. How much is that bond worth now?

11. You are to receive $100 a year for the next 40 years. How much is it worth now if the current interest rate in the economy is 6 percent? (Use Table A11-1.)

12. You are to receive $200 in 30 years. About how much is it worth now? (The interest rate is 3 percent.)

13. A salesperson calls you up and offers you $200 a year for life. If the interest rate is 9 percent, how much should you be willing to pay for that annuity?

14. The same salesperson offers you a lump sum of $20,000 in 10 years. How much should you be willing to pay? (The interest rate is still 9 percent.)

15. What is the present value of a cash flow of $100 per year forever (a perpetuity), assuming:

    The interest rate is 10 percent.

    The interest rate is 5 percent.

    The interest rate is 20 percent.

    a. Working with those same three interest rates, what are the future values of $100 today in one year? How about in two years?
    b. Working with those same three interest rates, how long will it take you to double your money?

16. State whether you agree or disagree with the following statements:
    a. If stock market prices go up, the economy is richer.
    b. A real asset worth $1 million is more valuable to an individual than a financial asset worth $1 million.
    c. Financial assets have no value to society since each has a corresponding liability.
    d. The United States has much more land than does Japan. Therefore, the value of all U.S. land should significantly exceed the value of land in Japan.
    e. U.S. GDP exceeds Japan's GDP; therefore, the stock market valuation of U.S.-based companies should exceed that of Japan-based companies.

APPENDIX B

Creation of Money Using T-Accounts

In this appendix I use T-accounts to demonstrate the example of the creation of money given in the text of the chapter.

The basis of financial accounting is the T-account presentation of balance sheets. The balance sheet is made up of assets on one side and liabilities and net worth on the other. By definition the two sides are equal; they balance (just as the T-account must).

To cement the money creation process in your mind, let's discuss how banks create money using transactions that affect the balance sheet. To keep the analysis simple, we limit the example to the case where only banks create money.

Table B11-1 shows the initial balance sheet of an imaginary Textland Bank, which we assume is the only bank in the country. As you can see, Textland has $500,000 in assets: $30,000 in cash, $300,000 in loans, and $170,000 in property. On the liabilities side, it has $150,000 in checking deposits and $350,000 in net worth. The two sides of the balance sheet are equal.

The first thing to notice about this balance sheet is that if all holders of checking accounts (demand deposits) wanted their currency, the bank couldn't give it to them. The currency it holds is only a portion—20 percent—of the total deposits:

$$\frac{\$30,000}{\$150,000} = 0.20$$

Banks rely on statistical averages and assume that not all people will want their money at the same time. Let's assume that Textland Bank has decided 20 percent is an appropriate reserve ratio.

TABLE B11-1 **Textland Bank Balance Sheet**

Beginning Balance

Assets		Liabilities and Net Worth	
Currency	$ 30,000	Checking deposits	$150,000
Loans	300,000	Net worth	350,000
Property	170,000		
Total assets	$500,000	Total liabilities and net worth	$500,000

TABLE B11-1 **(continued)**

Transaction 1

Assets		Liabilities and Net Worth	
Currency (beginning balance)	$30,000	Checking deposits (beginning balance)	$150,000
Currency from John	10,000	John's deposit	10,000
Total currency	$ 40,000	Total demand deposits	$160,000
Loans	300,000	Net worth	350,000
Property	170,000		
Total assets	$510,000	Total liabilities and net worth	$510,000

TABLE B11-1 **(continued)**

Transaction 2

Assets		Liabilities and Net Worth	
Currency (after Trans. 1)	$ 40,000	Checking deposits (after Trans. 1)	$160,000
Currency loaned to Fred	− 8,000	Net worth	350,000
Total currency	$ 32,000		
Loans (beginning balance)	300,000		
Loans to Fred	8,000		
Total loans	308,000		
Property	170,000		
Total assets	$510,000	Total liabilities and net worth	$510,000

TABLE B11-1   (continued)

Transaction 3				
Assets			**Liabilities and Net Worth**	
Currency (after Trans. 2).	$32,000		Checking deposits	$160,000
Currency from Mary	8,000		Mary's deposit	8,000
Total currency.		$ 40,000	Total demand deposits	$168,000
Loans		308,000	Net worth	350,000
Property		170,000		
Total assets.		$518,000	Total liabilities and net worth	$518,000

Now let's say that John Finder finds $10,000 in currency. He deposits that $10,000 into Textland Bank. After he does so, what will happen to the money supply? The first step is seen in Transaction 1, which shows the effect of John Finder's deposit on the bank's account. The bank gains $10,000 in currency, but its liabilities also increase by $10,000, so, as you can see, the two sides of the balance sheet are still equal. At this point no additional money has been created; $10,000 currency has simply been changed to a $10,000 checking deposit.

Now let's assume the bank uses a reserve ratio of 20 percent, meaning it lends out 80 percent of the currency it receives in new deposits. Say it lends out 80% × $10,000 = $8,000 to Fred Baker, keeping 20 percent × $10,000 = $2,000 in reserve. The change in the bank's balance sheet is seen in Transaction 2. This step creates $8,000 in money. Why? Because John Finder still has $10,000 in his checking account, while Fred Baker has $8,000 currency, so, combining John's checking account

balance with Fred's currency, the public has $8,000 in money. As you can see, loans have increased by $8,000 and currency in Textland Bank has decreased by $8,000.

Fred Baker didn't borrow the money to hold onto it. He spends it buying a new oven from Mary Builder, who, in turn, deposits the $8,000 into Textland Bank (the only bank according to our assumptions). Textland's balance sheet now looks like Transaction 3.

Mary Builder has a demand deposit of $8,000 and John Finder has a demand deposit of $10,000. But Textland bank has excess reserves of $6,400, since it must keep only $1,600 of Mary's $8,000 deposit as reserves:

$$80\% \times \$8,000 = \$6,400$$

So the bank is looking to make a loan.

At this point the process continues in the fashion described in the chapter text. A good exercise to see that you understand T-accounts is to use T-accounts to demonstrate the next two rounds of the process.

Questions for Thought and Review

1. Assume that there's only one bank in the country, that the reserve requirement is 10 percent, and that the ratio of individuals' currency holdings to their bank deposits is 20 percent. The bank begins with $20,000 in currency, $225,000 in loans, $105,000 in physical assets, $200,000 in demand deposits, and $150,000 in net worth.
   a. An immigrant comes into the country and deposits $10,000 in the bank. Show this deposit's effect on the bank's balance sheet.
   b. The bank keeps enough of this money to satisfy its reserve requirement, and loans out the rest to Ms. Entrepreneur. Show the effect on the bank's balance sheet.

   c. Ms. Entrepreneur uses the money to pay Mr. Carpenter, who deposits 80 percent of what he gets in the bank. Show the effect on the bank's balance sheet.
   d. Show the bank's balance sheet after the money multiplier is all through multiplying (based on the appendix).

2. Assume there is one bank in the country whose reserve requirement is 20 percent. It has $10,000 in currency; $100,000 in loans; $50,000 in physical assets; $50,000 in demand deposits; and $110,000 in net worth. Mr. Aged withdraws $1,000 from the bank and dies

on the way home without spending a penny. He is buried with the currency still in his pocket.

a. Show this withdrawal's effect on the bank's balance sheet.

b. What happened to the bank's reserve ratio and what must the bank do to meet reserve requirements?

c. What is the money multiplier? (Assume no currency holdings.)

d. What will happen to total money supply because of this event after the money multiplier is through multiplying?

3. Assume reserve requirements are 15 percent. Textland Bank's balance sheet looks like this:

Assets		Liabilities	
Currency	$ 30,000	Deposits	$150,000
Loans	320,000	Net worth	550,000
Property	350,000		
Total	$700,000	Total	$700,000

a. How much is the bank holding in excess reserves?

b. If the bank eliminates excess reserves by making new loans, how much new money would be created (assuming no currency holdings)? Show, using T-accounts.

12 Monetary Policy

There have been three great inventions since the beginning of time: fire, the wheel and central banking.

—*Will Rogers*

When Ben Bernanke speaks, people listen. That's because he's chairman of the U.S. central bank—the Federal Reserve Bank (the Fed)—and it is the Fed that determines monetary policy for the United States. **Monetary policy** is *a policy of influencing the economy through changes in the banking system's reserves that influence the money supply and credit availability in the economy.* Unlike fiscal policy, which is controlled by the government directly, monetary policy is controlled by the central bank in the United States, the Federal Reserve Bank (the Fed).

AFTER READING THIS CHAPTER, YOU SHOULD BE ABLE TO:

1. Explain how monetary policy works in the *AS/AD* model.
2. Summarize the structure and duties of the Fed.
3. Describe how the Fed changes the supply of money primarily through open market operations.
4. Define the Federal funds rate and discuss how the Fed uses it as an intermediate target.
5. State the Taylor rule and explain its relevance to monetary policy.
6. Define the yield curve and explain how its shape reflects the limit of the Fed's ability to control the economy.

How Monetary Policy Works in the Models

Monetary policy works through its influence on credit conditions and the interest rate in the economy. As shown in Figure 12-1(a), expansionary monetary policy shifts the *AD* curve out to the right and contractionary monetary policy shifts it in to the left. Changes in nominal income will be split between changes in real income and changes in the price level.

If the economy is significantly above potential output, once long-run equilibrium is reached, monetary policy affects only nominal income and the price level, as shown in Figure 12-1(b). Real output remains unchanged. Suppose the economy begins at potential output Y_P (point A), and expansionary monetary policy shifts the *AD* curve from AD_0 to AD_1. Because the economy is beyond potential, rising factor cost pressures very quickly shift the *SAS* curve up from SAS_0 to SAS_1. Once the long-run equilibrium has been reached, the price level rises from P_0 to P_1 and real output returns to potential output (point B). So, beyond potential output, expansionary monetary policy does not affect real output.

The general rule is: Expansionary monetary policy increases nominal income. Its effect on real income depends on how the price level responds:

$$\%\Delta\text{Real income} = \%\Delta\text{Nominal income} - \%\Delta\text{Price level}$$

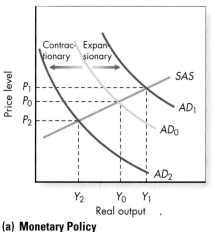

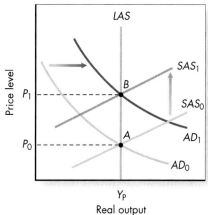

(a) **Monetary Policy**

(b) **Expansionary Monetary Policy beyond Potential Output**

FIGURE 12-1 (A AND B) The Effect of Monetary Policy in the *AS/AD* Model

Expansionary monetary policy shifts the *AD* curve to the right; contractionary monetary policy shifts the *AD* curve to the left. In (**a**) we see how monetary policy affects both real output and the price level. If the economy is at or above potential, as in (**b**), expansionary monetary policy will cause input costs to rise, which will eventually shift the *SAS* curve up enough so that real output remains unchanged. The only long-run effect of expansionary monetary policy when the economy is above potential is to increase the price level.

Thus, if nominal income rises by 5 percent and the price level rises by 2 percent, real income will rise by 3 percent.

In this chapter I explore how monetary policy changes aggregate expenditures, shifting the aggregate demand curve out to the right or in to the left. The effect of monetary policy on aggregate demand is not direct; rather it affects aggregate demand indirectly through the short-term and long-term interest rates. To see the indirect effect, consider Figure 12-2. Figure 12-2(a) shows the supply and demand for money graph that I presented in the last chapter. Recall that the interest rate in the money market is determined by the supply of money and the demand for money. The demand for money comes from people's desire to hold money, which is affected by the short-term interest rate. The Fed undertakes monetary policy by changing the supply of money. When it conducts expansionary monetary policy, it increases the supply of money from M_0 to M_1. In response, the interest rate in the money market falls from i_0 to i_1. That increase in the supply of money leads to a

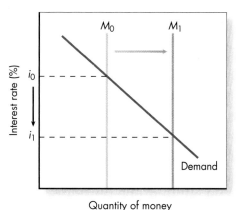

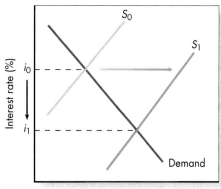

(a) **Money Market**

(b) **Loanable Funds Market**

FIGURE 12-2 (A AND B) Monetary Policy and the Money Market

Monetary policy affects the interest rate in the money market. When conducting expansionary monetary policy, the Fed increases the money supply from M_0 to M_1 as shown in (**a**). The increase in the supply of money leads to a parallel increase in the supply of loanable funds as shown in (**b**). The decline in interest rates increases investment spending, which shifts the aggregate demand curve out to the right.

parallel increase in the supply of loanable funds, shown in Figure 12-2(b), which lowers the interest rate that firms pay to borrow.

That lower interest rate for loanable funds increases the quantity of loanable funds demanded, which increases investment. Since investment is a component of aggregate demand, that increase in investment shifts out the aggregate demand curve, as we saw in Figure 12-1(a).

Summarizing, **expansionary monetary policy** is *a policy that increases the money supply and decreases the interest rate*. It tends to *increase* both investment and output.

Expansionary monetary policy is monetary policy aimed at reducing interest rates and raising the level of aggregate demand.

Contractionary monetary policy works in the opposite direction. **Contractionary monetary policy** is *a policy that decreases the money supply and increases the interest rate*. It tends to *decrease* both investment and output.

Contractionary monetary policy is monetary policy aimed at increasing interest rates and thereby restraining aggregate demand.

How Monetary Policy Works in Practice

Models make it all look so easy. Would that it were so easy. The reality of monetary policy is much messier and more complicated, and in this section, I discuss some of the institutional details that make monetary policy so complicated. I begin with a short summary of structure and workings of the Federal Reserve Bank of the United States—generally called, "the Fed."

Q-1 Demonstrate the effect of expansionary monetary policy in the *AS/AD* model.

Monetary Policy and the Fed

Monetary policy is conducted by a country's **central bank**—*a type of banker's bank whose financial obligations underlie an economy's money supply*. The central bank in the United States is the Fed. If commercial banks (the banks you and I use) need to borrow money, they go to the central bank. If there's a financial panic and a run on banks, the central bank is there to make loans to the banks until the panic goes away. Since its IOUs (I owe you's) are cash, the Fed can create money simply by issuing an IOU. It is this ability to create money that gives the central bank the power to control monetary policy. (A central bank also serves as a financial adviser to government. As is often the case with financial advisers, the government sometimes doesn't like the advice and doesn't follow it.)

In many countries, such as Great Britain, the central bank is a part of the government, just as this country's Department of the Treasury and the Department of Commerce are part of the U.S. government. In the United States, the central bank is not part of the government in the same way. The box "Central Banks in Other Countries" on page 669 gives you an idea of some differences.

It is the central bank's ability to create money that gives it the power to control monetary policy.

Web Note 12.1
Other Central Banks

Structure of the Fed   The Fed is not just one bank; it is composed of 12 regional banks along with the main Federal Reserve Bank whose headquarters are in Washington, D.C. The Fed is governed by a seven-member Board of Governors. Members of the Board of Governors, together with the president of the New York Fed and a rotating group of four presidents of the other regional banks, are voting members of the **Federal Open Market Committee (FOMC),** *the Fed's chief body that decides monetary policy.* All 12 regional bank presidents attend, and can speak at, FOMC meetings. The financial press and business community follow their discussions closely. There are even Fed watchers whose sole occupation is to follow what the Fed is doing and to tell people what it will likely do.

Q-2 What group of the Fed decides monetary policy?

Central Banks in Other Countries

In the United States, the central bank is the Fed, and much of this chapter is about its structure. But the Fed is only one of many central banks in the world. Let's briefly introduce you to some of the others.

The People's Bank of China

The People's Bank of China (PBOC) was established in 1948, shortly after the communist victory and the establishment of the People's Republic of China, by nationalizing all Chinese banks and incorporating them into a single bank. (The former Chinese central bank, named the Central Bank of China, was relocated to Taipei in 1949 and is the central bank for Taiwan.) From 1949 to 1978, the PBOC was the only bank in the People's Republic of China.

In the 1980s the commercial banking functions of the PBOC were split off into state-owned independent banks, and the PBOC began focusing on central bank functions such as monetary policy and regulation of the financial sector. In 1995, it was restructured and consciously modeled after the U.S. Fed. It opened nine regional branches and focused its operations on foreign reserve issues, monetary policy, and financial regulation.

European Central Bank

In the late 1990s a number of European Union countries formed a monetary union, creating a common currency called the euro, and a new central bank called the European Central Bank (ECB), whose structure is still evolving. As of 2007, the governing council had 21 members, including 6 permanent members and up to 15 rotating members.

The primary objective of the ECB is different from the Fed's; the ECB is focused solely on maintaining price stability, as was the former German central bank, the Bundesbank, after which it was modeled. Some economists have considered the ECB an expansion of the Bundesbank for the entire EU.

Most economists hold a wait-and-see attitude about the bank. They point out that the ECB is a new bank and it will take time for its operating procedures to become established. We can expect significant political infighting as the various countries attempt to influence the decisions of the ECB to favor them.

People's Bank of China

The Bank of England

The Bank of England is sometimes called the Old Lady of Threadneedle Street (because it's located on that street, and the British like such quaint characterizations). It does not use a required reserve mechanism. Instead, individual banks determine their own needed reserves, so any reserves they have would, in a sense, be excess reserves. Needless to say, bank reserves are much lower in England than they are in the United States.

How does the Old Lady control the money supply? With the equivalent of open market operations and with what might be called "tea control." Since England has only a few large banks, the Old Lady simply passes on the word at tea as to which direction she thinks the money supply should be going. Alas for sentimentalists, "tea control" is fading in England, as are many of the quaint English ways.

The Bank of Japan

Like the People's Bank of China, the Bank of Japan is quite similar to the Fed. It uses primarily open market operations to control the money supply. Reserve requirements are similar to the Fed's, but because it allows banks a longer period in which to do their averaging, and Japan does not have the many small banks that the United States does—banks that often hold excess reserves—excess reserves are much lower in Japan than in the United States. The Japanese financial system exhibits more interdependence between the central bank, commercial banks, and industry than does the U.S. system, which means that Japanese companies get more of their funding from commercial banks, which in turn borrow more from the Bank of Japan than U.S. commercial banks borrow from the Fed. The financial position of many Japanese commercial banks was questionable over the past decade, and the Bank of Japan worked with the banks to restructure loans without causing a breakdown of the financial system.

Clearly, there's more to be said about each of these central banks, but this brief introduction should give you a sense of both the similarities and the diversities among the central banks of the world.

The president of the United States appoints each governor for a term of 14 years, although most governors choose not to complete their terms. The president also designates one of the governors to be the chairperson of the Fed (in 2008, this was Ben Bernanke) for a four-year term. A chairperson can serve multiple terms, and the Fed chairperson is sometimes referred to as the second most powerful person in Washington (the most powerful being the president of the United States).

The Fed's general structure reflects its political history. Figure 12-3 demonstrates that structure. Notice in Figure 12-3(a) that most of the 12 regional Fed banks are in

---

FIGURE 12-3 (A AND B)   The Federal Reserve System

The Federal Reserve System is composed of 12 regional banks. It is run by the Board of Governors. The Federal Open Market Committee (FOMC) is the most important policy-making body.

Source: The Federal Reserve System (www.federalreserve.gov).

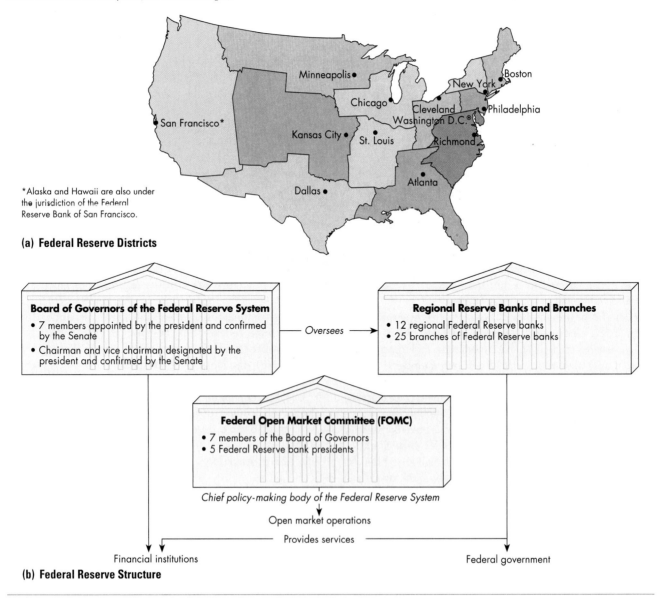

*Alaska and Hawaii are also under the jurisdiction of the Federal Reserve Bank of San Francisco.

(a) Federal Reserve Districts

Board of Governors of the Federal Reserve System
- 7 members appointed by the president and confirmed by the Senate
- Chairman and vice chairman designated by the president and confirmed by the Senate

Oversees

Regional Reserve Banks and Branches
- 12 regional Federal Reserve banks
- 25 branches of Federal Reserve banks

Federal Open Market Committee (FOMC)
- 7 members of the Board of Governors
- 5 Federal Reserve bank presidents

Chief policy-making body of the Federal Reserve System

Open market operations

Provides services

Financial institutions

Federal government

(b) Federal Reserve Structure

How Independent Should the Central Bank Be?

The Fed is relatively independent, but not all central banks are. One of the big debates in the early 2000s concerned how independent the central bank should be. Advocates of central bank independence argued that independence allows central banks to make the hard political decisions that a government influenced by political pressures cannot make. Increasing interest rates hurts—it slows down the economy and causes unemployment. But if the economy is above its sustainable level, it needs to be slowed down, or inflation will accelerate. As former Fed chairman William Martin said, "The job of the Federal Reserve is to take away the punch bowl just when the party is getting good." Independence, such as exists with the U.S. central bank, gives the Fed the ability to do that.

In some developing countries, the central bank is part of the government—and economists have found that when that is the case, the punch bowl tends to remain out longer. The result is that the money supply is more expansionary, and there tend to be higher levels of inflation.

There are many dimensions of independence—one is *goal independence* and another is *policy instrument independence*. Goal independence is having the freedom to determine what ultimate goals, such as low unemployment or low inflation, take priority. Policy instrument independence is having the freedom to determine how to achieve those goals. Many economists point out that goal independence is not necessarily a good thing. In a democracy goals are determined in the political process, and in a well-functioning democracy, the central bank is accountable for achieving the goals set by the political process, and does not set the goals itself. Once the goals are set, then one can talk about policy instrument independence.

Alan Blinder, former vice chairman of the Fed, put it this way:

> The independence of the Fed means, to me, two things. First, that we have very broad latitude to pursue our goals as we see fit; we decide what to do in pursuit of those goals.
>
> Second, it means that once our monetary policy decisions are made, they cannot be reversed by anybody in the U.S. government—except under extreme circumstances. (Congress would have to pass a law limiting the power of the Fed.) But although we are free to choose the means by which we achieve our goals, the goals themselves are given to us by statute, by the U.S. Congress. And that is how it should be in a democracy.

In the United States, the Fed has policy instrument independence, but not goal independence. By federal law, the goals of the Federal Reserve Bank are "maximum employment," "stable prices," and "moderate long-term interest rates." Those are different goals than the goals of the European Central Bank (ECB); the ECB's goal is only "stable prices." These different goals, however, become almost identical if one believes, as a number of economists do, that the only way to achieve maximum employment and moderate long-term interest rates is by achieving stable prices.

the East and Midwest. The South and West have only three banks: Atlanta, Dallas, and San Francisco. The reason is that in 1913, when the Fed was established, the West and South were less populated and less important economically than the rest of the country, so fewer banks were established there.

As these regions grew, the original structure remained because no one wanted to go through the political wrangling that restructuring would bring about. Instead, the southern and western regional Feds established a number of branches to handle their banking needs.

Even though each of the 12 geographic districts has a separate regional Federal Reserve bank, these regional banks have little direct power over the banking system. District banks and their branch banks handle administrative matters and gather information about business and banking conditions in their geographic regions for the Fed.

Duties of the Fed   In legislation establishing the Fed, Congress gave it six explicit functions:

1. Conducting monetary policy (influencing the supply of money and credit in the economy).
2. Supervising and regulating financial institutions.
3. Serving as a lender of last resort to financial institutions.
4. Providing banking services to the U.S. government.
5. Issuing coin and currency.
6. Providing financial services (such as check clearing) to commercial banks, savings and loan associations, savings banks, and credit unions.

Of these functions, the most important one is conducting monetary policy, which is why I presented that first and will spend most of the chapter discussing it.

The Conduct of Monetary Policy

Web Note 12.2
The FOMC

You've already seen that monetary policy shifts the *AD* curve. Let's now consider how it does so in practice. To do so, we need to look more specifically at the institutional structure of the banking system and the role of the Fed in that institutional structure.

Think back to our discussion of the banking system in the last chapter. Banks take in deposits, make loans, and buy other financial assets, keeping a certain percentage of reserves for those transactions. Those reserves are IOUs of the Fed—either vault cash held by banks or deposits at the Fed. *Vault cash, deposits at the Fed, plus currency in circulation* make up the **monetary base.** The monetary base held at banks serves as legal reserves of the banking system. By controlling the monetary base, the Fed can influence the amount of money in the economy and the activities of banks. The money supply is determined directly by the monetary base—the amount of IOUs that the Fed has outstanding, and, indirectly, by the amount of credit that banks extend.

> Allowable reserves are either banks' vault cash or deposits at the Fed.

Open Market Operations   The primary way that the Fed changes the amount of reserves in the system is through **open market operations**—*the Fed's buying and selling of government securities* (the only type of asset the Fed is allowed by law to hold in any appreciable quantity). These open market operations are the primary tool of monetary policy.

> The Fed's buying and selling of government securities is called open market operations.

When the Fed buys Treasury bills or bonds (government securities), it pays for them with IOUs that serve as reserves for banks. These IOUs don't have to be a written piece of paper. They may simply be a computer entry credited to the bank's account, say $1 billion. An IOU of the Fed is money.

Because the IOU the Fed uses to buy a government security serves as reserves to the banking system, with the simple act of buying a Treasury bond and paying for it with its IOU, the Fed can increase the money supply (since this creates reserves for the bank). To increase the money supply, the Fed goes to the bond market, buys a bond, and pays for it with its IOU. The individual or firm that sold the bond now has an IOU of the Fed. When the individual or firm deposits the IOU in a bank—presto!—the reserves of the banking system are increased. If the Fed buys $1 million worth of bonds, it increases reserves by $1 million and the total money supply by $1 million times the money multiplier.

When the Fed sells Treasury bonds, it collects back some of its IOUs, reducing banking system reserves and decreasing the money supply. Thus,

> To expand the money supply, the Fed buys bonds.

> To contract the money supply, the Fed sells bonds.

> **Q.3** When the Fed buys bonds, is it expanding or contracting the money supply?

Inside an FOMC Meeting

Let's go inside one of the eight regular Federal Open Market Committee (FOMC) meetings to gain some insight into how the Fed actually conducts monetary policy. The meeting consists of FOMC members and top Fed staff sitting around a large table debating what should be done. There's been enormous preparation for the meeting. The economists on the Federal Reserve staff have tracked the economy, and have made economic forecasts. Based on their studies, they've briefed the FOMC members, and the high-level staff get to sit in on the meeting. (Getting to sit in on the meeting is seen as a real perk of the job.)

The information they've put together is gathered in three books, which are distinguished by colors. The Beige Book is prepared by each of the 12 regional Federal Reserve banks and summarizes regional business conditions based on local surveys and conversations with local business people. The Green Book is prepared by the staff of the Federal Reserve in Washington, D.C.; it presents a two-year forecast of the U.S. economy as a whole. The Blue Book, also prepared by the Fed staff in Washington, analyzes three possible monetary policy options. This Blue Book is the central policy document, and one of the three options it presents will be selected by the FOMC.

The meeting begins with a summary of monetary policy actions since the committee last met, followed by a forecast of the economy. The Fed governors and regional bank presidents also present their forecasts. Once current economic conditions and forecasts are discussed, the director of monetary affairs presents the three monetary policy proposals in the Blue Book. Then there is open discussion of the various policy proposals. The committee meeting ends with a vote on what policy to follow, along with a policy directive on what open market operations to execute. At that point, the FOMC also makes a public announcement regarding current policy actions as well as what future actions they may take. For example, on March 21, 2007, the FOMC issued the following statement:

> The Federal Open Market Committee decided today to keep its target for the federal funds rate at 5¼ percent. Recent indicators have been mixed and the adjustment in the housing sector is ongoing.

Nevertheless, the economy seems likely to continue to expand at a moderate pace over coming quarters. Recent readings on core inflation have been somewhat elevated. Although inflation pressures seem likely to moderate over time, the high level of resource utilization has the potential to sustain those pressures. In these circumstances, the Committee's predominant policy concern remains the risk that inflation will fail to moderate as expected. Future policy adjustments will depend on the evolution of the outlook for both inflation and economic growth, as implied by incoming information.

The announcement was made at about 2:15 PM and within the next hour, the interest rate in the economy fell and the stock market shot up, with the Dow Jones Industrial Average rising 1.3 percent as you can see in the graph below.

MINUTE-BY-MINUTE
Dow Jones Industrial Average
Yesterday's close: **12447.52, up 1.3%**

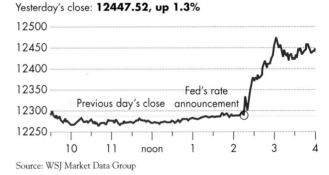

Source: WSJ Market Data Group

Why did this happen? The statement did not announce a change of interest rates. It said only that future policy adjustments are uncertain. What caused the change was what was *not* said in the statement. Previous statements had said that the Fed was leaning toward raising interest rates. This one did not, which led many in the stock market to believe that the Fed might lower interest rates in the future. Since traders saw that as good for the stock market, they bought stocks, pushing their prices up.

Tools of Monetary Policy

Understanding open market operations is essential to understanding monetary policy as it is actually practiced in the United States. So let's go through some examples.[1]

Open market operations involve the purchase or sale of federal government securities (bonds). When the Fed buys bonds, it deposits the funds in federal government accounts at a bank. Bank cash reserves rise. Banks don't like to hold excess reserves, so they lend out the excess, thereby expanding the deposit base of the economy. The money supply rises. Thus, an open market purchase is an example of *expansionary monetary policy* (monetary policy that tends to reduce interest rates and raise income), since it raises the money supply (as long as the banks strive to minimize their excess reserves).

An open market sale has the opposite effect. Here, the Fed sells bonds. In return for the bond, the Fed receives a check drawn against a bank. The bank's reserve assets are reduced (since the Fed "cashes" the check and takes the money away from the bank), and the money supply falls. That's an example of *contractionary monetary policy* (monetary policy that tends to raise interest rates and lower income).

The Reserve Requirement and the Money Supply   As I discussed in the previous chapter, the total amount of money created from a given amount of currency depends on the percentage of deposits that a bank keeps in reserves (the bank's reserve ratio). By law, the Fed controls the minimum percentage of deposits banks keep in reserves by controlling the reserve requirement of all U.S. banks. That minimum is called the **reserve requirement**—*the percentage the Federal Reserve System sets as the minimum amount of reserves a bank must have.*

For checking accounts (also called *demand deposits*), the amount banks keep in reserves depends partly on the Federal Reserve requirements and partly on how much banks feel they need for safety (the cash they need to keep on hand at any time to give to depositors who claim some of their deposits in the form of cash). The amount most banks need for safety is much smaller than what the Fed requires. For them, it's the Fed's reserve requirement that determines the amount they hold as reserves.

Banks hold as little in reserves as possible. Why? Because reserves earn no interest for a bank. And we all know that banks are in business to earn profits. How much is as little as possible? That depends on the type of liabilities the bank has. In the early 2000s, required reserves for large banks for their checking accounts were about 10 percent. The reserve requirement for all other accounts was zero, making the reserve requirement for total liabilities somewhat under 2 percent.

In the early 2000s, total reserves were about $45 billion and required reserves were about $43 billion. This means excess reserves (reserves in excess of requirements) were about $2 billion.

The total money supply, which includes checking account deposits in banks, depends upon the reserve requirement. Thus, by changing the reserve requirements, the Fed can increase or decrease the money supply. If the Fed increases the reserve requirement, it contracts the money supply; banks have to keep more reserves so they have less money to lend out; the decreased money multiplier contracts the money supply. If the Fed decreases the reserve requirement, it expands the money supply; banks have more money to lend out; the increased money multiplier further expands the money supply.

The total effect on the money supply of changing the reserve requirement can be determined by thinking back to the money multiplier, which, as you saw in the previous chapter, equals $(1 + c)/(r + c)$ where r is the percentage of each dollar that banks hold in reserves and c is the ratio of people's cash to deposits. When banks hold no excess

Banks hold as little in reserves as possible.

The money multiplier is $(1 + c)/(r + c)$.

---

[1]A discussion of the effects of open market operations on the supply of money using T-accounts is presented in Appendix A of this chapter.

Using the Money Multiplier in Practice

The money multiplier has been a staple of the macro principles course since its inception, and it remains an important concept in understanding how the monetary base is related to the aggregate supply of money in the economy. But recent changes in the financial system have made the operational use of the multiplier less important. For the most part, central banks don't determine how much to change the monetary base to get a desired change in the money supply using an assumed fixed multiplier. Instead, they adjust the monetary base to target either a desired amount of bank credit in the economy or a short-term interest rate.

The money multiplier relationship continues to be true by definition, but it is not the operational concept that it once was. The reasons include the decrease in the reserve requirement (in many countries, required reserves are zero); financial innovations that have increased the ways in which individuals can hold money; the increase in the amount of cash that individuals hold; and the decline in the stability of the relationship between the money supply and output. Each of these makes it harder to use the money multiplier as an operational variable, which is why much of the monetary policy discussion today focuses more on the interest rate than on the money supply.

reserves and face a reserve requirement of 15 percent, and people's cash-to-deposit ratio is 35 percent, the approximate money multiplier will be 1.35/0.5 = 2.7, so $1 million in reserves will support a total $2.7 million money supply. In reality, the cash-to-deposit ratio is about 0.4 ($c = 0.4$), the average reserve requirement for demand deposits is about 0.1 ($r = 0.1$), and banks hold little in the way of excess reserves. So the realistic money multiplier for demand deposits (M_1) is

$$\frac{1 + 0.4}{(0.1 + 0.4)} = \frac{1.4}{0.5} = 2.8$$

A $100 increase of reserves will support a $280 increase in demand deposits. For other deposits the reserve requirement is zero, so the money multiplier is larger for those.

What does a bank do if it comes up short of reserves? It can borrow from another bank that has excess reserves in what's called the Federal funds market. (The rate of interest at which these reserves can be borrowed is called the *Fed funds rate*. As I will discuss below, this Fed funds rate is a significant indicator of monetary policy.)

Another option that the bank has if it is short of reserves is to stop making new loans and to keep as reserves the proceeds of loans that are paid off. Still another option is to sell Treasury bonds to get the needed reserves. (Banks often hold some of their assets in Treasury bonds so that they can get additional reserves relatively easily if they need them.) Treasury bonds are sometimes called *secondary reserves*. They do not count as bank reserves—only IOUs of the Fed count as reserves. But Treasury bonds can be easily sold and transferred into cash that does count as reserves. Banks use all these options.

It is important to note that while these options are open to the individual banks, they are not open to the entire system of banks. The total amount of reserves is controlled by the Fed, and if the entire banking system is short of reserves, the banking system will have to figure out a way of either reducing the need for reserves or borrowing reserves from the Fed.

Borrowing from the Fed and the Discount Rate As I stated at the beginning of the chapter, a central bank is a banker's bank, and if the entire banking system is short of reserves, banks can go to the Federal Reserve and take out a loan. The **discount rate** is *the rate of interest the Fed charges for loans it makes to banks*. An increase in the

Q-4 If the cash-to-deposit ratio is 0.2 and the reserve requirement is 0.1, what happens to the money supply when the Fed sells $100 of bonds?

discount rate makes it more expensive for banks to borrow from the Fed. A discount rate decrease makes it less expensive for banks to borrow.

Up until 2002, the Fed set the discount rate slightly lower than the cost of reserves for banks from other sources, relying on moral suasion to stop banks from borrowing unless they really needed to. Beginning in 2003, the Fed changed this policy and now it sets the discount rate slightly higher than the banks' other costs of funds. An increase in the discount rate discourages banks from borrowing and contracts the money supply; a decrease in the discount rate encourages the banks to borrow and increases the money supply.

The Fed Funds Market

Web Note 12.3
Fed Funds

To get an even better sense of the way monetary policy works, let's look at it from the perspective of a bank. The bank will review its books, determine how many reserves it needs to meet its reserve requirement, and see if it has excess reserves or a shortage of reserves.

Say your bank didn't make as many loans as it expected to, so it has a surplus of reserves (excess reserves). Say also that another bank has made a few loans it didn't expect to make, so it has a shortage of reserves. The bank with surplus reserves can lend money to the bank with a shortage, and it can lend it overnight as **Fed funds**—*loans of excess reserves banks make to one another.* At the end of a day, a bank will look at its balances and see whether it has a shortage or surplus of reserves. If it has a surplus, it will call a Federal funds dealer to learn the **Federal funds rate**—*the interest rate banks charge one another for Fed funds.* Say the rate is 6 percent. The bank will then agree to lend its excess reserves overnight to the other bank for the daily equivalent of 6 percent per year. It's all simply done electronically, so there's no need actually to transfer funds. In the morning the money (plus overnight interest) is returned. The one-day interest rate is low, but when you're dealing with millions or billions, it adds up.

The **Federal funds market,** *the market in which banks lend and borrow reserves,* is highly efficient. The Fed can reduce reserves, and thereby increase the Fed funds rate, by selling bonds. Alternatively, when the Fed buys bonds, it increases reserves, causing the Fed funds rate to fall. Generally, large city banks are borrowers of Fed funds; small country banks are lenders of Fed funds.

Figure 12-4 shows the Fed funds rate and the discount rate since 1990. As you can see, in 2001 and 2002 the Fed funds rate fell from 6 to 1.25 percent as the Fed followed

The Federal funds rate is the interest rate banks charge one another for overnight reserve loans.

FIGURE 12-4 **The Fed Funds Rate and the Discount Rate Since 1990**

The Federal Reserve Bank follows expansionary or contractionary monetary policy by targeting a lower or higher Fed funds rate. The discount rate generally follows the Fed funds rate closely. Before 2003, it was kept lower than the Fed funds rate. Since 2003, the discount rate has been set slightly above the Fed funds rate target.

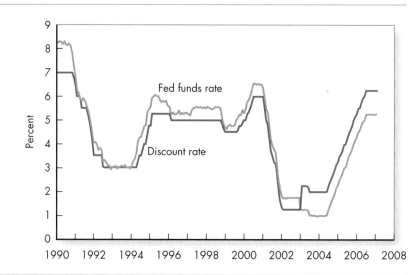

Will the Reserve Requirement Be Eliminated?

In 2006, President Bush signed the Financial Services Regulatory Relief Act of 2006 to improve the efficiency of the banking system. The Act allows the Fed, beginning in 2011, to reduce the reserve ratio to zero and to pay interest on reserves that banks maintain at the Fed. Currently, the Fed does not pay interest on reserves. If the Fed makes this change, it would be following the practices of central banks of other industrialized nations such as Canada, the United Kingdom, New Zealand and Japan. The reason for the change is that financial institutions are changing. More and more financial transactions take place outside the banking system, and distinguishing banks from other financial institutions is becoming harder and harder.

In practice, the change will make all reserves excess reserves, and make the interest rate paid on reserve balances a key element in the determination of reserves and hence of the money supply. Thus, the Fed will be able to affect reserves through the discount rate, open market operations, and the interest rate paid on reserves.

The transition to the new system will likely involve some changes in the amount of reserves held by banks, but it is unlikely to have a significant effect on the actual conduct of monetary policy. In practice, central banks conduct monetary policy largely by targeting short-term interest rates through open market operations. If the system changes, the Fed will establish a relationship between the discount rate (the rate the Fed charges banks for lending reserves), the interest rate on reserves, and the targeted Fed funds rate. Which of these will become the lead indicator of Fed policy will depend on the relative differentials that the Fed chooses for these interest rates.

---

an expansionary monetary policy. Starting in mid-2004, the Fed began to raise the Federal funds rate as it switched to a contractionary monetary policy, and in 2007 the target Fed funds rate was 5.25 percent. Notice also that the Fed funds rate tended to be slightly above the discount rate until 2003, when the Fed changed its operating procedures and began setting the discount rate slightly above the Fed funds rate.

Offensive and Defensive Actions   Economists keep a close eye on the Federal funds rate in determining the state of monetary policy. It has become an important intermediate target of the Fed in determining what monetary policy to conduct. Remember, the Fed sets minimum reserve requirements, but the actual amount of reserves available to banks is influenced by the amount of cash people hold and excess reserves that banks may choose to hold. That changes daily. For example, say there's a storm, and businesses don't make it to the bank with their cash. Bank reserves will fall even though the Fed didn't do anything. The Fed can, and does, offset such changes—by buying and selling bonds. Such actions are called *defensive actions*. They are designed to maintain the current monetary policy. These defensive actions are to be contrasted with *offensive actions*, which are actions meant to make monetary policy have expansionary or contractionary effects on the economy.

Q-5   There's been a big storm and cash held by individuals has increased. Should the Fed buy or sell bonds? Why?

The Fed Funds Rate as an Operating Target   How does the Fed decide whether its buying and selling of bonds is having the desired effect? It has to look at other targets—and in recent years the Federal funds rate has been the operating target of the Fed. Thus, the Fed determines whether monetary policy is tight or loose depending on what is happening to the Federal funds rate. In practice, it targets a range for that rate, and buys and sells bonds to keep the Federal funds rate within that range. If the Federal funds rate rises above the Fed's target range, it buys bonds, which increases reserves and lowers the Federal funds rate. If the Federal funds rate falls below the Fed's target range, it sells bonds, which decreases reserves and raises the Federal funds rate.

Monetary policy affects interest rates such as the Federal funds rate. The Fed looks at the Federal funds rate to determine whether monetary policy is tight or loose.

The Complex Nature of Monetary Policy

While the Fed focuses on the Fed funds rate as its operating target, it also has its eye on its ultimate targets: stable prices, acceptable employment, sustainable growth, and moderate long-term interest rates. But those ultimate targets are only indirectly affected by changes in the Fed funds rate, so the Fed watches what are called *intermediate targets:* consumer confidence, stock prices, interest rate spreads, housing starts, and a host of others. Intermediate targets are not always good guides for the Fed's ultimate targets. The Federal Reserve Bank of San Francisco once had an exhibit of an electronic video game in its lobby.[2] The object of the game was to hit a moving target with a dart from a moving arm. With both the arm and the target moving, most visitors missed the target.

The game was there to demonstrate the difficulties of implementing monetary policy. Monetary policy "shoots from a moving arm." Ultimately, policy actions of the Fed influence output and inflation but the influence is not direct, and many other factors also influence output and inflation.

In reality, the Fed's problem is even more complicated than the video game suggests. A more telling game would be one modeled after a Rube Goldberg cartoon. If you hit the first moving target, it releases a second dart when hit. That second dart is supposed to hit a second moving target, which in turn releases a third dart aimed at yet another moving target. Given the complicated path that monetary policy follows, it should not be surprising that the Fed often misses its ultimate targets. Small wonder that the Fed often doesn't have the precise effect it wants.

The following diagram summarizes the tools and targets of the Fed:

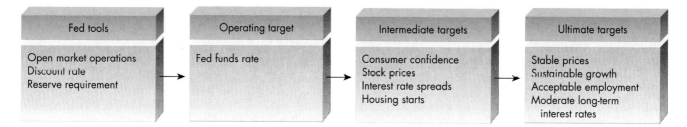

The Taylor Rule

U.S. Treasury economist John Taylor has summarized a rule that, in the late 1990s and early 2000s, described Fed policy relatively well. The rule, which has become known as the **Taylor rule,** can be stated as follows: *Set the Fed funds rate at 2 percent plus current inflation if the economy is at desired output and desired inflation. If the inflation rate is higher than desired, increase the Fed funds rate by 0.5 times the difference between desired and actual inflation. Similarly, if output is higher than desired, increase the Fed funds rate by 0.5 times the percentage deviation.*

Formally the Taylor rule is

Fed funds rate = 2 percent + Current inflation

+ 0.5 × (actual inflation less desired inflation)

+ 0.5 × (percent deviation of aggregate output from potential)

Let's consider some examples. Say that inflation is 2.5 percent, the Fed's target rate of inflation is 2 percent, and the aggregate output exceeds potential output by 1 percent.

Q-6 If inflation is 1 percent and the Fed wants 2 percent inflation and output is 2 percent below potential, what would the Taylor rule predict for a Fed funds rate target?

That means that the Fed would set the Fed funds rate at 5.25 percent (2 + 2.5 + 0.5(2.5 − 2) + 0.5(1)). The first row in the table below shows the calculations. The second row shows another example with different numbers.

Federal Funds Rate	=	2 Percent	+	Current Inflation	+	0.5 (Actual less targeted inflation)	+	0.5 (Deviation from potential output)
5.25	=	2	+	2.5	+	0.5(2.5 − 2)	+	0.5(1)
4.5	=	2	+	2	+	0.5(2 − 2)	+	0.5(1)

The Fed does not always slavishly follow the Taylor rule. For example, in late 2000 and early 2001, the economy was 1 percent over potential output by most estimates and inflation was 2 percent, which was equal to the target rate. The Taylor rule predicted that the Fed would set the Fed funds rate at 4.5 percent. (See the calculations in row 2 of the table.) Instead, it targeted a 6 percent rate, because it was especially concerned about the economy overheating. Then right after September 11, the Fed became concerned about the economy going into a severe recession and it lowered the Fed funds rate significantly—close to zero—even though little else had changed. Despite the fact that the Fed considers more issues than just inflation and potential output in determining interest rate targets, the Taylor rule provides a useful first guide to understanding Fed policy choices.

Controlling the Interest Rate   Notice how the Taylor rule focuses the discussion of monetary policy on the interest rate (specifically, the Fed funds rate), not the money supply. On the surface, this may seem inconsistent with the discussions of monetary policy that focused on the money supply, but it is not. It is simply a difference in focus. The Fed does control the amount of money in the economy, but it uses that control to target an interest rate, not to control the money supply. Specifically, as the demand for money shifts, the Fed adjusts the money supply (through open market operations) so that the market equilibrates at the targeted interest rate. Essentially, the Fed is choosing a monetary rule that creates an *effective supply curve of money* that is perfectly flat at the target interest rate. How it does so is shown in Figure 12-5.

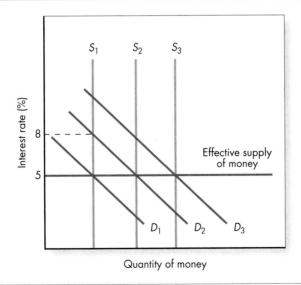

FIGURE 12-5 The Effective Supply Curve for Money

When the Fed chooses a monetary rule that targets the interest rate, it creates an effective supply curve of money that is flat at the target rate. To create a flat effective supply of money, the Fed adjusts the supply of money to changes in the demand for money at the targeted rate.

The Fed targets the interest rate by adjusting the money supply so that its targeted interest rate will equalize the supply and demand for money.

Q-7 How does the Fed create a flat effective money supply curve?

Say that we start with an interest rate of 5 percent, a money supply of S_1, and a money demand of D_1. Then, the demand for money rises to D_2. If the Fed held the money supply constant, the interest rate would rise to 8 percent. However, if in response to the increase in demand the Fed automatically raises the money supply to S_2, the interest rate remains at 5 percent. Similarly, if money demand rises to D_3, the Fed increases the money supply to S_3. As long as the Fed is willing to change the money supply to whatever level is necessary to achieve the targeted interest rate, it can determine the interest rate in the money market.

Limits to the Fed's Control of the Interest Rate   The above discussion makes it sound as if the Fed can control the interest rate, and it can, if by interest rate we mean the short-term interest rate. But, as we discussed in the last chapter, the economy has more than one interest rate. The long-term interest rate in the economy is determined in the *loanable funds market*, not the money market. As long as the short-term interest rate and the long-term interest rate move in tandem, then the Fed can also control the long-term interest rate. Unfortunately, they do not always move in tandem, and that has made the study of the relationship between the short-term and long-term rates an important part of discussions of monetary policy. Economists carefully follow this relationship in a graph called the **yield curve**—*a curve that shows the relationship between interest rates and bonds' time to maturity*. I show two alternative yield curves in Figure 12-6. As you can see, as you move out along the yield curve, bonds' time to maturity increases. Figure 12-6(a) demonstrates what is called a standard yield curve. It is a yield curve in which the short-term rates are lower than the long-term rate. Thus, if you invest in a one-year bond, you would earn 4 percent interest, and if you invest in a 30-year bond, you would earn 6 percent interest. This is considered a standard yield curve because long-term bonds are riskier than short-term bonds, so it is reasonable that they generally have a slightly higher interest rate.

The yield curve is a curve that shows the relationship between interest rates and bonds' time to maturity.

FIGURE 12-6 (A AND B)   **The Yield Curve**

The standard yield curve shown in (**a**) is upward-sloping: as the time to maturity increases, so does the interest rate. An inverted yield curve shown in (**b**) is downward-sloping: as the time to maturity increases, the interest rate decreases.

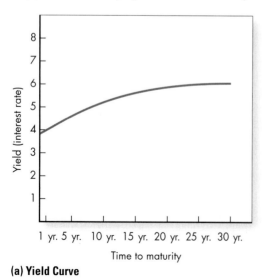

(a) Yield Curve

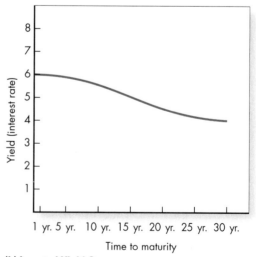

(b) Inverted Yield Curve

That relationship between short-term and long-term interest rates does not always hold. Figure 12-6(b) shows what is called an **inverted yield curve**—*a yield curve in which the short-term rate is higher than the long-term rate.* In the graph, you can see that a one-year bond pays 6 percent interest and a 30-year bond pays a lower, 4 percent, interest rate.

Why is the shape of the yield curve important? Because the standard discussion of monetary policy is based on the assumption that when the Fed pushes up the short-term rate, the long-term rate moves up as well. If the long-term rate doesn't move with the short-term rate, then investment won't respond, and monetary policy won't have any significant effect. Think of the issue as one of pushing a pea along a plate with a noodle. If the noodle is dry, you can do it easily, but if the noodle is wet, when you move one end, the other end doesn't move, and it is much more difficult.

As financial markets have become more liquid, and as technological changes in financial markets have provided firms with many alternative sources of credit, the Fed has found that its ability to control the long-term rate has lessened, and that monetary policy is becoming more and more like controlling the economy with a wet noodle rather than a dry noodle. When it uses contractionary monetary policy, as opposed to shifting the entire yield curve up the policy simply causes an inverted yield curve. That's why policy makers pay close attention to the yield curve.

The monetary influence is not gone; economists have found that if the Fed is willing to push the short-term rate high enough, it is able to pull the long-term rate with it, but the Fed's control of the long-term rate is more like the control parents have over their kids—they can influence (and hope) but cannot control.

Maintaining Policy Credibility

Policy makers are very concerned about establishing policy credibility. The reason why is that they believe that it is necessary to prevent inflationary expectations from becoming built into the system. They fear that if inflationary expectations become built into the system, the long-term interest rate, which is the rate that primarily influences investment, will be pushed up, making the yield curve steeper and requiring even stronger contractionary monetary policy to eliminate the inflation. To see why the long-term rate will rise if inflationary expectations become built into the system, it is important to remember that the long-term interest rate has two components: a real interest rate component and an inflationary expectations component, which means that you must distinguish the real interest rate from the nominal interest rate.

You learned about this real/nominal interest rate distinction in an earlier chapter. Recall, **nominal interest rates** are *the rates you actually see and pay.* When a bank pays 7 percent interest, that 7 percent is a nominal interest rate. What affects the economy is the real interest rate. **Real interest rates** are *nominal interest rates adjusted for expected inflation.*

For example, say you get 7 percent interest from the bank, but the price level goes up 7 percent. At the end of the year you have $107 instead of $100, but you're no better off than before because the price level has risen—on average, things

Q-8 What is the difference between a standard yield curve and an inverted yield curve?

Q.9 If the nominal interest rate is 10 percent and expected inflation is 3 percent, what is the real interest rate?

cost 7 percent more. What you would have paid $100 for last year now costs $107. (That's the definition of *inflation*.) Had the price level remained constant, and had you received 0 percent interest, you'd be in the equivalent position to receiving 7 percent interest on your $100 when the price level rises by 7 percent. That 0 percent is the *real interest rate*. It is the interest rate you would expect to receive if the price level remains constant.

The real interest rate cannot be observed because it depends on expected inflation. To calculate the real interest rate, you must subtract what you believe to be the expected rate of inflation from the nominal interest rate:

$$\text{Real interest rate} = \text{Nominal interest rate} - \text{Expected inflation rate}$$

For example, if the nominal interest rate is 7 percent and expected inflation is 4 percent, the real interest rate is 3 percent. The relationship between real and nominal interest rates is important both for your study of economics and for your own personal finances.

Q.10 How does the distinction between nominal and real interest rates add uncertainty to the effect of monetary policy on the economy?

What does this distinction between nominal and real interest rates mean for monetary policy? It adds yet another uncertainty to the effect of monetary policy. In the *AS/AD* model, we assumed that expansionary monetary policy lowers the interest rate and contractionary monetary policy increases the interest rate. However, if the expansionary monetary policy leads to expectations of increased inflation, expansionary monetary policy can increase nominal interest rates (the ones you see) and leave real interest rates (the ones that affect borrowing decisions) unchanged. Why? Because of expectations of increasing inflation. Lenders will want to be compensated for the inflation (which will decrease the value of the money they receive back) and will push the nominal interest rate up to get the desired real rate of interest.

Monetary Policy Regimes   The distinction between nominal and real interest rates and the possible effect of monetary policy on expectations of inflation has led most economists to conclude that a monetary regime, not a monetary policy, is the best approach to policy. A **monetary regime** is *a predetermined statement of the policy that will be followed in various situations*. A monetary policy, in contrast, is a response to events; it is chosen without a predetermined framework.

Monetary regimes are now favored because rules can help generate the expectations that even though in certain instances the Fed is increasing the money supply, that increase is not a signal that monetary expansion and inflation are imminent. The monetary regime that the Fed currently uses involves feedback rules that center on the Federal funds rate. If inflation is above its target, the Fed raises the Federal funds rate (by selling bonds, thereby decreasing the money supply) in an attempt to slow inflation down. If inflation is below its target, and if the economy is going into a recession, the Fed lowers the Fed funds rate (by buying bonds, thereby increasing the money supply). The Taylor rule discussed above is a quantification of this general feedback rule.

Problems with Monetary Policy Regimes   Establishing an explicit monetary policy regime to hold down expectations of inflation is not without its problems. Inevitably, special circumstances arise where it makes sense to deviate from the regime. The problem is analogous to the problem faced by parents. All parenting manuals tell parents to maintain credibility and to set fair and firm rules. Most parents attempt to do so. But as all, or at least most, parents know, sometimes exceptions are necessary. Not all contingencies can be planned for. So I suspect that both parents and monetary policy

Conventional Wisdom about Monetary Policy

Option	Advantages	Disadvantages
Expansionary	1. Interest rates may fall. 2. Economy may grow. 3. Decreases unemployment.	1. Inflation may worsen. 2. Capital outflow. 3. Trade deficit may increase.
Contractionary	1. Helps fight inflation. 2. Trade deficit may decrease. 3. Capital inflow.	1. Risks recession. 2. Increases unemployment. 3. Slows growth. 4. May help cause short-run political problems. 5. Interest rates may rise.

makers will consistently emphasize their firm rules and state that they will follow them no matter what, but that inevitably they will trade some credibility for some short-term gain, or in the belief that the initial rule did not take into account the particular situation that arose.

To make its commitment to a monetary regime clear to the public, even as it deviates slightly from that commitment in specific instances, the Fed has been trying, over the past decade, to increase the degree of *transparency* that accompanies its monetary policy decisions. Specifically, the Fed is releasing the minutes of its FOMC meetings much sooner after the meetings adjourn than it did in the past, and is going out of its way to explain its decisions. The hope is that the greater degree of transparency will demonstrate the Fed's general resolve to fight inflation, and show that any possible deviation from that resolve can be explained by special circumstances.

Conclusion

The above discussion should give you a good sense that conducting monetary policy is not a piece of cake. It takes not only a sense of the theory but also a feel for the economy. (See the box "Conventional Wisdom about Monetary Policy" for a summary of the standard view of monetary policy.) In short, the conduct of monetary policy is not a science. It does not allow the Fed to steer the economy as it might steer a car. It does work well enough to allow the Fed to *influence* the economy—much as an expert rodeo rider rides a bronco bull.

The Fed can influence, not steer, the economy.

Summary

- Monetary policy is the policy of influencing the economy through changes in the banking system's reserves that affect the money supply.

- In the *AS/AD* model, contractionary monetary policy works as follows:
$$M \downarrow \rightarrow i \uparrow \rightarrow I \downarrow \rightarrow Y \downarrow$$

- Expansionary monetary policy works as follows:
$$M \uparrow \rightarrow i \downarrow \rightarrow I \uparrow \rightarrow Y \uparrow$$

- The Federal Open Market Committee (FOMC) makes the actual decisions about monetary policy.

- The Fed is a central bank; it conducts monetary policy for the United States and regulates financial institutions.

- The Fed changes the money supply through open market operations:

    To expand the money supply, the Fed buys bonds.
    To contract the money supply, the Fed sells bonds.

- When the Fed buys bonds, the price of bonds rises and interest rates fall. When the Fed sells bonds, the price of bonds falls and interest rates rise.

- A change in reserves changes the money supply by the change in reserves times the money multiplier.

- The Federal funds rate is the rate at which one bank lends reserves to another bank. It is the Fed's primary operating target.

- The Taylor rule is a feedback rule that states: Set the Fed funds rate at 2 plus current inflation plus one-half the difference between actual and desired inflation plus one-half the percent difference between actual and potential output.

- The yield curve shows the relationship between interest rates and bonds' time to maturity.

- The Fed's direct control is on short-term interest rates; its effect on long-term interest rates is indirect. Fed policy intended to shift the yield curve might instead change its shape, and therefore not have the intended impact on investment.

- Nominal interest rates are the interest rates we see and pay. Real interest rates are nominal interest rates adjusted for expected inflation: Real interest rate = Nominal interest rate − Expected inflation.

- Because monetary policy can affect inflation expectations as well as nominal interest rates, the effect of monetary policy on interest rates can be uncertain. This uncertainty has led the Fed to follow monetary regimes.

Key Terms

central bank (*292*)
contractionary monetary policy (*292*)
discount rate (*299*)
expansionary monetary policy (*292*)
Fed funds (*300*)

Federal funds market (*300*)
Federal funds rate (*300*)
Federal Open Market Committee (FOMC) (*292*)
inverted yield curve (*305*)

monetary base (*296*)
monetary policy (*290*)
monetary regime (*306*)
nominal interest rate (*305*)
open market operations (*296*)

real interest rate (*305*)
reserve requirement (*298*)
Taylor rule (*302*)
yield curve (*304*)

Questions for Thought and Review

1. Investment increases by 20 for each interest rate drop of 1 percent. The expenditures multiplier is 3. If the money multiplier is 4, and each change of 5 in the money supply changes the interest rate by 1 percent, what open market policy would you recommend to increase income by 240? LO1, LO4

2. Demonstrate the effect of contractionary monetary policy in the *AS/AD* model.   LO1

3. Demonstrate the effect of expansionary monetary policy in the money and loanable funds markets.   LO1

4. Is the Fed a private or a public agency?   LO2

5. Why are there few regional Fed banks in the western part of the United States?   LO2

6. What are the six explicit functions of the Fed?   LO2

7. How does the Fed use open market operations to increase the money supply?   LO3

8. Write the formula for the money multiplier. If the Fed eliminated the reserve requirement, what would happen to the money multiplier and the supply of money?   LO3

9. If a bank is unable to borrow reserves from the Fed funds market to meet its reserve requirement, where else might it borrow reserves? What is the name of the rate it pays to borrow these reserves?   LO3

10. What happens to interest rates and the price of bonds when the Fed buys bonds?   LO3

11. If the Federal Reserve announces a change in the direction of monetary policy, is it describing an offensive or defensive action? Explain your answer.   LO3

12. "The effects of open market operations are somewhat like a stone cast in a pond." After the splash, discuss the first three ripples.   LO1, LO3

13. Why would a bank hold Treasury bills as secondary reserves when it could simply hold primary reserves—cash?   LO3

14. Define the *Federal funds rate* and explain why it is the interest rate that the Fed most directly controls.   LO4

15. Explain the relationship between tools, operating targets, intermediate targets, and ultimate targets. Give examples of each.   LO4

16. The table below gives the Fed funds rate target at the end of each year shown.

Year	Federal Funds Target Rate
2003	1.00%
2004	1.75
2005	5.00
2006	5.25

Using these figures, describe how the monetary policy directions changed from 2003 through 2006.   LO5

17. Target inflation is 2 percent; actual inflation is 3 percent. Output equals potential output. What does the Taylor rule predict will be the Fed funds rate?   LO5

18. Why is the effective supply curve for money horizontal?   LO6

19. You can lead a horse to water, but you can't make it drink. How might this adage be relevant to expansionary (as opposed to contractionary) monetary policy?   LO6

20. If the nominal interest rate is 6 percent and inflation is 5 percent, what's the real interest rate?   LO6

21. What is an inverted yield curve? Are you more likely to see one when the Fed is implementing contractionary or expansionary monetary policy?   LO6

22. Why would policy makers pay attention to the shape of the yield curve?   LO6

23. Does it matter to policy makers how people form expectations?   LO6

24. How does a policy regime differ from a policy?   LO6

25. How might an inflation target policy impair the ability of the Fed?   LO6

26. How are transparency and credibility related?   LO6

Problems and Exercises

27. Demonstrate the effect of expansionary monetary policy in the *AS/AD* model when the economy is
   a. Below potential output.
   b. Significantly above potential output.   LO1

28. The Fed wants to increase the money supply (which is currently 4,000) by 200. The money multiplier is 3 and people hold no cash. For each 1 percentage point the discount rate falls, banks borrow an additional 20. Explain how the Fed can achieve its goals using the following tools:
   a. Change the reserve requirement.
   b. Change the discount rate.
   c. Use open market operations.   LO3

29. Suppose the Fed decides it needs to pursue an expansionary policy. Assume people hold no cash, the reserve requirement is 20 percent, and there are no excess reserves.
   a. Show how the Fed would increase the money supply by $2 million by changing the reserve requirement.
   b. Show how the Fed would increase the money supply by $2 million through open market operations.   LO3

30. Suppose the Fed decides that it needs to pursue a contractionary policy. It wants to decrease the money supply by $2 million. Assume people hold 20 percent of their money in the form of cash balances, the reserve requirement is 20 percent, and there are no excess reserves.
   a. Show how the Fed would decrease the money supply by $2 million by changing the reserve requirement.
   b. Show how the Fed would decrease the money supply by $2 million through open market operations.
   c. Go to your local bank and find out how much excess reserves it holds. Recalculate *a* and *b* assuming all banks held that percentage in excess reserves.   LO3

31. Some individuals have suggested raising the required reserve ratio for banks to 100 percent.
    a. What would the money multiplier be if this change were made?
    b. What effect would such a change have on the money supply?
    c. How could that effect be offset?
    d. Would banks likely favor or oppose this proposal? Why? LO3

32. One of the proposals to reform monetary policy has been to have the central bank pay interest on reserves held at the bank.
    a. What effect would that proposal have on excess reserves?
    b. Would banks generally favor or oppose this proposal? Why?
    c. Would central banks generally favor or oppose this proposal? Why?
    d. What effect would this proposal probably have on interest rates paid by banks? LO3

33. Congratulations! You have been approved adviser to the Federal Reserve Bank.
    a. The Federal Open Market Committee decides that it must increase the money supply by 60. Committee members tell you the reserve ratio is 0.1 and the cash-to-deposit ratio is 0.3. They ask you what directive they should give to the open market desk. You tell them, being as specific as possible, using the money multiplier.
    b. They ask you for two other ways they could have achieved the same end. You tell them.
    c. Based on the AS/AD model, tell them what you think the effect on the price level of your policy will be. LO3

34. The "Check 21" Act, which went into effect in 2004, allows banks to transfer check images instead of paper checks. This act makes check processing much quicker. What will be the likely effect on the following?
    a. Float.
    b. Variability of float.
    c. Defensive Fed actions.   LO4

35. State the Taylor rule. What does the rule predict will happen to the Fed funds rate in each of the following situations?
    a. Inflation is 2 percent, the inflation target is 3 percent, and output is 2 percent below potential.
    b. Inflation is 4 percent, the inflation target is 2 percent, and output is 3 percent above potential.
    c. Inflation is 4 percent, the inflation target is 3 percent, and output is 2 percent below potential.   LO5

36. What would the Fed have to do in the following instances to keep the interest rate constant? Demonstrate graphically.
    a. A significant number of people begin to use credit cards for daily transactions, reducing the amount of money they hold.
    b. Bond traders expect bond prices to fall, and therefore increase their cash holdings.   LO5

37. Fill in the blanks in the following table: LO6

	Real Interest Rate	Nominal Interest Rate	Expected Inflation
a.	5	?	2
b.	?	3	4
c.	3	6	?
d.	?	5	1

Questions from Alternative Perspectives

1. Fisher Black, an economist who designed a famous options pricing model, argued that because of developments in financial markets, central banks would soon have no ability to control the economy with monetary policy, and that the price level would be indeterminant rather than determined by the money supply. What do you think his argument was? (Austrian)

2. The quotation at the beginning of this chapter, and those for almost all the chapters, is from a man not a woman.
    a. Does this suggest anything about the author's viewpoint or about the economics profession?
    b. Should we be concerned about the lack of quotations from women? (Feminist)

3. Monetary policy is difficult when interest rates are low. For example, in the early 2000s the Bank of Japan lowered the interest rate to 0.01 percent with little effect on investment.

a. Why is it difficult for monetary policy to be effective when interest rates are very low?
b. How might institutions be changed to make monetary policy effective under these circumstances? (Institutionalist)

4. Monetarists believe that money is neutral in that it has no real effect on interest rates, output, or employment. Keynes, alternatively, believed that money is not neutral in both the short and long run. For Keynesians, money supply can affect real decision making, providing liquidity when firms need it. How would a belief in the nonneutrality of money affect the policy discussion in the book? (Post-Keynesian)

5. As radical economists see it, when it comes to making monetary policy, the Fed consistently puts the interests of bondholders ahead of people seeking work. It regularly moves to protect the value of their stocks and bonds by

keeping inflation low even at the expense of maintaining employment growth.

a. In your opinion, does the Fed use monetary policy to direct the economy to everyone's benefit?

b. Should the Fed serve the interests of the holders of financial assets or the interests of workers? (Radical)

Web Questions

1. Go to the Federal Reserve's home page at www.federalreserve.gov.
   a. Who is the chairman of the board? For how long has he or she served?
   b. Who are the governors of the board?
   c. The site publishes a short biography for each governor. What experiences and/or degrees do all members have? What experiences and/or degrees differ among members?

2. Go to the New York Fed's Web site at www.ny.frb.org/research/current_issues/ci2-7.pdf to read "The Yield Curve as a Predictor of Recessions." Then answer the following questions:
   a. Why should the steepness of the yield curve be a predictor of recessions?
   b. Is the economy more likely to be headed for recession if there is a standard yield curve or if the yield curve is flat or inverted? Explain your answer.
   c. What is the current yield curve spread? What does this mean for future economic activity?

Answers to Margin Questions

1. Expansionary monetary policy makes more money available to banks for lending. Banks lower their interest rates to attract more borrowers. With lower interest rates, businesses will borrow more money and increase investment expenditures. The multiplier shifts the AD curve to the right by a multiple of the increase in investment expenditures. Real output increases to Y_1, and the price level rises to P_1. What ultimately happens to output and the price level depends on where the economy is relative to potential. (292)

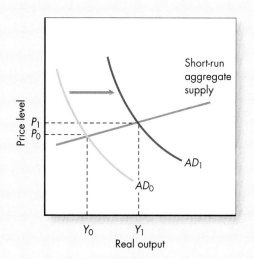

2. The Federal Open Market Committee (FOMC) decides on monetary policy (292).

3. When the Fed buys bonds, it is expanding the money supply. (296)

4. The money multiplier in this case is 4, so the money supply declines by $400. (299)

5. The Fed should buy bonds to offset the unintended decline in reserves. (301)

6. The Taylor rule predicts a Fed funds rate target of 1.5 percent. (302)

7. The Fed adjusts the money supply so that the targeted interest rate equilibrates the demand and supply for money. When demand increases, the Fed increases supply to maintain the interest rate target. It does the opposite when demand decreases. (304)

8. In a standard yield curve, bonds with greater time to maturity pay higher interest rates. In an inverted yield curve, bonds with greater time to maturity pay *lower* interest rates. (305)

9. The real interest rate is 7 percent, the nominal interest rate (10) less expected inflation (3). (306)

10. Because expansionary monetary policy can lead to expectations of higher inflation, expansionary monetary policy can lead to higher nominal interest rates. Because real interest rates cannot be observed directly, interest rates are not always a good guide for the direction of monetary policy. (306)

APPENDIX A

The Effect of Monetary Policy Using T-Accounts

The Fed uses the discount rate, the reserve requirement, and open market operations to change the money supply. Each of these tools works initially by affecting the amount of reserves in the banking system. Here I will show you exactly how the Fed changes the money supply using T-accounts. To simplify things, say there's only one bank, Textland Bank, with branches all over the country. Textland is fully loaned out at a 10 percent reserve requirement. For simplicity, assume people hold no cash. Textland's beginning balance sheet is presented below in Table A12-1.

Now say the Fed sells $10,000 worth of Treasury bonds to individuals. The person who buys them pays with a check to the Fed for $10,000. The Fed, in turn, presents that check to the bank, getting $10,000 in cash from the bank. This step is shown in Table A12-2.

As you can see, bank reserves are now $290,000, which is too low to meet requirements on demand deposits of $2,990,000. With a 10 percent reserve requirement,

$2,990,000 in deposits would require ¹⁄₁₀ × $2,990,000 = $299,000, so the bank is $9,000 short of reserves. It must figure out a way to meet its reserve requirement. Let's say that it calls in $9,000 of its loans. After doing so it has assets of $299,000 in cash and $2,990,000 in demand deposits, so it looks as if the bank has met its reserve requirement.

If the bank could meet its reserve requirement that way, its balance sheet would be as shown in Table A12-3. Loans would decrease by $9,000 and cash would increase by the $9,000 necessary to meet the reserve requirement.

Unfortunately for the bank, meeting its reserve requirement isn't that easy. That $9,000 in cash had to come from somewhere. Most likely, the person who paid off the loans in cash did it partly by running down her checking account, borrowing all the cash she could from others, and using whatever other options she had. Since, by assumption in this example, people don't hold cash,

TABLE A12-1 Textland Bank Balance Sheet

Beginning Balance

Assets		Liabilities and Net Worth	
Cash (reserves)	$ 300,000	Demand deposits	$3,000,000
Loans	2,000,000	Net worth	1,000,000
Treasury bonds	400,000		
Property	1,300,000		
Total assets	$ 4,000,000	Total liabilities and net worth	$4,000,000

TABLE A12-2

Transaction 1

Assets		Liabilities and Net Worth	
Cash (reserves)	$ 300,000	Demand deposits	$3,000,000
Payment to Fed (person's Treasury purchase)	(10,000)	Deposits for cash (person's check)	(10,000)
Total cash	$ 290,000	Total deposits	$2,990,000
Loans	2,000,000	Net worth	1,000,000
Treasury bonds	400,000		
Property	1,300,000		
Total assets	$3,990,000	Total liabilities and net worth	$3,990,000

TABLE A12-3

| | | Transaction 2 | | |
Assets			Liabilities and Net Worth	
Cash (reserves)...........	$ 290,000		Demand deposits	$2,990,000
Loans (repaid)............	9,000		Net worth............................	1,000,000
Total cash.................		$ 299,000		
Loans	2,000,000			
Loans called in	(9,000)			
Total loans		1,991,000		
Treasury bonds.............		400,000		
Property		1,300,000		
Total assets		$ 3,990,000	Total liabilities and net worth..............	$3,990,000

the banking system was initially fully loaned out, and Textland Bank was the only bank, the only cash in the economy was in Textland Bank's vaults! So that $9,000 in cash had to come from its vaults. Calling in the loans cannot directly solve its reserve problem. It still has reserves of only $290,000.

But calling in its loans did *indirectly* help solve the problem. Calling in loans decreased investment, which, because it decreased aggregate demand, decreased the income in the economy. (If you're not sure why this is the case, think back to the macro policy model.) That decrease in income decreases the amount of demand deposits people want to hold. As demand deposits decrease, the bank's need for reserves decreases.

Contraction of the money supply in this example works in the opposite way to an expansion of the money supply. Banks keep trying to meet their reserve requirement by getting cash, only to find that for the banking system as a whole the total cash is limited. Thus, the banking system as a whole must continue to call in loans until that decline in loans causes income to fall sufficiently to cause demand deposits to fall to a level that can be supported by the smaller reserves. In this example, with a money multiplier of 10, when demand deposits have fallen by $100,000 to $2.9 million, total reserves available to the system ($290,000) will be sufficient to meet the reserve requirement.

Questions for Thought and Review

1. Demonstrate, using T-accounts, the effect of the Fed selling $1 million of Treasury bonds when the reserve requirement is 10 percent and people hold no cash.

2. Demonstrate, using T-accounts, the effect of the Fed buying $2 million of Treasury bonds when the reserve requirement is 10 percent and people hold no cash.

13 Inflation and the Phillips Curve

The first few months or years of inflation, like the first few drinks, seem just fine. Everyone has more money to spend and prices aren't rising quite as fast as the money that's available. The hangover comes when prices start to catch up.

—*Milton Friedman*

AFTER READING THIS CHAPTER, YOU SHOULD BE ABLE TO:

1. State some of the distributional effects of inflation.
2. Explain how inflation expectations are formed.
3. Outline the quantity theory of money and its theory of inflation.
4. Outline the institutionalist theory of inflation.
5. Differentiate between long-run and short-run Phillips curves.
6. Explain the different views on the relationship between inflation and growth.

Politicians tend to get reelected when the economy is doing well. Thus, it should not surprise you that political pressures exert a strong bias toward lowering taxes and increasing spending, and expanding the money supply. What prevents politicians and the Fed from implementing expansionary policies is inflation, or at least the fear of generating an accelerating inflation. It is for that reason that inflation and its relationship to unemployment and growth come to center stage in any discussion of macro policy. Hence this chapter. It extends our earlier consideration of inflation and considers the trade-offs between inflation, unemployment, and growth.

Some Basics about Inflation

I introduced you to inflation in an earlier chapter. There, you saw the definition of *inflation* (a continuous rise in the price level) and how inflation is measured (with price indexes). I also explained that expectations of inflation can become built into individuals' behavior and economic institutions and cause a small inflation to accelerate, and that inflation creates feelings of injustice and destroys the informational value of prices and the market. (If any of those concepts seem a bit vague to you, a review might be a good idea.) I now build on that information to give you more insight into inflation.

The Distributional Effects of Inflation

Who wins and who loses in an inflation? The answer to that is simple: The winners are people who can raise their wages or prices and still keep their jobs or sell their goods. The losers are people who can't raise their wages or prices or who lose their jobs because their wage is too high. Consider a worker who has entered a contract to receive 4 percent annual wage increases for three years. If the worker expected inflation to be 2 percent at the time of the agreement, she was expecting her real wage to rise 2 percent each year. If instead inflation is 6 percent, her real wage will *fall* 2 percent. The worker loses, but the firm gains because it can charge 4 percent more for its products than it anticipated. The worker's wage was fixed by contract, but the firm could raise its prices. On average, winners and losers balance out; inflation does not make the population richer or poorer. Most people, however, worry about their own position, not what happens to the average person.

Lenders and borrowers, because they often enter into fixed nominal contracts, are also affected by inflation. If lenders make loans at 5 percent interest and expect inflation to be 2 percent, they plan to earn a 3 percent real rate of return on their loan. If, however, inflation turns out to be 4 percent, lenders will only earn a 1 percent real rate of return, and borrowers, who were expecting to pay a real interest rate of 3 percent, end up paying only 1 percent. Lenders will lose; borrowers will gain. In other words, unexpected inflation redistributes income from lenders to borrowers.

The composition of the group winning or losing from inflation changes over time. For example, before 1975, people on Social Security and pensions lost out during inflation since Social Security and pensions were, on the whole, fixed in nominal terms. Inflation lowered recipients' real income. Starting in 1975 Social Security payments and many pensions were changed to adjust automatically for changes in the cost of living, so Social Security recipients are no longer losers. Their real income is independent of inflation. (Actually, because of the adjustment method, some say that Social Security recipients actually now gain from inflation since the adjustment more than compensates them for the rise in the price level.)

What we can say about the distributional consequences of inflation is that people who don't expect inflation or who are tied to fixed nominal contracts will likely lose during an inflationary period. However, if these people are rational, they probably won't let it happen again; they'll be prepared for a subsequent inflation. That is, they will change their expectations of inflation.

Expectations of Inflation

Expectations of inflation play a key role in the inflationary process. When expectations of inflation are high, people tend to raise their wages and prices, causing inflation. So, in fact, expectations can become self-fulfilling. Because of the importance of expectations in perpetuating, and perhaps even in creating, inflation, economists have looked carefully at how individuals form expectations. Almost all economists believe that the expectations that people have of inflation are in some sense rational, by which I mean they are based on the best information available, given the cost of that information. But economists differ on what is meant by rational and thus on how those expectations are formed. Some economists argue that rational people will expect the same inflation that is predicted by the economists' model. That is, they form **rational expectations**—*the expectations that the economists' model predicts.* If inflation was, say, 2 percent last year and is 4 percent this year, but the economists' model predicts 0 percent inflation for the coming year, individuals will rationally expect 0 percent inflation.

Other economists argue that rational expectations cannot be defined in terms of economists' models. These economists instead focus on the process by which people develop their expectations. One way people form expectations is to look at conditions that already exist, or have recently existed. Such expectations are called **adaptive expectations**—*expectations based in some way on the past.* Thus, if inflation was 2 percent last year and 4 percent this year, the prediction for inflation will be somewhere around 3 percent. Adaptive

Q.1 True or false? Inflation makes an economy poorer. Explain your answer.

Unexpected inflation redistributes income from lenders to borrowers.

Web Note 13.1
Forecasting Inflation

Deflation

The low inflation of the early 2000s brought fear of a new problem—deflation (a sustained fall in the price level). Deflation is the opposite of inflation and is associated with a number of problems in the economy. One problem is that it may prevent the central bank from lowering the real interest rate as much as it wants to, since with deflation the real interest rate is the sum of the nominal interest rate and the rate of deflation. Thus, if the nominal interest rate is 2 percent and the rate of deflation is 3 percent, the real interest rate is 5 percent. But because people can always hold money rather than bonds, the nominal interest rate cannot fall below 0 percent. Since in a deflationary economy the real interest rate is higher than the nominal interest rate, deflation places a limit on how low the Fed can push the real interest rate. For example, the Fed cannot achieve a goal of 1 percent for real interest rates when the rate of deflation is 3 percent. Even if it lowers the nominal interest rate to 0 percent—the lowest level it can—the Fed cannot reduce the real rate of interest below 3 percent—the

rate of deflation. This means that monetary policy might not be able to lower interest rates enough to stimulate the economy as much as desired.

Another problem of deflation is that it is often associated with large falls in asset prices—specifically stock and real estate prices. Declines in these asset prices can cause serious problems for an economy for two reasons. First, as people see their wealth evaporating, they may cut their current spending, which can decrease aggregate demand and slow the economy. Second, since these assets often serve as collateral for loans, large falls in asset prices can make many financial institutions' liabilities exceed their assets, causing them to become insolvent. Thus, deflation can undermine a country's financial system. This happened in the early 2000s in Japan, making it difficult for the Japanese government to stimulate its economy. It left the Japanese government wondering how to save its banking system from a large-scale default, because such a default would totally undermine any recovery efforts.

Q-2 Name three different types of expectations.

expectations aren't the only type that people use. Sometimes they use **extrapolative expectations**—*expectations that a trend will continue.* For example, say that inflation was 2 percent last year and 4 percent this year; extrapolative expectations would predict 6 percent inflation next year. These are only three of the many reasonable ways people form expectations. Because there is no one economic model that predicts the economy perfectly, there is no way of specifying one rational expectation; there are only reasonable expectations. Individuals use various ways of forming expectations, often shifting suddenly from one way to another.

Since expectations play a key role in policy, shifts in the process of forming expectations can change the way the economy operates. It was precisely such a shift in the formation of expectations that played a key role in the late 1990s, when the economy expanded significantly without generating inflation. Sometime in the early 1990s in the United States, individuals stopped expecting high inflation (which, at the time, meant inflation greater than about 6 percent) and began expecting low inflation (which, at the time, meant inflation lower than 2 percent), and those expectations became self-fulfilling. The United States has continued to have relatively low inflation through the early 2000s.[1]

---

[1]The meaning of the terms "high inflation" and "low inflation" can change over time as people's beliefs about what is "normal inflation" change. This means that the terms high and low, which we will use throughout the chapter, must be interpreted in the context of the time and country being talked about. In the United States in 2008, inflation under 2 percent was still considered low, but because inflation had been within the lower range for a few years, what was considered "high inflation" had changed; in 2008 inflation over 4 percent was considered high. In developing countries, where inflation has often exceeded 50 percent, "high" and "low" inflation have quite different meanings from "high" and "low" inflations in developed countries; for example, 15 percent inflation could be considered low in a developing country.

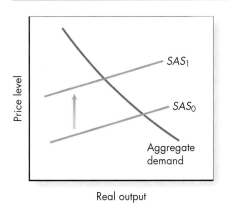

FIGURE 13-1 **Nominal Wages, Productivity, and Inflation**

When nominal wages increase by more than the growth of productivity, the *SAS* curve shifts up, resulting in inflation. When nominal wages increase by less than the growth of productivity, the *SAS* curve shifts down, resulting in deflation.

Productivity, Inflation, and Wages

Two key measures that policy makers use to determine whether inflation may be coming are changes in productivity and changes in wages. Together these measures determine whether or not the short-run aggregate supply curve will be shifting up. The rule of thumb is that wages can increase by the amount that productivity increases without generating any inflationary pressure:

$$\text{Inflation} = \text{Nominal wage increase} - \text{Productivity growth}$$

For example, if productivity is increasing at 2 percent, as it has been in the early 2000s, wages can go up by 2 percent without generating any inflationary pressure. Let's consider another example—the mid-1970s, when productivity growth slowed to 1 percent while wages went up by 6 percent. Inflation was 6 percent −1 percent = 5 percent.

You probably recognize this relationship from an earlier chapter. This is the same relationship that explains how the short-run aggregate supply curve shifts. When nominal wages increase by more than the growth of productivity, the *SAS* curve shifts up as shown in Figure 13-1, resulting in inflation. When nominal wages increase by less than the growth of productivity, the *SAS* curve shifts down, resulting in deflation (a sustained fall in the price level).

Theories of Inflation

Economists hold two slightly different theories of inflation: the quantity theory and the institutional theory. The quantity theory emphasizes the connection between money and inflation; the institutional theory emphasizes the relationship between market structure and price-setting institutions and inflation. The two theories overlap significantly, but because they come to different policy conclusions, it is helpful to consider them separately.

The Quantity Theory of Money and Inflation

The quantity theory of money can be summed up in one sentence: *Inflation is always and everywhere a monetary phenomenon.* If the money supply rises, the price level will rise. If the money supply doesn't rise, the price level won't rise. Forget all the other stuff—it just obscures the connection between money and inflation.

The Quantity Theory of Money

In the quantity theory model, inflation is caused by growth in the money supply. It focuses on the equation of exchange:

$MV = PQ$

The Equation of Exchange   The quantity theory of money centers on the **equation of exchange,** *an equation stating that the quantity of money times the velocity of money equals the price level times the quantity of real goods sold.* This equation is

$$MV = PQ$$

where:

    M = Quantity of money

    V = Velocity of money

    P = Price level

    Q = Quantity of real goods sold

Q is the real output of the economy (real GDP) and P is the price level, so PQ is the economy's nominal output (nominal GDP). V, the **velocity of money,** is *the number of times per year, on average, a dollar goes around to generate a dollar's worth of income.* Put another way, velocity is the amount of income per year generated by a dollar of money. Since $MV = PQ$, MV also equals nominal output. Thus, if there's $100 of money in the economy and velocity is 20, nominal GDP is $2,000. We can calculate V by dividing nominal GDP by the money supply. Let's take the United States as an example. In the United States in 2006, nominal GDP was approximately $13 trillion and M was approximately $1,300 billion (using M_1), so velocity was about GDP/M = 10, meaning each dollar in the economy circulated enough to support approximately $10 in total income.

Velocity Is Constant   The equation of exchange is a tautology, meaning it is true by definition. What changes it from a tautology to the quantity theory are three assumptions. The first assumption is that velocity remains constant (or changes at a predictable rate). Money is spent only so fast; how fast is determined by the economy's institutional structure, such as how close individuals live to stores, how people are paid (weekly, biweekly, or monthly), and what sources of credit are available. (Can you go to the store and buy something on credit, that is, without handing over cash?) This institutional structure changes slowly, quantity theorists argue, so velocity won't fluctuate very much. Next year, velocity will be approximately the same as this year.

If velocity can be predicted, the quantity theory can be used to predict how much nominal GDP will grow if we know how much the money supply grows. For example, if the money supply goes up 6 percent and velocity is predicted to be constant, the quantity theory of money predicts that nominal GDP will go up by 6 percent.

Something that is determined outside the model is called autonomous.

Three assumptions of quantity theory:

1. Velocity is constant.
2. Real output is independent of money supply.
3. Causation goes from money to prices.

Real Output Is Independent of the Money Supply   The second assumption is that Q is independent of the money supply. That is, Q is autonomous, meaning real output is determined by forces outside those forces in the quantity theory. If Q grows, it is because of factors that affect the real economy. Thus, policy analysis about the real economy based on the quantity theory focuses on the real economy—the supply side of the economy, not the demand side.

This assumption makes analyzing the economy a lot easier than if the financial and real sectors are interrelated and if real economic activity is influenced by financial changes. It separates two puzzles: how the real economy works and how the price level and financial sector work. Instead of having two different jigsaw puzzles all mixed up, each puzzle can be worked separately. The quantity theory doesn't say there aren't interconnections between the real and financial sectors, but it does say that most of these interconnections involve short-run considerations. The quantity theory is primarily concerned with the long run.

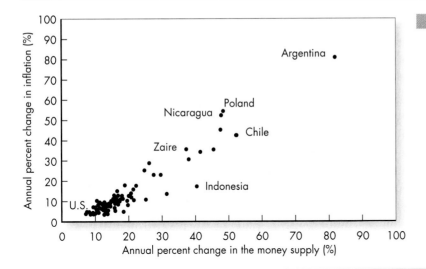

FIGURE 13-2 **Inflation and Money Growth, 1960–1990**

The empirical evidence that supports the quantity theory of money is most convincing in countries that experience significant inflation. Argentina and Chile are examples where high money growth has accompanied high rates of inflation.

Source: Federal Reserve Bank of Minneapolis.

Causation Goes from Money to Prices   With both V (velocity) and Q (quantity of output) unaffected by changes in M (money supply), the only thing that can change is P (price level). Given the two assumptions so far, either prices or money could be the driving force. The quantity theory makes the additional assumption that causation goes from money to prices.

With these three assumptions, the equation of exchange becomes the quantity theory of money:

$$M\overline{V} \rightarrow P\overline{Q}$$

In its simplest terms, the **quantity theory of money** says that *the price level varies in response to changes in the quantity of money.* Another way to write the quantity theory of money is: $\%\Delta M \rightarrow \%\Delta P$. If the money supply goes up 20 percent, prices go up 20 percent. If the money supply goes down 5 percent, the price level goes down 5 percent.

Examples of Money's Role in Inflation   As you can see in Figure 13-2, which plots inflation against the money supply for 110 countries from 1960 to 1990, there is a relationship between money supply growth and inflation. The connection between growth in the money supply and inflation is especially evident for large inflations such as in Argentina, Poland, Chile, and Zaire. For example, in Argentina inflation and money supply growth were both growing at about 85 percent per year. Russia in the 1990s, when the Russian government was forced to print enormous amounts of money to pay its bills, is another example. As a result, in both cases inflation blew up into hyperinflation.

In Figure 13-2, you can also see a large cluster of countries where inflation is below 10 percent. When inflation is 10 percent or below, the relationship in the short run between money and inflation isn't so clear. Consider the United States. Beginning in the mid-1970s, both inflation and money supply rose, with inflation exceeding 8 percent in some years. Inflation remained high for about six years and people began to expect that the high inflation would continue. However, in late 1979 and the early 1980s, the Fed began to fight inflation by decreasing the growth of the money supply significantly. But initially inflation did not decline; instead, unemployment jumped from 7 to 10 percent and inflation remained high. So the short-run connection between inflation and money did not exist. Eventually inflation did fall—to 4 percent in 1984 and to below 2 percent in the early 2000s—even though the money supply kept growing quite fast.

Q₃ What's the difference between the equation of exchange and the quantity theory of money?

Q₄ According to the quantity theory of money, what should the Fed do to lower inflation?

The Keeper of the Classical Faith: Milton Friedman

One of the most important economists of the 20th century is Milton Friedman, who died in 2006 at the age of 94. In macroeconomics, Friedman is best known for his support of the quantity theory.

By most accounts, Friedman was a headstrong student. He didn't simply accept the truths his teachers laid out. If he didn't agree, he argued strongly for his own belief. He was very bright, and his ideas were generally logical and convincing. He needed to be both persistent and intelligent to maintain and promote his views in spite of strong opposition.

Throughout the Keynesian years of the 1950s and 1960s, Friedman stood up and argued for the quantity theory, keeping it alive. During this period, Classical economics was called *mon-*

Nobel Prize Winner Milton Friedman

etarism, and because Friedman was such a strong advocate of the quantity theory, he was considered the leader of the monetarists.

Friedman argued that fiscal policy simply didn't work. It led to expansions in the size of government. He also opposed an activist monetary policy. The effects of monetary policy, he said, were too variable for it to be useful in guiding the economy. He called for a steady growth in the money supply, and argued consistently for a laissez-faire policy by government.

Friedman has made his mark in both microeconomics and macroeconomics. In the 1970s, his ideas caught hold and helped spawn a renewal of the quantity theory. He was awarded the Nobel Prize in economics in 1976.

The quantity theory view that printing money causes inflation is seen in the 18th-century satirical drawing.

Germany is another example. In the early 1990s, the German central bank felt Germany's inflation was too high. It cut the growth of the money supply considerably. The German economy fell into recession and remained in that recession through 1996. Again, inflation eventually did fall, but not until the late 1990s. Experiences like this are why economists emphasize that *there can be a long and variable lag in the connection between money growth and inflation.* For inflations below 10 percent, then, policy maker's conventional wisdom is that, in the short run, a change in money supply growth initially affects output and only later, possibly, does it affect inflation.

Why Central Banks Increase the Money Supply If the connection between large increases in the money supply and inflation are so well known, you may well be wondering why some central banks continue to increase the money supply at such high rates. Consider Zimbabwe, which has had inflation well above 1,000 percent through much of the early 2000s. Why doesn't the central bank simply stop increasing the money supply? The answer lies in the political structure of the country and the failure of the government to control spending. The Zimbabwe government is running huge budget deficits. To pay for the goods it is buying, it has to issue bonds, but no one wants to buy the bonds. If the government cannot sell its bonds, it will be in default, which would result in what many believe would be a complete breakdown of the economy. So the central bank of Zimbabwe has chosen to buy the bonds, which it does by printing money. So the underlying cause of the inflation in Zimbabwe is really the government budget deficit, which forces the central bank to buy the bonds to finance the deficit, which in turn leads to hyperinflation.

Financing the deficit by expansionary monetary policy is not costless. The inflation that results from the increases in the money supply works as a type of tax on individuals and is often called an **inflation tax** *(an implicit tax on the holders of cash and the holders of any obligations specified in nominal terms).* Inflation is considered a tax because it reduces the value of cash and other nominal obligations.

A New Inflation Equation?

The quantity theory has not done such a good job of predicting inflation in recent years, which has sent economists out searching for the reasons why. One reason is that financial innovations have caused the velocity of money to change in ways that cannot be easily predicted, making it impossible to predict inflation based on money supply growth. A second reason is globalization, which has changed the nature of competitive institutions. To take account of that globalization, researchers at the Federal Reserve Bank of Dallas have developed a new variation of the quantity theory that considers how globalization affects the relationship between money and inflation, and output growth. They find that inflation varies inversely with output growth not only in the domestic economy, but also with growth of global output—output growth in all countries. This means that even if the domestic money supply increases

and domestic output doesn't grow much, if global output is increasing significantly, then the result will not be significant inflation.

The relative importance of domestic and global output depends on country size, consumers' preference for domestic goods, ease of substitution of domestic for foreign goods, and the ability of a country to redeploy its workers who face global competition. Dallas Fed researchers argue that "had we understood the links between foreign output growth, trade, and inflation, we might have contemplated the booming 1990s with less anxiety about inflation."

The revised equation they are working on is still a work in progress, but it shows the way that economists work—they continually test their models against the empirical evidence, and when the models and evidence don't match, they work on modifying the models in a reasonable way to make them match.

The point of this example is that central banks know that issuing large quantities of money will cause inflation. What they don't know, and what the policy discussions are about, is whether it's worse to have the inflation or the unpleasant alternatives of a recession, or perhaps even a breakdown of the entire economy. Thus, the debate about monetary policy is not about whether the inflation is caused by the issuance of too much money, but whether countries' budget deficits can be ended.

Q-5 Why do some central banks issue large quantities of money if they know that doing so will cause inflation?

The Institutional Theory of Inflation

The alternative to the quantity theory is the institutional theory of inflation. Supporters of the institutional theory of inflation accept much of the quantity theory—money and inflation do move together. Where they differ is in what they see as the cause and the effect. According to the quantity theory of money, changes in the money supply cause changes in the price level. The direction of causation goes from left to right:

$$MV \rightarrow PQ$$

Institutional theorists see it the other way around. Increases in prices force government to increase the money supply or cause unemployment. The direction of causation goes from right to left:

$$MV \leftarrow PQ$$

According to the institutional theory of inflation, the source of inflation is in the price-setting process of firms. When setting prices, firms and individuals find it easier to raise prices than to lower them and do not take into account the effect of their pricing decisions on the price level.

Q-6 Use the equation of exchange to demonstrate the difference between the quantity theory and the institutional theory of inflation.

The institutional theory of inflation focuses on the institutional and structural aspects of an economy, as well as the money supply, as important causes of inflation.

Inflation Targeting

One of the big debates about Fed policy concerns whether the Fed should preannounce a policy about what it will do if inflation is at different levels. Such announcements are known as inflation targeting. With inflation targeting, the Fed commits itself to tightening the money supply and raising interest rates if inflation exceeds a certain level. Advocates of inflation targeting argue that it provides better assurances for investors that the central bank will fight inflation, and thus holds inflationary expectations down. They point to the success of countries such as New Zealand, which introduced inflation targeting in 1989 when a law was passed that required the Reserve Bank of New Zealand to keep consumer price inflation between 0 and 3 percent a year, a target agreed on by the government and the central bank. After averaging 10 percent a year in the 1980s, New Zealand's inflation rate fell in the early 1990s and averaged below 3 percent per year thereafter.

Advocates of inflation targeting argue that this experience, and ones like it, show that inflation targeting helps central banks establish credibility in their resolve to fight inflation. Critics of inflation targeting argue that explicit inflation targeting has problems. Inflation is hard to measure, and sometimes the price level goes up because of reasons that have little to do with forces creating sustainable pressure for inflation. According to critics, having an inflation target could force the central bank to raise interest rates and cut money supply growth when there was no need to do so, because it is too hard for the bank to distinguish the differences between sustainable and temporary inflation pressures. They argue that it is better to have an *implicit inflation target*, which can be adjusted slightly for the particular situation, which allows the bank to establish credibility, while at the same time giving it a bit of "wiggle room" to take account of particular situations. To date, the Fed has followed the critics, and has not adopted an explicit inflation target, but it has an implicit target, which is to keep inflation below about 2.5 percent.

Institutional theorists see the nominal wage- and price-setting process as generating inflation.

Put slightly differently, the institutional theory sees the nominal wage- and price-setting process as generating inflation. As one group pushes up its nominal wage or price, another group responds by doing the same. More groups follow until, finally, the first group finds that its relative wage or price hasn't increased. Then the entire process starts again. Once the nominal wage and price levels have risen, government has two options: It can either ratify the increase by increasing the money supply, thereby accepting the inflation, or it can refuse to ratify it. If it refuses to ratify it, firms will not be able to sell all they want at the higher price and will cut production and lay off workers (firms generally don't lower nominal wages). Unemployment will rise.

Supporters of the institutional theory of inflation argue that in most sectors of the economy, competition works slowly. Social pressures, as well as the invisible hand, influence wages and prices. The result is that even when there is substantial unemployment and considerable excess supply of goods, existing workers can still put an upward push on nominal wages, and existing firms can put an upward push on nominal prices.

Q-7 How would a quantity theorist likely respond to an insider/outsider model of inflation?

To get a better picture of how existing workers can push up wages despite substantial unemployment, let's consider the **insider/outsider model,** *an institutionalist story of inflation where insiders bid up wages and outsiders are unemployed.* Insiders are current business owners and workers who have good jobs with excellent long-run prospects. Outsiders are everyone else. Insiders receive above-equilibrium wages, profits, and rents. If the world were competitive, their wages, profits, and rents would be pushed down to the equilibrium level. To prevent this from happening, according to the insider/outsider model, insiders develop sociological and institutional barriers that prevent outsiders from competing away those above-equilibrium wages, profits, and rents. Such barriers include unions, laws restricting the firing of workers, and brand recognition. Because of those barriers, outsiders (often minorities) must take low-paying dead-end jobs or attempt to undertake marginal businesses that pay little return for many hours worked. Even when outsiders do find better jobs or business opportunities, they are first to be fired and their businesses are the first to suffer in a recession. Thus, outsiders have much higher unemployment rates than insiders. For example, in the United States, blacks tend to be outsiders; black unemployment rates have consistently been twice as high as white unemployment rates for the same age groups.

In short, the institutional theories of inflation emphasize that our economy is only partially competitive. The invisible hand is often thwarted by social and political forces. Such partially competitive economies are often characterized by insiders' monopolies. Insiders get the jobs and are paid monopoly wage levels. Outsiders are not employed at those higher wages. Imperfect competition allows workers (and firms) to raise nominal wages (and prices) even as unemployment (and excess supply of goods) exists. Then, as other insiders do likewise, the price level rises. This increase in the price level lowers workers' real wages. In response, workers further raise their nominal wages to protect their real wages. The result is an ongoing chase in which the insiders protect their real wages, while outsiders (the unemployed) suffer. (If the ideas of nominal and real are unclear to you, a review of earlier chapters may be in order.)

> Institutionalists believe that, under current conditions, the costs of unemployment are borne more heavily by minorities and other outsiders.

> Web Note 13.2
> WWII Income Policies

Demand-Pull and Cost-Push Inflation

Quantity and institutional theories of inflation are sometimes differentiated as demand-pull inflation and cost-push inflation. When the majority of industries are at close to capacity and they experience increases in demand, we say there's demand-pull pressure. The inflation that results is called **demand-pull inflation**—*inflation that occurs when the economy is at or above potential output*. Demand-pull inflation is generally characterized by shortages of goods and shortages of workers. Because there's excess demand, firms know that if they raise their prices, they'll still be able to sell their goods and workers know if they raise their wages, they will still be employed.

When significant proportions of markets (or one very important market, such as the labor market or the oil market) experience price rises not related to demand pressure, we say that there is cost-push pressure. The resulting inflation is **cost-push inflation**—*inflation that occurs when the economy is below potential output*. In cost-push inflation, because there is no excess demand (there may actually be excess supply), firms that raise their prices are not sure demand will be sufficient to sell off their goods and workers are not sure that after raising their wage they will all be employed. But the ones who actually do the pushing are fairly sure they won't be the ones who can't sell off their goods or the ones fired. A classic cost-push example occurred in the 1970s when the Organization of Petroleum Exporting Countries raised its price on oil, triggering cost-push inflation.

Notice that in much of the discussion of inflation I did not use these distinctions. The reason is that although demand-pull and cost-push pressures can be catalysts for starting inflation, they are not causes of continued inflation. The reality is that in an ongoing inflation, cost-push or demand-pull forces become intertwined. As Alfred Marshall (the 19th century English economist who originated supply and demand analysis) said, it is impossible to separate the roles of supply and demand in influencing price, just as it is impossible to say which blade of the scissors is cutting a sheet of paper.

> In an ongoing inflation, cost-push and demand-pull forces become intertwined.

Inflation and Unemployment: The Phillips Curve

Now that we've been through two main theories of inflation, let's talk about anti-inflation policy—how do policy makers keep inflation down? One obvious policy is to keep aggregate demand low—hold down growth of the money supply and run

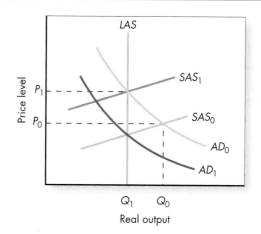

FIGURE 13-3 **Addressing Inflation with Monetary Policy**

When aggregate demand and short-run aggregate supply intersect at a level of output that is greater than potential output, inflationary pressures rise. Government can either keep output high and have low unemployment but higher inflation or lower aggregate demand to keep inflation low but accept higher unemployment. This illustrates the trade-off some policy makers believe exists between inflation and unemployment.

contractionary fiscal policy. This policy can be seen in our standard AS/AD model. Figure 13-3 shows a situation where with aggregate demand at AD_0 and aggregate supply at SAS_0, the quantity of aggregate demand exceeds potential output, a situation with inflationary pressures.

Short-run equilibrium is at a price level of P_0 and output Q_0, which means that output exceeds potential output. This creates upward pressure on the price level toward P_1. To hold down inflationary pressures, the government must shift the AD curve back to AD_1. But governments are also under pressure to hold output high, and the government likely doesn't realize that output is above potential. Often, the only way government can know for sure is that inflation starts increasing. So, government can either keep aggregate demand high at AD_0 (and keep output high and unemployment low but accept higher inflation) or lower aggregate demand to AD_1 to keep inflation low but accept lower output and higher unemployment.

Since higher output and lower unemployment are often associated with higher inflation, some policy makers have suggested that there is a trade-off between inflation and unemployment.

That trade-off can be represented graphically, as shown in Figure 13-4(a). The **short-run Phillips curve** is *a downward-sloping curve showing the relationship between inflation and unemployment when expectations of inflation are constant.* In a Phillips curve diagram, unemployment is measured on the horizontal axis; inflation is on the vertical axis. The Phillips curve shows us the possible short-run combinations of those two phenomena. It tells us that when unemployment is low, say 4 percent, inflation tends to be high, say 4 percent (point A in Figure 13-4(a)). It also tells us that if we want to lower inflation, say to 1 percent, we must be willing to accept high unemployment, say 7 percent (point B in Figure 13-4(a)).

History of the Phillips Curve

The Phillips curve began as an empirical relationship and was discovered by, you guessed it, an economist named Phillips. In the 1950s and 1960s, when unemployment was high, inflation was low; when unemployment was low, inflation was high. Figure 13-4(b) shows this empirical relationship for the United States for the years 1954–1968, when the short-run Phillips curve became part of how economists looked at the economy.

Because the short-run Phillips curve seemed to represent a relatively stable trade-off, in the 1960s the short-run Phillips curve began to play a central role in discussions

FIGURE 13-4 (A AND B) **The Phillips Curve Trade-Off**

Analyzing the empirical relationship between unemployment and inflation from 1954 to 1968—shown in (**b**)—led economists to believe there was the relatively stable Phillips curve which, for policy choices, could be represented by the smooth Phillips curve in (**a**). Source: Economic Report of the President.

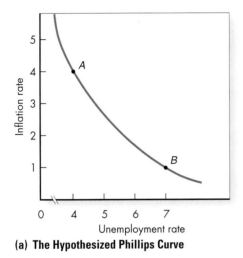

(a) **The Hypothesized Phillips Curve**

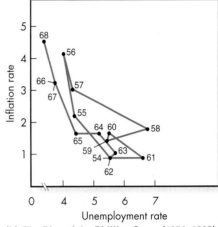

(b) **The Rise of the Phillips Curve (1954–1968)**

of macroeconomic policy. Republicans (often advised by supporters of the quantity theory) generally favored contractionary monetary and fiscal policy, which maintained high unemployment and low inflation (a point like B in Figure 13-4(a)). Democrats (often advised by supporters of the institutional theory) generally favored expansionary monetary and fiscal policies, which brought about low unemployment but high inflation (a point like A in Figure 13-4(a)).

In the early 1970s, however, the empirical short-run Phillips curve relationship seemed to break down. The data no longer seemed to show a trade-off between unemployment and inflation. Instead, when unemployment was high, inflation was also high. This phenomenon is termed **stagflation**—*the combination of high and accelerating inflation and high unemployment.* Since that time, the Phillips curve has been ephemeral—sometimes seeming as if it were reappearing, and then disappearing again.

The Long-Run and Short-Run Phillips Curves

Economists have explained this constantly changing relationship between inflation and unemployment by incorporating expectations of inflation into the analysis. They argue that actual inflation depends both on supply and demand forces and on how much inflation people expect. If people expect a lot of inflation, they will ask for higher nominal wage and price increases. To incorporate expectations into the Phillips curve it is necessary to distinguish between a short-run Phillips curve and a long-run Phillips curve.

At all points on the short-run Phillips curve, expectations of inflation (the rise in the price level that the average person expects) are fixed. Thus, on the short-run Phillips curve, expectations of inflation can differ from actual inflation. *At all points on the long-run Phillips curve, expectations of inflation are equal to actual inflation.* The **long-run Phillips curve** is thought to be *a vertical curve at the unemployment rate consistent with potential output.* (See the vertical curve in the margin.) It shows the trade-off (or complete lack thereof) when expectations of inflation equal actual inflation. Economists argue

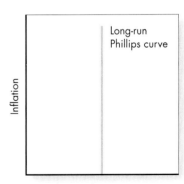

The long-run Phillips curve is vertical; it shows the lack of a trade-off between inflation and unemployment when expectations of inflation equal actual inflation. Expectations of inflation do not change along a short-run Phillips curve.

FIGURE 13-5 (A AND B)   **Inflation Expectations and the Phillips Curve**

Both (a) and (b) show how an increase in aggregate demand can increase output initially. Eventually, however, the economy will return to potential output but with a higher rate of inflation. The economy begins at point A. Initially, the aggregate demand curve moves from AD_0 to AD_1, pushing output above its potential in (a). As firms compete for labor, wages increase. To cover increasing costs, firms raise their prices. The combination of lower unemployment and higher inflation is shown by point B in (b). As workers realize that inflation is not 0 percent, but rather 4 percent, they will ask for further wage increases. Ultimately this process shifts the SAS curve to SAS_2 and the short-run Phillips curve to PC_1 (along which expected inflation equals 4 percent) and the economy to point C. The economy is once again in equilibrium. Unemployment has returned to 5.5 percent, but inflation is now 4 percent.

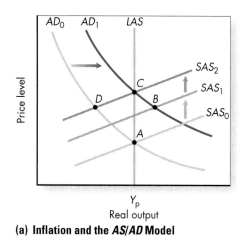

(a) **Inflation and the *AS/AD* Model**

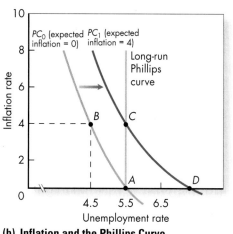

(b) **Inflation and the Phillips Curve**

Draw the long-run Phillips curve. Why does it have its shape?

The Long-Run and Short-Run Phillips Curves

that expectations of inflation to explain why the short-run Phillips curve relationship broke down in the 1970s.

Let's consider how expectations of inflation can explain high inflation and high un-employment in reference to both our *AS/AD* model and the Phillips curve model. Say the economy starts out with a rate of unemployment consistent with potential output. So there is no inflation, and the economy is at its potential output. (Wages can still be going up by the rate of productivity growth, say it's 3 percent, but the price level is not rising.) Further assume that individuals are expecting zero inflation; that is, if they get a 3 percent wage increase, they expect their real income to rise by 3 percent. This starting point is represented by point A in Figure 13-5 (a and b).

In Figure 13-5(a) you can see that short-run aggregate supply and aggregate demand intersect at potential income at point A. Since the economy is in both short-run and long-run equilibrium, there are no forces moving the economy away from point A in the *AS/AD* model. Point A in Figure 13-5(b) is also on both the long-run and short-run Phillips curve. This means that point A is a sustainable combination of inflation and unemployment—the situation can continue indefinitely. The only sustainable combi-nation of inflation and unemployment rates on the short-run Phillips curve is where it intersects the long-run Phillips curve, because that is the only unemployment rate consistent with the economy's potential income.

Moving Off the Long-Run Phillips Curve   Now let's say that the government decides to increase aggregate demand, shifting the AD curve from AD_0 to AD_1. This pushes output above its potential, Y_p, as in Figure 13-5(a). That will increase the de-mand for labor, and that competition for labor will push wages up by more than the increase in productivity as firms compete for the small pool of unemployed workers.

Say wages rise by 7 percent. Initially that increase is enough to satisfy workers who are still assumed to expect zero inflation. But notice that, unless potential output increases, there is a problem—their expectation will not be met. Since productivity is still rising by only 3 percent while wages are rising by 7 percent, the higher wage costs force firms to raise their prices by 4 percent, shifting the SAS curve up from SAS_0 to SAS_1. The economy moves to point B. This same point B is shown in the Phillips curve diagram where the economy is still on the short-run Phillips curve. Unemployment falls from 5.5 to 4.5 percent and inflation rises from 0 to 4 percent. But point B is not on the long-run Phillips curve and actual inflation exceeds expected inflation.

Moving Back onto the Long-Run Phillips Curve   Since expectations of inflation differ from actual inflation, point B is not a sustainable position. Since it is beyond potential income, Y_p, the SAS curve will continue to shift up. Eventually workers realize that their real wages aren't increasing by 7 percent; they are rising by only 3 percent. As workers come to expect the 4 percent inflation, they ask for higher wages to compensate for that inflation. The short-run Phillips curve will shift up from PC_0 to PC_1 since each short-run Phillips curve represents the trade-off for a given level of inflationary expectation. As wages increase, the SAS curve shifts up to SAS_2. As the price level rises, the dollars that people hold are worth less, causing the quantity of aggregate demand to decline and the economy to move to point C. Output returns to its potential, unemployment returns to its target rate, and the economy returns to a long-run equilibrium at point C on the long-run Phillips curve. Unemployment is once again at its target rate, but inflation, and expectations of inflation, are now 4 percent.

The general relationship is the following: Any time unemployment is lower than the target level of unemployment consistent with potential output, inflation and expectations of inflation will be increasing. That means that the short-run Phillips curve will be shifting up. The short-run Phillips curve will continue to shift up until output is no longer above potential. Thus, any level of inflation is consistent with the target level of unemployment if the cause of that inflation is expectations of inflation. Economists used these expectations of inflation to explain the experience in the 1970s. The economy had been pushed beyond its potential, which had caused inflation to accelerate. (This explanation was supplemented with discussions of supply-side inflationary pressures caused by the large rise in oil prices that occurred at that time.)

Stagflation and the Phillips Curve

The problem with point C is that although the economy is back at potential output, inflationary expectations are built into people's price-setting behavior. That expectational inflation can be eliminated only if aggregate demand falls, pushing the economy to a higher level of unemployment that exceeds the target rate. That is how economists explained the stagflation in the late 1970s and early 1980s. To end stagflation, the government attempted to push down the inflation through contractionary aggregate demand policy. The lower aggregate demand (shifting aggregate demand back from AD_1 to AD_0) pushed the economy to a position such as point D in Figure 13-5. At point D, unemployment exceeds the target rate. The higher unemployment puts downward pressure on wages and prices, shifting the short-run Phillips curve down.

As you can see, the long-run Phillips curve tells us whether there will be upward pressure on the price level (when the economy is to the left of the long-run Phillips curve, and unemployment is below the target rate) or downward pressure on the price level (when the economy is to the right of the long-run Phillips curve, and unemployment is above the target rate).

Q.9 If the economy is at point A on the Phillips curve below, what prediction would you make for unemployment and inflation?

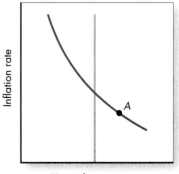

The Relationship between Inflation and Growth

The on-going debates about macro policy can be understood by thinking back to our discussion of low and high potential output and their relation to inflationary pressure. A graph of these is shown in Figure 13-6(a). Economists generally agree that below low potential output there will be no inflationary, and possibly some deflationary, pressures. They also agree that above high potential output there will be significant inflationary pressures. The degree of inflationary pressure between these two extremes is ambiguous. Since no one knows precisely where potential output is, there is usually a debate within this range.

The government wants to choose as high an output level as possible yet keep inflation low and prevent it from accelerating. At what point it can do that is the subject of much debate. Supporters of the institutional theory of inflation tend to argue that it is best to err on the high side, with policy aiming for high potential output as in Figure 13-5(a). Economists who focus on the quantity theory tend to argue that it is best to err on the low side, with policy aiming at low potential output.

Quantity Theory and the Inflation/Growth Trade-Off

I suspect many of you will agree that erring on the high side in terms of real output makes the most sense. If that were the entire trade-off, such a reaction is probably right. But supporters of the quantity theory point out a problem with that reasoning, which might be called the "little bit pregnant problem." At the beginning of a pregnancy, it's true you are only a little bit pregnant, but that "little bit" has initiated a set of cellular changes that will fundamentally alter your life. Supporters of the quantity theory say it is the same with a small rise in the price level: You can't have a "little bit" of inflation. That little bit is setting in motion a series of events that will make the inflation grow and grow, unless the government gives up its attempt to achieve a high rate of output. Their solution to prevent inflation is abstinence—just say no to any rise in the price level.

Those who support the quantity theory argue that erring on the low side pays off—it stops any chance of inflation. It establishes credibility of the Fed's resolve not to increase the money supply. If some inflation is allowed and the Fed loses credibility, that

Q.10 Why do quantity theorists believe that government should err on the side of lower output and a lower chance of inflation?

FIGURE 13-6 (A AND B) The Inflation/Growth Trade-Off

Quantity theorists are much more likely to err on the side of preventing inflation, arguing that an ongoing inflation will begin at low potential output. They emphasize the trade-off shown in (b). Institutionalists are more likely to argue that the inflation threshold is at high potential output.

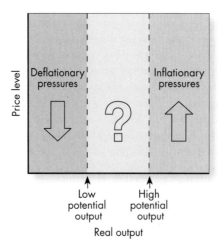

(a) Inflationary Pressures

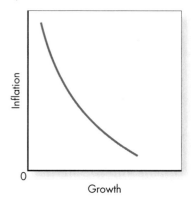

(b) Growth/Inflation Trade-Off

inflation undermines the long-run growth prospects of the economy, and hence causes future levels of potential income to be lower than they otherwise would be. Put another way, inflation undermines long-run growth; abstinence creates the environment for long-run growth. Thus, for quantity theorists, while there is no long-run trade-off between inflation and unemployment, there is a long-run trade-off between inflation and growth: High inflation leads to lower growth.

Low inflation leads to higher growth for a variety of reasons. Low inflation reduces price uncertainty, making it easier for businesses to invest in future production. Businesses can more easily enter into long-term contracts when inflation is low, which lowers the cost of doing business. Low inflation also makes using money much easier. When inflation is high, people spend more time trying to avoid the costs of inflation, which diverts their energies away from productive activities that would lead to growth.

The hypothesized relationship between inflation and growth is shown in Figure 13-6(b). For quantity theorists, even if there is a short-run relationship between inflation and unemployment, it is precarious for government to try to take advantage of it, because doing so can undermine the long-run growth potential of the economy. For quantity theorists, government policy creating an environment of price-level stability is the policy most likely to lead to high rates of growth. They suggest that the reason for the success of the economy in the late 1990s and early 2000s was that people believed that the Fed would fight inflation should it appear. Solid empirical evidence one way or the other, however, does not yet exist.

Institutional Theory and the Inflation/Growth Trade-Off

Other economists, mainly supporters of the institutional theory of inflation, are less sure about this negative relationship between inflation and growth. They agree that price-level rises have the potential of generating inflation, and that high accelerating inflation undermines growth, but they do not agree that all price-level increases start an inflationary process. The lower unemployment rate accompanying the inflation is so nice, and if the government is really careful—I mean really, really careful—it can avoid reaching the point where the little bit of rise in price level starts the monster of inflation growing within the economy. And besides, if inflation gets started, the government has some medicine that will rid the economy of the inflation relatively easily.

The real-world difference between the two views can be seen in the debate about monetary policy in the early 2000s, when the unemployment rate fell to around 4 percent. Until then, potential income had been estimated at an unemployment rate of 5.5 to 6 percent. So it seemed as if the economy was operating significantly beyond low-level potential output. But inflation remained low, at about 2–3 percent. Economists who focus on the quantity theory argued that inflation was just around the corner, and that unless the government instituted contractionary aggregate demand policy, the seeds of inflation would be sown. Other economists argued that institutional changes in the labor market had reduced the inflation threat and that more expansionary policy was called for. The Fed followed a path between the two. Initially, inflation did not rise, but instead fell as the economy slowed and unemployment rose. It was at that point that, for some economists, the policy concern changed from inflation to deflation. Whether inflation would have risen had growth continued was unclear. Then in 2004, inflation began to reappear, and some economists complained that the Fed had been too expansionary. Inflation of about 2–3 percent continued through 2008, and the Fed had critics on both sides—some saying that its monetary policy was too tight and others saying it was too loose.

Web Note 13.3
The Fed and Growth

Conclusion

The quantity and institutional theories of inflation, growth, and unemployment reflect two consistent but different worldviews. The institutional theorists see a world in which sociological and institutional factors interact with market forces, keeping the economy in a perpetual disequilibrium when considered in an economic framework. The quantity theorists see a world in which market forces predominate and institutional and sociological factors are insignificant. The overall economy is in continual equilibrium. These two theories carry over to economists' analyses of the central policy issue facing most governments as they decide on their monetary and fiscal policies: the trade-off between inflation and unemployment and growth. These different worldviews are an important reason why there are disagreements about policy, and the debate will likely continue for a long time.

Summary

- The winners in inflation are people who can raise their wages or prices and still keep their jobs or sell their goods. The losers are people who can't raise their wages or prices. On average, winners and losers balance out.

- People form expectations in many ways. Three ways are to base expectations on economic models, on an average of the past, and on a trend.

- A basic rule of thumb to predict inflation is: Inflation equals nominal wage increases minus productivity growth.

- The equation of exchange is $MV = PQ$; it becomes the quantity theory when velocity is constant, real output is independent of the money supply, and causation goes from money to prices. The quantity theory says that the price level varies in direct response to changes in the quantity of money. That is,

$$\%\Delta M \to \%\Delta P$$

- Central banks sometimes print money knowing that it will lead to inflation because the alternative might be a breakdown of the economy.

- The institutional theory of inflation sees the source of inflation in the wage-and-price setting institutions; it sees the direction of causation going from price increases to money increases.

- The long-run Phillips curve allows expectations of inflation to change; it is generally seen as vertical.

- The short-run Phillips curve holds expectations constant. It is generally seen as downward-sloping and shifts up when expectations of inflation rise and shifts down when expectations of inflation fall.

- Quantity theorists see a long-run trade-off between inflation and growth; the higher inflation, the lower the growth rate. Institutional theorists are less sure about this trade-off.

Key Terms

adaptive
  expectations (*315*)
cost-push inflation (*323*)
demand-pull
  inflation (*323*)
equation of
  exchange (*318*)

extrapolative
  expectations (*316*)
inflation tax (*320*)
insider/outsider
  model (*322*)
long-run Phillips
  curve (*325*)

quantity theory
  of money (*319*)
rational
  expectations (*315*)

short-run Phillips
  curve (*324*)
stagflation (*325*)
velocity of money (*318*)

Questions for Thought and Review

1. Why do lenders lose out in inflation? Under what conditions would they not lose out?   LO1

2. If you base your expectations of inflation on what has happened in the past, what kind of expectations are you demonstrating?   LO2

3. If productivity growth is 3 percent and wage increases are 5 percent, what would you predict inflation would be?   LO2

4. What three assumptions turn the equation of exchange into the quantity theory of money?   LO3

5. What does the quantity theory predict will happen to inflation if the money supply rises 10 percent?   LO3

6. Why did the relationship between growth in the money supply and inflation break down in the 1990s?   LO3

7. For what countries is the connection between the growth in the money supply and inflation still evident? What accounts for this?   LO3

8. If governments are aware that increases in the money supply cause inflation, why do some countries increase the money supply by significant amounts anyway?   LO3

9. Define the inflation tax. Who pays it?   LO3

10. Who is more likely to support monetary rules—a quantity theorist or an institutionalist? Explain your answer.   LO3

11. What is the direction of causation between money and prices according to the institutional theory of inflation?   LO4

12. What is the insider/outsider theory of inflation? Would quantity or institutional theorists likely believe this theory?   LO4

13. What would Alfred Marshall likely say about the cost-push/demand-pull distinction?   LO4

14. Draw both a short-run and a long-run Phillips curve. What does each say about the relationship between inflation and unemployment?   LO5

15. If people's expectations of inflation didn't change, would the economy move from a short-run to a long-run Phillips curve?   LO5

16. The Phillips curve is just a figment of economists' imagination. True or false?   LO5

17. What is the reasoning behind the view that there is a trade-off between inflation and growth?   LO6

Problems and Exercises

18. People's perception of inflation often differs from actual inflation.
    a. List five goods that you buy relatively frequently.
    b. Looking in old newspapers (found in the library on microfiche), locate sales prices for these goods since

1950, finding one price every five years or so. Determine the average annual price rise for each good from 1950 to today.
    c. Compare that price with the rise in the consumer price index.   LO2

19. Assume the money supply is $500, the velocity of money is 8, and the price level is $2. Using the quantity theory of money:
    a. Determine the level of real output.
    b. Determine the level of nominal output.
    c. Assuming velocity remains constant, what will happen if the money supply rises 20 percent?
    d. If the government established price controls and also raised the money supply 20 percent, what would happen?
    e. How would you judge whether the assumption of fixed velocity is reasonable?   LO3

20. In the early 1990s, Argentina stopped increasing the money supply and fixed the exchange rate of the Argentine austral at 10,000 to the dollar. It then renamed the Argentine currency the "peso" and cut off four zeros so that one peso equaled one dollar. Inflation slowed substantially. After this was done, the following observations were made. Explain why these observations did not surprise economists. (Difficult)
    a. The golf courses were far less crowded.
    b. The price of goods in dollar-equivalent pesos in Buenos Aires, the capital of the country, was significantly above that in New York City.
    c. Consumer prices—primarily services—rose relative to other goods.
    d. Luxury auto dealers were shutting down.   LO3

21. Grade inflation is widespread. In 1990, 81 percent of the students who took the SATs had an A or B average, but 40 percent of them scored less than 390 on the verbal SAT. Students' grades are increasing but what they are learning is decreasing. Some economists argue that grade inflation should be dealt with in the same way that price inflation should be dealt with—by creating a fixed standard and requiring all grades to be specified relative to that standard. One way to accomplish this is to index the grades professors give: specify on the grade report both the student's grade and the class average, and deflate (or inflate) the grade to some common standard. Discuss the advantages and disadvantages of such a proposal. (Difficult)   LO3, LO4

22. In the mid-1990s and through the early 2000s, Japan's annual money supply growth rate fell to 1–2 percent from an average annual rate of 10–11 percent in the late 1980s. What effect did this decline have on
    a. Japanese real output?
    b. Japanese unemployment?
    c. Japanese inflation?   LO5

23. Congratulations. You've just been appointed finance minister of Inflationland. Inflation has been ongoing for the past five years at 5 percent. The target rate of unemployment, 5 percent, is also the actual rate.
    a. Demonstrate the economy's likely position on both short-run and long-run Phillips curves.
    b. The president tells you she wants to be reelected. Devise a monetary policy strategy for her that might help her accomplish her goal.
    c. Demonstrate that strategy graphically, including the likely long-run consequences.   LO5

24. European Community Bank (ECB) governing council member Erkki Liikanen was quoted in a 2004 *Wall Street Journal* article as saying, "The stronger we get the produc-tivity growth . . . the more room we will get in monetary policy (to keep interest rates low)."
    a. Demonstrate his argument using the *AS/AD* model.
    b. Demonstrate his argument using the Phillips curve model.   LO5

25. Wayne Angell, a former Fed governor, stated in an edito-rial, "The Federal Reserve should get back on track get-ting inflation rates so low that inflation would no longer be a determining factor in household and business invest-ment decisions." Mr. Angell believes inflation lowers long-term growth. (Difficult)
    a. Is Wayne Angell most likely a quantity theorist or institutionalist? Explain your answer.
    b. How does inflation affect household decisions and, consequently, growth?   LO6

Questions from Alternative Perspectives

1. According to the quantity theory of money, the govern-ment controls inflation through the supply of money.
   a. Does that mean that the government can stop inflation if it wants to do so?
   b. What reasons might government have not to stop inflation? (Austrian)

2. The Book of Leviticus states, "You shall do no injustice in judgment, in measurement of length, weight, or vol-ume. You shall have just balances, just weights, a just ephah, a just hin. I am the Lord your God, who brought you out of the land of Egypt." When the Israelites began using shekels for money, a just weight meant that the silver coin had a particular weight and therefore an intrinsic value.
   a. If U.S. currency is not backed by gold, how do we know the dollar is a "just weight"?
   b. How is inflation an injustice in measurement?
   c. Who bears the injustice of inflation? (Religious)

3. When it comes to understanding inflation, and even other aspects of the business cycle, ecological economists will often emphasize the role of energy, and especially oil, in shaping macroeconomic outcomes. In this chapter, you were briefly introduced to the analytical concepts of demand-pull and cost-push inflation. To decide how important oil prices are in shaping macroeconomic outcomes such as inflation, do the following:
   a. Graph the average annual CPI inflation rate from 1970–2000s (www.bls.gov has the data); graph the world price of oil over the same time period (www.eia.doe.gov/emeu/cabs/chron.html has these data); overlay the graphs (this is sometimes called "tear drop analysis") and move them forward and backward a bit to create leads and lags. What kind of a pattern do you see?
   b. Use the *AD/AS* model to analyze the impact of an oil shock on the economy.
   c. What is the necessary consequence of using fiscal policy to stimulate the economy after a supply-side oil shock? What conclusions do you draw from the analysis? (Institutionalist)

4. This chapter discusses causes of inflation.
   a. Do you believe the cause of inflation is to be found in the institutional structure of wage- and price-setting institutions or in excess demand for goods and services?
   b. If you believe inflation is caused by wage- and price-setting institutions, what type of policy would Keynesian and Classical economists recommend?
   c. If you believe that inflation is caused by excess demand, would their policy recommendations be the same? (Post-Keynesian)

5. Radicals see the trade-off between inflation and unemployment as one that pits inflation-phobic investors—out to protect the value of their assets and the corporate profits in which they invest—against workers who are out for employment and wage growth. Lower unemployment rates and more jobs bolster the bargaining power of workers, pushing up wages, which either leads to inflation or eats into corporate profit margins. The trade-off changed in the 1990s as global-ization put workers in no position to push for higher wages even as unemployment rates declined. Compare this explanation of change in the trade-off between unemployment and inflation during the 1990s with the one in your textbook.
   a. Where do they agree and where do they differ?
   b. Which do you find more convincing? (Radical)

Web Questions

1. Economagic is a comprehensive site of free, easily available economic time series data useful for economic research, in particular economic forecasting. Go to the site www.economagic.com and find annual data for M_1 and nominal GDP from 1959 to the most recently available year. You will be able to find both by selecting the St. Louis Fed database. Use the tool called "transform this series" to calculate annual averages. Use these data to answer the following questions:
   a. Use a spreadsheet to calculate the velocity of money for each year from 1959 to the most recent year available.
   b. How much income did $1 support in 1960? In 1970? In 1980? In 1990? In 2000?
   c. What happened to the velocity of money over this time period?

d. What implications does the variability of the velocity of money have for the quantity theory of money?

2. The National Bureau of Economic Research publishes nontechnical summaries of economic papers. Go to www.nber.org/digest/dec97/w6062.html to read the summary of "Does Inflation Harm Growth?" to answer the following questions:
   a. How does inflation affect growth?
   b. What is the gain of reducing inflation by one percentage point?
   c. When does a one-percentage-point reduction in inflation affect growth more—when inflation is high or low?

Answers to Margin Questions

1. False. Inflation does not make an economy poorer. It redistributes income from those who do not raise their prices to those who do raise their prices. *(315)*

2. Three types of expectations are rational expectations, adaptive expectations, and extrapolative expectations. *(316)*

3. The equation of exchange, $MV = PQ$, is a tautology. What changes it to the quantity theory are three assumptions about the variables, specifically that velocity remains constant, that real output is determined separately, and that the causation flows from money to prices. With these assumptions added, the equation of exchange implies that changes in the money supply are reflected in changes in the price level—which is what the quantity theory of money says. *(319)*

4. According to the quantity theory of money, the Fed should decrease the growth of the money supply to lower inflation. *(319)*

5. Some central banks issue large quantities of money for a number of reasons. One reason is that, in their estimation, the benefit of doing so (avoiding a breakdown of the government and perhaps the entire economy) exceeds the cost (starting an inflation). Another reason is that some central banks lack the independence to maintain low inflation as a goal. *(321)*

6. According to the quantity theory, the direction of causation goes from money to prices ($MV \rightarrow PQ$)—increases in the money supply lead to increases in the price level.

According to institutional theory, the direction of causation goes from prices to money ($MV \leftarrow PQ$)—increases in the price level are ratified by government, which increases the money supply. *(321)*

7. A quantity theorist would likely say that the insider/outsider model of inflation tends to obscure the central cause of inflation—increases in the money supply. *(322)*

8. As you can see in the graph below, the long-run Phillips curve is perfectly vertical. That is, inflation is independent of the unemployment rate. Its shape is dependent on the assumption that people's expectations of inflation completely adjust to inflation in the long run, and that adjustment is not institutionally constrained. *(326)*

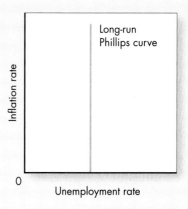

9. If the economy is at point A on the Phillips curve below, inflation is below expected inflation and unemployment is higher than the target rate of unemployment. If this were the only information I had about the economy, I would expect both unemployment and inflation to fall. *(327)*

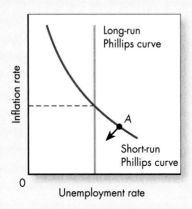

10. Quantity theorists believe that government should err on the side of low output and a lower chance of inflation because any amount of inflation sets into motion a series of changes in the economy that will likely lead to higher inflation. *(328)*

Fiscal Policy and Public Finance

14

An economist's lag may be a politician's catastrophe.

—*George Schultz*

If you listen to the news, or just everyday conversation, you will hear lots of discussion about government's taxing and spending policies. "We have to cut taxes; no, we need to cut spending . . . yes, but we need more funding for research on global warming and to support our troops." Inevitably, economists find themselves entwined in these discussions. Where economists come out on these questions has varied over time, and our changing views have led to the following joke that is often told about economists. It concerns a student who goes back to visit his economics teacher after 20 years. He sees the professor printing up the final exam. The student, who has a phenomenal memory, looks at the exam and remarks, "That's the same exam you gave us!" The professor replies, "In economics the questions always remain the same; it's only the answers that change."

Perhaps nowhere is that joke more appropriate than in macro policy, since views on **public finance**—*government's taxing and spending policies*—in general, and **fiscal policy**—*the changing of taxes and spending to affect the level of output in the economy*—in particular, have changed considerably over time. Despite these changes, there are some deeper truths about public finance and fiscal policy that almost all economists hold. In this chapter, we try to give you a sense of those deeper truths, and of the reasons for the changing views.

Classical Economics and Sound Finance

Let's begin by looking at how economists' views of public finance and fiscal policy have changed over time. Before the 1930s, economists generally supported a policy that was described as "sound finance." **Sound finance** was *a view of public finance and fiscal policy that the government budget should always be balanced except in wartime.* Economists held this view based on a combination of political and economic grounds, but primarily on political grounds. (Before 1930, economic analysis and political analysis were not as separate as they are today, and it is hard to separate out positions held on political as opposed to economic grounds.) The reason politics

AFTER READING THIS CHAPTER, YOU SHOULD BE ABLE TO:

1. Explain the logic of the Ricardian equivalence theorem.
2. Distinguish sound finance from functional finance.
3. List six assumptions of the *AS/AD* model that lead to potential problems with the use of fiscal policy.
4. Explain how automatic stabilizers work.
5. Distinguish the "nuanced functional finance view" of fiscal policy from the New Classical view of fiscal policy.

was important is that the Classical liberal tradition, which was the dominant tradition of economists at the time, viewed government with suspicion, so any policy that would make it easier to increase government spending during peacetime was seen as undesirable.

Ricardian Equivalence Theorem

Although the theoretical economists believed in the principle of sound finance, they also recognized that pure economic arguments for balancing the budget were weak or nonexistent. For example, David Ricardo, one of the most famous economists in the 19th century, pointed out that, in a purely theoretical sense, government spending financed by selling government bonds (the government running a budget deficit) was no different from government spending financed by taxes (the government running a balanced budget). The reason was that the government would have to increase taxes in the future both to pay the interest on the bonds and to repay the bonds when they came due. Those future taxes would make the taxpayers poorer in the same way that paying taxes now would make them poorer. Assuming people can borrow and save, and thereby shift spending between now and the future, people would save more now to pay for those future taxes. So, there is no reason why financing spending with a deficit should affect the aggregate level of income differently than financing spending with taxes. The difference between the two is simply a matter of who does the borrowing. It followed that a government deficit would not lead to an expansion of output in the economy. This *theoretical proposition that deficits do not affect the level of output in the economy because individuals increase their savings to account for expected future tax payments to repay the deficit* has become known as the **Ricardian equivalence theorem.**

Despite economists' recognition of the logical truth of the Ricardian equivalence theorem, most economists, including Ricardo, felt that, in practice, deficits could affect output and that it mattered a lot, politically, whether government financed its spending by bonds (ran deficits) or by taxes (balanced the budget). Based on their political ideology, economists of the time strongly pushed government to finance its spending with taxes, not bonds. Hence, their principle of sound finance. The reason they supported the principle of sound finance was because they felt that, politically, requiring government to follow the principle of sound finance made increasing government spending more difficult, and brought home to the politicians the central economic lesson that there is no free lunch. They argued that adhering to a policy of sound finance forced government to face the costs of a spending decision simultaneously with the benefits of that spending decision, something that bond finance—financing government spending by borrowing—did not do.

Because of their advocacy of sound finance, through the 1930s fiscal policy—the deliberate running of a deficit or surplus to guide the level of aggregate output in the economy—was not part of the economist's lexicon. Although economists of the time recognized that government spending could impact the level of output in the economy, they felt that, except in wartime, the long-run fiscal integrity of the government that sound finance led to should override such concerns. So through the 1930s economists' answer to the exam question about what government should do if there was a recession was that the government should maintain a balanced budget.

Nuanced Sound Finance

That view started to change in the 1920s in Europe, and in the 1930s in the United States, as the world economies fell into a sustained depression from which there seemed to be no escape. In response, major economists of the time such as A. C. Pigou, F. Knight, and J. M. Keynes started questioning the sound-finance principles. The

Q₁ Does the Ricardian equivalence theorem lead to a policy of sound finance?

Q₂ What would a pre-1930s Classical economist recommend government do if there is a recession?

reason was that they felt that the depressed state of the economy had created a vicious cycle in which the expectations of a continued depression kept investment spending low, which kept total spending low, and that low spending led to low output and high unemployment. They believed that the market would get out of the depression eventually, but as the depression continued, they came to believe that "eventually" was longer than was politically acceptable.

Given this collapse of economic expectations, many economists of the time favored giving up the principle of sound finance, at least temporarily, and using government spending to stimulate the economy. For example, numerous economists favored government public works programs such as the Federal Emergency Relief Program, which provided funds for unemployed workers, and the Works Progress Administration (WPA), which built roads and bridges. So, faced with a serious depression, economists were quite willing to support spending on these programs without tax increases, which essentially meant that they were willing to support deficit financing to stimulate the economy.

Their arguments for deficit spending were based on simple commonsense reasoning, not any complex underlying models (remember, their reasoning told them that, theoretically, Ricardian equivalence held, and deficits wouldn't expand the economy). But their theory also told them that depressions, such as the one in which the economy was stuck in the 1930s, shouldn't happen either. Given the depression that the economy was stuck in, they were willing to entertain the notion that it was possible that if the government spent more than it collected in taxes—ran a deficit—the economy would be jump-started: income would increase; the recipients of that increased income would spend more, creating a virtuous circle that ultimately would help pull the economy out of the recession. At least it was worth a try.

At the time, economists debated how much of the government spending stimulus would be offset by increased savings as bonds were sold to finance the deficit. But despite theoretical concerns, policy-making economists of the time generally felt that expansionary fiscal policy—government spending exceeding government tax revenues—could be of some use in helping pull an economy out of a severe recession. So, in the 1930s, economists' answer to the exam question, what to do if the economy is in a recession, changed from "do nothing" to a more nuanced answer. If the recession is small, maintain a policy of sound finance, but if it is a very bad recession—a depression—then consider trying to stimulate the economy with some government programs and deficit financing. But such deficit financing was a last resort that was inappropriate to small or moderate recessions.

Q-3 What would an economist who believes in nuanced sound finance recommend government do if there is a recession?

Keynesian Economics and Functional Finance

The textbook presentation of the economist's view of public finance and fiscal policy changed significantly in the late 1940s, as the ideas of J. M. Keynes' *The General Theory* worked their way into the principles of economics texts. Keynes' book was enormously important; it set in motion a series of events that influenced the way in which economists looked at the aggregate economy for about 50 years, and that still have some lingering effects on both the textbook presentation and applied policy. In fact, it was that book that created the field of macroeconomics and led to fiscal policy being seen as a method of controlling the level of income in the economy, rather than as just a practical policy that might be helpful in serious depressions.

Actually, what became known as Keynesian economics does not all follow from Keynes' work; *The General Theory* is a theoretical book, which is open to many interpretations about policy. The book does not mention fiscal policy as a policy tool; Keynes' support of fiscal policy as a practical tool predated his writing of *The General Theory* and was not dependent on it.[1] Instead, what became known as Keynesian economics was developed by his students together with a group of economists who were influenced by those students. In terms of what shows up in the textbook presentations, the ideas of one of those students, Abba Lerner, stands out. Lerner's book, *The Economics of Control*, spelled out what he called a *functional finance* view of public finance and fiscal policy. That functional finance view became the principles textbook view when Nobel Prize-winning economist Paul Samuelson incorporated it into his famous textbook, which established the template for all texts that followed.

Functional Finance

Q₄ How does functional finance differ from sound finance?

Functional finance held that, *as a theoretical proposition, governments should make spending and taxing decisions on the basis of their effect on the economy, not on the basis of some moralistic principle that budgets should be balanced.* Under functional finance, if spending in the economy was too low, the government should run a deficit; if spending was too high, the government should run a surplus.

To explain why functional finance was preferred to sound finance, Lerner gave the following famous analogy.

> Imagine yourself in a Buck Rogers interplanetary adventure, looking at a highway in a City of Tomorrow. The highway is wide and straight, and its edges are turned up so that it is almost impossible for a car to run off the road. What appears to be a runaway car is speeding along the road and veering off to one side. As it approaches the rising edge of the highway, its front wheels are turned so that it gets back onto the road and goes off at an angle, making for the other side, where the wheels are turned again. This happens many times, the car zigzagging but keeping on the highway until it is out of sight. You are wondering how long it will take for it to crash, when another car appears which behaves in the same fashion. When it comes near you, it stops with a jerk. A door is opened, and an occupant asks whether you would like a lift. You look into the car and before you can control yourself you cry out, "Why, there's no steering wheel." Want a ride?

For Lerner, the aggregate economy was subject to wild fluctuations and it needed a steering wheel to guide it. Fiscal policy was that steering wheel. Notice that the total focus here is on the government steering the economy; there is no discussion of politics or whether the recession is a major one or a minor one as there was in the nuanced view of sound finance. Lerner's functional finance had no nuances about policy.

Functional finance nicely fits the *AS/AD* model you learned in Chapter 9 and the multiplier model in Chapter 10. In these models, there was a desired level of output—potential output—but the economy fluctuated around it. However, by using its fiscal (and monetary) policy steering wheel, the government could increase or decrease either expenditures or taxes, thereby shifting the *AD* curve to the right or left to steer the economy to the desired level of output. (A good review exercise is to go through various changes in government spending and taxes in the *AS/AD* model.)

So in functional finance, the economist's answer to the question, what to do if there is a recession, is to run a deficit to return the economy to its potential output. Policy followed directly from the model.

In functional finance, if there is a recession, the government should run a deficit.

---

[1]Although the book was primarily about theory, Keynes never followed up on his theoretical arguments; he was an adviser to the British government and, with World War II and the economic problems following the war, that advising took up most of his time, and then after the war he had a heart attack that left him out of the debate about his work.

Nuanced Functional Finance

Lerner's stark presentation of functional finance did not last long as a guiding principle for practical macro public finance and fiscal policy. The reason was that the model made a number of assumptions that, in practice, did not hold, and the model did not deal with the difficult practical problems of implementing fiscal policy. These problems don't mean that functional finance models are wrong; they simply mean that for fiscal policy to work, the policy conclusions drawn from the model must be modified to reflect the real-world problems. Let's consider how the reality might not fit the model. The multiplier model assumes

1. Financing the deficit doesn't have any offsetting effects. (In reality, it often does.)

2. The government knows what the situation is—for instance, the size of the *mpe*, and other exogenous variables. (In reality, the government must estimate them.)

3. The government knows the economy's potential income level—the highest level of income that doesn't cause accelerating inflation. (In reality, the government may not know what this level is.)

4. The government has flexibility in changing spending and taxes. (In reality, government cannot change them quickly.)

5. The size of the government debt doesn't matter. (In reality, the size of the government debt often does matter.)

6. Fiscal policy doesn't negatively affect other government goals. (In reality, it often does.)

Let's consider each assumption a bit further.

> Six assumptions of the multiplier model that could lead to problems with fiscal policy are
>
> 1. Financing the deficit doesn't have any offsetting effects.
> 2. The government knows what the situation is.
> 3. The government knows the economy's potential income level.
> 4. The government has flexibility in changing spending and taxes.
> 5. The size of the government debt doesn't matter.
> 6. Fiscal policy doesn't negatively affect other government goals.

1. Financing the Deficit Doesn't Have Any Offsetting Effect

One of the limitations of the functional finance approach embodied in the AS/AD and multiplier models is that they assume that financing the deficit has no offsetting effects on income. Some economists argue that that is not the case, that the government financing of deficit spending will offset the deficit's expansionary effect.

The AS/AD and multiplier models assume that saving and investment can be unequal, and that the government can increase its expenditures without at the same time causing a decrease in private expenditures. Some economists object to that assumption. They believe the interest rate equilibrates saving and investment. They argue that when the government borrows to finance the deficit, that borrowing will increase interest rates and crowd out private investment.

Interest rate **crowding out**—*the offsetting of a change in government expenditures by a change in private expenditures in the opposite direction*—occurs as follows: When the government runs a budget deficit, it must sell bonds (that is, it must borrow) to finance that deficit. To get people to buy and hold the bonds, the government must make them attractive. That means the interest rate the bonds pay must be higher than it otherwise would have been. This tends to push up the interest rate in the economy, which makes it more expensive for private businesses to borrow, so they reduce their borrowing and their investment. That private investment is crowded out by expansionary fiscal policy. Hence the name *crowding out*. Increased government spending crowds out private spending.

> Crowding out is the offsetting effect on private expenditures caused by the government's sale of bonds to finance expansionary fiscal policy.

Figure 14-1(a) shows the supply and demand for loanable funds. Since any increase in government spending not financed by taxes has to be financed by bonds, deficit spending increases the demand for loanable funds; the demand for loanable funds increases from D_0 to D_1 and the interest rate rises from i_0 to i_1. That rise in interest rate will cause investment to decrease, which will offset the shift of aggregate demand in response to a deficit. Figure 14-1(b) shows the effect of this offset in the *AS/AD* model.

FIGURE 14-1 (A AND B)   **Crowding Out**

An increase in government spending will expand income, but it will also cause interest rates to rise, as is shown in (a), thereby causing investment to decrease, which will tend to decrease income, as is shown in (b). This is called *interest rate crowding out*. The net effect of fiscal policy depends on the degree of crowding out that takes place.

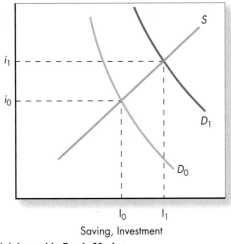

(a) Loanable Funds Market

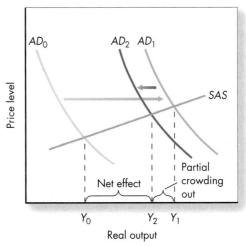

(b) The Goods Market

Q.5 If interest rates had no effect on investment or consumption, how much crowding out would occur?

Initially, income in the economy is Y_0 and government has decided to expand income to Y_1 by increasing its spending. If financing government spending were not an issue, expansionary fiscal policy would shift the AD curve to the right by a multiple of the increase in government spending, increasing income from Y_0 to Y_1. However, as we saw in Figure 14-1(a), financing is an issue. Financing the deficit increases interest rates and decreases investment. This shifts the AD curve to the left to AD_2. Income falls back to Y_2. How much it shifts back is a matter of debate; it depends upon how responsive the interest rate is to shifts in the demand for loanable funds and how responsive investment is to changes in the interest rate.

Because of crowding out, the net expansionary effect of fiscal policy is smaller than it otherwise would have been. Some economists argue that crowding out can totally offset the expansionary effect of fiscal policy, so the net effect is zero, or even negative, since they consider private spending more productive than government spending. This is the view taken by some of those who focus on the supply-side effects of fiscal policy. Larger deficits decrease the pool of savings available for investment by raising interest rates. The result is that potential output does not increase as much as it otherwise would, and thus deficits lead to slower growth.

The crowding out effect also works in reverse with contractionary fiscal policy. Say the government runs a budget surplus. That surplus will slow the economy since it shifts the AD curve back to the left. But it also means the U.S. Treasury (the U.S. government department that issues bonds to finance the deficit) can buy back some of its outstanding bonds, which, as we discussed in earlier chapters, will have a tendency to push bond prices up and interest rates down. Lower interest rates will stimulate investment, which in turn will have an offsetting expansionary effect on the economy. So when we include financing the deficit in our consideration of fiscal policy, the shift in AD from the surplus is partially offset.

Q.6 Demonstrate graphically what would happen if government expenditures policy stimulated private investment.

How large this financing offset to fiscal policy will be is a matter of debate. The empirical evidence about the degree of crowding out is mixed and has not resolved the debate.

Both sides see some crowding out occurring as the debt is financed by selling bonds. The closer to the potential income level the economy is, the more crowding out is likely to occur.

Even as the U.S. government ran large budget deficits in the early 2000s, the U.S. interest rate did not rise substantially. Some economists consequently downplayed the importance of crowding out. Other economists argued that crowding out did not occur because foreign governments and private sources were willing to finance the U.S. deficit by purchasing U.S. bonds. The increase in the supply of savings from foreign sources held the U.S. interest rate down. However, they point out that eventually foreigners will find other places to invest and will be less willing to buy U.S. bonds, and when they do, the U.S. interest rate could rise substantially if the U.S. budget deficits persist.

2. The Government Knows What the Situation Is The numbers we use to demonstrate fiscal policy in the *AS/AD* model were chosen arbitrarily. In reality, the numbers used in models must be estimated or based on preliminary figures subject to revision. Most economic data are published quarterly, and it usually takes six to nine months of data to indicate, with any degree of confidence, the state of the economy and which way it is heading. Thus, we could be halfway into a recession before we even know it is happening. For example, data revisions showed GDP fell for three consecutive quarters in 2001, whereas the preliminary figures had shown only a one-quarter decline. (Data are already three months old when published; then we need two or three quarters of such data before we have enough information to work with.)

In an attempt to deal with this problem, the government relies on large macroeconomic models and leading indicators to predict what the economy will be like six months or a year from now. As part of the input to these complex models, the government must predict economic factors that determine the size of the multiplier. These predictions are imprecise, so the forecasts are imprecise. Economic forecasting is still an art, not a science.

Economists' data problems limit the use of fiscal policy for fine tuning. There's little sense in recommending expansionary or contractionary policy until you know what policy is called for.

3. The Government Knows the Economy's Potential Income Level The problem of not knowing the level of potential income is related to the problem we just discussed. The target rate of unemployment and the potential level of income are not easy concepts to define. At one time it was thought 3 percent unemployment meant full employment. Some time later it was generally thought that 6.5 percent unemployment meant full employment. About that time economists stopped calling the potential level of income the *full-employment* level of income.

Any variation in potential income can make an enormous difference in the policy prescription that could be recommended. To see how big a difference, let's translate a 1 percent change in unemployment into a change in income. According to *Okun's rule of thumb* (defined in an earlier chapter as the general rule of thumb economists use to translate changes in the unemployment rate into changes in income), a 1 percentage point fall in the unemployment rate is associated with a 2 percent increase in income. Thus, in 2008 with income at about $14 trillion, a 1 percentage point fall in the unemployment rate would have increased income by about $280 billion.

Now let's say that one economist believes 5.5 percent is the long-run achievable target rate of unemployment, while another believes it's 4 percent. That's a 1.5 percentage point difference. Since a 1 percent decrease in the unemployment rate means an increase of $280 billion in national income, their views of the income level we should

Web Note 14.1
What's the Speed Limit?

target differ by over $420 billion (1.5 × $280 = $420). Yet both views are reasonable. Looking at the same economy (the same data), one economist may call for expansionary fiscal policy while the other may call for contractionary fiscal policy.

In practice, differences in estimates of potential income often lead to different policy recommendations. Empirical estimates suggest that the size of the multiplier is somewhere between 1.5 and 2.5. Let's say it's 2.5. That means autonomous expenditures must be predicted to increase or decrease by more than $168 billion before an economist who believes the target rate of unemployment is 4 percent would agree with the same policy recommendation put forward by an economist who believes the rate is 5.5 percent. Since almost all fluctuations in autonomous investment and autonomous consumption are less than this amount, there's no generally agreed-on policy prescription for most fluctuations. Some economists will call for expansionary policy; some will call for contractionary policy; and the government decision makers won't have any clear-cut policy to follow.

You might wonder why the range of potential income estimates is so large. Why not simply see whether the economy has inflation at the existing rate of unemployment and income level? Would that it were so easy. Inflation is a complicated process. Seeds of inflation are often sown years before inflation results. The main problem is that establishing a close link between the level of economic activity and inflation is a complicated statistical challenge to economists, one that has not yet been satisfactorily met. That leads to enormous debate as to what the causes are.

Almost all economists believe that outside some range (perhaps 3.5 percent unemployment on the low side and 10 percent on the high side), too much spending causes inflation and too little spending causes a recession. That 3.5 to 10 percentage point range is so large that, in most cases, the U.S. economy is in an ambiguous state where some economists are calling for expansionary policy and others are calling for contractionary policy.

Once the economy reaches the edge of the range of potential income or falls outside it, the economists' policy prescription becomes clearer. For example, in the Depression, when this multiplier model was developed, unemployment was 25 percent—well outside the range. Should the economy ever go into such a depression again, economists' policy prescriptions will be clear. The call will be for expansionary fiscal policy. Most times the economy is within the ambiguous range, so there are disagreements among economists.

4. The Government Has Flexibility in Changing Spending and Taxes
For argument's sake, let's say economists agree that contractionary policy is needed and that's what they advise the government. Will the government implement it? And, if so, will it implement contractionary fiscal policy at the right time? The answer to both questions is: probably not. There are also problems with implementing economists' calls for expansionary fiscal policy. Even if economists are unanimous in calling for expansionary fiscal policy, putting fiscal policy in place takes time and has serious implementation problems.

Numerous political and institutional realities in the United States today make it a difficult task to implement fiscal policy. Government spending and taxes cannot be changed instantaneously. The budget process begins more than a year and a half before the government's fiscal year begins. President George W. Bush's plans for tax relief that culminated in the Economic Growth and Tax Relief Reconciliation Act of 2001 were written months before the economy went into recession and many more months before the September 11, 2001, terrorist attacks, which deepened the recession. When the tax relief was first implemented, it looked to most economists as if it would be too expansionary and that it was not needed. That's why initially President Bush emphasized its supply-side effects. However, as I mentioned above, in this case the timing of

---

Differences in estimates of potential income often lead to different policy recommendations.

Q.7 Why don't economists have an accurate measure of potential income?

In most cases, the U.S. economy is in an ambiguous state where some economists are calling for expansionary policy and others are calling for contractionary policy.

Fighting the Vietnam War Inflation

In the chapter I described a 2001 case study in which fiscal policy worked the way it was supposed to through luck. Usually that isn't the case, and many times fiscal policy's effect comes at the wrong time and affects the economy in the wrong way. For example, one time that economists were united in their views on appropriate fiscal policy was during the Vietnam War, from the early 1960s until 1975, when the economy was pushed to its limits. About 1965,

The Vietnam War led to inflationary pressures.

President Lyndon B. Johnson's economic advisers started to argue strongly that a tax increase was needed to slow the economy and decrease inflationary pressures. President Johnson wouldn't hear of it. He felt a tax increase would be political suicide. Finally in mid-1968, after Johnson had decided not to run for reelection, a temporary income tax increase was passed. By then, however, many economists felt that the seeds of the 1970s inflation had already been sown.

the reductions in taxes was just about right. It helped boost consumer spending in a slowing economy and played an important demand-side role, even though countercyclical policy was not the motivation for passing the act.

Another difficulty is that nearly two-thirds of the government budget is mandated by government programs such as Medicare and Social Security and by interest payments on government debt. Even the remaining one-third, called discretionary spending, is difficult to change. Defense programs are generally multiyear spending commitments. Discretionary spending also includes appropriations to fund established government agencies such as the Department of Agriculture, the Department of Transportation, and the Internal Revenue Service. Changing their budgets is politically difficult.

Politicians face intense political pressures; their other goals may conflict with the goals of fiscal policy. For example, few members of Congress who hope to be reelected would vote to raise taxes in an election year. Similarly, few members would vote to slash defense spending when military contractors are a major source of employment in their districts, even when there's little to defend against. Squabbles between Congress and the president may delay initiating appropriate fiscal policy for months, even years. By the time the fiscal policy is implemented, what may have once been the right fiscal policy may have ceased to be right, and some other policy may have become right.

Imagine trying to steer a car at 60 miles an hour when there's a five-second delay between the time you turn the steering wheel and the time the car's wheels turn. Imagining that situation will give you a good sense of how fiscal policy works in the real world.

Real-world fiscal policy is similar to steering a car with a 5-second delay from turning the steering wheel to turning the wheels.

5. The Size of the Government Debt Doesn't Matter There is no inherent reason why adopting activist policies should have caused the government to run deficits year after year and hence to incur ever-increasing debt—accumulated deficits less accumulated surpluses. Activist functional finance policy is consistent with running deficits some years and surpluses other years. In practice, the introduction of activist functional finance policy has been accompanied by many deficits and few surpluses, and by a large increase in government debt.

There are two reasons why activist government policies have led to an increase in government debt. First, early activist economists favored large increases in government spending as well as favoring the government's using fiscal policy. These early activist economists employed the multiplier model to justify increasing spending without increasing taxes. A second reason is political. Politically it's much easier for government to increase spending and decrease taxes than to decrease spending and increase taxes. Due to political pressure, expansionary fiscal policy has predominated over contractionary fiscal policy.

Whether debt is a problem is an important and complicated issue, as we'll see in the next chapter. For now, all you need remember is that if one believes that the debt is harmful, then there might be a reason not to conduct expansionary fiscal policy, even when the model calls for it.

6. Fiscal Policy Doesn't Negatively Affect Other Government Goals   A society has many goals; achieving potential income is only one of them. So it's not surprising that those goals often conflict. When the government runs expansionary fiscal policy, the trade deficit tends to increase. As the economy expands and income rises, exports remain constant but imports rise. If a nation's international considerations do not allow a balance of trade deficit to become larger, as is true in many countries, those governments cannot run expansionary fiscal policies—unless they can somehow prevent this balance of trade deficit from becoming larger.

Summary of the Problems   So where do these six problems leave fiscal policy? While they don't eliminate its usefulness, they severely restrict it. Fiscal policy is a sledgehammer, not an instrument for fine-tuning. When the economy goes into a depression, the appropriate fiscal policy is clear. Similarly, when the economy has a hyperinflation, the appropriate policy is clear. But in less extreme cases, there will be debate on what the appropriate fiscal policy is—a debate economic theory can't answer conclusively.

Integrating these practical problems in running deficits has led modern economists to a much more nuanced view of deficit finance than found in the functional finance view. The modern view held by applied macro policy economists is that deficits can have stimulative effects on aggregate output, but they also agree with earlier Classical economists that there are political reasons for having balanced budgets, and not for relying on governments to control spending and taxes to achieve the desired level of output. As a tool, discretionary fiscal policy is not very helpful. But that does not mean that modern macro policy economists have discarded fiscal policy altogether. Instead of advocating discretionary fiscal policy in which government responds to fluctuations in income with changes in government spending and taxes, modern economists rely much more on building fiscal policy into institutions.

Fiscal policy is a sledgehammer, not an instrument for fine-tuning.

Building Fiscal Policies into Institutions

Economists quickly recognized the political problems with instituting direct countercyclical fiscal policy. To avoid these problems, they suggested policies that built fiscal policy into U.S. institutions so that it wouldn't require any political decisions. They called a built-in fiscal policy an **automatic stabilizer**—*a government program or policy that will counteract the business cycle without any new government action*. Automatic stabilizers include welfare payments, unemployment insurance, and the income tax system.

An automatic stabilizer is any government program or policy that will counteract the business cycle without any new government action.

Web Note 14.2
Unemployment
Compensation

How Automatic Stabilizers Work

To see how automatic stabilizers work, consider the unemployment insurance system. When the economy is slowing down or is in a recession, the unemployment rate will rise. When people lose their jobs, they will reduce their consumption, starting the multiplier process, which decreases income. Unemployment insurance immediately helps offset the decrease in individuals' incomes as the government pays benefits to the unemployed. Thus, government spending increases, and part of the fall in income is stopped without any explicit act by the government. Automatic stabilizers also work in reverse. When income increases, government spending declines automatically.

Another automatic stabilizer is our income tax system. Tax revenue fluctuates as income fluctuates. When the economy expands, tax revenues rise, slowing the economy; when the economy contracts, tax revenues decline, providing a stimulus to the economy. Let's go through the reasoning why. When the economy is strong, people have more income and thus pay higher taxes. This increase in tax revenue reduces consumption expenditures from what they would have been and moderates the economy's growth. When the economy goes into a recession, the opposite occurs.

Automatic Stabilizers

State Government Finance and Procyclical Fiscal Policy

Automatic stabilizers are sometimes offset by other institutional structures that work as a type of automatic *destabilizer*. Examples of such destabilizers are states' constitutional provisions to maintain balanced budgets. These provisions mean that whenever a recession hits, states are faced with declining tax revenue. To maintain balanced budgets, the states must cut spending, increase tax rates, or both. For example, during the 2001 recession, state governments struggled to balance their budgets by cutting expenditures on education, transportation, health care, and a variety of other programs while raising income and sales taxes. These actions deepened the recession. Similarly, during the previous 10-year expansion, state revenue rose; and states increased spending and decreased tax rates. The expansionary effect of these changes further increased total income. The result is what economists call **procyclical fiscal policy**—*changes in government spending and taxes that increase the cyclical fluctuations in the economy instead of reducing them*.

Countercyclical vs. Procyclical Policies

To reduce the procyclical nature of state financing, economists have suggested states establish *rainy-day funds*—reserves kept in good times, to be used to offset declines in revenue during recessions. Large rainy-day funds (which some economists have called rainy-season funds) would decrease the destabilizing aspect of state government spending. But politics usually keep rainy-day funds small; the funds are targets that are just too tempting for spending proposals or tax cuts.

An alternative way of building countercyclical policies into institutions would be for states to use a five-year rolling-average budgeting procedure (with a built-in underlying trend rate of increase) as the budget they are required to balance. With a rolling-average budget, revenues available for spending would be determined from a growth-adjusted average of revenues for the past five years. When revenues increase substantially in a year, the surplus available to be spent would build up only slowly and would therefore be much less politically tempting to raid. When revenues fall, the measured deficit would grow much more slowly, and the constitutional budget-balancing requirements would be much less procyclical.

Balancing a rolling-average budget, rather than the current-year budget, would counterbalance the balanced-budget requirement and would remove much of the procyclical aspect of current state budgeting procedures. In fact, if the federal government started using a similar five-year rolling-average budget, it too could build a more reasonable fiscal policy into its accounting procedures and reduce the need for discretionary stimulus packages.

The Negative Side of Automatic Stabilizers

Automatic stabilizers may seem like the solution to the economic woes we have discussed, but they, too, have their shortcomings. One problem is that when the economy is first starting to climb out of a recession, automatic stabilizers will slow the process, rather

Q-8 What effect do automatic stabilizers have on the size of the multiplier?

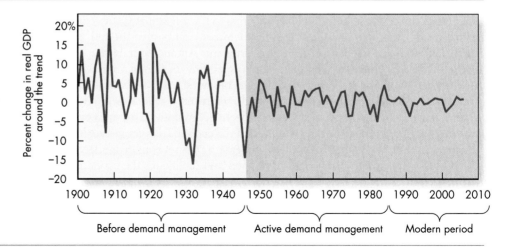

FIGURE 14-2   **Decrease in Fluctuations in the Economy**

Compared to the early 1900s, fluctuations in the economy have decreased; this suggests that policy makers have done something right.

Source: Federal Reserve Historical Charts and Economic Report of the President (www.doc.gov).

than help it along, for the same reason they slow the contractionary process. As income increases, automatic stabilizers increase government taxes and decrease government spending, and as they do, the discretionary policy's expansionary effects are decreased.

Despite these problems, most economists believe that automatic stabilizers have played an important role in reducing fluctuations in our economy. They point to the kind of data we see in Figure 14-2, which they say show a significant decrease in fluctuations in the economy. Other economists aren't so sure; they argue the apparent decrease in fluctuations is an optical illusion. As usual, economic data are sufficiently ambiguous to give both sides strong arguments. The jury is still out.

What Should Government Do about a Recession?

Q-9   What should government do if there is a recession? (nuanced functional finance answer)

Taking all the qualifications into account, the nuanced functional finance macro policy answer to the question, "What should the government do about a recession?" is generally: Do nothing in terms of specific tax or spending policy, but to let the automatic stabilizers in the economy do the adjustment. The reason for not undertaking specific policies is not because of a lack of concern about recession, but because, theoretically, it is unclear what effect a deficit would have and, practically and politically, it is very difficult to implement the control via fiscal policy at the right time. If, however, the economy falls into a depression, then you should consider running expansionary fiscal policy.

The New Classical Approach to Public Finance

The above discussion of a nuanced functional finance limited by practical and political problems was an adequate discussion of much of the macro policy economist's view of fiscal policy through the mid 1980s, and is still the predominant view of many macro policy economists. But it is an incomplete view; what it doesn't take into account is that there was a revolution in macroeconomic theory in the 1980s. In this revolution, Keynesian economics, of which the functional finance view of deficits and the practical approach to fiscal policy are to be found, was theoretically overthrown and replaced with what came to be known as **New Classical macroeconomics**—*a theoretical approach to macroeconomics that revived many pre-Keynesian theoretical ideas of the macro economy.* Specifically, New Classical economics reverted back to the theoretical Classical way of looking at public finance that I discussed at the beginning of this chapter, which centered on the Ricardian equivalence theorem. According to that theorem, whether a government deficit is financed by bonds (deficit spending) or by taxes (balanced budget) is irrelevant. The method of funding government spending does not affect aggregate output.

There was, however, a major difference between the New Classical view and the old Classical view. Unlike the old Classical view, which concentrated on political problems of spending and gave little emphasis to Ricardian equivalence in its advocacy of sound finance, the New Classical view focused on the Ricardian equivalence theorem as a guiding principle of its policy views. This meant that the New Classical view of government financing of spending—whether government runs a deficit or not—is that it doesn't matter; individuals will adjust their spending to account for future tax payments and that adjustment will offset any effect the deficit might have had on total output.

New Classicals recognize that there can be political reasons against deficit spending, but they argue that macroeconomists are not trained to make judgments about politics—they can simply report what economic theory states, and what the implications of that theory for policy are. Since economic theory states that deficit spending does not affect output, then, they argue, that is what economists' recommendations should be based upon. Of course, what theory states depends on what assumptions the theory is based upon, and modern macroeconomic literature is filled with debates about what are the appropriate assumptions.

Critics of New Classical economics argue specifically that the New Classical model, and the modern variation of it, the Dynamic Stochastic General Equilibrium Model, are too unrealistic to be the basis of any policy.[2] One of their most specific complaints is that the New Classical model is based on an assumption that the aggregate economy has only a single individual, who is called the representative agent, whereas almost all the problems in the macro economy come from interactions of many agents making different choices. That interaction creates coordination problems that the New Classical model simply assumes away. Models that do not seriously take into account these coordination failures are not relevant for an analysis of stabilization issues.[3]

New Classical economists respond, "yes, we agree," but then they ask the critics for their alternative models, and critics have not yet come up with a generally accepted alternative, although many models are beginning to deal with heterogeneity. With the lack of a generally accepted heterogeneous agent macro model, much of the critics' applied analysis has focused on empirical work—studying the patterns in the data, and seeing if one can draw some tentative conclusions from that empirical evidence. Unfortunately, the empirical evidence is difficult to interpret, and does not clearly indicate the effects of deficits on aggregate income. Just too many things change simultaneously and too little data are available to draw definitive conclusions. So the debate continues.

To make sure you understand the difference between the New Classical view of deficits and the nuanced functional finance view of deficits, consider Figure 14-3. In Figure 14-3(a), we show the effect of a deficit in the nuanced functional finance view. In it, expansionary fiscal policy shifts the AD curve out to the right; the rise in the interest rates from financing the deficit shifts the AD curve back to the left (crowding out) from AD_1 to AD_2, and if the interest rate crowding out is strong enough, then it could shift the AD curve all the way back to AD_0. But generally, the expectation is that there will be some stimulative effect of the government running a deficit.

Q-10 What would a New Classical economist recommend government do if there is a recession?

---

[2]I should mention that I am one of the critics of the New Classical and DSGE models, so even though I am trying to be fair to both sides in the presentation, I have taken a side in the debate, so the presentation here may be biased, even though I am trying to provide a balanced view.
[3]You might wonder why, if heterogeneous agent models are more relevant, we don't have such models in macro. The answer is that, mathematically, developing such models is very difficult, especially if one wants definitive results. Simply solving the Dynamic Stochastic General Equilibrium model for a representative agent is quite a mathematical feat.

Nuanced Functional Finance and New Classical Views

In the nuanced functional finance view shown in (a), deficit spending shifts the *AD* curve to the right. This causes a rise in interest rates that can reduce investment spending and shift the *AD* back to the left. In the New Classical view shown in (b), deficit spending does not shift the *AD* curve at all. Taxpayers reduce their spending by the exact amount of the deficit spending in expectation of future tax increases.

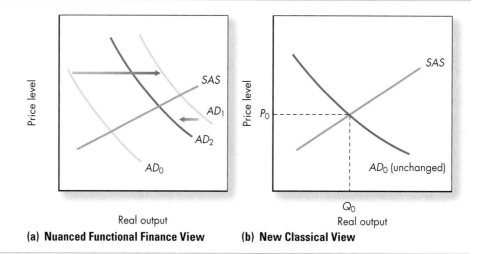

(a) **Nuanced Functional Finance View**   (b) **New Classical View**

In Figure 14-3(b), I show the New Classical view of deficits. When the government runs a deficit, the *AD* curve does not shift. It stays right where it is, as consumers reduce their expenditures so that they can save money to pay the taxes needed to pay the interest on that deficit and eventually to pay the bonds back. So when government rearranges its spending and taxes over time, individuals rearrange their spending and saving in the opposite direction, offsetting most of the effects that deficit spending might have had on aggregate output.

So, in terms of its countercyclical effect, the New Classical answer to what government should do in response to the economy falling into a recession is: Do nothing, because there is little you can do, since any attempt to do something would simply provoke a response in the private sector that would offset it.

If the size of the government deficit makes no difference to aggregate demand, what should guide government decisions on spending and taxes? New Classical economists argue that the incentive effects of taxes should. Specifically, lower tax rates provide greater incentives for firms and workers to produce. So whenever possible, one should cut taxes and government spending to encourage production. They argue that the focus of government policy should be on achieving growth and not on countercyclical aggregate demand policy.

So the New Classical answer to the question of "what to do about a recession?" is to cut taxes and government spending, not because of the recession, but instead because tax cuts will encourage growth and government spending is unproductive.

New Classical economists have justified this position by arguing that growth is much more central to the well-being of individuals than is stabilization. For example, University of Chicago economist Robert Lucas calculated that individuals would give up only 0.1 percent of their lifetime consumption to live in a world not subject to the degree of macroeconomic volatility that the U.S. experienced in the last 50 years. He concluded that there was little benefit in "devising ever more subtle policies to remove the residual amount of business cycle risk." Policy, he argued, should focus on growth, which does substantially affect the well-being of society.

Lucas's argument provoked much debate; critics argued that much of the stability in the macro economy existed because the government stood ready to implement stabilization policy and that Lucas significantly underestimated the true cost of instability. We will not resolve these debates here, but you should know that they exist as you put the New Classical view into perspective.

The New Classical answer to the question of "what to do about a recession?" is to cut taxes and government spending.

Incentive and Supply-Side Effects of Public Finance

The various political parties' views of public finance have changed significantly over the past 50 years. In the 1950s and early 1960s, the political parties' views on deficit finance were clear. The Democrats were Keynesian; they were the party of the deficits. Republicans were Classical; they were the party of sound finance. Consistent with these positions, Democrats pushed for increases in government programs and government spending, in part justifying these programs as a way to increase the size of the government budget and thereby increase effectiveness of fiscal policy as a tool of stabilization.

The push by Democrats for increased spending was partly offset by Republicans who pushed for tax decreases, but that push was often overwhelmed by their support of sound finance. Ultimately, Republicans found that they had to compromise on their support for sound finance and accept some level of deficits because of the political difficulty of cutting government programs once they were started. During this time, the relative size of the government increased, and government ran almost continual deficits. However, these deficits were not especially large relative to GDP, and no serious economist felt that these deficits were raising questions about the long-run financial viability of the government.

Just about the time that the New Classical revolution was taking hold in the early 1980s, Republicans were giving up their support for a balanced budget. Instead of supporting a balanced budget, they began to support cutting taxes whenever possible. Part of the justification for that position was the New Classical policy view of deficits and the Ricardian equivalence theorem. Supply-side economics emphasized the incentive effects of tax cuts, which they argued would lead to growth in output and hence would increase tax revenue. Some even argued the tax cuts would more than finance themselves, increasing, not decreasing, total tax revenues. The lay-public name for these views was *supply-side economics*. Most economists are hesitant about such claims. While all economists believe that incentive effects are important in the long run, most believe that the short-run incentive effects are relatively small.

That does not mean the Republican view could not be supported. Most economists felt that the reasoning for the Republican view on public finance was subtler and more political than the view presented in supply-side economics. Essentially, the Republican view could be supported if one believed that government spending was enormously inefficient and needed to be kept down, and that political forces would work to spend whatever money was available. If these views were true, it means that a budget surplus, or even a deficit that does not exceed a certain level of GDP that would alarm the public, is an invitation for increased government spending. These two propositions led Republicans to eliminate their support of sound finance and a balanced budget. The new Republican supply-side position became one of "always cut taxes" and "never raise taxes." This might be called the "starve the beast" approach to public finance. It is a public finance policy designed to reduce government spending in whatever way possible. To achieve that end, Republicans favor cutting taxes whenever they can to "starve the beast" and prevent the growth in any government program. In this view, any policy that does that, and tax cuts are one such policy, is a good policy.

This Republican position came into being with the Reagan era; George Bush the Elder violated it and his loss to Clinton in the 1992 election was attributed to that violation, making the "tax-cut" philosophy deeply entrenched in the Republican view. This left a few fiscally conservative Democrats, and a few maverick Republicans, as the few reluctant supporters of sound finance, and made large fiscal deficits the norm.

Conclusion

As should be clear from the above discussion, there is much debate in the economics profession about what the appropriate public finance and fiscal policy are. My sense is that the most prevalent modern view is the *nuanced sound functional finance* view. Considering all issues—practical, economic, and political—this view allows that there might be some gain from expansionary fiscal policy, but that, politically and practically, for government to use discretionary fiscal policy to steer the economy is close to impossible. It is even difficult to use fiscal policy in recessions. It is better to rely on automatic stabilizers that have been installed in the budget process. With automatic stabilizers in place, the budget will automatically swing into deficit when the economy goes into a recession, and this swing probably helps reduce the intensity of the recession. While this consensus view would be challenged by New Classical economists who hold that any focus on stabilization and the demand side of public finance is likely to miss the important supply-side incentive effects of policy, it will likely remain the view until the next big shift in macroeconomic policy thinking.

The above discussion of the changing views of fiscal policy may make it look as if economic policy is totally subjective. That isn't true. While economic policy is not a cut-and-dried topic, neither is it totally subjective. As Keynes once said, economics is a method rather than a doctrine, an apparatus of the mind, a technique of thinking that helps the possessor to draw correct conclusions. The operative word there is *method*, not *doctrine*.

In economics you don't learn correct economic policy; what you learn is a method for thinking about economic policy that others have found useful. That method is to learn some models and then to judiciously apply them to a variety of situations. Past applications of these models have found that expectations and the policy process are often more important than the particular policy, which has led economists to talk about credibility and policy regimes when discussing policy. In such an uncertain world, tools, not rules, are what's needed for guiding policy.

Summary

- Sound finance is a view that the government budget should always be balanced except in wartime.

- The Ricardian equivalence theorem states that it doesn't matter whether government spending is financed by taxes or deficits; neither would affect the economy.

- Although proponents of sound finance believed the logic of the Ricardian equivalence theorem, they believed that in reality, deficit spending could affect the economy. Still, because of political and moral issues, proponents of sound finance promoted balanced budgets.

- Functional finance is the theoretical proposition that governments should make spending and taxing decisions based on their effect on the economy, not moralistic principles.

- Six problems that make functional finance difficult to implement are
  1. Interest rate crowding out.
  2. The government knowing what the situation is.
  3. The government knowing the economy's potential income.
  4. Government's inability to respond quickly enough.
  5. The size of government debt not mattering.
  6. Conflicting goals.

- Activist fiscal policy is now built into U.S. economic institutions through automatic stabilizers.

- The New Classical view is that the Ricardian equivalence theorem is not only theoretically true, it is also true in practice and, therefore, government should not use deficit spending.

- The nuanced Keynesian view is that deficit spending can crowd out private investment, reducing the effect of deficit spending on the economy, but deficit spending will increase output in the economy.

- New Classicals believe that growth is much more central to the well-being of individuals.

Key Terms

automatic stabilizer (344)   functional finance (338)   procyclical fiscal   Ricardian equivalence
crowding out (339)   New Classical   policy (345)   theorem (336)
fiscal policy (335)   macroeconomics (346)   public finance (335)   sound finance (335)

Questions for Thought and Review

1. Why does sound finance not depend on the Ricardian equivalence theorem?   LO2

2. According to the Ricardian equivalence theorem, why is government spending offset by a reduction in private spending?   LO1

3. What is functional finance?   LO2

4. Why is functional finance difficult to implement?   LO2

5. According to crowding out, how is government spending offset by a reduction in private spending?   LO2

6. If interest rates have no effect on investment, how much crowding out will occur?   LO2

7. How does the budget process make fiscal policy difficult to implement?   LO3

8. How are state balanced-budget requirements procyclical?   LO4

9. Suppose one economist believes the target rate of unemployment is 4.5 percent while another believes it is 5.5 percent. Using Okun's rule of thumb, by how much would you expect their estimates of potential GDP to differ in a $10 trillion economy?   LO3

10. How do automatic stabilizers work? How can they slow an economic recovery?   LO4

11. Use the AS/AD model to explain why most presidents advocate government spending programs when running for reelection.   LO3

12. Use the AS/AD model to explain the maxim in politics that if you are going to increase taxes, the time to do it is right after your election, when reelection is far off.   LO3

13. How do New Classicals today differ from economists who promoted sound finance in the 1930s? How are they the same?   LO5

14. Why are incentive effects particularly important considerations for New Classical economists?   LO5

Problems and Exercises

15. Demonstrate the effect of the following on output and the price level in the AS/AD model and on the interest rate and investment in using the supply and demand for loanable funds:
    a. Full crowding out.
    b. Partial crowding out.

    c. Full crowding out and private investment is more productive than government investment.   LO3

16. According to the Ricardian equivalence theorem what is the effect of deficit spending on each of the following:
    a. The interest rate and private investment. Demonstrate your answer using the supply and demand for loanable funds.
    b. Output in the economy. Demonstrate your answer with the AS/AD model.   LO1

17. Explain the place of activist fiscal policy in directing the economy according to each of the following points of view:
    a. Sound finance.
    b. Functional finance.
    c. Nuanced functional finance.
    d. New Classical.   LO2, LO5

18. The economy is below potential. Demonstrate with the AS/AD model what an economist from each of the following schools of thought believes should be done to address an economy that is below potential.
    a. Nuanced functional finance.
    b. New Classical.   LO5

19. Congratulations! You've just been appointed chairman of the Council of Economic Advisers in Textland. The mpe is .8. There is a recessionary gap of $400.
    a. The government wants to eliminate the gap by changing expenditures. What policy would you suggest?
    b. Your research assistant comes running in and tells you that instead of changing expenditures, the government wants to achieve the same result by decreasing taxes. What policy would you recommend now? (Requires reading and using the math in Appendix A of the chapter "The Multiplier Model.")
    c. Your research assistant has a worried look on her face. "What's the problem?" you ask. "I goofed," she confesses. "I thought taxes were exogenous when actually there's a marginal tax rate of .2." Before she can utter another word, you say, "No problem, I'll simply recalculate my answers to parts a and b and change them before I send them in." What are your corrected answers? (Requires reading Appendix A of the chapter "The Multiplier Model.")
    d. She still has a pained expression, "What's wrong?" you ask. "You didn't let me finish," she says. "Not only was there a marginal tax rate of .2; there's also a marginal

propensity to import of .1." Again you interrupt to make sure she doesn't feel guilty. Again you say, "No problem," and recalculate your answers to parts a and b to account for the new information. What are your new answers? (Requires reading Appendix A of the chapter "The Multiplier Model.")

e. That pained look is still there, but this time you don't interrupt. You let her finish. She says, "And they want to see the answers graphically." You do the right thing. *Review question*

20. A tax cut has just been announced. Congressman Growth states that its effect will be on the supply side. Congressman Stable states that its effect will be on the demand side.

a. Demonstrate graphically the effect of the tax cut on the price level and output in the standard *AS/AD* model. Which of the two congressmen's views better fits the model?

b. Demonstrate the effect graphically of the tax cut on the price level and output if the other congressman is correct.

c. In the short run, which of the two congressmen is more likely correct?

d. How might the existence of significant crowding out change your answer to c? *Review question*

21. The government has just increased taxes.

a. Demonstrate the effect on the price level and output in the standard model.

b. How would your answer to a differ if there were partial crowding out?

c. How would your answer to a differ if there were complete crowding out?   LO3

22. When Professor Robert Gordon lowered his estimate of the target unemployment rate from 6 percent to 5.5 percent in early 1995, he quipped, "I've just created 600,000 jobs."

a. What events in the 1990s most likely motivated his revision of the target unemployment rate?

b. Show the effect this revision would have on the *AS/AD* model.

c. The unemployment rate at the time of the revision was 5.5 percent. Income was $7.3 trillion. Within 18 months the unemployment rate had fallen to 5 percent without signs of accelerating inflation. How much higher would the level of potential income have been in 1995 if the target unemployment rate were 5 percent rather than 5.5 percent?   LO3

23. President Bill Clinton's policy in 1993 was designed to reduce the deficit but increase employment.

a. Why would such a policy not fit well in the multiplier model?

b. Explain in words how such a policy might achieve the desired effect.

c. Graphically demonstrate your answer in b.

d. What data would you look at to see if your explanation in b and c is appropriate? *Review question*

Questions from Alternative Perspectives

1. It is often argued that savings should be encouraged. If one believes in the free market, does encouraging savings make sense? Why or why not? (Austrian)

2. During the Depression, unemployment rose to 25 percent. The *AS/AD* model presented in the book suggests that a fall in the price level would have solved the problem. Keynesians are not so convinced and believe that a fall in the price level would have lowered income, which would have shifted aggregate demand back further.

a. Demonstrate the standard argument graphically.

b. How does it deal (or not deal) with that interconnection between a fall in the price level and aggregate demand? (Post-Keynesian)

3. In this chapter you learned the importance of automatic stabilizers. At the state level, "rainy day" funds play a crucial role in maintaining services when state revenues decrease during a recession. While this may appear to be a rational institution, institutions are social constructs and what appears rational depends upon individual belief systems. The existence of a rainy day fund can be interpreted as definitive proof of excess taxation and, in states that allow voter referendums, this fund can be eliminated by a majority vote. What vested interests— those seeking something for nothing—benefit from such decisions? (Institutionalist)

4. The economy has often been far from full employment.

a. What would it take to run a regime of continuous full employment?

b. How would the establishment of a full employment regime alter the relations between workers and capitalists?

c. Is such a regime politically feasible? (Radical)

5. Any policy has both advantages and disadvantages, implying that policy makers must weigh both the advantages and disadvantages when deciding what policy to follow.

a. Does society share absolute, objective values that guide the weighing of the alternatives?

b. What role should religious beliefs play in establishing these values? (Religious)

Web Questions

1. The Virtual Economy home page provides a model of the British economy in which you can play the role of Chancellor, the person who helps determine levels of taxation and spending in Britain. Go to its home page at www.bized.ac.uk/virtual/economy and answer the following questions:
   a. Visit the Chancellor's office on the ground floor. What are the four key economic targets?
   b. What are the main policy tools at the Chancellor's disposal? Provide a brief description of each.
   c. Find the economic model on the fourth floor. Use the model to predict what will happen to each of the policy targets within the first three to four years if income taxes are raised 9 percentage points. Report your results.
   d. What does the model predict will happen within the first three to four years if government spending is increased 10 percent?

2. One of the problems with fiscal policy is the delay between the time government recognizes that the economy is in a recessionary gap (or inflationary gap) and the time it takes to change spending or taxes. Go to the home page of the White House's Office of Management and Budget at www.whitehouse.gov/omb to read about the budgetary process. This information can be found under "Circulars" on the left sidebar. Answer the following questions:
   a. What are the major steps in the budget process?
   b. How much time elapses between the time the president formulates his budget and the time that data are available to indicate what were the actual expenditures made and actual revenue collected?
   c. What percentage of total spending *must* the president and Congress act upon each year? What accounts for the remaining expenditures?

Answers to Margin Questions

1. No; the Ricardian equivalence theorem states that the method of financing a deficit does not matter; sound finance argues that it does matter and that deficits should not be run. (*336*)

2. Pre-1930 economists believed that government should maintain a balanced budget even if there was a recession. (*336*)

3. An economist who believes in nuanced sound finance would say that government should maintain a balanced budget for a small recession, but if there were a large recession or depression, they should be open to running deficits. (*337*)

4. They are fundamentally different; sound finance states that you should always balance the government budget; functional finance states that you should use the government budget balance as a steering wheel to control the economy, and that the state of the economy should determine whether you have a deficit or surplus. (*338*)

5. If interest rates did not affect investment or consumption expenditures, there would be no crowding out. (*340*)

6. If government spending stimulated private spending, the phenomenon of what might be called *crowding in* might occur. The increase in government spending would shift the *AD* from AD_0 to AD_1 as in the accompanying diagram. The resulting increase in income would cause a further increase in investment, shifting the aggregate demand curve out further to AD_2. Income would increase from Y_0 to Y_2—by more than what the simple *AS/AD* model would predict. (*340*)

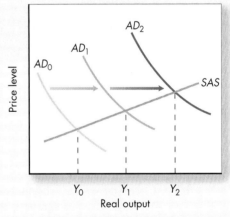

7. Potential income is not a measurable number. It is a conceptual number that must be estimated based on observable information about such phenomena as inflation, productivity, and unemployment. Estimating potential income is a challenge. (*342*)

8. Automatic stabilizers tend to decrease the size of the multiplier, decreasing the fluctuations in the economy. (*345*)

9. The nuanced functional finance answer to what to do if there is a recession is, generally, do nothing in terms of specific tax or spending policy, but let the automatic stabilizers in the economy do the adjustment for you. (*346*)

10. The New Classical answer to what to do is to do nothing, because the Ricardian equivalence theorem tells us that deficit spending will be offset by a decline in private spending. However, always cut taxes to stimulate growth. (*347*)

15 Politics, Deficits, and Debt

Any government, like any family, can for a year spend a little more than it earns. But you and I know that a continuance of that habit means the poorhouse.

—*Franklin D. Roosevelt*

In 2008 the United States was running a large budget deficit, as it had for the past six years. Those deficits were a substantial change from the U.S. budget surpluses that the U.S. government had run from 1998 to 2001, during which time economists had predicted future budget surpluses that cumulatively would exceed $5.9 trillion over the next 15 years. How can the budget picture change so fast? And what do such changes mean for the economy? This chapter considers these and other questions from an economist's perspective in order to give you some deeper insight into policy debates that you will likely hear about in the news media.

Let's begin by reviewing what economic theory has to say about deficits and surpluses. In the long-run framework, surpluses are good because they provide additional saving for an economy and deficits are bad because they reduce saving, growth, and income. In the short-run framework, the view of deficits and surpluses depends on the state of the economy relative to its potential. If the economy is operating below its potential output, deficits are good and surpluses are bad because deficits increase expenditures, moving output closer to potential.

Combining the two frameworks gives us the following policy directive: Whenever possible, run surpluses, or at least a balanced budget, to help stimulate long-run growth. That recommendation is made even stronger when the economy is booming—that is, when it is above its level of potential income. Should the economy fall into a recession, however, policy makers must choose between the different policies suggested by the long-run and short-run frameworks.

At the beginning of 2000, the U.S. economy was booming, unemployment was at historic lows, and there was general agreement that the economy was at its potential output. If ever there was a time to let government build up a surplus and cut debt, it was then; that was the policy both the short- and long-run economic frameworks recommended. What policy did the government follow? It increased spending and cut taxes—precisely the opposite of what economic theory suggested was needed.

In 2001, the situation changed and the economy fell into a mild recession. When the World Trade Center and the Pentagon were attacked on September 11, many feared that the mild recession, which had begun March 2001, would become a severe recession and possibly a depression because consumers would lose confidence in the economy. Suddenly, that earlier tax cut didn't look so bad in economists' short-run framework, and the tax cut played a role in making the recession of 2001 the shortest on record.

So what's going on here? The answer is complicated. To explain it, we need some background on accounting issues that pertain to deficits, some specifics about the demography and institutions of the United States, and some knowledge of politics as it relates to surpluses, deficits, and debt. This chapter is intended to provide you with that background.

Q-1 How can deficits be both good and bad for an economy?

Defining Deficits and Surpluses

The definitions of *deficit, surplus,* and *debt* are simple, but this simplicity hides important aspects that will help you understand current debates about deficits and debt. Thus, it's necessary to look carefully at some ambiguities in the definitions.

A **deficit** is *a shortfall of revenues under payments.* A **surplus** is *an excess of revenues over payments*; both are flow concepts. If your income (revenue) is $20,000 per year and your expenditures (payments) are $30,000 per year, you are running a deficit. This definition tells us that a government budget deficit occurs when government expenditures exceed government revenues. The table below shows federal government total expenditures, total revenue, and the difference between the two for various years since 1980.

A deficit is a shortfall of incoming revenues under payments. A surplus is an excess of revenues over payments.

(Billions of Dollars)	1980	1990	2000	2001	2002	2005	2006
Revenues	517.1	1,032.1	2,025.5	1,991.0	1,839	2,153.9	2,406.7
Expenditures	590.9	1,253.1	1,789.2	1,863.9	1,956	2,472.2	2,654.3
(−) Deficit/(+) surplus	−73.8	−221.0	236.2	127.1	−158	−318.3	−247.6

Source: Congressional Budget Office, *The Economic and Budget Outlook,* January 2007 (www.cbo.gov).

The federal government ran deficits through the 1980s and most of the 1990s. It began to run surpluses in 1998, and returned to running deficits in 2002.

Financing the Deficit

Just like private individuals, the government must pay for the goods and services it buys. This means that whenever the government runs a deficit, it has to finance that deficit. It does so by selling *bonds*—promises to pay back the money in the future—to private individuals and to the central bank. There's a whole division of the U.S. Treasury devoted to managing the government's borrowing needs.

The United States is fortunate to have people who want to buy its bonds. Some developing countries have few people who want to buy their bonds (lend them money) and therefore have trouble financing their deficits. However, countries have an option that individuals don't have. Their central banks can loan them the money (buy their bonds). Since the central bank's IOUs are money, the loans can be made simply by printing money; in principle, therefore, the central bank has a potentially unlimited source of funds. But, as we saw in earlier chapters, printing too much money can lead to serious inflation problems, which have negative effects on the economy. So, whenever possible, governments try not to use the "print money" option to finance their deficits.

The government finances its deficits by selling bonds to private individuals and to the central bank.

Arbitrariness of Defining Deficits and Surpluses

Whether or not you have a deficit or surplus depends on what you count as a revenue and what you count as an expenditure. These decisions can make an enormous difference in whether you have a surplus or deficit. For example, consider the problem of a firm with annual revenues of $8,000 but no expenses except a $10,000 machine expected to last five years. Should the firm charge the $10,000 to this year's expenditures? Should it split the $10,000 evenly among the five years? Or should it use some other approach? Which method the firm chooses makes a big difference in whether its current budget will be in surplus or deficit.

Accounting is central to the debate about whether we should be concerned about a deficit. Say, for example, that the government promises to pay an individual $1,000 ten years from now. How should government treat that promise? Since the obligation is incurred now, should government count as a current expense an amount that, if saved, would allow it to pay that $1,000 later? Or should government not count the amount as an expenditure until it actually pays out the money? The **Social Security system**—*a social insurance program that provides financial benefits to the elderly and disabled and to their eligible dependents and/or survivors*—is based on promises to pay, and thus the accounting procedures used for Social Security play an important role in how big the government's budget deficit actually is.

Many Right Definitions

There are many ways to measure expenditures and receipts, so there are many ways to measure deficits and surpluses.

Many accounting questions must be answered before we can determine the size of a budget deficit. Some have no right or wrong answer. For others, the answers vary according to the wording of the question. For still others, an economist's "right way" is an accountant's "wrong way." In short, there are many ways to measure expenditures and receipts, so there are many ways to measure surpluses and deficits.

To say that there are many ways to measure deficits is not to say that all ways are correct. Pretending to have income that you don't have is wrong by all standards. Similarly, inconsistent accounting practices—such as measuring an income flow sometimes one way and sometimes another—are wrong. Standard accounting practices rule out a number of "creative" but improper approaches to measuring deficits. But even eliminating these, there remain numerous reasonable ways of defining deficits, which accounts for some of the debate.

Deficits and Surpluses as Summary Measures

Deficit and surplus figures are simply summary measures of the financial health of the economy. To understand the summary, you must understand the methods that were used to calculate it.

The point of the previous discussion is that a deficit is simply a summary measure of a budget. As a summary, a surplus or deficit figure reduces a complicated set of accounting relationships to one figure. To understand what that summary measure is telling us, you've got to understand the accounting procedures used to calculate it. Only then can you make an informed judgment about whether a deficit is something to worry about. What's important is not whether a budget is in surplus or deficit but whether the economy is healthy.

Structural and Passive Deficits and Surpluses

The discussion of fiscal policy in earlier chapters emphasized the effect of the deficit on total income. But when thinking about such policies, it is important to remember that many government revenues and expenditures depend on the level of income in the economy. For example, say that the multiplier is 2 and the government is running expansionary policy. Say that that government increases its spending by $100 (increasing the budget deficit by $100), which causes income to rise by $200. If the tax rate is 20 percent, tax revenues will increase by $40 and the net effect of the policy will be to increase the budget deficit by $60, not $100. So as income changes, the deficit changes.

One implication of this feedback effect of changes in income on the deficit is the need to distinguish a deficit caused by a recessionary fall in income and a deficit brought about by government policy actions. Economists' method of distinguishing these is to differentiate between structural deficits and passive deficits.

To differentiate between a budget deficit being used as a policy instrument to affect the economy and a budget deficit that is the result of income deviating from its potential, economists ask the question: "Would the economy have a budget deficit if it were at its potential level of income?" If it would, that portion of the budget deficit is said to be a **structural deficit**—*the part of a budget deficit that would exist even if the economy were at its potential level of income.* In contrast, if an economy is operating below its potential, the actual deficit will be larger than the structural deficit. In such an economy, that part of the total budget deficit is a **passive deficit**—*the part of the deficit that exists because the economy is operating below its potential level of output.* The passive deficit is also known as the cyclical deficit. When an economy is operating above its potential, it has a passive surplus.

The actual deficit is always made up of the structural deficit and the passive, or cyclical, deficit.

The structural deficit is the deficit that remains when the cyclical elements of the deficit have been removed.

Actual deficit = Structural deficit + Passive deficit

This distinction has policy importance because economists believe that an economy can eliminate a passive budget deficit through growth in income, whereas it can't grow out of a structural deficit. Because the economy can't grow out of them, structural budget deficits are of more concern to policy makers than are passive budget deficits.

Let me give an example. Say potential income is $14 trillion and actual income is $13.8 trillion, a shortfall of $200 billion. Say also that the actual budget deficit is $250 billion and the marginal tax rate is 25 percent. If the economy were at its potential income, tax revenue would be $50 billion higher and the deficit would be $200 billion. That $200 billion is the structural deficit. The $50 billion (25 percent multiplied by the $200 billion shortfall) is the passive portion of the deficit.

As you can see from this example, assuming government spending doesn't change with income, you can calculate the passive deficit in the following way:

An economy's actual income is $1 trillion; its potential income is also $1 trillion. Its actual deficit is $100 billion. What is its passive deficit?

Passive deficit = Tax rate × (Potential output − Actual output)

Once you know the passive deficit, you can also calculate the structural deficit:

Structural deficit = Actual deficit − Passive deficit

Passive deficit = Tax rate × (Potential output − Actual output)
Structural deficit = Actual deficit − Passive deficit

Often there is significant debate about what an economy's potential income level is, and hence there is disagreement about what percentage of a deficit is structural and what percentage is passive. Nonetheless, the distinction is often used and is important to remember. For example, the passive/structural distinction plays a key role in explaining the sudden movement from predictions of surpluses to predictions of deficits that I discussed in the opening part of this chapter. The 2001 recession decreased the passive surplus, because, as income fell, tax revenues fell. The terrorist attacks in late 2001 also caused economists to lower their predictions of potential output, which lowered the estimate of the structural surplus. These changes alone reduced trillions of dollars in the predicted surplus. Take these changes, combine them with the tax cut that had previously been passed by Congress, and with the expected increases in government expenditures associated with the war on terror, and—*poof*—the expected $5.9 trillion surplus disappeared and turned into a large expected deficit.

In recent years there has been little debate about the U.S. budget deficit. Taxes have been cut, reducing revenues; defense expenditures have ballooned; and few cuts have been made in domestic government spending programs. In 2007, with GDP at or above potential output and unemployment at 4.5 percent, which is below most economists' estimate of the target rate of unemployment, most of the recent U.S. deficits are considered to be structural.

Nominal and Real Deficits and Surpluses

Another distinction that economists make when discussing the budget deficit and surplus picture is the real/nominal distinction. A **nominal deficit** is *the deficit determined by looking at the difference between expenditures and receipts.*[1] It's what most people think of when they think of the budget deficit; it's the value that is generally reported. The **real deficit** is *the nominal deficit adjusted for inflation.* To understand this distinction, it is important to recognize that inflation wipes out debt (accumulated deficits less accumulated surpluses). How much does it wipe out? Consider an example: If inflation is 4 percent per year, the real value of all assets denominated in dollars is declining by 4 percent each year. If you had $100, that $100 will be worth 4 percent less at the end of the year—the equivalent of $96 without inflation. By the same reasoning, when there's 4 percent inflation, the value of the debt is declining 4 percent each year. If a country has a debt of $2 trillion, 4 percent inflation will eliminate $80 billion of the real value of the debt each year.

The larger the debt and the larger the inflation, the more debt will be eliminated by inflation. For example, with 10 percent inflation and a $2 trillion debt, $200 billion of the debt will be eliminated by inflation each year. With 10 percent inflation and a $4 trillion debt, $400 billion of the debt would be eliminated.

If inflation is wiping out debt, and the deficit is equal to the increases in debt from one year to the next, inflation also affects the deficit. Economists take this into account by differentiating nominal deficits from real deficits.

We can calculate the real deficit by subtracting the decrease in the value of the government's total outstanding debts due to inflation. Specifically:[2]

$$\text{Real deficit} = \text{Nominal deficit} - (\text{Inflation} \times \text{Total debt})$$

Let's consider an example. Say that the nominal deficit is $280 billion, inflation is 4 percent, and total debt is $3 trillion. Substituting into the formula gives us a real deficit of $160 billion [$280 billion − (0.04 × $3 trillion) = $280 billion − $120 billion = $160 billion].

This insight into debt is directly relevant to the budget situation in the United States. For example, back in 1990, the nominal U.S. deficit was about $221 billion, while the real deficit was about one-third of that—$79 billion; in 2006 the U.S. government deficit was about $248 billion; there was 2.9 percent inflation and a

Q-3 Explain how inflation can wipe out debt.

Inflation reduces the value of the debt. That reduction is taken into account when the real deficit is calculated.

Real deficit = Nominal deficit − (Inflation × Total debt)

Q-4 The nominal deficit is $40 billion, inflation is 2 percent, and the total debt is $4 trillion. What is the real deficit?

---

[1] In this section I will discuss deficits only. Since a surplus is a negative deficit, the discussion can be easily translated into a discussion of surpluses.
[2] This is an approximation for low rates of inflation. When inflation becomes large, total debt is multiplied by Inflation /(1 + Inflation), rather than just by inflation.

total debt of about \$8.5 trillion. That means the real deficit was only \$1 billion.[3] The table below shows the U.S. nominal and real deficits and surpluses for selected years.

(Billions of Dollars)	1980	1990	2000	2006
Nominal (−)deficit/(+)surplus	−74	−221	+236	−248
Plus Inflation × Total debt	86	142	125	247
Government debt	930	3,233	5,674	8,530
Inflation	9.3	4.4	2.2	2.9
Equals Real (−)deficit/(+)surplus	+12	−79	+361	−1

Source: *The Economic and Budget Outlook*, Congressional Budget Office, January 2007 (www.cbo.gov); and *The Economic Report of the President*, 2007.

Because the United States has had both debt and inflation for the years shown, the real deficits are smaller than the nominal deficits and the real surpluses are greater than the nominal surpluses.

The lowering of the real deficit by inflation is not costless to the government. Persistent inflation becomes built into expectations and causes higher interest rates. When inflationary expectations were low, as they were in the 1950s, the U.S. government paid 3 or 4 percent on its bonds that financed the debt. In 1990, when inflationary expectations were high, the government paid 8 or 9 percent interest, which is about 5 percentage points more than it paid in the 1950s. With its \$3.2 trillion debt, this meant that the United States was paying about \$160 billion more in interest than it would have had to pay if no inflation had been expected and the nominal interest rate had been 3 rather than 8 percent. That reduced the amount it could spend on current services by \$160 billion. In other words, \$160 billion of the 1990 nominal U.S. deficit existed because of the rise in interest payments necessary to compensate bondholders for the expected inflation. As inflationary expectations and nominal interest rates fell through the 1990s and early 2000s, the difference between the real and nominal deficit (surplus) decreased, but the inflation that remained left bondholders requiring a small inflation premium, meaning that interest rates paid by government were higher than they otherwise would have been.

The Definition of Debt and Assets

Debt is *accumulated deficits minus accumulated surpluses*. Whereas deficits and surpluses are flow measures (they are defined for a period of time), debt is a stock measure (it is defined at a point in time). For example, say you've spent \$30,000 a year for 10 years and have had annual income of \$20,000 for 10 years. So you've had a deficit of \$10,000 per year—a flow. At the end of 10 years, you will have accumulated a debt of \$100,000 (10 × \$10,000 = \$100,000)—a stock. (Spending more than you have in income means that you need to borrow the extra \$10,000 per year from someone, so in later years much of your expenditure will be for interest on your previous debt.) If a country has been running more surpluses than deficits, the accumulated surpluses minus accumulated deficits are counted as part of its assets.

Debt is accumulated deficits minus accumulated surpluses. Whereas *deficit* is a flow concept, *debt* is a stock concept.

Q-5 Distinguish between *deficit* and *debt*.

[3]Because a surplus is the opposite of a deficit, you must add inflation times total debt to the nominal surplus to arrive at the real surplus.

Social Security and the U.S. Deficit

If you listen to *Car Talk* on PBS, you know that Tom and Ray Magliozzi often leave readers with a puzzler. In economics we also have puzzlers, and here's one of them for you to ponder. If debt is accumulated deficits, then the change in the debt in a particular year should be the size of the deficit or surplus. So if the U.S. debt is $7,956 billion as it was in 2005, and the deficit in 2006 is $248 billion, then the U.S. debt in 2006 should be 248 + 7,956 = $8,204 billion. When we look at the data however, we see that debt in 2006 was $8,530 billion. Why is this?

Car Talk makes you wait a week for the answer, but we don't have a week, so here's the answer. The deficit that the government reports is the deficit on what is called the unified budget, which is comprised of "off-budget" accounts (government trust funds, including the Social Security system) and "on-budget" accounts (most other government tax revenues and expenditures). The debt the government reports, however, does not include other government accounts, such

as the Social Security system account, which are currently running surpluses. The only asset that Social Security can hold is government bonds. So it is buying government debt (bonds) with its surplus revenues, building up a trust fund of assets to pay benefits to future retirees. In effect, the government on-budget account owes the Social Security and other trust funds 3.7 trillion dollars.

So the answer to the puzzler is that the reported government debt is on the on-budget accounts only while the reported deficit is on the unified account. Since the government is reporting different concepts, there is no reason that the debt in one year plus the deficit should equal the debt in the following year unless the Social Security and other government trust accounts are in balance. Of course, the larger debt reported is offset by the assets in the trust fund, but as I will discuss that later in the chapter, this method of accounting should leave you wondering how much trust you should have in the Social Security trust fund.

Debt Management

Web Note 15.1
Treasury Securities

The U.S. government, through its Treasury Department, must continually refinance the bonds that are coming due by selling new bonds, as well as sell new bonds when running a deficit. This makes for a very active market in U.S. government bonds, and the interest rate paid on government bonds is a closely watched statistic in the economy. If the government runs a surplus, it can either retire some of its previously issued bonds by buying them back or simply not replace the previously issued bonds when they come due.

To judge a country's debt, we must view its debt in relation to its assets.

The Need to Judge Debt Relative to Assets   Debt is also a summary measure of a country's financial situation. As a summary measure, debt has even more problems than deficit. Unlike a deficit, which is the difference between outflows and inflows, and hence provides both sides of the ledger, debt by itself is only half of a picture. The other half of the picture is assets. For a country, assets include its skilled workforce, its natural resources, its factories, its housing stock, and its holdings of foreign assets. For a government, assets include not only the buildings and land it owns but also, and more important, a portion of the assets of the people in the country, since government gets a portion of all earnings of those assets in tax revenue.

Why is debt only half the picture of a country's financial situation?

To get an idea of why the addition of assets is necessary to complete the debt picture, consider two governments: one has debt of $3 trillion and assets of $50 trillion; the other has only $1 trillion in debt but only $1 trillion in assets. Which is in a better financial position? The government with the $3 trillion debt is, because its debt is significantly exceeded by its assets. The point is simple: To judge a country's debt, we must view its debt in relation to all its assets.

This need to judge debt relative to assets adds an important caveat to the long-run position that government budget deficits are bad. When the government runs a deficit, it might be spending on projects that increase its assets. If the assets are valued at more

Generational Accounting

As I have emphasized in the text, different accounting procedures shed light on slightly different issues. Each provides a different perspective of the financial situation, and the combination of them provides you with a full understanding of the issues. One accounting procedure that some economists use is generational accounting. Generational accounting shows government deficits in terms of each generation's net lifetime tax payments and benefits received. Economists such as Larry Kotlikoff and Alan Auerbach have shown that our current system of taxation and transfers results in an intergenerational transfer of resources from younger to older generations. With the older generation becoming larger as the baby boomers age, these transfers are likely to put a severe strain on the tax system and the political foundations of our tax and transfer policies over the next couple of decades.

than their costs, then the deficit is making the society better off. Government investment can be as productive as private investment or even more productive.

To distinguish between expenditures that are building up assets and those that are not, many businesses have separate capital and expenditures budgets. When they run deficits in their capital account, we do not say that they are spending recklessly; we say that they are investing in the future, and generally we applaud that investment. We say they are running a deficit only in reference to their expenditures budget. While the U.S. government budget separates out investment from noninvestment expenditures, it does not have a separate capital account; it reports a consolidated budget, so it does not take into account the asset accumulation or the depreciation of its assets in determining its deficit.

Why aren't government finances generally discussed in relation to separate current and capital budgets? Because with government expenditures it is extraordinarily difficult to determine what an investment is. Business's investments will earn income that allows the business to pay off those investments. Most government goods earn no income; they are supplied free to individuals and are paid for by taxes. Impossible-to-answer questions arise such as: Are expenditures on new teachers an investment in better knowledge? Or: Are expenditures on a poverty program an investment in a better social environment? There are no unambiguous answers to these and similar questions; government accountants believe it is best to avoid such questions altogether.

Arbitrariness in Defining Debt and Assets   Like income and revenues, assets and debt are subject to varying definitions. Say, for example, that an 18-year-old is due to inherit $1 million at age 21. Should that expected future asset be counted as an asset now? Or say that the government buys an aircraft for $1 billion and discovers that it doesn't fly. What value should the government place on that aircraft? Or say that a country owes $1 billion, due to be paid 10 years from now, but inflation is ongoing at 20 percent per year. The inflation will reduce the value of the debt when it comes due by so much that its current real value will be $162 million—the approximate present value of $1 billion in 10 years with 20 percent inflation. It will be like paying about $162 million today. Should the country list the debt as a $1 billion debt or a $162 million debt?

Assets and debt are subject to varying definitions.

As was the case with income, revenues, and deficits, there's no single answer to how assets and debts should be valued. So even after you take assets into account, you still have to be careful when deciding whether or not to be concerned about debt.

The arbitrariness of the debt figure can be seen by considering the holdings of U.S. debt more carefully. In 2006, the U.S. government had a total of $8.5 trillion in debt, but the actual amount held by people and organizations outside the federal government

Ownership of the Debt

This pie chart shows that the debt is held by U.S. citizens, foreign citizens, financial institutions, and other government entities including state and local governments.

Source: *Treasury Bulletin*, U.S. Department of the Treasury, December 2006 (www.fms.treas.gov).

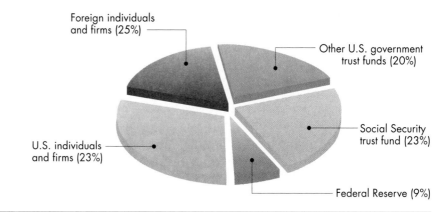

The government holds about 52 percent of its own debt.

is much less than that, as shown in Figure 15-1. There you can see that 52 percent of the debt is internal to the government (including the Fed's holdings)—one branch of the federal government owes another branch of the government the debt. It is an asset of one part of government and a debt of another part. When we net out these offsetting debts and assets, the total federal debt decreases from about $8.5 trillion to $4.1 trillion. Of that $4.1 trillion, about 48 percent is held by U.S. individuals and firms and about 52 percent is held by foreign individuals and firms.

Many of the bonds to finance the current deficit are being bought by the Social Security trust fund, a fund managed by the Social Security Administration in order to meet its future obligations. By law, the Social Security trust fund must be held in the form of nonmarketable government bonds. This means that one agency of government (the Social Security Administration) is buying the bonds of another agency (the Treasury Department). Until about 2017, when the Social Security system's outlays are predicted to exceed its revenues, the percentage of debt held by government agencies will continue to increase. In 2006, the Social Security trust fund owned 23 percent of the debt. By 2012, the fund is expected to own 50 percent of the debt. (The Social Security system will be discussed in more detail later in this chapter.)

Difference between Individual and Government Debt

The final point I want to make concerns the quotation from the beginning of the chapter, by Franklin D. Roosevelt, about deficit spending leading to the poorhouse. Roosevelt may have been a great president, but based on that comment, he probably would have failed his economics course. All debt is not the same. In particular, government debt is different from an individual's debt. There are three reasons for this.

Three reasons government debt is different from individual debt are

1. The government lives forever; people don't.

2. The government can print money to pay its debt; people can't.

3. Government owes much of its debt to itself—to its own citizens.

First, government is ongoing. Government never has to pay back its debt. An individual's life span is limited; when a person dies, there's inevitably an accounting of assets and debt to determine whether anything is left to go to heirs. Before any part of a person's estate is passed on, all debts must be paid. The government, however, doesn't ever have to settle its accounts.

Second, government has an option that individuals don't have for paying off a debt. Specifically, it can pay off a debt by creating money. As long as people will accept a country's currency, a country can always exchange money (non-interest-bearing debt) for bonds (interest-bearing debt).

Third, 75 percent of total government debt is **internal debt** (*government debt owed to other governmental agencies or to its own citizens*). Paying interest on the internal debt involves a redistribution among citizens of the country, but it does not involve a net reduction in income of the average citizen. For example, say that a country has $3 trillion in internal debt. Say also that the government pays $150 billion in interest on its debt each year. That means the government must collect $150 billion in taxes, so people are $150 billion poorer; but it pays out $150 billion in interest to them, so, on average, people in the country are neither richer nor poorer because of the debt. **External debt** (*government debt owed to individuals in foreign countries*) is more like an individual's debt. Paying interest on external debt involves a net reduction in domestic income. U.S. taxpayers will be poorer; foreign holders of U.S. bonds will be richer.

Web Note 15.2
External Debts

U.S. Government Deficits and Debt: The Historical Record

Now that we have been through the basics of deficits and debt, let's look at the historical record. From World War II until recently, the U.S. government ran almost continual deficits. From the 1950s to the early 1970s, the government budget balance fluctuated between small $3 billion surpluses to $25 billion deficits. Beginning in the mid-1970s, deficits grew considerably, from $53 billion in 1975 to $290 billion in 1992, before declining in the mid-1990s, disappearing in 1998, but then reappearing in 2002. Over most of that time, total debt has increased. It doubled in the 30 years from 1946 to 1975 and grew more quickly beginning in the mid-1970s, rising by a multiple of 30 to $8.5 trillion by 2006. Most economists, however, are much more concerned with deficits and debt relative to GDP than with the absolute figures.

Figure 15-2 graphs the budget deficit and debt as a percentage of GDP. From this perspective, as you can see in Figure 15-2(a), deficits as a percentage of GDP did not rise significantly in the 1970s and the 1980s, as they did when we considered them in absolute terms. And it's the same with debt. As you can see in Figure 15-2(b), debt, relative to GDP, has not been continually increasing. Instead, from the end of World War II to the 1970s, and from 1988 to 1990, the debt/GDP ratio actually decreased. In the mid-1990s it stabilized at somewhat under 70 percent of GDP, and in the late 1990s and early 2000s it fell to about 60 percent. Then, it started to rise again to 66 percent in 2007.

FIGURE 15-2 (A AND B)   **U.S. Budget Deficits and Debt Relative to GDP**

The size of the deficits and the size of the debt look somewhat different when considered relative to the GDP. Notice specifically how the total debt-to-GDP ratio declined substantially from the 1950s to the 1980s and how it increased in the 1980s and early 1990s. It declined in the late 1990s and early 2000s.

Source: *The Economic and Budget Outlook*, Congressional Budget Office, 2007 (www.cbo.gov); and U.S. Bureau of the Census, *Historical Statistics*.

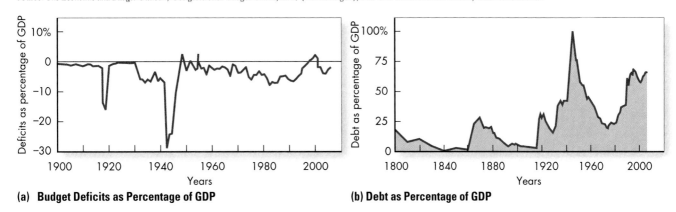

(a) **Budget Deficits as Percentage of GDP**   (b) **Debt as Percentage of GDP**

Deficits and debt relative to GDP provide measures of a country's ability to pay off a deficit and service its debt.

Economists prefer the "relative to GDP" measure because it better measures the government's ability to handle the deficit; a nation's ability to pay off a debt depends on its productive capacity (the asset side of the picture). GDP serves the same function for government as income does for an individual. It provides a measure of how much debt, and how large a deficit, government can handle. So when GDP grows, so does the debt the government can reasonably carry.

The Debt Burden

Most of the decrease in the debt-to-GDP ratio in U.S. history occurred through growth in GDP. Growth in GDP can occur in two ways: through inflation (a rise in nominal but not real GDP) or through real growth. Both ways reduce the problem of the debt. As I discussed above, inflation wipes out the value of existing debt; with inflation, there can be large nominal budget deficits but a small real deficit.

When an economy experiences real growth, the ability of the government to incur debt is increased; the economy becomes richer and, being richer, can handle more debt. As noted in an earlier chapter, real growth in the United States has averaged about 2.5 to 3.5 percent per year, which means that U.S. debt can grow at a rate of 2.5 to 3.5 percent without increasing the debt/GDP ratio. But for debt to grow, government must run a deficit, so a constant debt/GDP ratio in a growing economy is consistent with a continual deficit.

How much of a deficit are we talking about? U.S. federal government debt in 2006 was about $8.5 trillion and GDP was about $13 trillion, so the government debt/GDP ratio was about 66 percent. A real growth rate of 2.5 percent means that real GDP is growing at about $325 billion per year. That means that government can run a deficit of $215 billion a year without increasing the debt/GDP ratio. Of course, for those who believe that the total U.S. government debt is already too large relative to GDP, this argument (that the debt/GDP ratio is remaining constant) is unsatisfying. They'd prefer the debt/GDP ratio to fall.

U.S. Debt Relative to Other Countries

When judged relative to other countries, the United States does not have an especially large debt burden, as can be seen in Figure 15-3. Notice that the U.S. debt is only 66 percent of GDP. If it were 109 percent, as it is in Italy, the U.S. debt would be approximately $5.6 trillion higher than it is. This international comparison, combined with the fact that much of the U.S. debt is held by other government agencies, suggests

Q-7 What annual deficit could a $5 billion economy growing at a real annual rate of 5 percent have without changing its debt-GDP ratio?

FIGURE 15-3 **U.S. Debt Compared to Foreign Countries' Debt**

The U.S. debt does not appear so large when compared to the debts of some other countries in the early 2000s.

Source: *World Economic Outlook*, International Monetary Fund (www.imf.org), and

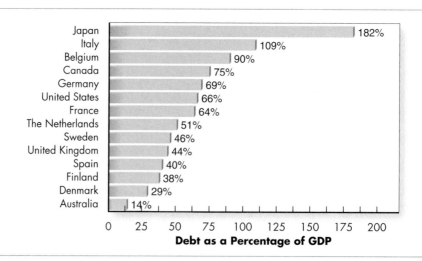

FIGURE 15-4 **Federal Interest Payments Relative to GDP**

Interest payments as a percentage of GDP remained relatively constant until the 1970s, after which they rose significantly due to high interest rates and large increases in debt. In the late 1990s, they fell as interest rates fell and surpluses reduced the total debt and started to rise slightly in the early 2000s.

Source: *The Economic and Budget Outlook*, Congressional Budget Office, 2007 (www.cbo.gov).

that the U.S. government can have trillions of dollars more in debt before there is significant need for concern.

Interest Rates and Debt Burden

Considering debt relative to GDP is still not quite sufficient to give an accurate picture of the debt burden. How much of a burden a given amount of debt imposes depends on the interest rate that must be paid on that debt. The annual **debt service** is *the interest rate on debt times the total debt*.

In 2006, the U.S. government paid out approximately $227 billion in interest. A larger debt would require even higher interest payments. The interest payment is government revenue that can't be spent on defense or welfare; it's a payment for past expenditures. Ultimately, the interest payments are the burden of the debt. That's what people mean when they say a deficit is burdening future generations.

Over the past 50 years, the interest rate has fluctuated considerably; when it has risen, the debt service has increased; when it has fallen, debt service has decreased. Figure 15-4 shows the federal interest payments relative to GDP. This ratio increased substantially in World War II and then again in the 1970s and early 1980s. In the mid 1990s it declined, but in the early 2000s it began to rise again and is currently between 1.5 and 2 percent. As long as the government has a debt, it will make interest payments.

The United States can afford its current debt in the sense that it can afford to pay the interest on that debt. In fact, as I discussed above, it could afford a much higher debt/GDP ratio, since U.S. government bonds are still considered one of the safest assets in the world. No one is worried about the U.S. government's defaulting; that's why we stated above that the U.S. debt can be increased by trillions of dollars without problems.

Projections for the Deficit

As mentioned earlier in the chapter, as recently as 2000, projections were for continual budget surpluses and a paying down of the debt. In 2001 Congress passed the Economic Growth and Tax Relief Reconciliation Act, which cut taxes significantly. Simultaneously, economic growth slowed and, with the war on terrorism, government

A REMINDER

Four Important Points about Deficits and Debt

1. Deficits are summary measures of the state of the economy. They are dependent on the accounting procedures used.

2. It is the health of the economy, not the deficit, with which we should be concerned.

3. Deficits and debt should be viewed relative to GDP to determine their importance.

4. Real deficit = Nominal deficit − (Inflation × Debt).

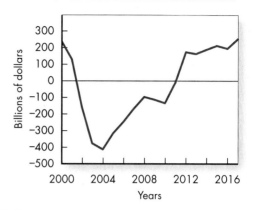

FIGURE 15-5 **Projections for the Budget Deficit**

After four years of budget surpluses from 1998 to 2001, budget surpluses turned into budget deficits beginning in 2002. According to CBO estimates, these deficits will turn to surpluses in 2012, assuming no changes in policy after 2012.

Source: Congressional Budget Office Budget Projections, January 2007.

Q.8 How did the Economic Growth and Tax Relief Reconciliation Act of 2001 contribute to the return of deficits?

expenditures increased significantly. Together, these factors reduced revenues and raised expenditures, turning the surpluses into deficits in 2002.

In 2003 and 2004, Congress cut taxes further and the war in Iraq lasted far longer and was far more costly than expected. As of 2007, the Congressional Budget Office estimated that the current budget deficits would continue at least for the next 5–7 years. The projected deficits are shown in Figure 15-5, but even these estimates may be low since additional funding for continued military operations in Iraq and Afghanistan do not show up in these estimates, and the estimates include the expiration of 2001 tax cuts in 2012, which Congress will not likely let expire. Since these are in large part structural deficits, difficult decisions lie ahead for the United States. We are not immune to the "no free lunch" law.

Social Security, Medicare, and Lockboxes

One of the debates about how concerned we should be about deficits involves the Social Security system. To understand this debate about Social Security and deficits, it is important to recognize that the United States uses a **cash flow accounting system**—*an accounting system entering expenses and revenues only when cash is received or paid out.* When it spends or collects money, these outflows or inflows show up on the budget. When the government doesn't have a cash inflow or outflow, nothing shows up on the budget. Thus, in 2004, when the government created a drug benefit for future retirees, the government incurred enormous future obligations; those obligations didn't show up as part of the deficit.

Because the government uses a cash flow accounting system, a number of obligations incurred by the government do not show up as part of expenditures.

Currently the Social Security system is running a large surplus in its portion of the budget. According to one projection, however, Social Security will be legally required to pay out benefits to retirees that far exceed its revenue. Some politicians have argued that to safeguard the current revenue needed to pay these future obligations, we should create a "lockbox" in which current Social Security revenue would be locked up for future retirees. (In reality there would be no physical lockbox; the word is a metaphor for an accounting rule that would require the government to dedicate the surpluses in the Social Security portion of the budget to pay down the debt held by the public.)

While this proposal has certain attractive attributes, they are not those most people identify with the lockbox concept. The proposal would only indirectly help future Social Security recipients. To see how, let's consider the Social Security system more carefully.

The Social Security system began with the passage of the Federal Insurance Contribution Act (FICA) in 1935; FICA requires employees and firms to pay taxes and, in return, gives the employees a pension after they retire.

A Pay-as-You-Go System

The Social Security system was set up as a **pay-as-you-go system** where *the payments to current beneficiaries are funded through current payroll taxes.* This means that the Social Security system is an unfunded pension system. A *funded pension system* is a system where the contributions paid by workers plus interest are used to fund those workers' pensions. An *unfunded pension system,* however, is not necessarily unsound. In an ongoing system, there will always be revenue coming in and payments going out. There are always current workers to support a system that pays the aged. The benefit of the unfunded system is that it allows initial payments to individuals to exceed what they paid in. As long as the population's age distribution, the annual death rate, the number of people working, and productivity, do not change much, an unfunded system runs smoothly.

The Social Security system is a partially unfunded pension system: payments to current beneficiaries are funded through current payroll taxes.

The Effect of the Baby Boom

An unfunded system does, however, present a potential problem if the amount paid in differs from the amount paid out. To see this, say we have only three groups of people: workers, the retired elderly, and the very young (who aren't yet working). Now suddenly we start a pension program. We use the money that we collect from the workers to pay pensions to the elderly retired people, who have paid nothing in because they retired before the system started up. In short, this group gets benefits without having paid anything into the system. In the next generation, the elderly die, the workers become elderly, and the young become workers. The new group of elderly gets paid by the new workers. As long as the three groups remain at equivalent relative sizes, the process works neatly—each generation will get paid when its time comes.

But what happens when there's a "baby boom"—when one group has an unusually large number of children in a short period of time? In this case, the sizes of the generations are significantly different. Initially things work out wonderfully. The baby boomers become workers, and there are lots of them relative to the elderly. There's plenty of

This lithograph, titled "Legislative assault (on the budget)," appeared in a French newspaper in 1835.

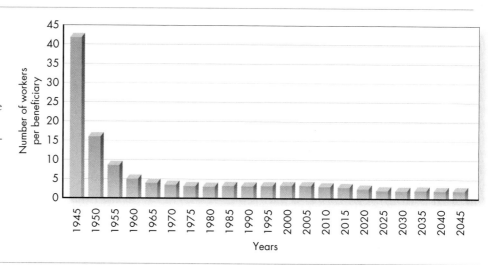

Q.9 How can a baby boom cause problems for an unfunded pension system?

money coming in and comparatively little going out. This allows for an increase in payments to the elderly, a decrease in the taxes paid in by the working group, an increase in the trust fund, or some combination of the three.

In the next generation, the baby-boom workers become elderly. Then, assuming the baby boomers have fewer children than their own parents had, the number of people collecting benefits becomes larger but the number of workers contributing to the system becomes smaller. In this case, payments per beneficiary must decrease, real contributions per worker coming in must increase, or some combination of the two must occur. None of these alternatives is particularly pleasant.

This example doesn't come out of nowhere. It represents the current situation in the U.S. Social Security system. From 1946 through the late 1960s, there was a baby boom, and these baby boomers are currently in the labor force. They'll start retiring in large numbers in the early 2010s and, when they do, the number of workers per retiree will decrease, so that around 2020 there will be about 2.5 workers per retiree instead of more than 15 workers per retiree as in the 1950s. Figure 15-6 shows these unpleasant projections.

The Social Security Trust Fund

In the 1970s and 1980s, economists pointed out that this problem would be occurring. In response, in 1983 the government passed an amendment to the Social Security Act of 1935. The age of eligibility was raised slightly, Social Security tax rates (FICA) were raised, and Social Security payments became subject to taxation for some beneficiaries. These measures were designed to create surpluses in the coming years.

Most of the current budget surpluses originate from a surplus generated from the Social Security system.

The Social Security Trust Fund

Currently, were it not for surpluses in the Social Security system, the budget deficit would be much larger. For example as discussed in an earlier box, in 2006 the Social Security system had a $190 billion surplus. Without this surplus and the surplus on other off-budget accounts, the government budget would have had a $574 billion deficit rather than a $248 billion deficit.

That portion of the surplus is not available for spending; it is earmarked for the Social Security trust fund, which holds special bonds issued by government that cannot be bought and sold on the bond market. The 1983 act was designed to produce surpluses that could be placed into a trust fund to make the payments coming due in the 2020 to 2040 period without requiring huge tax increases or massive borrowing then. The lockbox proposals are designed to ensure that those surpluses held in the trust fund would be available. In the early 2000s, the Social Security Administration estimated that surpluses would continue until about 2020. At that time, outlays will begin to exceed revenue, and by about 2040, the Social Security trust fund will be used up and the system will either have to begin borrowing, increase revenue, or reduce benefits. This doesn't mean the system is in crisis; it is far from a crisis, but it does mean that some adjustments need to be made.

The Social Security system is not the only government spending program that will experience significant funding problems in the future. The Medicare program will face more serious problems; since the elderly use significantly more medical services than younger individuals, these expenses will be substantial. The problem of future funding of the system was exacerbated in 2004 when the government expanded the Medicare program to include partial coverage of drugs for the elderly. Since the elderly are heavy users of drugs, the cost of this coverage is likely to spiral as baby boomers retire. This Medicare program is far closer to crisis than is the Social Security program. It has been estimated that in 2030, 60 or even 65 percent of the government budget will be spent on Social Security and Medicare, compared to the current 35 percent.

The bottom line is that the U.S. budget, considered separately from the Social Security budget, is having to borrow much more than the amount of its current official deficit. Its borrowing offsets the saving represented by the trust fund, which exists to pay future Social Security claims.

Why should a student care about these issues? Because there is no such thing as a free lunch, and someone is going to have to pay. When the baby boomers retire but continue consuming, those who are students today but will be workers in the future (that's you) are the ones who will pay.

The Real Problem and the Real Solution

While the conventional wisdom is for government to run a surplus when the economy is booming, it does not suggest that the trust fund will provide the complete answer to the Social Security funding problem. Even if we had a fully funded trust fund, it would not solve the Social Security problem. The reason is that the trust fund is simply a financial solution; the actual solution must be a "real" solution—a solution that deals with the supply and demand of real resources, not with nominal amounts.

To understand why this is the case, it is helpful to think of the problem in terms of the *AS/AD* model, which tells us that, in equilibrium, real aggregate demand must equal real aggregate supply—the amount of real goods available to consume must equal the amount of real goods for sale, as is true at point A in Figure 15-7. Herein lies the problem. When baby boomers, such as myself, retire in between 2010 and 2030, we will stop producing real goods, *but we will continue consuming* real goods. And given our medical needs, we will likely consume quite heavily—medicine, travel, and all that good stuff. Real goods must be provided to us. Our Social Security and Medicare payments, our other pensions, and our savings will give us significant nominal income to spend. In terms of the *AS/AD* model, the *AD* curve will shift to the right from AD_0 to AD_1. If that shift is not matched by a shift of the LAS curve, the quantity of aggregate demand will exceed the quantity of aggregate supply and the result will be inflation. That is, there will be pressure for the *SAS* curve to shift up and for inflation to rise. The problem is that someone has to produce the goods that we're spending on. That's where you and your fellow workers come in. Put bluntly, starting in 2010, you must produce not only enough real goods for yourself and your family but also enough for the retired baby boomers. Put another way, *the real output per worker must increase, but the real*

The real problem that is created by the baby boom is that as baby boomers retire, they will cease to contribute to production but will continue to consume. Workers will have to produce enough both for themselves and for the large number of retirees.

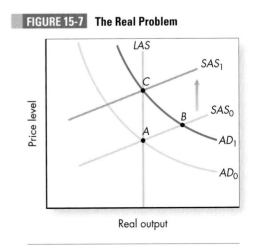

FIGURE 15-7 **The Real Problem**

consumption of workers must not increase as much if the increasing number of retired baby boomers are to have real goods to consume.

The Trust Fund Illusion   If this real problem—the need to match aggregate supply and aggregate demand—exists whether or not the Social Security trust fund exists, what does the trust fund do? The answer is "not much" directly, but it does have a positive indirect effect. The trust fund, like the lockbox policy meant to protect the trust fund, is an accounting illusion. When the United States created the Social Security system, it created obligations to individuals. What the trust fund does is to back that obligation with government bonds—an obligation of the government to pay a certain amount in the future. It backs one government obligation with another.

As I emphasized in the beginning of this chapter, the concepts of *deficit* and *surplus* are creatures of the accounting system used. Placing money into the Social Security trust fund essentially changes an unbooked obligation into a booked obligation. Given the political fear of deficits, this change may lead government to spend less now, and to keep taxes higher now, than it otherwise would. To the degree the government does this, the trust fund decreases the debt in private hands, making the interest burden of the debt less than it otherwise would have been. The holders of debt will not have the interest payments to spend on real goods in the future, making more real goods available for consumption in the future. So, the trust fund might help, even if it does not completely solve the problem.

Politics and Economic Policy[4]   Politics generally mixes illusions with reality, and both Republicans and Democrats have avoided discussing real solutions—solutions that match real production with real expenditures. They either want to assume that the Social Security trust fund will solve the problem, or they want to obfuscate (hide) the problem with rhetoric that doesn't really explain what the problem is. The real solution requires them to deal with the "real" problem that there is no free lunch.

Privatizing Social Security   One proposal being put forward is to privatize at least part of Social Security, creating what its advocates call an "ownership society." This may or may not be a good idea, but it will not solve the Social Security funding problem that the United States is facing. The reason is that the Social Security system is in large part a pay-as-you-go system. If younger people pull out of the system and move to private accounts, someone must pay the retirees who have been promised benefits. That can be done through either more government borrowing (the politically most-likely solution) or higher taxes. Privatization that does not reduce benefits or increase contributions does not solve the problem.

So what policy does provide a real solution? Any policy that brings the real forces of aggregate demand and aggregate supply into equilibrium. The matching of real production with real expenditures could be accomplished if you and your fellow workers save a large portion of your income rather than consume it; if you increase your productivity without increasing your pay; if the government taxes you more heavily starting in 2010, so you don't have income to spend; if Social Security recipients choose to save rather than spend their income; or if even more foreign saving flows in than has already been flowing into the United States. Policies that lead to these results will alleviate the problem.

All real policies achieve one of two ends: They increase future workers' contributions to real production more than they increase their consumption, or they reduce the real amount I and my fellow baby boomers spend when we retire. There are a number of ways such reductions can be accomplished, none of them politically attractive, which is

Q.10 Why won't a fully funded Social Security trust fund solve the real problem the U.S. economy will face as more and more baby boomers retire?

Web Note 15.3
The Social Security Debate

---

[4]This section reflects my particular view, so treat it as a stimulant for thought, not as the correct view. Your teacher, who grades your exam, will tell you the "correct" view.

why they are not much talked about. If not accomplished through policy, the spending reduction will be accomplished through inflation.

One policy is to increase taxes on workers. Another is to cut benefits once baby boomers start retiring. One way to cut benefits is to make Social Security "means tested," so that high-income individuals do not receive as much as they were promised. Another way to cut benefits is to increase the standard retirement age to 72. (It's now 65 to 68.)[5] This increase could be justified by the fact that the elderly live longer and are in better health now than in the past. Since many of us baby boomers will die off between 65 and 72, the savings would be considerable. Moreover, with the delayed Social Security benefits, many of us would work longer, increasing the number of people working and decreasing the number of people consuming without producing.

Neither of these benefit-cutting policies would affect the current budget picture, but both would significantly improve the U.S. economic picture because future real commitments would be decreased. I doubt that either of these policies will be considered, but they are the type of policies that will deal with the "real" macro problem facing the United States in the future.

Policies that would help to match real production to real expenditures in 2020 are

1. Increase taxes on workers to reduce their consumption.
2. Reduce Social Security payments to reduce consumption by retirees.
3. Increase the retirement age to 72 to increase real production.

Conclusion

This has been a relatively short chapter, but the points in it are important. Deficits, debts, and surpluses are all accounting measures. Whether a budget is in surplus or deficit is not especially important. What is important is the health of the economy. The economic framework tells us that if the economy is in a recession, you shouldn't worry much about deficits—they can actually be good for the economy. If you are in an expansion, surpluses make much more sense. It is the state of the economy that we need to consider when making decisions about whether deficits or surpluses are good.

Economics also tells us that there are limits to how much real output one can transfer with financial assets over time. In each time period, the real aggregate demand must equal the real aggregate supply; otherwise inflation or deflation will result. When demographic changes cause real supply and demand to differ substantially, as they will begin to do in the 2020s, there will be a real problem that financial transfers cannot solve. The AS/AD model tells us that that "real" problem must have a "real" solution. Politically we are unlikely to hear much discussion of such solutions, which is why the future economic health of the United States can be precarious even if the U.S. budget is in surplus.

---

[5]Government pension systems were started by the 19th-century German leader Otto von Bismarck. He reportedly chose 65 as the retirement age because his advisers told him that vital statistics for the country showed most people died before age 65.

Summary

- A deficit is a shortfall of revenues under payments. A surplus is the excess of revenues over payments. Debt is accumulated deficits minus accumulated surpluses.

- Budget deficits and surpluses should be judged in light of economic and political conditions.

- Deficits and surpluses are summary measures of a budget. Whether a budget is a problem depends on the budgeting procedures that measure it.

- A passive deficit is that part of the deficit that exists because the economy is below or above potential:

  Passive deficit =

  Tax rate × (Potential output − Actual output)

- A structural deficit is that part of a budget deficit that would exist even if the economy were at its potential level of income.

  Structural deficit = Actual deficit − Passive deficit

- A real deficit is a nominal deficit adjusted for the effect of inflation:

  Real deficit = Nominal deficit − (Inflation × Debt)

- A country's debt must be judged in relation to its assets. What is counted as a debt and as an asset can be arbitrary.

- Government debt and individual debt differ in three major ways: (1) government is ongoing and never needs to repay its debt, (2) government can pay off its debt by printing money, and (3) most of government debt is internal—owed to its own citizens.

- Deficits, surpluses, and debt should be viewed relative to GDP because this ratio better measures the government's ability to handle the deficit and pay off the debt. Compared to many countries, the United States has a low debt-to-GDP ratio.

- The Economic Growth and Tax Relief Reconciliation Act of 2001, an economic slowdown, and the war on terrorism contributed to a return to budget deficits in 2002.

- The Social Security system makes the surplus look bigger than it is. Beginning in 2020, the Social Security system will run deficits.

- The real problem is not the solvency of the Social Security system but the future mismatch between real production and real expenditures.

Key Terms

cash flow accounting system (366)
debt (359)
debt service (365)

deficit (355)
external debt (363)
internal debt (362)
nominal deficit (358)

passive deficit (357)
pay-as-you-go system (367)
real deficit (358)

Social Security system (356)
structural deficit (357)
surplus (355)

Questions for Thought and Review

1. "Budget deficits should be avoided, even if the economy is below potential, because they reduce saving and lead to lower growth." Does this policy directive follow from the short-run or the long-run framework? Explain your answer.   LO1

2. What are the two ways government can finance a budget deficit?   LO1

3. Your income is $40,000 per year; your expenditures are $45,000. You spend $10,000 of that $45,000 for tuition. Is your budget in deficit or surplus? Why?   LO1

4. If the structural budget deficit is $100 billion, the actual deficit is $300 billion, what is the size of the passive or cyclical deficit?   LO2

5. If the actual budget deficit is $100 billion, the economy is operating $250 billion above its potential, and the marginal tax rate is 20 percent, what are the structural deficit and the passive deficit?   LO2

6. Two economists are debating whether the target rate of unemployment is 4 percent or 6 percent. Mr. A believes it's 4 percent; Ms. B believes it's 6 percent. One says the structural deficit is $40 billion; the other says it's $20 billion. Which one says which? Why? (Difficult)   LO2

7. Inflation is 20 percent. Debt is $2 trillion. The nominal deficit is $300 billion. What is the real deficit?   LO3

8. How would your answer to question 5 differ if you knew that expected inflation was 15 percent?   LO3

9. "The debt should be of concern." What additional information do you need to undertake a reasonable discussion of this statement?   LO4

10. List three ways in which individual debt differs from government debt.   LO4

11. If all of the government's debt were internal, would financing that debt make the nation poorer?   LO4

12. How can a government that isn't running a deficit still get itself into financial trouble?   LO4

13. Why is debt service an important measure of whether debt is a problem?   LO4

14. How did the Social Security system contribute to the surpluses of the late 1990s? LO6

15. What are two solutions to the "real" problem posed by the growing number of retiring baby boomers beginning in 2020? LO6

16. Economist Paul W. McCracken stated, "A decision to go with budgets that involve deficits is a decision to have a future economy delivering lower incomes." Do you agree or disagree? Why? (Difficult) LO6

Problems and Exercises

17. Canada's debt was $576 billion at the end of 2001. Using the information below (in billions of Canadian dollars), fill in the blanks for Canada's budget balance and debt for the following years: LO1

	Revenues	Expenditures	Debt
2002	$192	$189	$___
2003	191	___	630
2004	212	201	___
2005	___	211	626
2006	225	216	___

18. Say the marginal tax rate is 30 percent and that government expenditures do not change with output. Say also that the economy is at potential output and that the deficit is $200 billion.
    a. What is the size of the passive deficit?
    b. What is the size of the structural deficit?
    c. How would your answers to a and b change if the deficit were still $200 billion but the output were $200 billion below potential?

    d. How would your answers to a and b change if the deficit were still $200 billion but output were $100 billion above potential?
    e. Which is likely of more concern to policy makers: a passive or a structural deficit? LO2

19. Calculate the real deficit or surplus in the following cases:
    a. Inflation is 10 percent. Debt is $3 trillion. Nominal deficit is $220 billion.
    b. Inflation is 2 percent. Debt is $1 trillion. Nominal deficit is $50 billion.
    c. Inflation is −4 percent. (Price levels are falling.) Debt is $500 billion. Nominal deficit is $30 billion.
    d. Inflation is 3 percent. Debt is $2 trillion. Nominal surplus is $100 billion. LO3

20. Assume a country's nominal GDP is $600 billion, government expenditures less debt service are $145 billion, and revenue is $160 billion. The nominal debt is $360 billion. Inflation is 3 percent and interest rates are 6 percent.
    a. Calculate debt service payments.
    b. Calculate the nominal deficit.
    c. Calculate the real deficit. LO3

21. Assume that a country's real growth is 2 percent per year, while its real deficit is rising 5 percent a year. Can the country continue to afford such deficits indefinitely? What problems might it face in the future? LO4

22. You've been hired by Creative Accountants, economic consultants. Your assignment is to make suggestions about how to structure a government's accounts so that the current deficit looks as small as possible. Specifically, they want to know how to treat the following: (Difficult)
    a. Government pensions.
    b. Sale of land.
    c. Social Security taxes.
    d. Proceeds of a program to allow people to prepay taxes for a 10 percent discount.
    e. Expenditures on F-52 bombers. LO4

Questions from Alternative Perspectives

1. International issues aside, what limits government's ability to undertake monetary or fiscal policy? (Austrian)

2. To help understand the distributional consequences of the tax cuts advocated by many conservative politicians, answer the following:
   a. What income groups have the largest marginal propensity to consume: high or low income?
   b. If your goal were to minimize the deficit cost of a tax stimulus, who should receive the tax cuts? Who received the tax cuts?
   c. What will the tax cut do, relatively speaking, to the debt? Who receives the interest payments on the debt?
   d. Is there a pattern here? (Institutionalist)

3. After President George W. Bush's election in 2000, he proposed cutting taxes.
   a. Would you consider that proposal Keynesian, Classical, or a combination of the two?
   b. From your response, how should President Bush deal with the U.S. deficit and be consistent with the school of thought that you chose? (Post-Keynesian)

4. If future economic growth rates average as little as 2.4 percent—far slower than the 3.0 percent average growth rate the U.S. economy posted over the last 75 years—the Social Security system will remain solvent long into the foreseeable future. A shortfall of 0.4 percent of GDP as projected by the CBO could be paid for merely by repealing the Bush tax cuts that go to the richest

1 percent of taxpayers. Those tax giveaways to the best off in our society will cost 0.6 percent of GDP if they are made permanent.

a. How does that position differ from your textbook's position that the real problem with Social Security is not its solvency but the future mismatch between real production and real expenditures?

b. What do both these positions suggest about the effectiveness of proposals to divert Social Security funds into private accounts? (Radical)

5. Over 40 countries in the world now report what has been called a "women's budget," analyzing public expenditures and revenue from a gender perspective.

a. What might be an example of a gender effect on the expenditure side of the budget?

b. On the revenue side?

c. Why are these effects important to consider? (Feminist)

Web Questions

1. The Social Security Network is a source of information on the current debate about Social Security. Go to its home page (www.socsec.org) to answer the following questions:

a. Summarize the current major proposal.

b. What's good about the proposal?

c. What's bad about the proposal?

2. The U.S. Department of Treasury maintains a learning vault at www.treasurydirect.gov. Go to this site and search for "faq about public debt" to answer the following questions:

a. What percent of the debt is held in each of the following: bills, notes, bonds, inflation-indexed notes, and inflation-indexed bonds?

b. What are intragovernmental holdings?

c. When would the debt decline?

Answers to Margin Questions

1. Deficits can be good when an economy is operating below its potential because they increase aggregate demand and total output. Deficits can be bad in the long run if they lead to lower investment, because lower investment will lead to lower growth. (355)

2. Since the economy is at its potential income, its passive deficit is zero. All of its budget deficit is a structural deficit. (357)

3. Inflation reduces the value of the dollars with which the debt will be repaid and hence, in real terms, wipes out a portion of the debt. (358)

4. The real deficit equals the nominal deficit minus inflation times the total debt. Inflation times the total debt in this case equals $80 billion (0.02 × $4 trillion). Since the nominal deficit is $40 billion, the real deficit is actually a surplus of $40 billion ($40 billion − $80 billion = −$40 billion). (358)

5. Deficit is a flow concept, the difference between income and expenditures. Debt—accumulated deficits minus accumulated surpluses—is a stock concept. (359)

6. To get a full picture of a country's financial situation, you have to look at assets as well as debt, since a large debt for a country with large assets poses no problem. (360)

7. A $5 billion economy growing at a real annual rate of 5 percent could have an annual deficit of $250 million (0.05 × $5 billion) and not increase its debt-GDP ratio. (364)

8. The act contributed to the return of deficits by lowering tax revenues and increasing government spending. (366)

9. An unfunded pension system is a pay-as-you-go system. It collects taxes from current workers and uses the proceeds to pay out benefits to current retirees. A baby boom changes the ratio between workers and retirees. Initially, it increases the number of workers in proportion to the number of retirees, lowering the tax rate that must be paid to meet given retirement goals per current retiree. However, when the baby boomers retire, it increases the necessary tax rate because there are so many more retirees for whom a retirement goal must be met, and there are fewer working taxpayers from whom the necessary amount of taxes must be collected. (368)

10. A fully funded trust fund wouldn't solve the real problem because the trust fund is a financial solution. The solution would make sure that the amount of real goods demanded equals the amount of real goods for sale without significant inflation. (370)

16 International Trade Policy, Comparative Advantage, and Outsourcing

One of the purest fallacies is that trade follows the flag. Trade follows the lowest price current. If a dealer in any colony wished to buy Union Jacks, he would order them from Britain's worst foe if he could save a sixpence.

—Andrew Carnegie

If economists had a mantra, it would be "Trade is good." Trade allows specialization and division of labor and thereby promotes economic growth. Consistent with that mantra, most economists oppose trade restrictions. Not everyone agrees with economists; almost every day we hear calls from some sector of the economy to restrict foreign imports to save U.S. jobs and protect U.S. workers from unfair competition. In this chapter we consider why economists generally favor free trade, and why, despite what economists tell them, countries impose trade restrictions.

Patterns of Trade

Before I consider these issues, let's look at some numbers to get a sense of the nature and dimensions of international trade.

Increasing but Fluctuating World Trade

In 1928, total world trade was about $500 billion (in today's dollars). U.S. gross domestic product (GDP) was about $830 billion, so world trade as a percentage of U.S. GDP was almost 60 percent. In 1935, that ratio had fallen to less than 30 percent. In 1950 it was 20 percent. Then it started rising. Today it is about 250 percent, with world trade amounting to about $32 trillion. As you can see, international trade has been growing, but with significant fluctuations in that growth. Sometimes international trade has grown rapidly; at other times it has grown slowly or has even fallen.

In part, fluctuations in world trade result from fluctuations in world output. When output rises, international trade rises; when output falls, international trade falls. Fluctuations in world trade are also in part explained by trade restrictions that countries have imposed from time to time. For example, decreases in world

AFTER READING THIS CHAPTER, YOU SHOULD BE ABLE TO:

1. Summarize some important data of trade.
2. Explain the principle of comparative advantage.
3. List three determinants of the terms of trade.
4. Explain why economists' and laypeople's views of trade differ.
5. Distinguish between inherent and transferable comparative advantages.
6. Explain three policies countries use to restrict trade.
7. Summarize why economists generally oppose trade restrictions.
8. Explain how free trade associations both help and hinder international trade.

income during the Depression of the 1930s caused a large decrease in trade, but that decrease was exacerbated by a worldwide increase in trade restrictions.

Differences in the Importance of Trade

The importance of international trade to countries' economies differs widely, as we can see in the table below, which presents the importance of the shares of exports—the value of goods and services sold abroad—and imports—the value of goods and services purchased abroad—for various countries.

	Total Output*	Export Ratio	Import Ratio
Netherlands	$ 710	63%	56%
Germany	3,036	38	31
Canada	1,357	32	28
Italy	1,950	24	24
France	2,370	22	24
United Kingdom	2,553	20	26
Japan	4,599	13	11
United States	13,247	8	14

*Numbers in billions.

Source: *World Development Indicators, 2006,* The World Bank.

Among the countries listed, the Netherlands has the highest amount of exports compared to total output; the United States has the lowest.

The Netherlands' imports are also the highest as a percentage of total output. Japan's are the lowest. The relationship between a country's imports and its exports is no coincidence. For most countries, imports and exports roughly equal one another, though in any particular year that equality can be rough indeed. For the United States in recent years, imports have generally significantly exceeded exports. But that situation can't continue forever, as I'll discuss.

Total trade figures provide us with only part of the international trade picture. We must also look at what types of goods are traded and with whom that trade is conducted.

What and with Whom the United States Trades

The majority of U.S. exports and imports involve significant amounts of manufactured goods. This isn't unusual, since much of international trade is in manufactured goods.

Figure 16-1 shows the regions with which the United States trades. Exports to Canada and Mexico made up the largest percentage of total U.S. exports to individual countries in 2006. The largest regions to whom the U.S. exports are the Pacific Rim and the European Union. Countries from which the United States imports major quantities include Canada and Mexico and the regions of the European Union and the Pacific Rim. Thus, the countries we export to are also the countries we import from.

The primary trading partners of the United States are Canada, Mexico, the European Union, and the Pacific Rim countries.

The Changing Nature of Trade   The nature of trade is continually changing, both in terms of the countries with which the United States trades and the goods and services traded. For example, U.S. imports from China, India, and other East Asian countries have increased substantially in recent years. In 1989 goods from China accounted for 2.5 percent of all U.S. merchandise imports. Today they account for 15 percent. Imports from India have increased tenfold over that time—from 0.1 percent to 1 percent of all goods imported.

FIGURE 16-1 (A AND B) **U.S. Exports and Imports by Region, 2006**

Major regions that trade with the United States include Canada, Mexico, the European Union, and the Pacific Rim.

Source: FT900 U.S. International Trade in Goods and Services 2006, U.S. Census Bureau (www.census.gov).

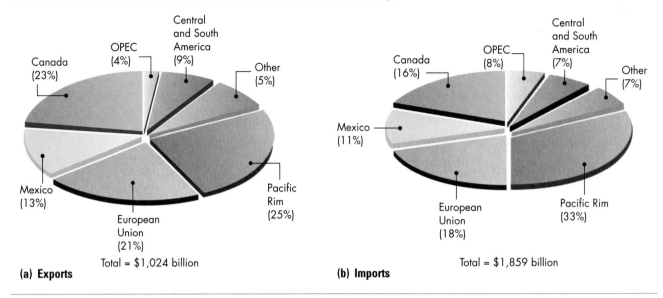

(a) Exports   Total = $1,024 billion

(b) Imports   Total = $1,859 billion

Q₁ How has the nature of U.S. imports from China changed in recent years?

The kind of goods and services the United States imports also has changed. Thirty years ago, the goods the United States imported from China and India were primarily basic manufacturing goods and raw commodities. Technologically advanced goods were produced here in the United States. That is changing. Today we are importing high-tech manufactured goods from these countries, and they are even developing their own new products that require significant research and development.

The change in the nature of the goods that a country produces and exports up the technological ladder is typical for developing countries. It characterized Japan, Korea, and Singapore in the post-World War II era, and today characterizes China and India. As this movement up the technological ladder occurs, foreign companies that had been subcontractors for U.S. companies become direct competitors of the U.S. companies. For example, the automaker Kia and the electronics producer Samsung have developed into major global firms, and in the future you can expect numerous Chinese companies to become household names.

We can expect the nature of trade to change even more in the future as numerous technological changes in telecommunications continue to reduce the cost of both voice and data communications throughout the world and expand the range of services that can be provided by foreign countries. Production no longer needs to occur in the geographic area where the goods are consumed. For example, financial accounting, compositing (typesetting) of texts, and research can now be done almost anywhere, and transferred with the click of a mouse. Even the customer service calls for a U.S. company can be answered almost anywhere at the same phone costs as if they were answered in the United States. (India, which has a sizeable well-educated, English-speaking population, even trains its employees to speak with a Midwest U.S. accent to make it less apparent to customers that the call is being answered in India.) This trade in services is what the press often refers to as *outsourcing*, but it is important to remember that outsourcing is simply a description of some aspects of trade.

Is Chinese and Indian Outsourcing Different Than Previous Outsourcing?

There has been a lot of discussion about outsourcing to China and India recently, and thus it is worthwhile to consider what is, and what is not, different about trade with China and India. First, what isn't new is trade. Manufacturers have used overseas suppliers for years. What is different about outsourcing to China and India today compared to earlier outsourcing to Japan, Singapore, and Korea in the 1980s and 1990s is the potential size of that outsourcing. China and India have a combined population of 2.5 billion people, a sizable number of whom are well educated and willing to work for much lower wages than U.S. workers. As technology opens up more areas to trade, and as India and China move up the technology chain, U.S.-based firms will likely experience much more competition than they have experienced to date. How U.S. companies deal with this competition will likely be the defining economic policy issue for the next decade. If they develop new technologies and new industries in which the United States has comparative advantages, then the United States' future can be bright. If they don't, significant, difficult adjustment will need to occur.

> How U.S. companies deal with new high-tech competition will likely be the defining economic policy issue for the next decade.

The rising competitiveness of Asian economies with the U.S. economy is manifested in the large deficit the United States is running on its **balance of trade**—*the difference between the value of exports and the value of imports*—as is shown in Figure 16-2(a). A trade deficit means that U.S. imports exceed U.S. exports. The United States has been running trade deficits since the 1970s, and in 2006 the U.S. trade deficit reached over $750 billion. The trade deficit looks a little less threatening when considered as a percentage of GDP, as is shown in Figure 16-2(b), but it is still of concern. This means that the United States is consuming a lot more than it is producing, and paying for current consumption with promises to pay in the future.

FIGURE 16-2 (A AND B) **The U.S. Trade Balance**

The United States has been running trade deficits since the 1970s. Panel (**a**) shows the trade deficit in billions of dollars. As (**b**) shows, the trade deficit looks slightly less threatening when considered as a percent of GDP.

Source: U.S. Department of Commerce: Bureau of Economic Analysis (www.bea.gov).

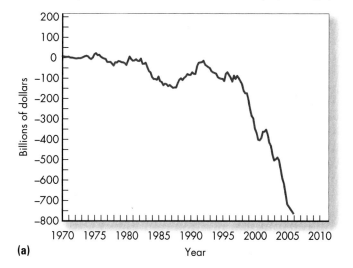

(a)

(b)

International Issues in Perspective

Since the 1970s, international issues have become increasingly important for the U.S. economy. That statement would be correct even if the reference period went back as far as the late 1800s. From the late 1800s through the first 40 years of the 1900s, the United States was in an isolationist period in which the country turned inward in both economic and foreign policies.

The statement would not be correct if the reference period were earlier than the late 1800s. In the 1600s, 1700s, and most of the 1800s, international trade was vital to the American economy—even more vital than now. The American nation grew from colonial possessions of England, France, and Spain. These "new world" colonial possessions were valued for their gold, agricultural produce, and natural resources. From a European standpoint, international trade was the colonies' reason for being.*

A large portion of the U.S. government's income during much of the 1800s came from tariffs. Our technology was imported from abroad, and international issues played a central role in wars fought here. (Many historians believe that the most important cause of the U.S. Civil War was the difference of views about tariffs on manufactured goods. The South opposed them because it wanted cheap manufactured goods, while the North favored them because it wanted to protect its manufacturing industries.) Up until the 1900s, no one would have studied the U.S. economy independently of international issues. Not only was there significant international trade; there was also significant immigration. The United States is a country of immigrants.

Only in the late 1800s did the United States adopt an isolationist philosophy in both politics and trade. So in reference to that isolationist period, the U.S. economy has become more integrated with the world economy. However, in a broader historical perspective, that isolationist period was an anomaly, and today's economy is simply returning international issues to the key role they've usually played.

Another important insight is that international trade has social and cultural dimensions. While much of the chapter deals with specifically economic issues, we must also remember the cultural and social implications of trade.

Let's consider an example from history. In the Middle Ages, Greek ideas and philosophy were lost to Europe when hordes of barbarians swept over the continent. These ideas and that philosophy were rediscovered in the Renaissance only as a by-product of trade between the Italian merchant cities and the Middle East. (The Greek ideas that had spread to the Middle East were protected from European upheavals.) *Renaissance* means rebirth: a rebirth in Europe of Greek learning. Many of our traditions and sensibilities are based on those of the Renaissance, and that Renaissance was caused, or at least significantly influenced, by international trade. Had there been no trade, our entire philosophy of life might have been different.

In economics courses we do not focus on these broader cultural issues but instead focus on relatively technical issues such as the reasons for trade and the implications of tariffs. But keep in the back of your mind these broader implications as you go through the various components of international economics. They add a dimension to the story that otherwise might be forgotten.

---

*The Native American standpoint was, I suspect, somewhat different.

Debtor and Creditor Nations

Running a trade deficit isn't necessarily bad.

Running a trade deficit isn't necessarily bad. In fact, while you're doing it, it's rather nice. If you were a country, you probably would be running a trade deficit now since, most likely, you're consuming (importing) more than you're producing (exporting). How can you do that? By living off past savings, getting support from your parents or a spouse, or borrowing.

Countries have the same options. They can live off foreign aid, past savings, or loans. The U.S. economy is currently financing its trade deficit by selling off assets—financial assets such as stocks and bonds, or real assets such as real estate and corporations. Since the assets of the United States total many trillions of dollars, it can continue to run trade deficits of a similar size for years to come, but in doing so it is reducing its wealth each year.

The United States has not always run a trade deficit. Following World War II it ran trade surpluses—an excess of exports over imports—with other countries, so it was an international lender. Thus, it acquired large amounts of foreign assets. Because of the large trade deficits the United States has run since the 1980s, now the United States is a large debtor nation. The United States has borrowed more from abroad than it has lent abroad.

As the United States has gone from being a large creditor nation to being the world's biggest debtor, international considerations have been forced on the nation. The cushion of being a creditor—of having a flow of interest income—has been replaced by the trials of being a debtor and having to pay out interest every year without currently getting anything for it when they pay that interest. Eventually, the United States will have to deal with this issue. Before we consider how it might do so, let's review the principle of comparative advantage, which is central to economists' understanding of trade.

Q-2 Will a debtor nation necessarily be running a trade deficit?

The Principle of Comparative Advantage

The reason two countries trade is that trade can make both countries better off. The reason that this is true is the principle of comparative advantage to which you were introduced in Chapter 2. It is, however, important enough to warrant an in-depth review. The basic idea of the principle of **comparative advantage** is that *as long as the relative opportunity costs of producing goods (what must be given up in one good in order to get another good) differ among countries, then there are potential gains from trade*. Let's review this principle by considering the story of I.T., an imaginary international trader, who convinces two countries to enter into trades by giving both countries some of the advantages of trade; he keeps the rest for himself.

The principle of comparative advantage states that as long as the relative opportunity costs of producing goods differ among countries, then there are potential gains from trade.

The Gains from Trade

Here's the situation. On his trips to the United States and Saudi Arabia, I.T. noticed that the two countries did not trade. He also noticed that the opportunity cost of producing a ton of food in Saudi Arabia was 10 barrels of oil and that the opportunity cost for the United States of producing a ton of food was 1/10 of a barrel of oil. At the time, the United States' production was 60 barrels of oil and 400 tons of food, while Saudi Arabia's production was 400 barrels of oil and 60 tons of food.

The choices for the United States can be seen in Figure 16-3(a), and the choices for Saudi Arabia can be seen in Figure 16-3(b). The tables give the numerical choices and the figures translate those numerical choices into graphs.

These graphs represent the two countries' production possibility curves. Each combination of numbers in the table corresponds to a point on the curve. For example, point B in each graph corresponds to the entries in row B, columns 2 and 3, in the relevant table.

Let's assume that the United States has chosen point C (production of 60 barrels of oil and 400 tons of food) and Saudi Arabia has chosen point D (production of 400 barrels of oil and 60 tons of food).

Q-3 If the opportunity cost of oil for food were the same for both the United States and Saudi Arabia, what should I.T. do?

FIGURE 16-3 (A AND B)   **Comparative Advantage: The United States and Saudi Arabia**

Looking at tables (**a**) and (**b**), you can see that if Saudi Arabia devotes all its resources to oil, it can produce 1,000 barrels of oil, but if it devotes all of its resources to food, it can produce only 100 tons of food. For the United States, the story is the opposite: Devoting all of its resources to oil, the United States can only produce 100 barrels of oil—10 times less than Saudi Arabia—but if it devotes all of its resources to food, it can produce 1,000 tons of food—10 times more than Saudi Arabia. Assuming resources are comparable, Saudi Arabia has a comparative advantage in the production of oil, and the United States has a comparative advantage in the production of food. The information in the tables is presented graphically below each table. These are the countries' production possibility curves. Each point on each country's curve corresponds to a row on that country's table.

Percentage of Resources Devoted to Oil	Oil Produced (barrels)	Food Produced (tons)	Row
100%	100	0	A
80	80	200	B
60	60	400	C
40	40	600	D
20	20	800	E
0	0	1,000	F

United States' Production Possibility Table

Percentage of Resources Devoted to Oil	Oil Produced (barrels)	Food Produced (tons)	Row
100%	1,000	0	A
80	800	20	B
60	600	40	C
40	400	60	D
20	200	80	E
0	0	100	F

Saudi Arabia's Production Possibility Table

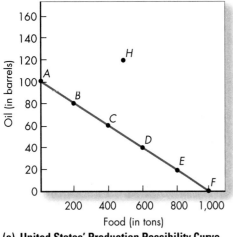

(a) United States' Production Possibility Curve

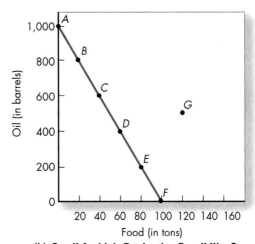

(b) Saudi Arabia's Production Possibility Curve

Now I.T., who understands the principle of comparative advantage, comes along and offers the following deal to the United States:

If you produce 1,000 tons of food and no oil (point *F* in Figure 16-3(a)) and give me 500 tons of food while keeping 500 tons for yourself, I'll guarantee you 120 barrels of oil, double the amount you're now getting. I'll put you on point *H*, which is totally above your current production possibility curve. You'll get more oil and have more food. It's an offer you can't refuse.

I.T. then flies off to Saudi Arabia, to whom he makes the following offer:

If you produce 1,000 barrels of oil and no food (point *A* in Figure 16-3(b)) and give me 500 barrels of oil while keeping 500 barrels for yourself, I guarantee you 120 tons of food, double the amount of food you're now getting. I'll put you on point G, which is totally above your current production possibility curve. You'll get more oil and more food. It's an offer you can't refuse.

Both countries accept; they'd be foolish not to. So the two countries' final consumption positions are as follows:

	Oil (barrels)	Food (tons)
Total production	1,000	1,000
U.S. consumption	120	500
U.S. gain in consumption	+60	+100
Saudi consumption	500	120
Saudi gain in consumption	+100	+60
I.T.'s profit	380	380

For arranging the trade, I.T. makes a handsome profit of 380 tons of food and 380 barrels of oil. I.T. has become rich because he understands the principle of comparative advantage.

Now obviously this hypothetical example significantly overemphasizes the gains a trader makes. Generally the person arranging the trade must compete with other traders and offer both countries a better deal than the one presented here. But the person who first recognizes a trading opportunity often makes a sizable fortune. The second and third persons who recognize the opportunity make smaller fortunes. Once the insight is generally recognized, the possibility of making a fortune is gone. Traders still make their normal returns, but the instantaneous fortunes are not to be made without new insight. In the long run, benefits of trade go to the producers and consumers in the trading countries, not the traders.

Dividing Up the Gains from Trade

As the above story suggests, when countries avail themselves of comparative advantage, there are high gains of trade to be made. Who gets these gains is unclear. The principle of comparative advantage doesn't determine how those gains of trade will be divided up among the countries involved and among traders who make the trade possible. While there are no definitive laws determining how real-world gains from trade will be apportioned, economists have developed some insights into how those gains are likely to be divided up. The first insight concerns how much the trader gets. The general rule is

> The more competition that exists among traders, the less likely it is that the trader gets big gains of trade; more of the gains from trade will go to the citizens in the two countries, and less will go to the traders.

What this insight means is that where entry into trade is unimpaired, most of the gains of trade will pass from the trader to the countries. Thus, the trader's big gains from trade occur in markets that are newly opened.

This insight isn't lost on trading companies. Numerous import/export companies exist whose business is discovering possibilities for international trade in newly opened markets. Individuals representing trading companies go around hawking projects or goods to countries. For example, at the end of the 1999 NATO bombing campaign in Kosovo, what the business world calls the *import/export contingent* flew to Kosovo with offers of goods and services to sell. Many of these same individuals had been in Iraq and

Three determinants of the terms of trade are

1. The more competition, the less the trader gets.

2. Smaller countries get a larger proportion of the gain than larger countries.

3. Countries producing goods with economies of scale get a larger gain from trade.

Iran in the early 1990s, in Saudi Arabia when oil prices rose in the 1970s, and in the Far East when China opened its doors to international trade in the 1980s.

A second insight is

> Once competition prevails, smaller countries tend to get a larger percentage of the gains of trade than do larger countries.

The reason, briefly, is that more opportunities are opened up for smaller countries by trade than for larger countries. The more opportunities, the larger the relative gains. Say, for instance, that the United States begins trade with Mali, a small country in Africa. Enormous new consumption possibilities are opened up for Mali—prices of all types of goods will fall. Assuming Mali has a comparative advantage in fish, before international trade began, cars were probably extraordinarily expensive in Mali, while fish was cheap. With international trade, the price of cars in Mali falls substantially, so Mali gets the gains. Because the U.S. economy is so large compared to Mali's, the U.S. price of fish doesn't change noticeably. Mali's fish are just a drop in the bucket. The price ratio of cars to fish doesn't change much for the United States, so it doesn't get much of the gains of trade. Mali gets almost all the gains from trade.

There's an important catch to this gains-from-trade argument. The argument holds only if competition among traders prevails. That means that Mali residents are sold cars at the same price (plus shipping costs) as U.S. residents. International traders in small countries often have little competition from other traders and keep large shares of the gains from trade for themselves. In the earlier food/oil example, the United States and Saudi Arabia didn't get a large share of the benefits. It was I.T. who got most of the benefits. Since the traders often come from the larger country, the smaller country doesn't get this share of the gains from trade; the larger country's international traders do.

A third insight is

> Gains from trade go to the countries producing goods that exhibit economies of scale.

Trade allows an increase in production. If there are economies of scale, that increase can lower the average cost of production of a good. Hence, an increase in production can lower the price of the good in the producing country. The country producing the good with the larger economies of scale has its costs reduced by more, and hence gains more from trade than does its trading partner.

Comparative Advantage in Today's Economy

The comparative advantage model conveys a story with the theme, "trade is good"; trade benefits both parties to the trade. This story doesn't fit much of the lay public's view of trade, nor the fears of outsourcing discussed above. If trade is good, why do so many people oppose it, and what accounts for the difference between economists' view of trade and the lay public's view? I suggest three reasons.

One reason for the difference is that laypeople often do not recognize the gains of trade—the gains are often stealth gains such as a decline in prices—while they easily identify the loss of jobs caused by the trade adjustments as countries shift production to take advantage of trade. For example, consider the price of clothing: A shirt today costs far less in real terms (in terms of the number of hours you have to work to buy it) than it did a decade or two ago. Much of the reason for that is trade. But how many people attribute that fall in price of shirts to trade? Not many; they just take it for granted. But the reality is that much of our current lifestyle in the United States has been made possible by trade.

Q-4   In what circumstances would a small country not get the larger percentage of the gains from trade?

Gains from trade are often stealth gains.

Much of our current lifestyle is made possible by trade.

Another reason for the difference between the lay view of trade and economists' view is that the lay public often believes that since countries such as China have lower wages, they must have a comparative advantage in just about everything, so that if we allow free trade, eventually we will lose all U.S. jobs. This belief is an internal logical contradiction; by definition comparative advantage refers to relative opportunity cost. If one country has a comparative advantage in one set of goods, the other country must have a comparative advantage in another set.

That said, economists also must admit that the lay public does have a point. The comparative advantage model assumes that a country's imports and exports are equal. As we saw above, U.S. imports and exports are not equal. Currently, the United States imports much more than it exports, and foreign countries are accepting our IOUs in exchange for those imports. As long as foreign countries are willing to accept those promises of the United States to pay some time in the future, they can have a comparative advantage in the production of many more goods than the United States.[1] Currently, people in other countries finance the U.S. trade deficit by buying U.S. assets. Once the other countries decide that it is no longer in their interests to finance the U.S. trade deficit, economic forces such as the adjustment of exchange rates will be set in motion to restore a more equal division of comparative advantages.

The comparative advantage model assumes that a country's imports and exports are equal.

A third reason accounting for the difference between the lay view of trade and the economists' view is that laypeople often think of trade as trade in just manufactured goods. Trade is much broader, and includes the services that traders provide. Countries can have comparative advantages in trade itself, and the gains the trader makes can account for the seeming differences in countries' comparative advantages.

Q-5 What are three reasons for the difference between laypeople's and economists' views of trade?

Notice in my example that the international traders who brought the trade about benefited significantly from trade. I included traders because trade does not take place on its own—markets and trade require entrepreneurs. The market is not about abstract forces; it is about real people operating to improve their position. Many of the gains from trade do not go to the countries producing or consuming the good but rather to the trader. And the gains that traders get can be enormous.

Consider, for example, the high-priced sneakers ($100) that many "with-it" students wear. Those sneakers are likely made in China, costing about $8 to make. So much of the benefits of trade do not go to the producer or the consumer; they go to the trader. However, not all of the difference is profit. The trader has other costs; there are, for example, costs of transportation and advertising—someone has to convince you that you need those "with-it" sneakers. (Just do it, right?) A portion of the benefits of the trade is accruing to U.S. advertising firms, which can pay more to creative people who think up those crazy ads.

The United States currently has a large comparative advantage in facilitating trade. Many of the firms that specialize in the role as trader are U.S.-based companies, and these companies buy many of the goods and services that support trade from their home country—the United States. Therefore, trade with China and India has been generating jobs in the United States. These are jobs that laypeople often do not associate with trade—jobs in research, management, advertising, and distribution of goods. What this means is that goods manufactured in China, India, and other Asian countries are creating demand for advertising, management, and distribution, and are therefore creating jobs and income in the United States. That's one reason for the large increase in service jobs in the U.S. economy.

Trade with China and India has been generating jobs in the United States.

---

[1]One could make the model fit reality if one thinks of the United States as having a comparative advantage in producing IOUs.

A final consideration to keep in mind is that trade increases income and wealth abroad, thereby creating additional demand for U.S. goods. Two billion consumers whose incomes are increasing offer many new growth opportunities for U.S. firms. Trade expands the total pie, and even when a country gets a smaller proportion of the new total pie, the absolute amount it gets can increase.

When one adds these considerations to the initial layperson's reaction to trade, a much more nuanced view emerges that makes trade look much better. This does not mean that trade presents no problems. One big policy problem is that the benefits of trade are quite uneven. The people whose jobs are outsourced are significantly hurt by trade and are very visible. The benefits of trade in lower prices and jobs created by trade are spread throughout the economy and are much less visible. It is the concentrated nature of the costs of trade and dispersed nature of the benefits that will continue to present a challenge to policy makers when dealing with the effects of trade.

The concentrated nature of the costs of trade and the dispersed nature of the benefits present a challenge for policy makers.

Other Sources of U.S. Comparative Advantage

When thinking about how the theory of comparative advantage relates to the current debate about outsourcing—what jobs are outsourced and what jobs are created in the United States—it is important to remember that comparative advantage is not determined by wages alone. Many other factors enter into comparative advantage and these other factors give the United States a comparative advantage in a variety of goods and services. Some of those other sources of U.S. comparative advantage include

1. *Skills of the U.S. labor force.* Our educational system and experience in production (learning by doing) has created a U.S. workforce that is highly productive, which means that it can be paid more and still be competitive.

2. *U.S. governmental institutions.* The United States has a stable, relatively noncorrupt government, which is required for effective production. These institutions give firms based in the United States a major comparative advantage.

3. *U.S. physical and technological infrastructure.* The United States has probably the best infrastructure for production in the world. This infrastructure includes extensive road systems, telecommunications networks, and power grids.

4. *English is the international language of business.* U.S. citizens learn English from birth. Chinese and Indian citizens must learn it as a second language. One is seldom as comfortable or productive working in one's second language as in one's first language.

5. *Wealth from past production.* The United States is extraordinarily wealthy, which means that the United States is the world's largest consumer. Production that supports many aspects of consumption cannot be easily transferred geographically, and thus the United States will maintain a comparative advantage in producing these nontransferable aspects of consumption.

6. *U.S. natural resources.* The United States is endowed with many resources: rich farmland, a pleasant and varied climate, beautiful scenery for tourism, minerals, and water. These give it comparative advantages in a number of areas.

7. *Cachet.* The United States continues to be a cultural trendsetter. People all over the world want to watch U.S. movies, want to have U.S. goods, and are influenced by U.S. advertising agencies to favor U.S. goods. As long as that is the case, the United States will have a comparative advantage in goods tied to that cachet.

8. *Inertia*. It takes time and costs money to change production. Companies will not move production to another country for a small cost differential. The difference has to be large, it has to be expected to continue for a long time, and it must be large enough to offset the risk of the unknown. Thus, the current place of production has an advantage over other potential places for production simply because the current location is known.

9. *U.S. intellectual property rights*. Currently, U.S. companies and individuals hold a large number of intellectual property rights, which require other countries that use their patented goods or methods to pay U.S. patent holders. Every time someone (legally) buys the Windows operating system for his or her computer, a portion of the purchase price covers a payment to a U.S. company. America's culture of embracing new ideas and questioning authority cultivates an environment of innovation that will likely continue to generate new intellectual property rights.

10. *A relatively open immigration policy*. Many of the brightest, most entrepreneurial students of developing countries immigrate and settle in the United States. They create jobs and help maintain U.S. comparative advantages in a number of fields, especially high-technology fields. More than 50 percent of the engineering degrees, for example, go to foreign students, many of whom remain in the United States.

The United States has numerous sources of comparative advantage.

Combined, these other sources of comparative advantage will maintain the United States' competitiveness in a variety of types of production for the coming decades.

Some Concerns about the Future

The above discussion of the sources of U.S. comparative advantage should have made those of you who are U.S. citizens feel a bit better about the future of the U.S. economy; the United States is not about to lose all its jobs to outsourcing. But that does not mean that there are not real issues of concern. The typical layperson's concern that the comparative advantage story does not capture what is going on with trade and outsourcing has some real foundations, and deserves to be considered seriously.

Inherent and Transferable Sources of Comparative Advantages   When David Ricardo first made the comparative advantage argument in the early 1800s, he was talking about an economic environment that was quite different than today's. His example was Britain and Portugal, with Britain producing wool and Portugal producing wine. What caused their differing costs of production was climate; Britain's climate was far less conducive to growing grapes than Portugal's but more conducive to raising sheep. Differing technologies or labor skills in the countries did not play a key role in their comparative advantages, and it was highly unlikely that the climates, and therefore comparative advantages, of the countries could change. Put another way, both countries have inherent sources of comparative advantages, which we will call **inherent comparative advantages**—*comparative advantages that are based on factors that are relatively unchangeable*, rather than transferable sources of comparative advantages, which we will call **transferable comparative advantages**—*comparative advantages based on factors that can change relatively easily*.

As the theory of comparative advantage developed, economists applied it to a much broader range of goods whose sources of comparative advantages were not due to climate. For example, some countries had land, specific resources, capital, types of labor, or technology as sources of comparative advantage. Extending the analysis to these other sources of comparative advantage makes sense, but it is important to keep in mind that only some of these comparative advantages are inherent; others are transferable. Comparative advantages due to resources or climate are unlikely to change; comparative advantages that depend on capital, technology, or education, however, can change. In fact, we would expect them to change.

The Law of One Price   Whether a country can maintain a much higher standard of living than another country in the long run depends in part on whether its sources of comparative advantages are transferable or inherent. Saudi Arabia will maintain its comparative advantage in producing oil, but the United States' comparative advantage based on better education is likely to be more fleeting. In cases where sources of comparative advantage are not inherent, economic forces will push to eliminate that comparative advantage. The reason is the law of one price: in a competitive market, there will be pressure for equal factors to be priced equally. If factor prices aren't equal, firms can reduce costs by redirecting production to countries where factors are priced lower. The tendency of economic forces to eliminate transferable comparative advantage is sometimes called the *convergence hypothesis*. Even seemingly inherent comparative advantages can be changed by technology. Consider oil. The development of cost-effective fuel cells may leave Saudi Arabia with a comparative advantage in oil but not necessarily with a comparative advantage in producing energy.

When markets are working, any country with a comparative advantage due only to transferable capital and technology will lose that comparative advantage as capital and technology spread to other countries. Ultimately, in the case of transferable comparative advantage, production will shift to the lower-wage country that has equivalent institutional structures. This is the law of one price in action: The same good—including equivalent labor—must sell for the same price, unless trade is restricted or other differences exist. That is what's happening now with the United States and outsourcing. Skills needed to do information technology work, for example, are transferable. Because an information technology professional with three to five years' experience earns about $75,000 in the United States and only $26,000 in India, those jobs are moving abroad. As long as wages differ, and the workers' productivities in countries are comparable, transferable comparative advantages of U.S. production will continue to erode, and as they erode, production and jobs will be moved abroad.

The question, therefore, is not: Why is outsourcing to China and India occurring today? The questions are: Why didn't it happen long ago, and how did U.S. productivity, and hence its standard of living, come to so exceed China's and India's productivity, and hence their standards of living? Or alternatively: How did the United States get in its current high-wage position, and is it likely to maintain that position into the indefinite future?

How the United States Gained and Is Now Losing Sources of Comparative Advantage   To better understand the current U.S. position, let's look at it historically. The United States developed its highly favorable position from the 1920s until the late 1940s when the two world wars directed production toward the United States. Those wars, the entrepreneurial spirit of the U.S. population, U.S. institutions conducive to production, and the flow of technology and capital into the United States gave the United States a big boost both during the two world wars and after. Coming out of World War II, at the then-existing exchange rates, the United States had a major cost advantage in producing a large majority of goods, just as China has a cost advantage in producing the large majority of goods today.

Such cost advantages in a majority of areas of production are not sustainable because the balance of trade will be highly imbalanced. In the absence of specific policy by governments, or large private flows of capital, eventually that imbalance will right itself. After World War II, the trade balance that favored the United States was maintained temporarily by U.S. companies, which invested heavily in Europe, and by the U.S. government, which transferred funds to Europe with programs such as the Marshall Plan. These flows of capital financed Europe's trade deficits and allowed the United States to run large trade surpluses, just as current flows of investment into the United States from a variety of countries, and the explicit policy of buying U.S. bonds by Chinese and Japanese central banks, are financing the U.S. trade deficits now, and allowing large Chinese trade surpluses with the United States.

Methods of Equalizing Trade Balances   Capital flows that sustain trade imbalances eventually stop, and when they do, adjustments in sources of comparative advantages must take place so that the trade surplus countries—such as China today—become less competitive (lose sources of comparative advantage) and the trade deficit countries—in this case, the United States—become more competitive (gain sources of comparative advantage). This adjustment can occur in a number of ways. The two most likely adjustments today are that wages in China rise relative to wages in the United States or the U.S. exchange rate falls. Both adjustments will make Chinese goods relatively more expensive and U.S. goods relatively cheaper, just as these adjustments did with countries such as Japan, Taiwan, and Korea in previous decades. Neither of these is especially pleasant for us, which is why we will likely hear continued calls for trade restrictions in the coming decade.

Unfortunately, as I will discuss below, the trade restriction policies that governments can undertake will generally make things worse. In a globalized free-trade economy, the U.S. wage advantage can only be maintained to the degree that total cost of production of a good in the United States (with all the associated costs) is no more expensive than the total cost of producing that same good abroad (with all the associated costs). The degree to which production shifts because of lower wages abroad depends on how transferable are the U.S. comparative advantages that we listed above. Some of them are generally nontransferable, and thus will support sustained higher relative U.S. wages. English as the language of business; the enormous wealth of the United States gained earlier; inertia; and U.S. political, social, and capital infrastructure will keep much production in the United States, and will maintain a comparative advantage for U.S. production even with significantly higher U.S. wages.

But in the coming decades, we can expect a narrowing of the wage gap between the United States and China and India. Given these strong market forces that cannot be prevented without undermining the entire international trading system, about the only available realistic strategy for the United States is to adapt to this new situation. Its best strategy is to work toward maintaining existing comparative advantages through investment in education and infrastructure, while continuing to provide an environment conducive to innovation so that we develop comparative advantages in new industries.

In the absence of specific policy by governments, or large private flows of capital, eventually any large trade imbalance will right itself.

Q-6   What are two likely adjustments that will reduce the wage gap between China and the United States?

The U.S. wage advantage can only be maintained to the degree that total cost of production of a good in the United States is no more than the total cost of that same good abroad.

Varieties of Trade Restrictions

The policies countries can use to restrict trade include tariffs and quotas, voluntary restraint agreements, embargoes, regulatory trade restrictions, and nationalistic appeals. I'll consider each in turn and also review the geometric analysis of each.

FIGURE 16-4 (A AND B)   **Selected Tariff Rates**

The tariff rates in **(a)** will be continually changing as the changes negotiated by the World Trade Organization come into effect. In **(b)** you see tariff rates for the United States since 1920.

Source: General Agreement on Tariffs and Trade (GATT) and the World Bank (www.worldbank.org).

Country	%	Country	%
Argentina	11.8	Norway	0.5
Australia	4.2	Peru	9.0
Canada	3.7	Philippines	5.1
Colombia	11.7	Poland	6.2
Czech Rep.	5.0	Singapore	0
European Union	2.5	South Africa	7.8
Hungary	8.9	Sri Lanka	13.4
India	22.2	Thailand	14.7
Indonesia	7.2	United States	1.7
Japan	2.7	Venezuela	12.4
Mexico	16.2	Zimbabwe	15.9

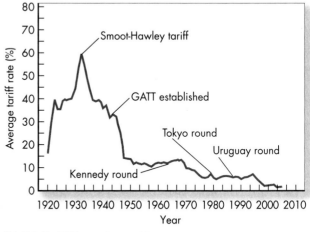

(a) Tariff Rates by Country

(b) U.S. Tariff Rates since 1920

Tariffs and Quotas

Three policies used to restrict trade are

1. Tariffs (taxes on internationally traded goods).
2. Quotas (quantity limits placed on imports).
3. Regulatory trade restrictions (government-imposed procedural rules that limit imports).

Tariffs and Quotas

Tariffs are *taxes governments place on internationally traded goods*—generally imports. (Tariffs are also called *customs duties*.) Tariffs are the most-used and most-familiar type of trade restriction. Tariffs operate in the same way a tax does: They make imported goods relatively more expensive than they otherwise would have been, and thereby encourage the consumption of domestically produced goods. On average, U.S. tariffs raise the price of imported goods by less than 3 percent. Figure 16-4(a) presents average tariff rates for industrial goods for a number of countries and the European Union, and Figure 16-4(b) shows the tariff rates imposed by the United States since 1920.

Probably the most infamous tariff in U.S. history is the Smoot-Hawley Tariff of 1930, which raised tariffs on imported goods to an average of 60 percent. It was passed at the height of the Great Depression in the United States in the hope of protecting American jobs. It didn't work. Other countries responded with similar tariffs. As a result of these trade wars, international trade plummeted from $60 billion in 1928 to $25 billion in 1938, unemployment worsened, and the international depression deepened. These effects of the tariff convinced many, if not most, economists that free trade is preferable to trade restrictions.

The dismal failure of the Smoot-Hawley Tariff was the main reason the **General Agreement on Tariffs and Trade (GATT),** *a regular international conference to reduce trade barriers,* was established in 1947 immediately following World War II. In 1995 GATT was replaced by the **World Trade Organization (WTO),** *an organization whose functions are generally the same as GATT's were—to promote free and fair trade among countries.* Unlike GATT, the WTO is a permanent organization with an enforcement system (albeit weak). Since its formation, rounds of negotiations have resulted in a decline in worldwide tariffs.

Quotas are *quantity limits placed on imports.* They have the same effect on equilibrium price and quantity as the quantity restrictions discussed in Chapter 5, and their effect in limiting trade is similar to the effect of a tariff. Both increase price and reduce quantity. Tariffs, like all taxes on suppliers, shift the supply curve up by the amount of the tax, as Figure 16-5 shows. A tariff, T, raises equilibrium price from P_0 to P_1 by an amount that is less than the tariff, and equilibrium quantity declines from Q_0 to Q_1. With a quota, Q_1, the equilibrium price also rises to P_1.

There is, however, a difference between tariffs and quotas. In the case of the tariff, the government collects tariff revenue represented by the shaded region. In the case of a quota, the government collects no revenue. The benefit of the increase in price goes to the importer as additional corporate revenue. So which of the two do you think import companies favor? The quota, of course—it means more profits as long as your company is the one to receive the rights to fill those quotas. In fact, once quotas are instituted, firms compete intensely to get them.

Tariffs affect trade patterns. For example, as of 2007 the United States imposes a tariff on light trucks from Japan, so the United States imports few light trucks from Japan. You will see Japanese-named trucks, but most of these are produced in the United States. Many similar examples exist, and by following the tariff structure, you can gain a lot of insight into patterns of trade.

The issues involved with tariffs and quotas can be seen in a slightly different way by assuming that the country being considered is small relative to the world economy and that imports compete with domestic producers. The small-country assumption means that the supply from the world to this country is perfectly elastic at the world price, $2, as in Figure 16-6(a).

The world price of the good is unaffected by this country's demand. This assumption allows us to distinguish the world supply from domestic supply. In the absence of any trade restrictions, the world price of $2 would be the domestic price. Domestic low-cost

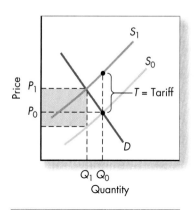

FIGURE 16-5 **The Effects of Tariffs and Quotas**

FIGURE 16-6 (A AND B) **Tariffs and Quotas When the Domestic Country Is Small**

This exhibit shows the effects of a tariff in (a) and of a quota in (b) when the domestic country is small. The small-country assumption means that the world supply is perfectly elastic, in this case at $2.00 a unit. With a tariff of 50 cents, world supply shifts up by 50 cents. Domestic quantity demanded falls to 175 and domestic quantity supplied rises to 125. Foreign suppliers are left supplying the difference, 50 units. The domestic government collects revenue shown in the shaded area. The figure in (b) shows how the same result can be achieved with a quota of 50. Equilibrium price rises to $2.50. Domestic firms produce 125 units and consumers demand 175 units. The difference between the tariff and the quota is that, with a tariff, the domestic government collects the revenue from the higher price. With a quota, the benefits of the higher price accrue to the foreign and domestic producers.

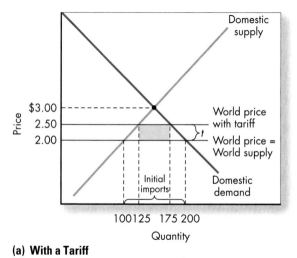

(a) With a Tariff

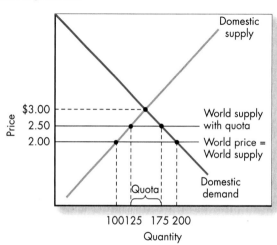

(b) With a Quota

suppliers would supply 100 units of the good at $2. The remaining 100 units demanded are being imported.

In Figure 16-6(a) I show the effect of a tariff of 50 cents placed on all imports. Since the world supply curve is perfectly elastic, all of this tax, shown by the shaded region, is borne by domestic consumers. Price rises to $2.50 and quantity demanded falls to 175. With a tariff, the rise in price will increase domestic quantity supplied from 100 to 125 and will reduce imports to 50. Now let's compare this situation with a quota of 50, shown in Figure 16-6(b). Under a quota of 50, the final price would be the same, but higher revenue would accrue to foreign and domestic producers rather than to the government. One final difference: Any increase in demand under a quota would result in higher prices because it would have to be filled by domestic producers. Under a tariff, any increase in demand would not affect price.

Voluntary Restraint Agreements

Imposing new tariffs and quotas is specifically ruled out by the WTO, but foreign countries know that WTO rules are voluntary and that, if a domestic industry brought sufficient political pressure on its government, the WTO rules would be forgotten. To avoid the imposition of new tariffs on their goods, countries often voluntarily restrict their exports. That's why Japan has agreed informally to limit the number of cars it exports to the United States.

The effect of such voluntary restraint agreements is similar to the effect of quotas: They directly limit the quantity of imports, increasing the price of the good and helping domestic producers. For example, when the United States encouraged Japan to impose "voluntary" quotas on exports of its cars to the United States, Toyota benefited from the quotas because it could price its limited supply of cars higher than it could if it sent in a large number of cars, so profit per car would be high. Since they faced less competition, U.S. car companies also benefited. They could increase their prices because Toyota had done so.

Embargoes

An **embargo** is *a total restriction on the import or export of a good*. Embargoes are usually established for international political reasons rather than for primarily economic reasons.

An example was the U.S. embargo of trade with Iraq prior to the U.S. invasion. The U.S. government hoped that the embargo would so severely affect Iraq's economy that Saddam Hussein would lose political power. It did make life difficult for Iraqis, but it did not bring about the downfall of the Hussein government. The United States has also imposed embargoes on Cuba, Iran, and Libya.

Regulatory Trade Restrictions

Tariffs, quotas, and embargoes are the primary *direct* methods to restrict international trade. There are also indirect methods that restrict trade in not-so-obvious ways; these are called **regulatory trade restrictions** (*government-imposed procedural rules that limit imports*). One type of regulatory trade restriction has to do with protecting the health and safety of a country's residents. For example, a country might restrict imports of all vegetables grown where certain pesticides are used, knowing full well that all other countries use those pesticides. The effect of such a regulation would be to halt the import of vegetables. Another example involves building codes. U.S. building codes require that plywood have fewer than, say, three flaws per sheet. Canadian building codes require that plywood have fewer than, say, five flaws per sheet. The different building codes are a nontariff barrier that makes trade in building materials between the United States and Canada difficult.

A second type of regulatory restriction involves making import and customs procedures so intricate and time-consuming that importers simply give up. For example, at one time France required all imported VCRs to be individually inspected in Toulouse. Since Toulouse is a provincial city, far from any port and outside the normal route for imports after they enter France, the inspection process took months.

Some regulatory restrictions are imposed for legitimate reasons; others are designed simply to make importing more difficult and hence protect domestic producers from international competition. It's often hard to tell the difference. A good example of this difficulty began in 1988, when the EU disallowed all imports of meat from animals that had been fed growth-inducing hormones. As the box "Hormones and Economics" on the next page details, the debate continues.

Q-7 How might a country benefit from having an inefficient customs agency?

Nationalistic Appeals

Finally, nationalistic appeals can help to restrict international trade. "Buy American" campaigns and Japanese xenophobia[2] are examples. Many Americans, given two products of equal appeal except that one is made in the United States and one is made in a foreign country, would buy the U.S. product. To get around this tendency, foreign and U.S. companies often go to great lengths to get a MADE IN THE U.S.A. classification on goods they sell in the United States. For example, components for many autos are made in Japan but shipped to the United States and assembled in Ohio or Tennessee so that the finished car can be called an American product.

Some regulatory restrictions are imposed for legitimate reasons; others are designed simply to make importing more difficult.

Web Note 16.2
Buy American

Reasons for Trade Restrictions

Let's now turn to a different question: If trade is beneficial, as it is in our example of I.T., why do countries restrict trade?

Unequal Internal Distribution of the Gains from Trade

One reason is that the gains of trade are not equally distributed. In the example of the argument for trade discussed at the beginning of the chapter, I.T. persuaded Saudi Arabia to specialize in the production of oil rather than food, and persuaded the United States to produce more food than oil. That means, of course, that some U.S. oil workers will have to become farmers, and in Saudi Arabia some farmers will have to become oil producers.

Often people don't want to make radical changes in the kind of work they do—they want to keep on producing what they're already producing. So when these people see the same kinds of goods that they produce coming into their country from abroad, they lobby to prevent the foreign competition.

Had I.T. been open about the difficulties of trading, he would have warned the countries that change is hard. It has very real costs that I.T. didn't point out when he made his offers. But these costs of change are relatively small compared to the gains from trade. Moreover, they're short-run, temporary costs, whereas gains from trade are permanent, long-run gains. Once the adjustment has been made, the costs will be gone but the benefits will still be there.

For most goods, the benefits for the large majority of the population so outweigh the small costs to some individuals that, decided on a strict cost/benefit basis, international

---

[2]*Xenophobia* is a Greek word meaning "fear of foreigners." Pronounce the *x* like *z*.

Hormones and Economics

Trade restrictions, in practice, are often much more complicated than they seem in textbooks. Seldom does a country say, "We're limiting imports to protect our home producers." Instead the country explains the restrictions in a more politically acceptable way. Consider the fight between the European Union (EU) and the United States over U.S. meat exports. In 1988 the EU, in line with Union-wide internal requirements, banned imports of any meat from animals treated with growth-inducing hormones, which U.S. meat producers use extensively. The result: the EU banned the meat exported from the United States.

The EU claimed that it had imposed the ban only because of public health concerns. The United States claimed that the ban was actually a trade restriction, pointing out that its own residents ate this kind of meat with confidence because a U.S. government agency had certified that the levels of hormones in the meat were far below any danger level.

The United States retaliated against the EU by imposing 100 percent tariffs on Danish and West German hams, Italian tomatoes, and certain other foods produced by EU member nations. The EU threatened to respond by placing 100 percent tariffs on $100 million worth of U.S. walnuts and dried fruits, but instead entered into bilateral meetings with the United States. Those meetings allowed untreated meats into the EU for human consumption and treated meats that would be used as dog food. In response, the United States removed its retaliatory tariff on hams and tomato sauce, but retained its tariffs on many other goods. In the 1990s, Europe's dog population seemed to be growing exponentially as Europe's imports of "dog food" increased by leaps and bounds. In 1996 the United States asked the WTO to review the EU ban. It did so in 1997, finding in favor of the United States. The EU appealed and in 1999 the WTO stood by its earlier ruling and the United States reimposed the 100 percent tariffs. Since then, the EU has stood firm and has conducted studies that, it says, show the use of growth hormones to be unsafe, but the WTO continues to rule that they are safe. In 2004, the EU replaced its ban on U.S. beef with a provisional ban until it collects more information, and argued that this provisional ban met the WTO rules. The United States disagreed and continued its retaliatory tariffs. So the dispute continues.

Which side is right in this dispute? The answer is far from obvious. Both the United States and the EU have potentially justifiable positions. As I said, trade restrictions are more complicated in reality than in textbooks.

trade is still a deal you can't refuse. The table below lists economists' estimates of the cost to consumers of saving a job in some industries through trade restrictions.

Industry	Cost of Production (per job saved)
Apparel	$297,550
Footwear	290,323
Sugar	108,900
Ceramic tiles	99,264
Canned tuna	74,000

Source: 2002 estimates based on *Economic Effects of Significant Import Restraints*, 2004, International Trade Commission (www.usit.gov).

With benefits so outweighing costs, it would seem that transition costs could be forgotten. But they can't.

Benefits of trade are generally widely scattered among the entire population. In contrast, costs of free trade often fall on small groups of people who loudly oppose the particular free trade that hurts them. This creates a political push against free trade.

It isn't only in the United States that the push for trade restrictions focuses on the small costs and not on the large benefits. For example, the European Union (EU) places large restrictions on food imports from nonmember nations. If the EU were to remove those barriers, food prices in EU countries would decline significantly—it is estimated that meat prices alone would fall by about 65 percent. Consumers would benefit, but farmers would be hurt. The farmers, however, have the political clout to see that the costs are considered and the benefits aren't. The result: The EU places high duties on foreign agricultural products.

The cost to society of relaxing trade restrictions has led to a number of programs to assist those who are hurt. Such programs are called **trade adjustment assistance programs**—*programs designed to compensate losers for reductions in trade restrictions.*

Governments have tried to use trade adjustment assistance to facilitate free trade, but they've found that it's enormously difficult to limit the adjustment assistance to those who are actually hurt by international trade. As soon as people find that there's assistance for people injured by trade, they're likely to try to show that they too have been hurt and deserve assistance. Losses from free trade become exaggerated and magnified. Instead of only a small portion of the gains from trade being needed for trade adjustment assistance, much more is demanded—often even more than the gains.

Telling people who claim to be hurt that they aren't really being hurt isn't good politics. That's why offering trade adjustment assistance as a way to relieve the pressure to restrict trade is a deal many governments can refuse.

> Benefits of trade are generally widely scattered among the entire population. In contrast, costs of free trade often fall on specific small groups.

> Telling people who claim to be hurt that they aren't really being hurt isn't good politics.

Haggling by Companies over the Gains from Trade

Many naturally advantageous bargains aren't consummated because each side is pushing for a larger share of the gains from trade than the other side thinks should be allotted.

To see how companies haggling over the gains of trade can restrict trade, let's reconsider the original deal that I.T. proposed. I.T. got 380 tons of food and 380 barrels of oil. The United States got an additional 100 tons of food and 60 barrels of oil. Saudi Arabia got an additional 100 barrels of oil and 60 tons of food.

Suppose the Saudis had said, "Why should we be getting only 100 barrels of oil and 60 tons of food when I.T. is getting 380 barrels of oil and 380 tons of food? We want an additional 300 tons of food and another 300 barrels of oil, and we won't deal unless we get them." Similarly the United States might have said, "We want an additional 300 tons of food and an additional 300 barrels of oil, and we won't go through with the deal unless we get them." If either the U.S. or the Saudi Arabian company that was involved in the trade for its country (or both) takes this position, I.T. might just walk—no deal. Tough bargaining positions can make it almost impossible to achieve gains from trade.

The side that drives the hardest bargain gets the most gains from the bargain, but it also risks making the deal fall through. Such strategic bargaining goes on all the time. **Strategic bargaining** means *demanding a larger share of the gains from trade than you can reasonably expect.* If you're successful, you get the lion's share; if you're not successful, the deal falls apart and everyone is worse off.

> Strategic bargaining can lead to higher gains from trade for the side that drives the hardest bargain, but it also can make the deal fall through.

Haggling by Countries over Trade Restrictions

Another type of trade bargaining that often limits trade is bargaining between countries. Trade restrictions and the threat of trade restrictions play an important role in that kind of haggling. Sometimes countries must go through with trade restrictions that they really don't want to impose, just to make their threats credible.

Once one country has imposed trade restrictions, other countries attempt to get those restrictions reduced by threatening to increase their own restrictions. Again, to make the threat credible, sometimes countries must impose or increase trade restrictions simply to show they're willing to do so. For example, in the mid-1990s China was allowing significant illegal copying of U.S. software without paying royalties. The United States exerted pressure to stop such copying but felt that China was not responding effectively. To force compliance, the United States made a list of Chinese goods that it threatened with 100 percent tariffs unless China complied. The United States did not want to put on these restrictions but felt that it would have more strategic bargaining power if it threatened to do so. Hence the name **strategic trade policies**—*threatening to implement tariffs to bring about a reduction in tariffs or some other concession from the other country.*

Ultimately, strategic bargaining power depends on negotiators' skills and the underlying gains from trade that a country would receive. A country that would receive only a small portion of the gains from trade is in a much stronger bargaining position than a country that would receive significant gains. It's easier for the former to walk away from trade.

The potential problem with strategic trade policies is that they can backfire. One rule of strategic bargaining is that the other side must believe that you'll go through with your threat. Thus, strategic trade policy can lead a country that actually supports free trade to impose trade restrictions, just to show how strongly it believes in free trade.

Specialized Production

My discussion of comparative advantage took it as a given that one country was inherently more productive than another country in producing certain goods. But when one looks at trading patterns, it's often not at all clear why particular countries have a productive advantage in certain goods. There's no inherent reason for Switzerland to specialize in the production of watches or for South Korea to specialize in the production of cars. Much in trade cannot be explained by inherent resource endowments. If they don't have inherent advantages, why are countries and places often so good at producing what they specialize in? Two important explanations are that they *learn by doing* and that *economies of scale* exist.

Learning by Doing   **Learning by doing** means *becoming better at a task the more often you perform it.* Take watches in Switzerland. Initially production of watches in Switzerland may have been a coincidence; the person who started the watch business happened to live there. But then people in the area became skilled in producing watches. Their skill made it attractive for other watch companies to start up. As additional companies moved in, more and more members of the labor force became skilled at watchmaking and word went out that Swiss watches were the best in the world. That reputation attracted even more producers, so Switzerland became the watchmaking capital of the world. Had the initial watch production occurred in Austria, not Switzerland, Austria might be the watch capital of the world.

When there's learning by doing, it's much harder to attribute inherent comparative advantage to a country. One must always ask: Does country A have an inherent comparative advantage, or does it simply have more experience? Once country B gets the experience, will country A's comparative advantage disappear? If it will, then country B has a strong reason to limit trade with country A in order to give its own workers time to catch up as they learn by doing.

Q-8 In strategic trade bargaining, it is sometimes reasonable to be unreasonable. True or false? Explain.

Strategic trade policies are threats to implement tariffs to bring about a reduction in tariffs or some other concession from the other country.

Learning by doing means becoming better at a task the more you perform it.

The Antiglobalization Forces

Often when the World Trade Organization or a similar type organization promoting free trade hosts a meeting, protests (sometimes violent ones) are held by a loosely organized collection of groups opposing globalization. The goals of these groups are varied. Some argue that trade hurts developed countries such as the United States; others argue that it hurts developing countries by exploiting poor workers so that Westerners can get luxuries cheaply. Still others argue against a more subtle Western economic imperialism in which globalization spreads Western cultural values and undermines developing countries' social structures.

Each of these arguments has some appeal, although making the first two simultaneously is difficult because it says that voluntary trade hurts both parties to the trade. But the arguments have had little impact on the views of most policy makers and economists.

Supporting free trade does not mean that globalization does not have costs. It does have costs, but many of the costs associated with free trade are really the result of technological changes. The reality is that technological developments, such as those in telecommunications and transportation, are pushing countries closer together and will involve difficult social and cultural changes, regardless of whether trade is free or not. Restricting trade might temporarily slow these changes but is unlikely to stop them.

Most empirical studies have found that, with regard to material goods, the workers in developing countries involved in trade are generally better off than those not involved in trade. That's why most developing countries work hard to encourage companies to move production facilities into their countries. From a worker's perspective, earning $4 a day can look quite good when the alternative is earning $3 a day. Would the worker rather earn $10 a day? Of course, but the higher the wages in a given country, the less likely it is that firms are going to locate production there.

Many economists are sympathetic to various antiglobalization arguments, but they often become frustrated at the lack of clarity of the antiglobalization groups' views. To oppose something is not enough; to effect positive change, one must not only understand how the thing one opposes works but also have a realistic plan for a better alternative.

Economies of Scale In determining whether an inherent comparative advantage exists, a second complication is **economies of scale**—*the situation in which costs per unit of output fall as output increases.* Many manufacturing industries (such as steel and autos) exhibit economies of scale. The existence of significant economies of scale means that it makes sense (that is, it lowers costs) for one country to specialize in one good and another country to specialize in another good. But who should specialize in what is unclear. Producers in a country can, and generally do, argue that if only the government will establish barriers, they'll be able to lower their costs per unit and eventually sell at lower costs than foreign producers.

Most countries recognize the importance of learning by doing and economies of scale. A variety of trade restrictions are based on these two phenomena. The most common expression of the learning-by-doing and economies-of-scale insights is the **infant industry argument,** which is that *with initial protection, an industry will be able to become competitive.* Countries use this argument to justify many trade restrictions. They argue, "You may now have a comparative advantage, but that's simply because you've been at it longer, or are experiencing significant economies of scale. We need trade restrictions on our _____ industry to give it a chance to catch up. Once an infant industry grows up, then we can talk about eliminating the restrictions."

In economies of scale, costs per unit of output go down as output increases.

Q.9 Is it efficient for a country to maintain a trade barrier in an industry that exhibits economies of scale?

The infant industry argument says that with initial protection, an industry will be able to become competitive.

Macroeconomic Aspects of Trade

The comparative advantage argument for free trade assumes that a country's resources are fully utilized. When countries don't have full employment, imports can decrease domestic aggregate demand and increase unemployment. Exports can stimulate domestic aggregate demand and decrease unemployment. Thus, when an economy is in a recession, there is a strong macroeconomic reason to limit imports and encourage exports. These macroeconomic effects of free trade play an important role in the public's view of imports and exports. When a country is in a recession, pressure to impose trade restrictions increases substantially.

National Security

Countries often justify trade restrictions on grounds of national security. These restrictions take two forms:

1. Export restrictions on strategic materials and defense-related goods.
2. Import restrictions on defense-related goods. For example, in a war we don't want to be dependent on oil from abroad.

For a number of goods, national security considerations make sense. For example, the United States restricts the sale of certain military items to countries that may be fighting the United States someday. The problem is where to draw the line about goods having a national security consideration. Should countries protect domestic agriculture? All high-technology items, since they might be useful in weapons? All chemicals? Steel? When a country makes a national security argument for trade, we must be careful to consider whether a domestic political reason may be lurking behind that argument.

International Politics

International politics frequently provides another reason for trade restrictions. Over the past decades, the United States restricted trade with Cuba to punish that country for trying to extend its Marxist political and economic policies to other Latin American countries. The United States also has trade restrictions on Iran for its position on nuclear power plants. The list can be extended, but you get the argument: Trade helps you, so we'll hurt you by stopping trade until you do what we want. So what if it hurts us too? It'll hurt you more than it hurts us.

Increased Revenue Brought in by Tariffs

A final argument made for one particular type of trade restriction—a tariff—is that tariffs bring in revenues. In the 19th century, tariffs were the U.S. government's primary source of revenue. They are less important as a source of revenue today for many developed countries because those countries have instituted other forms of taxes. However, tariffs remain a primary source of revenue for many developing countries. They're relatively easy to collect and are paid by people rich enough to afford imports. These countries justify many of their tariffs with the argument that they need the revenues.

Why Economists Generally Oppose Trade Restrictions

Each of the preceding arguments for trade restrictions has some validity, but most economists discount them and support free trade. The reason is that, in their considered judgment, the harm done by trade restrictions outweighs the benefits. This is true, even

Reasons for restricting trade include

1. Unequal internal distribution of the gains from trade.
2. Haggling by companies over the gains from trade.
3. Haggling by countries over trade restrictions.
4. Specialized production: learning by doing and economies of scale.
5. Macroeconomic aspects of trade.
6. National security.
7. International politics.
8. Increased revenue brought in by tariffs.

though, from the U.S. perspective, transferable comparative advantages are likely to place significant pressures on jobs to leave the United States, and hold down U.S. wages in the coming decades. Most economists believe that the United States will be better off if it allows free trade than it would be if it did not.

Free Trade Increases Total Output

Economists' first argument for free trade is that, viewed from a global perspective, free trade increases total output. From a national perspective, economists agree that particular instances of trade restrictions may actually help one nation, even as most other nations are hurt. But they argue that the country imposing trade restrictions can benefit *only if the other country doesn't retaliate* with trade restrictions of its own. Retaliation is the rule, not the exception, however, and when there is retaliation, trade restrictions cause both countries to lose. Thus, if the United States were to place a tariff on goods from China, those aspects of production that depend on Chinese goods would be hurt, and, as I discussed above, there are many such goods. Moreover, China would likely place tariffs on goods from the United States, hurting both countries. Such tariffs would cut overall production, making both countries worse off.

International Trade Provides Competition

A second reason most economists support free trade is that trade restrictions reduce international competition. International competition is desirable because it forces domestic companies to stay on their toes. If trade restrictions on imports are imposed, domestic companies don't work as hard and therefore become less efficient.

For example, in the 1950s and 1960s, the United States imposed restrictions on imported steel. U.S. steel industries responded to this protection by raising their prices and channeling profits from their steel production into other activities. By the 1970s, the U.S. steel industry was using outdated equipment to produce overpriced steel. Instead of making the steel industry stronger, restrictions made it a flabby, uncompetitive industry.

In the 1980s and 1990s, the U.S. steel industry became less and less profitable. Larger mills closed or consolidated, while nonunion minimills, which made new steel out of scrap steel, did well. By the late 1990s, minimills accounted for 45 percent of total U.S. steel production. In 2002 it looked as if a number of larger mills were going to declare bankruptcy, and enormous pressure was placed on the federal government to bail them out by taking over their pension debt and instituting tariffs. The U.S. government responded by imposing 20–30 percent tariffs on foreign steel imports. Most economists opposed the tariffs and pointed out that they were unlikely to lead to a rebuilding of the U.S. steel industry because other countries had a comparative advantage in steel production. Moreover, other countries would retaliate with tariffs on U.S. goods. Despite their opposition, the tariffs were instituted. Major U.S. trading partners—including EU countries, Japan, and China—responded by threatening to implement tariffs on U.S. goods worth about $335 million, and in 2003, the U.S. government withdrew the tariffs.

The benefits of international competition are not restricted to mature industries like steel; they can also accrue to young industries wherever they appear. Economists dispose of the infant industry argument by reference to the historical record. In theory the argument makes sense. But very few of the infant industries protected by trade restrictions have ever grown up. What tends to happen instead is that infant industries become dependent on the trade restrictions and use political pressure to keep that protection. As a result, they often remain immature and internationally uncompetitive. Most economists would support the infant industry argument only if the trade restrictions included definite conditions under which the restrictions would end.

Economists generally oppose trade restrictions because

1. From a global perspective, free trade increases total output.
2. International trade provides competition for domestic companies.
3. Restrictions based on national security are often abused or evaded.
4. Trade restrictions are addictive.

Very few of the infant industries protected by trade restrictions have ever grown up.

Web Note 16.3
Protection and
Industrialization

Restrictions Based on National Security Are Often Abused or Evaded

Most economists agree with the national security argument for export restrictions on goods that are directly war related. Selling bombs to Iran, whom the United States has called a member of the Axis of Evil, doesn't make much sense. Economists point out that the argument is often carried far beyond goods directly related to national security. For example, in the 1980s the United States restricted exports of sugar-coated cereals to the Soviet Union purportedly for reasons of national security. Sugar-frosted flakes may be great, but they were unlikely to help the Soviet Union in a war.

Another argument that economists give against the national security rationale is that trade restrictions on military sales can often be evaded. Countries simply have another country buy the goods for them. Such third-party sales—called *transshipments*—are common in international trade and limit the effectiveness of any absolute trade restrictions for national security purposes.

Economists also argue that by fostering international cooperation, international trade makes war less likely—a significant contribution to national security.

Trade Restrictions Are Addictive

Economists' final argument against trade restrictions is: Yes, some restrictions might benefit a country, but almost no country can limit its restrictions to the beneficial ones. Trade restrictions are addictive—the more you have, the more you want. Thus, a majority of economists take the position that the best response to such addictive policies is "Just say no."

Yes, some restrictions might benefit a country, but almost no country can limit its restrictions to the beneficial ones.

Institutions Supporting Free Trade

Web Note 16.4
Export Promotion

As I have stated throughout the text, economists generally like markets and favor trade being as free as possible. They argue that trade allows specialization and the division of labor. When each country follows its comparative advantage, production is more efficient and the production possibility curve shifts out. These views mean that most economists, liberal and conservative alike, generally oppose international trade restrictions.

Despite political pressures to restrict trade, governments have generally tried to follow economists' advice and have entered into a variety of international agreements and organizations. The most important is the World Trade Organization (WTO), which has about 150 members, and is the successor to the General Agreement on Tariffs and Trade (GATT). You will still occasionally see references to GATT, even though the WTO has taken its place. One of the differences between the WTO and GATT is that the WTO includes some enforcement mechanisms.

Important international economic organizations include the WTO, which took the place of GATT.

Achieving agreement on trade barrier reductions is politically difficult, as is demonstrated by the latest WTO negotiations, called the Doha Development Round. Begun in 2001, it was meant to lead to fairer trade rules for developing countries, especially in agriculture. The Round did not go well; the United States and Europe were unwilling to eliminate subsidies to their farmers that the developing countries said made it impossible for them to compete fairly, and hence would not reduce their tariffs on manufactured goods. As of 2007, there was still no agreement.

The push for free trade has a geographic dimension, which includes **free trade associations**—*groups of countries that have reduced or eliminated trade barriers among themselves*. The European Union (EU) is the most famous free trade association. All barriers to trade among the EU's member countries were removed in 1992. In the coming

A free trade association is a group of countries that allows free trade among its members and puts up common barriers against all other countries' goods.

Dumping

The WTO allows countries to impose trade restrictions on imports if they can show that the goods are being dumped. *Dumping* is selling a good in a foreign country at a lower price than in the country where it's produced. On the face of it, who could complain about someone who wants to sell you a good cheaply? Why not just take advantage of the bargain price? The first objection is the learning-by-doing argument. To stay competitive, a country must keep on producing. Dumping by another country can force domestic producers out of business. Having eliminated the competition, the foreign producer has the field to itself and can raise the price. Thus, dumping can be a form of predatory pricing.

The second argument against dumping involves the short-term macroeconomic and political effects it can have on the importing country. Even if one believes that dumping is not a preliminary to predatory pricing, it can displace workers in the importing country, causing political pressure on that government to institute trade restrictions. If that country's economy is in a recession, the resulting unemployment will have substantial macroeconomic repercussions, so pressure for trade restrictions will be amplified.

decade more European countries can be expected to join the EU. In 1993, the United States and Canada agreed to enter into a similar free trade union, and they, together with Mexico, created the North American Free Trade Association (NAFTA). Under NAFTA, tariffs and other trade barriers among these countries are being gradually reduced. Some other trading associations include Mercosur (among South American countries) and ASEAN (among Southeast Asian countries).

Economists have mixed reactions to free trade associations. They see free trade as beneficial, but they are concerned about the possibility that these regional free trade associations will impose significant trade restrictions on nonmember countries. They also believe that bilateral negotiations between member nations will replace multilateral efforts among members and nonmembers. Whether the net effect of these bilateral negotiations is positive or negative remains to be seen.

Groups of other countries have loose trading relationships because of cultural or historical reasons. These loose trading relationships are sometimes called trading zones. For example, many European countries maintain close trading ties with many of their former colonies in Africa where they fit into a number of overlapping trading zones. European companies tend to see that central area as their turf. The United States has close ties in Latin America, making the Western hemisphere another trading zone. Another example of a trading zone is that of Japan and its economic ties with other Far East countries; Japanese companies often see that area as their commercial domain.

These trading zones overlap, sometimes on many levels. For instance, Australia and England, Portugal and Brazil, and the United States and Saudi Arabia are tied together for historical or political reasons, and those ties lead to increased trade between them that seems to deviate from the above trading zones. Similarly, as companies become more and more global, it is harder and harder to associate companies with particular countries. Let me give an example: Do you know who the largest exporters of cars from the United States are? The answer is: Japanese automobile companies!

Thus, there is no hard-and-fast specification of trading zones, and knowing history and politics is important to understanding many of the relationships.

One way countries strengthen trading relationships among groups of countries is through a most-favored-nation status. The term **most-favored nation** refers to *a country that will be charged as low a tariff on its exports as any other country.* Thus, if the United

Q-10 What is economists' view of limited free trade associations such as the EU or NAFTA?

A most-favored nation is a country that will pay as low a tariff on its exports as will any other country.

States lowers tariffs on goods imported from Japan, which has most-favored-nation status with the United States, it must lower tariffs on those same types of goods imported from any other country with most-favored-nation status.

Conclusion

International trade, and changing comparative advantages, will become more and more important for the United States in the coming decades. With international transportation and communication becoming easier and faster, and with other countries' economies growing, the U.S. economy will inevitably become more interdependent with the other economies of the world. As international trade becomes more important, the push for trade restrictions will likely increase. Various countries' strategic trade policies will likely conflict, and the world could find itself on the verge of an international trade war that would benefit no one.

Concern about that possibility leads most economists to favor free trade. As often happens, economists advise politicians to follow a politically unpopular policy—to take the hard course of action. Whether politicians follow economists' advice or whether they follow the politically popular policy will play a key role in determining the course of the U.S. economy in the 2000s.

Summary

- The nature of trade is continually changing. The United States is importing more and more high-tech goods and services from India and China and other East Asian countries.

- Outsourcing is a type of trade. Outsourcing is a larger phenomenon today compared to 30 years ago because China and India are so large, enormous outsourcing is possible.

- According to the principle of comparative advantage, as long as the relative opportunity costs of producing goods (what must be given up in one good in order to get another good) differ among countries, there are potential gains from trade.

- Three insights into the terms of trade include

  1. The more competition exists in international trade, the less the trader gets and the more the involved countries get.

  2. Once competition prevails, smaller countries tend to get a larger percentage of the gains from trade than do larger countries.

  3. Gains from trade go to countries that produce goods that exhibit economies of scale.

- The gains from trade in the form of low consumer prices tend to be widespread and not easily recognized, while the costs in jobs lost tend to be concentrated and readily identifiable.

- The United States has comparative advantages based on its skilled workforce, its institutions, and its language, among other things.

- Inherent comparative advantages are based on factors that are relatively unchangeable. They are not subject to the law of one price.

- Transferable comparative advantages are based on factors that can change relatively easily. The law of one price can eliminate these comparative advantages.

- Trade restrictions include tariffs and quotas, embargoes, voluntary restraint agreements, regulatory trade restrictions, and nationalistic appeals.

- Reasons that countries impose trade restrictions include unequal internal distribution of the gains from trade, haggling by companies over the gains from trade, haggling by countries over trade restrictions, learning by doing and economies of scale, macroeconomic aspects of trade, national security, international political reasons, and increased revenue brought in by tariffs.

- Economists generally oppose trade restrictions because of the history of trade restrictions and their understanding of the advantages of free trade.

- The World Trade Organization is an international organization committed to reducing trade barriers.

- Free trade associations help trade by reducing barriers to trade among member nations. Free trade associations could hinder trade by building up barriers to trade with nations outside the association; negotiations among members could replace multilateral efforts to reduce trade restrictions among members and nonmembers.

Key Terms

balance of trade (379)
comparative advantage (381)
economies of scale (397)
embargo (392)
free trade association (400)
General Agreement on Tariffs and Trade (GATT) (390)

infant industry argument (397)
inherent comparative advantage (387)
learning by doing (396)
most-favored nation (401)
quota (390)

regulatory trade restriction (392)
strategic bargaining (395)
strategic trade policy (396)
tariff (390)
trade adjustment assistance program (395)

transferable comparative advantage (387)
World Trade Organization (WTO) (390)

Questions for Thought and Review

1. Will a country do better importing or exporting a good for which it has a comparative advantage? Why?   LO1

2. Widgetland has 60 workers. Each worker can produce 4 widgets or 4 wadgets. Each resident in Widgetland currently consumes 2 widgets and 2 wadgets. Wadgetland also has 60 workers. Each can produce 3 widgets or 12 wadgets. Wadgetland's residents consume 1 widget and 9 wadgets. Is there a basis for trade? If so, offer the countries a deal they can't refuse.   LO2

3. Why does competition among traders affect how much of the gains from trade are given to the countries involved in the trade?   LO3

4. Why do smaller countries usually get most of the gains from trade? What are some reasons why a small country might not get the gains of trade?   LO3

5. Which country will get the larger gain from trade: a country with economies of scale or diseconomies of scale? Explain your answer.   LO3

6. How is outsourcing to China and India today different than U.S. outsourcing in the past?   LO4

7. What are three reasons why economists' and laypeople's view of trade differ?   LO4

8. List at least three sources of comparative advantages that the United States has and will likely maintain over the coming decade.   LO5

9. How do inherent comparative advantages differ from transferable comparative advantages? From the standpoint of adjustment costs to trade, which would a country prefer and why?   LO5

10. What is the law of one price and why is it important to any discussion of the future of the U.S. economy?   LO5

11. Which is the law of one price likely to eliminate: a transferable or an inherent comparative advantage? Explain your answer.   LO5

12. What are two methods by which the wage gap between Chinese and U.S. workers will likely narrow?   LO5

13. Suggest an equitable method of funding trade adjustment assistance programs. Why is it equitable? What problems might a politician have in implementing such a method?   LO6

14. Demonstrate graphically how the effects of a tariff differ from the effects of a quota.   LO6

15. How do the effects of voluntary restraint agreements differ from the effects of a tariff? How are they the same?   LO6

16. Mexico exports many vegetables to the United States. These vegetables are grown using chemicals that are not allowed in U.S. vegetable agriculture. Should the United States restrict imports of Mexican vegetables? Why or why not? (Difficult)   LO6, LO7

17. When the United States placed a temporary price floor on tomatoes imported from Mexico, U.S. trade representative Mickey Kantor said, "The agreement will provide strong relief to the tomato growers in Florida and other states, and help preserve jobs in the industry." What costs did Americans bear from the price floor? (Difficult)   LO6

18. If you were economic adviser to a country that was following your advice about trade restrictions and that country fell into a recession, would you change your advice? Why, or why not? (Difficult)   LO7

19. What are two reasons economists support free trade?   LO7

20. A study by the World Bank on the effects of Mercosur, a regional trade pact among four Latin American countries, concluded that free trade agreements "might confer significant benefits, but there are also significant dangers." What are those benefits and dangers? (Difficult)   LO8

21. What is the relationship between GATT and WTO?   LO8

Problems and Exercises

22. Suppose there are two states that do not trade: Iowa and Nebraska. Each state produces the same two goods: corn and wheat. For Iowa the opportunity cost of producing 1 bushel of wheat is 3 bushels of corn. For Nebraska the opportunity cost of producing 1 bushel of corn is 3 bushels of wheat. At present, Iowa produces 20 million bushels of wheat and 120 million bushels of corn, while Nebraska produces 20 million bushels of corn and 120 million bushels of wheat.
   a. Explain how, with trade, Nebraska can end up with 40 million bushels of wheat and 120 million bushels of corn while Iowa can end up with 40 million bushels of corn and 120 million bushels of wheat.
   b. If the states ended up with the numbers given in *a*, how much would the trader get?   LO2

23. Country A can produce, at most, 40 olives or 20 pickles, or some combination of olives and pickles such as the 20 olives and 10 pickles it is currently producing. Country B can produce, at most, 120 olives or 60 pickles, or some combination of olives and pickles such as the 100 olives and 50 pickles it is currently producing.
   a. Is there a basis for trade? If so, offer the two countries a deal they can't refuse.
   b. How would your answer to *a* change if you knew that there were economies of scale in the production of pickles and olives rather than the production possibilities described in the question? Why? If your answer is yes, which country would you have produce which good?   LO2, LO3

24. The world price of textiles is P_w, as in the accompanying figure of the domestic supply and demand for textiles.

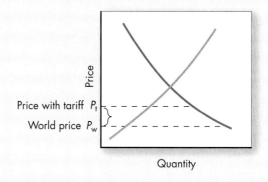

The government imposes a tariff *t*, to protect the domestic producers. For this tariff:
   a. Label the gains to domestic producers.
   b. Label the revenue to government.
   c. Label the costs to domestic producers.
   d. Are the gains greater than the costs? Why?   LO6

25. In 2005 the hourly compensation for manufacturing employees in Germany was $33.00. In the United States it was $23.65, while in Taiwan it was $6.38. (Difficult)
   a. Give three reasons why firms produce in Germany rather than in a lower-wage country.
   b. Germany has just entered into an agreement with other EU countries that allows people in any EU country, including Greece and Italy, which have lower wage rates, to travel and work in any EU country, including high-wage countries. Would you expect a significant movement of workers from Greece and Italy to Germany right away? Why or why not?
   c. Workers in Thailand are paid significantly less than workers in Taiwan. If you were a company CEO, what other information would you want before you decided where to establish a new production facility?   LO2, LO4

26. Suppose that two countries, Machineland and Farmland, have the following production possibility curves.

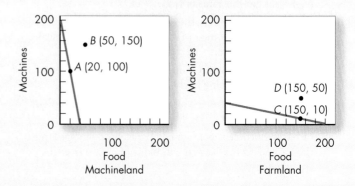

a. Explain how these two countries can move from points A and C, where they currently are, to points B and D.

b. If possible, state by how much total production for the two countries has risen.

c. If you were a trader, how much of the gains from trade would you deserve for discovering this trade?

d. If there were economies of scale in the production of both goods, how would your analysis change? LO2

27. Suppose there are two countries, Busytown and Lazyasiwannabe, with the following production possibility tables:

% of Resources Devoted to Cars	Busytown	
	Cars Produced (thousands)	Gourmet Meals Produced (thousands)
100%	60	0
80	48	10
60	36	20
40	24	30
20	12	40
0	0	50

% of Resources Devoted to Cars	Lazyasiwannabe	
	Cars Produced (thousands)	Gourmet Meals Produced (thousands)
100%	50	0
80	40	10
60	30	20
40	20	30
20	10	40
0	0	50

a. Draw the production possibility curves for each country.

b. Which country has the comparative advantage in producing cars? In producing gourmet meals?

c. Suppose each country specializes in the production of one good. Explain how Busytown can end up with 36,000 cars and 22,000 meals and Lazyasiwannabe can end up with 28,000 meals and 24,000 cars. LO2

28. One of the basic economic laws is "the law of one price." It says that given certain assumptions one would expect that if free trade is allowed, the price of goods in countries should converge.

a. Can you list what three of those assumptions likely are?

b. Should the law of one price hold for labor also? Why or why not?

c. Should it hold for capital more so or less so than for labor? Why or why not? LO5

29. On January 1, 2005, quotas on clothing imports to the United States first instituted in the 1960s to protect the U.S. garment industry were eliminated.

a. Demonstrate graphically how this change affected equilibrium price and quantity of imported garments.

b. Demonstrate graphically how U.S. consumers benefited from the end of the quota system.

c. What was the likely effect on profits of foreign companies that sold clothing in the U.S. market? LO6, LO7

30. The U.S. government taxes U.S. companies for their overseas profits, but it allows them to deduct from their U.S. taxable income the taxes that they pay abroad and interest on loans funding operations abroad, with no limits on the amount deducted. (Difficult)

a. Is it possible that the overseas profit tax produces no net revenue?

b. What would you suggest to the government about this tax if its desire were to increase corporate income tax revenue?

c. Why might the government keep this tax even if it were not collecting any net revenue? LO6, LO7

31. In the 1930s Clair Wilcox of Swarthmore College organized a petition by economists "that any measure which provided for a general upward revision of tariff rates be denied passage by Congress, or if passed, be vetoed." It was signed by one-third of all economists in the United States at the time, of all political persuasions. A month later, the Smoot-Hawley Tariff was passed.

a. Why did economists oppose the tariff?

b. Demonstrate the effect of the tariff on the price of goods.

c. How would the tariff help the economy if other countries did not institute a retaliatory tariff?

d. What would be the effect on the macro economy if other countries did institute a retaliatory tariff? LO6, LO7

Questions from Alternative Perspectives

1. Evaluate the following statement: Comparative advantage will benefit all people because everyone has a comparative advantage in something. Therefore, trade based on comparative advantage should be facilitated without undue government intervention. (Austrian)

2. In the 10th century B.C., King Solomon brought the Israelites into great economic wealth through specialization and trade. It was difficult when faced with the practices and beliefs of their trading partners, however, for Israel to maintain its identity as a people of one God. King Solomon, for example, provided a place for each of his wives to worship the gods of her own people. If such syncretism (adoption of foreign practices and beliefs) is inevitable with increased globalization, should trade be encouraged, even today? (Religious)

3. Global outsourcing has cost the U.S. economy far over one million jobs since 2001, or somewhere between 15 and 35 percent of the total decline in employment since the onset of the 2001 recession.
   a. How does outsourcing affect the bargaining power of U.S. workers and the bargaining power of U.S. employers?
   b. What will it likely do to the overall level of U.S. workers' wages?
   c. What will it likely do to lawyers' wages?
   d. If you stated that it affected lawyers' wages differently, do you believe that the U.S. policy response to outsourcing would be different? (Post-Keynesian)

4. In David Ricardo's original example of comparative advantage in his *Principles of Political Economy*, written in

1817, Portugal possesses an absolute advantage in both the production of cloth and the production of wine. But England has a comparative advantage in the production of cloth, while Portugal's comparative advantage is in wine production. According to Ricardo, an English political economist, England should specialize in the production of cloth and Portugal in wine making.
   a. Was Ricardo's advice self-serving?
   b. Knowing that light manufacturing, such as clothing and textile production, has led most industrialization processes, would you have advised 19th century Portugal to specialize in wine making? (Radical)

5. The text presents free trade as advantageous for developing countries. However, in its period of most rapid development, the half century following the Civil War, the United States imposed tariffs on imports that averaged around 40 percent, a level higher than those in all but one of today's developing economies.
   a. Why did so many of today's industrialized countries not follow those policies as they were developing?
   b. What does this insight into economic history suggest about the doctrine of free trade and whose interests it serves? (Radical)

Web Questions

1. Go to the WTO's home page at www.wto.org to find out how trade disputes are settled.
   a. What is the procedure for settling disputes?
   b. What is the timetable for the settlement procedure?
   c. What happens if one of the countries does not abide by the settlement?

2. Go to the National Center for Policy Analysis Web site (www.ncpa.org). Select "Policy Issues," then "Trade" and finally "Tariffs and other Trade Barriers" to answer the following:
   a. List three trade barriers mentioned in the articles.
   b. What are the reasons the trade barriers were instituted?
   c. According to the articles, what was the result of those trade barriers?

3. Go to the home page of free trade association ASEAN (www.aseansec.org) and answer the following questions:
   a. What countries belong to the trade association?
   b. When was the association established?
   c. What is the association's stated objective?
   d. What is the combined gross domestic product of all members?

4. Choose a country, and using *The Economist* magazine's country site (www.economist.com/countries), answer the following questions:
   a. Using export and import shares, how globalized is your country?
   b. What goods does your country export and import?
   c. What are the probable goods for which your country has a comparative advantage?

Answers to Margin Questions

1. The type of goods being imported has changed from primarily low-tech goods to technologically advanced goods. (378)

2. A debtor nation will not necessarily be running a trade deficit. *Debt* refers to accumulated past deficits. If a country had accumulated large deficits in the past, it could run a surplus now but still be a debtor nation. (381)

3. He should walk away because there is no basis for trade. (381)

4. The percentage of gains from trade that goes to a country depends upon the change in the price of the goods being traded. If trade led to no change in prices in a small country, then that small country would get no gains from trade. Another case in which a small country gets a small

percentage of the gains from trade would occur when its larger trading partner was producing a good with economies of scale and the small country was not. A third case is when the traders who extracted most of the surplus or gains from trade come from the larger country; then the smaller country would end up with few of the gains from trade. (384)

5. Three reasons for the difference are (1) gains from trade are often stealth gains, (2) comparative advantage is determined by more than wages, and (3) nations trade more than just manufactured goods. (385)

6. Two likely adjustments that will reduce the wage gap are a fall in the value of the dollar (U.S. exchange rate) and a rise in Chinese wages relative to U.S. wages. (389)

7. An inefficient customs agency can operate with the same effect as a trade restriction, and if trade restrictions would help the country, then it is possible that an inefficient customs agency could also help the country. (393)

8. True. In strategic trade bargaining it is sometimes reasonable to be unreasonable. The belief of the other bargainer that you will be unreasonable leads you to be able to extract larger gains from trade. Of course, this leads to the logical paradox that if "unreasonable" is "reasonable," unreasonable really is reasonable, so it is only reasonable to be reasonable. Sorting out that last statement can be left for a philosophy or logic class. (396)

9. Whether or not it is efficient for a country to maintain barriers to trade in an industry that exhibits economies of scale depends upon the marginal costs and marginal benefits of maintaining those barriers. Having significant economies of scale does mean that average costs of production will be lower at higher levels of production; however, trade restrictions might mean that the industry might be able to inflate its costs. (397)

10. Most economists have a mixed view of limited free trade associations such as NAFTA or the EU. While they see free trade as beneficial, they are concerned about the possibility that these limited trade associations will impose trade restrictions on nonmember countries. Whether the net effect of these will be positive or negative is a complicated issue. (401)

17 International Financial Policy

A foreign exchange dealer's office during a busy spell is the nearest thing to Bedlam I have struck.

—Harold Wincott

In 2007 a euro that had cost 80 cents a few years earlier cost about $1.35, and there were expectations that the value of the dollar might fall further. The dollar had, however, fallen far less against the Chinese yuan, because the Chinese government was holding the value of its currency down. Earlier, in 2001, Argentina went through five presidents in two weeks as it struggled to adjust from a fixed to a flexible exchange rate, and in the late 1990s the international financial system almost broke down as Asian currency values fell substantially.

To understand what's happening in these events, you must understand exchange rates and the balance of payments. This chapter gives you that understanding. The chapter starts with an in-depth consideration of the balance of payments, showing how it relates to the trade balance and exchange rates. That discussion is then tied to a consideration of the supply of and demand for currencies and how monetary and fiscal policy affect exchange rates. Finally I discuss exchange rate policy in some depth and present the arguments for and against various exchange rate regimes.

The Balance of Payments

The best door into an in-depth discussion of exchange rates and international financial considerations is a discussion of **balance of payments** (*a country's record of all transactions between its residents and the residents of all foreign nations*).[1] These include a country's buying and selling of goods and services (imports and exports) and interest and profit payments from previous investments, together with all the capital inflows and outflows. Table 17-1 presents the 1987 and 2006 balance of payments accounts for the United States. These accounts record all payments made by foreigners to U.S. citizens and all payments made by U.S. citizens to foreigners in those years.

---

[1]Balance of payments records are not very good. Because of measurement difficulties, many transactions go unrecorded and many numbers must be estimated, leaving a potential for large errors.

TABLE 17-1	The Balance of Payments Account, 1987 and 2006			
		1987 (billions of dollars)		2006 (billions of dollars)
1.	**Current account**			
2.	Merchandise			
3.	Exports	+250		+1,024
4.	Imports	−410		−1,860
5.	Balance of merchandise trade		−160	−836
6.	Services			
7.	Exports	+ 99		+ 413
8.	Imports	− 91		− 342
9.	Balance on services		+ 8	+ 71
10.	Balance of trade		+152	−765
11.	Net investment income	+ 14		− 7
12.	Net transfers	− 23		− 85
13.	Invest. trans. balance		− 9	− 92
14.	**Balance on current account**		**−161**	**−857**
15.	**Financial and capital account**			
16.	Capital balance		1	− 4
17.	Private financial account			
18.	Private financial inflows	+203		+1,464
19.	Private financial outflows	− 90		−1,053
20.	Balance on private financial account		+113	+411
21.	Government financial account			
22.	Foreign government financial bal.	+ 45		+ 301
23.	U.S. government financial bal.	+ 10		+ 2
24.	Balance on government financial acct.		+ 55	+303
25.	**Balance on financial and capital account**		**+169**	**+710**
26.	Statistical Discrepancy		− 8	−147
27.	**Total**		**0**	**0**

Goods the United States exports must be paid for in dollars so, in order to buy U.S. exports, foreigners must exchange their currencies for dollars. Exports involve a flow of payments into the United States, so in the balance of payments accounts they have a plus sign. Similarly, U.S. imports must be paid for in foreign currency; they involve a flow of dollars out of the United States, and thus they have a minus sign. Notice that the bottom line of the balance of payments is $0. By definition, the bottom line (which includes all supplies and demands for currencies, including those of the government) must add up to zero.

As you can see in Table 17-1, the balance of payments account is broken down into the current account and the financial and capital account. The **current account** (lines 1–14) is *the part of the balance of payments account in which all short-term flows of payments are listed.* It includes exports and imports, which are what we normally mean when we talk about the trade balance. The **financial and capital account** (lines 15–25) is *the part of the balance of payments account in which all long-term flows of payments are listed.* If a U.S. citizen buys a German stock, or if a Japanese company buys a U.S. company, the transaction shows up on this account.

The U.S. government can influence the exchange rate (the rate at which one currency trades for another) by buying and selling **official reserves**—*government holdings*

The balance of payments is a country's record of all transactions between its residents and the residents of all foreign countries.

The current account is the part of the balance of payments account that lists all short-term flows of payments.

The financial and capital account is the part of the balance of payments account that lists all long-term flows of payments.

of foreign currencies—or by buying and selling other international reserves, such as gold. Such buying and selling is recorded in the government financial balance (line 23)—the part of the balance of payments account that records the amount of its own currency or foreign currencies that a nation buys or sells. Foreign governments can also influence the U.S. exchange rate by buying and selling reserves. Such buying and selling is recorded in the foreign government financial balance (line 22).

To get a better idea of what's included in these accounts, let's consider each of them more carefully.

The Current Account

Looking at Table 17-1, you can see that the current account is composed of the merchandise (or goods) account (lines 2–5), the services account (lines 6–9), the net investment income account (line 11), and the net transfers account (line 12).

Starting with the merchandise account, notice that in 1987 the United States imported $410 billion worth of goods and exported $250 billion worth of goods. *The difference between the value of goods exported and the value of goods imported* is called the **balance of merchandise trade.** Looking at line 5, you can see that the United States had a balance of merchandise trade deficit of $160 billion in 1987 and $836 billion in 2006.

The merchandise trade balance is often discussed in the press as a summary of how the United States is doing in the international markets. It's not a good summary. Trade in services is just as important as trade in merchandise, so economists pay more attention to the combined balance of goods and services.

Thus, the **balance of trade**—*the difference between the value of goods and services exported and imported*—(line 10) becomes a key statistic for economists. Notice that in both 1987 and 2006 most of the U.S. trade deficit resulted from an imbalance in the merchandise account. The service account worked in the opposite direction. It was slightly positive in 1987; in 2006 the services account reduced the trade deficit by $71 billion. Such services include tourist expenditures and insurance payments by foreigners to U.S. firms. For instance, when you travel in Japan, you spend yen, which you must buy with dollars; this is an outflow of payments, which is a negative contribution to the services account.

There is no reason that in a particular year the goods and services sent into a country must equal the goods and services sent out, even if the current account is in equilibrium, because the current account also includes payments from past investments and net transfers. When you invest, you expect to make a return on that investment. The payments to foreign owners of U.S. capital assets are a negative contribution to the U.S. balance of payments. The payment to U.S. owners of foreign capital assets is a positive contribution to the U.S. balance of payments. These payments on investment income are a type of holdover from past trade and services imbalances. So even though they relate to investments, they show up on the current account.

The final component on the current account is net transfers, which include foreign aid, gifts, and other payments to individuals not exchanged for goods or services. If you send a $1,000 bond to your aunt in Mexico, it shows up with a minus sign here.

Adding up the pluses and minuses on the current account, we arrive at line 14, the current account balance. Notice that in 1987 the United States ran a $161 billion deficit on the current account, and in 2006 the United States had a deficit of $857 billion (line 14). That means that, in the current account, the supply of dollars greatly exceeded the demand for dollars. If the current account represented the total supply of and demand for dollars, the value of the dollar would have fallen. But it doesn't represent the total. There are also the financial account and statistical discrepancies.

The balance of trade is the difference between the value of goods and services exported and imported.

Q₋₁ If you, a U.S. citizen, are traveling abroad, where will your expenditures show up in the balance of payments accounts?

Payments on investment income show up on the current account.

The Financial and Capital Account

The financial and capital account measures the flow of payments between countries for financial assets such as stocks, bonds, and ownership rights to real estate. It is broken into two subcategories: (1) the capital account, which includes debt forgiveness, migrant's transfers, and transfers related to the sale of fixed assets; and (2) the financial account, which includes trade in assets such as business firms, bonds, stocks, and ownership right to real estate.[2] As you can see, the capital account transactions are rather small on balance. As you can also see in Table 17-1, in both years there was a significant inflow of financial assets into the United States in excess of outflows of assets from the United States. In 1987, financial inflows (payments by foreigners for U.S. real and financial assets) were $169 billion more than financial outflows (payments by U.S. citizens for foreign assets). In 2006, inflows exceeded outflows by $710 billion.

To buy these U.S. assets, foreigners needed dollars, so these net financial inflows represent a demand for dollars. In 1987 and 2006, the demand for dollars to buy real and financial assets offset the excess supply of dollars on the current account. Because of the importance of financial flows, when you think about what's likely to happen to a currency's value, it's important to remember both the demand for dollars to buy goods and services and the demand for dollars to buy assets.

> In thinking about what determines a currency's value, it's important to remember both the demand for dollars to buy goods and services and the demand for dollars to buy assets.

If we added up the current account balance and the financial account balance, the two would not completely balance because of measurement errors. Line 26 takes care of that problem; it is the sum of all the above items with the sign reversed, and thus is a measure of the statistical discrepancy in the figures. In 1987 there was a small −$8 billion discrepancy, and in 2006 there was a +$147 billion discrepancy. These discrepancies arise because many international transactions, especially on the capital account, go unrecorded and hence must be estimated. Including line 26, the net balance of payments, including all government payments, is always zero.

When economists say that a country is running a balance of payments deficit or surplus, they are excluding its government's financial transactions (line 23). Thus, if line 23 is positive, the United States is running a balance of payments deficit and, if it is negative, it is running a balance of payments surplus. Government financial transactions represent its buying and selling of currencies. Foreign governments also may be buying up U.S. currency, which they did substantially in 2006, as you can see by the large positive entry on line 22. These foreign countries are increasing their holding of U.S. dollars, and their purchases of U.S. dollars allow the U.S. balance of payments accounts to remain in equilibrium even as private quantities supplied and demanded for these currencies differ.

While the current and financial accounts offset each other, there is a difference between the long-run effects of the demand for dollars to buy currently produced goods and services and the demand for dollars to buy assets. Assets earn profits or interest, so when foreigners buy U.S. assets, they earn income from those assets just for owning them. The net investment income from foreigners' previous asset purchases shows up on line 11 of the current account. It's the difference between the income U.S. citizens receive from their foreign assets and the income foreigners receive from their U.S. assets. If assets earned equal returns, we would expect that when foreigners own more U.S. capital assets than U.S. citizens own foreign capital assets, net investment income should be negative. And when U.S. citizens own more foreign capital assets than

---

[2]The separation of the financial and capital accounts is a recent change; earlier, both were simply called the capital account.

foreigners own U.S. capital assets, net investment income should be positive. Why is this? Because net investment income is simply the difference between the returns on U.S. citizens' assets held abroad and foreign citizens' assets held in the United States.

Since the 1980s, the inflow of capital into the United States has greatly exceeded the outflow of capital from the United States. As a result, the United States has become a net debtor nation; the amount foreigners own in the United States now exceeds the amount U.S. citizens own abroad by well over $1 trillion. So we would expect that U.S. investment income would be highly negative. But looking at line 11 of Table 17-1, we see that was not the case. The reason? Foreigners' returns have been low, and many of the foreign assets owned by U.S. citizens abroad are undervalued. For example, the Japanese bought a lot of U.S. real estate at very high prices and have been losing money on those investments. While this trend has continued much longer than expected, we cannot expect it to continue forever.

Q-2 How can net investment income be positive if a country is a net debtor nation?

Exchange Rates

Supply and demand are two central forces of economics, so it shouldn't be surprising that our initial discussion of the determination of exchange rates uses supply and demand curves. As I stated above, an exchange rate is the rate at which one country's currency can be traded for another country's currency. The exchange rate is determined in what is called the **forex market** *(foreign exchange market)*. In the forex markets, traders buy and sell currencies, taking orders from banks, which in turn take orders for currencies from individuals and companies that want to exchange one currency for another. It is a very busy market with nearly $2 trillion traded every day.

The exchange rate will tell you the price of a foreign currency. Below is an exchange rate table from March 5, 2007. It tells you how much a dollar was worth in terms of other currencies on that day.

Exchange Rates, March 5, 2007

	U.S. $ Equivalent	Currency per U.S. $
Argentina (peso)	0.3226	3.1000
Canada (dollar)	0.8490	1.1779
China (renminbi)	0.1290	7.7500
Denmark (krone)	0.1759	5.6855
Israel (shekel)	0.2370	4.2200
Japan (yen)	0.0086	116.5400
Pakistan (rupee)	0.0165	60.7170
Philippines (peso)	0.0206	48.5670
Russia (ruble)	0.0381	26.2483
Saudi Arabia (riyal)	0.2668	3.7481
U.K. (pound)	1.9222	0.5202
European Union (euro)	1.3093	0.7638

The second column reports the U.S. dollar equivalent. It tells you the price of foreign currencies in terms of dollars. For example, one Argentinean peso costs about 32 cents. You also can look at exchange rates from the viewpoint of the foreign currency. For example, how many pesos are needed to buy one U.S. dollar? The third column tells you that one U.S. dollar costs 3.10 pesos.

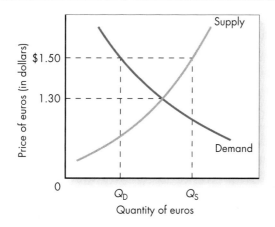

FIGURE 17-1 **The Supply of and Demand for Euros**

As long as you keep quantities and prices *of what* straight, the standard, or fundamental, analysis of the determination of exchange rates is easy. Just remember that if you're talking about the supply of and demand for euros, the price will be measured in dollars and the quantity will be in euros.

As you learned in Chapter 5, people exchange currencies to buy goods or assets in other countries. For example, an American who wants to buy stock of a company that trades on the EU stock exchange first needs to buy euros with dollars. If the stock costs 150 euros, he will need to buy 150 euros. With an exchange rate of $1.30 for 1 euro, he will need to pay $195 to buy 150 euros ($1.30 × 150). Only then can he buy the stock.

Let's now turn to the graphs. At first glance, the graphical analysis of foreign exchange rates seems simple: You have an upward-sloping supply curve and a downward-sloping demand curve. But what goes on the axes? Obviously price and quantity, but what price? And what quantity? Because you are talking about the prices of currencies relative to each other, you have to specify which currencies you are using.

In Figure 17-1, I present the supply of and demand for euros in terms of dollars. Notice that the quantity of euros goes on the horizontal axis and the dollar price of euros goes on the vertical axis. When you are comparing currencies of only two countries the supply of one currency equals the demand for the other currency. To demand one currency, you must supply another. In this figure, I am assuming that there are only two trading partners: the United States and the European Union. This means that the supply of euros is equivalent to the demand for dollars. The Europeans who want to buy U.S. goods or assets supply euros to buy dollars. Let's consider an example. Say a European wants to buy an IBM computer made in the United States. She has euros, but IBM wants dollars. So, to buy the computer, she or IBM must somehow exchange euros for dollars. She is *supplying* euros in order to *demand* dollars.

The supply curve of euros is upward-sloping because the more dollars European citizens get for their euros, the cheaper U.S. goods and assets are for them and the greater the quantity of euros they want to supply for those goods. Say, for example, that the dollar price of one euro rises from $1.30 to $1.35. That means that the price of a dollar to a European has fallen from 0.78 euro to 0.74 euro. For a European, a good that cost $100 now falls in price from 78 euros to 74 euros. U.S. goods are cheaper, so the Europeans buy more U.S. goods and more dollars, which means they supply more euros.

The demand for euros comes from Americans who want to buy European goods or assets. The demand curve is downward-sloping because the lower the dollar price of euros, the more euros U.S. citizens want to buy, using the same reasoning I just described.

The market is in equilibrium when the quantity supplied equals the quantity demanded. In my example, equilibrium occurs at a dollar price of $1.30 for one euro. If the price of euros is above or below $1.30, quantity supplied won't equal the quantity

To demand one currency, you must supply another currency.

Q-3 Show graphically the effect on the price of euros of an increase in the demand for dollars by Europeans.

demanded and there will be pressure for the exchange rate to move to equilibrium. Say, for example, that the price is $1.50. The quantity of euros supplied will be greater than the quantity demanded. People who want to sell euros won't be able to sell them. To find buyers, they will offer to sell their euros for less. As they do, the price of euros falls.

Exchange Rates and the Balance of Payments

The total balance of payments (including government financial flows) is always in equilibrium, so we know that the quantity of a currency supplied always equals the quantity demanded. That does not mean, however, that foreign or domestic governments did not buy or sell currencies to maintain that equilibrium. If a government wants to keep its exchange rate higher than what would be supported by the market, the government must remove the excess supply of its currency. Its purchase of domestic currency would be recorded as a positive entry in the government financial account. Without that entry, the balance of payments would be in deficit. Thus, in Figure 17-1, when the price of euros is $1.50, the quantity of euros supplied exceeds the quantity demanded, so without the government's purchase of euros, Europe is running a balance of payments deficit. When the price of euros is below $1.30, the quantity of euros demanded exceeds the quantity supplied, so excluding government sale of euros, Europe is running a balance of payments surplus.

A deficit in the balance of payments means that the private quantity supplied of a currency exceeds the private quantity demanded. A surplus in the balance of payments means the opposite.

Fundamental Forces Determining Exchange Rates

Exchange rate analysis is usually broken down into fundamental analysis and short-run analysis. In this section, I discuss fundamental analysis—a consideration of the fundamental forces that determine the supply of and demand for currencies, and hence cause them to shift. These fundamental forces include a country's income, a country's prices, the interest rate in a country, and the country's trade policy. That means that changes in a country's income, changes in a country's prices, changes in interest rates, and changes in trade policy can cause the supply of and demand for a currency to shift. Let's consider how they do so.

Changes in a Country's Income The demand for imports depends on the income in a country. When a country's income falls, demand for imports falls. Hence, demand for foreign currency to buy those imports falls, which means that the supply of the country's currency to buy the foreign currency falls. That's why, in my presentation of the AS/AD model, I said that imports depend on income.

How important is this relationship? Very important. For example, in the early 2000s, strong economic growth in the United States relative to its primary trading partners led to increased imports, which increased the supply of U.S. dollars. The increase in the supply tended to lower the price of the dollar relative to foreign currencies.

Four important fundamental determinants of exchange rates are income, prices, interest rates, and trade policy.

Changes in a Country's Prices The United States' demand for imports and foreign countries' demand for U.S. exports depend on prices of U.S. goods compared to prices of foreign competing goods. If the United States has more inflation than other countries, foreign goods will become cheaper, U.S. demand for foreign currencies will tend to increase, and foreign demand for dollars will tend to decrease. This rise in U.S. inflation will shift the dollar supply outward and the dollar demand inward.

Changes in Interest Rates People like to invest their savings in assets that will yield the highest return. Other things equal, a rise in U.S. interest rates relative to those abroad will increase demand for U.S. assets. As a result, demand for dollars will increase, while simultaneously the supply of dollars will decrease as fewer Americans sell their dollars to buy foreign assets. A fall in the U.S. interest rate or a rise in foreign interest rates will have the opposite effect.

Changes in Trade Policy   The demand for imports is affected by a government's trade policy. An increase in trade restrictions, such as the 30 percent tariff President George W. Bush imposed on imported steel in 2002, increases the price of imports, reducing the quantity of imports demanded. Consequently, the demand for foreign currency to buy those imports declines so that the supply of a country's currency falls. A number of other countries threatened to impose retaliatory tariffs on American goods, which they were allowed to do under WTO rules. These retaliatory tariffs would have reduced U.S. exports and reduced the demand for the U.S. dollar. To avoid these retaliatory tariffs, President Bush repealed the tariffs on steel in late 2003.

Some Examples   To make sure that you've understood the analysis, let's consider some examples. First, the U.S. economy goes into recession with interest rates remaining constant—what will likely happen to exchange rates? Second, the Mexican economy has runaway inflation—what will likely happen to exchange rates? And third, the interest rate on yen-denominated assets increases—what will likely happen to the exchange rate? If you answered: The value of the dollar will rise, the value of the peso will fall, and the value of the yen will rise, you're following the argument. If those weren't your answers, a review is in order.

Indirect Methods of Influencing Exchange Rates

The government can influence the price of its currency either directly through market intervention or indirectly through monetary and fiscal policy. Let's begin with the indirect method of monetary and fiscal policy.

Monetary Policy's Effect on Exchange Rates   Monetary policy affects exchange rates in three primary ways: (1) through its effect on the interest rate, (2) through its effect on income, and (3) through its effect on price levels and inflation.

The Effect on Exchange Rates via Interest Rates   Expansionary monetary policy pushes down the U.S. interest rate, which decreases the financial inflow into the United States, decreasing the demand for dollars, pushing down the value of the dollar, and decreasing the U.S. exchange rate. Contractionary monetary policy does the opposite. It raises the U.S. interest rate, which tends to bring in financial capital flows from abroad, increasing the demand for dollars, increasing the value of the dollar, and increasing the U.S. exchange rate. This interest rate effect is the dominant short-run effect, and it often overwhelms the other effects.

To see why these effects take place, consider a person in Japan in the early 2000s, when the Japanese interest rate was close to 0 percent. He or she reasoned, "Why should I earn 0 percent return in Japan? I'll save (buy some financial assets) in the United States where I'll earn 3 percent." If the U.S. interest rate goes up due to contraction in the money supply, other things equal, the advantage of holding one's financial assets in the United States will become even greater and more people will want to save here. People in Japan hold yen, not dollars, so in order to save in the United States they must buy dollars. Thus, a rise in U.S. interest rates increases demand for dollars and, in terms of yen, pushes up the U.S. exchange rate. This example illustrates that it is relative interest rates that govern the flow of financial assets.

Q-4   What effect does the lowering of a country's interest rates have on exchange rates?

The interest rate effect on exchange rates is the dominant short-run effect.

Iceland's Struggle to Slow Inflation

In 2006, the Icelandic inflation rate exceeded its target inflation rate, and investors became worried. The financial press began to issue comments such as this: "The negative outlook has been triggered by a material deterioration in Iceland's macro-prudential risk indicators, accompanied by an unsustainable current account deficit and soaring net external indebtedness." A group of developed countries, the Organisation for Economic Co-operation and Development (OECD), warned that that failure to bring inflation down could damage the country's international credibility, and that "[i]n the absence of swift and vigorous policy action, financial market stability could be at risk."

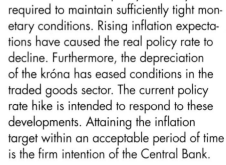

In response to these and other warnings, foreign exchange traders began selling króna, the Icelandic currency. The króna's value started to decline, which led the Icelandic Central Bank to tighten the money supply and raise interest rates. In 2006 the Icelandic Central Bank issued the following statement:

Economic developments since the end of March indicate that a considerable increase in the policy rate may be required to maintain sufficiently tight monetary conditions. Rising inflation expectations have caused the real policy rate to decline. Furthermore, the depreciation of the króna has eased conditions in the traded goods sector. The current policy rate hike is intended to respond to these developments. Attaining the inflation target within an acceptable period of time is the firm intention of the Central Bank.

The Central Bank of Iceland continued raising interest rates by substantial amounts, to 12 percent and then to 13.5 percent, stating that "further rises were unavoidable." They continued raising interest rates and, in mid-2007, the interest rate was about 15 percent while inflation had decreased to less than 6 percent.

Countries are continually taking into account the effect of monetary policy on exchange rates. For example, in the mid-1990s, Taiwan kept its money supply tight, raising its interest rates to keep the new Taiwan dollar high. In 1997 Taiwan cut reserve ratios; interest rates fell and the value of the new Taiwan dollar fell.

The Effect on Exchange Rates via Income   Monetary policy also affects income in a country. As money supply rises, income expands; when money supply falls, income contracts.[3] This effect on income provides another way in which the money supply affects the exchange rate. As we saw earlier, when income rises, imports rise while exports are unaffected. To buy foreign products, U.S. citizens need foreign currency, which they must buy with dollars. So when U.S. imports rise, the supply of dollars to the foreign exchange market increases as U.S. citizens sell dollars to buy foreign currencies to pay for those imports. This decreases the dollar exchange rate. This effect through income and imports provides a second path through which monetary policy affects the exchange rate: Expansionary monetary policy causes U.S. income to rise,

---

[3]When there's inflation, it's the rate of money supply growth relative to the rate of inflation that's important. If inflation is 10 percent and money supply growth is 10 percent, the rate of increase in the real money supply is zero. If money supply growth falls to, say, 5 percent while inflation stays at 10 percent, there will be a contractionary effect on the real economy.

imports to rise, and the U.S. exchange rate to fall via the income path. Contraction-ary monetary policy causes U.S. income to fall, imports to fall, and the U.S. exchange rate to rise via the income path.

The Effect on Exchange Rates via Price Levels

A third way in which monetary policy can affect exchange rates is through its effect on prices in a country. Expansion-ary monetary policy pushes the U.S. price level up. As the U.S. price level rises relative to foreign prices, U.S. exports become more expensive, and goods the United States imports become relatively cheaper, decreasing U.S. competitiveness. This increases de-mand for foreign currencies and decreases demand for dollars. Thus, via the price path, expansionary monetary policy pushes down the dollar's value for the same reason that an expansion in income pushes it down.

Contractionary monetary policy puts downward pressure on the U.S. price level and slows down any existing inflation. As the U.S. price level falls relative to foreign prices, U.S. exports become more competitive and the goods the United States imports, relatively more expensive. Thus, contractionary monetary policy pushes up the value of the dollar via the price path.

Q.5 What effect would contractionary monetary policy have on a country's exchange rates?

The Net Effect of Monetary Policy on Exchange Rates

Notice that all these effects of monetary policy on exchange rates are in the same direction. Expansion-ary monetary policy pushes a country's exchange rate down; contractionary monetary policy pushes a country's exchange rate up. Summarizing these effects, we have the fol-lowing relationships for expansionary and contractionary monetary policy:

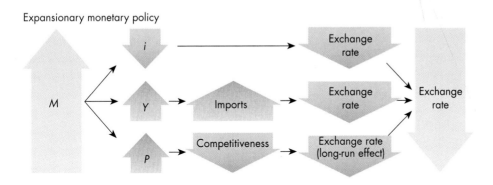

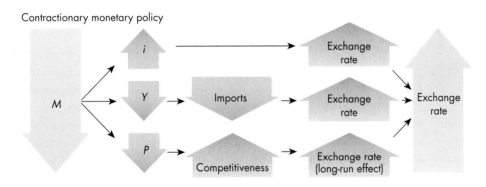

Monetary policy affects exchange rates through the interest rate path, the income path, and the price level path, as shown in the accompanying diagram.

There are, of course, many provisos to the relationship between monetary policy and the exchange rate. For example, as the exchange rate falls, the price of imports goes up and there is some inflationary pressure from that rise in price and hence some pressure for the price level to rise as well as fall. Monetary policy affects exchange rates in subtle ways, but if an economist had to give a quick answer to what effect monetary policy would have on exchange rates, it would be

Expansionary monetary policy lowers exchange rates. It decreases the relative value of a country's currency.

Contractionary monetary policy increases exchange rates. It increases the relative value of a country's currency.

Expansionary monetary policy lowers exchange rates. It decreases the relative value of a country's currency.

Contractionary monetary policy increases exchange rates. It increases the relative value of a country's currency.

Fiscal Policy's Effect on Exchange Rates   The effect of fiscal policy on exchange rates is not so clear. The reason why can be seen by considering its effects on income, the price level, and interest rates.

The Effect on Exchange Rates via Income   Expansionary fiscal policy expands income and therefore increases imports, increasing the trade deficit and lowering the exchange rate. Contractionary fiscal policy contracts income, thereby decreasing imports and increasing the exchange rate. These effects of expansionary and contractionary fiscal policies via the income path are similar to the effects of monetary policy, so if it's not intuitively clear to you why the effect is what it is, it may be worthwhile to review the slightly more complete discussion of monetary policy's effect presented previously.

The Effect on Exchange Rates via Price Levels   Let's turn to the effect of fiscal policy on exchange rates through prices. Expansionary fiscal policy increases aggregate demand and increases prices of a country's exports; hence, it decreases the competitiveness of a country's exports, which pushes down the exchange rate. Contractionary fiscal policy works in the opposite direction. These are the same effects that monetary policy had. And, as was the case with monetary policy, the price path is a long-run effect.

The Effect on Exchange Rates via Interest Rates   Fiscal policy's effect on the exchange rate via the interest rate path is different from monetary policy's effect. Let's first consider the effect of expansionary fiscal policy. Whereas expansionary monetary policy lowers the interest rate, expansionary fiscal policy raises interest rates because the government sells bonds to finance that budget deficit. The higher U.S. interest rate causes foreign capital to flow into the United States, which pushes up the U.S. exchange rate. Therefore, expansionary fiscal policy's effect on exchange rates via the interest rate effect is to push up a country's exchange rate.

Contractionary fiscal policy decreases interest rates since it reduces the bond financing of that deficit. Lower U.S. interest rates cause capital to flow out of the United States, which pushes down the U.S. exchange rate. Thus, the U.S. government budget surplus in the late 1990s put downward pressure on the interest rate and downward pressure on the exchange rate value of the dollar, while the deficits in the early 2000s put upward pressure on the interest rate and exchange rate.

The Net Effect of Fiscal Policy on Exchange Rates   Of these three effects, the interest rate effect and the income effect are both short-run effects. These two work in opposite directions, so the net effect of fiscal policy on the exchange rate is, in general, ambiguous, although in specific instances either the interest rate effect or

Q-6   What is the net effect of expansionary fiscal policy on the exchange rate?

the income effect may swamp the other. The following diagram summarizes these three effects.

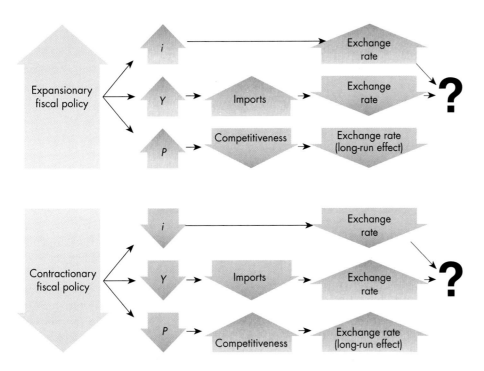

Fiscal policy affects exchange rates through the income path, the interest rate path, and the price level path, as shown in the accompanying diagram.

As you can see, it's unclear what the effect of expansionary or contractionary fiscal policy will be on exchange rates.

Direct Methods of Influencing Exchange Rates

The supply/demand analysis may have made it look like exchange rates are driven by fundamentals. Unfortunately, that is not the case. In day-to-day trading, fundamentals can be overwhelmed by expectations of how a currency will change in value. The supply and demand curves for currencies can shift around rapidly in response to rumors, expectations, and expectations of expectations. As they shift, they bring about large fluctuations in exchange rates that make trading difficult and have significant real effects on economic activity.

Let me outline just one potential problem. Say you expect the price of the currency to fall one-half of 1 percent tomorrow. What should you do? The correct answer is: Sell that currency quickly. Why? One-half of 1 percent may not sound like much, but, annualized, it is equivalent to a rate of interest per year of 617 percent. Based on that expectation, if you're into making money (and you're really sure about the fall), you will sell all of that currency that you hold, and borrow all you can so you can sell some more. You can make big money if you guess small changes in exchange rates correctly. (Of course, if you're wrong, you can lose big money.) This means that if the market generally believes the exchange rates will move, those expectations will tend to be self-fulfilling. Self-fulfilling expectations undermine the argument in favor of letting markets determine exchange rates: When expectations rule, the exchange rate may not reflect actual demands and supplies of goods. Instead, the exchange rate can reflect expectations and rumors. The resulting fluctuations serve no real purpose, and cause problems for international trade and the country's economy. Let's consider an example.

Q-7 Why don't most governments leave determination of the exchange rate to the market?

Suppose that a firm decides to build a plant in the United States because costs in the United States are low. But suppose also that the value of the dollar then rises significantly; the firm's costs rise significantly too, making it uncompetitive. When currencies fluctuate, companies find it harder to make good decisions on where to produce.

In a real-world example, from July to September 1997, the value of the Thai baht fell nearly 40 percent. Goodyear (Thailand), which had been one of the five most profitable companies on the Stock Exchange of Thailand, suddenly faced a 20 percent rise in the costs of raw materials because it paid for those raw materials in dollars. It also faced a decline in tire prices because the demand for tires had fallen 20 to 40 percent when the Thai economy contracted. Within just two months, a highly profitable venture had become unprofitable. Other firms were closing shop because they were unable to pay the interest on loans that were denominated in dollars. In summary, large fluctuations make real trade difficult and cause serious real consequences.

The problems caused by fluctuating exchange rates have led to calls for government to intervene and either stabilize or fix its exchange rate directly by buying or selling its currency. It can increase the value of its currency by buying its currency, assuming it has international reserves to buy it with. Alternatively, it can decrease the value of its currency by selling its currency. This ability of a country to buy and sell its currency means that, assuming it has sufficient reserves, a country can fix its currency at a specific level.

Currency Support   Let's consider currency support. Suppose that, given the interaction of private supply and demand forces, the equilibrium value of the euro is $1.30 a euro, but the European Union wants to maintain a value of $1.50 a euro. This is shown in Figure 17-2. At $1.50 a euro, quantity supplied exceeds quantity demanded. The European Union must buy the surplus, $Q_2 - Q_1$, using official reserves (foreign currency holdings). In doing so, it shifts the total demand for euros to D_1, making the equilibrium market exchange rate (including the European government's demand for euros) equal to $1.50. This process is called **currency support**—the *buying of a currency by a government to maintain its value at above its long-run equilibrium value*. It is a direct exchange rate policy. If a government has sufficient official reserves, or if it can convince other governments to lend it reserves, it can fix the exchange rate at the rate it wants, no matter what the private level of supply and demand is. In reality, governments have no such power to support currencies in the long run, since their reserves are limited. For example, in 2002 the Argentinean government tried to keep its currency fixed to the

A country fixes the exchange rate by standing ready to buy and sell its currency anytime the exchange rate is not at the fixed exchange rate.

A country can maintain a fixed exchange rate above its market price only as long as it has the reserves.

FIGURE 17-2 **A Demonstration of Direct Exchange Rate Policy**

If the government chooses to hold the exchange rate at $1.50, when the equilibrium is $1.30, there is an excess supply given by $Q_2 - Q_1$. The government purchases this excess (using official reserves) and closes the difference, thus maintaining equilibrium.

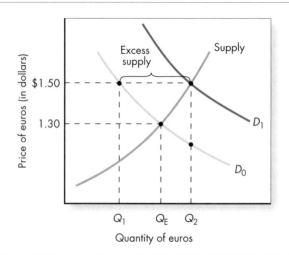

U.S. dollar, but it ran out of foreign reserves and was forced to let its currency decline in value.

A country has more power to prevent the value of its currency from rising since it can create its own money. Thus, throughout the early 2000s, China used yuan to buy large amounts of dollars, thereby preventing the value of the yuan from rising relative to the dollar.

Currency Stabilization   A more viable long-run exchange rate policy is **currency stabilization**—the *buying and selling of a currency by the government to offset temporary fluctuations in supply and demand for currencies*. In currency stabilization, the government is not trying to change the long-run equilibrium; it is simply trying to keep the exchange rate at that long-run equilibrium. The government sometimes buys and sometimes sells currency, so it is far less likely to run out of reserves.

Successful currency stabilization requires the government to choose the correct long-run equilibrium exchange rate. A policy of stabilization can become a policy of support if the government chooses too high a long-run equilibrium. Unfortunately, government has no way of knowing for sure what the long-run equilibrium exchange rate is, so how much stabilizing it can do depends on its access to reserves. If it has sufficient reserves, the government buys up sufficient quantities of its currency to make up the difference.

Once the government has dried up the sources of borrowing foreign currencies, if it wants to hold its exchange rate above the private equilibrium exchange rate, it must move to indirect methods of monetary and fiscal policy to affect private supplies and demands for its currency.

The same argument about running out of reserves cannot be made for a country that wants to maintain a below-market exchange rate. Since a government can create all the domestic currency it wants, it's easier for the European Union to push the value of its currency down by selling euros than it is for the government to hold it up by buying euros. By the same token, it's easier for another country (say, Japan) to push the value of the euro up (by pushing the value of the yen down). Thus, if the two governments can decide which way they want their exchange rates to move, they have a large incentive to cooperate. Of course, cooperation requires an agreement on the goals, and often countries' goals conflict. One role of the various international economic organizations is to provide a forum for reaching agreement on exchange rate goals and a vehicle through which cooperation can take place.

Notice that, in principle, any trader could establish a fixed exchange rate by guaranteeing to buy or sell a currency at a given rate. Any "fix," however, is only as good as the guarantee, and to fix an exchange rate would require many more resources than an individual trader has; only governments have sufficient resources to fix an exchange rate, and often even governments run out of resources.

In reality, given the small level of official reserves compared to the enormous level of private trading, significant amounts of stabilization are impossible. Instead, governments use *strategic currency stabilization*—buying and selling at strategic moments to affect expectations of traders, and hence to affect their supply and demand. Such issues are discussed in depth in international finance courses.

Stabilizing Fluctuations versus Deviating from Long-Run Equilibrium
The key to whether or not exchange rate intervention is a viable option involves the long-run equilibrium exchange rate. Direct exchange rate policy can succeed if the problem is one of stabilization. If, however, the problem is long run, or if the government estimates the wrong equilibrium, eventually the government will run out of official reserves. Here's the rub: While in theory it is important to make the distinction, in practice it is difficult to do so. The government can only guess at the

Q-8   In general, would it be easier for the United States to push the value of the dollar down or up? Why?

Strategic currency stabilization is the process of buying and selling at strategic moments to affect the expectations of traders, and hence affect their supply and demand.

Determining the Causes of Fluctuations in the Dollar's Value

As you can see on the graph, the dollar's value has fluctuated considerably since 1973. A good exercise to see if you understand movements in the value of the dollar is to try to choose which factors caused the fluctuation.

Let's start with the relatively small fluctuations in 1973 and 1974. These probably reflected expectational bubbles—in which speculators were more concerned with short-run fluctuations than long-run fundamentals—while the dollar's low value in 1979 and 1980 reflected high inflation, relatively low real interest rates, and the booming U.S. economy during this period.

The rise of the dollar in the early 1980s reflected higher real U.S. interest rates and the falling U.S. inflation rate, although the rise was much more than expected and probably reflected speculation, as did the sudden fall in the dollar's value in 1985. Similarly, the fluctuations in the late 1980s and early 1990s reflected both changing interest rates in the United States and changing foreign interest rates, as well as changing relative inflation rates.

In the late 1990s, the value of the dollar rose substantially. Part of the explanation for this lies in the weakness of the Japanese economy, which led the Japanese central bank to increase the Japanese money supply, thereby lowering the Japanese interest rate. That weakness also was

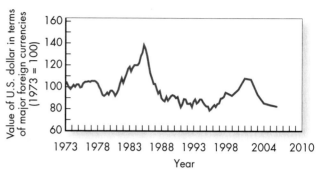

Source: Board of Governors, Federal Reserve System (www.federalreserve.gov).

reflected in the fall in the prices of Japanese stocks. That fall led investors to shift out of Japanese stocks and into U.S. stocks, thereby increasing the demand for the dollar, and pushing up the U.S. effective exchange rate. Since the early 2000s, the value of the dollar has been declining slowly as its trade deficit has expanded.

As you can see, after the fact we economists are pretty good at explaining the movements in the exchange rates. Alas, before the fact we aren't so good because often speculative activities make the timing of the movements unpredictable.

long-run equilibrium rate, since no definitive empirical measure of this rate exists. The long-run equilibrium must be estimated. If that estimate is wrong, a sustainable stabilization policy becomes an unsustainable deviation from long-run equilibrium policy. Thus, a central issue in exchange rate intervention policy is estimating the long-run equilibrium exchange rate.

Purchasing Power Parity and Real Exchange Rates

Purchasing power parity is one way economists have of estimating the long-run equilibrium rate. **Purchasing power parity (PPP)** is *a method of calculating exchange rates that attempts to value currencies at rates such that each currency will buy an equal basket of goods.* It is based on the idea that the exchange of currencies reflects the exchange of real goods. If you are able to exchange a basket of goods from country X for an equivalent basket of goods from country Z, you should also be able to exchange the amount of currency from country X that is needed to purchase country X's basket of goods for the amount of currency from country Z that is needed to purchase country Z's basket of goods. For example, say that the yen is valued at 100 yen to $1. Say also that you can buy the same basket of goods for 1,000 yen that you can buy for $7. In that case, the purchasing power parity exchange rate would be 143 yen to $1 (1,000/7 = 143) compared

TABLE 17-2 Actual and Purchasing Power Parity Exchange Rates for 2006

Country	Actual Exchange Rate (currency per dollar)	PPP Exchange Rate (currency per dollar)	Under (−)/ Over (+) valuation
Switzerland	1.253	1.950	+56
United Kingdom	0.54	0.66	+22
Japan	116.31	136.39	+17
United States	1	1	0
Brazil	2.1738	1.11	−49
Russia	26.305	9.87	−62
China	7.97	1.81	−77
India	44.05	8.803	−80
Mozambique	26,140	5,051	−81
Uganda	1,753	316	−82

Source: *World Economic Outlook Database*, 2006. International Monetary Fund (www.imf.org).

to an actual exchange rate of 100 yen to $1. An economist would say that at 100 to the dollar the yen is overvalued—with 100 yen you could not purchase a basket of goods equivalent to the basket of goods you could purchase with $1.

Table 17-2 shows various calculations for purchasing power parity for a variety of countries. The second column shows the 2006 actual exchange rates. The third column shows purchasing power parity exchange rates. The fourth column shows the difference between the two, or the 2006 distortion in the exchange rates (if you believe the PPP exchange rates are the correct ones).

Purchasing power parity is a method of calculating exchange rates such that various currencies will each buy an equal basket of goods and services.

Criticisms of the Purchasing Power Parity Method

For many economists, estimating exchange rates using PPP has serious problems. If the currency is overvalued and will eventually fall, why don't traders use that information and sell that currency now, making it fall now? After all, they are out after a profit. So if there is open trading in a currency, any expected change in the exchange rate will affect exchange rates now. If traders don't sell now when there are expectations that a currency's overvaluation will eventually make its value fall, they must believe there is some reason that its value won't, in fact, fall.

Critics argue that the difficulty with PPP exchange rates is the complex nature of trade and consumption. They point out that the PPP will change as the basket of goods changes. This means that there is no one PPP measure. They also point out that, since all PPP measures leave out asset demand for a currency, the measures are missing an important element of the demand. Critics ask: Is there any reason to assume that in the long run the asset demand for a currency is less important than the goods demand for a currency? Because the asset demand for a currency is important, critics of PPP argue that there is little reason to assume that the short-run actual exchange rate will ever adjust to the PPP exchange rates. And if that rate doesn't adjust, then PPP does not provide a good estimate of the equilibrium rate. These critics further contend that the existing exchange rate is the best estimate of the long-run equilibrium exchange rate.

Web Note 17.1
The Big Mac Index

Purchasing power parity exchange rates may or may not be appropriate long-run exchange rates.

Real Exchange Rates

Regardless of one's view of the usefulness of purchasing power parity, the concept gets at the importance of prices in the determination of exchange rates. Say, for example, that the

A real exchange rate is an exchange rate adjusted for differential inflation or differential changes in the price level.

price level in the United States goes up by 10 percent while the price level in Europe stays constant. In such a situation, we would expect some change in the exchange rate—the most likely effect would be that the U.S. dollar falls by 10 percent relative to the euro. To capture the distinction between changes in exchange rates caused by changes in price levels and changes in exchange rates caused by other things, economists differentiate between nominal and real exchange rates. A **real exchange rate** is *an exchange rate adjusted for differential inflation or differential changes in the price level*. A nominal exchange rate is the exchange rate you see in the papers—it is the rate you'd get when exchanging currencies.

Let's consider the above example: The U.S. price level rises by 10 percent, the European price level remains constant, and the nominal U.S. exchange rate falls by 10 percent. In that case, the real exchange rate will have remained constant. More generally, the change in the real exchange rate (foreign/domestic or in this case euro/$) can be approximately calculated by adding the difference in the rates of inflation between the two countries (domestic inflation − foreign inflation) to the percentage change in the nominal exchange rate.

Q-9 If U.S. inflation is 2 percent, the European Union's inflation rate is 4 percent, and the nominal U.S. dollar exchange rate rises by 3 percent relative to the euro, what happens to the real exchange rate of the dollar?

$$\%\Delta \text{ real exchange rate} =$$
$$\%\Delta \text{ nominal exchange rate} + [\text{domestic inflation} - \text{foreign inflation}]$$

For example, say the U.S. price level had risen only by 8 percent and Europe's had remained constant, but the U.S. nominal exchange rate had fallen by 10 percent. In that case, we would say that the real U.S. exchange rate had fallen by 2 percent.

$$\%\Delta \text{ real exchange rate} = -10 + (8 - 0) = -2 \text{ percent}$$

Advantages and Disadvantages of Alternative Exchange Rate Systems

The problems of stabilizing exchange rates have led to an ongoing debate about whether a fixed exchange rate, a flexible exchange rate, or a combination of the two is best. This debate nicely captures the macro issues relevant to exchange rate stabilization, so in this section I consider that debate. First, a brief overview of the three alternative regimes:

Fixed exchange rate: *When the government chooses a particular exchange rate and offers to buy and sell its currency at that price.* For example, suppose the U.S. government says it will buy euros at $1.30 per euro and sell dollars at 0.78 euro per dollar. In that case, we say that the United States has a fixed exchange rate of 0.78 euro to the dollar.

Flexible exchange rate: *When the government does not enter into foreign exchange markets at all, but leaves the determination of exchange rates totally up to currency traders.* The price of its currency is allowed to rise and fall as market forces dictate.

Partially flexible exchange rate: *When the government sometimes buys or sells currencies to influence the exchange rate, while at other times letting private market forces operate.* A partially flexible exchange rate is sometimes called a dirty float because it isn't purely market-determined or government-determined.

Three exchange rate regimes are

1. Fixed exchange rate: The government chooses an exchange rate and offers to buy and sell currencies at that rate.

2. Flexible exchange rate: Determination of exchange rates is left totally up to the market.

3. Partially flexible exchange rate: The government sometimes affects the exchange rate and sometimes leaves it to the market.

Fixed Exchange Rates

The advantages of a fixed exchange rate system are

1. Fixed exchange rates provide international monetary stability.

2. Fixed exchange rates force governments to make adjustments to meet their international problems.

The disadvantages of a fixed exchange rate system are

1. Fixed exchange rates can become unfixed. When they're expected to become unfixed, they create enormous monetary instability.

2. Fixed exchange rates force governments to make adjustments to meet their international problems. (Yes, this is a disadvantage as well as an advantage.)

Let's consider each in turn.

Fixed Exchange Rates and Exchange Rate Stability   The advantage of fixed exchange rates is that firms know what exchange rates will be, making trade easier. However, to maintain fixed exchange rates, the government must choose an exchange rate and have sufficient official reserves to support that rate. If the rate it chooses is too high, its exports lag and the country continually loses official reserves. If the rate it chooses is too low, it is paying more for its imports than it needs to and is building up official reserves.

The difficulty is that as soon as the country gets close to its official reserves limit, foreign exchange traders begin to expect a drop in the value of the currency, and they try to get out of that currency because anyone holding that currency when it falls will lose money. For example, in December 1997, when traders found out that South Korea had only $10 billion in reserves instead of the official government announcement of $30 billion, they sold the Korean won and its value dropped. False rumors of an expected depreciation or decrease in a country's fixed exchange rate can become true by causing a "run on a currency," as all traders sell that currency. Thus, at times fixed exchange rates can become highly unstable because expectation of a change in the exchange rate can force the change to occur. As opposed to small movements in currency values, under a fixed rate regime these movements occur in large, sudden jumps.

Fixed Exchange Rates and Policy Independence   Maintaining a fixed exchange rate places limitations on a central bank's actions. In a country with fixed exchange rates, the central bank must ensure that the international quantities of its currency supplied and demanded are equal at the existing exchange rate.

Say, for example, that the United States and the Bahamas have fixed exchange rates: $1 B = $1 U.S. The Bahamian central bank decides to run an expansionary monetary policy, lowering the interest rate and stimulating the Bahamian economy. The lower interest rates will cause financial capital to flow out of the country, and the higher income will increase imports. Demand for Bahamian dollars will fall. To prop up its dollar and to maintain the fixed exchange rate, the Bahamian government will have to buy its own currency. It can do so only as long as it has sufficient official reserves of other countries' currencies.

Because most countries' official reserves are limited, a country with fixed exchange rates is limited in its ability to conduct expansionary monetary and fiscal policies. It loses its freedom to stimulate the economy in response to a recession. That's why, when a serious recession hits, many countries are forced to abandon fixed exchange rates. They run out of official reserves, and choose expansionary monetary policy to achieve their domestic goals over contractionary monetary policy to achieve their international goals.

Flexible Exchange Rates

The advantages and disadvantages of a flexible exchange rate (exchange rates totally determined by private market forces) are the reverse of those of fixed exchange rates. The advantages are

1. Flexible exchange rates provide for orderly incremental adjustment of exchange rates rather than large, sudden jumps.

2. Flexible exchange rates allow government to be flexible in conducting domestic monetary and fiscal policies.

Fixed exchange rates provide international monetary stability and force governments to make adjustments to meet their international problems. (This is also a disadvantage.) If they become unfixed, they create monetary instability.

The disadvantages are

1. Flexible exchange rates allow speculation to cause large jumps in exchange rates, which do not reflect market fundamentals.
2. Flexible exchange rates allow government to be flexible in conducting domestic monetary and fiscal policies. (This is a disadvantage as well as an advantage.)

Let's consider each in turn.

Flexible Exchange Rates and Exchange Rate Stability　　Advocates of flexible exchange rates argue as follows: Why not treat currency markets like any other market and let private market forces determine a currency's value? There is no fixed price for TVs; why should there be a fixed price for currencies? The opponents' answer is based on the central role that international financial considerations play in an economy and the strange shapes and large shifts that occur in the short-run supply and demand curves for currencies.

When expectations shift supply and demand curves around all the time, there's no guarantee that the exchange rate will be determined by long-run fundamental forces. The economy will go through real gyrations because of speculators' expectations about other speculators. Thus, the argument against flexible exchange rates is that they allow far too much fluctuation in exchange rates, making trade difficult.

Flexible Exchange Rates and Policy Independence　　The policy independence arguments for and against flexible exchange rates are the reverse of those given for fixed exchange rates. Individuals who believe that national governments should not have flexibility in setting monetary policy argue that flexible exchange rates don't impose the discipline on policy that fixed exchange rates do. Say, for example, that a country's goods are uncompetitive. Under a fixed exchange rate system, the country would have to contract its money supply and deal with the underlying uncompetitiveness of its goods. Under a flexible exchange rate system, the country can maintain an expansionary monetary policy, allowing inflation simply by permitting the value of its currency to fall.

Advocates of policy flexibility argue that it makes no sense for a country to go through a recession when it doesn't have to; flexible exchange rates allow countries more flexibility in dealing with their problems. True, policy flexibility may lead to inflation, but inflation is better than a recession.

Partially Flexible Exchange Rates

Faced with the dilemma of choosing between these two unpleasant policies, most countries have opted for a policy in between: partially flexible exchange rates. With such a policy, they try to get the advantages of both fixed and flexible exchange rates.

When policy makers believe there is a fundamental misalignment in a country's exchange rate, they will allow private forces to determine it—they allow the exchange rate to be flexible. When they believe that the currency's value is falling because of speculation, or that too large an adjustment in the currency is taking place, and that that adjustment won't achieve their balance of payments goals, they step in and fix the exchange rate, either supporting or pushing down their currency's value. Countries that follow a currency stabilization policy have partially flexible exchange rates.

If policy makers are correct, this system of partial flexibility works smoothly and has the advantages of both fixed and flexible exchange rates. If policy makers are incorrect, however, a partially flexible system has the disadvantages of both fixed and flexible systems.

Flexible exchange rate regimes provide for orderly incremental adjustment of exchange rates rather than large sudden jumps, and allow governments to be flexible in conducting domestic monetary and fiscal policies. (This is also a disadvantage.)

Partially flexible exchange rate regimes combine the advantages and disadvantages of fixed and flexible exchange rates.

Which View Is Right?

Which view is correct is much in debate. Most foreign exchange traders I know tell me that the possibility of government intervention increases the amount of private speculation in the system. In the private investors' view, their own assessments of what exchange rates should be are better than those of policy makers. If private investors knew the government would not enter in, private speculators would focus on fundamentals and would stabilize short-run exchange rates. When private speculators know government might enter into the market, they don't focus on fundamentals; instead they continually try to outguess government policy makers. When that happens, private speculation doesn't stabilize; it destabilizes exchange rates as private traders try to guess what the government thinks.

Many of my economics colleagues who work for the Fed aren't convinced by private investors' arguments. They maintain that some government intervention helps stabilize currency markets. I don't know which group is right—private foreign exchange traders or economists at the Fed. But to decide, it is necessary to go beyond the arguments and consider how the various exchange rate regimes have worked in practice. Appendix A to this chapter gives you an introduction into the history of exchange rate regimes.

Q-10 Does government intervention stabilize exchange rates?

Fixed vs. Flexible vs. Partially Flexible Exchange Rates

The Euro: A Common Currency for Europe

If you think of countries with a fixed exchange rate as being in a marriage, you can think of a common currency as in a marriage for life, from which it is almost impossible to escape. In 2002 12 European nations consummated their fixed exchange rate regime established under the EU's plan for monetary union and adopted the euro as their common currency. Slovenia joined in 2007; those countries using the euro as their currency are shown in Figure 17-3 with the euro symbol (€). (Other members of the EU are considering joining in the near future.) They adopted the euro for a number of reasons, some political and some economic; but regardless of why they did it, the euro will have significant effects on international finance and trade over the next decade.

First, let's consider the advantages the EU countries get from adopting a common currency. The first advantage is that, politically, a common currency ties the countries closely together. World Wars I and II started from fights among European countries. An important motive behind the increasing integration of Europe—from initial creation of a common market, to the establishment of the European Union with reduced border controls, to the establishment of the monetary union—has been to prevent large-scale war from ever happening again. Many feel that political reasons drove the countries toward union.

There are, however, also economic reasons. One is to eliminate the cost of exchanging currencies when trading among members, and thereby provide an incentive to increase trade within the EU countries. A second is price transparency. With the adoption of a single currency, consumers and businesses can more easily see price differentials, resulting in greater competition. For example, instead of having to compare a pair of German shoes priced at 60 marks with an Italian pair priced at 48,000 lire, a consumer just needs to compare 30 euros with 25 euros. A third advantage is that the common currency makes it more likely that companies will think of Europe as a single market. Producing for that market would give European consumers more clout and make Europe, as well as the United States, the reference market when new goods are planned. It would also allow European firms to take advantage of economies of scale when producing for the European market. Finally, planners hoped that the importance of the euro would lead individuals throughout the world to hold their assets in euros rather than in dollars. That would mean lower interest rates for Europe relative to

Web Note 17.2
Multinational Money

Three economic advantages of a common currency are that it:
1. eliminates the cost of exchanging currencies,
2. facilitates price comparisons, and
3. creates a larger market.

FIGURE 17-3 **Map of EU Countries**

Members of the European Union as of 2007 included Austria, Belgium, Bulgaria, Cyprus, Czech Republic, Denmark, Estonia, Finland, France, Germany, Greece, Hungary, Ireland, Italy, Latvia, Lithuania, Luxembourg, Malta, Poland, Portugal, Romania, Slovakia, Slovenia, Spain, Sweden, The Netherlands, and the United Kingdom. Those countries that also share a common currency are marked with a €, the symbol of the euro.

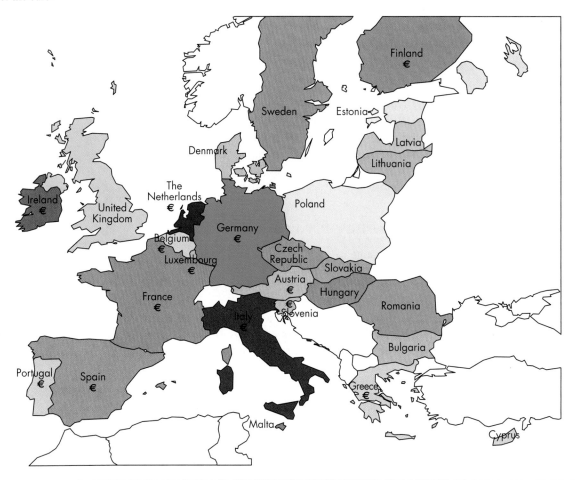

what they would have been, and the possibility that the euro will be used as an international reserve currency along with the dollar. An international reserve currency is a currency in which people and firms hold their savings. This means that the EU could create euros and exchange them for other currencies to buy products without increasing the money supply and risking inflation. (For the EU, it would be like getting an interest-free loan.) Because the U.S. dollar has been the world's reserve currency, the United States has been getting those interest-free loans, which is one of the reasons it's been able to run continual large trade deficits. If the euro partially replaces the dollar as the world reserve currency, there will likely be a large fall in demand for the dollar and a decrease in its relative value.

One major disadvantage of the common currency area is that members of the EU will no longer have independent monetary policies. So if an external shock hurts one region worse than another, the region hit hard cannot increase the money supply to offset the effect on output. For example, in the early 2000s, Ireland's economy was growing

A major disadvantage of a common currency is the loss of independent monetary policy for member countries.

quickly while Germany's economy was contracting, but the two countries shared the same interest rate and monetary policy. A common currency also presents nationalism problems. A country's currency is a symbol to people of their country, and giving it up means losing part of their identity. Loss of nationalism is one reason Britain has been reluctant to adopt the euro.

The initial adoption of the euro has gone relatively smoothly, although realization of its advantages is still in the future. It will be an experiment that will be followed carefully over the next decade.

Conclusion

This chapter began with a quotation suggesting that a foreign exchange dealer's office can be the nearest thing to bedlam that there is. Seeing some order within that bedlam is not easy, but understanding the balance of payments and its relation to the determination of exchange rates is a good first step. And it is a necessary step. With international transportation and communication becoming easier and faster and other countries' economies growing, the U.S. economy will become more interdependent with the global economy in the upcoming decades, making understanding these issues more and more necessary to understanding macroeconomics.

Summary

- The balance of payments is made up of the current account and the financial and capital account.

- Exchange rates in a perfectly flexible exchange rate system are determined by the supply of and demand for a currency.

- An increase in a country's income increases the demand for foreign currency and leads to a decline in the value of the country's own currency.

- An increase in a country's price level reduces the demand for one's currency and increases the demand for foreign currency and leads to a decline in the value of one's own currency.

- A decrease in a country's interest rates reduces the demand for that country's currency and increases the demand for foreign currency, leading to a decline in the value of one's own currency.

- Increased trade restrictions on imports reduce the demand for foreign currencies, leading to an increase in the value of one's own currency.

- To raise the price of its currency, a country can either increase private demand through contractionary

monetary policy or decrease private supply through contractionary monetary policy.

- Expansionary monetary policy, through its effect on interest rates, income, and the price level, tends to lower a country's exchange rate.

- Fiscal policy has an ambiguous effect on a country's exchange rate.

- A country can stabilize or fix its exchange rate by either directly buying and selling its own currency or adjusting its monetary and fiscal policy to achieve its exchange rate goal.

- It is easier technically for a country to bring the value of its currency down than it is to support its currency.

- It is extraordinarily difficult to correctly estimate the long-run equilibrium exchange rate; one method of doing so is the purchasing power parity approach.

- Fixed exchange rates provide international monetary stability but can create enormous monetary instability if they become unfixed. Fixed exchange rates force governments to make adjustments to meet their international problems.

- Flexible exchange rates allow exchange rates to make incremental changes, but are also subject to large jumps in value as a result of speculation. Flexible exchange rates give governments flexibility in conducting domestic monetary and fiscal policy.

- A real exchange rate is an exchange rate adjusted for differences in inflation:

  %Δ real exchange rate = %Δ nominal exchange rate + [domestic inflation − foreign inflation]

- A common currency creates strong political ties, reduces the cost of trade, facilitates price comparisons, and creates a larger single market. A common currency also makes it impossible to have an independent monetary policy. The 13 countries that share the euro gave up their own national currencies and gave up independent monetary policies.

Key Terms

balance of merchandise
    trade *(410)*
balance of payments *(408)*
balance of trade *(410)*
currency
    stabilization *(421)*

currency support *(420)*
current account *(409)*
financial and capital
    account *(409)*
fixed exchange
    rate *(424)*

flexible exchange
    rate *(424)*
forex market *(412)*
official reserves *(409)*
partially flexible
    exchange rate *(424)*

purchasing power
    parity (PPP) *(422)*
real exchange rate *(424)*

Questions for Thought and Review

1. If a country is running a balance of trade deficit, will its current account be in deficit? Why? LO1

2. When someone sends 100 British pounds to a friend in the United States, will this transaction show up on the financial or current account? Why? LO1

3. Support the following statement: "It is best to offset a capital and financial account surplus with a current account deficit." LO1

4. Support the following statement: "It is best to offset a capital and financial account deficit with a current account surplus." LO1

5. In Figure 17-2, a foreign government chooses to maintain an equilibrium market exchange rate of U.S. $1.30 per unit of its own currency. Discuss the implications of the government trying to maintain a higher fixed rate—say at $1.50. LO3

6. In the early 1980s, the U.S. economy fell into a recession (the government faced the problem of both a high federal deficit and a high trade deficit, called the twin deficits), and the dollar was very strong. Can you provide an explanation for this sequence of events? (Difficult) LO1

7. Ms. Economist always tries to travel to a country where the purchasing power parity exchange rate is lower than the market exchange rate. Why? LO5

8. Throughout the early 2000s, the U.S. trade gap widened, spurred by a surge of imports. What was likely happening to income in the U.S. economy? LO3

9. Draw the schematics to show the effect of expansionary monetary policy on the exchange rate. LO3

10. What effect on the U.S. trade deficit and exchange rate would result if Japan ran an expansionary monetary policy? LO3

11. What would be the effect on the U.S. exchange rate if Japan ran a contractionary fiscal policy? LO3

12. If expansionary monetary policy immediately increases inflationary expectations and the price level, how might the effect of monetary policy on the exchange rate be different than that presented in this chapter? LO3

13. What effect will a combination of expansionary fiscal policy and contractionary monetary policy have on the exchange rate? LO3

14. If you were the finance minister of Never-Never Land, how would you estimate the long-run exchange rate of your currency, the neverback? Defend your choice as well as discuss its possible failings. (Difficult) LO5

15. If U.S. inflation is 4 percent and Japan's inflation is 1 percent, and the nominal U.S. dollar exchange rate falls by 3 percent relative to the yen, what happens to the real exchange rate? LO5

16. Which is preferable: a fixed or a flexible exchange rate? Why? LO6

17. Dr. Dollar Bill believes price stability is the main goal of central bank policy. Is the doctor more likely to prefer fixed or flexible exchange rates? Why? (Difficult) LO6

18. If currency traders expect the government to devalue a currency, what will they likely do? Why? LO6

19. A country eliminates all tariffs. Would you expect the value of its currency to rise or fall? Explain your answer. LO6

20. During the 1995–96 Republican presidential primaries, Patrick Buchanan wrote an editorial in *The Wall Street Journal* beginning, "Since the Nixon era the dollar has fallen 75 percent against the yen, 60 percent against the mark." What trade policies do you suppose he was promoting? He went on to outline a series of tariffs. Agree or disagree with his policies. (Difficult) LO3

21. In an op-ed article, Paul Volcker, former chairman of the Board of Governors of the Federal Reserve, asked the following question: "Is it really worth spending money in the exchange markets, modifying monetary policy, and taking care to balance the budget just to save another percentage or two [of value of exchange rates]?" What's your answer to this question? (Difficult) LO3

22. In mid-1994 the value of the dollar fell sufficiently to warrant coordinated intervention among 17 countries. Still, the dollar went on falling. One economist stated, "[The intervention] was clearly a failure . . . It's a good indication something else has to be done." Why would the United States and foreign countries want to keep up the value of the dollar? LO6

23. What are three advantages of the euro for Europe? LO7

24. What are two disadvantages of the euro for Europe? LO7

25. Should Canada, the United States, and Mexico adopt a common currency? Why or why not? LO7

Problems and Exercises

26. In the early 2000s, China was running a large current account surplus.
    a. What did this suggest about its capital account?
    b. China's private balance of payments was in surplus. What does this suggest about its exchange rate regime?
    c. What actions was the Chinese central bank likely undertaking in the foreign exchange markets? Demonstrate the situation with supply and demand graphs.
    d. If the Chinese central bank pulled out of the forex market, what would likely happen to the yuan?
    e. In May 2004, inflation picked up in China; what effect did that likely have on the value of the yuan? LO2

27. Draw the fundamental analysis of the supply and demand for the British pound in terms of dollars. Show what will happen to the exchange rate with those curves in response to each of the following events:
    a. The U.K. price level rises.
    b. The United States reduces tariffs.
    c. The U.K. economy experiences a boom.
    d. The U.K. interest rates rise. LO2

28. The government of Never-Never Land, after much deliberation, finally decides to switch to a fixed exchange rate policy. It does this because the value of its currency, the neverback, is so high that the trade deficit is enormous. The finance minister fixes the rate at $10 a neverback, which is lower than the equilibrium rate of $20 a neverback.
    a. Discuss the trade or traditional macro policy options that could accomplish this lower exchange rate.
    b. Using the laws of supply and demand, show graphically how possible equilibria are reached. LO2

29. Will the following be suppliers or demanders of U.S. dollars in foreign exchange markets?
    a. A U.S. tourist in Latin America.
    b. A German foreign exchange trader who believes that the dollar exchange rate will fall.
    c. A U.S. foreign exchange trader who believes that the dollar exchange rate will fall.
    d. A Costa Rican tourist in the United States.
    e. A Russian capitalist who wants to protect his wealth from expropriation.
    f. A British investor in the United States. LO1

30. You've been hired as an economic adviser to Yamaichi Foreign Exchange Traders. What buy or sell recommendations for U.S. dollars would you make in response to the following news?
    a. Faster economic growth in the EU.
    b. Expectations of higher interest rates in the United States.
    c. The U.S. interest rate rises, but less than expected.
    d. Expected loosening of U.S. monetary policy.
    e. Higher inflationary predictions for the United States.
    f. The U.S. government imposes new trade restrictions on imports. LO2

31. State whether the following will show up on the current account or the capital and financial account:
    a. IBM's exports of computers to Japan.
    b. IBM's hiring of a British merchant bank as a consultant.
    c. A foreign national living in the United States repatriates money.
    d. Ford Motor Company's profit in Hungary.
    e. Ford Motor Company uses that Hungarian profit to build a new plant in Hungary. LO1

32. One of the basic laws of economics is the law of one price. It says that given certain assumptions one would expect that if free trade is allowed, the prices of goods in multiple countries should converge. This law underlies purchasing power parity.
    a. Can you list what three of those assumptions likely are?
    b. Should the law of one price hold for labor also? Why or why not?
    c. Should it hold for capital more so or less so than for labor? Why or why not? LO5

33. A *Wall Street Journal* article, "As Fear of Deficits Falls, Some See a Larger Threat," describes the following threat of a high U.S. budget deficit:

    [T]he investors who finance our deficits by buying Treasury bonds and bills, especially the foreigners who buy a larger share of them than ever, will question our ability to repay them, and balk at lending more—

triggering a big drop in the dollar and much higher interest rates.

a. Why would a drop in foreign confidence in the U.S. ability to repay debt lead to a drop in the dollar and much higher interest rates?

b. In what way are higher interest rates and a lower value of the dollar bad for the U.S. economy?   LO5

Questions from Alternative Perspectives

1. If all currencies were on a gold standard, there would be no exchange rates between currencies and we would not face the difficulties presented by fluctuating exchange rates.
   a. What would be the benefit of having all currencies on a gold standard?
   b. What would be the cost? (Austrian)

2. According to Gary North in *Priorities and Dominion: An Economic Commentary on Matthew*, in the book of Matthew, Jesus teaches about the rate of exchange between earthly wealth and eternal wealth.
   a. Would Jesus argue for a high or low exchange rate for earthly riches? Explain your answer.
   b. Do wealthy people believe the exchange rate is high or low?
   c. Do you believe the perceived exchange rate falls or rises as one approaches death? (Religious)

3. Most traders in currencies are men.
   a. Why is this?
   b. Why has it remained even though there is supposed to be no discrimination in employment?
   c. The language of traders is often quite coarse; does this fact provide a possible answer to both *a* and *b*?
   d. Did you think of it before you read *c*? (Feminist)

4. Nobel Prize–winning economist James Tobin has suggested that a method of decreasing unwanted sudden

capital flows among countries would be to place a small tax on such flows. Post-Keynesian economist Paul Davidson argued against doing so because it won't solve the problem, suggesting that it is like using a pebble when a boulder is needed. What might Davidson's argument be? (Hint: It is related to the role of expectations.) (Post-Keynesian)

5. Most economists favor lowering barriers to trade. But even among mainstream economists there is far less support for financial liberalization—the removal of government regulation of financial and capital markets—than for trade liberalization. "It is a seductive idea," says free-trader Jagdish Bhagwati, "but the claims of enormous benefit from free capital mobility are not persuasive." In addition, capital market liberalization entails substantial risks because it strips away the regulations intended to control the flow of short-term loans and contracts in and out of a country. The IMF, on the other hand, remains an unabashed supporter of free financial markets, arguing that they are a precondition for a developing country attracting long-term foreign investment.
   a. Who has it right?
   b. Is financial liberalization a good or bad policy, especially for developing countries? (Radical)

Web Questions

1. The Big Mac index is an index of purchasing power parity created by a magazine called *The Economist*. *The Economist* publishes the exchange rate value of various currencies that would make the Big Mac cost the same as in the United States. Go to www.economist.com and search for its Big Mac index. Look up the purchasing power parity of the dollar for five currencies and compare them with the actual exchange rates.
   a. Which currencies were undervalued? Which were overvalued?
   b. What are the shortcomings of the Big Mac index?
   c. If you were to design your own index, what types of goods would you use in your basket of goods? Explain your answer.
   d. How could you check the validity of the Big Mac index?

2. Pick a foreign currency and answer the following questions using www.oanda.com.
   a. What is the name of your country's currency?
   b. In the last year, has the currency risen or fallen in value against the dollar?
   c. Using information from *The Economist* magazine (www.economist.com/countries) about your country, explain why the currency's price rose or fell.

3. Go to the IMF's Web site at www.imf.org/external/np/exr/center/action/eng/devalue/index.htm to find out how the IMF can help a country facing a shortage of official reserves.
   a. Describe the problem facing the fictitious African economy.
   b. What course of action did you recommend?
   c. What was the outcome of your recommendations?

Answers to Margin Questions

1. The expenditures of a U.S. citizen traveling abroad will show up as a debit on the services account. As tourism or traveling, it is a service. *(410)*

2. Net investment income is the return a country gets on its foreign investment minus the return foreigners get on their investment within a country. A country is a net debtor nation if the value of foreign investment within a country exceeds the value of its investment abroad. A country can be a net debtor nation and still have its net investment income positive if its foreign investment is undervalued at market values (valuation is generally done at book value), or if its foreign investment earns a higher rate of return than foreigners' investment within that country. *(412)*

3. An increase in the demand for dollars is the equivalent of an increase in the supply of euros, so an increase in the demand for dollars pushes down the price of euros in terms of dollars, as in the following diagram. *(413)*

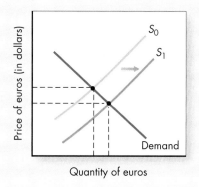

Quantity of euros

4. A fall in a country's interest rate will push down its exchange rate. *(415)*

5. Contractionary monetary policy pushes up the interest rate, decreases income and hence imports, and has a tendency to decrease inflation. Therefore, through these paths, contractionary monetary policy will tend to increase the exchange rate. *(417)*

6. The net effect of expansionary fiscal policy on exchange rates is uncertain. Through the interest rate effect it pushes up the exchange rate, but through the income and price level effects it pushes down the exchange rate. *(418)*

7. In the short run, normal market forces have a limited, and possibly even perverse, effect on exchange rates, which is why most governments don't leave determination of exchange rates to the market. *(419)*

8. In general, it would be easier for the United States to push the value of the dollar down because doing so involves the United States buying up foreign currencies, which it can pay for simply by printing more dollars. To push the dollar up requires foreign reserves. *(421)*

9. The real exchange rate of the dollar relative to the euro rises 1 percent.

   %Δ real exchange rate = %Δ nominal exchange rate + [domestic inflation − foreign inflation] = 3 + (2 − 4) = 1. *(424)*

10. There is much debate about whether government intervention stabilizes exchange rates—private traders tend to believe it does not; government economists tend to believe that it does. *(427)*

APPENDIX A

History of Exchange Rate Systems

A good way to give you an idea of how the various exchange rate systems work is to present a brief history of international exchange rate systems.

The Gold Standard: A Fixed Exchange Rate System

Governments played a major role in determining exchange rates until the 1930s. Beginning with the Paris Conference of 1867 and lasting until 1933 (except for the period around World War I), most of the world economies had a system of relatively fixed exchange rates under what was called a **gold standard**—*a system of fixed exchange rates in which the value of currencies was fixed relative to the value of gold and gold was used as the primary reserve asset.*

Under a gold standard, the amount of money a country issued had to be directly tied to gold, either because gold coin served as the currency in a country (as it did in the United States before 1914) or because countries were required by law to have a certain percentage of gold backing their currencies. Gold served as currency or backed all currencies. Each country participating in a gold standard agreed to fix the price of its currency relative to gold. That meant a country would agree to pay a specified amount of gold on demand to anyone who wanted to exchange that country's currency for gold. To do so, each country had to maintain a stockpile of gold. When a country fixed the price of its currency relative to gold, it fixed its currency's price in relation to other currencies as a result of the process of arbitrage.

Under the gold standard, a country made up the difference between the quantity supplied and the quantity demanded of its currency by buying or selling gold to hold the price of its currency fixed in terms of gold. How much a country would need to buy and sell depended on its balance of payments deficit or surplus. If the country ran a surplus in the balance of payments, it was required to sell its currency—that is, buy gold—to stop the value of its currency from rising. If a country ran a deficit, it was required to buy its currency—that is, sell gold—to stop the value of its currency from falling.

The gold standard enabled governments to prevent short-run instability of the exchange rate. If there was a speculative run on its currency, the government would buy its currency with gold, thereby preventing the exchange rate from falling.

But for the gold standard to work, there had to be a method of long-run adjustment; otherwise countries would have run out of gold and would no longer have been able to fulfill their obligations under the gold standard. The **gold specie flow mechanism** was *the long-run adjustment mechanism that maintained the gold standard*. Here's how it worked: Since gold served as official reserves to a country's currency, a balance of payments deficit (and hence a downward pressure on the exchange rate) would result in a flow of gold out of the country and hence a decrease in the country's money supply. That decrease in the money supply would contract the economy, decreasing imports, lowering the country's price level, and increasing the interest rate, all of which would work toward eliminating the balance of payments deficit.

Similarly a country with a balance of payments surplus would experience an inflow of gold. That flow would increase the country's money supply, increasing income (and hence imports), increasing the price level (making imports cheaper and exports more expensive), and lowering the interest rate (increasing capital outflows). These would work toward eliminating the balance of payments surplus.

Thus, the gold standard determined a country's monetary policy and forced it to adjust any international balance of payments disequilibrium. Adjustments to a balance of payments deficit were often politically unpopular; they often led to recessions, which, because the money supply was directly tied to gold, the government couldn't try to offset with expansionary monetary policy.

The gold specie flow mechanism was called into play in the United States in late 1931 when the Federal Reserve, in response to a shrinking U.S. gold supply, decreased the amount of money in the U.S. economy, deepening the depression that had begun in 1929. The government's domestic goals and responsibilities conflicted with its international goals and responsibilities.

That conflict, which was rooted in the after-effects of World War I and the Depression, led to partial abandonment of the gold standard in 1933. At that time the United States made it illegal for individual U.S. citizens to own gold. Except for gold used for ornamental and certain medical and industrial purposes, all privately owned gold had to be sold to the government. Dollar bills were no longer backed by gold in the sense that U.S. citizens could exchange dollars for a prespecified amount of gold. Instead, dollar bills were backed by silver, which meant that any U.S. citizen could change dollars for a prespecified amount of silver. In the late 1960s, that changed also. Since that time, for U.S. residents, dollars have been backed only by trust in the soundness of the U.S. economy.

Gold continued to serve, at least partially, as international backing for U.S. currency. That is, other countries could still exchange dollars for gold. However, in 1971, in response to another conflict between international and domestic goals, the United States totally cut off the relationship between dollars and gold. After that, a dollar could be redeemed only for another dollar, whether it was a U.S. citizen or a foreign government who wanted to redeem the dollar.

The Bretton Woods System: A Fixed Exchange Rate System

As World War II was coming to an end, the United States and its allies met to establish a new international economic order. After much wrangling, they agreed upon a system called the **Bretton Woods system,** *an agreement about fixed exchange rates that governed international financial relationships from the period after the end of World War II until 1971.* It was named after the resort in New Hampshire where the meeting that set up the system was held.

The Bretton Woods system established the International Monetary Fund (IMF) to oversee the international economic order. The IMF was empowered to arrange short-term loans between countries. The Bretton Woods system also established the World Bank, which was empowered to make longer-term loans to developing countries. Today the World Bank and IMF continue their central roles in international financial affairs.

The Bretton Woods system was based on mutual agreements about what countries would do when experiencing balance of payments surpluses or deficits. It was essentially a fixed exchange rate system. For example, under the Bretton Woods system, the exchange rate of the dollar for the British pound was set at slightly over $4 to the pound.

The Bretton Woods system was not based on a gold standard. When countries experienced a balance of payments surplus or deficit, they did not necessarily buy or sell gold to stabilize the price of their currency. Instead they bought and sold other currencies. To ensure that participating countries would have sufficient reserves, they established a stabilization fund from which a country could obtain a short-term loan. It was hoped that this stabilization fund would be sufficient to handle all short-run adjustments that did not reflect fundamental imbalances.

In those cases where a misalignment of exchange rates was determined to be fundamental, the countries involved agreed that they would adjust their exchange rates. The IMF was empowered to oversee an orderly adjustment. It could authorize a country to make a one-time adjustment of up to 10 percent without obtaining formal approval from the IMF's board of directors. After a country had used its one-time adjustment, formal approval was necessary for any change greater than 1 percent.

The Bretton Woods system reflected the underlying political and economic realities of the post–World War II period in which it was set up. European economies were devastated; the U.S. economy was strong. To rebuild, Europe was going to have to import U.S. equipment and borrow large amounts from the United States. There was serious concern over how high the value of the dollar would rise and how low the value of European currencies would fall in a free market exchange. The establishment of fixed exchange rates set limits on currencies' relative movements; the exchange rates that were chosen helped provide for the rebuilding of Europe.

In addition, the Bretton Woods system provided mechanisms for long-term loans from the United States to Europe that could help sustain those fixed exchange rates. The loans also eliminated the possibility of competitive depreciation of currencies, in which each country tries to stimulate its exports by lowering the relative value of its currency.

One difficulty with the Bretton Woods system was a shortage of official reserves and international liquidity. To offset that shortage, the IMF was empowered to create *a type of international money* called **special drawing rights (SDRs).** But SDRs never became established as an international currency and the U.S. dollar kept serving as official reserves for individuals and countries. To get the dollars to foreigners, the United States had to run a deficit in its current account. Since countries could exchange the dollar for gold at a fixed price, the use of dollars as a reserve currency meant that, under the Bretton Woods system, the world was on a gold standard once removed.

The number of dollars held by foreigners grew enormously in the 1960s. By the early 1970s, those dollars far exceeded in value the amount of gold the United States had. Most countries accepted this situation; even though they could legally demand gold for their dollars, they did not. But Charles de Gaulle, the nationalistic president of France, wasn't pleased with the U.S. domination of international affairs at that time. He believed Europe deserved a much more prominent position. He demanded gold for the dollars held by the French central bank, knowing that the United States didn't have enough gold to meet his demand. As a result of his and other countries' demands, on August 15, 1971, the United States ended its policy of exchanging gold for dollars at $35 per ounce. With that change, the Bretton Woods system was dead.

The Present U.S. System: A Partially Flexible Exchange Rate System

International monetary affairs were much in the news in the early 1970s as countries groped for a new exchange rate system. The makeshift system finally agreed on involved partially flexible exchange rates. Most Western countries' exchange rates are allowed to fluctuate, although at various times governments buy or sell their own currencies to affect the exchange rate.

Under the present partially flexible exchange rate system, countries must continually decide when a balance of payments surplus or deficit is a temporary phenomenon and when it is a signal of a fundamental imbalance. If they believe the situation is temporary, they enter into the foreign exchange market to hold their exchange rate at what they believe is an appropriate level. If, however, they believe that the balance of payments imbalance is a fundamental one, they let the exchange rate rise or fall.

While most Western countries' exchange rates are partially flexible, certain countries have agreed to fixed exchange rates of their currencies in relation to rates of a group of certain other currencies. For example, a group of European Union countries adopted irreversible fixed exchange rates among their currencies, by electing to have one currency—the euro, which was introduced in 2002. Other currencies are fixed relative to the dollar (not by the United States but by the other countries).

Deciding what is, and what is not, a fundamental imbalance is complicated, and such decisions are considered at numerous international conferences held under the auspices of the IMF or governments. A number of organizations such as the Group of Eight focus much discussion on this issue. Often the various countries meet and agree, formally or informally, on acceptable ranges of exchange rates. Thus, while the present system is one of partially flexible exchange rates, the range of flexibility is limited.

Key Terms

Bretton Woods
    system (434)

gold specie flow
    mechanism (434)

gold standard (433)

special drawing rights
    (SDRs) (435)

Macro Policy in a Global Setting

> *The actual rate of exchange is largely governed by the expected behavior of the country's monetary authority.*
>
> —Dennis Robertson

In the early 2000s, the U.S. exchange rate fell, the U.S. trade deficit reached an all-time high, and newspapers were full of stories of outsourcing and loss of American jobs. Such issues are likely to be much in the news throughout the coming years. In this chapter, we pull together what we have learned about monetary and fiscal policy, comparative advantage, trade deficits, and exchange rates, and talk about macro policy in a global setting. To begin, we need to discuss our international macro goals.

"We design them here, but the labor is cheaper in Hell."

The Ambiguous International Goals of Macroeconomic Policy

Macroeconomic international goals are less straightforward than domestic goals. There is general agreement about the domestic goals of macroeconomic policy: We want low inflation, low unemployment, and high growth. There's far less agreement on what a country's international goals should be.

Most economists agree that the international goal of U.S. macroeconomic policy is to maintain the U.S. position in the world economy. But there's enormous debate about what achieving that goal means. Do we want a high or a low exchange rate? Do we want a balance of trade surplus? Or would it be better to have a balance of trade deficit? Or should we not even pay attention to the balance of trade? Let's consider the exchange rate goal first.

The Exchange Rate Goal

The U.S. exchange rate has fluctuated significantly over the past 30 years. There is a debate over whether a country should have a high or a low exchange rate. A high exchange rate for the dollar makes foreign currencies cheaper, lowering the price of imports. Lowering import prices places competitive pressure on U.S. firms and helps to hold down inflation. All of this benefits U.S. residents' living

AFTER READING THIS CHAPTER, YOU SHOULD BE ABLE TO:

1. Discuss why there is significant debate about what U.S. international goals should be.
2. Describe the paths through which monetary policy affects the trade balance.
3. Explain the paths through which fiscal policy affects the trade balance.
4. Summarize the reasons why governments try to coordinate their monetary and fiscal policies.
5. State the potential problem of internationalizing a country's debt.
6. Explain how restoring U.S. competitiveness will likely affect U.S. policy in the future.

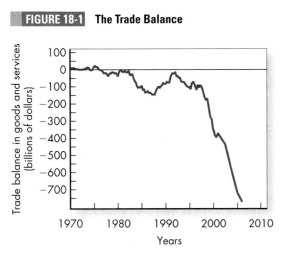

FIGURE 18-1 **The Trade Balance**

standard. But a high exchange rate encourages imports and discourages exports. In doing so, it can cause a balance of trade deficit that can exert a contractionary effect on the economy by decreasing aggregate demand for U.S. output. So a high exchange rate also has a cost to U.S. residents.

A low exchange rate has the opposite effect. It makes imports more expensive and exports cheaper, and it can contribute to inflationary pressure. But, by encouraging exports and discouraging imports, it can cause a balance of trade surplus and exert an expansionary effect on the economy.

Many economists argue that a country should have no exchange rate policy because exchange rates are market-determined prices that are best left to the market. These economists question whether the government should even worry about the effect of monetary policy and fiscal policy on exchange rates. According to them, government should simply accept whatever exchange rate exists and not consider it in its conduct of monetary and fiscal policies.

The Trade Balance Goal

Figure 18-1 shows the U.S. trade balance over the past 40 years. You can see that the United States has consistently run a trade deficit over that period, and that that trade deficit has generally increased. A deficit in the trade balance (the difference between imports and exports) means that, as a country, we're consuming more than we're producing. Imports exceed exports, so we're consuming more than we could if we didn't run a deficit. A surplus in the trade balance means that exports exceed imports—we're producing more than we're consuming. Since consuming more than we otherwise could is kind of nice, it might seem that a trade deficit is preferred to a trade surplus.

But wait. A trade deficit isn't without costs, and a trade surplus isn't without benefits. We pay for a trade deficit by selling off U.S. assets to foreigners—by selling U.S. companies, factories, land, and buildings to foreigners, or selling them financial assets such as U.S. dollars, stocks, and bonds. All the future interest and profits on these assets will go to foreigners, not U.S. citizens. That means eventually, sometime in the future, we will have to produce more than we consume so we can pay them *their* profit and interest on *their* assets. Thus, while in the short run a trade deficit allows more current consumption, in the long run it presents potential problems.

As long as a country can borrow, or sell assets, a country can have a trade deficit. But if a country runs a trade deficit year after year, eventually the long run will arrive and the country will run out of assets to sell and run out of other countries from whom to borrow. When that happens, the trade deficit problem must be faced.

The debate about whether a trade deficit should be of concern to policy makers involves whether these long-run effects should be anticipated and faced before they happen.

Opinions differ greatly. Some say not to worry—just accept what's happening. These "not-to-worry" economists argue that the trade deficit will end when U.S. citizens don't want to borrow from foreigners anymore and foreigners don't want to buy any more of our assets. They argue that the inflow of financial capital (money coming into the United States to buy our assets) from foreigners is financing new investment that will make the U.S. economy strong enough in the long run to reverse the trade deficit without serious disruption to the U.S. economy. So why deal with the trade deficit now, when it will take care of itself in the future?

Q-1 What effect does a low exchange rate have on a country's exports and imports?

Exchange rates have conflicting effects and, depending on the state of the economy, there are arguments for both high and low exchange rates.

The trade balance is the difference between a country's exports and imports.

Running a trade deficit is good in the short run but presents problems in the long run.

Q-2 Why do some people argue that we should not worry about a trade deficit?

The U.S. Trade Deficit and the Value of the Dollar

The continued U.S. trade deficit from the 1970s into the early 2000s has confounded many analysts. Why has it remained so high? Why are other countries willing to give the United States many more real goods and services than they require in return? The answer is that they want to buy U.S. assets. There are a number of reasons why. First, the value of U.S. assets has increased. For example, Japan's stock market and real estate markets were falling while the U.S. stock market was rising, which gave Japanese investors a strong incentive to invest in the United States. Second, the United States is considered a safe haven—a solid economy that is safer than any other. If you want safety, you buy U.S. government bonds. Third, Japan and China have been buying

large amounts of dollars in order to prevent the value of the dollar from falling relative to their currencies. At some point, however, the demand for U.S. assets is expected to end and the U.S. trade deficit will have to fall.

If a majority of economic analysts are correct, we should see a continued fall in the price of the dollar, which will lower the relative price of U.S. exports and increase the cost of imports. Because people don't want to hold assets in currencies whose values are falling, this fall could be much more sudden than policy makers would like, creating serious questions about whether they can do anything to prevent it.

Others argue that, yes, the trade deficit will eventually take care of itself, but the accompanying economic distress will be great. By dealing with the problem now, the United States can avoid a highly unpleasant solution in the future.

Both views are reasonable, which is why there's no consensus on what a country's trade balance goal should be.

International versus Domestic Goals

In the real world, when there's debate about a goal, that goal is generally less likely to guide policy than goals about which there's general agreement. Since there's general agreement about our country's domestic goals (low inflation, low unemployment, and high growth), domestic goals generally dominate the U.S. political agenda.

Even if a country's international goals weren't uncertain, domestic goals would likely dominate the political agenda. The reason is that inflation, unemployment, and growth affect a country's citizens directly. Trade deficits and exchange rates affect them indirectly—and in politics, indirect effects take a back seat.

Often a country responds to an international goal only when the international community forces it to do so. For example, in the 1980s when Brazil couldn't borrow any more money from other countries, it reluctantly made resolving its trade deficit a key goal. Similarly, when other countries threatened to limit Japanese imports, Japan took steps to increase the value of the yen and decrease its trade surplus. Currently China is facing international pressure to let its exchange rate rise. When a country is forced to face certain economic facts, international goals can become its primary goals. As countries become more economically integrated, these pressures from other countries become more important.

Domestic goals generally dominate international goals.

Web Note 18.1
Putting Exchange Rates First

FIGURE 18-2 Targeting an Exchange Rate with Monetary and Fiscal Policy

To increase the exchange rate value of the euro, the European Central Bank (ECB) could run contractionary monetary policy to increase interest rates and increase the private demand for euros or induce a recession and decrease the private supply of euros, or a combination of the two.

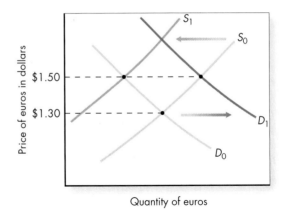

Balancing the Exchange Rate Goal with Domestic Goals

In the last chapter we talked about monetary and fiscal policy's effect on the exchange rate. In it we saw that while fiscal policy's effect on exchange rates was ambiguous, monetary policy had a predictable effect: Expansionary monetary policy tended to push the exchange rate down; contractionary monetary policy tended to push the exchange rate up.[1] What this means is that in principle, the government can control the exchange rate with monetary policy. The problem with doing so is that monetary policy also affects the domestic economy—contractionary monetary policy decreases income and jobs. Contractionary monetary policy is not a policy that countries generally want to follow.

The way in which monetary policy affects the exchange rate is by affecting the supply and demand for the country's currency. To review this, let's consider the case of Europe that we examined in the previous chapter. That case is shown in Figure 18-2. Europe's problem here is that it wants the exchange rate for the euro to be $1.50, not $1.30. The EU has three options for raising the value of the euro: decrease the private supply of euros (shifting the supply curve in from S_0 to S_1), increase the private demand for euros (shifting the demand curve out from D_0 to D_1), or use some combination of the two. Let's see how it could accomplish its goal with monetary or fiscal policy.

To increase the demand for euros, the EU must create policies that increase the private foreign demand for EU assets, or for EU goods and services. In the short run, the European Central Bank (ECB) can increase the interest rate by running contractionary monetary policy. A higher interest rate increases the foreign demand for the EU's interest-bearing assets. The problem with this approach is that to maintain an exchange rate at a certain level, a country must give up any attempt to target its interest rate to achieve domestic goals. To put it another way: A country can achieve an interest rate target or an exchange rate target, but generally it cannot achieve both at the same time.

Contractionary monetary policy also slows down the domestic economy and induces a recession. This recession decreases the demand for imports and thereby decreases the private supply of euros. Governments are usually loath to use this contractionary policy because politically induced recessions are not popular. It is because of the constraints that fixed exchange rates, or any policy designed to hold its exchange rate up, place on domestic monetary and fiscal policy that many countries choose flexible, or at least partially flexible, exchange rate regimes.

Q-3 If a country wants to fix its exchange rate at a rate that is higher than the market rate, what monetary or fiscal policy must it use?

Q-4 If a country runs a contractionary monetary policy, what effect will that likely have on its exchange rate?

---

[1] We don't discuss fiscal policy as a control policy for exchange rates because fiscal policy has an ambiguous effect on the exchange rate, as the interest rate effect of fiscal policy pushes the exchange rate one way and the income effect pushes it another. (See the previous chapter if you are not clear on this effect.)

Monetary and Fiscal Policy and the Trade Deficit

Since a major policy issue for the United States in the coming years is likely to be its large trade deficit, and the pressures that will likely decrease that deficit, let's now turn to a consideration of how monetary and fiscal policy affect the trade deficit. We begin with monetary policy.

Monetary Policy's Effect on the Trade Balance

When a country's international trade balance is negative (in deficit), the country is importing more than it is exporting. When a country's international trade balance is positive (in surplus), the country is exporting more than it is importing.

Monetary policy affects the trade balance primarily through its effect on income. Specifically, expansionary monetary policy increases income. When income rises, imports rise, while exports are unaffected. As imports rise, the trade balance shifts in the direction of deficit. So expansionary monetary policy shifts the trade balance toward a deficit.

Contractionary policy works in the opposite direction. It decreases income. When income falls, imports fall (while exports are unaffected), so the trade balance shifts in the direction of surplus. Thus, expansionary monetary policy increases the trade deficit; contractionary monetary policy decreases the trade deficit.

Monetary policy will also affect the trade balance in a variety of other ways—for example, through its effect on the price level and the exchange rate. These other effects tend to be more long-run effects and tend to offset one another. So we will not consider them here. While many complications can enter the trade balance picture, most economists would summarize monetary policy's short-run effect on the trade balance as follows:

Expansionary monetary policy makes a trade deficit larger.

Contractionary monetary policy makes a trade deficit smaller.

Q-5 What effect will contractionary monetary policy have on the trade balance?

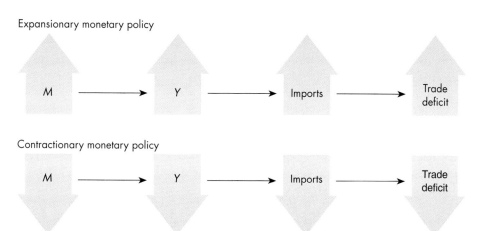

Expansionary monetary policy

M → Y → Imports → Trade deficit

Expansionary monetary policy makes a trade deficit larger.

Contractionary monetary policy

M → Y → Imports → Trade deficit

Contractionary monetary policy makes a trade deficit smaller.

Fiscal Policy's Effect on the Trade Balance

Fiscal policy, like monetary policy, works on the trade deficit primarily through its effects on income. (Again, there are other paths by which fiscal policy affects the trade deficit, but this one is the largest since changes in income are quickly reflected in a change in imports.) So if asked for a quick answer, economists would say that contractionary fiscal policy decreases a trade deficit.

Summarizing the effects of expansionary and contractionary fiscal policy schematically, we have

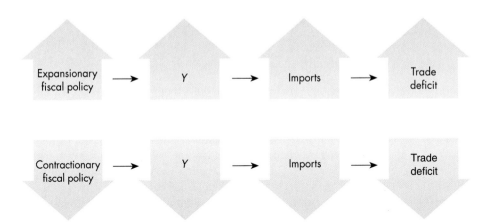

Contractionary fiscal policy decreases a trade deficit.

International Phenomena and Domestic Goals

So far, we've focused on the effect of monetary and fiscal policies on international goals. But often the effect is the other way around: International phenomena change and have significant influences on the domestic economy and on the ability to achieve domestic goals.

For example, say that Japan ran contractionary monetary policy. That would increase the Japanese exchange rate and increase Japan's trade surplus, which means it would decrease the U.S. exchange rate and increase the U.S. trade deficit, both of which would affect U.S. domestic goals.

Alternatively, let's consider how the current situation is likely to play out for the United States in the coming decade. Currently, the United States is running a large trade deficit, which will be difficult to sustain. If the United States chooses to reduce that trade deficit with monetary or fiscal policy, it will have to run contractionary monetary and fiscal policy, keeping the economy from growing as fast as it otherwise would. That is not a politically attractive option, which is an important reason why the United States has not chosen to deal with the trade deficit with monetary or fiscal policy.

But what if other countries stop buying the large amount of dollar-denominated assets that they are currently buying? The dollar exchange rate will fall, possibly precipitously, unless the trade deficit is reduced. In the long run, that fall in the exchange rate will improve the competitiveness of the U.S. economy, decrease imports, and increase exports. But in the short run, the dollar's decline will place the U.S. economy in a bind, since it will push up prices of imports, creating inflationary pressure, and make Americans worse off. Too fast of a decline will likely create severe financial problems that can reverberate through the economy. Thus, the U.S. government will feel pressure to cut some of the trade deficit with contractionary monetary and fiscal policy, policies imposed on the United States by its international position.

International Goals and Policy Alternatives

The table on the next page provides a summary of how alternative policy actions achieve international goals.

International Goal	Policy Alternatives
Lower exchange rate	• Contractionary foreign monetary policy • Expansionary domestic monetary policy
Lower trade deficit	• Contractionary domestic fiscal policy • Expansionary foreign fiscal policy • Contractionary domestic monetary policy • Expansionary foreign monetary policy

You can see in the table why coordination of monetary and fiscal policies is much in the news, since a foreign country's policy can eliminate, or reduce, the need for domestic policies to be undertaken.

International Monetary and Fiscal Coordination

Unless forced to do so because of international pressures, most countries don't let international goals guide their macroeconomic policy. But for every effect that monetary and fiscal policies have on a country's exchange rates and trade balance, there's an equal and opposite effect on the combination of other countries' exchange rates and trade balances. When one country's exchange rate goes up, by definition another country's exchange rate must go down. Similarly, when one country's balance of trade is in surplus, another's must be in deficit. This interconnection means that other countries' fiscal and monetary policies affect the United States, while U.S. fiscal and monetary policies affect other countries, so pressure to coordinate policies is considerable.

Governments try to coordinate their monetary and fiscal policies because their economies are interdependent.

Coordination Is a Two-Way Street

Policy coordination—*the integration of a country's policies to take account of their global effects*—of course, works both ways. If other countries are to take the U.S. economy's needs into account, the United States must take other countries' needs into account in determining its goals. Say, for example, the U.S. economy is going into a recession. This domestic problem calls for expansionary monetary policy. But expansionary monetary policy will increase U.S. income and U.S. imports and lower the value of the dollar. Say that, internationally, the United States has agreed that it must work toward eliminating the U.S. trade deficit in the short run. Does it forsake its domestic goals? Or does it forsake its international commitment?

Q₈ If domestic problems call for expansionary monetary policy and international problems call for contractionary monetary policy, what policy will a country likely adopt?

There's no one right answer to those questions. It depends on political judgments (how long until the next election?), judgments about what foreign countries can do if the United States doesn't meet its international commitments, and similar judgments by foreign countries about the United States.

Each country will likely do what's best for the world economy as long as it's also best for itself.

Despite the complications, the above discussion gives you an understanding of many events that may have previously seemed incomprehensible. To show you the relevance of what I have said above about international considerations, let's look at two situations.

Let's consider the example of Argentina in the early 2000s. In the early 1990s, Argentina established a fixed exchange rate between the peso and the U.S. dollar and promised to maintain that exchange rate under all circumstances. Numerous international investors relied on that promise. In the late 1990s, the Argentinean economy went into recession and domestic political pressures called for expansionary aggregate

Monetary and Fiscal Policy's Effect on International Goals

The effect of expansionary monetary and fiscal policy on international goals in the short run is summarized in the diagram. In the short run, expansionary monetary policy tends to increase a trade deficit and decrease the exchange rate. Expansionary fiscal policy tends to increase the trade deficit. Its effect on the exchange rate is ambiguous. The effects of contractionary policy work in the opposite direction.

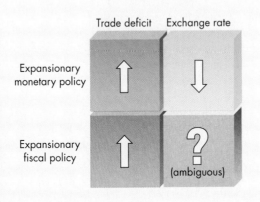

Trade deficit   Exchange rate

Expansionary monetary policy   ↑   ↓

Expansionary fiscal policy   ↑   ? (ambiguous)

demand policy. Maintaining the fixed exchange rate required contractionary aggregate demand policy. The internal political pressures won, and Argentina abandoned its fixed exchange rate in early 2002.

The second concerns Japan in 1993 and early 1994. Japan was experiencing a recession, in part because its tight monetary policy had pushed up interest rates and hence pushed up the exchange rate for the yen. Other countries, especially the United States and European countries, put enormous pressure on Japan to run expansionary fiscal policy, which would keep the relative value of the yen high but simultaneously increase Japanese income, and hence Japanese demand for imports. In response, Japan ran expansionary fiscal policy and this helped to keep the value of the yen higher than it otherwise would have been. Soon thereafter, Japan simultaneously ran expansionary monetary policy, thereby lowering the interest rate and the exchange rate. There are many more examples, but these two should give you a good sense of the relevance of the issues.

Crowding Out and International Considerations

Let's reconsider the issue of crowding out that we considered in an earlier chapter, only this time we'll take into account international considerations. Say a government is running a budget deficit and the central bank has decided it won't increase the money supply to help finance the deficit. (This happened in the 1980s with the Fed and the U.S. government.) What will be the result?

The basic idea of crowding out is that the budget deficit will cause the interest rate to go up. But wait. There's another way to avoid the crowding out that results from financing the deficit: Foreigners could buy the debt at the existing interest rate. This is called *internationalizing the debt*, and that is what happened to the U.S. economy in recent years.

There have been massive inflows to the United States of financial capital from abroad. These inflows held down the U.S. interest rate even as the federal government ran large budget deficits. Thus, large U.S. budget deficits didn't push up interest rates because foreigners, not U.S. citizens, were buying U.S. debt.

But, as we discussed, internationalization of the U.S. debt is not costless. While it helps in the short run, it presents problems in the long run. Today more than 50 percent of privately held U.S. government debt is held by foreigners. Foreign ownership of U.S. debt means that the United States must pay foreigners interest each year on that debt. To do so, the United States must export more than it imports, which means that the United States must consume less than it produces at some time in the future to pay for the trade deficits it's running now. As you can see, the issues quickly become complicated.

Q-9 How does internationalizing the debt reduce crowding out?

While internationalizing a country's debt may help in the short run, in the long run it presents potential problems since foreign ownership of a country's debts means the country must pay interest to those foreign countries and that debt may come due.

444

Globalization, Macro Policy, and the U.S. Economy

We began this book stating that the United States operates in a global economy and that policy today must consider global issues. As a conclusion to the chapter, let's pull our various discussions together and review the likely problems that international considerations are creating for the U.S. economy over the coming decades. I start with some general points about the relationship of international issues to macro policy.

International Issues and Macro Policy

The first point is that the more globally connected a country is, the less flexibility it has with its monetary and fiscal policy. Global issues restrict the use of monetary and fiscal policy to achieve domestic goals. How much they do so, and the manner in which they do so, depend on the country's exchange rate regime, which leads to our second point: How fast a country must respond to international pressure depends on the exchange rate regime it follows. If an economy sets fixed exchange rates, its monetary and fiscal policies are much more restricted than they are with flexible exchange rates. The reason is that the amount of currency stabilization that can be achieved with direct intervention is generally quite small, since a country's foreign reserves are limited. When this is the case, to keep its currency fixed at the desirable level, it must adjust the economy to the exchange rate. Specifically, it must undertake policies that will change either the private supply of its currency or the private demand for its currency. It can do so by traditional macro policy—monetary and fiscal policy—influencing the economy, or by trade policy to affect the level of exports and imports. This means that if monetary and fiscal policies are being used to achieve exchange rate goals, they cannot also be used to achieve domestic goals.

The second point is that with flexible exchange rates, countries have more freedom with monetary and fiscal policy, but then they have to accept whatever happens to their exchange rate, and there are often strong political forces that do not want to do that. That is the position in which the United States will find itself if foreigners significantly reduce their demand for U.S. assets.

The third point is that an alternative to using monetary and fiscal policy to guide the economy toward meeting its international goals is trade policy designed to affect the level of exports and imports. As discussed in a previous chapter, specific use of tariffs and quotas is limited by international conventions, but indirect policies to affect imports and exports are used all the time. For example, U.S. tax laws can be designed to make it more costly for companies to produce abroad. Implicit subsidies can be given for exports and implicit constraints can be placed on imports. We can expect such programs to continue and to expand in the coming decade as the United States attempts to reduce its trade deficit by means other than a fall in the exchange rate of the dollar, which is the alternative path to reducing its trade deficit.

The fourth point is that macro policy is short-run policy, which must be conducted within a longer-range setting of the country's overall **competitiveness**—*the ability of a country to sell its goods to other countries*. That longer-range setting for the United States in the coming decade is not likely to be conducive to expansionary macro policy, which is a change from the past. Following World War II, the long-run setting did allow expansionary macro policy. The United States had a strong competitive position and a trade surplus even though the value of the dollar was high. (During that time, the United States had a fixed exchange rate; see Appendix A of the previous chapter for a brief history of the period.)

Web Note 18.3
Foreign Exchange Futures

Q-10 If a country has a fixed exchange rate, does it have more or less flexibility in choosing its monetary and fiscal policy to achieve domestic goals?

In the 1970s, economic development and investment abroad reduced U.S. competitiveness. Fortunately for the United States, foreign individuals and countries had an enormous demand for U.S. assets. (The capital and financial account surplus discussed in the last chapter reflects that demand.) Had foreign individuals and countries not wanted to increase their holdings of U.S. assets, the long-run setting for macro policy would have been far less conducive to expansionary macro policy. The trade deficit would have lowered the value of the dollar, which would have offset the declining U.S. competitiveness. If this had happened, however, and the United States had also wanted to hold the value of the dollar up, U.S. monetary and fiscal policy would have had to have been contractionary.

Because foreign individuals and countries have been willing to increase their holdings of dollars through the early 2000s, international issues have not limited U.S. macro policy. Thus, President Bush was able to run highly expansionary fiscal policies and large government budget deficits in the early 2000s without causing U.S. interest rates to rise because inflows of foreign financial assets bought the bonds to finance the deficit. In fact, from 2005 to 2006, the privately held U.S. government debt rose by $209 billion; foreign holdings of U.S. debt rose by $97 billion.

Restoring International Trade Balance to the U.S. Economy

When we think about the likely future direction of the U.S. economy, we have to integrate the theory of comparative advantage into our discussion, because it provides the long-run setting within which short-run policy is conducted. The theory of comparative advantage focuses on the case where trade is balanced—where the comparative advantages of both countries in various goods are balanced. If that is not the case, economic theory assumes something will adjust to bring them into balance.[2] But when the demand for a country's assets is large, those adjustments do not have to take place. That's what happened to the United States. The large demand for U.S. assets allowed U.S. production in a variety of goods and services to lose their competitiveness. U.S. comparative advantage was not in produced goods but in assets; the demand for its assets meant that the United States did not need a demand for its goods and services. Thinking only in terms of goods and services, at current exchange rates, the United States doesn't have a comparative advantage in as many different goods and services as do other countries. That's what it means to be running a trade deficit.

As long as other countries are willing to accept U.S. currency or U.S. assets in payment for the goods that they produce, the United States can continue to run a trade deficit at the current exchange rate. We've seen the beginning of the downward pressure on the value of the dollar, but as of 2007, the dollar has not fallen much against the Chinese yuan or Indian rupee, because their central banks have bought dollars to stop their own currencies from appreciating. (A good review of the last chapter is to discuss, using supply and demand curves, how the Central Bank of China is preventing the appreciation of the yuan.)

At some point, foreigners will likely stop wanting to accumulate more U.S. currency or assets and foreign government support will likely slow. When this happens, assuming nothing else changes, the dollar will depreciate, especially relative to the rupee and

---

[2]When David Ricardo first developed the comparative advantage argument, he discussed how, if there were trade imbalances between the two countries, those imbalances would be quickly eliminated by changes in the two countries' price levels as money followed from the deficit country to the surplus country. When he was writing, countries based their currencies on gold, and it was probably a reasonable assumption. Today, capital markets are much more developed, and capital flows in the opposite direction can offset the need for quick adjustment based on imbalances of trade.

yuan, until the United States regains comparative advantage in enough goods to create a balance in the balance of payments without the inflow of foreign financial assets. Until that happens, we can expect further outsourcing of U.S. jobs and weak U.S. economic growth.

The fall in the value of the dollar is not absolutely certain. Many events could temporarily change the situation. For example, political uncertainty in China or India could slow the process enormously, and even possibly reverse it. Similarly, large inflation in China or India would serve the same purpose as a rise in their exchange rates, and eliminate the need for the value of the dollar to fall. Even if those events don't happen, a sudden collapse of the U.S. economy is not likely to be in the cards because the collapse of the U.S. economy is not in the interest of other countries. Global economies are interconnected; if the U.S. economy were to collapse, so would other world economies. Thus, we can expect foreign governments to step in to support the dollar and slow its fall if the private demand for U.S. assets decreases. Just as the United States does not want its currency to fall too precipitously, China and India do not want their currencies to rise too quickly. This suggests that international pressures on U.S. macro policy will keep U.S. growth slower than what it otherwise would be, and place continual downward pressure on U.S. wages for workers producing an expanding number of tradable goods.

Global economies are interconnected; if the U.S. economy were to collapse, so would other world economies.

A Conclusion

It's time to conclude the chapter and our consideration of global macro policy. Both have been just an introduction. You shouldn't think of them as any more than that. In no way has this brief chapter exhausted the international topics relevant to macro policy. But the chapter has, I hope, made you aware of the international dimensions of our economic goals—and of the problems that international issues pose for macro policy—and the book has made you aware of the central insights of economics. That awareness is absolutely necessary if you are to understand the ongoing debates about economic policy.

Summary

- The international goals of a country are often in dispute.

- Domestic goals generally dominate international goals, but countries often respond to an international goal when forced to do so by other countries.

- Expansionary monetary policy, through its effect on income, increases its trade deficit.

- Contractionary fiscal policy tends to decrease its trade deficit.

- For every effect that monetary and fiscal policies have on a country's exchange rate and trade balance, there is an equal and opposite effect on the combination of

foreign countries' exchange rates and trade balances. Therefore, countries try to coordinate their policies.

- International financial inflows can reduce crowding out.

- Internationalizing a country's debt means that at some time in the future the country must consume less than it produces.

- The United States has lost its competitiveness in the production of many goods. Unless foreigners continue to demand U.S. assets, the U.S. trade deficit will put downward pressure on the dollar and U.S. policy makers will face implementing contractionary policies and/or trade restrictions.

Key Terms

competitiveness *(445)*   policy coordination *(443)*

Questions for Thought and Review

1. Look up the current U.S. exchange rate relative to the yen. Would you suggest raising it or lowering it? Why? (Difficult)   LO1

2. Look up the current U.S. trade balance. Would you suggest raising it or lowering it? Why? (Difficult)   LO1

3. What effect on the U.S. trade deficit would result if China and Japan ran an expansionary monetary policy?   LO2

4. What would be the effect on the U.S. trade deficit if China and Japan ran a contractionary fiscal policy?   LO2

5. Is the United States justified in complaining of Japan's and China's use of an export-led growth policy? Why?   LO3

6. In the 1990s, Japan's economic recession was much in the news. What would you suspect was happening to its trade balance during this time? What policies would you guess other countries (such as those in the Group of Eight) were pressuring Japan to implement?   LO3

7. Why might a sudden large drop in the value of the dollar put pressure on the United States to run contractionary monetary and fiscal policy?   LO1

8. How does internationalizing the debt reduce crowding out?   LO5

9. What are the costs of internationalizing the debt?   LO5

10. What would likely happen to exchange rates if one country has a comparative advantage in production of most goods and the financial and capital account was balanced? (Difficult)   LO6

Problems and Exercises

11. Draw the schematics to show the effect of expansionary monetary policy on the trade deficit.   LO2

12. If the value of the dollar is expected to fall:
    a. Would you rather be holding dollars or other currencies?
    b. Would the same argument you used to answer *a* also hold for the Chinese government?
    c. Why might the Chinese government buy dollars even though it expects the value of the dollar to fall?   LO1

13. You observe that over the past decade a country's competitiveness has been continually eroded and its trade deficit has risen.

a. What monetary or fiscal policies might have led to such results? Why?
    b. You also observe that interest rates have steadily risen along with a rise in the exchange rate. What policies would lead to this result?
    c. What policy might you suggest to improve the country's competitiveness? Explain how that policy might work.   LO2

14. Congratulations! You have been appointed an adviser to the IMF. A country that has run trade deficits for many years now has difficulty servicing its accumulated international debt and wants to borrow from the IMF to meet its obligations. The IMF requires that the country set a target trade surplus.
    a. What monetary and fiscal policies would you suggest the IMF require of that country?
    b. What would be the likely effect of that plan on the country's domestic inflation and growth?
    c. How do you think the country's government will respond to your proposals? Why?   LO2

15. Congratulations! You've been hired as an economic adviser to a country that has perfectly flexible exchange rates. State what monetary and fiscal policy you might suggest in each of the following situations, and explain why you would suggest those policies.
    a. You want to lower the interest rate, decrease inflationary pressures, and lower the trade deficit.
    b. You want to lower the interest rate, decrease inflationary pressures, and lower a trade surplus.
    c. You want to lower the interest rate, decrease unemployment, and lower the trade deficit.
    d. You want to raise the interest rate, decrease unemployment, and lower the trade deficit.   LO2

16. According to a study done at J.P. Morgan, as world trade has increased from about 12 percent of world output in the 1970s to about 25 percent of world output in the early 2000s, global dispersion of growth rates has been decreasing, from around 3 percent dispersion in the 1970s to about 1 percent dispersion in the early 2000s.
    a. If that is true, would one expect more or less stabilization coming from trade with other countries?
    b. What does this convergence of growth rates suggest about the possibility of a global recession?
    c. If a global recession occurred, what policy recommendation would you put forward?   LO4

Questions from Alternative Perspectives

1. In developed countries, it is highly questionable whether an activist monetary and fiscal policy is of any use. Why is it even more questionable in developing countries? (Austrian)

2. Your text talks about how the United States has been consuming more than it has been producing for more than 30 years, making it the largest debtor nation in the world. Deuteronomy 28:43–44 warns against such indebtedness to foreigners. "Aliens residing among you shall ascend above you higher and higher, while you shall descend lower and lower. They shall lend to you but you shall not lend to them; they shall be the head and you shall be the tail."
   a. Is the trade deficit bad even if it can continue indefinitely?
   b. Are there biblical ethics against living beyond one's means that suggests any trade deficit is bad?
   c. In what way is the Deuteronomist's saying true for America today? (Religious)

3. In 2002, the U.S. federal budget deficit (how much greater government spending was than taxes) was about 2.6 percent of GDP. That year the trade deficit (how much imports surpassed exports) was even larger, about 4.1 percent of GDP. Also in 2002, investment in the U.S. economy exceeded U.S. private savings by about 1.5 percent of GDP.
   a. What is the relationship among these three balances?
   b. What do they tell us about who financed the U.S. budget deficit in 2002?
   c. And what do they suggest about the extent of crowding out of private investment in the U.S. economy in 2002? (Institutionalist)

4. The U.S. trade deficit reached $765 billion, or 5.8 percent of GDP, in 2006. Some economists argue that this gap is truly frightening because the current account deficit is the amount of money the United States must attract from abroad. If foreign investors stop buying U.S. bonds and stocks, then skyrocketing interest rates, plummeting stock values, and an economic downturn will surely follow. Others see the gaping current account deficit as a sign of economic vitality. The flipside of a large trade deficit is, after all, a surplus of capital flowing into your country.
   a. Is the U.S. current account deficit a sign of impending disaster or a sign of economic health or something in between?
   b. How has this unprecedented shortfall affected the U.S. economy and how will it affect our economic future? (Post-Keynesian)

5. What has happened to world income inequality is a matter of sharp dispute. Many analysts claim that world incomes have converged in the second half of the twentieth century, leading to a sharp reduction in world inequality. Many others report that the gap between the poorest and the richest people and countries has continued to widen over the last two decades. When a friend of mine who writes about global inequality sorted through these studies, he came to this conclusion: "The wide range of different results of respected studies of world inequality in the last two decades casts doubt on the idea that world inequality has sharply and unambiguously declined or increased during the epoch of neoliberalism." Assuming my friend has read them correctly and fairly, what do these studies imply about the convergence hypothesis and about the globalization process? (Radical)

Web Questions

1. The Census Bureau has an interactive program that reports the top trading partners of the United States. Go to www.census.gov/foreign-trade/top/index.html#top_partners and answer the following questions:
   a. What are the United States' five largest trading partners?
   b. With what five countries does the United States have the largest trade deficits?
   c. What policies could the United States encourage those countries to implement to reduce those deficits?
   d. With what five countries does the United States have the largest trade surpluses?

2. The International Monetary Fund (IMF), which has 183 member countries, was established to promote international monetary cooperation, exchange stability, and orderly exchange arrangements. In the late 1990s, it came under increasing criticism. The Hoover Institution launched a public policy inquiry on the IMF in 1999. Go to the official site of this inquiry (www.imfsite.org) to answer the following questions:
   a. What is conditionality?
   b. What are some typical IMF financing preconditions? If implemented, what would be the effect of these preconditions on the country's (a) exchange rate, (b) trade deficit, (c) domestic economy?
   c. Name five countries that have recently received IMF financing.
   d. What is mission creep?

Answers to Margin Questions

1. A low exchange rate value of a country's currency will tend to stimulate exports and curtail imports. *(438)*

2. A trade deficit means a country is consuming more than it is producing. Consuming more than you produce is pleasant. It also means that capital is flowing into the country, which can be used for investment. So why worry? *(438)*

3. To increase the value of its currency, a country can increase the private demand for its currency by implementing contractionary monetary policy or it could decrease private supply of its currency by implementing contractionary monetary and fiscal policy. *(440)*

4. Contractionary monetary policy will likely lead to an increase in its exchange rate. *(440)*

5. Contractionary monetary policy will tend to decrease income, decreasing imports and decreasing the trade deficit. *(441)*

6. The effect of expansionary fiscal policy on the trade deficit is to increase the trade deficit. *(442)*

7. If other countries stop buying dollar-denominated assets, the value of the dollar will likely fall. *(442)*

8. Generally, when domestic policies and international policies conflict, a country will choose to deal with its domestic problems. Thus, it will likely use expansionary monetary policy if domestic problems call for that. *(443)*

9. Because foreigners buy U.S. bonds that finance the U.S. debt, the demand for bonds is higher than it otherwise would be and the interest rate is lower than it otherwise would be. *(444)*

10. If a country has a fixed exchange rate, it has less flexibility in choosing its monetary and fiscal policies to achieve domestic goals. *(445)*

Macro Policies in Developing Countries

19

Rise up, study the economic forces which oppress you . . . They have emerged from the hand of man just as the gods emerged from his brain. You can control them.

—*Paul LaFargue*

Throughout this book, I have emphasized that macro policy is an art in which one takes the abstract principles learned in *positive economics*—the abstract analysis and models that tell us how economic forces direct the economy—and examines how those principles work out in a particular institutional structure to achieve goals determined in *normative economics*—the branch of economics that considers what goals we should be aiming for. In this chapter, we see another aspect of that art.

Most of this book has emphasized the macroeconomics of Western industrialized economies, the United States in particular. That means I have focused on their goals and their institutions. In this chapter, I shift focus and discuss the macroeconomic problems of developing economies.

Developing Countries in Perspective

There are nearly 6.6 billion people in the world. Of these, 5 billion (about 75 percent) live in developing, rather than developed, countries. Per capita income in developing countries is around $500 per year; in the United States, per capita income is about $40,000.

These averages understate the differences between the poorest country and the richest. Consider the African country of Chad—definitely one of the world's poorest. Its per capita income is about $250 per year—less than 1/100 of the per capita income in the United States. Moreover, income in Chad goes primarily to the rich, so Chad's poor have per capita income of significantly less than $250.

How does a person live on that $250 per year, as many people in the world do? To begin with, that person can't

Go out for Big Macs.

Use Joy perfume (or any type of perfume).

Wear designer clothes.

What to Call Developing Countries

In this chapter, following common usage, I call low-income countries *developing countries*. They have not always been called *developing*. In the 1950s they were called *backward*, but it was eventually realized that *backward* carried with it significant negative value judgments. Then these countries were called *underdeveloped*, but it was eventually realized that *underdeveloped* also suggested significant negative value judgments. More recently they have been called *developing*, but eventually everyone will realize that *developing* implies significant negative value judgments. After all, in what sense are these countries "developing" any more than the United States? All countries are evolving or developing countries. Many so-called developing countries have highly refined cultures, which they don't want to lose; they may want to develop economically but not at the cost of cultural change.

What should one call these countries? That remains to be seen, but whatever one calls them, bear in mind that language can conceal value judgments.

And that person must

> Eat grain—usually rice or corn—for all meals, every day.
>
> Mix fat from meat—not meat itself—with the rice on special occasions (maybe).
>
> Live in one room with 9 or 10 other people.
>
> Work hard from childhood to old age (if there is an old age). Those too old to work in the fields stay at home and care for those too young to work in the fields. (But children go out to work in the fields when they're about six years old.)
>
> Go hungry, because no matter how many family members can work in the fields, probably the work and soil don't yield enough to provide the workers with an adequate number of calories per day.

In a poor person's household, it's likely that a couple of the older children have gone into the city to find work that pays money wages. If they were lucky and found jobs, they can send money home each month. That money may be the only cash income their family back in the village has. The family uses the money to buy a few tools and cooking utensils.

The preceding is, of course, only one among billions of different stories. Even Americans and Europeans who are classified as poor find it hard to contemplate what life is really like in a truly poor country.

Don't Judge Society by Its Income Alone

Poor people in developing countries survive and often find pleasure in their hard lives. In many poor countries, there are far fewer suicides than in the United States. For example, the U.S. suicide rate for men is approximately 18 per 100,000 people. In Costa Rica it's 9.7; in Mexico it's 5.1; and in Peru it's 0.6. Who has time for suicide? You're too busy surviving. There's little ambiguity and few questions about the meaning of life. Living! That's what life's all about. There's no "Mom, what am I going to do today?" You know what you're going to do: survive if you can. And survival is satisfying.

Often these economically poor societies have elaborate cultural rituals and networks of intense personal relationships that provide individuals with a deep sense of fulfillment and satisfaction.

Often economically poor societies have cultures that provide individuals with a deep sense of fulfillment and satisfaction.

Are people in these societies as happy as Americans are? If your immediate answer is no, be careful to understand the difficulty of making such a judgment. The answer isn't clear-cut. For us to say, "My God! What a failure their system is!" is wrong. It's an inappropriate value judgment about the relative worth of cultures. All too often Americans have gone into another country to try to make people better off but have ended up making them worse off.

An economy is part and parcel of a culture. You can't judge just an economy; you must judge the entire culture. Some developing countries have cultures that, in many people's view, are preferable to ours. If one increases a country's income but takes away its culture in doing so, its people arguably may be worse off.

That said, if we asked people in developing countries if they believe that they would be better off if they had more income, most would definitely answer yes!

Even culturally sensitive people agree that economic growth within the context of a developing country's culture would be a good thing, if only because those countries exist simultaneously with market economies. Given market societies' expansionary tendencies, without economic growth, cultures in economically poor countries would simply be overrun and destroyed by the cultures of market societies. Their land would be taken, their agricultural patterns would be changed, their traditional means of subsistence would be destroyed, and their cultures would be obliterated. So, generally, the choice isn't between development and preservation of the existing culture (and its accompanying ancient ways to which the poor have adjusted). Rather, the choice is between development (with its attendant wrenching cultural transitions) and continuing poverty and slower, but still painful, cultural transitions.

An economy is part and parcel of a culture.

Q₁ In what way is economic development the only choice for developing countries?

Some Comparative Statistics on Rich and Poor Nations

The low average income in poor countries has its effects on people's lives. Life expectancy is about 60 years in most very economically poor countries (compared to about 80 years in the United States). In economically poor countries, most people drink contaminated water, consume about half the number of calories the World Health Organization has determined is minimal for good health, and do physical labor (often of the kind done by machine in developed countries). Table 19-1 compares developing countries, middle-income countries, and developed countries.

As with all statistics, care must be taken in interpreting the figures in Table 19-1. For example, the income comparisons were all made on the basis of current exchange rates. But relative prices between rich and poor countries often differ substantially; the cost of goods relative to total income tends to be much lower for people in developing countries than for those in developed countries.

To allow for these differences, some economists have looked at the domestic purchasing power of money in various countries and have adjusted the comparisons accordingly. Rather than comparing incomes by using exchange rates, they use **purchasing power parity (PPP)**—*a method of comparing income by looking at the domestic purchasing power of money in different countries.* That is, purchasing power parity equalizes the cost of an identical basket of goods among countries. Using purchasing power parity, the World Bank found that income differences among countries are cut by half. In other words, when one uses the World Bank's PPP method of comparison, it's as if the people in developing countries had twice as much income as they had when their incomes were compared using market exchange rates.

A similar adjustment can be made with the life expectancy rates. A major reason for the lower life expectancies in developing countries is their high infant mortality rates. Once children survive infancy, however, their life expectancies are much closer to those

Purchasing power parity exchange rates are calculated by determining what a specified basket of consumer goods will cost in various countries.

TABLE 19-1 Statistics on Selected Developing, Middle-Income, and Developed Countries

Country	Physicians per Thousand People	Daily Calorie Supply	Life Expectancy	Infant Mortality (per 1,000)	Labor Force in Agriculture (%)	Labor Force in Industry (%)	Adult Literacy Rate	Land and Mobile Phones (per 1,000)	GDP per Capita ($)
Developing									
Bangladesh	0.26	2,205	67	56	63%	11%	43%	37	$ 470
Ethiopia	0.03	1,857	42	110	80	8	43	8	160
Haiti	0.25	2,086	52	74	66	9	53	64	450
Middle-Income									
Brazil	1.15	3,050	71	32	20	14	89	587	3,460
Iran	0.45	3,085	71	32	30	25	79	270	2,770
Republic of Korea	1.57	3,058	77	5	6	26	98	1,168	15,830
Thailand	0.37	2,467	71	24	49	14	93	365	2,190
Developed									
Japan	1.98	2,761	82	3	5	28	99	1,176	38,980
Sweden	3.28	3,185	80	3	2	24	99	1,743	41,060
United States	2.56	3,774	77	7	1	13	99	1,223	43,740

Sources: *World Development Report, 2007*, The World Bank (www.worldbank.org); *CIA World Factbook, 2006*. Because of reporting lags, some data are for earlier years.

of children in developed countries. Say life expectancy at birth is 50 years and that 10 percent of all infants die within their first year. As a person grows older, at each birthday the person's life expectancy is higher. So if a child lives to the age of 3 years, then at that point the child has an actual life expectancy of close to 60 years, rather than 50 years.

Growth versus Development

Growth occurs because of an increase in inputs, given a production function; development occurs through a change in the production function.

Economists use the term *developing*, rather than *growing*, to emphasize that the goals of these countries involve more than simply an increase in output; these countries are changing their underlying institutions. Put another way, these economies are changing their production functions; they are not increasing inputs given a production function. Thus, *development* refers to an increase in productive capacity and output brought about by a change in the underlying institutions, and *growth* refers to an increase in output brought about by an increase in inputs.

Q-2 Why does restructuring in developed countries suggest that the distinction between growth and development can be overdone?

The distinction can be overdone. Institutions, and hence production functions, in developed as well as in developing countries are continually changing, and output changes are a combination of changes in production functions and increases in inputs. For example, in the 1990s and early 2000s, the major Western economies have been **restructuring** their economies—*changing the underlying economic institutions*—as they work to compete better in the world economy. As they restructure, they change their methods of production, their laws, and their social support programs. Thus, in some ways, they are doing precisely what developing countries are doing—developing rather than just growing. Despite the ambiguity, the distinction between growth and development can be a useful one if you remember that the two blend into each other.

While the lessons of abstract theory do not change when we shift our attention to developing economies, the institutions and goals change enormously.

The reason economists separate out developing economies is that these economies have (1) different institutional structures and (2) a different weighting of goals than do Western developed economies. These two differences—in institutional structure and in goals—change the way in which the lessons of abstract theory are applied and discussed.

Differing Goals

When discussing macro policy within Western developed economies, I did not dwell on questions of normative goals of macroeconomics. Instead, I used generally accepted goals in the United States as the goals of macro policy—achieving low inflation, low unemployment, and an acceptable growth rate—with a few caveats. You may have noticed that the discussion focused more on what might be called stability goals—achieving low unemployment and low inflation—than it did on the acceptable growth rate goal. I chose that focus because growth in Western developed countries is desired because it holds unemployment down, and because it avoids difficult distributional questions, as much as it is desired for its own sake. Our economy has sufficient productive capacity to provide its citizens, on average, with a relatively high standard of living. The problem facing Western societies is as much seeing that all members of those societies share in that high standard of living as it is raising the standard.

In the developing countries, the weighting of goals is different. Growth and development are primary goals. When people are starving and the economy isn't fulfilling people's **basic needs**—*adequate food, clothing, and shelter*—a main focus of macro policy will be on how to increase the economy's growth rate through development so that the economy can fulfill those basic needs.

There are differences in normative goals between developing and developed countries because their wealth differs. Developing countries face basic economic needs whereas developed countries' economic needs are considered by most people to be normatively less pressing.

Differing Institutions

Developing countries differ from developed countries not only in their goals but also in their macroeconomic institutions. These macroeconomic institutions are qualitatively different from institutions in developed countries. Their governments are different; their financial institutions—the institutions that translate savings into investment—are different; their fiscal institutions—the institutions through which government collects taxes and spends its money—are different; and their social and cultural institutions are different. Because of these differences, the way in which we discuss macroeconomic policy is different.

One of the differences concerns very basic market institutions—such as Western-style property rights and contract law. In certain groups of developing countries, most notably sub-Saharan Africa, these basic market institutions don't exist; instead, communal property rights and tradition structure economic relationships. How can one talk about market forces in such economies?[1] On a more mundane level, consider the issue of monetary policy. Talking about monetary policy via open market operations (the buying and selling of bonds by the central bank) is not all that helpful when there is no market for government bonds, as is the case in many developing countries.

Let's now consider some specific institutional differences more carefully.

Economies at different stages of development have different institutional needs because the problems they face are different.

Political Differences and Laissez-Faire   Views of how activist macroeconomic policy should be are necessarily contingent on the political system an economy has. One of the scarcest commodities in developing countries is socially minded leaders. Not that developed countries have any overabundance of them, but most developed countries have at least a tradition of politicians seeming to be fair and open-minded, and a set of institutionalized checks and balances that limit leaders using government for their personal benefit. In many developing countries, those institutionalized checks and balances on governmental leaders often do not exist.

Let's consider a few examples. First, let's look at Saudi Arabia, which, while economically rich, maintains many of the institutions of a developing country. It is an

In many developing countries, institutional checks and balances on government leaders often do not exist.

---

[1]One can, of course, talk about economic forces. But, as discussed in Chapter 1, economic forces become market forces only in a market institutional setting.

absolute monarchy in which the royal family is the ultimate power. Say a member of that family comes to the bank and wants a loan that, on economic grounds, doesn't make sense. What do you think the bank loan officer will do? Grant the loan, if the banker is smart. Thus, despite the wealth of the country, it isn't surprising that many economists believe the Saudi banking system reflects that political structure—and may find itself in serious trouble if oil prices fall significantly.

A second example is Nigeria, which had enormous possibilities for economic growth in the 1980s because of its oil riches. It didn't develop. Instead, politicians fought over the spoils, and bribes became a major source of their income. Corruption was rampant, and the Nigerian economy went nowhere. I will stop there, but, unfortunately, there are many other examples.

Because of the structure of government in many developing countries, many economists who, in Western developed economies favor activist government policies, may well favor Classical laissez-faire policies for the same reasons that early Classical economists did—because they have a profound distrust of the governments. That distrust, however, must have limits. As I discussed in Chapter 3, even a laissez-faire policy requires some government role in setting the rules. So there is no escaping the need for socially minded leaders.

The Dual Economy   A second institutional difference between developed and developing countries is the dual nature of developing countries' economies. Whereas it often makes sense to talk about a Western economy as a single economy, it does not for most developing countries. A developing country's economy is generally characterized by a **dual economy**—*the existence of two sectors: a traditional sector and an internationally oriented modern market sector.*[2]

Often, the largest percentage of the population participates in the traditional economy. It is a local currency, or no currency, sector in which traditional ways of doing things take precedence. The second sector—the internationally oriented modern market sector—is often indistinguishable from a Western economy. Activities in the modern sector are often conducted in foreign currencies, rather than domestic currencies, and contracts are often governed by international law. This dual economy aspect of developing countries creates a number of dilemmas for policy makers and affects the way they think about macroeconomic problems.

For example, take the problem of unemployment. Many developing countries have a large subsistence-farming economy. Subsistence farmers aren't technically unemployed, but often there are so many people on the land that, in economic terms, their contribution to output is minimal or even negative, so for policy purposes one can consider the quantity of labor that will be supplied at the going wage unlimited. But to call these people unemployed is problematic. These subsistence farmers are simply outside the market economy. In such cases, one would hardly want, or be able, to talk of an unemployment problem in the same way we talk in the United States.

Fiscal Structure of Developing Economies   A third institutional difference concerns developing countries' fiscal systems. To undertake discretionary fiscal policy—running a deficit or surplus to affect the aggregate economy—the government must be able to determine expenditures and tax rates, with a particular eye toward the difference between the two. As discussed in an earlier chapter, discretionary fiscal policy is difficult for Western developed countries to undertake; it is almost impossible for developing economies.

The term dual economy refers to the existence of the two sectors in most developing countries: a traditional sector and an internationally oriented modern market sector.

Q-3   What is meant by the term *dual economy?*

Web Note 19.1
The Modern Sector

---

[2]I discuss these two sectors as if they were separate, but in reality they are interrelated. Portions of the economy devoted to the tourist trade span both sectors, as do some manufacturing industries. Still, there is sufficient independence of the two sectors that it is reasonable to treat them as separate.

In the traditional sector of many developing countries, barter or cash transactions predominate, and such transactions are especially difficult to tax. Often, the governments in these economies don't have the institutional structures with which to collect taxes (or, when they have the institutional structure, it is undermined by fraud and evasion), so their taxing options are limited; that's why they often use tariffs as a primary source of revenue.

Often developing countries do not have the institutional structures with which to collect taxes.

Similar problems exist with government expenditures. Many expenditures of developing countries are mandated by political considerations—if the government doesn't make them, it will likely be voted out of office. Within such a setting, to talk about activist fiscal policy—choosing a deficit for its macroeconomic implications—even if it might otherwise be relevant, is not much help since the budget deficit is not a choice variable, but instead is a result of other political decisions.

Many government expenditures in developing countries are mandated by political considerations.

The political constraints facing developing countries can, of course, be overstated. The reality is that developing countries do institute new fiscal regimes. Take, for example, Mexico. In the early 1980s, Mexico's fiscal problems seemed impossible to solve, but in the late 1980s and early 1990s, Carlos de Salinas, a U.S.-trained economist, introduced a fiscal austerity program and an economic liberalization program that lowered Mexico's budget deficit and significantly reduced its inflation. But such changes are better called a **regime change**—*a change in the entire atmosphere within which the government and the economy interrelate*—rather than a **policy change**—*a change in one aspect of government's actions, such as monetary policy or fiscal policy*. Regimes can change suddenly. For example, in Mexico soon after President Salinas left office, his brother was implicated in a murder and drug scandal. Foreign investors became worried and pulled money out of Mexico. The peso fell, inflation and interest rates rose, and the Mexican economy fell into a serious recession. In one day, the regime of confidence had changed to a regime of uncertainty and confusion, full of questions about what policy actions the Mexican government would take.

A regime change is a change in the entire atmosphere within which the government and the economy interrelate; a policy change is a change in one aspect of government's actions.

Financial Institutions of Developing Economies   I spent two chapters discussing the complex financial systems of developed countries because you had to understand those financial systems in order to understand macro policy. While some parts of that discussion carry over to developing countries, other parts don't, since financial systems in developing countries are often quite different than those in developed countries.

The primary difference arises from the dual nature of developing countries' economies. In the traditional part of developing economies, the financial sector is embryonic; trades are made by barter, or with direct payment of money; trades requiring more sophisticated financial markets, such as mortgages to finance houses, just don't exist.

The primary difference between financial institutions in developing countries and developed countries arises from the dual nature of developing countries' economies.

In the modern international part of developing economies, that isn't the case. Developing countries' international financial sectors are sometimes as sophisticated as Western financial institutions. A currency trading room in Ecuador or Nigeria looks similar to one in New York, London, or Frankfurt. That modern financial sector is integrated into the international economy (with pay rates that often approach or match those of the West). This dual nature of developing countries' financial sectors constrains the practice of monetary policy and changes the regulatory and control functions of central banks.

The above is one of many institutional examples of differences that exist and that change the nature of the macro problem. What's important is not so much the specifics of the example but, rather, the general point it brings home. Economies at different stages of development have different institutional, and policy, needs. Institutions with the same names in different countries can have quite different roles. Such institutions can differ in subtle ways, making it important to have specific knowledge of a country's institutions before one can understand its economy and meaningfully talk about policy.

It is important to have specific knowledge of a country's institutions before one can understand its economy and meaningfully talk about policy.

A Real, Real-World Application: The Traditional Economy Meets the Internet

San Juana Hernandez, of Acuna, Mexico, wanted to borrow some money to paint her grocery store and order some more goods to stock. Marco Apaza, of La Paz, Bolivia, needed some money to expand his sporting goods wholesale business and to build an addition on his parents' home, where he lives, so that he has a bit more room. They needed only small amounts—under $1,000 each. In the traditional economy, the possibilities for loans didn't exist; banks generally don't make the type of small loans that they needed, and there were no good methods of providing the loans. But both got their loans, in part because I loaned them some of the money. How did I do it from up here in Vermont? I went to the Web site, Kiva.org, found their loan request (along with thousands of others) and sent some money via PayPal. Kiva.org combined my money with that of another 40 or so people, and made the loan to them.

This innovative program, which is a modern variation on the micro credit programs discussed in earlier chapters, allows a type of international micro credit, in which individuals throughout the world can make loans to individuals in developing countries. The people go to a microfinance agency in their home city, which checks them out to see that they are legitimate borrowers, and which then posts their loan request on the Kiva Web site. Individuals with money to lend can go to the Web site and choose to make loans to whomever they want. There is no guarantee that the loans will be paid back, but the experience to date about repayments has been, as it has with most micro credit lending, very good. Such programs show that technology can help break down the barrier between the traditional and the market sector.

Monetary Policy in Developing Countries

Now that I've discussed some of the ways in which financial institutions differ in developing countries, let's consider some issues of central banking and monetary policy for those economies.

Central Banks Are Less Independent

The first thing to note about central banking in developing countries is that its primary goal is often different than a central bank's primary goal in developed countries. The reason is that, while all central banks have a number of goals, at the top of them all is the goal of keeping the economy running. Western central banks have the luxury of assuming away the problem of keeping the economy running—inertia, institutions, and history hold Western industrial economies together, and keep them running. Central banks in developing countries can't make that assumption.

What this means in practice is that central banks in developing countries generally have far less independence than do central banks in developed countries. With a political and fiscal system that generates large deficits and that cannot exist without these deficits, the thought of an independent monetary policy goes out the window.

A second difference concerns the institutional implementation of monetary policy. In a developing country, a broad-based domestic government bond market often does not exist. So if the government runs a deficit and is financing it domestically, the central bank usually must buy the bonds, which means that it must increase the money supply.

Central banks in developing countries generally have far less independence than do central banks in developed countries.

As you know, increasing the money supply leads to higher inflation. And developing countries on the whole have experienced high inflation, as the table below shows.

| | **Annual Inflation Rates** | | | | | | |
	1991–2000	2001	2002	2003	2004	2005	2006
United States	2.4	2.8	1.6	2.3	2.7	3.4	3.9
World	12.7	4.4	3.9	4.1	3.8	4.2	4.0
Developed countries	3.0	3.0	2.2	2.3	2.2	2.7	2.8
Former Soviet countries	101.7	16.0	9.9	8.5	8.2	8.3	6.2
Latin America and Caribbean	50.0	6.1	9.3	10.9	6.8	6.6	5.8
Asia and Pacific	7.0	4.9	4.1	3.6	4.2	5.3	6.2
Sub-Saharan Africa	16.8	11.8	12.8	14.8	11.0	11.5	6.5
Middle-East and North Africa	9.7	3.8	4.7	5.7	7.6	5.5	4.4

Source: International Labor Statistics (LABORSTA).

Central banks recognize that increasing the money supply will cause inflation, but often central banks feel as if they have no choice because of the political consequences of not issuing the money.

As I discussed above, often, in developing countries, the government's sources of tax revenue are limited, and the low level of income in the economy makes the tax base small. A government attempting to collect significantly more taxes might risk being overthrown. Similarly, its ability to cut expenditures is limited. If it cuts expenditures, it will almost certainly be overthrown. With new tax sources unavailable and with no ability to cut expenditures, the government uses its only other option to meet its obligations—it issues debt. And, if the central bank agrees with the conclusion that the government is correct in its assessment that it has no choice, then if the central bank doesn't want the government to be overthrown, it has no choice but to monetize that debt (print money to pay that debt). Sometimes the central bank's choices are even more limited; dictatorships simply tell the central bank to provide the needed money, or be eliminated.

Issuing money to finance budget deficits may be a short-term solution, but it is not a long-term solution. It is an accounting identity that real resources consumed by the economy must equal the real resources produced or imported. If the government deficit doesn't increase output, the real resources the government is getting because the central bank is monetizing its debt must come from somewhere else. Where do those real resources come from? From the *inflation tax*—an implicit tax on the holders of cash and the holders of any obligations specified in nominal terms. Inflation works as a type of tax on these individuals.

Faced with the prospect of a collapse of government, the central banks generally choose to keep the governments operating (which isn't surprising, since they are often branches of the government). To do that, they increase the money supply enormously, causing hyperinflation in many of these countries. These hyperinflations soon take on a life of their own. The expectation of accelerating inflation creates even more inflationary pressure as individuals try to spend any money they have quickly, before the prices go up. This increases velocity, nominal demand for goods, and inflationary pressures.

One problem with using an inflation tax is that in an inflation, the government is not the only recipient of revenue; any issuer of fixed-interest-rate debt denominated in domestic currency also gains. And the holder of any fixed-interest-rate debt denominated in domestic currency loses. This income redistribution caused by an inflation can temporarily stimulate real output, but it can also undermine the country's financial institutions.

Q-4 If everyone knows that the cause of inflation in developing countries is the creation of too much money, why don't these countries stop inflation?

Central banks recognize that printing too much money causes inflation, but often feel compelled to do so for political reasons.

The Importance of an Independent Central Bank

Inflation works as a tax on holders of obligations specified in nominal terms.

Q-5 In an inflation, who else, besides government, gets revenue from an inflation tax?

The point of the above discussion is that the central banks know that issuing large quantities of money will cause inflation. What they don't know, and what the policy discussions are about, is which is worse: the inflation or the unpleasant alternatives. Should the central bank bail out the government? There are legitimate questions about whether countries' budget deficits are absolutely necessary or not. It is those assessments in which the debate about developing countries' inflation exists; the debate is not about whether the inflation is caused by the issuance of too much money.

Opponents of any type of bailout point out that any "inflation solution" is only a temporary solution that, if used, will require ever-increasing amounts of inflation to remain effective. Proponents of bailouts agree with this argument but argue that inflation buys a bit more time, and the alternative is the breakdown of the government and the economy. Because of the unpleasant alternative, the fact that inflation is only a temporary solution doesn't stop developing countries' leaders from using it. They don't have time for the luxury of long-run solutions and are often simply looking for policies that will hold their governments together for a month at a time.

Focus on the International Sector and the Exchange Rate Constraint

Another difference between the monetary policies of developed and developing countries concerns the policy options they consider for dealing with foreign exchange markets. Developed countries are generally committed to full exchange rate convertibility. With full exchange rate convertibility, individuals can exchange their currency for any other country's currency without significant government restrictions.

Developing countries often do not have fully convertible currencies. Individuals and firms in these countries face restrictions on their ability to exchange currencies—sometimes general restrictions and sometimes restrictions that depend on the purpose for which they wish to use the foreign exchange.

Various Types of Convertibility   Since convertibility plays such a central role in developing countries' macro policies, let's review the various types of convertibility. The United States has **full convertibility**—*individuals may change dollars into any currency they want for whatever legal purpose they want.* (There are, however, reporting laws about movements of currency.) Most Western developed countries have full convertibility.

A second type of convertibility is **convertibility on the current account**—*a system that allows people to exchange currencies freely to buy goods and services, but not to buy assets in other countries.* The third type of convertibility is **limited capital account convertibility**—*a system that allows full current account convertibility and partial capital account convertibility.* There are various levels of restrictions on what types of assets one can exchange, so there are many types of limited capital account convertibility.

Almost no developing country allows full convertibility. Why? One reason is that they want to force their residents to keep their savings, and to do their investing, in their home country, not abroad. Why don't their citizens want to do that? Because when there is a chance of a change in governments—and government seizure of assets as there often is in developing countries—rich individuals generally prefer to have a significant portion of their assets abroad, away from the hands of their government.

These limits on exchange rate convertibility explain a general phenomenon found in most developing countries—the fact that much of the international part of the dual economy in developing countries is "dollarized"—contracts are framed, and accounting is handled, in dollars, not in the home country's currency. Dollarization exists almost completely in the international sectors of countries that have nonconvertible currencies, and largely in the international sectors of countries where

The fact that inflation is only a temporary solution doesn't stop developing countries' leaders from using it.

Q-6 Distinguish between convertibility on the current account from full convertibility.

Almost no developing country has full convertibility.

the currency is convertible on the current account but not on the capital account. This dollarization exists because of nonconvertibility, or the fear of nonconvertibility. Thus, ironically, nonconvertibility increases the focus on dollarized contracts in the international sector, and puts that sector beyond effective control by the central bank.

Nonconvertibility does not halt international trade—it merely complicates it, since it adds another layer of uncertainty and bureaucracy to the trading process. Each firm that is conducting international trade must see that it will have sufficient foreign exchange to carry on its business. Developing governments will often want to encourage this international trade, while preventing outflows of their currencies for other purposes.

When developing countries have partially convertible exchange rates, exchange rate policy—buying and selling foreign currencies in order to help stabilize the exchange rate—often is an important central bank function. This is such an important function because trade in most of these countries' currencies is *thin*—there is not a large number of traders or trades. When trading is thin, large fluctuations in exchange rates are possible in response to a change in a few traders' needs. Even the uncertainties of the weather can affect traders. Say an expected oil tanker is kept from landing in port because of bad weather. The financial exchange—paying for that oil—that would have taken place upon landing does not take place, and the supply/demand conditions for a country's currency could change substantially. In response, the value of the country's currency could rise or fall dramatically unless it were stabilized. The central bank often helps provide exchange rate stabilization.

Conditionality and the Balance of Payments Constraint   In designing their policies, developing countries often rely on advice from the International Monetary Fund (IMF). One reason is that the IMF has economists who have much experience with these issues. A second reason is that, for these countries, the IMF is a major source of temporary loans that they need to stabilize their currencies.

These loans usually come with conditions that the country meet certain domestic monetary and fiscal stabilization goals. Specifically, these goals are that government deficits be lowered and money supply growth be limited. Because of these requirements, IMF's loan policy is often called **conditionality**—*the making of loans that are subject to specific conditions*. These goals have been criticized by economists such as Joseph Stiglitz, who argues that the contractionary monetary and fiscal policies often required by conditionality tend to be procyclical and only worsen the recession. The IMF responds that in a developing country, the long-run fiscal and monetary goals must take precedence to establish a basis for development.

Even a partially flexible exchange rate regime presents the country with the **balance of payments constraint**—*limitations on expansionary domestic macroeconomic policy due to a shortage of international reserves*. Attempts to expand the domestic economy with expansionary monetary policy continually push the economy to its balance of payments constraint. To meet both its domestic goals and international balance of payments constraints, many developing countries turn to loans from the IMF, not only for the exchange rate stabilization reasons discussed above but also for a more expansionary macro policy than otherwise would be possible. Because of the IMF's control of these loans, macro policy in developing countries is often conducted with one eye toward the IMF, and sometimes with a complete bow.

The Need for Creativity

The above discussion may have made it seem as if conducting domestic macro policy in developing countries is almost hopelessly dominated by domestic political concerns and international constraints. If by macro policy one means using traditional monetary and fiscal policy tools as they are used in standard ways, that's true. But macro policy, interpreted

Nonconvertibility does not halt international trade; it merely makes it more difficult.

The basis for most IMF loans is conditionality.

The balance of payments constraint consists of limitations on expansionary domestic macro policy due to a shortage of international reserves.

broadly, is much more than using those tools. It is the development of new institutions that expand the possibilities for growth. It is creating a new production function, not operating within an existing one. Macro policy, writ large to include the development of new institutions, can have enormous effects. To undertake such policies requires an understanding of the role of institutions, the specific nature of the problem in one's country, and creativity.

Obstacles to Economic Development

What stops countries from developing economically? Economists have discovered no magic potion that will make a country develop. We can't say, "Here are steps 1, 2, 3, 4. If you follow them you'll grow, but if you don't follow them you won't grow."

What makes it so hard for developing countries to devise a successful development program is that social, political, and economic problems blend into one another and cannot be considered separately. The institutional structure that we take for granted in the United States often doesn't exist in those countries. For example economists' analysis of production assumes that a stable government exists that can enforce contracts and supply basic services. In most developing countries, that assumption can't be made. Governments are often anything but stable; overnight, a coup d'état can bring a new government into power, with a whole new system of rules under which businesses have to operate. Imagine trying to figure out a reasonable study strategy if every week you had a new teacher who emphasized different things and gave totally different types of tests from last week's teacher. Firms in developing countries face similar problems.

While economists can't say, "Here's what you have to do in order to grow," we have been able to identify some general obstacles that all developing countries seem to face:

1. Political instability.
2. Corruption.
3. Lack of appropriate institutions.
4. Lack of investment.
5. Inappropriate education.
6. Overpopulation.
7. Health and disease.

I consider each in turn.

Political Instability

A student's parents once asked me why their son was doing poorly in my economics class. My answer was that he could not read well and he could hardly write. Until he could master those basics, there was no use talking about how he could better learn economics.

Roughly the same reasoning can be applied to the problem of political instability in developing countries. Unless a country achieves political stability (acceptance within a country of a stable system of government), it's not going to develop economically, no matter what it does.

All successful development strategies require a stable government. A mercantilist or a socialist development strategy requires an elaborate government presence. A market-based strategy requires a much smaller government role, but even with markets, a stable environment is needed for a market to function and for contracts to be made with confidence.

Many developing countries don't have that stability. Politically they haven't established a tradition of orderly governmental transition. Coups d'état or armed insurrections always remain possible.

Web Note 19.2
Development Economists

Seven problems facing developing countries are
1. Political instability.
2. Corruption.
3. Lack of appropriate institutions.
4. Lack of investment.
5. Inappropriate education.
6. Overpopulation.
7. Health and disease.

All successful development strategies require a stable government.

One example is Somalia. There, a civil war among competing groups in 1990 led to famine and enormous hardship, which provoked the sympathy of the world. But attempts by the UN and the United States to establish a stable government by sending troops there caused as many, or more, problems than they resolved, and in 1995 the United States withdrew its troops. Today Somalia continues to lack a unified central government. Political instability exists in most developing countries, but it is strongest in Africa, which in large part accounts for Africa's low rate of economic growth relative to that of the other geographic areas.

Even countries whose governments aren't regularly toppled face threats of overthrow, and those threats are sufficient to prevent individual economic activity. To function, an economy needs some rules—any rules—that will last.

The lack of stability is often exacerbated by social and cultural differences among groups within a country. Political boundaries often reflect arbitrary decisions made by former colonial rulers, not the traditional cultural and tribal boundaries that form the real-life divisions. The result is lack of consensus among the population as a whole as well as inter-tribal suspicion and even warfare.

For example, Nigeria is a federation established under British colonial rule. It comprises three ethnic regions: the northern, Hausa Fulan, region; the western, Yoruba, region; and the eastern, Ibo, region. These three regions are culturally distinct and so are in continual political and military conflict. Nigeria has experienced an endless cycle of military coups, attempts at civilian rule, and threats of secession by the numerically smaller eastern region. Had each region been allowed to remain separate, economic development might have been possible; but because the British lumped the regions together and called them a country, economic development is next to impossible.

The Influence of Political Instability on Development   Do these political considerations affect economic questions? You bet. As I will discuss shortly, any development plan requires financial investment from somewhere—either external or internal. Political instability closes off both sources of investment funds.

Any serious potential investor takes political instability into account. Foreign companies considering investment in a developing country hire political specialists who analyze the degree of risk involved. Where the risk is too great, foreign companies simply don't invest.

Political instability also limits internal investment. Income distribution in many developing countries is highly skewed. There are a few very rich people and an enormous number of very poor people, while the middle class is often small.

Whatever one's view of the fairness of such income inequality, it has a potential advantage for society. Members of the wealthy elite in developing countries have income to spare, and their savings are a potential source of investment funds. But when there is political instability, that potential isn't realized. Fearing that their wealth may be taken from them, the rich often channel their investment out of their own country so that, should they need to flee a revolution, they'll still be able to live comfortably. Well-off people in developing countries provide major inflows of investment into the United States and other Western countries.

Political Instability and Unequal Distribution of Income   The highly skewed distribution of income in most developing countries contributes in another way to political instability. It means that the poor majority has little vested interest in maintaining the current system. A coup? Why not? What have they got to lose? The economic prospects for many people in developing countries are so bleak that they are quite willing to join or at least support a guerrilla insurgency that promises to set up a new, better system. The resulting instability makes development almost impossible.

Q-7 Why does political instability present an economic problem for developing countries?

Q-8 Income inequality leads to higher levels of savings by the rich and therefore has significant advantages for developing countries. True or false? Explain your answer.

Corruption

Bribery, graft, and corruption are ways of life in most developing countries. In Egypt it's called *baksheesh* (meaning "gift of money"); in Mexico it's called *la mordida* ("the bite"). If you want to park in a parking spot in Mexico City, you'd better pay the policeman, or your car will get a ticket. If you want to take a photograph of the monument to Ramses II in front of the Cairo railroad station, you'd better slip the traffic officer a few bucks, or else you may get run over.

Without a well-developed institutional setting and a public morality that condemns corruption, economic forces function in a variety of areas that people in developed countries would consider inappropriate. In any country, the government has the right to allow imports, to allow development, to determine where you can park your car, to say whether you can take photographs of public buildings, to decide who wins a lawsuit, and so forth. In developing countries, however, those rights can be, and often are, sold. The litigant who pays the judge the most wins. How about the right to import? Want to import a new machine? That will be 20 percent of the cost, please.

Such graft and corruption quickly become institutionalized to the degree that all parties involved feel they have little choice but to take part. Government officials say that graft and bribery are built into their pay structure, so unless they take bribes, they won't have enough income to live on. Businesspeople say that if they want to stay in business, they have to pay bribes. Similarly, workers must bribe business in order to get a job, and labor leaders must be bribed not to cause trouble for business.

I'm not claiming that such payments are wrong. Societies decide what is right and wrong; economists don't. The term *bribery* in English has a pejorative connotation. In many other languages, the terms people use for this type of activity don't have such negative connotations.

But I am claiming that such payments—with the implied threat that failure to pay will have adverse consequences—make it more difficult for a society's economy to grow. Knowing that those payments must be made prevents many people from undertaking actions that might lead to growth. For example, a friend of mine wanted to build a group of apartments in the Bahamas, but when he discovered the payoffs he'd have to make to various people, he abandoned the whole idea.

Limiting an activity makes the right to undertake that limited activity valuable to the person doing the limiting. When bribery is an acceptable practice, it creates strong incentives to limit an ever-increasing number of activities—including many activities that could make a country grow.

Lack of Appropriate Institutions

Almost all economists agree that, to develop, a country should establish markets. Markets require the establishment of property rights. In a recent book, *The Mystery of Capital*, Hernando DeSoto argued that developing countries' main problem is that their assets, such as houses, do not have the legal standing to be used as collateral or to be bought and sold easily, so markets cannot work. Unfortunately, establishing property rights is a difficult political process. That is the problem of a number of African countries: how to establish property rights with an undeveloped political process.

Creating markets is not enough. The markets must be meshed with the cultural and social fabric of the society. Thus, questions of economic development inevitably involve much more than supply and demand. They involve broader questions about the cultural and social institutions in a society.

Let me give an example of cultural characteristics not conducive to development. Anyone who has traveled in developing countries knows that many of these countries operate on what they call "_____ time," where the "_____" is the name of the particular country one is in. What is meant by "_____ time" is that in that country, things get done when they get done, and it is socially inappropriate to push for things to get done at specific times. Deadlines are demeaning (many students operate on "_____ time").

As a self-actualizing mentality, "_____ time" may be high-level mental development, but in an interdependent economic setting, "_____ time" doesn't fit. Economic development requires qualities such as extreme punctuality and a strong sense of individual responsibility. People who believe their being two minutes late will make the world come to an end fit far better with a high-production country than do people who are more laid back. The need to take such cultural issues into account explains why development economics tends to be far less theoretical and far more country- and region-specific than other branches of economics.

> As a self-actualizing mentality, "_____ time" may be a high-level mental development, but in an interdependent economic setting, "_____ time" doesn't fit.

Lack of Investment

Even if a country can overcome the political, social, and institutional constraints on development, there are also economic constraints. If a country is to grow, it must somehow invest, and funds for investment must come from savings. These savings can be either brought in from abroad (as private investment or foreign government aid) or generated internally (as domestic savings). Each source of investment capital has its problems.

Investment Funded by Domestic Savings   In order to save, a person must first have enough to live on. With per capita incomes of $250 per year, poor people in developing countries don't have a whole lot left over to put into savings. Instead, you rely on your kids, if they live, to take care of you in your old age. As for the rich, the threat of political instability often makes them put their money into savings abroad, as I discussed before. For the developing country, it's as if the rich didn't save. In fact, it's even worse because when they save abroad, the rich don't even spend the money at home as do poor people, so the rich generate less in the way of short-run income multiplier effects in their home country than do the poor.

> With per capita incomes of as low as $250 per year, poor people in developing countries don't have a lot left over to put into savings.

That leaves the middle class (small as it is) as the one hope these countries have for domestic savings. For them, the problem is: Where can they put their savings? Often these countries have an underdeveloped financial sector; there's no neighborhood bank, no venture capital fund, no government-secured savings vehicle. The only savings vehicle available may be the government savings bond. But savings bonds finance the government deficit, which supports the government bureaucracy, which is limiting activities that could lead to growth. Few middle-class people invest in those government bonds. After all, what will a government bond be worth after the next revolution? Nothing!

Some governments have taxed individuals (a type of forced savings) and channeled that money back into investment. But again, politics and corruption are likely to interfere. Instead of going into legitimate productive investment, the savings—in the form of "consulting fees," outright payoffs, or "sweetheart contracts"—go to friends of those in power. Before you get up on your high horse and say, "How do the people allow that to happen?" think of the United States, where it's much easier to prevent such activities but where scandals in government spending are still uncovered with depressing regularity.

Investment Funded from Abroad   The other way to generate funds for investment is from external savings, either foreign aid or foreign investment.

Foreign Aid   The easiest way to finance development is with **foreign aid** (*funds that developed countries lend or give to developing countries*). The problem is that foreign aid

The Doha Round and Development Aid

Say you are a cotton farmer in Africa. Since your labor costs are much lower than U.S. labor costs, you figure you can compete, even though U.S. technology and capital far exceeds yours. Taking technology and labor into account, you figure you have a 20 percent cost advantage, so that even taking into account higher shipping costs, your cotton is cost competitive. Unfortunately for you, that cost advantage disappears because U.S. cotton farmers have a benefit that you don't have—they get substantial subsidies from the U.S. government, which allows them to outcompete you. It isn't only in cotton, and it isn't only in the United States that the subsidies undermine your ability to compete on the world market. Farmers get help in a large number of agricultural goods, and the European and Japanese governments also give their farmers large subsidies. African and other develop-

ing nations argue that these subsidies undermine their ability to compete, and to develop. They argue that they don't want foreign aid as much as they want a level playing field so that they can compete.

It was precisely such arguments that led the World Trade Organization to organize the Doha round of trade negotiations. It was designed to reduce tariffs and other trade barriers that developing countries place on developed countries' goods, and in return reduce subsidies and other assistance that developed countries give to their own agricultural production. These trade negotiations started in 2001 and in mid-2007 were still ongoing as political pressures in developed countries made governments unable to reduce farm subsidies that the developing countries argued were needed to create a level playing field in trade of agricultural goods.

generally comes with strings attached; funds are earmarked for specific purposes. For example, most foreign aid is military aid; helping a country prepare to fight a war isn't a good way to help it develop.

Total foreign aid from all countries comes to about $14 per person in developing countries.

As you can see in the table below, the United States gives about $23 billion (about $80 per U.S. citizen) per year in foreign aid.

Country	Development Aid 2006 (millions of U.S. dollars)	Percent of GDP
Sweden	$ 3,967	1.03%
United Kingdom	12,607	0.52
Austria	1,513	0.48
France	10,448	0.47
Germany	10,351	0.36
Canada	3,713	0.30
Japan	11,608	0.25
Italy	3,672	0.20
United States	22,739	0.17

Source: *OECD DAC Chairman's Report* (www.oecd.org).

For the 5.5 billion people in developing countries, total foreign aid from all countries comes to about $19 per person. That isn't going to finance a lot of economic development, especially when much of the money is earmarked for military purposes.

Foreign Investment   If a global or multinational company believes that a country has a motivated, cheap workforce; a stable government supportive of business; and sufficient **infrastructure investment**—*investment in the underlying structure of the economy*, such as transportation or power facilities—it has a strong incentive to invest in the country. That's a lot of ifs, and generally the poorest countries don't measure up. What they have to offer instead are raw materials that the global corporation can develop.

Countries at the upper end of the group of developing countries (such as Mexico and Brazil) may meet all these requirements, but large amounts of foreign investment often result in political problems as citizens of these countries complain about imperialist exploitation, outside control, and significant outflows of profits. Developing countries have tried to meet such complaints by insisting that foreign investment come in the form of joint development projects under local control, but that cuts down the amount that foreign firms are willing to invest.

When the infrastructure doesn't exist, as is the case in the poorest developing countries, few firms will invest in that country, no matter how cheap the labor or how stable the government. Firms require infrastructure investment such as transportation facilities, energy availability, and housing and amenities for their employees before they will consider investing in a country. And they don't want to pay to establish this infrastructure themselves.

Competition for Investment among Developing Countries   The world is made up of about 30 highly industrial countries and about 160 other countries at various stages of development. Global companies have a choice of where to locate, and often developing countries compete to get the development located in their country. In their efforts to get the development, they may offer tax rebates, free land, guarantees of labor peace, or loose regulatory environments within which firms can operate.

This competition can be keen, and can result in many of the benefits of development being transferred from the developing country to the global company and ultimately to the Western consumer, since competition from other firms will force the global company to pass on the benefits in the form of lower prices.

An example of the results of such competition can be seen in the production of chemicals. Say a company is planning to build a new plant to produce chemicals. Where does it locate? Considering the wide-ranging environmental restrictions in the United States and Western Europe, a chemical company will likely look toward a developing country that will give it loose regulation. If one country will not come through, the chemical firm will point out that it can locate elsewhere. Concern about Mexico's relatively loose environmental regulatory environment was one of the sticking points of U.S. approval of NAFTA.

Competition for global company investment often leads to the benefits of that investment being passed on to the Western consumer.

Focal Points and Takeoff   The scope of competition among developing countries can be overstated. Most companies do not consider all developing countries as potential production and investment sites. To decide to produce in a developing country requires a knowledge of that country—its legal structure, its political structure, and its infrastructure. Gaining this information involves a substantial initial investment, so most companies tend to focus on a few developing countries about which they have specific knowledge, or that they know other companies have chosen as development sites. (If company X chose it, it must meet the appropriate criteria.)

Because of this informational requirement, developing countries that have been successful in attracting investment often get further investment. Eventually they reach a stage called **economic takeoff**—*a stage when the development process becomes self-sustaining*. Other developing countries fall by the wayside. This means that economic development is not evenly spread over developing countries, but rather is concentrated in a few.

Millennium Development Goals

In 2000, leaders from around the world gathered at the United Nations and adopted the UN Millennium Declaration that set specific goals to combat poverty, hunger, disease, illiteracy, environmental degradation, and discrimination against women to be achieved within a specific time frame. The goals have come to be known as the Millennium Development Goals. They include

1. Cut extreme poverty and hunger in half by 2015.

2. Achieve universal primary education.

3. Empower women and promote equality between women and men.

4. Reduce under-five mortality by two-thirds.

5. Reduce material mortality by three-quarters.

6. Reverse the spread of disease, especially HIV/AIDS and malaria.

7. Ensure environmental sustainability.

8. Create a global partnership for development, with targets for aid, trade, and debt relief.

Support for these goals has been boosted by the endorsement of high-profile celebrities such as U2's Bono. In 2002, for example, the then-U.S. Treasury secretary Paul O'Neill and Bono generated a lot of press by traveling to Africa together to highlight the importance of development and foreign aid. Bono was instrumental in getting President George W. Bush to establish the Millennium Challenge Corporation (see www.mcc.gov), a government-owned corporation responsible for overseeing additional foreign aid to countries meeting requirements such as political and economic freedom, investments in education and health, control of corruption, and respect for civil liberties and the rule of law. As of 2006, the MCC has declared 23 countries to be eligible and 10 countries have received aid.

No one would argue about the desirability of achieving these goals. But economists have debated how to achieve those goals. Economist Jeffrey Sachs wrote a book called *The End of Poverty* where he argues that extreme poverty, defined as living on less than $1 a day, can be eliminated by 2025 by doubling foreign aid and using that aid to address the multiplicity of problems extremely poor countries

Bono and Paul O'Neill on their trip to Africa in 2002.

face, from the very simple problem of lacking mosquito nets to prevent malaria to more complicated issues of drinkable water. Sachs argues that we can eliminate extreme poverty and disease if we just try.

Not all economists agree with Sachs about what should be done about the problem. Economist William Easterly wrote a book called *The White Man's Burden* where he argues that extreme poverty is caused by a complicated interplay of politics, society, technology, geography, and economic systems; therefore, the cures are also necessarily complicated. He argues that we have doubled foreign aid in the past with no measurable result, and that Sachs' "End of Poverty program" will lead to little success. Easterly is not opposed to eradicating poverty, but he promotes a slower piecemeal approach, that will (1) allow policy makers and economists to evaluate the success of specific programs, (2) hold institutions accountable for how funds are spent, and (3) be based on a good understanding of which programs work.

So, have the UN Millennium Declaration and Sachs' "End of Poverty program" been successful? Success has been slow and not universal across countries. For example, from 1990 to 2002, the proportion of the world's population living in extreme poverty dropped from 29 to 19 percent. But most of this was in southeastern Asia and Oceania, which had already experienced economic growth. Extreme poverty fell very little in sub-Saharan Africa and Latin America.

Inappropriate Education

The right education is a necessary component of any successful development strategy. The wrong education is an enormous burden. Developing countries tend to have too much of the wrong education and too little of the right education.

Often educational systems in developing countries resemble Western educational systems. The reason is partly the colonial heritage of developing countries and partly what might be described as an emulation factor. The West defines what an educated person is, and developing countries want their citizens to be seen as educated. An educated person should be able to discuss the ideas of Vladimir Nabokov, the poetry of Lord Byron, the intricacies of chaos theory, the latest developments in fusion technology, the nuances of the modern Keynesian/Classical debate, and the dissociative properties of Andy Warhol's paintings. So saith Western scholars; so be it.

But, put bluntly, that type of education is almost irrelevant to economic growth and may be a serious detriment to growth. Basic skills—reading, writing, and arithmetic, taught widely—are likely to be more conducive to growth than is high-level education. When education doesn't match the needs of the society, the degrees—the credentials—become more important than the knowledge learned. The best jobs go to those with the highest degrees, not because the individuals holding the degrees are better able to do the job, but simply because they hold the credentials. **Credentialism,** in which *the degrees, or credentials, become more important than the knowledge learned,* serves to preserve the monopoly position of those who manage to get the degree.

If access to education is competitive, credentialism has its advantages. Even irrelevant education, as long as it is difficult, serves a screening or selection role. Those individuals who work hardest at getting an education advance and get the good jobs. Since selecting hardworking individuals is difficult, even irrelevant education serves this selection role.

But developing countries' current educational practices may be worse than irrelevant. Their educational systems often reflect Western culture, not their own cultures. The best students qualify for scholarships abroad, and their education in a different tradition makes it difficult for them to return home.

In my studies in Europe and the United States, I've come to know a large number of the best and the brightest students from developing countries. They're superb students and they do well in school. But as they near graduation, most of them face an enormously difficult choice. They can return to their home country—to material shortages, to enormous challenges for which they have little training, and to an illiterate society whose traditional values are sometimes hostile to the values these new graduates have learned. Or they can stay in the West, find jobs relevant to their training, enjoy an abundance of material goods, and associate with people to whom they've now learned to relate. Which would you choose?

The choice many of them make results in a **brain drain** (*the outflow of the best and brightest students from developing countries to developed countries*). Many of these good students don't return to the developing country. Those that do go home take jobs as government officials, expecting high salaries and material comforts far beyond what their society can afford. Instead of becoming the dynamic entrepreneurs of growth, they become impediments to growth.

There are, of course, many counter examples to the arguments presented here. Many developing countries try to design their education system to fit their culture. And many of the dynamic, selfless leaders who make it possible for the country to develop do return home. As with most issues, there are both positive and negative attributes to the way something is done. I emphasize the problems with educational systems in developing economies because the positive attributes of education are

The right education is a necessary component of any successful development strategy. The wrong education is an enormous burden.

Many good students from developing countries who study abroad don't return to the developing country.

Q-10 How could too much education cause problems for development?

generally accepted. Without education, development is impossible. The question is how that education should be structured.

Overpopulation

Two ways a country can increase per capita income are

1. Decrease the number of people in the country (without decreasing the total income in the country).
2. Increase the income (without increasing the population).

In each case, the qualifier is important, because income and population are related in complicated ways: People earn income; without people there would be no income. But often the more people there are, the less income per person there is, because the resources of the country become strained.

A country's population can never be higher than the natural resources that it has, or can import, can support. But that doesn't mean that overpopulation can't be an obstacle to development. Nature has its own ways of reducing populations that are too large: Starvation and disease are the direct opposite to development. That control system works in nature, and it would work with human societies. The problem is that we don't like it.

Thomas Carlyle gave economics the name *the dismal science* as he was verbally sparring about a number of issues with economists of his period. The name stuck with economics in large part because of the writings of Thomas Malthus, who in the early 1800s said that society's prospects are dismal because population tends to outrun the means of subsistence. (Population grows geometrically—that is, at an increasing rate; the means of subsistence grow arithmetically—that is, at a constant rate.) The view was cemented into economic thinking in the law of diminishing marginal productivity: As more and more people are added to a fixed amount of land, the output per worker gets smaller and smaller.

Through technological progress, most Western economies have avoided the fate predicted by Malthus because growth in output has exceeded growth in population. In contrast, many developing economies have not avoided the Malthusian fate because diminishing marginal productivity has exceeded technological change, and limited economic growth isn't enough to offset the increase in population. The result is a constant or falling output per person.

That doesn't mean that developing countries haven't grown economically. They have. But population growth makes per capita output growth small or negative.

Population grows for a number of reasons, including

1. As public health measures are improved, infant mortality rates and death rates for the population as a whole both decline.
2. As people earn more income, they believe they can afford to have more children.
3. In rural areas, children are useful in working the fields.

What to do? Should the government reduce the population growth rate? If it should, how can it do so? Various measures have been tried: advertising campaigns, free condoms, forced sterilization, and economic incentives. For example, in China the government has tried imposing severe economic penalties on couples who have more than one child, while providing material incentives such as a free television set to couples who agreed not to have more than one child.

China's vigorous population control campaign has had a number of effects. First, it created so much anger at the government that in rural areas the campaign was dropped. Second, it led to the killing of many female babies because, if couples were to have only

> Many developing economies have not avoided the Malthusian fate because diminishing marginal productivity has exceeded technological change.

one baby, strong cultural and economic pressures existed to ensure that the baby was a male. Third, it led to an enormous loss of privacy. Dates of women's menstrual periods were posted in factories and officials would remind them at appropriate times that they should take precautions against getting pregnant. Only a very strong government could impose such a plan.

Even successful population control programs have their problems. In Singapore a population control campaign was so successful among educated women that the government became concerned that its "population quality" was suffering. It began a selective campaign to encourage college-educated women to have children. They issued "love tips" to men (since some college-educated women complained that their male companions were nerds and had no idea how to be romantic) and offered special monetary bonuses to college-educated women who gave birth to children. As you might imagine, the campaign provoked a backlash, and it was eventually dropped by the government.

Individuals differ substantially in their assessment of the morality of these programs, but even if one believes that population control is an appropriate government concern, it does not seem that such programs will be successful, by themselves, in limiting population growth.

Even successful population control programs have their problems.

Health and Disease

Before a country can hope to develop, it must have a reasonably healthy population. If you are sick, it's hard to think, to work, or even to do standard daily tasks like growing food. In many developing countries, large portions of the population are undernourished or sick. Disease hits young children particularly hard. Millions of children die from pneumonia, diarrhea, malaria, and measles, all of which, because of the children's general malnutrition, are often aggravated by intestinal worms. Older individuals suffer from HIV/AIDS, tuberculosis, and malaria. For example, more than 30 million people now have AIDS in Africa, and about one-third of today's 15-year-olds in Africa will likely die of AIDS.

Web Note 19.3
Fighting Disease

These diseases make it difficult for people to work, or even to take care of their kids, and create a vicious cycle. You're sick, you can't work, and so you and your family become victims of malnutrition. You get even more prone to disease, and less able to work and contribute to development. Thus, maintaining public health is more than a humanitarian issue; it is a key development issue.

What to do? Most of these diseases can be alleviated with drugs, but developing the infrastructure to provide these drugs is often difficult or impossible, even when the money for the drugs becomes available. Thus, one must not only get the drugs but also create the cultural and physical environment in which those drugs can be effective. Drug companies have little incentive to work on developing low-cost medicines to treat diseases in developing countries because the people there don't have much money to pay for them, so the return would be low. Instead, pharmaceutical companies focus their research on providing high-priced drugs to be sold in rich countries. Drug companies created anti-AIDS drugs, but their focus was on markets in wealthy developed countries. Only later, and under significant social and political pressure, did they start offering treatment for AIDS at low cost to developing countries.

Mission Impossible

At this point in my course, I inevitably throw my hands up and admit that I don't know what makes it possible for a country to develop. Nor, judging from what I have read, do the development experts. The good ones (that is, the ones I agree with) admit that they don't know; others (that is, the ones I don't agree with) simply don't know that they don't know.

My gut feeling is that there are no definitive general answers that apply to all developing countries. The appropriate answer varies with each country and each situation. Each

Economic development is a complicated problem because it is entwined with cultural and social issues.

proposed solution to the development problem has a right time and a right place. Only by having a complete sense of a country, its history, and its cultural, social, and political norms can one decide whether it's the right time and place for this or that policy.

Summary

- While policies in developed countries focus on stability, developing countries struggle to provide basic needs.

- Development refers to an increase in productive capacity and output brought about by a change in underlying institutions, while growth refers to an increase in output brought about by an increase in inputs.

- Many developing economies have serious political problems that make it impossible for government to take an active, positive role in the economy.

- Many developing countries have dual economies—one a traditional, nonmarket economy and the other an internationalized market economy.

- Many developing countries need a change in the entire atmosphere within which the government and economy relate. They need regime changes rather than policy changes.

- Although developing countries know that printing too much money leads to inflation, their choices are limited. Some central banks lack independence and for others the only alternative is the collapse of government.

- Most monetary policies in developing countries focus on the international sector and are continually dealing with the balance of payments constraint.

- Most developing countries have some type of limited convertibility to limit the outflow of saving.

- Macro policies in developing countries are more concerned with institutional policies and regime changes than are macro policies in developed countries.

- Seven obstacles to economic development are political instability, corruption, lack of appropriate institutions, lack of investment, inappropriate education, overpopulation, and poor health and disease.

Key Terms

balance of payments
   constraint (461)
basic needs (455)
brain drain (469)
conditionality (461)

convertibility on the
   current account (460)
credentialism (469)
dual economy (456)
economic takeoff (467)

foreign aid (465)
full convertibility (460)
infrastructure
   investment (467)
limited capital account
   convertibility (460)

policy change (457)
purchasing power
   parity (PPP) (453)
regime change (457)
restructuring (454)

Questions for Thought and Review

1. If you suddenly found yourself living as a poor person in a developing country, what are some things that you now do that you would no longer be able to do? What new things would you have to do? LO1

2. What is wrong with saying that people in developing countries are worse off than people in the United States? LO1

3. Does the fact that suicide rates are lower in developing countries than in the United States imply that Americans would be better off living in a developing country? Why? LO1

4. How does the exchange rate method of comparing incomes differ from the purchasing power method of comparing incomes? LO1

5. What is the difference between development and growth?   LO2

6. What are three ways in which the institutions of developing countries differ from those in developed countries?   LO3

7. Why do governments in developing countries often seem more arbitrary and oppressive than governments in developed countries?   LO3

8. Why might an economist favor activist policies in developed countries and laissez-faire policies in developing countries?   LO3

9. What is meant by "the dual economy"?   LO4

10. How does a regime change differ from a policy change?   LO5

11. What is the inflation tax?   LO6

12. Why doesn't the fact that the "inflation solution" is only a temporary solution stop many developing countries from using it?   LO6

13. What is conditionality, and how does it relate to the balance of payments constraint?   LO7

14. Why are investment and savings so low in developing countries?   LO8

15. If developing countries are so unstable and offer such a risky environment for investment, why do foreigners invest any money in them at all?   LO8

16. If you were a foreign investor thinking of making an investment in a developing country, what are some things that you would be concerned about?   LO8

17. Should developing countries send their students abroad for an education?   LO8

18. How does corruption limit investment and economic growth?   LO8

19. Should a country control the size and makeup of its population? Why?   LO8

20. A United Nations study reported that more than 300 million low-income women owned businesses in developing countries, but only 5 million had access to credit other than from money lenders. How might the UN alleviate this obstacle to growth? What other obstacles might exist for women entrepreneurs in developing nations? (Difficult)   LO8

Problems and Exercises

21. Interview a foreign student in your class or school. Ask about each of the seven obstacles to economic development and how his or her country is trying to overcome them.   LO2

22. Spend one day living like someone in a developing country. Eat almost nothing and work lifting stones for 10 hours. Then, that same evening, study this chapter and contemplate the bootstrap strategy of development.   LO1

23. In the 1990s, Germany passed a law requiring businesses to take back and recycle all forms of packaging. A large group of businesses formed a company to collect and recycle these packages. Its costs are 4.5 cents per pound for glass, 9.5 cents per pound for paper, and 74 cents per pound for plastic. This accounts for a recycling cost of about $100 per ton for glass and $2,000 per ton for plastic, and the average recycling cost is $500 per ton. A developing country has offered to create a giant landfill and accept Germany's waste at a cost of $400 per ton, which includes $50 per ton sorting and transport costs and a $350-per-ton fee to be paid to the developing country.
    a. Should Germany accept this proposal?
    b. Will the proposal benefit the developing country?
    c. What alternative or modification to the proposal might you suggest?   LO1, LO2, LO3

24. Choose any developing country and answer the following questions about it:
    a. What is its level of per capita income?
    b. What is its growth potential?
    c. What is the exchange rate of its currency in relation to the U.S. dollar?
    d. What policy suggestions might you make to the country?   LO1, LO2, LO3

25. It has been argued that development economics has no general theory; it is instead the application of common sense to real-world problems.
    a. Do you agree or disagree with that statement? Why?
    b. Why do you think this argument about the lack of generality of theories is made for developing countries more than it is made for developed countries?   LO2

26. Say that you have been hired to design an education system for a developing country.
    a. What skills would you want it to emphasize?
    b. How might it differ from an ideal educational system here in the United States?
    c. How much of the U.S. educational system involves credentialism, and how much involves the learning of relevant skills?   LO8

27. According to the Peruvian economist Hernando de Soto, in the 1980s, getting a deed for property in Peru involved 207 bureaucratic steps, took 43 months, and cost 10 weeks' worth of the official minimum wage.
    a. What problems would that create for economic development?
    b. What problems would the lack of titling create for public utilities?   LO8

Questions from Alternative Perspectives

1. Christians are called to be Christ-like, a "light to lighten the nations" (Luke 2:32).
   a. In light of the basic biblical norms of justice, righteousness, and stewardship, how should a nation decide how much development aid to provide developing countries?
   b. Is it within Christian norms to make that aid conditional? (Hint: Consider the biblical concept of forgiveness, which includes repentance and the restoration of right relationships.) (Religious)

2. When thinking about development, it is often presented as an analytic exercise, but development policies have very real consequences.
   a. Who is responsible for economies that fail to develop?
   b. Who will primarily suffer the consequences from a failure at economic development?
   c. If your answers to *a* and *b* differ, how might that difference affect the development policies chosen? How does this difference possibly affect the choice of development policies? (Institutionalist)

3. In an earlier chapter, the book described the Grameen bank as an example of a successful micro credit reform.
   a. Why do many of the micro credit policies focus on women rather than men?
   b. Does your answer in *a* suggest anything about other policies that might help developing countries develop? (Feminist)

4. Islam considers the interest on loans to be an instrument of oppression of the poor by the wealthy. That is why interest is banned by the Qur'an. In 2003, member countries of the Islamic Development Bank owed $883 billion in external debt and paid $14 billion in interest.
   a. How could loans be an instrument of oppression?
   b. How could loans be an instrument of development?
   c. The Islamic Development Bank makes loans that remain within Islamic law. What do you suppose are the conditions for those loans? (You might want to look at its Web site at www.isdb.org for help.) (Religious)

5. The brief for globalization goes something like this. Countries that trade a lot grow quickly and poverty rates decline in rapidly growing countries. Therefore, globalization promotes rapid growth and alleviates poverty and is far superior to economic isolation. Radicals believe that the globalization debate is not about economic isolation vs. integration into the world economy; rather, the real debate is about what policies allow a developing economy to successfully engage with the world economy. The advocates' case tells us about a country's degree of engagement with the world economy but not the manner of that engagement. From the radical perspective, knowing that international trade and faster economic growth rates are positively correlated hardly constitutes an endorsement of the neo-liberal policy of lower barriers for trade and the movement of international capital.
   a. How should a developing economy engage with global economy: through free trade and financial liberalization policies?
   b. Would the strategies promoted by the opponents of globalization—more national control and limits on the movement of foreign and domestic capital—be better polices for engaging with the world economy? (Radical)

Web Questions

1. Go to the World Bank's student challenge, Build It!, at www.worldbank.org/challenge to answer the following questions.
   a. What three social challenges face developing countries?
   b. What three economic challenges face developing countries?
   c. What three environmental challenges face developing countries?
   d. What additional challenges to promote sustainable development could have been listed?

2. The Bretton Woods Project is an IMF and World Bank watchdog. Go to its home page at www.brettonwoodsproject.org to answer the following questions:
   a. What is the Bretton Woods Project?
   b. Under the tab "Topics," select "World Bank/IMF roles" to read criticisms of the IMF World Bank. Provide a brief summary of one criticism.

Answers to Margin Questions

1. Given market societies' expansionary tendencies, the cultures in economically poor countries that do not grow would simply be overrun and destroyed by cultures of market societies. This means that the choice is not between development and preservation of existing culture; rather, the choice is between economic development with its attendant wrenching cultural transitions and continued poverty with exploitation by developed countries and its attendant wrenching cultural transitions. *(453)*

2. Restructuring in developed countries suggests that the distinction between growth and development can be overdone since it is an example of developed countries' growth occurring through changing institutions—development—rather than through increasing inputs—growth. *(454)*

3. *Dual economy* refers to a developing country's tendency to have two economies that have little interaction: one a traditional nonmarket economy and the other an internationally oriented modern market economy. *(456)*

4. While everyone agrees that inflation in developing countries is caused by the central bank issuing too much money, the real policy question concerns what the political consequences of not issuing too much money may be. Sometimes the cure for inflation can be worse than the problem. *(459)*

5. In an inflation, any issuers of fixed-interest-rate debt denominated in the domestic currency gain from the holders of these debts. *(459)*

6. Full convertibility includes convertibility on the capital account as well as on the current account. It means that people are allowed to buy foreign financial assets—to save abroad. Convertibility on the current account means that people are allowed to buy foreign currencies to buy foreign goods, but not necessarily to buy foreign financial assets. *(460)*

7. In order for a market to operate, a set of rules—any rules—is needed. Lack of stability undermines the existence of any rules and leads to a failure of cooperation among people. *(463)*

8. It depends, but the answer is probably false. Often the wealthy elite in a developing country fear that if they invest in their country, their money will be taken away, so they often invest out of their country—meaning that the benefits of their savings go to other countries, not to the investors' own developing country. *(463)*

9. The more it costs to undertake economic activities, the fewer economic activities individuals undertake. *(464)*

10. Education is absolutely necessary for development, but it is most helpful if it is the right type of education—focusing on basic skills such as reading, writing, and arithmetic. When education focuses on abstract issues, determined by different cultures and having little relevance to the country's problems, "too much" education can lead to a brain drain and a diversion of people's talent away from the central development issues. *(469)*

A

Adaptive Expectations Expectations based in some way on the past.

Aggregate Demand (AD) Curve A curve that shows how a change in the price level will change aggregate expenditures on all goods and services in an economy.

Aggregate Demand Management Government's attempt to control the aggregate level of spending in the economy.

Aggregate Expenditures The total amount of spending on final goods and services in the economy; consumption (spending by consumers), investment (spending by business), spending by government, and net foreign spending on U.S. goods (the difference between U.S. exports and U.S. imports).

Aggregate Production (AP) The total amount of goods and services produced in every industry in an economy.

Annuity Rule The present value of any annuity is the annual income it yields divided by the interest rate.

Art of Economics The application of the knowledge learned in positive economics to the achievement of the goals one has determined in normative economics.

Asset Management How a bank handles its loans and other assets.

Automatic Stabilizer Any government program or policy that will counteract the business cycle without any new government action.

Autonomous Expenditures Expenditures that do not systematically vary with income.

B

Balance of Merchandise Trade The difference between the value of goods exported and the value of goods imported.

Balance of Payments A country's record of all transactions between its residents and the residents of all foreign nations.

Balance of Payments Constraint Limitations on expansionary domestic macroeconomic policy due to a shortage of international reserves.

Balance of Trade The difference between the value of the goods and services a country imports and the value of the goods and services it exports.

Bank A financial institution whose primary function is accepting deposits for, and lending money to, individuals and firms.

Bar Graph A graph where the area under each point is filled in to look like a bar.

Basic Needs Adequate food, clothing, and shelter.

Bond A promise to pay a certain amount of money plus interest in the future.

Brain Drain The outflow of the best and brightest students from developing countries to developed countries.

Bretton Woods System An agreement about fixed exchange rates that governed international financial relationships from the period after the end of World War II until 1971.

Business A private producing unit in our society.

Business Cycle The upward or downward movement of economic activity, or real GDP, that occurs around the growth trend.

C

Capitalism An economic system based on the market in which the ownership of the means of production resides with a small group of individuals called capitalists.

Cash Flow Accounting System An accounting system entering expenses and revenues only when cash is received or paid out.

Central Bank A type of bankers' bank whose financial obligations underlie an economy's money supply.

Classical Growth Model A model of growth that focuses on the role of capital accumulation in the growth process.

Classicals Macroeconomists who generally favor laissez-faire or nonactivist policies.

Comparative Advantage The ability to be better suited to the production of one good than to the production of another good.

Competitiveness The ability of a country to sell its goods to other countries.

Conditionality The making of loans that are subject to specific conditions.

Constant Returns to Scale A situation in which long-run average total costs do not change with an increase in output. Also: Output will rise by the same proportionate increase as all inputs.

Consumer Price Index (CPI) A measure of prices of a fixed basket of consumer goods, weighted according to each component's share of an average consumer's expenditures.

Consumer Sovereignty The principle that the consumer's wishes determine what's produced.

Consumption Spending by households on goods and services.

Contractionary Monetary Policy Monetary policy that decreases the money supply and increases interest rates.

Contractual Intermediary A financial institution that holds and stores individuals' financial assets.

Convergence Hypothesis The hypothesis that per capita income in countries with similar institutional structures will grow toward the same level of income per person.

Convertibility on the Current Account An exchange rate system that allows people to exchange currencies freely to buy goods and services, but not to buy assets in other countries.

Coordinate System A two-dimensional space in which one point represents two numbers.

Corporation A business that is treated as a person, legally owned by its stockholders. Its stockholders are not liable for the actions of the corporate "person."

Cost-Push Inflation Inflation that occurs when the economy is below potential output.

Countercyclical Fiscal Policy Fiscal policy in which the government offsets any change in aggregate expenditures that would create a business cycle.

Credentialism When the academic degrees, or credentials, become more important than the knowledge learned.

Crowding Out The offsetting of a change in government expenditures by a change in private expenditures in the opposite direction.

Currency Stabilization Buying and selling of a currency by the government to offset temporary fluctuations in supply and demand for currencies.

Currency Support Buying of a currency by a government to maintain its value at above its long-run equilibrium value.

Current Account The part of the balance of payments account in which all short-term flows of payments are listed.

Cyclical Unemployment Unemployment resulting from fluctuations in economic activity.

D

Debt Accumulated deficits minus accumulated surpluses.

Debt Service The interest rate on debt times the total debt.

Decreasing Returns to Scale A situation when output rises by a smaller proportionate increase than all inputs.

Deficit A shortfall of revenues under payments.

Deflation A continuous fall of the price level.

Demand A schedule of quantities of a good that will be bought per unit of time at various prices, other things constant.

Demand Curve The graphic representation of the relationship between price and quantity demanded.

Demand-Pull Inflation Inflation that occurs when the economy is at or above potential output.

Demerit Good or Activity Good or activity that government believes is bad for people even though they choose to use the good or engage in the activity.

Depository Institution A financial institution whose primary financial liability is deposits in checking or savings accounts.

Depreciation A measure of the decline in value of an asset that occurs over time through use. Also: A decrease in the value of a currency.

Depression A large recession.

Direct Relationship A relationship in which when one variable goes up, the other goes up too.

Discount Rate The rate of interest the Fed charges for loans it makes to banks.

Division of Labor The splitting up of a task to allow for specialization of production.

Dual Economy The existence of two sectors: a traditional sector and an internationally oriented modern market sector.

E

E-commerce Buying and selling over the Internet.

Economic Decision Rule If the marginal benefits of doing something exceed the marginal costs, do it. If the marginal costs of doing something exceed the marginal benefits, don't do it.

Economic Force The necessary reaction to scarcity.

Economic Model A framework that places the generalized insights of a theory in a more specific contextual setting.

Economic Policy An action (or inaction) taken by government to influence economic actions.

Economic Principle A commonly held economic insight stated as a law or general assumption.

Economic Takeoff A stage when the development process becomes self-sustaining.

Economics The study of how human beings coordinate their wants and desires, given the decision-making mechanisms, social customs, and political realities of the society.

Economies of Scale Situation when long-run average total costs decrease as output increases.

Efficiency Achieving a goal as cheaply as possible. Also: using as few inputs as possible.

Embargo A total restriction on the import or export of a good.

Employment–Population Ratio The number of people who are working as a percentage of people available to work.

Entrepreneurship The ability to organize and get something done. Also: Labor services that involve high degrees of organizational skills, concern, oversight responsibility, and creativity.

Equation of Exchange An equation stating that the quantity of money times the velocity of money equals the price level times the quantity of real goods sold.

Equilibrium A concept in which opposing dynamic forces cancel each other out.

Equilibrium Income　The level of income toward which the economy gravitates in the short run.

Equilibrium Price　The price toward which the invisible hand drives the market.

Equilibrium Quantity　The amount bought and sold at the equilibrium price.

Euro　The currency used by the 12 members of the European Union.

Excess Demand　Situation when quantity demanded is greater than quantity supplied.

Excess Reserves　Reserves held by banks in excess of what banks are required to hold.

Excess Supply　Situation when quantity supplied is greater than quantity demanded.

Exchange Rate　The price of one country's currency in terms of another currency.

Excise Tax　A tax that is levied on a specific good.

Expansion　An upturn that lasts for at least two consecutive quarters of a year.

Expansionary Monetary Policy　Monetary policy that increases the money supply and decreases the interest rate.

Expected Inflation　Inflation people expect to occur.

Expenditures Multiplier　A number that tells how much income will change in response to a change in autonomous expenditures.

External Debt　Government debt owed to individuals in foreign countries.

Externality　An effect of a decision on a third party not taken into account by the decision maker.

Extrapolative Expectations　Expectations that a trend will continue.

F

Fallacy of Composition　The false assumption that what is true for a part will also be true for the whole.

Fed Funds　Loans of excess reserves banks make to one another.

Federal Funds Market　The market in which banks lend and borrow reserves.

Federal Funds Rate　The interest rate banks charge one another for Fed funds.

Federal Open Market Committee (FOMC)　The Fed's chief body that decides monetary policy.

Federal Reserve Bank (the Fed)　The U.S. central bank whose liabilities (Federal Reserve notes) serve as cash in the United States.

Feudalism　An economic system in which traditions rule.

Final Output　Goods and services purchased for their final use.

Financial and Capital Account　The part of the balance of payments account in which all long-term flows of payments are listed.

Financial Assets　Assets such as stocks or bonds, whose benefit to the owner depends on the issuer of the asset meeting certain obligations.

Financial Institution　A business whose primary activity is buying, selling, or holding financial assets.

Financial Liabilities　Liabilities incurred by the issuer of a financial asset to stand behind the issued asset.

Fine-Tuning　Fiscal policy designed to keep the economy always at its target or potential level of income.

Fiscal Policy　The deliberate change in either government spending or taxes to stimulate or slow down the economy. Also, the changing of taxes and spending to affect the level of output in the economy.

Fixed Exchange Rate　When the government chooses a particular exchange rate and offers to buy and sell its currency at that price.

Flexible Exchange Rate　When the government does not enter into foreign exchange markets at all, but leaves the determination of exchange rates totally up to market forces.

Foreign Aid　Funds that developed countries lend or give to developing countries.

Forex Market　The foreign exchange market.

Free Rider　A person who participates in something for free because others have paid for it.

Free Trade Association　A group of countries that have reduced or eliminated trade barriers among themselves.

Frictional Unemployment　Unemployment caused by people entering the job market and people quitting a job just long enough to look for and find another one.

Full Convertibility　An exchange rate system in which individuals may change dollars into any currency they want for whatever legal purpose they want.

Functional Finance　A theoretical proposition that governments should make spending and taxing decisions on the basis of their effect on the economy, not on the basis of some moralistic principle that budgets should be balanced.

G

GDP Deflator　An index of the price level of aggregate output, or the average price of the components of GDP, relative to a base year.

General Agreement on Tariffs and Trade (GATT)　A regular international conference to reduce trade barriers held from 1947 to 1995. It has been replaced by the World Trade Organization (WTO).

Global Corporation　Corporation with substantial operations on both the production and sales sides in more than one country.

Globalization　The integration of world economies.

Gold Specie Flow Mechanism　The long-run adjustment mechanism that maintained the gold standard.

Gold Standard   The system of fixed exchange rates in which the value of currencies was fixed relative to the value of gold and gold was used as the primary reserve asset.

Government Failure   A situation in which the government intervention in the market to improve market failure actually makes the situation worse.

Government Spending   Goods and services that government buys.

Graph   A picture of points in a coordinate system in which points denote relationships between numbers.

Gross Domestic Product (GDP)   The total market value of all final goods and services produced in an economy in a one-year period.

Gross National Product (GNP)   The aggregate final output of citizens and businesses of an economy in a one-year period.

H

Households   Groups of individuals living together and making joint decisions.

Human Capital   The skills that are embodied in workers through experience, education, and on-the-job training, or, more simply, people's knowledge.

Hyperinflation   Inflation that hits triple digits—100 percent or more per year.

I–J

Increasing Returns to Scale   A situation when output rises by a greater proportionate increase than all inputs.

Induced Expenditures   Expenditures that change as income changes.

Industrial Revolution   A time when technology and machines rapidly modernized industrial production and mass-produced goods replaced handmade goods.

Inefficiency   Getting less output from inputs that, if devoted to some other activity, would produce more output.

Inefficient   Achieving a goal in a more costly manner than necessary.

Infant Industry Argument   The argument that with initial protection, an industry will be able to become competitive.

Inflation   A continual rise in the price level.

Inflation Tax   An implicit tax on the holders of cash and the holders of any obligations specified in nominal terms.

Inflationary Gap   A difference between equilibrium income and potential income when equilibrium income exceeds potential income.

Infrastructure Investment   Investment in the underlying structure of the economy.

Inherent Comparative Advantage   Comparative advantage that is based on factors that are relatively unchangeable.

Input   What is put into a production process to achieve an output.

Insider/Outsider Model   An institutionalist story of inflation where insiders bid up wages and outsiders are unemployed.

Institutions   The formal and informal rules that constrain human behavior.

Interest Rate   The price paid for the use of a financial asset.

Interest Rate Effect   The effect that a lower price level has on investment expenditures through the effect that a change in the price level has on interest rates.

Intermediate Products   Products used as inputs in the production of some other product.

Internal Debt   Government debt owed to other governmental agencies or to its own citizens.

International Effect   As the price level falls (assuming the exchange rate does not change), net exports will rise.

Interpolation Assumption   The assumption that the relationship between variables is the same between points as it is at the points.

Inverse Relationship   A relationship between two variables in which when one goes up, the other goes down.

Inverted Yield Curve   A yield curve in which the short-term rate is higher than the long-term rate.

Investment   Spending for the purpose of additional production.

Invisible Hand   The price mechanism; the rise and fall of prices that guides our actions in a market.

Invisible Hand Theory   A market economy, through the price mechanism, will tend to allocate resources efficiently.

K

Keynesians   Macroeconomists who generally favor activist government policy.

L

Labor Force   Those people in an economy who are willing and able to work.

Labor Force Participation Rate   The percentage of the total population at least 16 years old who either work or are actively looking for work.

Laissez-Faire   An economic policy of leaving coordination of individuals' actions to the market.

Law of Demand   Quantity demanded rises as price falls, other things constant. Also can be stated as: Quantity demanded falls as price rises, other things constant.

Law of Diminishing Marginal Productivity   As more and more of a variable input are added to an existing fixed input, eventually the additional output one gets from that additional input is going to fall. Also, increasing one input, keeping all others constant, will lead to smaller and smaller gains in output.

Law of One Price The wages of workers in one country will not differ significantly from the wages of (equal) workers in another institutionally similar country.

Law of Supply Quantity supplied rises as price rises, other things constant. Also can be stated as: Quantity supplied falls as price falls, other things constant.

Learning by Doing As we do something, we learn what works and what doesn't, and over time we become more proficient at it. Also: To improve the methods of production through experience.

Liability Management How a bank attracts deposits and what it pays for them.

Limited Capital Account Convertibility An exchange rate system that allows full current account convertibility and partial capital account convertibility.

Limited Liability The liability of a stockholder (owner) in a corporation; it is limited to the amount the stockholder has invested in the company.

Line Graph A graph where the data are connected by a continuous line.

Linear Curve A curve that is drawn as a straight line.

Long-Run Aggregate Supply (LAS) Curve A curve that shows the long-run relationship between output and the price level.

Long-Run Phillips Curve A vertical curve at the unemployment rate consistent with potential output. (It shows the trade-off [or complete lack thereof] when expectations of inflation equal actual inflation.)

M

M_1 Currency in the hands of the public, checking account balances, and traveler's checks.

M_2 M1 plus savings deposits, small-denomination time deposits, and money market mutual fund shares, along with some esoteric financial instruments.

Macroeconomic Externality An externality that affects the levels of unemployment, inflation, or growth in the economy as a whole.

Macroeconomics The study of the economy as a whole, which includes inflation, unemployment, business cycles, and growth.

Marginal Benefit Additional benefit above the benefits already derived.

Marginal Cost Additional cost over and above the costs already incurred.

Marginal Propensity to Expend (*mpe*) The ratio of the change in aggregate expenditures to a change in income.

Market Demand Curve The horizontal sum of all individual demand curves.

Market Economy An economic system based on private property and the market in which, in principle, individuals decide how, what, and for whom to produce.

Market Failure A situation in which the invisible hand pushes in such a way that individual decisions do not lead to socially desirable outcomes.

Market Force An economic force that is given relatively free rein by society to work through the market.

Market Supply Curve The horizontal sum of all individual supply curves. Also: Horizontal sum of all the firms' marginal cost curves, taking account of any changes in input prices that might occur.

Mercantilism An economic system in which government determines the what, how, and for whom decisions by doling out the rights to undertake certain economic activities.

Merit Good or Activity A good or activity that government believes is good for you, even though you may not choose to consume the good or engage in the activity.

Microeconomics The study of individual choice, and how that choice is influenced by economic forces.

Minimum Wage Law A law specifying the lowest wage a firm can legally pay an employee.

Monetary Base Vault cash, deposits at the Fed, plus currency in circulation.

Monetary Policy A policy of influencing the economy through changes in the banking system's reserves that influence the money supply and credit availability in the economy.

Monetary Regime A predetermined statement of the policy that will be followed in various situations.

Money A highly liquid financial asset that's generally accepted in exchange for other goods, is used as a reference in valuing other goods, and can be stored as wealth.

Money Multiplier $(1 + c)/(r + c)$, where r is the percentage of deposits banks hold in reserve and c is the ratio of money people hold in currency to the money they hold as deposits.

Monopoly Power The ability of individuals or firms currently in business to prevent other individuals or firms from entering the same kind of business.

Mortgage A special name for a secured loan on real estate.

Most-Favored Nation A country that will be charged as low a tariff on its exports as any other country.

Movement along a Demand Curve The graphical representation of the effect of a change in price on the quantity demanded.

Movement along a Supply Curve The graphical representation of the effect of a change in price on the quantity supplied.

Multiplier Effect The amplification of initial changes in expenditures.

Multiplier Equation An equation that tells us that income equals the multiplier times autonomous expenditures.

N

Net Domestic Product (NDP) The sum of consumption expenditures, government expenditures, net exports, and investment less depreciation. That is, GDP less depreciation.

Net Exports Spending on goods and services produced in the United States that foreigners buy (exports) minus goods and services produced abroad that U.S. citizens buy (imports).

Net Foreign Factor Income Income from foreign domestic factor sources minus foreign factor income earned domestically.

Net Investment Gross investment less depreciation.

New Classical Macroeconomics A theoretical approach to macroeconomics that revived many pre-Keynesian theoretical ideas of the macro economy.

New Growth Theory A theory that emphasizes the role of technology rather than capital in the growth process.

Nominal Deficit The deficit determined by looking at the difference between expenditures and receipts.

Nominal GDP GDP calculated at existing prices.

Nominal Interest Rate The interest rate you actually see and pay when borrowing, or receive when lending.

Nominal Output The total amount of goods and services measured at current prices.

Nonlinear Curve A curve that is drawn as a curved line.

Normative Economics The study of what the goals of the economy should be.

O

Official Reserves Government holdings of foreign currencies.

Okun's Rule of Thumb (sometimes called Okun's Law) A 1 percentage-point change in the unemployment rate will be associated with a 2 percent change in output in the opposite direction.

Open Market Operations The Fed's buying and selling of government securities.

Opportunity Cost The benefit you might have gained from choosing the next-best alternative.

Output A result of a productive activity.

Outsourcing The relocation of production once done in the United States to foreign countries.

P

Partially Flexible Exchange Rate When the government sometimes buys or sells currencies to influence the exchange rate, while at other times the government simply accepts the exchange rate determined by supply and demand forces, that is, letting private market forces operate.

Partnership A business with two or more owners.

Passive Deficit The part of the deficit that exists because the economy is operating below its potential level of output.

Patent The legal protection of a technical innovation that gives the person holding it sole right to use that innovation. (Note: A patent is good for only a limited time.)

Pay-as-You-Go System A system in which payments to current beneficiaries are funded through current payroll taxes.

Per Capita Growth Producing more goods and services per person.

Per Capita Real Output Real GDP divided by the total population.

Permanent Income Hypothesis A proposition that expenditures are determined by permanent or lifetime income.

Personal Consumption Expenditure (PCE) Deflator A measure of prices of goods that consumers buy that allows yearly changes in the basket of goods that reflect actual consumer purchasing habits.

Phillips Curve A representation of the relationship between inflation and unemployment. (Note: There is both a short-run and a long-run relationship.)

Pie Chart A circle divided into "pie pieces," where the undivided pie represents the total amount and the pie pieces reflect the percentage of the whole pie that the various components make up.

Policy Change A change in one aspect of government's actions, such as monetary policy or fiscal policy.

Policy Coordination The integration of a country's policies to take account of their global effects.

Positive Economics The study of what is, and how the economy works.

Positive Externality The positive effect of a decision on others not taken into account by the decision maker. Also, when the effects of a decision not taken into account by the decision maker are beneficial to others.

Potential Income The level of income that the economy technically is capable of producing without generating accelerating inflation.

Potential Output Output that would materialize at the target rate of unemployment and the target rate of capacity utilization. Also, the highest amount of output an economy can produce from existing production processes and resources.

Precautionary Motive Holding money for unexpected expenses and impulse buying.

Present Value A method of translating a flow of future income or savings into its current worth.

Price Ceiling A government-imposed limit on how high a price can be charged. In other words, a government-set price below the market equilibrium price.

Price Floor A government-imposed limit on how low a price can be charged. In other words, a government-set price above equilibrium price.

Price Index A number set at 100 in the base year that summarizes what happens to a weighted composite of prices of a selection of goods (often called a market basket of goods) over time.

Principle of Increasing Marginal Opportunity Cost In order to get more of something, one must give up ever-increasing quantities of something else.

Private Good A good that, when consumed by one individual, cannot be consumed by another individual.

Private Property Right Control a private individual or firm has over an asset.

Procyclical Fiscal Policy Changes in government spending and taxes that increase the cyclical fluctuations in the economy instead of reducing them.

Producer Price Index (PPI) An index of prices that measures average change in the selling prices received by domestic producers of goods and services over time.

Production Function The relationship between the inputs (factors of production) and outputs.

Production Possibility Curve A curve measuring the maximum combination of outputs that can be obtained from a given number of inputs.

Production Possibility Table A table that lists a choice's opportunity costs by summarizing what alternative outputs can be achieved with given inputs.

Productive Efficiency Achieving as much output as possible from a given amount of inputs or resources.

Productivity Output per unit of input.

Profit What's left over from total revenues after all the appropriate costs have been subtracted. Also, a return on entrepreneurial activity and risk taking.

Public Finance Government's taxing and spending policies.

Public Good A good that if supplied to one person must be supplied to all and whose consumption by one individual does not prevent its consumption by another individual. That is, a good that is nonexclusive and nonrival.

Purchasing Power Parity (PPP) A method of calculating exchange rates that attempts to value currencies at rates such that each currency will buy an equal basket of goods. Also, a method of comparing income by looking at the domestic purchasing power in different countries.

Q

Quantity-Adjusting Markets Markets in which firms respond to changes in demand primarily by changing production instead of changing their prices.

Quantity Demanded A specific amount that will be demanded per unit of time at a specific price, other things constant, other thangs constant.

Quantity Supplied A specific amount that will be supplied at a specific price, other things constant.

Quantity Theory of Money A theory that the price level varies in response to changes in the quantity of money.

Quota Quantity limit placed on imports.

R

Rational Expectations Expectations that the economists' model predicts. Also: Forward-looking expectations that use available information.

Real-Business-Cycle Theory A theory that fluctuations in the economy reflect real phenomena—simultaneous shifts in supply and demand, not simply supply responses to demand shifts.

Real Deficit The nominal deficit adjusted for inflation.

Real Exchange Rate The nominal exchange rate adjusted for differential inflation or differential changes in the price level.

Real Gross Domestic Product (real GDP) The market value of final goods and services produced in an economy, stated in the prices of a given year. Also: Nominal GDP adjusted for inflation.

Real Interest Rate Nominal interest rate adjusted for expected inflation.

Real Output The total amount of goods and services produced, adjusted for price-level changes.

Recession A decline in real output that persists for more than two consecutive quarters of a year.

Recessionary Gap The amount by which equilibrium output is below potential output.

Regime Change A change in the entire atmosphere within which the government and the economy interrelate.

Regulatory Trade Restrictions Government-imposed procedural rules that limit imports.

Rent Control A price ceiling on rents, set by government.

Reserve Ratio The ratio of reserves to total deposits.

Reserve Requirement The percentage the Federal Reserve System sets as the minimum amount of reserves a bank must have.

Reserves Currency and deposits a bank keeps on hand or at the Fed or central bank, enough to manage the normal cash inflows and outflows.

Restructuring Changing the underlying economic institutions.

Ricardian Equivalence Theory The theoretical proposition that deficits do not affect the level of output in the economy because individuals increase their savings to account for expected future tax payments to repay the deficit.

Rule of 72 The number of years it takes for a certain amount to double in value is equal to 72 divided by its annual rate of interest.

S

Say's Law A law that states that supply creates its own demand.

Scarcity The goods available are too few to satisfy individuals' desires.

Shift in Demand The graphical representation of the effect of anything other than price on demand.

Shift in Supply The graphical representation of the effect of a change in a factor other than price on supply.

Short-Run Aggregate Supply (SAS) Curve A curve that specifies how a shift in the aggregate demand curve affects the price level and real output in the short run, other things constant.

Short-Run Phillips Curve A downward-sloping curve showing the relationship between inflation and unemployment when expectations of inflation are constant.

Simple Money Multiplier The measure of the amount of money ultimately created per dollar deposited in the banking system, when people hold no currency.

Slope The change in the value on the vertical axis divided by the change in the value on the horizontal axis.

Social Capital The habitual way of doing things that guides people in how they approach production.

Social Security System A social insurance program that provides financial benefits to the elderly and disabled and to their eligible dependents and/or survivors.

Socialism An economic system based on individuals' goodwill toward others, not on their own self-interest, and in which, in principle, society decides what, how, and for whom to produce.

Sole Proprietorship A business that has only one owner.

Sound Finance A view of public finance and fiscal policy that the government budget should always be balanced except in wartime.

Special Drawing Rights (SDRs) A type of international money.

Specialization The concentration of individuals in certain aspects of production.

Speculative Motive Holding cash to avoid holding financial assets whose prices are falling.

Stagflation The combination of high and accelerating inflation and high unemployment.

Stock A financial asset that conveys ownership rights in a corporation. Also, certificates of ownership in a company.

Strategic Bargaining Demanding a larger share of the gains from trade than you can reasonably expect.

Strategic Trade Policy Threatening to implement tariffs to bring about a reduction in tariffs or some other concession from the other country.

Structural Deficit The part of a budget deficit that would exist even if the economy were at its potential level of income.

Structural Unemployment Unemployment caused by the institutional structure of an economy or by economic restructuring making some skills obsolete.

Sunk Cost Cost that has already been incurred and cannot be recovered.

Supply A schedule of quantities a seller is willing to sell per unit of time at various prices, other things constant.

Supply Curve A graphical representation of the relationship between price and quantity supplied.

Surplus An excess of revenues over payments.

T

Target Rate of Unemployment The lowest sustainable rate of unemployment that policy makers believe is achievable given existing demographics and the economy's institutional structure.

Tariff An excise tax on an imported (internationally traded) good.

Taylor Rule The rule is: Set the Fed funds rate at 2 percent plus current inflation if the economy is at desired output and desired inflation. If the inflation rate is higher than desired, increase the Fed funds rate by 0.5 times the difference between desired and actual inflation. Similarly, if output is higher than desired, increase the Fed funds rate by 0.5 times the percentage deviation.

Technological Agglomeration The tendency of technological advances to spawn further technological advances, creating a concentration of new technologies in a specific location.

Technology The way we make goods and supply services.

Third-Party-Payer Market A market in which the person who receives the good differs from the person paying for the good.

Trade Adjustment Assistance Programs Programs designed to compensate losers for reductions in trade restrictions.

Transactions Motive The need to hold money for spending.

Transfer Payments Payments to individuals by government that do not involve production by those individuals.

Transferable Comparative Advantage Comparative advantage based on factors that can change relatively easily.

U

Unemployment Rate The percentage of people in the economy who are willing and able to work but who are not working.

Unexpected Inflation   Inflation that surprises people.

V

Value Added   The increase in value that a firm contributes to a product or service.

Velocity of Money   The number of times per year, on average, a dollar goes around to generate a dollar's worth of income.

W–X

Wealth Accounts   A balance sheet of an economy's stock of assets and liabilities.

Wealth Effect   A fall in the price level will make the holders of money and of other financial assets richer, so they buy more.

World Trade Organization (WTO)   Organization committed to getting countries to agree not to impose new tariffs or other trade restrictions except under certain limited conditions. See also *General Agreement on Tariffs and Trade*.

Y–Z

Yield Curve   A curve that shows the relationship between interest rates and bonds' time to maturity.

A

Ain't (verb)   An ungrammatical form of "isn't," sometimes used to emphasize a point although the speaker knows that "isn't" is the correct form.

All the Rage (descriptive phrase)   Extremely popular, but the popularity is likely to be transitory.

Armada (proper noun)   Historic term for the Spanish navy. Now obsolete.

Automatic Pilot (noun)   To be on automatic pilot is to be acting without thinking.

B

Baby Boom (noun)   Any period when more than the statistically predicted number of babies are born. Originally referred to a specific group: those born in the years 1945–1964.

Baby Boomers (descriptive phrase)   Americans born in the years 1945 through 1964. An enormous and influential group of people whose large number is attributed to the "boom" in babies that occurred when military personnel, many of whom had been away from home for four or five years, were discharged from military service after the end of World War II.

Back to the Drawing Board (descriptive phrase)   To start all over again after having your plan or project turn out to be useless.

Bailed Out (descriptive phrase)   To be rescued. It has other colloquial meanings as well, but they do not appear in this book.

Bailout (noun)   The action of having been bailed out. (See "Bailed Out")

Bear Market (noun)   Stock market dominated by people who are not buying (i.e., are hibernating). Opposite of a bull market, where people are charging ahead vigorously to buy.

Bedlam (noun)   Chaotic and apparently disorganized activity. Today the word is not capitalized. A few hundred years ago in England, the noun meant the Hospital of St. Mary's of Bethlehem, an insane asylum. The hospital was not in Bethlehem; it was in London. "Bedlam" was the way "Bethlehem" was pronounced by the English.

Bidding (or Bid) (verb sometimes used as a noun)   Has two different meanings. (1) Making an offer, or a series of offers, to compete with others who are making offers. Also the offer itself. (2) Ordering or asking a person to take a specified action.

Big Mac (proper noun)   Brand name of a kind of hamburger sold at McDonald's restaurants.

Bind (noun)   To "be in a bind" means to be in a situation where one is forced to make a difficult decision one does not want to make—where any decision seems as if it would be wrong, or at least undesirable.

Blow It (verb; past tense: blew it)   To do a poor job, to miss an opportunity, to perform unsatisfactorily.

Blow Off (verb)   To treat as inconsequential; to deal superficially with something.

Blowout (noun)   Serious release of pent-up emotions or of control over one's actions.

Booming (adjective)   Being extraordinarily and quickly successful.

Botched Up (adjective)   Operated badly; spoiled.

Bottleneck (noun)   Situation in which no action can be taken because a large number of people or actions are confronted by a very small opening or opportunity.

Brainteaser (noun)   Question or puzzle that intrigues the brain, thus "teasing" it to answer the question or solve the puzzle.

Broke (adjective)   (1) To "go broke" or to "be broke" is to become insolvent, to lose all one's money and assets. (2) Usually not as bad as to have gone broke—just to be (hopefully) temporarily out of money or short of funds.

Bronco Bull   A bull ridden in a rodeo. The rider's object is to stay on the bull until he wrestles it to the ground or is thrown off. (See also "Rodeo.")

Buck Rogers (proper name)   American comic strip character popular in the first three-quarters of the 20th century.

Bucks (noun)   American slang for "dollars."

Bust (noun) (as in "housing bust")   A sudden decline in the price of an asset. (Opposite of boom)

C

Cachet (noun)   Prestige, distinction, high quality. This word is borrowed from French and is pronounced "ca-SHAY."

Catch (noun)   A proviso; an unexpected complication.

Caveat (noun)   In English, this noun means "caution" or "warning." It comes from Latin, where it is a whole little sentence: "Let him beware."

Center Stage (noun)   A dominant position.

Chit (noun)   Type of IOU (which see) or coupon with a designated value that can be turned in toward the purchase or acquisition of some item.

Clear-cut (adjective)   Precisely defined.

Coffer (noun)   A box or trunk used to hold valuable items; hence, "coffers" has come to mean a vault or other safe storage place to hold money or other valuable items.

Coin Flip (noun)   The decision made by flipping, or tossing, a coin after agreeing, with others, or with oneself, to choose one of two alternatives based on which side of the coin is facing up after the flip. (Also see "flipside.")

Come Through (verb)   Satisfy someone's demands or expectations.

Come Up Short (descriptive phrase)   To be deficient.

Corvette (noun)   A type of expensive sports car.

Cut and Dried (descriptive phrase)   Simple, obvious, and settled.

D

Decent (adjective)   One of its specialized meanings is "of high quality."

Down Pat (descriptive phrase)   To have something down pat is to know it precisely, accurately, and without needing to think about it.

E

Elmo (proper noun)   Character in the television show *Sesame Street*.

Energizer Bunny (noun)   Character in a television commercial for Energizer batteries. Just as the batteries are alleged to do, the Energizer bunny keeps going and going.

Esperanto (noun)   An artificial language invented in the 1880s, intended to be "universal." It is based on words from the principal European languages, and the theory was that all speakers of these European languages would effortlessly understand Esperanto. It never had a big following and today is almost unknown.

F

Fake (verb)   To fake is to pretend or deceive; to try to make people believe that you know what you're doing or talking about when you don't know or aren't sure.

Fire (verb)   To discharge an employee permanently. It's different from "laying off" an employee, an action taken when a temporary situation makes the employee superfluous but the employer expects to take the employee back when the temporary situation is over.

Fit to a T (verb)   Suit perfectly.

Fix (verb)   To prepare, as in "fixing a meal." This is only one of the multiplicity of meanings of this verb.

Flipside (noun)   The other side of a two-sided object or of a two-sided argument or situation. Origin: In the days before tape and DVD, we used to have large disks, made of vinyl or other material, upon which music was recorded, using both sides of the disk.

Forest for the Trees (descriptive phrase)   To be so focused on details that you don't see the overall situation.

Form Follows Function (description)   A phrase borrowed from architecture, where it means that the architect determines what a building is to be used for, and then designs the building to meet the demands of that use, or function.

Free Lunch (descriptive phrase)   Something you get without paying for it in any way. Usually applied negatively: There is no "free lunch."

Front (noun and verb)   Activity undertaken to divert attention from what is.

Funky (adjective)   Eccentric in style or manner.

G

Gee (expletive)   Emphatic expression signaling surprise or enthusiasm.

Giveaways (noun)   Something, usually valuable, that you confer without receiving anything tangible in return. In this book, it refers to Congress enacting tax cuts that are insignificant to all but people who are already rich.

Glitch (noun)   Trivial difficulty.

Go-between (noun)   A person or firm that carries out the contact between two people or firms who are not able, or do not wish, to communicate directly with each other.

Go-Cart (noun)   A small engine-powered vehicle that is used for racing and recreation.

Good and Ready (descriptive phrase)   Really, really ready.

Good Cop/Bad Cop (noun)   Alternating mood shifts. It comes from the alleged practice of having two police officers interview a suspect—one officer is kind and coaxing while the other is mean and nasty. This is supposed to make the suspect feel that the nice cop is a safe person to confide in.

Good Offices (descriptive phrase)   An expression common in 18th-century England, meaning "services."

Gooey (adjective)   Sticky or slimy.

Goofed (verb)   Past tense of the verb *goof*, meaning to make a careless mistake.

GOP   This acronym stands for "Grand Old Party." The GOP is the Republican political party.

Got It Made (descriptive phrase)   Succeeded.

Greek (noun)   See "Like Greek."

Groucho Marx (proper name)   A famous U.S. comedian (1885–1977).

Guns and Butter (descriptive phrase)   Metaphor describing the dilemma whether to devote resources to war or to peace.

Guzzle, Guzzler (verb and noun)   Verb: to consume something greedily, wastefully, and rapidly. Noun: an object (or a person) that guzzles.

H

Handout (noun)   Unearned offering (as distinct from a gift); charity.

Handy (adjective)   Convenient.

Hangover (noun)   The queasy feeling, usually accompanied by a headache, that can afflict a person who has gotten drunk. The feeling can last for hours after the person is no longer actually drunk.

Hard Up (adjective)   Seriously worried.

Hassle (noun and verb)   Noun: unreasonable obstacle. Verb: to place unreasonable obstacles or arguments in the way of someone.

Heat (noun)   Anger, blame, outrage, and pressure to change.

High Horse, Getting on Your (descriptive phrase)   Adopting a superior attitude; looking down (from your high horse) on other people's opinions or actions.

Hog Bellies (noun)   Commercial term for the part of a pig that becomes bacon and pork chops. (Also called *pork bellies*.)

Hot Air (descriptive phrase)   An empty promise. Also, bragging.

How Come (expression)   Why? That is, "How has it come about that . . . ?"

I

IOU (noun)   A nickname applied to a formal acknowledgment of a debt, such as a U.S. Treasury bond. Also an informal but written acknowledgment of a debt. Pronounce the letters and you will hear "I owe you."

Iron Curtain (noun)   Imaginary but daunting line between Western Europe and adjacent communist countries. After the political abandonment of Communism in these countries, the Curtain no longer exists.

J

Jolt (noun)   A sudden blow.

Jumpstart (verb and noun)   Verb: to give a sudden, sharp impetus to an object or person in order to elicit an immediate response. Noun: the action that elicits an immediate response. A small portable cable device, called "a jumper," can be carried in your car for emergency use if a battery goes dead.

Just Say No (admonition)   Flatly refuse. This phrase became common in the 1970s after Nancy Reagan, the wife of the then-president of the United States, popularized it in a campaign against the use of addictive drugs.

K

Klutz (noun)   Awkward, incompetent person.

L

Lag Time (noun)   The time between when you perform an action and the time you see results from having performed the action.

Laid Back (adjective)   Casual; calm; free from worry and feelings of pressure.

Late Victorian (adjective or noun)   Embodying some concept typical of the late period of Queen Victoria. Also, a person from that period or who acts like someone from that period. (Queen Victoria was queen of England from 1837 to 1901.)

Lay Off (verb)   To discharge a worker temporarily.

Leads (noun)   Persons or institutions that you think will be interested in whatever you have to sell. Also, the information you have that makes you think someone or something is worth pursuing.

Left the Nest (descriptive phrase)   To have left one's parental home, usually because one has grown up and become self-sufficient.

Levi's (noun)   Popular brand of jeans.

Like Greek (descriptive phrase)   Incomprehensible (because in the United States, classical Greek is considered to be a language that almost no one learns).

Limbo (noun)   To be "in limbo" is to be in a place or situation from which there is no escape.

Lord Tennyson (proper name)   Alfred Tennyson, 19th-century English poet who wrote a poem, *Ulysses*, about the nobility of effort ("To strive, to seek, to find and not to yield").

Losing Ground (verb)   Regressing.

Lousy (adjective)   Incompetent or distasteful.

M

Make It (verb)   To succeed in doing something; for instance, "make it to the bank" means to get to the bank before it closes.

Mall (noun)   Short for "shopping mall." A variety of stores grouped on one piece of land, with ample parking for all the mall's shoppers and often with many amenities such as covered walkways, playgrounds for children, fountains, and so on.

MasterCard (proper noun)   Brand name of a widely issued credit card.

Medicare (proper noun)   U.S. government health insurance program for people who are disabled or age 65 and over. There is no means test.

Mind Your Ps and Qs (expression)   Pay close attention to distinctions. It comes from the similarity of the small printed letters "p" and "q" where the only visual distinction is the location of the downstroke. Also, the letters are right next to each other in our alphabet.

Mob (noun)   Organized criminal activity. Also, the group to which organized criminals belong.

Mother of Necessity   A witty remark that reverses the terms of a famous saying, "Necessity is the mother of invention."

N

NASDAQ (also sometimes spelled "Nasdaq") (noun)   Stock market operated by the National Association of Securities Dealers. The "AQ" stands for "Automated Quotations."

Nature of the Beast (descriptive phrase)   Character of whatever you are describing (need not have anything to do with a "beast").

Nerd (noun)   An insignificant and uninteresting person or a person so absorbed in a subject that he or she thinks of nothing else and is therefore boring.

Nicholas Apert (proper name) Nineteenth-century French experimenter who discovered how to preserve food by canning or bottling it.

No Way (exclamation) Emphatic expression denoting refusal, denial, or extreme disapproval.

Not to Worry (admonition; also, when hyphenated, used as an adjective) Don't worry; or, it's nothing to worry about.

O

Off the Books (descriptive phrase) Not officially recorded (and hence it's an untaxed transaction).

Off-the-Cuff (adjective) A quick, unthinking answer for which the speaker has no valid authority (comes from the alleged practice of writing an abbreviated answer on the cuff of your shirt, to be glanced at during an examination).

On Her (His) Own (descriptive phrase) By herself (himself); without any help.

Op-Ed (adjective) Describes an article that appears on the "op-ed" page of a newspaper, which is **OP**posite the **ED**itorial page.

P

Pain, Real (noun) This real pain is not a *real* pain; rather, it is something—anything—that gives you a lot of trouble and that you dislike intensely. For instance, some people think balancing a checkbook is a real pain.

Park Avenue (noun) Expensive and fashionable street in New York City.

Part and Parcel (noun) An integral element of a concept, action, or item.

Peer Pressure (descriptive phrase) Push to do what everyone else in your particular group is doing.

Penny-Pincher (noun) Person who is unusually careful with money, sometimes to the point of being stingy.

Philharmonic (adjective) A philharmonic orchestra is an orchestra that specializes in classical music. Sometimes used as a noun, as in "I heard the Philharmonic."

Phoenix from the Ashes (descriptive phrase) Metaphor for coming to life after having been thought to be dead. In ancient Greek mythology, the phoenix was a bird said to (really) rise from the ashes after a fire. (Phoenix, Arizona, was so named because of the hot climate that prevails there.)

Pick Up Steam (verb) As steam pressure increases, the speed of a steam engine increases. When this happens, we say the engine has "picked up steam."

Pickle (noun) Dilemma.

Picky (adjective) Indulging in fine distinctions when making a decision.

Pie (noun) Metaphor for the total amount of a specific item that exists.

Piece of Cake (descriptive phrase) Simple; easy to achieve without much effort or thought.

Pinch (noun, used as part of a phrase) "In a pinch" means in a tough spot; in an emergency; in a situation calling for improvisation.

Pitt, (Sir) William (historical figure) Chief financial officer and prime minister of Britain in the 1780s. He is usually designated "the younger" to distinguish him from his father, who was also a high British government official.

Poof! (exclamation) Spoken emphatically to mean that something has suddenly and inexplicably disappeared.

Poorhouse (noun) Public institution where impoverished individuals were housed. These institutions were purposely dreary and unpleasant. They no longer officially exist, but they have a modern manifestation: shelters for the homeless.

Pound (noun) Unit of British currency.

Powers That Be (expression) People or institutions that have power such that there is nothing one can do to influence those people or institutions—or at least nothing easy.

Presto! (exclamation) Immediately.

Ps and Qs See under *Mind*.

Pub (noun) Short for "public house," a commercial establishment where alcoholic drinks are served, usually with refreshments and occasionally with light meals.

Q

Queen Elizabeth (proper noun) Here the author means Queen Elizabeth the first (reigned in England from 1558 to 1603).

Quip (noun and verb) Noun: a jocular remark. Verb: to make a jocular remark.

Quote (noun) Seller's statement of what he or she will charge for a good or service.

R

R&D (noun) Research and development.

Rainy Day (noun) Period when you (hopefully) temporarily have an income shortage.

Rainy Day Fund (descriptive phrase) Money set aside when you are doing well financially—that is, in a financially sunny period—to use in case you have a period when you are doing less well financially—that is, when you run into a financially rainy period.

Raise Your Eyebrows (verb) To express surprise, usually by a facial expression rather than vocally.

Red Flag (noun) A red flag warns you to be very alert to a danger or perceived danger. (Ships in port that are loading fuel or ammunition raise a red flag to signal danger.)

Red-Lined (adjective) On a motor vehicle's tachometer, a red line that warns at what speed an engine's capacity is being strained.

Relief (noun)   This term was an informal one, applied specifically to the financial assistance people in the United States received from the government during the Great Depression (1929 until about 1941). It arose because of a government program administered by the Works Progress Administration (WPA) formed to create jobs, and hence to employ people who otherwise would have been unemployed.

Ring Up (verb)   Before the introduction of computer-type machines that record each payment a retail customer makes—say at the supermarket or a restaurant—a "cash register" was used. When you pressed the keys representing the amount offered by the customer, a drawer sprang open and a bell rang.

Robin Hood (proper name)   Semifictional English adventurer of the 12th or 13th century. He "stole from the rich and gave to the poor."

Rock Bottom (noun)   To reach the absolute limit of one's endurance or resources.

Rodeo (noun)   Entertainment where a person rides a bull that is wildly trying to throw the rider off. Horses are often exhibited similarly.

Rolodex File (noun)   Manual—as opposed to electronic—device for organizing names, addresses, phone numbers, and e-numbers.

Rube Goldberg (proper name)   A famous cartoonist whose cartoons depicted complicated methods of doing simple things.

Rule of Thumb (descriptive phrase)   An estimate that is quick and easy to make and is reliable enough for rough calculations. Comes from using the space from the tip of your thumb to the thumb's first joint to represent an inch.

S

Saks (proper name)   A midsize department store that sells expensive, fashionable items. There are very few stores in the Saks chain, and Saks stores are considered exclusive.

Scab (noun)   Person who takes a job, or continues in a job, even though workers at that firm are on strike.

Scrooge (proper name)   Character in Charles Dickens' *Christmas Carol*, an English story written in the mid 1850s. He was unbelievably miserly and disagreeable (but in the story he reformed).

Shivering in Their Sandals (descriptive phrase)   Adaptation of standard English idiom *shivering in their shoes*, which means being afraid.

Shorthand (noun)   Any of several systems of abbreviated writing or writing that substitutes symbols for words and phrases. Shorthand was widely used in business until the introduction of mechanical and electronic devices for transmitting the human voice gradually made shorthand obsolete. Today it means to summarize very briefly or to substitute a short word or phrase for a long description.

Show Up (verb)   To put in an appearance, to arrive.

Silk Stockings (noun)   Silk stockings for women denoted luxury and extravagance, almost like caviar or pearls. With the development of nylon in 1940, silk stockings for anyone, let alone the queens or factory girls mentioned in this book, joined the dinosaurs in oblivion.

Skyrocket (verb and noun)   Verb: to rise suddenly and rapidly. Noun: the type of fireworks that shoot into the sky and explode suddenly in a shower of brilliant sparks.

Slow as Molasses (descriptive phrase)   Very slow. Molasses is a thick, sweet syrup made from sugar cane (known as "treacle" in the United Kingdom) that pours with agonizing slowness from its container.

Small Potatoes (noun)   An expression meaning insignificant or trivial.

Snitch (verb)   To engage in petty theft. (This verb has another meaning, which is to betray a person by divulging a secret about that person. If you do that, you are not only snitching, you are a snitch.)

Snowball (verb)   To increase rapidly, like a ball of wet snow that grows and grows when it is rolled rapidly in more wet snow.

Spending a Penny (descriptive phrase)   Spending any money at all. Do not confuse with usage in England, where the phrase means to go to the bathroom.

Spoils (noun)   Rewards or advantages gained through illegal or unethical activity.

Squirrel Away (verb)   To hide or conceal in a handy but secret place (as a squirrel stores nuts).

Star Trek (title)   Famous U.S. TV series about life in outer space.

Stay on Their Toes (idiom)   To be alert.

Steady (noun)   A person to whom you are romantically committed and with whom you spend a lot of time, especially in social activities.

Stealth Gains (noun)   Gains that occur unbeknownst to you.

Strings Attached (descriptive phrase)   A gift that comes with strings attached comes with certain conditions set forth by the donor.

T

Tacky (adjective)   In very poor taste.

Take a Flier (expression)   To take a chance; to undertake a risky action in the hope that you will be lucky.

Take Title (verb)   Legal term meaning to acquire ownership.

Tea Control (noun)   A method of resolving differences by informal but powerful social mechanisms, such as inviting your opponents to tea and settling matters while passing teacups and plates of cake around.

Temp (noun) Worker whose job is temporary and who accepts the job with that understanding.

Tidy (adjective) Neat, advantageous, profitable. "A tidy sum" is a really nice amount of money that you may not have expected to acquire.

Tough (adjective) Very difficult.

Trendy (adjective) A phenomenon that is slightly ahead of traditional ways and indicates a trend. Something trendy may turn into something traditional, or it may fade away without ever becoming mainstream.

Truck (verb) To exchange one thing for another. This was Adam Smith's definition in 1776 and it is still one of the meanings of the verb.

Tune In (verb) To become familiar with.

Turf (noun) Territory, especially the figurative territory of a firm.

Twinkies (noun) Brand name of an inexpensive small cake.

U

Under-the-Counter (adjective) Secret or concealed by an unscrupulous person. Also See *under the table* below.

Under the Table (descriptive phrase) To accept money surreptitiously in order to avoid paying taxes on it or to conceal the income for other reasons. Also, to proffer such money to avoid having it known that you are making a particular deal.

V

Village Watchman (descriptive phrase) Before modern communication technology, in small communities local news was gathered and reported by an official, the village watchman or town crier, who walked around collecting facts and gossip.

W–Z

Wampum (noun) String of beads made of polished shells, formerly used by North American Indians as money.

Whatever (noun) Designates an unspecified generic item or action when the speaker wants to let you know that it doesn't matter whether you know the exact item or place.

White Elephant (noun) Property requiring expensive care but yielding little profit; trinket without value to most people but esteemed by a few. There are real white elephants, which are albinos. They are rare and therefore expensive and high-maintenance.

Whiz (noun) An expert.

Wild About (descriptive phrase) Extremely enthusiastic about undertaking a particular action or admiring a particular object or person.

Wind Up (descriptive phrase) To discover that you have reached a particular conclusion or destination.

Working Off the Books (descriptive phrase) Being paid wages or fees that are not reported to the tax or other authorities by either the payer or the payee.

World War I (proper noun) 1914–1918. The United States did not enter until 1917.

World War II (proper noun) 1938–1945. The United States did not enter until 1941.

Writ Large (adjective) Strongly emphasized; defined broadly. ("Writ" is an obsolete form of the word "written.")

ABOUT THE AUTHOR

page iv: Tad Merrick.

CHAPTER 1

page 4: © Hulton-Deutsch Collection/CORBIS; **page 9:** Bleichroeder Print Collection, Baker Library, Harvard Business School; **page 11:** © Rachel Epstein/PhotoEdit; **page 13:** © Bettmann/Corbis; **page 15:** © Steve Cole/Getty Images; **page 17:** © Time & Life Pictures/Getty Images.

CHAPTER 2

page 23: © Royalty-Free/Corbis; **page 32:** © PhotoDisc/Getty Images; **page 33:** © Jon Riley/Getty Images; **page 36:** © Michael Newman/PhotoEdit; **page 37:** © AFP/Getty Images; **page 38:** Image courtesy of the Foresight Institute and the Institute for Molecular Manufacturing (IMM), www.imm.org.

CHAPTER 3

page 53: © Marianna Day Massey/ZUMA/Corbis; **page 56:** © Jess Alford/Getty Images; **page 67:** © Digital Vision/Getty Images.

CHAPTER 4

page 81: © Mike Ditz/2007 Transtock.com; **page 90:** © Royalty-Free/Corbis; **page 93:** © McGraw-Hill Companies, Inc./Gary He, photographer.

CHAPTER 5

page 104: © National Oceanic and Atmospheric Administration/Department of Commerce; **page 112:** © Rachel Epstein/PhotoEdit.

CHAPTER 6

page 133: Courtesy of National Bureau of Economic Research, Inc; **page 139:** © Andy Sacks/Getty Images.

CHAPTER 7

page 156: © Getty Images; **page 157:** Bleichroeder Print Collection, Baker Library, Harvard Business School; **page 170:** © Getty Images.

CHAPTER 8

page 176: © Medioimages/Getty Images; **page 186:** © AP Images; **page 196:** © John Van Hasselt/Corbis Sygma.

CHAPTER 9

page 201: © AP Photo/Beth A. Keiser; **page 202:** © Bettmann/Corbis; **page 217:** © PhotoDisc/Getty Images.

CHAPTER 10

page 227: Courtesy of Dr. Danylo Kozub; **page 228:** © Anthony Ise/Getty Images; **page 243:** © Science Museum/Science & Society Picture Library, London.

CHAPTER 11

page 257: © Collection of The New-York Historical Society, accession number 1971.104; **page 264:** © C. Sherburne/PhotoLink; **page 265:** © PhotoLink/Getty Images; **page 266:** © AP Photo/Doug Mills; **page 271:** © PhotoDisc/Getty Images; **page 272:** Bleichroeder Print Collection, Baker Library, Harvard Business School.

CHAPTER 12

page 290: © AP Photo/Paul Sakuma; **page 293:** © Yuan Xuejun/Panorama/The Image Works; **page 297:** Federal Reserve Photo–Britt Leckman.

CHAPTER 13

page 314: © Bettmann/Corbis; **page 320:** © Time & Life Pictures/Getty Images; **page 320:** Bleichroeder Print Collection, Baker Library, Harvard Business School.

CHAPTER 14

page 335: © AP Photo/Dennis Cook; **page 343:** Photo courtesy of U.S. Army Center of Military History/NARA/Signal Corps Photo # CC045191; **page 349:** © Denis Scott/Corbis.

CHAPTER 15

page 354: © AP Photo/Mark Lennihan; **page 367:** Bleichroeder Print Collection, Baker Library, Harvard Business School.

CHAPTER 16

page 376: © Mike Nelson/AFP/Getty Images; **page 394:** © C. Sherburne/PhotoLink/Getty Images; **page 397:** © Paul Conklin/PhotoEdit.

CHAPTER 17

CHAPTER 18

CHAPTER 19

Page numbers followed by n indicate material found in notes.

A